RING AROUND
THE BASES

◇

RING AROUND THE BASES

◇

The Complete Baseball Stories
of Ring Lardner

◇

Edited and with an Introduction by

MATTHEW J. BRUCCOLI

Foreword by Ring Lardner, Jr.

UNIVERSITY OF SOUTH CAROLINA PRESS

© 1992 Estate of Ring Lardner
Foreword © 1992 Ring Lardner, Jr.
Introduction © 1992 Matthew J. Bruccoli

Published in Columbia, South Carolina, by the
University of South Carolina Press

Manufactured in the United States of America

07 06 05 04 03   5 4 3 2 1

Library of Congress Cataloging-in-Publication Data

Lardner, Ring, 1885–1933.
  Ring around the bases : the complete baseball stories of Ring Lardner / edited and
with an introduction by Matthew J. Bruccoli ; foreword by Ring Lardner, Jr.
    p. cm.
  ISBN 1-57003-531-8 (pbk. : alk. paper)
  1. Baseball stories, American. I. Bruccoli, Matthew Joseph, 1931– II. Title.
PS3523.A7 A6 2003
813'.52—dc22

                                                          2003016348

CONTENTS

◇

FOREWORD

by Ring Lardner, Jr.

◊

TODAY, if someone referred to baseball as the national game, you might stop and compare it in your head with other organized sports to decide if it deserved the title. A hundred years ago, when my father was growing up, there would have been no such hesitation. Professional football, basketball, golf, tennis and hockey were non-existent, as were such sedentary pastimes as radio, television and the movies. Baseball, both as a participatory and a spectator sport, was practically the only game in town.

In Southwestern Michigan, where Ring Lardner was born and raised, there were "bush" leagues close at hand and National League games within easy access by train in Chicago. (He was fifteen by the time the American League was founded in 1900.) He enjoyed playing baseball himself, without showing any notable skill at it, but it was the professional sport that became almost as important a part of his life as music and literature. As a boy he kept track of team ranking and other important statistics, and between the ages of twenty and twenty-eight, his major activity as a newspaperman was reporting the game, first for the *South Bend*, [Indiana], *Times* and then for a series of Chicago papers.

Traveling with the Chicago teams, especially the White Sox, he made friends with many players, among them Guy "Doc" White, an outstanding pitcher and a semi-professional musician, with whom he wrote three songs. One of them was a quite sentimental celebration of baseball called "Gee, It's a Wonderful Game."

I still have my father's Life Pass to the American League made of 14-karat gold and signed by Charles E. Comiskey, White Sox owner at the time of the infamous World Series of 1919. The John Sayles movie *Eight Men Out* shows him singing his parody *I'm Forever Blowing Ball Games* in the Chicago railway car returning from Cincinnati after the first two games, and it is true that his attachment to the sport never quite recovered from the shock of those events. But he continued to go to games when he could and to cover the World Series almost every year during the 1920s. Sometimes one or more of my brothers and I would sit with him in a box in the newly built Yankee Stadium and be introduced to the players, including Ruth and Gehrig, who came over to pay their respects. We were presented with so many autographed balls that I don't think we ever played with one at home that wasn't decorated with one or more famous signatures.

Among his four sons, I was the only southpaw and the most seriously overweight. After a display of my inability to run for a fly ball when I was about eight, my mother suggested hopefully that perhaps I should be given a try behind the plate. "You ever hear of a left-handed catcher?" my father asked rhetorically. There was a touch of scorn in his voice and, while it may have been directed at her, I felt it more than she did.

RING LARDNER, JR.

INTRODUCTION

by Matthew J. Bruccoli

◇

RINGGOLD WILMER LARDNER (1885–1933) grew up in Niles, Michigan, in a genteel atmosphere of nineteenth-century small-town respectability. Like most American writers of his generation, he served his literary apprenticeship on newspapers. In 1905 he broke in with the *South Bend* [Indiana] *Times* as "society reporter, courthouse man, dramatic critic and sporting editor." He moved to Chicago in 1907 where he covered the Cubs and the White Sox for the *Inter-Ocean*, the *Examiner*, and the *Tribune*. America was crowded with competing newspapers, and the sports writers were the journalistic stars. In 1913, when he was 28, Lardner took over the widely read *Tribune* column, "In the Wake of the News."

The next year he published his first work of magazine fiction, "A Busher's Letters Home"—the first Jack Keefe story—in *The Saturday Evening Post*. A busher is a player from the minor leagues (the bush leagues, so-designated from the rural locations of the teams)—hence someone who is inexperienced, ignorant, crude, immature, or unprofessional. Bushers were expected to improve on and off the field; but Jack Keefe is a life-long busher.

By the end of 1914 the *Post* had published nine Lardner baseball stories, including the six Busher installments that were collected as *You Know Me Al* (1916). These stories achieved an immediate popularity; there had been nothing else like them in sports literature. They had an inside quality absent from the baseball fiction of the era, most of which was hero-worship stuff written for boys.*

Lardner's custom of populating his stories with fictional characters and actual figures buttressed the authenticity of his fiction, which dealt with men working at their trade. His athletes were not un-

*There were Gilbert Patten / Burt L. Standish, creator of Frank Meriwell; Ralph Henry Barbour; Edward Stratemeyer, creator of Baseball Joe; and Zane Grey.

blemished knights in shining flannel. Lardner employed exaggeration and humor to indicate the truth about the limitations of his characters who were mostly uneducated men with no skills off the field. For most of these celebrities there was no life after baseball. A star's salary was $10,000, and many players got less than $3000; there were no pensions and no lucrative public-relations jobs. At a time when it was impossible to write openly about athletes and alcoholism, Lardner conveyed the impression that his characters were familiar with the interiors of saloons and the contents of the bottles therein.

Lardner's baseball stories began appearing more than seventy-five years ago, but they present no difficulties for contemporary readers. Not even television has altered baseball, although John Lardner— one of Ring's four writer sons—observed that it slowed down the game because the players were posing for the cameras. The chief difference in baseball before and after 1920 resulted from the introduction of the lively ball and the eminence of the home-run hitter.

The *Post* and its readers wanted all the Busher stories that Lardner could deliver. More than he wanted to write, for he tired of the character and the requirements of the epistolary form. The letter format restricted Lardner to the point of view of Jack Keefe, who is stupid at best. But Keefe became an American stereotype, as well as a dependable money-maker. When the Busher series terminated in 1919 there were twenty-five stories that recorded Keefe's history from his rookie season with the White Sox, through the Sox-Giants world tour (five uncollected stories) and his World War I army service (nine stories collected in *Treat 'em Rough* and *The Real Dope*), ending in "The Busher Pulls a Mays" with his banishment to the Philadelphia Athletics. This volume omits the Jack Keefe stories set during the world tour and the war because they are not baseball stories. After he stopped writing about Keefe, Lardner reluctantly provided the continuity for a syndicated *You Know Me Al* comic strip from 1922 to 1925.[1]

Lardner alternated the Busher letters with other story types. Although his second story, "My Roomy," is about a baseball player, the character is a psychopath. In 1915 Lardner began writing stories that did not deal with sports; between the last Keefe story in 1919 and the 1932 *Lose With a Smile* sequence he wrote only two baseball stories. In "Ring," his eloquent tribute to his dead friend, F. Scott Fitzgerald asserted that Lardner's achievement was limited by his material: "A boy's game, with no more possibilities in it than a boy could master, a game bound by walls which kept out novelty or danger, change or adventure." Fitzgerald regretfully concluded that "Ring got less percentage of himself on paper than any other American of the first flight."² Yet Lardner's 130 short stories, 34 of which are baseball stories, show a remarkable range—wider, in fact, than Fitzgerald's material. *Ring Around the Bases* presents an incomplete and therefore distorted view of Lardner's fiction. For example, it omits his examinations of the post-war middle class and the new leisure class. Anyone who has not read "There Are Smiles," the 1928 story about a New York City traffic cop, has an imperfect understanding of Lardner's genius.

The foregoing comments bear on the issue of Ring Lardner's "permanent stature"—AKA "his position in the canon of American literature." Lardner has been excluded from the top rank of American fiction writers because he did not write novels. Allegedly, the short-story form restricted the scope and development of his work. But a serious writer writes about the subjects that have meaning for him in the best way—perhaps the only way—that he can. If he is good enough, readers share his concerns. If readers keep reading him because they want to, the writer has staying power. Reputations fluctuate during a writer's working life and posthumously. A constant process of preservation and recovery operates apart from the activities of the official stature-determiners and canon-makers. Literature is what lasts—apart from the influence of fashion.

Despite the exposure of Lardner's magazine stories—*The Saturday Evening Post* had a weekly circulation of 2,000,000 copies when he wrote for it—he did not reach a large book readership. *You Know Me Al* required one printing in 1916 and was not reprinted until 1925 as part of the Scribners program of launching Lardner as a serious writer. During the Twenties he was a member of the legendary Maxwell Perkins stable at Charles Scribner's Sons that included Fitzgerald, Hemingway, and Wolfe; but his primary readers were not book-buyers. Most of Lardner's readership and income resulted from his magazine and newspaper work.* He received increasing respect during his lifetime, especially from other writers. His admirers included Fitzgerald, Dorothy Parker, John O'Hara, Gilbert Seldes, Harold Ross, H. L. Mencken, and Virginia Woolf. Ernest Hemingway denied that Lardner had influenced him, which

---

*He wrote "Ring Lardner's Weekly Letter" for the Bell Syndicate from 1919 to 1927, as well as syndicated coverage of sporting events (baseball, boxing, and political conventions).

is proof of the influence; he had written imitations of Lardner for the Oak Park High School *Trapeze*. Lardner was one of the most copied and parodied writers of his time.

It is impossible to verify the theory that Lardner was trapped by his popularity: that the necessity of satisfying his markets prevented him from writing ambitious books. Yet there is no evidence that he regarded himself as anything but a professional writer, as defined by William Charvat:

> The terms of professional writing are these: that it provides a living for the author, like any other job; that it is a main and prolonged, rather than intermittent or sporadic, resource for the writer; that it is produced with the hope of extended sale in the open market, like any article of commerce; and that it is written with reference to buyers' tastes and reading habits.[3]

Writers write what they can, how they can; and publication is the essential act of authorship. Writing to satisfy the requirements of a market does not necessarily constitute selling out. There are many literary pots and many ways of boiling them.

As happens with most writers who made literature out of what was regarded as sub-literary material, Lardner's career has inspired a full ration of guesswork. Thus:

Lardner as misanthrope. It is claimed that his fiction began as good-humored entertainment and grew progressively bitter. Read the stories. Jack Keefe is not an innocent boob; he is dumb, dishonest, mean, and vain. The Busher is a grotesque, as are many of Lardner's characters. (A scholar might be moved to assert that Lardner practiced Ben Jonson's "comedy of humours," which portrays characters motivated by a single exaggerated trait.) Nonetheless, an argument can be made that Lardner's misanthropy determined his view of his craft: that his pain limited his ambition.

Lardner's ear. Writers who report speech accurately are praised for their auditory equipment, as though they were some sort of recording device. Lardner commented that he listened "hard"; but more than listening was required. H. L. Mencken's *The American Language* cites this instruction on the dropped g sound at the ends of words:

> Lardner calls my attention to the fact that *anything* and *everything* are almost always excepted. He says: "I used, occasionally, to sit on the players' bench at baseball games, and it was there that I noted the exceptions made in favor of these two words. A player, returning to

the bench after batting, would be asked, 'Has he got *anything* in there?' ('He —— in there' always means the pitcher). The answer would be 'He's got *everything*.' On the other hand, the player might return and (usually after striking out) say, 'He hasn't got nothin'.' And the manager: 'Looks like he must have somethin'."[4]

Lardner was in control of his prose—an especially difficult requirement in vernacular writing—and eschewed nonfunctional "funny" misspellings. He was the last notable figure in the tradition of American vernacular literature and would have endorsed Mark Twain's claim about the dialogue in *Huckleberry Finn*: "The shadings have not been done in a haphazard fashion, or by guesswork; but painstakingly, and with the trustworthy guidance and support of personal familiarity with these several forms of speech."

Apart from linguistic or stylistic considerations, these stories merit a safe place in the big leagues of American literature—not in the bush league of "sport fiction, baseball." Great fiction is always great social history. Ring Lardner provided a trustworthy record of American society. That he employed the tools of wit and irony does not mitigate the value of his testimony.

NOTES

1. *Ring Lardner's You Know Me Al: The Comic Strip Adventures of Jack Keefe*, preface by Al Capp. New York & London: Harcourt Brace Jovanovich / Bruccoli Clark, 1979.

2. *The New Republic*, 76 (11 October 1933), 254–255. Reprinted in Fitzgerald's *The Crack-Up* (New York: New Directions, 1945).

3. *The Profession of Authorship in America*, ed. Bruccoli (Columbus: Ohio State University Press, 1968), p. 3.

4. Second Edition (New York: Knopf, 1926), p. 276. See also Lardner's "Baseball-American," pp. 392–393.

EDITOR'S NOTE

◇

Ring Around the Bases is the first complete collection of Ring Lardner's baseball short stories. It includes thirteen stories that have not appeared in any Lardner volume: "The Busher Reënlists," "The Battle of Texas," "The Busher Pulls a Mays," "Sick 'Em," "Back to Baltimore," "The Poor Simp," "Where Do You Get That Noise?" "Good for the Soul," "The Crook," "The Hold-Out," "The Yellow Kid," "Take a Walk," "The Courtship of T. Dorgan." The previously uncollected stories are printed here from their magazine texts. The others are reprinted from Lardner's own story collections. No silent editorial alterations have been made in these stories.

RING AROUND
THE BASES

◇

Gee! It's A Wonderful Game

Words by
R. N. LARDNER

Music by
G. HARRIS (Doc) WHITE
Arranged by Chas. Miller

Who dis - cov - erd the land of the brave and the
Who lost out in the bat - tle of old Wa - ter -

free? I don't know, _____ I don't know. _____ 'Twas
loo? I don't know, _____ I don't know. _____ They

Chris - ty Col - um - bus is what they tell me; May be
say 'twas Nap - o - le - on, may be it's true; May be

so,_____ I don't know._____ There's on - ly one
so,_____ I don't know._____ The pink sheets don't

Chris - ty that I know at all, One Chris - ty that I ev - er
print Mis - ter Bon - a - parte's face, No sto - ries a - bout him to

saw,_____ He's the one who dis - cov - ered the fade a - way
day,_____ 'Cause he nev - er could hold down that old sec - ond

Gee! It's A W.G. 4

ball, And he pitch-es for Mugg-sy Mc Graw.
base, Like his name sake, Big Nap Laz-o - way.

CHORUS *p-ff*

Base - ball, Base - ball aint it a
Base - ball, Base - ball aint it a

won - der - ful game? Old Chris - ty Col um' found this
dan - dy old game? The Gen'-'ral of France could - n't

coun - try, by gum But the ex - tras don't car - ry his
lead 'em like Chance, So no won - der 'his Wat - er - loo

name. _____ If old man Col‑um‑bus had sat in the
came. _____ If down in his pock‑et Nap‑o‑leon had

stand, Had seen Mat‑ty pitch‑ing that "fa‑der" so
dug, Had paid his five francs to see Ty‑rus Cobb

grand, He'd have said "Boys I'm glad I dis‑cov‑ered this land
slug, He'd have said I give up, I'm a bug, I'm a bug

Gee! it's a won‑der‑ful game.   game. _____
Gee! it's a won‑der‑ful game.   game. _____

Gee! It's A W. G. 4

A BUSHER'S
LETTERS HOME

◊

Terre Haute, Indiana, September 6.

FRIEND AL: Well, Al old pal I suppose you seen in the paper where I been sold to the White Sox. Believe me Al it comes as a surprise to me and I bet it did to all you good old pals down home. You could of knocked me over with a feather when the old man come up to me and says Jack I've sold you to the Chicago Americans.

I didn't have no idea that anything like that was coming off. For five minutes I was just dum and couldn't say a word.

He says We aren't getting what you are worth but I want you to go up to that big league and show those birds that there is a Central League on the map. He says Go and pitch the ball you been pitching down here and there won't be nothing to it. He says All you need is the nerve and Walsh or no one else won't have nothing on you.

So I says I would do the best I could and I thanked him for the treatment I got in Terre Haute. They always was good to me here and though I did more than my share I always felt that my work was appresiated. We are finishing second and I done most of it. I can't help but be proud of my first year's record in professional baseball and you know I am not boasting when I say that Al.

Well Al it will seem funny to be up there in the big show when I never was really in a big city before. But I guess I seen enough of life not to be scared of the high buildings eh Al?

I will just give them what I got and if they don't like it they can send me back to the old Central and I will be perfectly satisfied.

I didn't know anybody was looking me over, but one of the boys told me that Jack Doyle the White Sox scout was down here looking

This story first appeared in *The Saturday Evening Post*, March 7, 1914. One of the six Jack Keefe stories collected in *You Know Me Al*, (New York: Doran, 1916).

at me when Grand Rapids was here. I beat them twice in that serious. You know Grand Rapids never had a chance with me when I was right. I shut them out in the first game and they got one run in the second on account of Flynn misjuding that fly ball. Anyway Doyle liked my work and he wired Comiskey to buy me. Comiskey come back with an offer and they excepted it. I don't know how much they got but anyway I am sold to the big league and believe me Al I will make good.

Well Al I will be home in a few days and we will have some of the good old times. Regards to all the boys and tell them I am still their pal and not all swelled up over this big league business.

Your pal,   JACK.

Chicago, Illinois, December 14.

OLD PAL: Well Al I have not got much to tell you. As you know Comiskey wrote me that if I was up in Chi this month to drop in and see him. So I got here Thursday morning and went to his office in the afternoon. His office is out to the ball park and believe me its some park and some office.

I went in and asked for Comiskey and a young fellow says He is not here now but can I do anything for you? I told him who I am and says I had an engagement to see Comiskey. He says The boss is out of town hunting and did I have to see him personally?

I says I wanted to see about signing a contract. He told me I could sign as well with him as Comiskey and he took me into another office. He says What salary did you think you ought to get? and I says I wouldn't think of playing ball in the big league for less than three thousand dollars per annum. He laughed and says You don't want much. You better stick round town till the boss comes back. So here I am and it is costing me a dollar a day to stay at the hotel on Cottage Grove Avenue and that don't include my meals.

I generally eat at some of the cafes round the hotel but I had supper downtown last night and it cost me fifty-five cents. If Comiskey don't come back soon I won't have no more money left.

Speaking of money I won't sign no contract unless I get the salary you and I talked of, three thousand dollars. You know what I was getting in Terre Haute, a hundred and fifty a month, and I know it's going to cost me a lot more to live here. I made inquiries round here and find I can get board and room for eight dollars a week but I will be out of town half the time and will have to pay for my room when I am away or look up a new one when I come back. Then I will have to buy cloths to wear on the road in places like New York. When Comiskey comes back I will name him three thousand dollars as my lowest figure and I guess he will come through when he sees I am in ernest. I heard that Walsh was getting twice as much as that.

The papers says Comiskey will be back here sometime to-morrow. He has been hunting with the president of the league so he ought to feel pretty good. But I don't care how he feels. I am going to get a contract for three thousand and if he don't want to give it to me he can do the other thing. You know me Al.

Yours truly,   JACK.

Chicago, Illinois, December 16.

DEAR FRIEND AL: Well I will be home in a couple of days now but I wanted to write you and let you know how I come out with Comiskey. I signed my contract yesterday afternoon. He is a great old fellow Al and no wonder everybody likes him. He says Young man will you have a drink? But I was to smart and wouldn't take nothing. He says You was with Terre Haute? I says Yes I was. He says Doyle tells me you were pretty wild. I says Oh no I got good control. He says Well do you want to sign? I says Yes if I get my figure. He asks What is my figure and I says three thousand dollars per annum. He says Don't you want the office furniture too? Then he says I thought you was a young ball-player and I didn't know you wanted to buy my park.

We kidded each other back and forth like that a while and then he says You better go out and get the air and come back when you feel better. I says I feel O. K. now and I want to sign a contract because I have got to get back to Bedford. Then he calls the secretary and tells him to make out my contract. He give it to me and it calls for two hundred and fifty a month. He says You know we always have a city serious here in the fall where a fellow picks up a good bunch of money. I hadn't thought of that so I signed up. My yearly salary will be fifteen hundred dollars besides what the city serious brings me. And that is only for the first year. I will demand three thousand or four thousand dollars next year.

I would of started home on the evening train but I ordered a suit of cloths from a tailor over on Cottage Grove and it won't be done till tomorrow. It's going to cost me twenty bucks but it ought to last a long time. Regards to Frank and the bunch.

Your Pal, JACK.

Paso Robles, California, March 2.

OLD PAL AL: Well Al we been in this little berg now a couple of days and its bright and warm all the time just like June. Seems funny to have it so warm this early in March but I guess this California climate is all they said about it and then some.

It would take me a week to tell you about our trip out here. We came on a Special Train De Lukes and it was some train. Every place we stopped there was crowds down to the station to see us go through and all the people looked me over like I was a actor or something. I guess my hight and shoulders attracted their attention. Well Al we finally got to Oakland which is across part of the ocean from Frisco. We will be back there later on for practice games.

We stayed in Oakland a few hours and then took a train for here. It was another night in a sleeper and believe me I was tired of sleepers before we got here. I have road one night at a time but this was four straight nights. You know Al I am not built right for a sleeping car birth.

The hotel here is a great big place and got good eats. We got in at breakfast time and I made a B line for the dining room. Kid Gleason who is a kind of asst. manager to Callahan come in and sat down with me. He says Leave something for the rest of the boys because they will be just as hungry as you. He says Ain't you afraid you will cut your throat with that knife. He says There ain't no extra charge for using the forks. He says You shouldn't ought to eat so much because you're overweight now. I says You may think I am fat, but it's all solid bone and muscle. He says Yes I suppose it's all solid bone from the neck up. I guess he thought I would get sore but I will let them kid me now because they will take off their hats to me when they see me work.

Manager Callahan called us all to his room after breakfast and give us a lecture. He says there would be no work for us the first day but that we must all take a long walk over the hills. He also says we must not take the training trip as a joke. Then the colored trainer give us our suits and I went to my room and tried mine on. I ain't a bad looking guy in the White Sox uniform Al. I will have my picture taken and send you boys some.

My roommate is Allen a lefthander from the Coast League. He don't look nothing like a pitcher but you can't never tell about them dam left handers. Well I didn't go on the long walk because I was tired out. Walsh stayed at the hotel too and when he seen me he says Why didn't you go with the bunch? I says I was too tired. He says Well when Callahan comes back you better keep out of sight or tell him you are sick. I says I don't care nothing for Callahan. He says No but Callahan is crazy about you. He says You better obey orders and you will git along better. I guess Walsh thinks I am some rube.

When the bunch come back Callahan never said a word to me but Gleason come up and says Where was you? I told him I was too tired to go walking. He says Well I will borrow a wheelbarrow some place and push you round. He says Do you sit down when you pitch? I let him kid me because he has not saw my stuff yet.

Next morning half the bunch mostly vetrans went to the ball park which isn't no better than the one we got at home. Most of them was vetrans as I say but I was in the bunch. That makes things look pretty good for me don't it Al? We tossed the ball round and hit fungos and run round and then Callahan asks Scott and Russell and I to warm up easy and pitch a few to the batters. It was warm and I felt pretty good so I warmed up pretty good. Scott pitched to them first and kept laying them right over with nothing on them. I don't believe a man gets any batting practice that way. So I went in and after I lobbed a few over I cut loose my fast one. Lord was to bat and he ducked out of the way and then throwed his bat to the bench. Callahan says What's the matter Harry? Lord says I forgot to pay up my life insurance. He says I ain't ready for Walter Johnson's July stuff.

Well Al I will make them think I am Walter Johnson before I get through with them. But Callahan come out to me and says What are you trying to do kill somebody? He says Save your smoke because you're going to need it later on. He says Go easy with the boys at first or I won't have no batters. But he was laughing and I guess he was pleased to see the stuff I had.

There is a dance in the hotel to-night and I am up in my room writing this in my underwear while I get my suit pressed. I got it all mussed up coming out here. I don't know what shoes to wear. I asked Gleason and he says Wear your baseball shoes and if any of the girls gets fresh with you spike them. I guess he was kidding me.

Write and tell me all the news about home.

Yours truly,   JACK.

Paso Robles, California, March 7.

FRIEND AL: I showed them something out there to-day Al. We had a game between two teams. One team was made up of most of the regulars and the other was made up of recruts. I pitched three innings for the recruts and shut the old birds out. I held them to one hit and that was a ground ball that the recrut shortstop Johnson ought to of ate up. I struck Collins out and he is one of the best batters in the bunch. I used my fast ball most of the while but showed them a few spitters and they missed them a foot. I guess I must of got Walsh's goat with my spitter because him and I walked back to the hotel together and he talked like he was kind of jealous. He says You will have to learn to cover up your spitter. He says I could stand a mile away and tell when you was going to throw it. He says Some of these days I will learn you how to cover it up. I guess Al I know how to cover it up all right without Walsh learning me.

I always sit at the same table in the dining room along with Gleason and Collins and Bodie and Fournier and Allen the young lefthander I told you about. I feel sorry for him because he never says a word. To-night at supper Bodie says How did I look to-day Kid? Gleason says Just like you always do in the spring. You looked like a cow. Gleason seems to have the whole bunch scared of him and they let him say anything he wants to. I let him kid me to but I ain't scared of him. Collins then says to me You got some fast ball there boy. I says I was not as fast today as I am when I am right. He says Well then I don't want to hit against you when you are right. Then Gleason says to Collins Cut that stuff out. Then he says to me Don't believe what he tells you boy. If the pitchers in this league weren't no faster than you I would still be playing ball and I would be the best hitter in the country.

After supper Gleason went out on the porch with me. He says Boy you have got a little stuff but you have got a lot to learn. He says You field your position like a wash woman and you don't hold the runners up. He says When Chase was on second base to-day he got such a lead on you that the little catcher couldn't of shot him out at third with a rifle. I says They all thought I fielded my position all right in the Central League. He says Well if you think you do it all right you better go back to the Central League where you are appresiated. I says You can't send me back there because you could not get waivers. He says Who would claim you? I says St. Louis and Boston and New York.

You know Al what Smith told me this winter. Gleason says Well if you're not willing to learn St. Louis and Boston and New York can have you and the first time you pitch against us we will steal fifty bases. Then he quit kidding and asked me to go to the field with him early to-morrow morning and he would learn me some things. I don't think he can learn me nothing but I promised I would go with him.

There is a little blonde kid in the hotel here who took a shine to me at the dance the other night but I am going to leave the skirts alone. She is real society and a swell dresser and she wants my picture. Regards to all the boys.   Your friend,   JACK.

P.S. The boys thought they would be smart to-night and put something over on me. A boy brought me a telegram and I opened it and it said You are sold to Jackson in the Cotton States League. For just a minute they had me going but then I happened to think that Jackson is in Michigan and there's no Cotton States League round there.

Paso Robles, California, March 9.

DEAR FRIEND AL: You have no doubt read the good news in the papers before this reaches you. I have been picked to go to Frisco with the first team. We play practice games up there about two weeks while the second club plays in Los Angeles. Poor Allen had to go with the second club. There's two other recrut pitchers with our part of the team but my name was first on the list so it looks like I had made good. I knowed they would like my stuff when they seen it. We leave here to-night. You got the first team's address so you will know where to send my mail. Callahan goes with us and Gleason goes with the second club. Him and I have got to be pretty good pals and I wish he was going with us even if he don't let me eat like I want to. He told me this morning to remember all he had learned me and to keep working hard. He didn't learn me nothing I didn't know before but I let him think so.

The little blonde don't like to see me leave here. She lives in Detroit and I may see her when I go there. She wants me to write but I guess I better not give her no encouragement.

Well Al I will write you a long letter from Frisco.
                         Yours truly,   JACK.

Oakland, California, March 19.

DEAR OLD PAL: They have gave me plenty of work here all right. I have pitched four times but have not went over five innings yet. I worked against Oakland two times and against Frisco two times and only three runs have been scored off me. They should only ought to of had one but Bodie misjuged a easy fly ball in Frisco and Weaver made a wild peg in Oakland that let in a run. I am not using much but my fast ball but I have got a world of speed and they can't foul me when I am right. I whiffed eight men in five innings in Frisco yesterday and could of did better than that if I had of cut loose.

Manager Callahan is a funny guy and I don't understand him sometimes. I can't figure out if he is kidding or in ernest. We road back to Oakland on the ferry together after yesterday's game and he says Don't you never throw a slow ball? I says I don't need no slow ball with my spitter and my fast one. He says No of course you don't need it but if I was you I would get one of the boys to learn it to me. He says And you better watch the way the boys fields their positions and holds up the runners. He says To see you work a man might think they had a rule in the Central League forbidding a pitcher from leaving the box or looking toward first base.

I told him the Central didn't have no rule like that. He says And I noticed you taking your wind up when What's His Name was on second base there to-day. I says Yes I got more stuff when I wind up. He says Of course you have but if you wind up like that with Cobb on base he will steal your watch and chain. I says Maybe Cobb can't get on base when I work against him. He says That's right and maybe San Francisco Bay is made of grapejuice. Then he walks away from me.

He give one of the youngsters a awful bawling out for something he done in the game at supper last night. If he ever talks to me like he done to him I will take a punch at him. You know me Al.

I come over to Frisco last night with some of the boys and we took in the sights. Frisco is some live town Al. We went all through China Town and the Barbers' Coast. Seen lots of swell dames but they was all painted up. They have beer out here that they call steam beer. I had a few glasses of it and it made me logey. A glass of that Terre Haute beer would go pretty good right now.

We leave here for Los Angeles in a few days and I will write you from there. This is some country Al and I would love to play ball round here.   Your Pal,   JACK.

P.S.—I got a letter from the little blonde and I suppose I got to answer it.

Los Angeles, California, March 26.

FRIEND AL: Only four more days of sunny California and then we start back East. We got exhibition games in Yuma and El Paso, Texas, and Oklahoma City and then we stop over in St. Joe, Missouri, for three days before we go home. You know Al we open the season in Cleveland and we won't be in Chi no more than just passing through. We don't play there till April eighteenth and I guess I will work in that serious all right against Detroit. Then I will be glad to have you and the boys come up and watch me as you suggested in your last letter.

I got another letter from the little blonde. She has went back to Detroit but she give me her address and telephone number and believe me Al I am going to look her up when we get there the twenty-ninth of April.

She is a stenographer and was out here with her uncle and aunt.

I had a run in with Kelly last night and it looked like I would have to take a wallop at him but the other boys separated us. He is a bush outfielder from the New England League. We was playing poker. You know the boys plays poker a good deal but this was the first time I got in. I was having pretty good luck and was about four bucks to the good and I was thinking of quitting because I was tired and sleepy. Then Kelly opened the pot for fifty cents and I stayed. I had three sevens. No one else stayed. Kelly stood pat and I drawed two cards. And I catched my fourth seven. He bet fifty cents but I felt pretty safe even if he did have a pat hand. So I called him. I took the money and told them I was through.

Lord and some of the boys laughed but Kelly got nasty and begun to pan me for quitting and for the way I played. I says Well I won the pot didn't I? He says Yes and he called me something. I says I got a notion to take a punch at you.

He says Oh you have have you? And I come back at him. I says Yes I have have I? I would of busted his jaw if they hadn't stopped me. You know me Al.

I worked here two times once against Los Angeles and once against Venice. I went the full nine innings both times and Venice beat me four to two. I could of beat them easy with any kind of support. I walked a couple of guys in the forth and Chase drops a throw and Collins lets a fly ball get away from him. At that I would of shut them out if I had wanted to cut loose. After the game Callahan says You didn't look so good in there to-day. I says I didn't cut loose. He says Well you been working pretty near three weeks now and you ought to be in shape to cut loose. I says Oh I am in shape all right. He says Well don't work no harder than you have to or you might get hurt and then the league would blow up. I don't know if he was kidding me or not but I guess he thinks pretty well of me because he works me lots oftener than Walsh or Scott or Benz.

I will try to write you from Yuma, Texas, but we don't stay there only a day and I may not have time for a long letter.

Yours truly,   JACK.

Yuma, Arizona, April 1.

DEAR OLD AL: Just a line to let you know we are on our way back East. This place is in Arizona and it sure is sandy. They haven't got no regular ball club here and we play a pick-up team this afternoon. Callahan told me I would have to work. He says I am using you because we want to get through early and I know you can beat them quick. That is the first time he has said anything like that and I guess he is wiseing up that I got the goods.

We was talking about the Athaletics this morning and Callahan says None of you fellows pitch right to Baker. I was talking to Lord and Scott afterward and I say to Scott How do you pitch to Baker? He says I use my fadeaway. I says How do you throw it? He says Just like you throw a fast ball to anybody else. I says Why do you call it a fadeaway then? He says Because when I throw it to Baker it fades away over the fence.

This place is full of Indians and I wish you could see them Al. They don't look nothing like the Indians we seen in that show last summer.

Your old pal,   JACK.

Oklahoma City, April 4.

FRIEND AL: Coming out of Amarillo last night I and Lord and Weaver was sitting at a table in the dining car with a old lady. None of us were talking to her but she looked me over pretty careful and seemed to kind of like my looks. Finally she says Are you boys with some football club? Lord nor Weaver didn't say nothing so I thought it was up to me and I says No mam this is the Chicago White Sox Ball Club. She says I knew you were athaletes. I says Yes I guess you could spot us for athaletes. She says Yes indeed and specially you. You certainly look healthy. I says You ought to see me stripped. I didn't see nothing funny about that but I thought Lord and Weaver would die laughing. Lord had to get up and leave the table and he told everybody what I said.

All the boys wanted me to play poker on the way here but I told them I didn't feel good. I know enough to quit when I am ahead Al. Callahan and I sat down to breakfast all alone this morning. He says Boy why don't you get to work? I says What do you mean? Ain't I working? He says You ain't improving none. You have got the stuff to make a good pitcher but you don't go after bunts and you don't cover first base and you don't watch the baserunners. He made me kind of sore talking that way and I says Oh I guess I can get along all right.

He says Well I am going to put it up to you. I am going to start you over in St. Joe day after to-morrow and I want you to show me something. I want you to cut loose with all you've got and I want you to get round the infield a little and show them you aren't tied in that box. I says Oh I can field my position if I want to. He says Well you better want to or I will have to ship you back to the sticks. Then he got up and left. He didn't scare me none Al. They won't ship me to no sticks after the way I showed on this trip and even if they did they couldn't get no waivers on me.

Some of the boys have begun to call me Four Sevens but it don't bother me none. Yours truly, JACK.

St. Joe, Missouri, April 7.

FRIEND AL: It rained yesterday so I worked to-day instead and St. Joe done well to get three hits. They couldn't of scored if we had played all week. I give a couple of passes but I catched a guy flatfooted off of first base and I come up with a couple of bunts and throwed guys out. When the game was over Callahan says That's the way I like to see you work. You looked better to-day than you looked on the whole trip. Just once you wound up with a man on but otherwise you was all O.K. So I guess my job is cinched Al and I won't have to go to New York or St. Louis. I would rather be in Chi anyway because it is near home. I wouldn't care though if they traded me to Detroit. I hear from Violet right along and she says she can't hardly wait till I come to Detroit. She says she is strong for the Tigers but she will pull for me when I work against them. She is nuts over me and I guess she has saw lots of guys to.

I sent her a stickpin from Oklahoma City but I can't spend no more dough on her till after our first payday the fifteenth of the month. I had thirty bucks on me when I left home and I only got about ten left including the five spot I won in the poker game. I have to tip the waiters about thirty cents a day and I seen about twenty picture shows on the coast besides getting my cloths pressed a couple of times.

We leave here to-morrow night and arrive in Chi the next morning. The second club joins us there and then that night we go to Cleveland to open up. I asked one of the reporters if he knowed who was going to pitch the opening game and he says it would be Scott or Walsh but I guess he don't know much about it.

These reporters travel all round the country with the team all season and send in telegrams about the game every night. I ain't seen no Chi papers so I don't know what they been saying about me. But I should worry eh Al? Some of them are pretty nice fellows and some of them got the swell head. They hang round with the old fellows and play poker most of the time.

Will write you from Cleveland. You will see in the paper if I pitch the opening game.   Your old pal,   JACK.

Cleveland, Ohio, April 10.

OLD FRIEND AL: Well Al we are all set to open the season this afternoon. I have just ate breakfast and I am sitting in the lobby of the hotel. I eat at a little lunch counter about a block from here and I saved seventy cents on breakfast. You see Al they give us a dollar a meal and if we don't want to spend that much all right. Our rooms at the hotel are paid for.

The Cleveland papers says Walsh or Scott will work for us this afternoon. I asked Callahan if there was any chance of me getting into the first game and he says I hope not. I don't know what he meant but he may surprise these reporters and let me pitch. I will beat them Al. Lajoie and Jackson is supposed to be great batters but the bigger they are the harder they fall.

The second team joined us yesterday in Chi and we practiced a little. Poor Allen was left in Chi last night with four others of the recruit pitchers. Looks pretty good for me eh Al? I only seen Gleason for a few minutes on the train last night. He says, Well you ain't took off much weight. You're hog fat. I says Oh I ain't fat. I didn't need to take off no weight. He says One good thing about it the club don't have to engage no birth for you because you spend all your time in the dining car. We kidded along like that a while and then the trainer rubbed my arm and I went to bed. Well Al I just got time to have my suit pressed before noon.

Yours truly, JACK.

Cleveland, Ohio, April 11.

FRIEND AL: Well Al I suppose you know by this time that I did not pitch and that we got licked. Scott was in there and he didn't have nothing. When they had us beat four to one in the eight inning Callahan told me to go out and warm up and he put a batter in for Scott in our ninth. But Cleveland didn't have to play their ninth so I got no chance to work. But it looks like he means to start me in one of the games here. We got three more to play. Maybe I will pitch this afternoon. I got a postcard from Violet. She says Beat them Naps. I will give them a battle Al if I get a chance.

Glad to hear you boys have fixed it up to come to Chi during the Detroit serious. I will ask Callahan when he is going to pitch me and let you know. Thanks Al for the papers.

Your friend, JACK.

St. Louis, Missouri, April 15.

FRIEND AL: Well Al I guess I showed them. I only worked one inning but I guess them Browns is glad I wasn't in there no longer than that. They had us beat seven to one in the sixth and Callahan pulls Benz out. I honestly felt sorry for him but he didn't have nothing, not a thing. They was hitting him so hard I thought they would score a hundred runs. A righthander name Bumgardner was pitching for them and he didn't look to have nothing either but we ain't got much of a batting team Al. I could hit better than some of them regulars. Anyway Callahan called Benz to the bench and sent for me. I was down in the corner warming up with Kuhn. I wasn't warmed up good but you know I got the nerve Al and I run right out there like I meant business. There was a man on second and nobody out when I come in. I didn't know who was up there but I found out afterward it was Shotten. He's the centerfielder. I was

cold and I walked him. Then I got warmed up good and I made
Johnston look like a boob. I give him three fast balls and he let two
of them go by and missed the other one. I would of handed him a
spitter but Schalk kept signing for fast ones and he knows more
about them batters than me. Anyway I whiffed Johnston. Then up
come Williams and I tried to make him hit at a couple of bad ones.
I was in the hole with two balls and nothing and come right across
the heart with my fast one. I wish you could of saw the hop on it.
Williams hit it right straight up and Lord was camped under it. Then
up come Pratt the best hitter on their club. You know what I done
to him don't you Al? I give him one spitter and another he didn't
strike at that was a ball. Then I come back with two fast ones and
Mister Pratt was a dead baby. And you notice they didn't steal no
bases neither.

In our half of the seventh inning Weaver and Schalk got on and
I was going up there with a stick when Callahan calls me back and
sends Easterly up. I don't know what kind of managing you call that.
I hit good on the training trip and he must of knew they had no
chance to score off me in the innings they had left while they were
liable to murder his other pitchers. I come back to the bench pretty
hot and I says You're making a mistake. He says If Comiskey had
wanted you to manage this team he would of hired you.

Then Easterly pops out and I says Now I guess you're sorry you
didn't let me hit. That sent him right up in the air and he bawled me
awful. Honest Al I would of cracked him right in the jaw if we hadn't
been right out where everybody could of saw us. Well he sent Cicotte
in to finish and they didn't score no more and we didn't neither.

I road down in the car with Gleason. He says Boy you shouldn't
ought to talk like that to Cal. Some day he will lose his temper and
bust you one. I says He won't never bust me. I says He didn't have
no right to talk like that to me. Gleason says I suppose you think
he's going to laugh and smile when we lost four out of the first five
games. He says Wait till to-night and then go up to him and let him
know you are sorry you sassed him. I says I didn't sass him and I
ain't sorry.

So after supper I seen Callahan sitting in the lobby and I went
over and sit down by him. I says When are you going to let me
work? He says I wouldn't never let you work only my pitchers are
all shot to pieces. Then I told him about you boys coming up from
Bedford to watch me during the Detroit serious and he says Well I
will start you in the second game against Detroit. He says But I

wouldn't if I had any pitchers. He says A girl could get out there and pitch better than some of them have been doing.

So you see Al I am going to pitch on the nineteenth. I hope you guys can be up there and I will show you something. I know I can beat them Tigers and I will have to do it even if they are Violet's team.

I notice that New York and Boston got trimmed to-day so I suppose they wish Comiskey would ask for waivers on me. No chance Al.   Your old pal,   JACK.

P.S.—We play eleven games in Chi and then go to Detroit. So I will see the little girl on the twenty-ninth.

Oh you Violet.

Chicago, Illinois, April 19.

DEAR OLD PAL: Well Al it's just as well you couldn't come. They beat me and I am writing you this so as you will know the truth about the game and not get a bum steer from what you read in the papers.

I had a sore arm when I was warming up and Callahan should never ought to of sent me in there. And Schalk kept signing for my fast ball and I kept giving it to him because I thought he ought to know something about the batters. Weaver and Lord and all of them kept kicking them round the infield and Collins and Bodie couldn't catch nothing.

Callahan ought never to of left me in there when he seen how sore my arm was. Why, I couldn't of threw hard enough to break a pain of glass my arm was so sore.

They sure did run wild on the bases. Cobb stole four and Bush and Crawford and Veach about two apiece. Schalk didn't even make a peg half the time. I guess he was trying to throw me down.

The score was sixteen to two when Callahan finally took me out in the eighth and I don't know how many more they got. I kept telling him to take me out when I seen how bad I was but he wouldn't do it. They started bunting in the fifth and Lord and Chase just stood there and didn't give me no help at all.

I was all O.K. till I had the first two men out in the first inning. Then Crawford come up. I wanted to give him a spitter but Schalk signs me for the fast one and I give it to him. The ball didn't hop much and Crawford happened to catch it just right. At that Collins ought to of catched the ball. Crawford made three bases and up come

Cobb. It was the first time I ever seen him. He hollered at me right off the reel. He says You better walk me you busher. I says I will walk you back to the bench. Schalk signs for a spitter and I gives it to him and Cobb misses it.

Then instead of signing for another one Schalk asks for a fast one and I shook my head no but he signed for it again and yells Put something on it. So I throwed a fast one and Cobb hits it right over second base. I don't know what Weaver was doing but he never made a move for the ball. Crawford scored and Cobb was on first base. First thing I knowed he had stole second while I held the ball. Callahan yells Wake up out there and I says Why don't your catcher tell me when they are going to steal. Schalk says Get in there and pitch and shut your mouth. Then I got mad and walked Veach and Moriarty but before I walked Moriarty Cobb and Veach pulled a double steal on Schalk. Gainor lifts a fly and Lord drops it and two more come in. Then Stanage walks and I whiffs their pitcher.

I come in to the bench and Callahan says Are your friends from Bedford up there? I was pretty sore and I says Why don't you get a catcher? He says We don't need no catcher when you're pitching because you can't get nothing past their bats. Then he says You better leave your uniform in here when you go out next inning or Cobb will steal it off your back. I says My arm is sore. He says Use your other one and you'll do just as good.

Gleason says Who do you want to warm up? Callahan says Nobody. He says Cobb is going to lead the league in batting and basestealing anyway so we might as well give him a good start. I was mad enough to punch his jaw but the boys winked at me not to do nothing.

Well I got some support in the next inning and nobody got on. Between innings I says Well I guess I look better now don't I? Callahan says Yes but you wouldn't look so good if Collins hadn't jumped up on the fence and catched that one off Crawford. That's all the encouragement I got Al.

Cobb come up again to start the third and when Schalk signs me for a fast one I shakes my head. Then Schalk says All right pitch anything you want to. I pitched a spitter and Cobb bunts it right at me. I would of threw him out a block but I stubbed my toe in a rough place and fell down. This is the roughest ground I ever seen Al. Veach bunts and for a wonder Lord throws him out. Cobb goes to second and honest Al I forgot all about him being there and first thing I knowed he had stole third. Then Moriarty hits a fly ball to

Bodie and Cobb scores though Bodie ought to of threw him out twenty feet.

They batted all round in the forth inning and scored four or five more. Crawford got the luckiest three-base hit I ever see. He popped one way up in the air and the wind blowed it against the fence. The wind is something fierce here Al. At that Collins ought to of got under it.

I was looking at the bench all the time expecting Callahan to call me in but he kept hollering Go on and pitch. Your friends wants to see you pitch.

Well Al I don't know how they got the rest of their runs but they had more luck than any team I ever seen. And all the time Jennings was on the coaching line yelling like a Indian. Some day Al I'm going to punch his jaw.

After Veach had hit one in the eight Callahan calls me to the bench and says You're through for the day. I says it's about time you found out my arm was sore. He says I ain't worrying about your arm but I'm afraid some of our outfielders will run their legs off and some of them poor infielders will get killed. He says The reporters just sent me a message saying they had run out of paper. Then he says I wish some of the other clubs had pitchers like you so we could hit once in a while. He says Go in the clubhouse and get your arm rubbed off. That's the only way I can get Jennings sore he says.

Well Al that's about all there was to it. It will take two or three stamps to send this but I want you to know the truth about it. The way my arm was I ought never to of went in there.

Yours truly,   JACK.

Chicago, Illinois, April 25.

FRIEND AL: Just a line to let you know I am still on earth. My arm feels pretty good again and I guess maybe I will work at Detroit. Violet writes that she can't hardly wait to see me. Looks like I got a regular girl now Al. We go up there the twenty-ninth and maybe I won't be glad to see her. I hope she will be out to the game the day I pitch. I will pitch the way I want to next time and them Tigers won't have such a picnic.

I suppose you seen what the Chicago reporters said about that game. I will punch a couple of their jaws when I see them.

Your pal,   JACK.

Chicago, Illinois, April 29.

DEAR OLD AL: Well Al it's all over. The club went to Detroit last night and I didn't go along. Callahan told me to report to Comiskey this morning and I went up to the office at ten o'clock. He give me my pay to date and broke the news. I am sold to Frisco.

I asked him how they got waivers on me and he says Oh there was no trouble about that because they all heard how you tamed the Tigers. Then he patted me on the back and says Go out there and work hard boy and maybe you'll get another chance some day. I was kind of choked up so I walked out of the office.

I ain't had no fair deal Al and I ain't going to no Frisco. I will quit the game first and take that job Charley offered me at the billiard hall.

I expect to be in Bedford in a couple of days. I have got to pack up first and settle with my landlady about my room here which I engaged for all season thinking I would be treated square. I am going to rest and lay round home a while and try to forget this rotten game. Tell the boys about it Al and tell them I never would of got let out if I hadn't worked with a sore arm.

I feel sorry for that little girl up in Detroit Al. She expected me there today.   Your old pal,   JACK.

P.S. I suppose you seen where that lucky lefthander Allen shut out Cleveland with two hits yesterday. The lucky stiff.

THE BUSHER
COMES BACK

◇

San Francisco, California, May 13.
FRIEND AL: I suppose you and the rest of the boys in Bedford
will be supprised to learn that I am out here, because I remember
telling you when I was sold to San Francisco by the White Sox that
not under no circumstances would I report here. I was pretty mad
when Comiskey give me my release, because I didn't think I had
been given a fair show by Callahan. I don't think so yet Al and I
never will but Bill Sullivan the old White Sox catcher talked to me
and told me not to pull no boner by refuseing to go where they sent
me. He says You're only hurting yourself. He says You must remember that this was your first time up in the big show and very
few men no matter how much stuff they got can expect to make
good right off the reel. He says All you need is experience and
pitching out in the Coast League will be just the thing for you.

So I went in and asked Comiskey for my transportation and he
says That's right Boy go out there and work hard and maybe I will
want you back. I told him I hoped so but I don't hope nothing of
the kind Al. I am going to see if I can't get Detroit to buy me,
because I would rather live in Detroit than anywheres else. The little
girl who got stuck on me this spring lives there. I guess I told you
about her Al. Her name is Violet and she is some queen. And then
if I got with the Tigers I wouldn't never have to pitch against Cobb
and Crawford, though I believe I could show both of them up if I
was right. They ain't got much of a ball club here and hardly any
good pitchers outside of me. But I don't care.

I will win some games if they give me any support and I will get

The Saturday Evening Post, May 23, 1914; *You Know Me Al.*

back in the big league and show them birds something. You know me, Al.   Your pal,   JACK.

Los Angeles, California, May 20.

AL: Well old pal I don't suppose you can find much news of this league in the papers at home so you may not know that I have been standing this league on their heads. I pitched against Oakland up home and shut them out with two hits. I made them look like suckers Al. They hadn't never saw no speed like mine and they was scared to death the minute I cut loose. I could of pitched the last six innings with my foot and trimmed them they was so scared.

Well we come down here for a serious and I worked the second game. They got four hits and one run, and I just give them the one run. Their shortstop Johnson was on the training trip with the White Sox and of course I knowed him pretty well. So I eased up in the last inning and let him hit one. If I had of wanted to let myself out he couldn't of hit me with a board. So I am going along good and Howard our manager says he is going to use me regular. He's a pretty nice manager and not a bit sarkastic like some of them big leaguers. I am fielding my position good and watching the baserunners to. Thank goodness Al they ain't no Cobbs in this league and a man ain't scared of haveing his uniform stole off his back.

But listen Al I don't want to be bought by Detroit no more. It is all off between Violet and I. She wasn't the sort of girl I suspected. She is just like them all Al. No heart. I wrote her a letter from Chicago telling her I was sold to San Francisco and she wrote back a postcard saying something about not haveing no time to waste on bushers. What do you know about that Al? Calling me a busher. I will show them. She wasn't no good Al and I figure I am well rid of her. Good riddance is rubbish as they say.

I will let you know how I get along and if I hear anything about being sold or drafted.   Yours truly,   JACK.

San Francisco, California, July 20.

FRIEND AL: You will forgive me for not writeing to you oftener when you hear the news I got for you. Old pal I am engaged to be married. Her name is Hazel Carney and she is some queen, Al—a great big stropping girl that must weigh one hundred and sixty lbs.

She is out to every game and she got stuck on me from watching me work.

Then she writes a note to me and makes a date and I meet her down on Market Street one night. We go to a nickel show together and have some time. Since then we been together pretty near every evening except when I was away on the road.

Night before last she asked me if I was married and I tells her No and she says a big handsome man like I ought to have no trouble finding a wife. I tells her I ain't never looked for one and she says Well you wouldn't have to look very far. I asked her if she was married and she said No but she wouldn't mind it. She likes her beer pretty well and her and I had several and I guess I was feeling pretty good. Anyway I guess I asked her if she wouldn't marry me and she says it was O.K. I ain't a bit sorry Al because she is some doll and will make them all sit up back home. She wanted to get married right away but I said No wait till the season is over and maybe I will have more dough. She asked me what I was getting and I told her two hundred dollars a month. She says she didn't think I was getting enough and I don't neither but I will get the money when I get up in the big show again.

Anyway we are going to get married this fall and then I will bring her home and show her to you. She wants to live in Chi or New York but I guess she will like Bedford O.K. when she gets acquainted.

I have made good here all right Al. Up to a week ago Sunday I had won eleven straight. I have lost a couple since then, but one day I wasn't feeling good and the other time they kicked it away behind me.

I had a run in with Howard after Portland had beat me. He says Keep on running round with that skirt and you won't never win another game.

He says Go to bed nights and keep in shape or I will take your money. I told him to mind his own business and then he walked away from me. I guess he was scared I was going to smash him. No manager ain't going to bluff me Al.

So I went to bed early last night and didn't keep my date with the kid. She was pretty sore about it but business before pleasure Al. Don't tell the boys nothing about me being engaged. I want to surprise them.   Your pal,   JACK.

Sacramento, California, August 16.

FRIEND AL: Well Al I got the surprise of my life last night. Howard called me up after I got to my room and tells me I am going back to the White Sox. Come to find out, when they sold me out here they kept a option on me and yesterday they exercised it. He told me I would have to report at once. So I packed up as quick as I could and then went down to say good-by to the kid. She was all broke up and wanted to go along with me but I told her I didn't have enough dough to get married. She said she would come anyway and we could get married in Chi but I told her she better wait. She cried all over my sleeve. She sure is gone on me Al and I couldn't help feeling sorry for her but I promised to send for her in October and then everything will be all O.K. She asked me how much I was going to get in the big league and I told her I would get a lot more money than out here because I wouldn't play if I didn't. You know me Al.

I come over here to Sacramento with the club this morning and I am leaveing to-night for Chi. I will get there next Tuesday and I guess Callahan will work me right away because he must of seen his mistake in letting me go by now. I will show them Al.

I looked up the skedule and I seen where we play in Detroit the fifth and sixth of September. I hope they will let me pitch there Al. Violet goes to the games and I will make her sorry she give me that kind of treatment. And I will make them Tigers sorry they kidded me last spring. I ain't afraid of Cobb or none of them now, Al.

Your pal,   JACK.

Chicago, Illinois, August 27.

AL: Well old pal I guess I busted in right. Did you notice what I done to them Athaletics, the best ball club in the country? I bet Violet wishes she hadn't called me no busher.

I got here last Tuesday and set up in the stand and watched the game that afternoon. Washington was playing here and Johnson pitched. I was anxious to watch him because I had heard so much about him. Honest Al he ain't as fast as me. He shut them out, but they never was much of a hitting club. I went to the clubhouse after the game and shook hands with the bunch. Kid Gleason the assistant manager seemed pretty glad to see me and he says Well have you learned something? I says Yes I guess I have. He says Did you see the game this afternoon? I says I had and he asked me what I thought of Johnson. I says I don't think so much of him. He says Well I guess you ain't learned nothing then. He says What was the matter with Johnson's work? I says He ain't got nothing but a fast ball. Then he says Yes and Rockefeller ain't got nothing but a hundred million bucks.

Well I asked Callahan if he was going to give me a chance to work and he says he was. But I sat on the bench a couple of days and he didn't ask me to do nothing. Finally I asked him why not and he says I am saving you to work against a good club, the Athaletics. Well the Athaletics come and I guess you know by this time what I done to them. And I had to work against Bender at that but I ain't afraid of none of them now Al.

Baker didn't hit one hard all afternoon and I didn't have no trouble with Collins neither. I let them down with five blows all though the papers give them seven. Them reporters here don't no more about scoreing than some old woman. They give Barry a hit on a fly ball that Bodie ought to of eat up, only he stumbled or something and they handed Oldring a two base hit on a ball that Weaver had to duck to get out of the way from. But I don't care nothing about reporters. I beat them Athaletics and beat them good, five to one. Gleason slapped me on the back after the game and says Well you learned something after all. Rub some arnicky on your head to keep the swelling down and you may be a real pitcher yet. I says I ain't got no swell head. He says No. If I hated myself like you do I would be a moveing picture actor.

Well I asked Callahan would he let me pitch up to Detroit and he says Sure. He says Do you want to get revenge on them? I says, Yes I did. He says Well you have certainly got some comeing. He says I never seen no man get worse treatment than them Tigers give you last spring. I says Well they won't do it this time because I will know how to pitch to them. He says How are you going to pitch to Cobb? I says I am going to feed him on my slow one. He says Well Cobb had ought to make a good meal off of that. Then we quit jokeing and he says You have improved a hole lot and I am going to work you right along regular and if you can stand the gaff I may be able to use you in the city serious. You know Al the White Sox plays a city serious every fall with the Cubs and the players makes quite a lot of money. The winners gets about eight hundred dollars a peace and the losers about five hundred. We will be the winners if I have anything to say about it.

I am tickled to death at the chance of working in Detroit and I can't hardly wait till we get there. Watch my smoke Al.

Your pal,   JACK.

P.S. I am going over to Allen's flat to play cards a while to-night. Allen is the left-hander that was on the training trip with us. He ain't got a thing, Al, and I don't see how he gets by. He is married and his wife's sister is visiting them. She wants to meet me but it won't do her much good. I seen her out to the game today and she ain't much for looks.

Detroit, Mich., September 6.

FRIEND AL: I got a hole lot to write but I ain't got much time because we are going over to Cleveland on the boat at ten P. M. I made them Tigers like it Al just like I said I would. And what do you think, Al, Violet called me up after the game and wanted to see me but I will tell you about the game first.

They got one hit off me and Cobb made it a scratch single that he beat out. If he hadn't of been so dam fast I would of had a no hit game. At that Weaver could of threw him out if he had of started after the ball in time. Crawford didn't get nothing like a hit and I whiffed him once. I give two walks both of them to Bush but he is such a little guy that you can't pitch to him.

When I was warming up before the game Callahan was standing beside me and pretty soon Jennings come over. Jennings says You ain't going to pitch that bird are you? And Callahan said Yes he was. Then Jennings says I wish you wouldn't because my boys is all tired out and can't run the bases. Callahan says They won't get no chance to-day. No, says Jennings I suppose not. I suppose he will walk them all and they won't have to run. Callahan says He won't give no bases on balls, he says. But you better tell your gang that he is liable to bean them and they better stay away from the plate. Jennings says He won't never hurt my boys by beaning them. Than I cut in. Nor you neither, I says. Callahan laughs at that so I guess I must of pulled a pretty good one. Jennings didn't have no comeback so he walks away.

Then Cobb come over and asked if I was going to work. Callahan told him Yes. Cobb says How many innings? Callahan says All the way. Then Cobb says Be a good fellow Cal and take him out early. I am lame and can't run. I butts in then and said Don't worry, Cobb. You won't have to run because we have got a catcher who can hold them third strikes. Callahan laughed again and says to me You sure did learn something out on that Coast.

Well I walked Bush right off the real and they all begun to holler

on the Detroit bench There he goes again. Vitt come up and Jennings
yells Leave your bat in the bag Osker. He can't get them over. But
I got them over for that bird all O.K. and he pops out trying to bunt.
And then I whiffed Crawford. He starts off with a foul that had me
scared for a minute because it was pretty close to the foul line and
it went clear out of the park. But he missed a spitter a foot and then
I supprised them Al. I give him a slow ball and I honestly had to
laugh to see him lunge for it. I bet he must of strained himself. He
throwed his bat way like he was mad and I guess he was. Cobb came
prancing up like he always does and yells Give me that slow one
Boy. So I says All right. But I fooled him. Instead of giveing him a
slow one like I said I was going I handed him a spitter. He hit it all
right but it was a line drive right in Chase's hands. He says Pretty
lucky Boy but I will get you next time. I come right back at him. I
says Yes you will.

Well Al I had them going like that all through. About the sixth
inning Callahan yells from the bench to Jennings What do you think
of him now? And Jennings didn't say nothing. What could he of said?

Cobb makes their one hit in the eighth. He never would of
made it if Schalk had of let me throw him spitters instead of fast
ones. At that Weaver ought to of threw him out. Anyway they
didn't score and we made a monkey out of Dubuque, or whatever
his name is.

Well Al I got back to the hotel and snuck down the street a ways
and had a couple of beers before supper. So I come to the supper
table late and Walsh tells me they had been several phone calls for
me. I go down to the desk and they tell me to call up a certain
number. So I called up and they charged me a nickel for it. A girl's
voice answers the phone and I says Was they some one there that
wanted to talk to Jack Keefe? She says You bet they is. She says
Don't you know me, Jack? This is Violet. Well, you could of knocked
me down with a peace of bread. I says What do you want? She says
Why I want to see you. I says Well you can't see me. She says Why
what's the matter, Jack? What have I did that you should be sore at
me? I says I guess you know all right. You called me a busher. She
says Why I didn't do nothing of the kind. I says Yes you did on that
postcard. She says I didn't write you no postcard.

Then we argued along for a while and she swore up and down that
she didn't write me no postcard or call me no busher. I says Well
then why didn't you write me a letter when I was in Frisco? She says
she had lost my address. Well Al I don't know if she was telling me

the truth or not but may be she didn't write that postcard after all. She was crying over the telephone so I says Well it is too late for I and you to get together because I am engaged to be married. Then she screamed and I hang up the receiver. She must of called back two or three times because they was calling my name round the hotel but I wouldn't go near the phone. You know me Al.

Well when I hang up and went back to finish my supper the dining room was locked. So I had to go out and buy myself a sandwich. They soaked me fifteen cents for a sandwich and a cup of coffee so with the nickel for the phone I am out twenty cents altogether for nothing. But then I would of had to tip the waiter in the hotel a dime.

Well Al I must close and catch the boat. I expect a letter from Hazel in Cleveland and maybe Violet will write me too. She is stuck on me all right Al. I can see that. And I don't believe she could of wrote that postcard after all.   Yours truly,   JACK.

Boston, Massachusetts, September 12.

OLD PAL: Well Al I got a letter from Hazel in Cleveland and she is comeing to Chi in October for the city serious. She asked me to send her a hundred dollars for her fare and to buy some cloths with. I sent her thirty dollars for the fare and told her she could wait till she got to Chi to buy her cloths. She said she would give me the money back as soon as she seen me but she is a little short now because one of her girl friends borrowed fifty off of her. I guess she must be pretty soft-hearted Al. I hope you and Bertha can come up for the wedding because I would like to have you stand up with me.

I all so got a letter from Violet and they was blots all over it like she had been crying. She swore she did not write that postcard and said she would die if I didn't believe her. She wants to know who the lucky girl is who I am engaged to be married to. I believe her Al when she says she did not write that postcard but it is too late now. I will let you know the date of my wedding as soon as I find out.

I guess you seen what I done in Cleveland and here. Allen was going awful bad in Cleveland and I relieved him in the eighth when we had a lead of two runs. I put them out in one-two-three order in the eighth but had hard work in the ninth due to rotten support. I walked Johnston and Chapman and Turner sacrificed them ahead.

Jackson come up then and I had two strikes on him. I could of whiffed him but Schalk makes me give him a fast one when I wanted to give him a slow one. He hit it to Berger and Johnston ought to of been threw out at the plate but Berger fumbles and then has to make the play at first base. He got Jackson all O.K. but they was only one run behind then and Chapman was on third base. Lajoie was up next and Callahan sends out word for me to walk him. I thought that was rotten manageing because Lajoie or no one else can hit me when I want to cut loose. So after I give him two bad balls I tried to slip over a strike on him but the lucky stiff hit it on a line to Weaver. Anyway the game was over and I felt pretty good. But Callahan don't appresiate good work Al. He give me a call in the clubhouse and said if I ever disobeyed his orders again he would suspend me without no pay and lick me too. Honest Al it was all I could do to keep from wrapping his jaw but Gleason winks at me not to do nothing.

I worked the second game here and give them three hits two of which was bunts that Lord ought to of eat up. I got better support in Frisco than I been getting here Al. But I don't care. The Boston bunch couldn't of hit me with a shovel and we beat them two to nothing. I worked against Wood at that. They call him Smoky Joe and they say he has got a lot of speed.

Boston is some town, Al, and I wish you and Bertha could come here sometime. I went down to the wharf this morning and seen them unload the fish. They must of been a million of them but I didn't have time to count them. Every one of them was five or six times as big as a blue gill.

Violet asked me what would be my address in New York City so I am dropping her a postcard to let her know all though I don't know what good it will do her. I certainly won't start no correspondents with her now that I am engaged to be married.

Yours truly,   JACK.

New York, New York, September 16.

FRIEND AL: I opened the serious here and beat them easy but I know you must of saw about it in the Chi papers. At that they don't give me no fair show in the Chi papers. One of the boys bought one here and I seen in it where I was lucky to win that game in Cleveland. If I knowed which one of them reporters wrote that I would punch his jaw.

Al I told you Boston was some town but this is the real one. I never seen nothing like it and I been going some since we got here. I walked down Broadway the Main Street last night and I run into a couple of the ball players and they took me to what they call the Garden but it ain't like the gardens at home because this one is indoors. We sat down to a table and had several drinks. Pretty soon one of the boys asked me if I was broke and I says No, why? He says You better get some lubricateing oil and loosen up. I don't know what he meant but pretty soon when we had had a lot of drinks the waiter brings a check and hands it to me. It was for one dollar. I says Oh I ain't paying for all of them. The waiter says This is just for that last drink.

I thought the other boys would make a holler but they didn't say nothing. So I give him a dollar bill and even then he didn't act satisfied so I asked him what he was waiting for and he said Oh nothing, kind of sassy. I was going to bust him but the boys give me the sign to shut up and not to say nothing. I excused myself pretty soon because I wanted to get some air. I give my check for my hat to a boy and he brought my hat and I started going and he says Haven't you forgot something? I guess he must of thought I was wearing a overcoat.

Then I went down the Main Street again and some man stopped me and asked me did I want to go to the show. He said he had a ticket. I asked him what show and he said the Follies. I never heard of it but I told him I would go if he had a ticket to spare. He says I will spare you this one for three dollars. I says You must take me for some boob. He says No I wouldn't insult no boob. So I walks on but if he had of insulted me I would of busted him.

I went back to the hotel then and run into Kid Gleason. He asked me to take a walk with him so out I go again. We went to the corner and he bought me a beer. He don't drink nothing but pop himself. The two drinks was only ten cents so I says This is the place for me. He says Where have you been? and I told him about paying one dollar for three drinks. He says I see I will have to take charge of you. Don't go round with them ball players no more. When you want to go out and see the sights come to me and I will stear you. So to-night he is going to stear me. I will write to you from Philadelphia.   Your pal,   JACK.

Philadelphia, Pa., September 19.

FRIEND AL: They won't be no game here to-day because it is raining. We all been loafing round the hotel all day and I am glad of it because I got all tired out over in New York City. I and Kid Gleason went round together the last couple of nights over there and he wouldn't let me spend no money. I seen a lot of girls that I would of liked to of got acquainted with but he wouldn't even let me answer them when they spoke to me. We run in to a couple of peaches last night and they had us spotted too. One of them says I'll bet you're a couple of ball players. But Kid says You lose your bet. I am a bellhop and the big rube with me is nothing but a pitcher.

One of them says What are you trying to do kid somebody? He says Go home and get some soap and remove your disguise from your face. I didn't think he ought to talk like that to them and I called him about it and said maybe they was lonesome and it wouldn't hurt none if we treated them to a soda or something. But he says Lonesome. If I don't get you away from here they will steal everything you got. They won't even leave you your fast ball. So we left them and he took me to a picture show. It was some California pictures and they made me think of Hazel so when I got back to the hotel I sent her three postcards.

Gleason made me go to my room at ten o'clock both nights but I was pretty tired anyway because he had walked me all over town. I guess we must of saw twenty shows. He says I would take you to the grand opera only it would be throwing money away because we can hear Ed Walsh for nothing. Walsh has got some voice Al a loud high tenor.

To-morrow is Sunday and we have a double header Monday on account of the rain to-day. I thought sure I would get another chance to beat the Athaletics and I asked Callahan if he was going to pitch me here but he said he thought he would save me to work against Johnson in Washington. So you see Al he must figure I am about the best he has got. I'll beat him Al if they get a couple of runs behind me.   Yours truly,   JACK.

P.S. They was a letter here from Violet and it pretty near made me feel like crying. I wish they was two of me so both them girls could be happy.

Washington, D.C., September 22.

DEAR OLD AL: Well Al here I am in the capital of the old United
States. We got in last night and I been walking round town all morn-
ing. But I didn't tire myself out because I am going to pitch against
Johnson this afternoon.

This is the prettiest town I ever seen but I believe they is more
colored people here than they is in Evansville or Chi. I seen the
White House and the Monumunt. They say that Bill Sullivan and
Gabby St. once catched a baseball that was threw off of the top of
the Monumunt but I bet they couldn't catch it if I throwed it.

I was in to breakfast this morning with Gleason and Bodie and
Weaver and Fournier. Gleason says I'm supprised that you ain't sick
in bed to-day. I says Why?

He says Most of our pitchers get sick when Cal tells them they
are going to work against Johnson. He says Here's these other fellows
all feeling pretty sick this morning and they ain't even pitchers. All
they have to do is hit against him but it looks like as if Cal would
have to send substitutes in for them. Bodie is complaining of a sore
arm which he must of strained drawing to two card flushes. Fournier
and Weaver have strained their legs doing the tango dance. Nothing
could cure them except to hear that big Walter had got throwed
out of his machine and wouldn't be able to pitch against us in this
serious.

I says I feel O.K. and I ain't afraid to pitch against Johnson and I
ain't afraid to hit against him neither. Then Weaver says Have you
ever saw him work? Yes, I says, I seen him in Chi. Then Weaver
says Well if you have saw him work and ain't afraid to hit against
him I'll bet you would go down to Wall Street and holler Hurrah
for Roosevelt. I says No I wouldn't do that but I ain't afraid of no
pitcher and what is more if you get me a couple of runs I'll beat him.
Then Fournier says Oh we will get you a couple of runs all right.
He says That's just as easy as catching whales with a angleworm.

Well Al I must close and go in and get some lunch. My arm feels
great and they will have to go some to beat me Johnson or no
Johnson.   Your pal,   JACK.

Washington, D.C., September 22.

FRIEND AL: Well I guess you know by this time that they didn't
get no two runs for me, only one, but I beat him just the same. I
beat him one to nothing and Callahan was so pleased that he give

me a ticket to the theater. I just got back from there and it is pretty late and I already have wrote you one letter to-day but I am going to sit up and tell you about it.

It was cloudy before the game started and when I was warming up I made the remark to Callahan that the dark day ought to make my speed good. He says Yes and of course it will handicap Johnson.

While Washington was takeing their practice their two coachers Schaefer and Altrock got out on the infield and cut up and I pretty near busted laughing at them. They certainly is funny Al. Callahan asked me what was I laughing at and I told him and he says That's the first time I ever seen a pitcher laugh when he was going to work against Johnson. He says Griffith is a pretty good fellow to give us something to laugh at before he shoots that guy at us.

I warmed up good and told Schalk not to ask me for my spitter much because my fast one looked faster than I ever seen it. He says it won't make much difference what you pitch to-day. I says Oh, yes, it will because Callahan thinks enough of me to work me against Johnson and I want to show him he didn't make no mistake. Then Gleason says No he didn't make no mistake. Wasteing Cicotte or Scotty would of been a mistake in this game.

Well, Johnson whiffs Weaver and Chase and makes Lord pop out in the first inning. I walked their first guy but I didn't give Milan nothing to bunt and finally he flied out. And then I whiffed the next two. On the bench Callahan says That's the way, boy. Keep that up and we got a chance.

Johnson had fanned four of us when I come up with two out in the third inning and he whiffed me to. I fouled one though that if I had ever got a good hold of I would of knocked out of the park. In the first seven innings we didn't have a hit off of him. They had got five or six lucky ones off of me and I had walked two or three, but I cut loose with all I had when they was men on and they couldn't do nothing with me. The only reason I walked so many was because my fast one was jumping so. Honest Al it was so fast that Evans the umpire couldn't see it half the time and he called a lot of balls that was right over the heart.

Well I come up in the eighth with two out and the score still nothing and nothing. I had whiffed the second time as well as the first but it was account of Evans missing one on me. The eighth started with Shanks muffing a fly ball off of Bodie. It was way out by the fence so he got two bases on it and he went to third while they was throwing Berger out. Then Schalk whiffed.

Callahan says Go up and try to meet one Jack. It might as well be you as anybody else. But your old pal didn't whiff this time Al. He gets two strikes on me with fast ones and then I passed up two bad ones. I took my healthy at the next one and slapped it over first base. I guess I could of made two bases on it but I didn't want to tire myself out. Anyway Bodie scored and I had them beat. And my hit was the only one we got off of him so I guess he is a pretty good pitcher after all Al.

They filled up the bases on me with one out in the ninth but it was pretty dark then and I made McBride and their catcher look like suckers with my speed.

I felt so good after the game that I drunk one of them pink cocktails. I don't know what their name is. And then I sent a post-card to poor little Violet. I don't care nothing about her but it don't hurt me none to try and cheer her up once in a while. We leave here Thursday night for home and they had ought to be two or three letters there for me from Hazel because I haven't heard from her lately. She must of lost my road addresses.

Your pal,   JACK.

P.S. I forgot to tell you what Callahan said after the game. He said I was a real pitcher now and he is going to use me in the city serious. If he does Al we will beat them Cubs sure.

Chicago, Illinois, September 27.

FRIEND AL: They wasn't no letter here at all from Hazel and I guess she must of been sick. Or maybe she didn't think it was worth while writeing as long as she is comeing next week.

I want to ask you to do me a favor Al and that is to see if you can find me a house down there. I will want to move in with Mrs. Keefe, don't that sound funny Al? sometime in the week of October twelfth. Old man Cutting's house or that yellow house across from you would be O.K. I would rather have the yellow one so as to be near you. Find out how much rent they want Al and if it is not no more than twelve dollars a month get it for me. We will buy our furniture here in Chi when Hazel comes.

We have a couple of days off now Al and then we play St. Louis two games here. Then Detroit comes to finish the season the third and fourth of October.

Your pal,   JACK.

Chicago, Illinois, October 3.

DEAR OLD AL: Thanks Al for getting the house. The one-year lease is O.K. You and Bertha and me and Hazel can have all sorts of good times together. I guess the walk needs repairs but I can fix that up when I come. We can stay at the hotel when we first get there.

I wish you could of came up for the city serious Al but anyway I want you and Bertha to be sure and come up for our wedding. I will let you know the date as soon as Hazel gets here.

The serious starts Tuesday and this town is wild over it. The Cubs finished second in their league and we was fifth in ours but that don't scare me none. We would of finished right on top if I had of been here all season.

Callahan pitched one of the bushers against Detroit this afternoon and they beat him bad. Callahan is saveing up Scott and Allen and Russell and Cicotte and I for the big show. Walsh isn't in no shape and neither is Benz. It looks like I would have a good deal to do because most of them others can't work no more than once in four days and Allen ain't no good at all.

We have a day to rest after to-morrow's game with the Tigers and then we go at them Cubs.   Your pal,   JACK.

P.S. I have got it figured that Hazel is fixing to surprise me by dropping in on me because I haven't heard nothing yet.

Chicago, Illinois, October 7.

FRIEND AL: Well Al you know by this time that they beat me to-day and tied up the serious. But I have still got plenty of time Al and I will get them before it is over. My arm wasn't feeling good Al and my fast ball didn't hop like it had ought to. But it was the rotten support I got that beat me. That lucky stiff Zimmerman was the only guy that got a real hit off of me and he must of shut his eyes and throwed his bat because the ball he hit was a foot over his head. And if they hadn't been makeing all them errors behind me they wouldn't of been nobody on bases when Zimmerman got that lucky scratch. The serious now stands one and one Al and it is a cinch we will beat them even if they are a bunch of lucky stiffs. They has been great big crowds at both games and it looks like as if we should ought to get over eight hundred dollars a peace if we win and we will win sure because I will beat them three straight if necessary.

But Al I have got bigger news than that for you and I am the happyest man in the world. I told you I had not heard from Hazel for a long time. To-night when I got back to my room they was a letter waiting for me from her.

Al she is married. Maybe you don't know why that makes me happy but I will tell you. She is married to Kid Levy the middle weight. I guess my thirty dollars is gone because in her letter she called me a cheap skate and she inclosed one one-cent stamp and two twos and said she was paying me for the glass of beer I once bought her. I bought her more than that Al but I won't make no holler. She all so said not for me to never come near her or her husband would bust my jaw. I ain't afraid of him or no one else Al but they ain't no danger of me ever bothering them. She was no good and I was sorry the minute I agreed to marry her.

But I was going to tell you why I am happy or maybe you can guess. Now I can make Violet my wife and she's got Hazel beat forty ways. She ain't nowheres near as big as Hazel but she's classier Al and she will make me a good wife. She ain't never asked me for no money.

I wrote her a letter the minute I got the good news and told her to come on over here at once at my expense. We will be married right after the serious is over and I want you and Bertha to be sure and stand up with us. I will wire you at my own expense the exact date.

It all seems like a dream now about Violet and I haveing our misunderstanding Al and I don't see how I ever could of accused her of sending me that postcard. You and Bertha will be just as crazy about her as I am when you see her Al. Just think Al I will be married inside of a week and to the only girl I ever could of been happy with instead of the woman I never really cared for except as a passing fancy. My happyness would be complete Al if I had not of let that woman steal thirty dollars off of me.

Your happy pal,   JACK.

P.S. Hazel probibly would of insisted on us takeing a trip to Niagara falls or somewheres but I know Violet will be perfectly satisfied if I take her right down to Bedford. Oh you little yellow house.

Chicago, Illinois, October 9.

FRIEND AL: Well Al we have got them beat three games to one now and will wind up the serious to-morrow sure. Callahan sent me in to save poor Allen yesterday and I stopped them dead. But I don't care now Al. I have lost all interest in the game and I don't care if Callahan pitches me to-morrow or not. My heart is just about broke Al and I wouldn't be able to do myself justice feeling the way I do.

I have lost Violet Al and just when I was figureing on being the happyest man in the world. We will get the big money but it won't do me no good. They can keep my share because I won't have no little girl to spend it on.

Her answer to my letter was waiting for me at home to-night. She is engaged to be married to Joe Hill the big lefthander Jennings got from Providence. Honest Al I don't see how he gets by. He ain't got no more curve ball than a rabbit and his fast one floats up there like a big balloon. He beat us the last game of the regular season here but it was because Callahan had a lot of bushers in the game.

I wish I had knew then that he was stealing my girl and I would of made Callahan pitch me against him. And when he come up to bat I would of beaned him. But I don't suppose you could hurt him by hitting him in the head. The big stiff. Their wedding ain't going to come off till next summer and by that time he will be pitching in the Southwestern Texas League for about fifty dollars a month.

Violet wrote that she wished me all the luck and happyness in the world but it is too late for me to be happy Al and I don't care what kind of luck I have now.

Al you will have to get rid of that lease for me. Fix it up the best way you can. Tell the old man I have changed my plans. I don't know just yet what I will do but maybe I will go to Australia with Mike Donlin's team. If I do I won't care if the boat goes down or not. I don't believe I will even come back to Bedford this winter. It would drive me wild to go past that little house every day and think how happy I might of been.

Maybe I will pitch to-morrow Al and if I do the serious will be over to-morrow night. I can beat them Cubs if I get any kind of decent support. But I don't care now Al.

Yours truly,   JACK.

Chicago, Illinois, October 12.

AL: Your letter received. If the old man won't call it off I guess I will have to try and rent the house to some one else. Do you know of any couple that wants one Al? It looks like I would have to come down there myself and fix things up someway. He is just mean enough to stick me with the house on my hands when I won't have no use for it.

They beat us the day before yesterday as you probibly know and it rained yesterday and to-day. The papers says it will be all O.K. to-morrow and Callahan tells me I am going to work. The Cub pitchers was all shot to peaces and the bad weather is just nuts for them because it will give Cheney a good rest. But I will beat him Al if they don't kick it away behind me.

I must close because I promised Allen the little lefthander that I would come over to his flat and play cards a while to-night and I must wash up and change my collar. Allen's wife's sister is visiting them again and I would give anything not to have to go over there. I am through with girls and don't want nothing to do with them.

I guess it is maybe a good thing it rained to-day because I dreamt about Violet last night and went out and got a couple of high balls before breakfast this morning. I hadn't never drank nothing before breakfast before and it made me kind of sick. But I am all O.K. now.   Your pal,   JACK.

Chicago, Illinois, October 13.

DEAR OLD AL: The serious is all over Al. We are the champions and I done it. I may be home the day after to-morrow or I may not come for a couple of days. I want to see Comiskey before I leave and fix up about my contract for next year. I won't sign for no less than five thousand and if he hands me a contract for less than that I will leave the White Sox flat on their back. I have got over fourteen hundred dollars now Al with the city serious money which was $814.30 and I don't have to worry.

Them reporters will have to give me a square deal this time Al. I had everything and the Cubs done well to score a run. I whiffed Zimmerman three times. Some of the boys say he ain't no hitter but he is a hitter and a good one Al only he could not touch the stuff I got. The umps give them their run because in the fourth inning I had Leach flatfooted off of second base and Weaver tagged him O.K. but the umps wouldn't call it. Then Schulte the lucky stiff happened to get a hold of one and pulled it past first base. I guess Chase must of been asleep. Anyway they scored but I don't care because we piled up six runs on Cheney and I drove in one of them myself with one of the prettiest singles you ever see. It was a spitter and I hit it like a shot. If I had hit it square it would of went out of the park.

Comiskey ought to feel pretty good about me winning and I guess he will give me a contract for anything I want. He will have to or I will go to the Federal League.

We are all invited to a show to-night and I am going with Allen and his wife and her sister Florence. She is O.K. Al and I guess she thinks the same about me. She must because she was out to the game to-day and seen me hand it to them. She maybe ain't as pretty as Violet and Hazel but as they say beauty isn't only so deep.

Well Al tell the boys I will be with them soon. I have gave up the idea of going to Australia because I would have to buy a evening full-dress suit and they tell me they cost pretty near fifty dollars.

Yours truly,   JACK.

Chicago, Illinois, October 14.

FRIEND AL: Never mind about that lease. I want the house after all Al and I have got the supprise of your life for you.

When I come home to Bedford I will bring my wife with me. I and Florence fixed things all up after the show last night and we are going to be married to-morrow morning. I am a busy man to-day Al because I have got to get the license and look round for furniture. And I have also got to buy some new cloths but they are haveing a sale on Cottage Grove Avenue at Clark's store and I know one of the clerks there.

I am the happyest man in the world Al. You and Bertha and I and Florence will have all kinds of good times together this winter because I know Bertha and Florence will like each other. Florence looks something like Bertha at that. I am glad I didn't get tied up with Violet or Hazel even if they was a little bit prettier than Florence.

Florence knows a lot about baseball for a girl and you would be supprised to hear her talk. She says I am the best pitcher in the league and she has saw them all. She all so says I am the best looking ball player she ever seen but you know how girls will kid a guy Al. You will like her O.K. I fell for her the first time I seen her.

Your old pal,   JACK.

P.S. I signed up for next year. Comiskey slapped me on the back when I went in to see him and told me I would be a star next year if I took good care of myself. I guess I am a star without waiting for next year Al. My contract calls for twenty-eight hundred a year which is a thousand more than I was getting. And it is pretty near a cinch that I will be in on the World Serious money next season.

P.S. I certainly am relieved about that lease. It would of been fierce to of had that place on my hands all winter and not getting any use out of it. Everything is all O.K. now. Oh you little yellow house.

THE BUSHER'S
HONEYMOON

◇

Chicago, Illinois, October 17.

FRIEND AL: Well Al it looks as if I would not be writeing so much to you now that I am a married man. Yes Al I and Florrie was married the day before yesterday just like I told you we was going to be and Al I am the happyest man in the world though I have spent $30 in the last 3 days incluseive. You was wise Al to get married in Bedford where not nothing is nearly half so dear. My expenses was as follows:

License	$ 2.00
Preist	3.50
Haircut and shave	.35
Shine	.05
Carfair	.45
New suit	14.50
Show tickets	3.00
Flowers	.50
Candy	.30
Hotel	4.50
Tobacco both kinds	.25

You see Al it costs a hole lot of money to get married here. The sum of what I have wrote down is $29.40 but as I told you I have spent $30 and I do not know what I have did with that other $0.60. My new brother-in-law Allen told me I should ought to give the preist $5 and I thought it should be about $2 the same as the license so I split the difference and give him $3.50. I never seen him before and probily won't never see him again so why should I give him

The Saturday Evening Post, July 11, 1914; *You Know Me Al*.

anything at all when it is his business to marry couples? But I like to do the right thing. You know me Al.

I thought we would be in Bedford by this time but Florrie wants to stay here a few more days because she says she wants to be with her sister. Allen and his wife is thinking about takeing a flat for the winter instead of going down to Waco Texas where they live. I don't see no sense in that when it costs so much to live here but it is none of my business if they want to throw their money away. But I am glad I got a wife with some sense though she kicked because I did not get no room with a bath which would cost me $2 a day instead of $1.50. I says I guess the clubhouse is still open yet and if I want a bath I can go over there and take the shower. She says Yes and I suppose I can go and jump in the lake. But she would not do that Al because the lake here is cold at this time of the year.

When I told you about my expenses I did not include in it the meals because we would be eating them if I was getting married or not getting married only I have to pay for six meals a day now instead of three and I didn't used to eat no lunch in the playing season except once in a while when I knowed I was not going to work that afternoon. I had a meal ticket which had not quite ran out over to a resturunt on Indiana Ave and we eat there for the first day except at night when I took Allen and his wife to the show with us and then he took us to a chop suye resturunt. I guess you have not never had no chop suye Al and I am here to tell you you have not missed nothing but when Allen was going to buy the supper what could I say? I could not say nothing.

Well yesterday and to-day we been eating at a resturunt on Cottage Grove Ave near the hotel and at the resturunt on Indiana that I had the meal ticket at only I do not like to buy no new meal ticket when I am not going to be round here no more than a few days. Well Al I guess the meals has cost me all together about $1.50 and I have eat very little myself. Florrie always wants desert ice cream or something and that runs up into money faster than regular stuff like stake and ham and eggs.

Well Al Florrie says it is time for me to keep my promise and take her to the moveing pictures which is $0.20 more because the one she likes round here costs a dime apeace. So I must close for this time and will see you soon.   Your pal,   JACK.

Chicago, Illinois, October 22.

AL: Just a note Al to tell you why I have not yet came to Bedford yet where I expected I would be long before this time. Allen and his wife have took a furnished flat for the winter and Allen's wife wants Florrie to stay here untill they get settled. Meentime it is costing me a hole lot of money at the hotel and for meals besides I am paying $10 a month rent for the house you got for me and what good am I getting out of it? But Florrie wants to help her sister and what can I say? Though I did make her promise she would not stay no longer than next Saturday at least. So I guess Al we will be home on the evening train Saturday and then may be I can save some money.

I know Al that you and Bertha will like Florrie when you get acquainted with her spesially Bertha though Florrie dresses pretty swell and spends a hole lot of time fusing with her face and her hair.

She says to me to-night Who are you writeing to and I told her Al Blanchard who I have told you about a good many times. She says I bet you are writeing to some girl and acted like as though she was kind of jealous. So I thought I would tease her a little and I says I don't know no girls except you and Violet and Hazel. Who is Violet and Hazel? she says. I kind of laughed and says Oh I guess I better not tell you and then she says I guess you will tell me. That made me kind of mad because no girl can't tell me what to do. She says Are you going to tell me? and I says No.

Then she says If you don't tell me I will go over to Marie's that is her sister Allen's wife and stay all night. I says Go on and she went downstairs but I guess she probily went to get a soda because she has some money of her own that I give her. This was about two hours ago and she is probily down in the hotel lobby now trying to scare me by makeing me believe she has went to her sister's. But she can't fool me Al and I am now going out to mail this letter and get a beer. I won't never tell her about Violet and Hazel if she is going to act like that. Yours truly, JACK.

Chicago, Illinois, October 24.

FRIEND AL: I guess I told you Al that we would be home Saturday evening. I have changed my mind. Allen and his wife has a spair bedroom and wants us to come there and stay a week or two. It won't cost nothing except they will probily want to go out to the moveing pictures nights and we will probily have to go along with them and I am a man Al that wants to pay his share and not be cheap.

I and Florrie had our first quarrle the other night. I guess I told you the start of it but I don't remember. I made some crack about Violet and Hazel just to tease Florrie and she wanted to know who they was and I would not tell her. So she gets sore and goes over to Marie's to stay all night. I was just kidding Al and was willing to tell her about them two poor girls whatever she wanted to know except that I don't like to brag about girls being stuck on me. So I goes over to Marie's after her and tells her all about them except that I turned them down cold at the last minute to marry her because I did not want her to get all swelled up. She made me sware that I did not never care nothing about them and that was easy because it was the truth. So she come back to the hotel with me just like I knowed she would when I ordered her to.

They must not be no mistake about who is the boss in my house. Some men let their wife run all over them but I am not that kind. You know me Al.

I must get busy and pack my suitcase if I am going to move over to Allen's. I sent three collars and a shirt to the laundrey this morning so even if we go over there to-night I will have to take another trip back this way in a day or two. I won't mind Al because they sell my kind of beer down to the corner and I never seen it sold nowheres else in Chi. You know the kind it is, eh Al? I wish I was lifting a few with you to-night.   Your pal,   JACK.

Chicago, Illinois, October 28.

DEAR OLD AL: Florrie and Marie has went downtown shopping because Florrie thinks she has got to have a new dress though she has got two changes of cloths now and I don't know what she can do with another one. I hope she don't find none to suit her though it would not hurt none if she got something for next spring at a reduckshon. I guess she must think I am Charles A. Comiskey or somebody. Allen has went to a colledge football game. One of the reporters give him a pass. I don't see nothing in football except a lot of scrapping between little slobs that I could lick the whole bunch of them so I did not care to go. The reporter is one of the guys that travled round with our club all summer. He called up and said he hadn't only the one pass but he was not hurting my feelings none because I would not go to no rotten football game if they payed me.

The flat across the hall from this here one is for rent furnished. They want $40 a month for it and I guess they think they must be lots of suckers running round loose. Marie was talking about it and says Why don't you and Florrie take it and then we can be right together all winter long and have some big times? Florrie says It would be all right with me. What about it Jack? I says What do you think I am? I don't have to live in no high price flat when I got a home in Bedford where they ain't no people trying to hold everybody up all the time. So they did not say no more about it when they seen I was in ernest. Nobody cannot tell me where I am going to live sister-in-law or no sister-in-law. If I was to rent the rotten old flat I would be paying $50 a month rent includeing the house down in Bedford. Fine chance Al.

Well Al I am lonesome and thirsty so more later.

Your pal, JACK.

Chicago, Illinois, November 2.

FRIEND AL: Well Al I got some big news for you. I am not comeing to Bedford this winter after all except to make a visit which I guess will be round Xmas. I changed my mind about that flat across the hall from the Allens and decided to take it after all. The people who was in it and owns the furniture says they would let us have it till the 1 of May if we would pay $42.50 a month which is only $2.50 a month more than they would of let us have it for for a short time. So you see we got a bargain because it is all furnished and everything and we won't have to blow no money on furniture besides the club goes to California the middle of Febuery so Florrie would not have no place to stay while I am away.

The Allens only subleased their flat from some other people till the 2 of Febuery and when I and Allen goes West Marie can come over and stay with Florrie so you see it is best all round. If we should of boughten furniture it would cost us in the neighborhood of $100 even without no piano and they is a piano in this here flat which makes it nice because Florrie plays pretty good with one hand and we can have lots of good times at home without it costing us nothing except just the bear liveing expenses. I consider myself lucky to of found out about this before it was too late and somebody else had of gotten the tip.

Now Al old pal I want to ask a great favor of you Al. I all ready have payed one month rent $10 on the house in Bedford and I want you to see the old man and see if he won't call off that lease. Why should I be paying $10 a month rent down there and $42.50 up here when the house down there is not no good to me because I am liveing up here all winter? See Al? Tell him I will gladly give him another month rent to call off the lease but don't tell him that if you don't have to. I want to be fare with him.

If you will do this favor for me, Al, I won't never forget it. Give my kindest to Bertha and tell her I am sorry I and Florrie won't see her right away but you see how it is Al.

Yours,   JACK.

Chicago, Illinois, November 30.

FRIEND AL: I have not wrote for a long time have I Al but I have been very busy. They was not enough furniture in the flat and we have been buying some more. They was enough for some people maybe but I and Florrie is the kind that won't have nothing but the best. The furniture them people had in the liveing room was oak but they had a bookcase bilt in in the flat that was mohoggeny and Florrie would not stand for no joke combination like that so she moved the oak chairs and table in to the spair bedroom and we went downtown to buy some mohoggeny. But it costs too much Al and we was feeling pretty bad about it when we seen some Sir Cashion walnut that was prettier even than the mohoggeny and not near so expensive. It is not no real Sir Cashion walnut but it is just as good and we got it reasonable. Then we got some mission chairs for the dining room because the old ones was just straw and was no good and we got a big lether couch for $9 that somebody can sleep on if we get to much company.

I hope you and Bertha can come up for the holidays and see how comfertible we are fixed. That is all the new furniture we have boughten but Florrie set her heart on some old Rose drapes and a red table lamp that is the biggest you ever seen Al and I did not have the heart to say no. The hole thing cost me in the neighborhood of $110 which is very little for what we got and then it will always be ourn even when we move away from this flat though we will have to leave the furniture that belongs to the other people but their part of it is not no good anyway.

I guess I told you Al how much money I had when the season ended. It was $1400 all told includeing the city serious money. Well

Al I got in the neighborhood of $800 left because I give $200 to Florrie to send down to Texas to her other sister who had a bad egg for a husband that managed a club in the Texas Oklahoma League and this was the money she had to pay to get the divorce. I am glad Al that I was lucky enough to marry happy and get a good girl for my wife that has got some sense and besides if I have got $800 left I should not worry as they say.   Your pal,   JACK.

Chicago, Illinois, December 7.

DEAR OLD AL: No I was in ernest Al when I says that I wanted you and Bertha to come up here for the holidays. I know I told you that I might come to Bedford for the holidays but that is all off. I have gave up the idea of comeing to Bedford for the holidays and I want you to be sure and come up here for the holidays and I will show you a good time. I would love to have Bertha come to and she can come if she wants to only Florrie don't know if she would have a good time or not and thinks maybe she would rather stay in Bedford and you come alone. But be sure and have Bertha come if she wants to come but maybe she would not injoy it. You know best Al.

I don't think the old man give me no square deal on that lease but if he wants to stick me all right. I am grateful to you Al for trying to fix it up but maybe you could of did better if you had of went at it in a different way. I am not finding no fault with my old pal though. Don't think that. When I have a pal I am the man to stick to him threw thick and thin. If the old man is going to hold me to that lease I guess I will have to stand it and I guess I won't starv to death for no $10 a month because I am going to get $2800 next year besides the city serious money and maybe we will get into the World Serious too. I know we will if Callahan will pitch me every 3d day like I wanted him to last season. But if you had of approached the old man in a different way maybe you could of fixed it up. I wish you would try it again Al if it is not no trouble.

We had Allen and his wife here for thanksgiveing dinner and the dinner cost me better than $5. I thought we had enough to eat to last a week but about six o'clock at night Florrie and Marie said they was hungry and we went downtown and had dinner all over again and I payed for it and it cost me $5 more. Allen was all ready to pay for it when Florrie said No this day's treat is on us so I had to pay for it but I don't see why she did not wait and let me do the talking. I was going to pay for it any way.

Be sure and come and visit us for the holidays Al and of coarse if Bertha wants to come bring her along. We will be glad to see you both. I won't never go back on a friend and pal. You know me Al.

Your old pal,   JACK.

Chicago, Illinois, December 20.

FRIEND AL: I don't see what can be the matter with Bertha because you know Al we would not care how she dressed and would not make no kick if she come up here in a night gown. She did not have no license to say we was to swell for her because we did not never think of nothing like that. I wish you would talk to her again Al and tell her she need not get sore on me and that both her and you is welcome at my house any time I ask you to come. See if you can't make her change her mind Al because I feel like as if she must of took offense at something I may of wrote you. I am sorry you and her are not comeing but I suppose you know best. Only we was getting all ready for you and Florrie said only the other day that she wished the holidays was over but that was before she knowed you was not comeing. I hope you can come Al.

Well Al I guess there is not no use talking to the old man no more. You have did the best you could but I wish I could of came down there and talked to him. I will pay him his rotten old $10 a month and the next time I come to Bedford and meet him on the street I will bust his jaw. I know he is a old man Al but I don't like to see nobody get the best of me and I am sorry I ever asked him to let me off. Some of them old skinflints has no heart Al but why should I fight with a old man over chicken feed like $10? Florrie says a star pitcher like I should not ought never to scrap about little things and I guess she is right Al so I will pay the old man his $10 a month if I have to.

Florrie says she is jealous of me writeing to you so much and she says she would like to meet this great old pal of mine. I would like to have her meet you to Al and I would like to have you change your mind and come and visit us and I am sorry you can't come Al.

Yours truly,   JACK.

Chicago, Illinois, December 27.

OLD PAL: I guess all these lefthanders is alike though I thought this Allen had some sense. I thought he was different from the most and was not no rummy but they are all alike Al and they are all lucky that somebody don't hit them over the head with a ax and kill them but I guess at that you could not hurt no lefthanders by hitting them over the head. We was all down on State St. the day before Xmas and the girls was all tired out and ready to go home but Allen says No I guess we better stick down a while because now the crowds is out and it will be fun to watch them. So we walked up and down State St. about a hour longer and finally we come in front of a big jewlry store window and in it was a swell dimond ring that was marked $100. It was a ladies' ring so Marie says to Allen Why don't you buy that for me? And Allen says Do you really want it? And she says she did.

So we tells the girls to wait and we goes over to a salloon where Allen has got a friend and gets a check cashed and we come back and he bought the ring. Then Florrie looks like as though she was getting all ready to cry and I asked her what was the matter and she says I had not boughten her no ring not even when we was engaged. So I and Allen goes back to the salloon and I gets a check cashed and we come back and bought another ring but I did not think the ring Allen had boughten was worth no $100 so I gets one for $75. Now Al you know I am not makeing no kick on spending a little money for a present for my own wife but I had allready boughten her a rist watch for $15 and a rist watch was just what she had wanted. I was willing to give her the ring if she had not of wanted the rist watch more than the ring but when I give her the ring I kept the rist watch and did not tell her nothing about it.

Well I come downtown alone the day after Xmas and they would not take the rist watch back in the store where I got it. So I am going to give it to her for a New Year's present and I guess that will make Allen feel like a dirty doose. But I guess you cannot hurt no left-hander's feelings at that. They are all alike. But Allen has not got nothing but a dinky curve ball and a fast ball that looks like my slow one. If Comiskey was not good hearted he would of sold him long ago.

I sent you and Bertha a cut glass dish Al which was the best I could get for the money and it was pretty high pricet at that. We was glad to get the pretty pincushions from you and Bertha and Florrie says to tell you that we are well supplied with pincushions

now because the ones you sent makes a even half dozen. Thanks Al
for remembering us and thank Bertha too though I guess you paid
for them.   Your pal,   JACK.

Chicago, Illinois, Januery 3.

OLD PAL: Al I been pretty sick ever since New Year's eve. We
had a table at 1 of the swell resturunts downtown and I never seen
so much wine drank in my life. I would rather of had beer but they
would not sell us none so I found out that they was a certain kind
that you can get for $1 a bottle and it is just as good as the kind that
has got all them fancy names but this left-hander starts ordering some
other kind about 11 oclock and it was $5 a bottle and the girls both
says they liked it better. I could not see a hole lot of difference
myself and I would of gave $0.20 for a big stine of my kind of beer.
You know me Al. Well Al you know they is not nobody that can
drink more than your old pal and I was all O.K. at one oclock but
I seen the girls was getting kind of sleepy so I says we better go
home.

Then Marie says Oh, shut up and don't be no quiter. I says You
better shut up yourself and not be telling me to shut up, and she
says What will you do if I don't shut up? And I says I would bust
her in the jaw. But you know Al I would not think of busting no
girl. Then Florrie says You better not start nothing because you had
to much to drink or you would not be talking about busting girls in
the jaw. Then I says I don't care if it is a girl I bust or a lefthander.
I did not mean nothing at all Al but Marie says I had insulted Allen
and he gets up and slaps my face. Well Al I am not going to stand
that from nobody not even if he is my brother-in-law and a lefthander
that has not got enough speed to brake a pain of glass.

So I give him a good beating and the waiters butts in and puts us
all out for fighting and I and Florrie comes home in a taxi and Allen
and his wife don't get in till about 5 oclock so I guess she must of
had to of took him to a doctor to get fixed up. I been in bed ever
since till just this morning kind of sick to my stumach. I guess I
must of eat something that did not agree with me. Allen come
over after breakfast this morning and asked me was I all right so I
guess he is not sore over the beating I give him or else he wants
to make friends because he has saw that I am a bad guy to monkey
with.

Florrie tells me a little while ago that she paid the hole bill at the resturunt with my money because Allen was broke so you see what kind of a cheap skate he is Al and some day I am going to bust his jaw. She won't tell me how much the bill was and I won't ask her to no more because we had a good time outside of the fight and what do I care if we spent a little money?

Yours truly,   JACK.

Chicago, Illinois, January 20.

FRIEND AL: Allen and his wife have gave up the flat across the hall from us and come over to live with us because we got a spair bedroom and why should they not have the bennifit of it? But it is pretty hard for the girls to have to cook and do the work when they is four of us so I have a hired girl who does it all for $7 a week. It is great stuff Al because now we can go round as we please and don't have to wait for no dishes to be washed or nothing. We generally almost always has dinner downtown in the evening so it is pretty soft for the girl too. She don't generally have no more than one meal to get because we generally run round downtown till late and don't get up till about noon.

That sounds funny don't it Al, when I used to get up at 5 every morning down home. Well Al I can tell you something else that may sound funny and that is that I lost my taste for beer. I don't seem to care for it no more and I found I can stand allmost as many drinks of other stuff as I could of beer. I guess Al they is not nobody ever lived can drink more and stand up better under it than me. I make the girls and Allen quit every night.

I only got just time to write you this short note because Florrie and Marie is giving a big party to-night and I and Allen have got to beat it out of the house and stay out of the way till they get things ready. It is Marie's berthday and she says she is 22 but say Al if she is 22 Kid Gleason is 30. Well Al the girls says we must blow so I will run out and mail this letter.   Yours truly,   JACK.

Chicago, Illinois, January 31.

AL: Allen is going to take Marie with him on the training trip to California and of course Florrie has been at me to take her along. I told her postivly that she can't go. I can't afford no stunt like that but still I am up against it to know what to do with her while we are on the trip because Marie won't be here to stay with her. I don't like to leave her here all alone but they is nothing to it Al I can't afford to take her along. She says I don't see why you can't take me if Allen takes Marie. And I says That stuff is all O.K. for Allen because him and Marie has been grafting off of us all winter. And then she gets mad and tells me I should not ought to say her sister was no grafter. I did not mean nothing like that Al but you don't never know when a woman is going to take offense.

If our furniture was down in Bedford everything would be all O.K. because I could leave her there and I would feel all O.K. because I would know that you and Bertha would see that she was getting along O.K. But they would not be no sense in sending her down to a house that has not no furniture in it. I wish I knowed somewheres where she could visit Al. I would be willing to pay her bord even.

Well Al enough for this time.   Your old pal,   JACK.

Chicago, Illinois, Febuery 4.

FRIEND AL: You are a real old pal Al and I certainly am greatful to you for the invatation. I have not told Florrie about it yet but I am sure she will be tickled to death and it is certainly kind of you old pal. I did not never dream of nothing like that. I note what you say Al about not excepting no bord but I think it would be better and I would feel better if you would take something say about $2 a week.

I know Bertha will like Florrie and that they will get along O.K. together because Florrie can learn her how to make her cloths look good and fix her hair and fix up her face. I feel like as if you had took a big load off of me Al and I won't never forget it.

If you don't think I should pay no bord for Florrie all right. Suit yourself about that old pal.

We are leaveing here the 20 of Febuery and if you don't mind I will bring Florrie down to you about the 18. I would like to see the old bunch again and spesially you and Bertha.

Yours,   JACK.

P.S. We will only be away till April 14 and that is just a nice visit. I wish we did not have no flat on our hands.

Chicago, Illinois, Febuery 9.

OLD PAL: I want to thank you for asking Florrie to come down there and visit you Al but I find she can't get away. I did not know she had no engagements but she says she may go down to her folks in Texas and she don't want to say that she will come to visit you when it is so indefanate. So thank you just the same Al and thank Bertha too.

Florrie is still at me to take her along to California but honest Al I can't do it. I am right down to my last $50 and I have not payed no rent for this month. I owe the hired girl 2 weeks' salery and both I and Florrie needs some new cloths.

Florrie has just came in since I started writeing this letter and we have been talking some more about California and she says maybe if I would ask Comiskey he would take her along as the club's guest. I had not never thought of that Al and maybe he would because he is a pretty good scout and I guess I will go and see him about it. The league has its skedule meeting here to-morrow and may be I can see him down to the hotel where they meet at. I am so worried Al that I can't write no more but I will tell you how I come out with Comiskey.   Your pal,   JACK.

Chicago, Illinois, Febuery 11.

FRIEND AL: I am up against it right Al and I don't know where I am going to head in at. I went down to the hotel where the league was holding its skedule meeting at and I seen Comiskey and got some money off of the club but I owe all the money I got off of them and I am still wondering what to do about Florrie.

Comiskey was busy in the meeting when I went down there and they was not no chance to see him for a while so I and Allen and some of the boys hung round and had a few drinks and fanned. This here Joe Hill the busher that Detroit has got that Violet is hooked up to was round the hotel. I don't know what for but I felt like busting his jaw only the boys told me I had better not do nothing because I might kill him and any way he probily won't be in the league much longer. Well finally Comiskey got threw the meeting and I seen him and he says Hello young man what can I do for you? And I says I would like to get $100 advance money. He says Have you been takeing care of yourself down in Bedford? And I told him I had been liveing here all winter and it did not seem to make no hit with him though I don't see what business it is of hisn where I live.

So I says I had been takeing good care of myself. And I have Al. You know that. So he says I should come to the ball park the next day which is to-day and he would have the secretary take care of me but I says I could not wait and so he give me $100 out of his pocket and says he would have it charged against my salery. I was just going to brace him about the California trip when he got away and went back to the meeting.

Well Al I hung round with the bunch waiting for him to get threw again and we had some more drinks and finally Comiskey was threw again and I braced him in the lobby and asked him if it was all right to take my wife along to California. He says Sure they would be glad to have her along. And then I says Would the club pay her fair? He says I guess you must of spent that $100 buying some nerve. He says Have you not got no sisters that would like to go along to? He says Does your wife insist on the drawing room or will she take a lower birth? He says Is my special train good enough for her?

Then he turns away from me and I guess some of the boys must of heard the stuff he pulled because they was laughing when he went away but I did not see nothing to laugh at. But I guess he ment that I would have to pay her fair if she goes along and that is out of the question Al. I am up against it and I don't know where I am going to head in at.   Your pal,   JACK.

Chicago, Illinois, Febuery 12.

DEAR OLD AL: I guess everything will be all O.K. now at least I am hopeing it will. When I told Florrie about how I come out with Comiskey she bawled her head off and I thought for a while I was going to have to call a doctor or something but pretty soon she cut it out and we sat there a while without saying nothing. Then she says If you could get your salery razed a couple of hundred dollars a year would you borrow the money ahead somewheres and take me along to California? I says Yes I would if I could get a couple hundred dollars more salery but how could I do that when I had signed a contract for $2800 last fall allready? She says Don't you think you are worth more than $2800? And I says Yes of coarse I was worth more than $2800. She says Well if you will go and talk the right way to Comiskey I believe he will give you $3000 but you must be sure you go at it the right way and don't go and ball it all up.

Well we argude about it a while because I don't want to hold nobody up Al but finally I says I would. It would not be holding nobody up anyway because I am worth $3000 to the club if I am worth a nichol. The papers is all saying that the club has got a good chance to win the pennant this year and talking about the pitching staff and I guess they would not be no pitching staff much if it was not for I and one or two others—about one other I guess.

So it looks like as if everything will be all O.K. now Al. I am going to the office over to the park to see him the first thing in the morning and I am pretty sure that I will get what I am after because if I do not he will see that I am going to quit and then he will see what he is up against and not let me get away.

I will let you know how I come out.   Your pal,   JACK.

Chicago, Illinois, Febuery 14.

FRIEND AL: Al old pal I have got a big supprise for you. I am going to the Federal League. I had a run in with Comiskey yesterday and I guess I told him a thing or 2. I guess he would of been glad to sign me at my own figure before I got threw but I was so mad I would not give him no chance to offer me another contract.

I got out to the park at 9 oclock yesterday morning and it was a hour before he showed up and then he kept me waiting another hour so I was pretty sore when I finally went in to see him. He says Well young man what can I do for you? I says I come to see about my contract. He says Do you want to sign up for next year all ready? I says No I am talking about this year. He says I thought I and you talked business last fall. And I says Yes but now I think I am worth more money and I want to sign a contract for $3000. He says If you behave yourself and work good this year I will see that you are took care of. But I says That won't do because I have got to be sure I am going to get $3000.

Then he says I am not sure you are going to get anything. I says What do you mean? And he says I have gave you a very fare contract and if you don't want to live up to it that is your own business. So I give him a awful call Al and told him I would jump to the Federal League. He says Oh, I would not do that if I was you. They are haveing a hard enough time as it is. So I says something back to him and he did not say nothing to me and I beat it out of the office.

I have not told Florrie about the Federal League business yet as I am going to give her a big supprise. I bet they will take her along with me on the training trip and pay her fair but even if they don't I should not worry because I will make them give me a contract for $4000 a year and then I can afford to take her with me on all the trips.

I will go down and see Tinker to-morrow morning and I will write you to-morrow night Al how much salery they are going to give me. But I won't sign for no less than $4000. You know me Al.

                                    Yours,   JACK.

Chicago, Illinois, Febuery 15.

OLD PAL: It is pretty near midnight Al but I been to bed a couple of times and I can't get no sleep. I am worried to death Al and I don't know where I am going to head in at. Maybe I will go out and buy a gun Al and end it all and I guess it would be better for everybody. But I cannot do that Al because I have not got the money to buy a gun with.

I went down to see Tinker about signing up with the Federal League and he was busy in the office when I come in. Pretty soon Buck Perry the pitcher that was with Boston last year come out and seen me and as Tinker was still busy we went out and had a drink together. Buck shows me a contract for $5000 a year and Tinker had allso gave him a $500 bonus. So pretty soon I went up to the office and pretty soon Tinker seen me and called me into his private office and asked what did I want. I says I was ready to jump for $4000 and a bonus. He says I thought you was signed up with the White Sox. I says Yes I was but I was not satisfied. He says That does not make no difference to me if you are satisfied or not. You ought to of came to me before you signed a contract. I says I did not know enough but I know better now. He says Well it is to late now. We cannot have nothing to do with you because you have went and signed a contract with the White Sox. I argude with him a while and asked him to come out and have a drink so we could talk it over but he said he was busy so they was nothing for me to do but blow.

So I am not going to the Federal League Al and I will not go with the White Sox because I have got a raw deal. Comiskey will be sorry for what he done when his team starts the season and is up against it for good pitchers and then he will probily be willing to give me

anything I ask for but that don't do me no good now Al. I am way
in debt and no chance to get no money from nobody. I wish I had
of stayed with Terre Haute Al and never saw this league.

Your pal,   JACK.

Chicago, Illinois, Febuery 17.

FRIEND AL: Al don't never let nobody tell you that these here
lefthanders is right. This Allen my own brother-in-law who married
sisters has been grafting and spongeing on me all winter Al. Look
what he done to me now Al. You know how hard I been up against
it for money and I know he has got plenty of it because I seen it on
him. Well Al I was scared to tell Florrie I was cleaned out and so I
went to Allen yesterday and says I had to have $100 right away
because I owed the rent and owed the hired girl's salery and could
not even pay no grocery bill. And he says No he could not let me
have none because he has got to save all his money to take his wife
on the trip to California. And here he has been liveing on me all
winter and maybe I could of took my wife to California if I had not
of spent all my money takeing care of this no good lefthander and
his wife. And Al honest he has not got a thing and ought not to be
in the league. He gets by with a dinky curve ball and has not got no
more smoke than a rabbit or something.

Well Al I felt like busting him in the jaw but then I thought No
I might kill him and then I would have Marie and Florrie both to
take care of and God knows one of them is enough besides paying
his funeral expenses. So I walked away from him without takeing a
crack at him and went into the other room where Florrie and Marie
was at. I says to Marie I says Marie I wish you would go in the other
room a minute because I want to talk to Florrie. So Marie beats it
into the other room and then I tells Florrie all about what Comiskey
and the Federal League done to me. She bawled something awful
and then she says I was no good and she wished she had not never
married me. I says I wisht it too and then she says Do you mean
that and starts to cry.

I told her I was sorry I says that because they is not no use fusing
with girls Al specially when they is your wife. She says No California
trip for me and then she says What are you going to do? And I says
I did not know. She says Well if I was a man I would do something.
So then I got mad and I says I will do something. So I went down

to the corner salloon and started in to get good and drunk but I could not do it Al because I did not have the money.

Well old pal I am going to ask you a big favor and it is this. I want you to send me $100 Al for just a few days till I can get on my feet. I do not know when I can pay it back Al but I guess you know the money is good and I know you have got it. Who would not have it when they live in Bedford? And besides I let you take $20 in June 4 years ago Al and you give it back but I would not have said nothing to you if you had of kept it. Let me hear from you right away old pal.   Yours truly,   JACK.

Chicago, Illinois, Febuery 19.

AL: I am certainly greatful to you Al for the $100 which come just a little while ago. I will pay the rent with it and part of the grocery bill and I guess the hired girl will have to wait a while for hern but she is sure to get it because I don't never forget my debts. I have changed my mind about the White Sox and I am going to go on the trip and take Florrie along because I don't think it would not be right to leave her here alone in Chi when her sister and all of us is going.

I am going over to the ball park and up in the office pretty soon to see about it. I will tell Comiskey I changed my mind and he will be glad to get me back because the club has not got no chance to finish nowheres without me. But I won't go on no trip or give the club my services without them giveing me some more advance money so as I can take Florrie along with me because Al I would not go without her.

Maybe Comiskey will make my salery $3000 like I wanted him to when he sees I am willing to be a good fellow and go along with him and when he knows that the Federal League would of gladly gave me $4000 if I had not of signed no contract with the White Sox.

I think I will ask him for $200 advance money Al and if I get it may be I can send part of your $100 back to you but I know you cannot be in no hurry Al though you says you wanted it back as soon as possible. You could not be very hard up Al because it don't cost near so much to live in Bedford as it does up here.

Anyway I will let you know how I come out with Comiskey and I will write you as soon as I get out to Paso Robles if I don't get no time to write you before I leave.   Your pal,   JACK.

P.S. I have took good care of myself all winter Al and I guess I ought to have a great season.

P.S. Florrie is tickled to death about going along and her and I will have some time together out there on the Coast if I can get some money somewheres.

Chicago, Illinois, Febuery 21.

FRIEND AL: I have not got the heart to write this letter to you Al. I am up here in my $42.50 a month flat and the club has went to California and Florrie has went too. I am flat broke Al and all I am asking you is to send me enough money to pay my fair to Bedford and they and all their leagues can go to hell Al.

I was out to the ball park early yesterday morning and some of the boys was there allready fanning and kidding each other. They tried to kid me to when I come in but I guess I give them as good as they give me. I was not in no mind for kidding Al because I was there on business and I wanted to see Comiskey and get it done with.

Well the secretary come in finally and I went up to him and says I wanted to see Comiskey right away. He says The boss was busy and what did I want to see him about and I says I wanted to get some advance money because I was going to take my wife on the trip. He says This would be a fine time to be telling us about it even if you was going on that trip.

And I says What do you mean? And he says You are not going on no trip with us because we have got wavers on you and you are sold to Milwaukee.

Honest Al I thought he was kidding at first and I was waiting for him to laugh but he did not laugh and finally I says What do you mean? And he says Cannot you understand no English? You are sold to Milwaukee. Then I says I want to see the boss. He says It won't do you no good to see the boss and he is to busy to see you. I says I want to get some money. And he says You cannot get no money from this club and all you get is your fair to Milwaukee. I says I am not going to no Milwaukee anyway and he says I should not worry about that. Suit yourself.

Well Al I told some of the boys about it and they was pretty sore and says I ought to bust the secretary in the jaw and I was going to do it when I thought No I better not because he is a little guy and I might kill him.

I looked all over for Kid Gleason but he was not nowheres round and they told me he would not get into town till late in the afternoon. If I could of saw him Al he would of fixed me all up. I asked 3 or 4 of the boys for some money but they says they was all broke.

But I have not told you the worst of it yet Al. When I come back to the flat Allen and Marie and Florrie was busy packing up and they asked me how I come out. I told them and Allen just stood there stareing like a big rummy but Marie and Florrie both begin to cry and I almost felt like as if I would like to cry to only I am not no baby Al.

Well Al I told Florrie she might just as well quit packing and make up her mind that she was not going nowheres till I got money enough to go to Bedford where I belong. She kept right on crying and it got so I could not stand it no more so I went out to get a drink because I still had just about a dollar left yet.

It was about 2 oclock when I left the flat and pretty near 5 when I come back because I had ran in to some fans that knowed who I was and would not let me get away and besides I did not want to see no more of Allen and Marie till they was out of the house and on their way.

But when I come in Al they was nobody there. They was not nothing there except the furniture and a few of my things scattered round. I sit down for a few minutes because I guess I must of had to much to drink but finally I seen a note on the table addressed to me and I seen it was Florrie's writeing.

I do not remember just what was there in the note Al because I tore it up the minute I read it but it was something about I could not support no wife and Allen had gave her enough money to go back to Texas and she was going on the 6 oclock train and it would not do me no good to try and stop her.

Well Al they was not no danger of me trying to stop her. She was not no good Al and I wisht I had not of never saw either she or her sister or my brother-in-law.

For a minute I thought I would follow Allen and his wife down to the deepo where the special train was to pull out of and wait till I see him and punch his jaw but I seen that would not get me nothing.

So here I am all alone Al and I will have to stay here till you send me the money to come home. You better send me $25 because I have got a few little debts I should ought to pay before I leave town.

I am not going to Milwaukee Al because I did not get no decent deal and nobody cannot make no sucker out of me.

Please hurry up with the $25 Al old friend because I am sick and tired of Chi and want to get back there with my old pal.

Yours,   JACK.

P.S. Al I wish I had of took poor little Violet when she was so stuck on me.

A NEW BUSHER
BREAKS IN

◇

Chicago, Illinois, March 2.
FRIEND AL: Al that peace in the paper was all O.K. and the right dope just like you said. I seen president Johnson the president of the league to-day and he told me the peace in the papers was the right dope and Comiskey did not have no right to sell me to Milwaukee because the Detroit Club had never gave no.wavers on me. He says the Detroit Club was late in fileing their claim and Comiskey must of tooken it for granted that they was going to wave but president Johnson was pretty sore about it at that and says Comiskey did not have no right to sell me till he was positive that they was not no team that wanted me.

It will probily cost Comiskey some money for acting like he done and not paying no attention to the rules and I would not be supprised if president Johnson had him throwed out of the league.

Well I asked president Johnson should I report at once to the Detroit Club down south and he says No you better wait till you hear from Comiskey and I says What has Comiskey got to do with it now? And he says Comiskey will own you till he sells you to Detroit or somewheres else. So I will have to go out to the ball park to-morrow and see is they any mail for me there because I probily will get a letter from Comiskey telling me I am sold to Detroit.

If I had of thought at the time I would of knew that Detroit never would give no wavers on me after the way I showed Cobb and Crawford up last fall and I might of knew too that Detroit is in the market for good pitchers because they got a rotten pitching staff but they won't have no rotten staff when I get with them.

If necessary I will pitch every other day for Jennings and if I do

The Saturday Evening Post, September 12, 1914; *You Know Me Al.*

we will win the pennant sure because Detroit has got a club that can get 2 or 3 runs every day and all as I need to win most of my games is 1 run. I can't hardly wait till Jennings works me against the White Sox and what I will do to them will be a plenty. It don't take no pitching to beat them anyway and when they get up against a pitcher like I they might as well leave their bats in the bag for all the good their bats will do them.

I guess Cobb and Crawford will be glad to have me on the Detroit Club because then they won't never have to hit against me except in practice and I won't pitch my best in practice because they will be teammates of mine and I don't never like to show none of my teammates up. At that though I don't suppose Jennings will let me do much pitching in practice because when he gets a hold of a good pitcher he won't want me to take no chances of throwing my arm away in practice.

Al just think how funny it will be to have me pitching for the Tigers in the same town where Violet lives and pitching on the same club with her husband. It will not be so funny for Violet and her husband though because when she has a chance to see me work regular she will find out what a mistake she made takeing that left-hander instead of a man that has got some future and soon will be makeing 5 or $6000 a year because I won't sign with Detroit for no less than $5000 at most. Of coarse I could of had her if I had of wanted to but still and all it will make her feel pretty sick to see me winning games for Detroit while her husband is batting fungos and getting splinters in his unie from slideing up and down the bench.

As for her husband the first time he opens his clam to me I will haul off and bust him one in the jaw but I guess he will know more than to start trouble with a man of my size and who is going to be one of their stars while he is just holding down a job because they feel sorry for him. I wish he could of got the girl I married instead of the one he got and I bet she would of drove him crazy. But I guess you can't drive a left-hander crazyer than he is to begin with.

I have not heard nothing from Florrie Al and I don't want to hear nothing. I and her is better apart and I wish she would sew me for a bill of divorce so she could not go round claiming she is my wife and disgraceing my name. If she would consent to sew me for a bill of divorce I would gladly pay all the expenses and settle with her for any sum of money she wants say about $75.00 or $100.00 and they is no reason I should give her a nichol after the way her and her sister Marie and her brother-in-law Allen grafted off of me.

Probily I could sew her for a bill of divorce but they tell me it costs money to sew and if you just lay low and let the other side do the sewing it don't cost you a nichol.

It is pretty late Al and I have got to get up early to-morrow and go to the ball park and see is they any mail for me. I will let you know what I hear old pal.   Your old pal,   JACK.

Chicago, Illinois, March 4.

AL: I am up against it again. I went out to the ball park office yesterday and they was nobody there except John somebody who is asst secretary and all the rest of them is out on the Coast with the team. Maybe this here John was trying to kid me but this is what he told me. First I says Is they a letter here for me? And he says No. And I says I was expecting word from Comiskey that I should join the Detroit Club and he says What makes you think you are going to Detroit? I says Comiskey asked wavers on me and Detroit did not give no wavers. He says Well that is not no sign that you are going to Detroit. If Comiskey can't get you out of the league he will probily keep you himself and it is a cinch he is not going to give no pitcher to Detroit no matter how rotten he is.

I says What do you mean? And he says You just stick round town till you hear from Comiskey and I guess you will hear pretty soon because he is comeing back from the Coast next Saturday. I says Well the only thing he can tell me is to report to Detroit because I won't never pitch again for the White Sox. Then John gets fresh and says I suppose you will quit the game and live on your saveings and then I blowed out of the office because I was scared I would loose my temper and break something.

So you see Al what I am up against. I won't never pitch for the White Sox again and I want to get with the Detroit Club but how can I if Comiskey won't let me go? All I can do is stick round till next Saturday and then I will see Comiskey and I guess when I tell him what I think of him he will be glad to let me go to Detroit or anywheres else. I will have something on him this time because I know that he did not pay no attention to the rules when he told me I was sold to Milwaukee and if he tries to slip something over on me I will tell president Johnson of the league all about it and then you will see where Comiskey heads in at.

Al old pal that $25.00 you give me at the station the other day is all shot to peaces and I must ask you to let me have $25.00 more which will make $75.00 all togegher includeing the $25.00 you sent me before I come home. I hate to ask you this favor old pal but I know you have got the money. If I am sold to Detroit I will get some advance money and pay up all my dedts incluseive.

If he don't let me go to Detroit I will make him come across with part of my salery for this year even if I don't pitch for him because I signed a contract and was ready to do my end of it and would of if he had not of been nasty and tried to slip something over on me. If he refuses to come across I will hire a attorney at law and he will get it all. So Al you see you have got a cinch on getting back what you lone me but I guess you know that Al without all this talk because you have been my old pal for a good many years and I have allways treated you square and tried to make you feel that I and you was equals and that my success was not going to make me forget my old friends.

Wherever I pitch this year I will insist on a salery of 5 or $6000 a year. So you see on my first pay day I will have enough to pay you up and settle the rest of my dedts but I am not going to pay no more rent for this rotten flat because they tell me if a man don't pay no rent for a while they will put him out. Let them put me out. I should not worry but will go and rent my old room that I had before I met Florrie and got into all this trouble.

The sooner you can send me that $35.00 the better and then I will owe you $85.00 incluseive and I will write and let you now how I come out with Comiskey.   Your pal,   JACK.

Chicago, Illinois, March 12.

FRIEND AL: I got another big supprise for you and this is it I am going to pitch for the White Sox after all. If Comiskey was not a old man I guess I would of lost my temper and beat him up but I am glad now that I kept my temper and did not loose it because I forced him to make a lot of consessions and now it looks like as though I would have a big year both pitching and money.

He got back to town yesterday morning and showed up to his office in the afternoon and I was there waiting for him. He would not see me for a while but finally I acted like as though I was getting tired of waiting and I guess the secretary got scared that I would beat it out of the office and leave them all in the lerch. Anyway he went in and spoke to Comiskey and then come out and says the boss was ready to see me. When I went into the office where he was at he says Well young man what can I do for you? And I says I want you to give me my release so as I can join the Detroit Club down South and get in shape. Then he says What makes you think you are going to join the Detroit Club? Because we need you here. I says Then why did you try to sell me to Milwaukee? But you could not because you could not get no wavers.

Then he says I thought I was doing you a favor by sending you to Milwaukee because they make a lot of beer up there. I says What do you mean? He says You been keeping in shape all this winter by trying to drink this town dry and besides that you tried to hold me up for more money when you allready had signed a contract allready and so I was going to send you to Milwaukee and learn you something and besides you tried to go with the Federal League but they would not take you because they was scared to.

I don't know where he found out all that stuff at Al and besides he was wrong when he says I was drinking to much because they is not nobody that can drink more than me and not be effected. But I did not say nothing because I was scared I would forget myself and call him some name and he is a old man. Yes I did say something. I says Well I guess you found out that you could not get me out of the league and then he says Don't never think I could not get you out of the league. If you think I can't send you to Milwaukee I will prove it to you that I can. I says You can't because Detroit won't give no wavers on me. He says Detroit will give wavers on you quick enough if I ask them.

Then he says Now you can take your choice you can stay here and pitch for me at the salery you signed up for and you can cut out the monkey business and drink water when you are thirsty or else you can go up to Milwaukee and drownd yourself in one of them brewrys. Which shall it be? I says How can you keep me or send me to Milwaukee when Detroit has allready claimed my services? He says Detroit has claimed a lot of things and they have even claimed the pennant but that is not no sign they will win it. He says And besides you would not want to pitch for Detroit because then you would not never have no chance to pitch against Cobb and show him up.

Well Al when he says that I knowed he appresiated what a pitcher I am even if he did try to sell me to Milwaukee or he would not of made that remark about the way I can show Cobb and Crawford up. So I says Well if you need me that bad I will pitch for you but I must have a new contract. He says Oh I guess we can fix that up

O.K. and he steps out in the next room a while and then he comes back with a new contract. And what do you think it was Al? It was a contract for 3 years so you see I am sure of my job here for 3 years and everything is all O.K.

The contract calls for the same salery a year for 3 years that I was going to get before for only 1 year which is $2800.00 a year and then I will get in on the city serious money too and the Detroit Club don't have no city serious and have no chance to get into the World's Serious with the rotten pitching staff they got. So you see Al he fixed me up good and that shows that he must think a hole lot of me or he would of sent me to Detroit or maybe to Milwaukee but I don't see how he could of did that without no wavers.

Well Al I allmost forgot to tell you that he has gave me a ticket to Los Angeles where the 2d team are practicing at now but where the 1st team will be at in about a week. I am leaveing to-night and I guess before I go I will go down to president Johnson and tell him that I am fixed up all O.K. and have not got no kick comeing so that president Johnson will not fine Comiskey for not paying no attention to the rules or get him fired out of the league because I guess Comiskey must be all O.K. and good hearted after all.

I won't pay no attention to what he says about me drinking this town dry because he is all wrong in regards to that. He must of been jokeing I guess because nobody but some boob would think he could drink this town dry but at that I guess I can hold more than anybody and not be effected. But I guess I will cut it out for a while at that because I don't want to get them sore at me after the contract they give me.

I will write to you from Los Angeles Al and let you know what the boys says when they see me and I will bet that they will be tickled to death. The rent man was round to-day but I seen him comeing and he did not find me. I am going to leave the furniture that belongs in the flat in the flat and allso the furniture I bought which don't amount to much because it was not no real Sir Cashion walnut and besides I don't want nothing round me to remind me of Florrie because the sooner her and I forget each other the better.

Tell the boys about my good luck Al but it is not no luck neither because it was comeing to me.   Yours truly,   JACK.

Los Angeles, California, March 16.

AL: Here I am back with the White Sox again and it seems to good
to be true because just like I told you they are all tickled to death
to see me. Kid Gleason is here in charge of the 2d team and when
he seen me come into the hotel he jumped up and hit me in the
stumach but he acts like that whenever he feels good so I could not
get sore at him though he had no right to hit me in the stumach. If
he had of did it in ernest I would of walloped him in the jaw.

He says Well if here ain't the old lady killer. He ment Al that I
am strong with the girls but I am all threw with them now but he
don't know nothing about the troubles I had. He says Are you in
shape? And I told him Yes I am. He says Yes you look in shape like
a barrel. I says They is not no fat on me and if I am a little bit bigger
than last year it is because my mussels is bigger. He says Yes your
stumach mussels is emense and you must of gave them plenty of
exercise. Wait till Bodie sees you and he will want to stick round
you all the time because you make him look like a broom straw or
something. I let him kid me along because what is the use of getting
mad at him? And besides he is all O.K. even if he is a little rough.

I says to him A little work will fix me up all O.K. and he says You
bet you are going to get some work because I am going to see to it
myself. I says You will have to hurry because you will be going up
to Frisco in a few days and I am going to stay here and join the 1st
club. Then he says You are not going to do no such a thing. You
are going right along with me. I knowed he was kidding me then
because Callahan would not never leave me with the 2d team no
more after what I done for him last year and besides most of the
stars generally allways goes with the 1st team on the training trip.

Well I seen all the rest of the boys that is here with the 2d team
and they all acted like as if they was glad to see me and why should
not they be when they know that me being here with the White Sox
and not with Detroit means that Callahan won't have to do no worrying about his pitching staff? But they is four or 5 young recrut
pitchers with the team here and I bet they is not so glad to see me
because what chance have they got?

If I was Comiskey and Callahan I would not spend no money on
new pitchers because with me and 1 or 2 of the other boys we got
the best pitching staff in the league. And instead of spending the
money for new pitching recruts I would put it all in a lump and buy
Ty Cobb or Sam Crawford off of Detroit or somebody else who can

hit and Cobb and Crawford is both real hitters Al even if I did make them look like suckers. Who wouldn't?

Well Al to-morrow A.M. I am going out and work a little and in the P.M. I will watch the game between we and the Venice Club but I won't pitch none because Gleason would not dare take no chances of me hurting my arm. I will write to you in a few days from here because no matter what Gleason says I am going to stick here with the 1st team because I know Callahan will want me along with him for a attraction.   Your pal,   JACK.

San Francisco, California, March 20.

FRIEND AL: Well Al here I am back in old Frisco with the 2d team but I will tell you how it happened Al. Yesterday Gleason told me to pack up and get ready to leave Los Angeles with him and I says No I am going to stick here and wait for the 1st team and then he says I guess I must of overlooked something in the papers because I did not see nothing about you being appointed manager of the club. I says No I am not manager but Callahan is manager and he will want to keep me with him. He says I got a wire from Callahan telling me to keep you with my club but of coarse if you know what Callahan wants better than he knows it himself why then go ahead and stay here or go jump in the Pacific Ocean.

Then he says I know why you don't want to go with me and I says Why? And he says Because you know I will make you work and won't let you eat everything on the bill of fair includeing the name of the hotel at which we are stopping at. That made me sore and I was just going to call him when he says Did not you marry Mrs. Allen's sister? And I says Yes but that is not none of your business. Then he says Well I don't want to butt into your business but I heard you and your wife had some kind of a argument and she beat it. I says Yes she give me a rotten deal. He says Well then I don't see where it is going to be very pleasant for you traveling round with the 1st club because Allen and his wife is both with that club and what do you want to be mixed up with them for? I says I am not scared of Allen or his wife or no other old hen.

So here I am Al with the 2d team but it is only for a while till Callahan gets sick of some of them pitchers he has got and sends for me so as he can see some real pitching. And besides I am glad to be here in Frisco where I made so many friends when I was pitching

here for a short time till Callahan heard about my work and called
me back to the big show where I belong at and nowheres else.

Yours truly,   JACK.

San Francisco, California, March 25.

OLD PAL: Al I got a supprise for you. Who do you think I seen
last night? Nobody but Hazel. Her name now is Hazel Levy because
you know Al she married Kid Levy the middleweight and I wish he
was champion of the world Al because then it would not take me
more than about a minute to be champion of the world myself. I
have not got nothing against him though because he married her and
if he had not of I probily would of married her myself but at that
she could not of treated me no worse than Florrie. Well they was
setting at a table in the cafe where her and I use to go pretty near
every night. She spotted me when I first come in and sends a waiter
over to ask me to come and have a drink with them. I went over
because they was no use being nasty and let bygones be bygones.

She interduced me to her husband and he asked me what was I
drinking. Then she butts in and says Oh you must let Mr. Keefe buy
the drinks because it hurts his feelings to have somebody else buy
the drinks. Then Levy says Oh he is one of these here spendrifts is
he? and she says Yes he don't care no more about a nichol than his
right eye does. I says I guess you have got no holler comeing on the
way I spend my money. I don't steal no money anyway. She says
What do you mean? and I says I guess you know what I mean. How
about that $30.00 that you borrowed off of me and never give it
back? Then her husband cuts in and says You cut that line of talk
out or I will bust you. I says Yes you will. And he says Yes I will.

Well Al what was the use of me starting trouble with him when
he has got enough trouble right to home and besides as I say I have
not got nothing against him. So I got up and blowed away from the
table and I bet he was relieved when he seen I was not going to start
nothing. I beat it out of there a while afterward because I was not
drinking nothing and I don't have no fun setting round a place and
lapping up ginger ail or something. And besides the music was rotten.

Al I am certainly glad I throwed Hazel over because she has grew
to be as big as a horse and is all painted up. I don't care nothing
about them big dolls no more or about no other kind neither. I am
off of them all. They can all of them die and I should not worry.

Well Al I done my first pitching of the year this P.M. and I guess

I showed them that I was in just as good a shape as some of them birds that has been working a month. I worked 4 innings against my old team the San Francisco Club and I give them nothing but fast ones but they sure was fast ones and you could hear them zip. Charlie O'Leary was trying to get out of the way of one of them and it hit his bat and went over first base for a base hit but at that Fournier would of eat it up if it had of been Chase playing first base instead of Fournier.

That was the only hit they got off of me and they ought to of been ashamed to of tooken that one. But Gleason don't appresiate my work and him and I allmost come to blows at supper. I was pretty hungry and I ordered some stake and some eggs and some pie and some ice cream and some coffee and a glass of milk but Gleason would not let me have the pie or the milk and would not let me eat more than ½ the stake. And it is a wonder I did not bust him and tell him to mind his own business. I says What right have you got to tell me what to eat? And he says You don't need nobody to tell you what to eat you need somebody to keep you from floundering yourself. I says Why can't I eat what I want to when I have worked good?

He says Who told you you worked good and I says I did not need nobody to tell me. I know I worked good because they could not do nothing with me. He says Well it is a good thing for you that they did not start bunting because if you had of went to stoop over and pick up the ball you would of busted wide open. I says Why? and he says because you are hog fat and if you don't let up on the stable and fancy groceries we will have to pay 2 fairs to get you back to Chi. I don't remember now what I says to him but I says something you can bet on that. You know me Al.

I wish Al that Callahan would hurry up and order me to join the 1st team. If he don't Al I believe Gleason will starve me to death. A little slob like him don't realize that a big man like I needs good food and plenty of it.   Your pal,   JACK.

Salt Lake City, Utah, April 1.

AL: Well Al we are on our way East and I am still with the 2d team and I don't understand why Callahan don't order me to join the 1st team but maybe it is because he knows that I am all right and have got the stuff and he wants to keep them other guys round where he can see if they have got anything.

The recrut pitchers that is along with our club have not got nothing and the scout that reckommended them must of been full of hops or something. It is not no common thing for a club to pick up a man that has got the stuff to make him a star up here and the White Sox was pretty lucky to land me but I don't understand why they throw their money away on new pitchers when none of them is no good and besides who would want a better pitching staff than we got right now without no raw recruts and bushers.

I worked in Oakland the day before yesterday but he only let me go the 1st 4 innings. I bet them Oakland birds was glad when he took me out. When I was in that league I use to just throw my glove in the box and them Oakland birds was licked and honest Al some of them turned white when they seen I was going to pitch the other day.

I felt kind of sorry for them and I did not give them all I had so they got 5 or 6 hits and scored a couple of runs. I was not feeling very good at that and besides we got some awful excuses for a ball player on this club and the support they give me was the rottenest I ever seen gave anybody. But some of them won't be in this league more than about 10 minutes more so I should not fret as they say.

We play here this afternoon and I don't believe I will work because the team they got here is not worth wasteing nobody on. They must be a lot of boobs in this town Al because they tell me that some of them has got ½ a dozen wives or so. And what a man wants with 1 wife is a misery to me let alone a ½ dozen.

I will probily work against Denver because they got a good club and was champions of the Western League last year. I will make them think they are champions of the Epworth League or something.

Yours truly,   JACK.

Des Moines, Iowa, April 10.

FRIEND AL: We got here this A.M. and this is our last stop and we will be in old Chi to-morrow to open the season. The 1st team gets home to-day and I would be there with them if Callahan was a real manager who knowed something about manageing because if I am going to open the season I should ought to have 1 day of rest at home so I would have all my strength to open the season. The Cleveland Club will be there to open against us and Callahan must know that I have got them licked any time I start against them.

As soon as my name is announced to pitch the Cleveland Club is licked or any other club when I am right and they don't kick the game away behind me.

Gleason told me on the train last night that I was going to pitch here to-day but I bet by this time he has got orders from Callahan to let me rest and to not give me no more work because suppose even if I did not start the game to-morrow I probily will have to finish it.

Gleason has been sticking round me like as if I had a million bucks or something. I can't even sit down and smoke a cigar but what he is there to knock the ashes off of it. He is O.K. and good-hearted if he is a little rough and keeps hitting me in the stumach but I wish he would leave me alone sometimes espesially at meals. He was in to breakfast with me this A.M. and after I got threw I snuck off down the street and got something to eat. This is not right because it costs me money when I have to go away from the hotel and eat and what right has he got to try and help me order my meals? Because he don't know what I want and what my stumach wants.

My stumach don't want to have him punching it all the time but he keeps on doing it. So that shows he don't know what is good for me. But is a old man Al otherwise I would not stand for the stuff he pulls. The 1st thing I am going to do when we get to Chi is I am going to a resturunt somewheres and get a good meal where Gleason or no one else can't get at me. I know allready what I am going to eat and that is a big stake and a apple pie and that is not all.

Well Al watch the papers and you will see what I done to that Cleveland Club and I hope Lajoie and Jackson is both in good shape because I don't want to pick on no cripples.

Your pal,   JACK.

Chicago, Illinois, April 16.

OLD PAL: Yesterday was the 1st pay day old pal and I know I promised to pay you what I owe you and it is $75.00 because when I asked you for $35.00 before I went West you only sent me $25.00 which makes the hole sum $75.00. Well Al I can't pay you now because the pay we drawed was only for 4 days and did not amount to nothing and I had to buy a meal ticket and fix up about my room rent.

And then they is another thing Al which I will tell you about. I come into the clubhouse the day the season opened and the 1st guy I seen was Allen. I was going to bust him but he come up and held his hand out and what was they for me to do but shake hands with him if he is going to be yellow like that? He says Well Jack I am glad they did not send you to Milwaukee and I bet you will have a big year. I says Yes I will have a big year O.K. if you don't sick another 1 of your sister-in-laws on to me. He says Oh don't let they be no hard feelings about that. You know it was not no fault of mine and I bet if you was to write to Florrie everything could be fixed up O.K.

I says I don't want to write to Florrie but I will get a attorney at law to write to her. He says You don't even know where she is at and I says I don't care where she is at. Where is she? He says She is down to her home in Waco, Texas, and if I was you I would write to her myself and not let no attorney at law write to her because that would get her mad and besides what do you want a attorney at law to write to her about? I says I am going to sew her for a bill of divorce.

The he says On what grounds? and I says Dessertion. He says You better not do no such thing or she will sew you for a bill of divorce for none support and then you will look like a cheap guy. I says I don't care what I look like. So you see Al I had to send Florrie $10.00 or maybe she would be mean enough to sew me for a bill of divorce on the ground of none suport and that would make me look bad.

Well Al, Allen told me his wife wanted to talk to me and try and fix things up between I and Florrie but I give him to understand that I would not stand for no meeting with his wife and he says Well suit yourself about that but they is no reason you and I should quarrel.

You see Al he don't want no mix-up with me because he knows he could not get nothing but the worst of it. I will be friends with him but I won't have nothing to do with Marie because if it had not of been for she and Florrie I would have money in the bank besides not being in no danger of getting sewed for none support.

I guess you must of read about Joe Benz getting married and I guess he must of got a good wife and 1 that don't bother him all the time because he pitched the opening game and shut Cleveland out with 2 hits. He was pretty good Al, better than I ever seen him and they was a couple of times when his fast ball was pretty near as fast as mine.

I have not worked yet Al and I asked Callahan to-day what was the matter and he says I was waiting for you to get in shape. I says I am in shape now and I notice that when I was pitching in practice this A.M. they did not hit nothing out of the infield. He says That was because you are so spread out that they could not get nothing past you. He says The way you are now you cover more ground than the grand stand. I says Is that so? And he walked away.

We go out on a trip to Cleveland and Detroit and St. Louis in a few days and maybe I will take my regular turn then because the other pitchers has been getting away lucky because most of the hitters has not got their batting eye as yet but wait till they begin hitting and then it will take a man like I to stop them.

The 1st of May is our next pay day Al and then I will have enough money so as I can send you the $75.00.   Your pal,   JACK.

Detroit, Michigan, April 28.

FRIEND AL: What do you think of a rotten manager that bawls me out and fines me $50.00 for loosing a 1 to 0 game in 10 innings when it was my 1st start this season? And no wonder I was a little wild in the 10th when I had not had no chance to work and get control. I got a good notion to quit this rotten club and jump to the Federals where a man gets some kind of treatment. Callahan says I throwed the game away on purpose but I did not do no such a thing Al because when I throwed that ball at Joe Hill's head I forgot that the bases was full and besides if Gleason had not of starved me to death the ball that hit him in the head would of killed him.

And how could a man go to 1st base and the winning run be forced in if he was dead which he should ought to of been the lucky left handed stiff if I had of had my full strenth to put on my fast one instead of being ½ starved to death and weak. But I guess I better tell you how it come off. The papers will get it all wrong like they generally allways does.

Callahan asked me this A.M. if I thought I was hard enough to work and I was tickled to death, because I seen he was going to give me a chance. I told him Sure I was in good shape and if them Tigers scored a run off me he could keep me setting on the bench the rest of the summer. So he says All right I am going to start you and if you go good maybe Gleason will let you eat some supper.

Well Al when I begin warming up I happened to look up in the grand stand and who do you think I seen? Nobody but Violet. She smiled when she seen me but I bet she felt more like crying. Well I smiled back at her because she probily would of broke down and made a seen or something if I had not of. They was not nobody warming up for Detroit when I begin warming up but pretty soon I looked over to their bench and Joe Hill Violet's husband was warming up. I says to myself Well here is where I show that bird up if they got nerve enough to start him against me but probily Jennings don't want to waste no real pitcher on this game which he knows we got cinched and we would of had it cinched Al if they had of got a couple of runs or even 1 run for me.

Well, Jennings come passed our bench just like he allways does and tried to pull some of his funny stuff. He says Hello are you still in the league? I says Yes but I come pretty near not being. I came pretty near being with Detroit. I wish you could of heard Gleason and Callahan laugh when I pulled that one on him. He says something back but it was not no hot comeback like mine.

Well Al if I had of had any work and my regular control I guess I would of pitched a o hit game because the only time they could touch me was when I had to ease up to get them over. Cobb was out of the game and they told me he was sick but I guess the truth is that he knowed I was going to pitch. Crawford got a couple of lucky scratch hits off of me because I got in the hole to him and had to let up. But the way that lucky left handed Hill got by was something awful and if I was as lucky as him I would quit pitching and shoot craps or something.

Our club can't hit nothing anyway. But batting against this bird was just like hitting fungos. His curve ball broke about ½ a inch and you could of wrote your name and address on his fast one while it was comeing up there. He had good control but who would not when they put nothing on the ball?

Well Al we could not get started against the lucky stiff and they could not do nothing with me even if my suport was rotten and I give a couple or 3 or 4 bases on balls but when they was men waiting to score I zipped them threw there so as they could not see them let alone hit them. Every time I come to the bench between innings I looked up to where Violet was setting and give her a smile and she smiled back and once I seen her clapping her hands at me after I had made Moriarty pop up in the pinch.

Well we come along to the 10th inning, o and o, and all of a sudden we got after him. Bodie hits one and Schalk gets 2 strikes and 2 balls and then singles. Callahan tells Alcock to bunt and he does it but Hill sprawls all over himself like the big boob he is and the bases is full with nobody down. Well Gleason and Callahan argude about should they send somebody up for me or let me go up there and I says Let me go up there because I can murder this bird and Callahan says Well they is nobody out so go up and take a wallop.

Honest Al if this guy had of had anything at all I would of hit 1 out of the park, but he did not have even a glove. And how can a man hit pitching which is not no pitching at all but just slopping them up? When I went up there I hollered to him and says Stick 1 over here now you yellow stiff. And he says Yes I can stick them over allright and that is where I got something on you.

Well Al I hit a foul off of him that would of been a fare ball and broke up the game if the wind had not of been against it. Then I swung and missed a curve that I don't see how I missed it. The next 1 was a yard outside and this Evans calls it a strike. He has had it in for me ever since last year when he tried to get funny with me and I says something back to him that stung him. So he calls this 3d strike on me and I felt like murdering him. But what is the use?

I throwed down my bat and come back to the bench and I was glad Callahan and Gleason was out on the coaching line or they probily would of said something to me and I would of cut loose and beat them up. Well Al Weaver and Blackburne looked like a couple of rums up there and we don't score where we ought to of had 3 or 4 runs with any kind of hitting.

I would of been all O.K. in spite of that peace of rotten luck if this big Hill had of walked to the bench and not said nothing like a real pitcher. But what does he do but wait out there till I start for the box and I says Get on to the bench you lucky stiff or do you want me to hand you something? He says I don't want nothing more of yourn. I allready got your girl and your goat.

Well Al what do you think of a man that would say a thing like that? And nobody but a left hander could of. If I had of had a gun I would of killed him deader than a doornail or something. He starts for the bench and I hollered at him Wait till you get up to that plate and then I am going to bean you.

Honest Al I was so mad I could not see the plate or nothing. I don't even know who it was come up to bat 1st but whoever it was I hit him in the arm and he walks to first base. The next guy bunts and Chase tries to pull off 1 of them plays of hisn instead of playing safe and he don't get nobody. Well I kept getting madder and madder and I walks Stanage who if I had of been myself would not foul me.

Callahan has Scotty warming up and Gleason runs out from the bench and tells me I am threw but Callahan says Wait a minute he is going to let Hill hit and this big stiff ought to be able to get him out of the way and that will give Scotty a chance to get warm. Gleason says You better not take a chance because the big busher is hogwild, and they kept argueing till I got sick of listening to them and I went back to the box and got ready to pitch. But when I seen this Hill up there I forgot all about the ball game and I cut loose at his bean.

Well Al my control was all O.K. this time and I catched him square on the fourhead and he dropped like as if he had been shot. But pretty soon he gets up and gives me the laugh and runs to first base. I did not know the game was over till Weaver came up and pulled me off the field. But if I had not of been ½ starved to death and weak so as I could not put all my stuff on the ball you can bet that Hill never would of ran to first base and Violet would of been a widow and probily a lot better off than she is now. At that I never should ought to of tried to kill a left-hander by hitting him in the head.

Well Al they jumped all over me in the clubhouse and I had to hold myself back or I would of gave somebody the beating of their life. Callahan tells me I am fined $50.00 and suspended without no pay. I asked him What for and he says They would not be no use in telling you because you have not got no brains. I says Yes I have to got some brains and he says Yes but they is in your stumach. And then he says I wish we had of sent you to Milwaukee and I come back at him. I says I wish you had of.

Well Al I guess they is no chance of getting square treatment on this club and you won't be supprised if you hear of me jumping to the Federals where a man is treated like a man and not like no white slave.   Yours truly,   JACK.

Chicago, Illinois, May 2.

AL: I have got to disappoint you again Al. When I got up to get my pay yesterday they held out $150.00 on me. $50.00 of it is what I was fined for loosing a 1 to 0 10-inning game in Detroit when I was so weak that I should ought never to of been sent in there and the $100.00 is the advance money that I drawed last winter and which I had forgot all about and the club would of forgot about it to if they was not so tight fisted.

So you see all I get for 2 weeks' pay is about $80.00 and I sent $25.00 to Florrie so she can't come no none support business on me.

I am still suspended Al and not drawing no pay now and I got a notion to hire a attorney at law and force them to pay my salery or else jump to the Federals where a man gets good treatment.

Allen is still after me to come over to his flat some night and see his wife and let her talk to me about Florrie but what do I want to talk about Florrie for or talk about nothing to a nut left hander's wife?

The Detroit Club is here and Cobb is playing because he knows I am suspended but I wish Callahan would call it off and let me work against them and I would certainly love to work against this Joe Hill again and I bet they would be a different story this time because I been getting something to eat since we been home and I got back most of my strenth.   Your old pal,   JACK.

Chicago, Illinois, May 5.

FRIEND AL: Well Al if you been reading the papers you will know before this letter is received what I done. Before the Detroit Club come here Joe Hill had win 4 strate but he has not win no 5 strate or won't neither Al because I put a crimp in his winning streek just like I knowed I would do if I got a chance when I was feeling good and had all my strenth. Callahan asked me yesterday A.M. if I thought I had enough rest and I says Sure because I did not need no rest in the 1st place. Well, he says, I thought maybe if I layed you off a few days you would do some thinking and if you done some thinking once in a while you would be a better pitcher.

Well anyway I worked and I wish you could of saw them Tigers trying to hit me Cobb and Crawford incluseive. The 1st time Cobb come up Weaver catched a lucky line drive off of him and the next time I eased up a little and Collins run back and took a fly ball off of the fence. But the other times he come up he looked like a sucker except when he come up in the 8th and then he beat out a bunt but allmost anybody is liable to do that once in a while.

Crawford got a scratch hit between Chase and Blackburne in the 2d inning and in the 4th he was gave a three-base hit by this Evans who should ought to be writeing for the papers instead of trying to umpire. The ball was 2 feet foul and I bet Crawford will tell you the same thing if you ask him. But what I done to this Hill was awful. I give him my curve twice when he was up there in the 3d and he missed it a foot. Then I come with my fast ball right past his nose and I bet if he had not of ducked it would of drove that big horn of hisn clear up in the press box where them rotten reporters sits and smokes their hops. Then when he was looking for another fast one I slopped up my slow one and he is still swinging at it yet.

But the best of it was that I practally won my own game. Bodie and Schalk was on when I come up in the 5th and Hill hollers to me and says I guess this is where I shoot one of them bean balls. I says Go ahead and shoot and if you hit me in the head and I ever find it out I will write and tell your wife what happened to you. You see what I was getting at Al. I was insinuateing that if he beaned me with his fast one I would not never know nothing about it if somebody did not tell me because his fast one is not fast enough to hurt nobody even if it should hit them in the head. So I says to him Go ahead and shoot and if you hit me in the head and I ever find it out I will write and tell your wife what happened to you. See, Al?

Of coarse you could not hire me to write to Violet but I did not mean that part of it in ernest. Well sure enough he shot at my bean and I ducked out of the way though if it had of hit me it could not of did no more than tickle. He takes 2 more shots and misses me and then Jennings hollers from the bench What are you doing pitching or trying to win a cigar? So then Hill sees what a monkey he is makeing out of himself and tries to get one over, but I have him 3 balls and nothing and what I done to that groover was a plenty. She went over Bush's head like a bullet and got between Cobb and Veach and goes clear to the fence. Bodie and Schalk scores and I would of scored to if anybody else besides Cobb had of been chaseing the ball. I got 2 bases and Weaver scores me with another wallop.

Say, I wish I could of heard what they said to that baby on the bench. Callahan was tickled to death and he says Maybe I will give you back that $50.00 if you keep that stuff up. I guess I will get that $50.00 back next pay day and if I do Al I will pay you the hole $75.00.

Well Al I beat them 5 to 4 and with good support I would of held them to 1 run but what do I care as long as I beat them? I wish though that Violet could of been there and saw it.

Yours truly,   JACK.

Chicago, Illinois, May 29.

OLD PAL: Well Al I have not wrote to you for a long while but it is not because I have forgot you and to show I have not forgot you I am incloseing the $75.00 which I owe you. It is a money order Al and you can get it cashed by takeing it to Joe Higgins at the P.O.

Since I wrote to you Al I been East with the club and I guess you know what I done in the East. The Athaletics did not have no right to win that 1 game off of me and I will get them when they come here the week after next. I beat Boston and just as good as beat New York twice because I beat them 1 game all alone and then saved the other for Eddie Cicotte in the 9th inning and shut out the Washington Club and would of did the same thing if Johnson had of been working against me instead of this left handed stiff Boehling.

Speaking of left handers Allen has been going rotten and I would not be supprised if they sent him to Milwaukee or Frisco or somewheres.

But I got bigger news than that for you Al. Florrie is back and we are liveing together in the spair room at Allen's flat so I hope they don't send him to Milwaukee or nowheres else because it is not costing us nothing for room rent and this is no more than right after the way the Allens grafted off of us all last winter.

I bet you will be supprised to know that I and Florrie has made it up and they is a secret about it Al which I can't tell you now but maybe next month I will tell you and then you will be more supprised than ever. But that is all I can tell you now.

We got in this A.M. Al and when I got to my room they was a slip of paper there telling me to call up a phone number so I called it up and it was Allen's flat and Marie answered the phone. And when I reckonized her voice I was going to hang up the phone but she says Wait a minute somebody wants to talk with you. And then Florrie come to the phone and I was going to hang up the phone again when she pulled this secret on me that I was telling you about.

So it is all fixed up between us Al and I wish I could tell you the secret but that will come later. I have tooken my baggage over to Allen's and I am there now writeing to you while Florrie is asleep. And after a while I am going out and mail this letter and get a glass of beer because I think I have got 1 comeing now on account of this secret. Florrie says she is sorry for the way she treated me and she cried when she seen me. So what is the use of me being nasty Al? And let bygones be bygones.   Your pal,   JACK.

Chicago, Illinois, June 16.

FRIEND AL: Al I beat the Athaletics 2 to 1 to-day but I am writeing to you to give you the supprise of your life. Old pal I got a baby and he is a boy and we are going to name him Allen which Florrie thinks is after his uncle and aunt Allen but which is after you old pal. And she can call him Allen but I will call him Al because I don't never go back on my old pals. The baby was born over to the hospital and it is going to cost me a bunch of money but I should not worry. This is the secret I was going to tell you Al and I am the happyest man in the world and I bet you are most as tickled to death to hear about it as I am.

The baby was born just about the time I was makeing McInnis look like a sucker in the pinch but they did not tell me nothing about it till after the game and then they give me a phone messige in the clubhouse. I went right over there and everything was all O.K. Little Al is a homely little skate but I guess all babys is homely and don't have no looks till they get older and maybe he will look like Florrie or I then I won't have no kick comeing.

Be sure and tell Bertha the good news and tell her everything has came out all right except that the rent man is still after me about that flat I had last winter. And I am still paying the old man $10.00 a month for that house you got for me and which has not never done me no good. But I should not worry about money when I got a real family. Do you get that Al, a real family?

Well Al I am to happy to do no more writeing to-night but I wanted you to be the 1st to get the news and I would of sent you a telegram only I did not want to scare you. Your pal,   JACK.

Chicago, Illinois, July 2.

OLD PAL: Well old pal I just come back from St. Louis this A.M. and found things in pretty fare shape. Florrie and the baby is out to Allen's and we will stay there till I can find another place. The Dr. was out to look at the baby this A.M. and the baby was waveing his arm round in the air. And Florrie asked was they something the matter with him that he kept waveing his arm. And the Dr. says No he was just getting his exercise.

Well Al I noticed that he never waved his right arm but kept waveing his left arm and I asked the Dr. why was that. Then the Dr. says I guess he must be left handed. That made me sore and I says I guess you doctors don't know it all. And then I turned round and beat it out of the room.

Well Al it would be just my luck to have him left handed and Florrie should ought to of knew better than to name him after Allen. I am going to hire another Dr. and see what he has to say because they must be some way of fixing babys so as they won't be left handed. And if nessary I will cut his left arm off of him. Of coarse I would not do that Al. But how would I feel if a boy of mine turned out like Allen and Joe Hill and some of them other nuts?

We have a game with St. Louis to-morrow and a double header on the 4th of July. I guess probily Callahan will work me in one of the 4th of July games on account of the holiday crowd.

Your pal,   JACK.

P.S. Maybe I should ought to leave the kid left handed so as he can have some of their luck. The lucky stiffs.

THE BUSHER'S KID

◇

Chicago, Illinois, July 31.

FRIEND AL: Well Al what do you think of little Al now? But I guess I better tell you first what he done. Maybe you won't believe what I am telling you but did you ever catch me telling you a lie? I guess you know you did not Al. Well we got back from the East this A.M. and I don't have to tell you we had a rotten trip and if it had not of been for me beating Boston once and the Athaletics two times we would of been ashamed to come home.

I guess these here other pitchers thought we was haveing a vacation and when they go up in the office to-morrow to get there checks they should ought to be arrested if they take them. I would not go nowheres near Comiskey if I had not of did better than them others but I can go and get my pay and feel all O.K. about it because I done something to ern it.

Me loseing that game in Washington was a crime and Callahan says so himself. This here Weaver throwed it away for me and I would not be surprised if he done it from spitework because him and Scott is pals and probily he did not want to see me winning all them games when Scott was getting knocked out of the box. And no wonder when he has not got no stuff. I wish I knowed for sure that Weaver was throwing me down and if I knowed for sure I would put him in a hospital or somewheres.

But I was going to tell you what the kid done Al. So here goes. We are still liveing at Allen's and his wife. So I and him come home together from the train. Well Florrie and Marie was both up and the baby was up too—that is he was not up but he was woke up. I beat it right into the room where he was at and Florrie come in with me. I says Hello Al and what do you suppose he done. Well Al he did

The Saturday Evening Post, October 3, 1914; *You Know Me Al.*

not say Hello pa or nothing like that because he is not only one
month old. But he smiled at me just like as if he was glad to see me
and I guess maybe he was at that.

I was tickled to death and I says to Florrie Did you see that. And
she says See what. I says The baby smiled at me. Then she says They
is something the matter with his stumach. I says I suppose because
a baby smiles that is a sign they is something the matter with his
stumach and if he had the toothacke he would laugh. She says You
think your smart but I am telling you that he was not smileing at all
but he was makeing a face because they is something the matter with
his stumach. I says I guess I know the difference if somebody is
smileing or makeing a face. And she says I guess you don't know
nothing about babys because you never had none before. I says How
many have you had. And then she got sore and beat it out of the
room.

I did not care because I wanted to be in there alone with him and
see would he smile at me again. And sure enough Al he did. Then
I called Allen in and when the baby seen him he begin to cry. It
don't take a man no time at all to get wise to these babys and it don't
take them long to know if a man is there father or there uncle.

When he begin to cry I chased Allen out of the room and called
Florrie because she should ought to know by this time how to make
him stop crying. But she was still sore and she says Let him cry or
if you know so much about babys make him stop yourself. I says
Maybe he is sick. And she says I was just telling you that he had a
pane in his stumach or he would not of made that face that you said
was smileing at you.

I says Do you think we should ought to call the doctor but she
says No if you call the doctor every time he has the stumach acke
you might just as well tell him he should bring his trunk along and
stay here. She says All babys have collect and they is not no use
fusing about it but come and get your breakfast.

Well Al I did not injoy my breakfast because the baby was crying
all the time and I knowed he probily wanted I should come in and
visit with him. So I just eat the prunes and drunk a little coffee and
did not wait for the rest of it and sure enough when I went back in
our room and started talking to him he started smileing again and
pretty soon he went to sleep so you see Al he was smileing and not
makeing no face and that was a hole lot of bunk about him haveing
the collect. But I don't suppose I should ought to find fault with

Florrie for not knowing no better because she has not never had no babys before but still and all I should think she should ought to of learned something about them by this time or ask somebody.

Well Al little Al is woke up again and is crying and I just about got time to fix him up and get him asleep again and then I will have to go to the ball park because we got a poseponed game to play with Detroit and Callahan will probily want me to work though I pitched the next to the last game in New York and would of gave them a good beating except for Schalk dropping that ball at the plate but I got it on these Detroit babys and when my name is announced to pitch they feel like forfiting the game. I won't try for no strike out record because I want them to hit the first ball and get the game over with quick so as I can get back here and take care of little Al.

Your pal,   JACK.

P.S. Babys is great stuff Al and if I was you I would not wait no longer but would hurry up and adopt 1 somewheres.

Chicago, Illinois, August 15.

OLD PAL: What do you think Al. Kid Gleason is comeing over to the flat and look at the baby the day after to-morrow when we don't have no game skeduled but we have to practice in the A.M. because we been going so rotten. I had a hard time makeing him promise to come but he is comeing and I bet he will be glad he come when he has came. I says to him in the clubhouse Do you want to see a real baby? And he says You're real enough for me Boy.

I says No I am talking about babys. He says Oh I thought you was talking about ice cream soda or something. I says No I want you to come over to the flat to-morrow and take a look at my kid and tell me what you think of him. He says I can tell you what I think of him without takeing no look at him. I think he is out of luck. I says What do you mean out of luck. But he just laughed and would not say no more.

I asked him again would he come over to the flat and look at the baby and he says he had troubles enough without that and kidded along for a while but finally he seen I was in ernest and then he says he would come if I would keep the missus out of the room while he was there because he says if she seen him she would probily be sorry she married me.

He was just jokeing and I did not take no excepshun to his remarks because Florrie could not never fall for him after seeing me because he is not no big stropping man like I am but a little runt and look at how old he is. But I am glad he is comeing because he will think more of me when he sees what a fine baby I got though he thinks a hole lot of me now because look what I done for the club and where would they be at if I had jumped to the Federal like I once thought I would. I will tell you what he says about little Al and I bet he will say he never seen no prettyer baby but even if he don't say nothing at all I will know he is kidding.

The Boston Club comes here to-morrow and plays 4 days includeing the day after to-morrow when they is not no game. So on account of the off day maybe I will work twice against them and if I do they will wish the grounds had of burned down.

Yours truly,   JACK.

Chicago, Illinois, August 17.

AL: Well old pal what did I tell you about what I would do to that Boston Club? And now Al I have beat every club in the league this year because yesterday was the first time I beat the Boston Club this year but now I have beat all of them and most of them several times.

This should ought to of gave me a record of 16 wins and 0 defeats because the only games I lost was throwed away behind me but instead of that my record is 10 games win and 6 defeats and that don't include the games I finished up and helped the other boys win which is about 6 more alltogether but what do I care about my record Al? because I am not the kind of man that is allways thinking about there record and playing for there record while I am satisfied if I give the club the best I got and if I win all O.K. And if I lose who's fault is it. Not mine Al.

I asked Callahan would he let me work against the Boston Club again before they go away and he says I guess I will have to because you are going better than anybody else on the club. So you see Al he is beginning to appresiate my work and from now on I will pitch in my regular turn and a hole lot offtener then that and probily Comiskey will see the stuff I am made from and will raise my salery next year even if he has got me signed for 3 years and for the same salery I am getting now.

But all that is not what I was going to tell you Al and what I was going to tell you was about Gleason comeing to see the baby and what he thought about him. I sent Florrie and Marie downtown and says I would take care of little Al and they was glad to go because

Florrie says she should ought to buy some new shoes though I don't
see what she wants of no new shoes when she is going to be tied up
in the flat for a long time yet on account of the baby and nobody
cares if she wears shoes in the flat or goes round in her bear feet.
But I was glad to get rid of the both of them for a while because
little Al acts better when they is not no women round and you can't
blame him.

The baby was woke up when Gleason come in and I and him went
right in the room where he was laying. Gleason takes a look at him
and says Well that is a mighty fine baby and you must of boughten
him. I says What do you mean? And he says I don't believe he is
your own baby because he looks humaner than most babys. And I
says Why should not he look human. And he says Why should he.

Then he goes to work and picks the baby right up and I was a-
scared he would drop him because even I have not never picked him
up though I am his father and would be a-scared of hurting him. I
says Here, don't pick him up and he says Why not? He says Are
you going to leave him on that there bed the rest of his life? I says
No but you don't know how to handle him. He says I have handled
a hole lot bigger babys than him or else Callahan would not keep
me.

Then he starts patting the baby's head and I says Here, don't do
that because he has got a soft spot in his head and you might hit it.
He says I thought he was your baby and I says Well he is my baby
and he says Well then they can't be no soft spot in his head. Then
he lays little Al down because he seen I was in ernest and as soon
as he lays him down the baby begins to cry. Then Gleason says See
he don't want me to lay him down and I says Maybe he has got a
pane in his stumach and he says I would not be supprised because
he just took a good look at his father.

But little Al did not act like as if he had a pane in his stumach and
he kept sticking his finger in his mouth and crying. And Gleason
says He acts like as if he had a toothacke. I says How could he have
a toothacke when he has not got no teeth? He says That is easy. I
have saw a lot of pitchers complane that there arm was sore when
they did not have no arm.

Then he asked me what was the baby's name and I told him Allen
but that he was not named after my brother-in-law Allen. And Gleason says I should hope not. I should hope you would have better
sense than to name him after a left hander. So you see Al he don't

like them no better then I do even if he does jolly Allen and Russell along and make them think they can pitch.

Pretty soon he says What are you going to make out of him, a ball player? I says Yes I am going to make a hitter out of him so as he can join the White Sox and then maybe they will get a couple of runs once in a while. He says If I was you I would let him pitch and then you won't have to give him no educasion. Besides, he says, he looks now like he would divellop into a grate spitter.

Well I happened to look out of the window and seen Florrie and Marie comeing acrost Indiana Avenue and I told Gleason about it. And you ought to of seen him run. I asked him what was his hurry and he says it was in his contract that he was not to talk to no women but I knowed he was kidding because I allready seen him talking to severel of the players' wifes when they was on trips with us and they acted like as if they thought he was a regular comeedion though they really is not nothing funny about what he says only it is easy to make women laugh when they have not got no grouch on about something.

Well Al I am glad Gleason has saw the baby and maybe he will fix it with Callahan so as I won't have to go to morning practice every A.M. because I should ought to be home takeing care of little Al when Florrie is washing the dishs or helping Marie round the house. And besides why should I wear myself all out in practice because I don't need to practice pitching and I could hit as well as the rest of the men on our club if I never seen no practice.

After we get threw with Boston, Washington comes here and then we go to St. Louis and Cleveland and then come home and then go East again. And after that we are pretty near threw except the city serious. Callahan is not going to work me no more after I beat Boston again till it is this here Johnson's turn to pitch for Washington. And I hope it is not his turn to work the 1st game of the serious because then I would not have no rest between the last game against Boston and the 1st game against Washington.

But rest or no rest I will work against this here Johnson and show him up for giveing me that trimming in Washington, the lucky stiff. I wish I had a team like the Athaletics behind me and I would loose about 1 game every 6 years and then they would have to get all the best of it from these rotten umpires.   Your pal,   JACK.

New York, New York, September 16.

FRIEND AL: Al it is not no fun running round the country no more
and I wish this dam trip was over so as I could go home and see how
little Al is getting along because Florrie has not wrote since we was
in Philly which was the first stop on this trip. I am a-scared they is
something the matter with the little fellow or else she would of wrote
but then if they was something the matter with him she would of
sent me a telegram or something and let me know.

So I guess they can't be nothing the matter with him. Still and all
I don't see why she has not wrote when she knows or should ought
to know that I would be worrying about the baby. If I don't get no
letter to-morrow I am going to send her a telegram and ask her what
is the matter with him because I am positive she would of wrote if
they was not something the matter with him.

The boys has been trying to get me to go out nights and see a
show or something but I have not got no heart to go to shows. And
besides Callahan has not gave us no pass to no show on this trip. I
guess probily he is sore on account of the rotten way the club has
been going but still he should ought not to be sore on me because
I have win 3 out of my last 4 games and would of win the other if
he had not of started me against them with only 1 day's rest and the
Athaletics at that, who a man should ought not to pitch against if he
don't feel good.

I asked Allen if he had heard from Marie and he says Yes he did
but she did not say nothing about little Al except that he was keeping
her awake nights balling. So maybe Al if little Al is balling they is
something wrong with him. I am going to send Florrie a telegram
to-morrow—that is if I don't get no letter.

If they is something the matter with him I will ask Callahan to
send me home and he won't want to do it neither because who else
has he got that is a regular winner. But if little Al is sick and Callahan
won't let me go home I will go home anyway. You know me Al.

                        Yours truly,   JACK.

Boston, Massachusetts, September 24.

AL: I bet if Florrie was a man she would be a left hander. What do
you think she done now Al? I sent her a telegram from New York
when I did not get no letter from her and she did not pay no atension
to the telegram. Then when we got up here I sent her another
telegram and it was not more then five minutes after I sent the 2d

telegram till I got a letter from her. And it said the baby was all O.K. but she had been so busy takeing care of him that she had not had no time to write.

Well when I got the letter I chased out to see if I could catch the boy who had took my telegram but he had went allready so I was spending $.60 for nothing. Then what does Florrie do but send me a telegram after she got my second telegram and tell me that little Al is all O. K., which I knowed all about then because I had just got her letter. And she sent her telegram c. o. d. and I had to pay for it at this end because she had not paid for it and that was $.60 more but I bet if I had of knew what was in the telegram before I read it I would of told the boy to keep it and would not of gave him no $.60 but how did I know if little Al might not of tooken sick after Florrie had wrote the letter?

I am going to write and ask her if she is trying to send us both to the Poor House or somewheres with her telegrams. I don't care nothing about the $.60 but I like to see a woman use a little judgement though I guess that is impossable.

It is my turn to work to-day and to-night we start West but we have got to stop off at Cleveland on the way. I have got a nosion to ask Callahan to let me go right on threw to Chi if I win to-day and not stop off at no Cleveland but I guess they would not be no use because I have got that Cleveland Club licked the minute I put on my glove. So probily Callahan will want me with him though it don't make no difference if we win or lose now because we have not got no chance for the pennant. One man can't win no pennant Al I don't care who he is.   Your pal,   JACK.

Chicago, Illinois, October 2.

FRIEND AL: Well old pal I am all threw till the city serious and it is all fixed up that I am going to open the serious and pitch 3 of the games if nessary. The club has went to Detroit to wind up the season and Callahan did not take me along but left me here with a couple other pitchers and Billy Sullivan and told me all as I would have to do was go over to the park the next 3 days and warm up a little so as to keep in shape. But I don't need to be in no shape to beat them Cubs Al. But it is a good thing Al that Allen was tooken on the trip to Detroit or I guess I would of killed him. He has not been going good and he has been acting and talking nasty to everybody because he can't win no games.

Well the 1st night we was home after the trip little Al was haveing
a bad night and was balling pretty hard and they could not nobody
in the flat get no sleep. Florrie says he was haveing the collect and
I says Why should he have the collect all the time when he did not
drink nothing but milk? She says she guessed the milk did not agree
with him and upsetted his stumach. I says Well he must take after
his mother if his stumach gets upsetted every time he takes a drink
because if he took after his father he could drink a hole lot and not
never be effected. She says You should ought to remember he has
only got a little stumach and not a great big resservoire. I says Well
if the milk don't agree with him why don't you give him something
else? She says Yes I suppose I should ought to give him weeny worst
or something.

Allen must of heard us talking because he hollered something and
I did not hear what it was so I told him to say it over and he says
Give the little X-eyed brat poison and we would all be better off. I
says You better take poison yourself because maybe a rotten pitcher
like you could get by in the league where you're going when you
die. Then I says Besides I would rather my baby was X-eyed then
to have him left handed. He says It is better for him that he is X-
eyed or else he might get a good look at you and then he would
shoot himself. I says Is that so? and he shut up. Little Al is not no
more X-eyed than you or I are Al and that was what made me sore
because what right did Allen have to talk like that when he knowed
he was lying?

Well the next morning Allen nor I did not speak to each other
and I seen he was sorry for the way he had talked and I was willing
to fix things up because what is the use of staying sore at a man that
don't know no better.

But all of a sudden he says When are you going to pay me what
you owe me? I says What do you mean? And he says You been
liveing here all summer and I been paying all the bills. I says Did
not you and Marie ask us to come here and stay with you and it
would not cost us nothing. He says Yes but we did not mean it was
a life sentence. You are getting more money than me and you don't
never spend a nichol. All I have to do is pay the rent and buy your
food and it would take a millionare or something to feed you.

Then he says I would not make no holler about you grafting off
of me if that brat would shut up nights and give somebody a chance
to sleep. I says You should ought to get all the sleep you need on
the bench. Besides, I says, who done the grafting all last winter and

without no invatation? If he had of said another word I was going
to bust him but just then Marie come in and he shut up.

The more I thought about what he said and him a rotten left hander
that should ought to be hussling freiht the more madder I got and
if he had of opened his head to me the last day or 2 before he went
to Detroit I guess I would of finished him. But Marie stuck pretty
close to the both of us when we was together and I guess she knowed
they was something in the air and did not want to see her husband
get the worst of it though if he was my husband and I was a woman
I would push him under a st. car.

But Al I won't even stand for him saying that I am grafting off of
him and I and Florrie will get away from here and get a flat of our
own as soon as the city serious is over. I would like to bring her
and the kid down to Bedford for the winter but she wont listen to
that.

I allmost forgot Al to tell you to be sure and thank Bertha for the
little dress she made for little Al. I don't know if it will fit him or
not because Florrie has not yet tried it on him yet and she says she
is going to use it for a dishrag but I guess she is just kidding.

I suppose you seen where Callahan took me out of that game down
to Cleveland but it was not because I was not going good Al but it
was because Callahan seen he was makeing a mistake wasteing me
on that bunch who allmost any pitcher could beat. They beat us that
game at that but only by one run and it was not no fault of mine
because I was tooken out before they got the run that give them the
game.   Your old pal,   JACK.

                                    Chicago, Illinois, October 4.
FRIEND AL: Well Al the club winds up the season at Detroit to-
morrow and the serious starts the day after to-morrow and I will be
in there giveing them a battle. I wish I did not have nobody but the
Cubs to pitch against all season and you bet I would have a record
that would make Johnson and Mathewson and some of them other
swell heads look like a dirty doose.

I and Florrie and Marie has been haveing a argument about how
could Florrie go and see the city serious games when they is not
nobody here that can take care of the baby because Marie wants to
go and see the games to even though they is not no more chance of
Callahan starting Allen than a rabbit or something.

Florrie and Marie says I should ought to hire a nurse to take care of little Al and Florrie got pretty sore when I told her nothing doing because in the first place I can't afford to pay no nurse a salary and in the second place I would not trust no nurse to take care of the baby because how do I know the nurse is not nothing but a grafter or a dope fiend maybe and should ought not to be left with the baby?

Of coarse Florrie wants to see me pitch and a man can't blame her for that but I won't leave my baby with no nurse Al and Florrie will have to stay home and I will tell her what I done when I get there. I might of gave my consent to haveing a nurse at that if it had not of been for the baby getting so sick last night when I was takeing care of him while Florrie and Marie and Allen was out to a show and if I had not of been home they is no telling what would of happened. It is a cinch that none of them bonehead nurses would of knew what to do.

Allen must of been out of his head because right after supper he says he would take the 2 girls to a show. I says All right go on and I will take care of the baby. Then Florrie says Do you think you can take care of him all O. K.? And I says Have not I tooken care of him before allready? Well, she says, I will leave him with you only don't run in to him every time he cries. I says Why not? And she says Because it is good for him to cry. I says You have not got no heart or you would not talk that way.

They all give me the laugh but I let them get away with it because I am not picking no fights with girls and why should I bust this Allen when he don't know no better and has not got no baby himself. And I did not want to do nothing that would stop him takeing the girls to a show because it is time he spent a peace of money on somebody.

Well they all went out and I went in on the bed and played with the baby. I wish you could of saw him Al because he is old enough now to do stunts and he smiled up at me and waved his arms and legs round and made a noise like as if he was trying to say Pa. I did not think Florrie had gave him enough covers so I rapped him up in some more and took a blanket off of the big bed and stuck it round him so as he could not kick his feet out and catch cold.

I thought once or twice he was going off to sleep but all of a sudden he begin to cry and I seen they was something wrong with him. I gave him some hot water but that made him cry again and I thought maybe he was to cold yet so I took another blanket off of Allen's bed and wrapped that round him but he kept on crying and trying to kick inside the blankets. And I seen then that he must have collect or something.

So pretty soon I went to the phone and called up our regular Dr. and it took him pretty near a hour to get there and the baby balling all the time. And when he come he says they was nothing the matter except that the baby was to hot and told me to take all them blankets off of him and then soaked me 2 dollars. I had a nosion to bust his jaw. Well pretty soon he beat it and then little Al begin crying again and kept getting worse and worse so finally I got a-scared and run down to the corner where another Dr. is at and I brung him up to see what was the matter but he did not charge me a cent so I thought he was not no robber like our regular doctor even if he was just as much of a boob.

The baby did not cry none while he was there but the minute he had went he started crying and balling again and I seen they was not no use of fooling no longer so I looked around the house and found the medicine the doctor left for Allen when he had a stumach acke once and I give the baby a little of it in a spoon but I guess he did not like the taste because he hollered like a Indian and finally I could not stand it no longer so I called that second Dr. back again and this time he seen that the baby was sick and asked me what I had gave it and I told him some stumach medicine and he says I was a fool and should ought not to of gave the baby nothing. But while he was talking the baby stopped crying and went off to sleep so you see what I done for him was the right thing to do and them doctors was both off of there nut.

This second Dr. soaked me 2 dollars the 2d time though he had not did no more than when he was there the 1st time and charged me nothing but they is all a bunch of robbers Al and I would just as leave trust a policeman.

Right after the baby went to sleep Florrie and Marie and Allen come home and I told Florrie what had come off but instead of giveing me credit she says If you want to kill him why don't you take a ax? Then Allen butts in and says Why don't you take a ball and throw it at him? Then I got sore and I says Well if I did hit him with a ball I would kill him while if you was to throw that fast ball of yours at him and hit him in the head he would think the musketoes was biteing him and brush them off. But at that, I says, you could not hit him with a ball except you was aiming at something else.

I guess they was no comeback to that so him and Marie went to there room. Allen should ought to know better than to try and get the best of me by this time and I would shut up anyway if I was him after getting sent home from Detroit with some of the rest of them

when he only worked 3 innings up there and they had to take him
out or play the rest of the game by electrick lights.

I wish you could be here for the serious Al but you would have
to stay at a hotel because we have not got no spair room and it would
cost you a hole lot of money. But you can watch the papers and you
will see what I done.   Yours truly,   JACK.

Chicago, Illinois, October 6.

DEAR OLD PAL: Probily before you get this letter you will of saw
by the paper that we was licked in the first game and that I was
tooken out but the papers don't know what really come off so I am
going to tell you and you can see for yourself if it was my fault.

I did not never have no more stuff in my life then when I was
warming up and I seen the Cubs looking over to our bench and
shakeing there heads like they knowed they did not have no chance.
O'Day was going to start Cheney who is there best bet and had him
warming up but when he seen the smoke I had when I and Schalk
was warming up he changed his mind because what was the use of
useing his best pitcher when I had all that stuff and it was a cinch
that no club in the world could score a run off of me when I had all
that stuff?

So he told a couple others to warm up to and when my name was
announced to pitch Cheney went and set on the bench and this here
lefthander Pierce was announced for them.

Well Al you will see by the paper where I sent there 1st 3 batters
back to the bench to get a drink of water and all 3 of them good
hitters Leach and Good and this here Saier that hits a hole lot of
home runs but would not never hit one off of me if I was O. K.
Well we scored a couple in our half and the boys on the bench all
says Now you got enough to win easy because they won't never score
none off of you.

And they was right to because what chance did they have if this
thing that I am going to tell you about had not of happened? We
goes along seven innings and only 2 of there men had got to 1st base
one of them on a bad peg of Weaver's and the other one I walked
because this blind Evans don't know a ball from a strike. We had
not did no more scoreing off of Pierce not because he had no stuff
but because our club could not take a ball in there hands and hit it
out of the infield.

Well Al I did not tell you that before I come out to the park I kissed little Al and Florrie good by and Marie says she was going to stay home to and keep Florrie Co. and they was not no reason for Marie to come to the game anyway because they was not a chance in the world for Allen to do nothing but hit fungos. Well while I was doing all this here swell pitching and makeing them Cubs look like a lot of rummys I was thinking about little Al and Florrie and how glad they would be when I come home and told them what I done though of coarse little Al is not only a little over 3 months of age and how could he appresiate what I done? But Florrie would.

Well Al when I come in to the bench after there ½ of the 7th I happened to look up to the press box to see if the reporters had gave Schulte a hit on that one Weaver throwed away and who do you think I seen in a box right alongside of the press box? It was Florrie and Marie and both of them claping there hands and hollering with the rest of the bugs.

Well old pal I was never so surprised in my life and it just took all the heart out of me. What was they doing there and what had they did with the baby? How did I know that little Al was not sick or maybe dead and balling his head off and nobody round to hear him?

I tried to catch Florrie's eyes but she would not look at me. I hollered her name and the bugs looked at me like as if I was crazy and I was to Al. Well I seen they was not no use of standing out there in front of the stand so I come into the bench and Allen was setting there and I says Did you know your wife and Florrie was up there in the stand? He says No and I says What are they doing here? And he says What would they be doing here—mending there stockings? I felt like busting him and I guess he seen I was mad because he got up off of the bench and beat it down to the corner of the field where some of the others was getting warmed up though why should they have anybody warming up when I was going so good?

Well Al I made up my mind that ball game or no ball game I was not going to have little Al left alone no longer and I seen they was not no use of sending word to Florrie to go home because they was a big crowd and it would take maybe 15 or 20 minutes for somebody to get up to where she was at. So I says to Callahan You have got to take me out. He says What is the matter? Is your arm gone? I says No my arm is not gone but my baby is sick and home all alone. He says Where is your wife? And I says She is setting up there in the stand.

Then he says How do you know your baby is sick? And I says I don't know if he is sick or not but he is left home all alone. He says Why don't you send your wife home? And I says I could not get word to her in time. He says Well you have only got two innings to go and the way your going the game will be over in 10 minutes. I says Yes and before 10 minutes is up my baby might die and are you going to take me out or not? He says Get in there and pitch you yellow dog and if you don't I will take your share of the serious money away from you.

By this time our part of the inning was over and I had to go out there and pitch some more because he would not take me out and he has not got no heart Al. Well Al how could I pitch when I kept thinking maybe the baby was dying right now and maybe if I was home I could do something? And instead of paying attension to what I was doing I was thinking about little Al and looking up there to where Florrie and Marie was setting and before I knowed what come off they had the bases full and Callahan took me out.

Well Al I run to the clubhouse and changed my cloths and beat it for home and I did not even hear what Callahan and Gleason says to me when I went by them but I found out after the game that Scott went in and finished up and they batted him pretty hard and we was licked 3 and 2.

When I got home the baby was crying but he was not all alone after all Al because they was a little girl about 14 years of age there watching him and Florrie had hired her to take care of him so as her and Marie could go and see the game. But just think Al of leaveing little Al with a girl 14 years of age that did not never have no babys of her own! And what did she know about takeing care of him? Nothing Al.

You should ought to of heard me ball Florrie out when she got home and I bet she cried pretty near enough to flood the basemunt. We had it hot and heavy and the Allens butted in but I soon showed them where they was at and made them shut there mouth.

I had a good nosion to go out and get a hole lot of drinks and was just going to put on my hat when the doorbell rung and there was Kid Gleason. I thought he would be sore and probily try to ball me out and I was not going to stand for nothing but instead of balling me out he come and shook hands with me and interduced himself to Florrie and asked how was little Al.

Well we all set down and Gleason says the club was depending on me to win the serious because I was in the best shape of all the pitchers. And besides the Cubs could not never hit me when I was right and he was telling the truth to.

So he asked me if I would stand for the club hireing a train nurse to stay with the baby the rest of the serious so as Florrie could go and see her husband win the serious but I says No I would not stand for that and Florrie's place was with the baby.

So Gleason and Florrie goes out in the other room and talks a while and I guess he was persuadeing her to stay home because pretty soon they come back in the room and says it was all fixed up and I would not have to worry about little Al the rest of the serious but could give the club the best I got. Gleason just left here a little while ago and I won't work to-morrow Al but I will work the day after and you will see what I can do when I don't have nothing to worry me.   Your pal,   JACK.

Chicago, Illinois, October 8.

OLD PAL: Well old pal we got them 2 games to one now and the serious is sure to be over in three more days because I can pitch 2 games in that time if nessary. I shut them out to-day and they should ought not to of had four hits but should ought to of had only 2 but Bodie don't cover no ground and 2 fly balls that he should ought to of eat up fell safe.

But I beat them anyway and Benz beat them yesterday but why should he not beat them when the club made 6 runs for him? All they made for me was three but all I needed was one because they could not hit me with a shuvvel. When I come to the bench after the 5th inning they was a note there from the boy that answers the phone at the ball park and it says that somebody just called up from the flat and says the baby was asleep and getting along fine. So I felt good Al and I was better than ever in the 6th.

When I got home Florrie and Marie was both there and asked me how did the game come out because I beat Allen home and I told them all about what I done and I bet Florrie was proud of me but I supose Marie is a little jellus because how could she help it when Callahan is depending on me to win the serious and her husband is wearing out the wood on the bench? But why should she be sore when it is me that is winning the serious for them? And if it was not for me Allen and all the rest of them would get about $500.00 apeace instead of the winners' share which is about $750.00 apeace.

Cicotte is going to work to-morrow and if he is lucky maybe he can get away with the game and that will leave me to finish up the day after to-morrow but if nessary I can go in to-morrow when they get to hitting Cicotte and stop them and then come back the following day and beat them again. Where would this club be at Al if I had of jumped to the Federal?   Yours truly,   JACK.

Chicago, Illinois, October 11.

FRIEND AL: We done it again Al and I guess the Cubs won't never want to play us again not so long as I am with the club. Before you get this letter you will know what we done and who done it but probily you could of guessed that Al without seeing no paper.

I got 2 more of them phone messiges about the baby dureing the game and I guess that was what made me so good because I knowed then that Florrie was takeing care of him but I could not help feeling sorry for Florrie because she is a bug herself and it must of been pretty hard for her to stay away from the game espesially when she knowed I was going to pitch and she has been pretty good to sacrifice her own plesure for little Al.

Cicotte was knocked out of the box the day before yesterday and then they give this here Faber a good beating but I wish you could of saw what they done to Allen when Callahan sent him in after the game was gone allready. Honest Al if he had not of been my brother in law I would of felt like laughing at him because it looked like as if they would have to call the fire department to put the side out. They had Bodie and Collins hollering for help and with there tongue hanging out from running back to the fence.

Anyway the serious is all over and I won't have nothing to do but stay home and play with little Al but I don't know yet where my home is going to be at because it is a cinch I won't stay with Allen no longer. He has not come home since the game and I suppose he is out somewheres lapping up some beer and spending some of the winner's share of the money which he would not of had no chance to get in on if it had not of been for me.

I will write and let you know my plans for the winter and I wish Florrie would agree to come to Bedford but nothing doing Al and after her staying home and takeing care of the baby instead of watching me pitch I can't be too hard on her but must leave her have her own way about something.   Your pal,   JACK.

Chicago, Illinois, October 13.

AL: I am all threw with Florrie Al and I bet when you hear about it you won't say it was not no fault of mine but no man liveing who is any kind of a man would act different from how I am acting if he had of been decieved like I been.

Al Florrie and Marie was out to all them games and was not home takeing care of the baby at all and it is not her fault that little Al is not dead and that he was not killed by the nurse they hired to take care of him while they went to the games when I thought they was home takeing care of the baby. And all them phone messiges was just fakes and maybe the baby was sick all the time I was winning them games and balling his head off instead of being asleep like they said he was.

Allen did not never come home at all the night before last and when he come in yesterday he was a sight and I says to him Where have you been? And he says I have been down to the Y. M. C. A. but that is not none of your business. I says Yes you look like as if you had been to the Y. M. C. A. and I know where you have been and you have been out lushing beer. And he says Suppose I have and what are you going to do about it? And I says Nothing but you should ought to be ashamed of yourself and leaveing Marie here while you was out lapping up beer.

Then he says Did you not leave Florrie home while you was getting away with them games, you lucky stiff? And I says Yes but Florrie had to stay home and take care of the baby but Marie don't never have to stay home because where is your baby? You have not got no baby. He says I would not want no X-eyed baby like yourn. Then he says So you think Florrie stayed to home and took care of the baby do you? And I says What do you mean? And he says You better ask her.

So when Florrie come in and heard us talking she busted out crying and then I found out what they put over on me. It is a wonder Al that I did not take some of that cheap furniture them Allens got and bust it over there heads, Allen and Florrie. This is what they done Al. The club give Florrie $50.00 to stay home and take care of the baby and she said she would and she was to call up every so often and tell me the baby was all O. K. But this here Marie told her she was a sucker so she hired a nurse for part of the $50.00 and then her and Marie went to the games and beat it out quick after the games was over and come home in a taxicab and chased the nurse out before I got home.

Well Al when I found out what they done I grabbed my hat and goes out and got some drinks and I was so mad I did not know where I was at or what come off and I did not get home till this A.M. And they was all asleep and I been asleep all day and when I woke up Marie and Allen was out but Florrie and I have not spoke to each other and I won't never speak to her again.

But I know now what I am going to do Al and I am going to take little Al and beat it out of here and she can sew me for a bill of divorce and I should not worry because I will have little Al and I will see that he is tooken care of because I guess I can hire a nurse as well as they can and I will pick out a train nurse that knows something. Maybe I and him and the nurse will come to Bedford Al but I don't know yet and I will write and tell you as soon as I make up my mind. Did you ever hear of a man getting a rottener deal Al? And after what I done in the serious too.   Your pal,   JACK.

Chicago, Illinois, October 17.

OLD PAL: I and Florrie has made it up Al but we are threw with Marie and Allen and I and Florrie and the baby is staying at a hotel here on Cottage Grove Avenue the same hotel we was at when we got married only of coarse they was only the 2 of us then.

And now Al I want to ask you a favor and that is for you to go and see old man Cutting and tell him I want to ree-new the lease on that house for another year because I and Florrie has decided to spend the winter in Bedford and she will want to stay there and take care of little Al while I am away on trips next summer and not stay in no high-price flat up here. And may be you and Bertha can help her round the house when I am not there.

I will tell you how we come to fix things up Al and you will see that I made her apollojize to me and after this she will do what I tell her to and won't never try to put nothing over. We was eating breakfast—I and Florrie and Marie. Allen was still asleep yet because I guess he must of had a bad night and he was snoreing so as you could hear him in the next st. I was not saying nothing to nobody but pretty soon Florrie says to Marie I don't think you and Allen should ought to kick on the baby crying when Allen's snoreing makes more noise than a hole wagonlode of babys. And Marie got sore and says I guess a man has got a right to snore in his own house and you and Jack has been grafting off of us long enough.

Then Florrie says What did Allen do to help win the serious and get that $750.00? Nothing but set on the bench except when they was makeing him look like a sucker the 1 inning he pitched. The trouble with you and Allen is you are jellous of what Jack has did and you know he will be a star up here in the big league when Allen is tending bar which is what he should ought to be doing because then he could get stewed for nothing.

Marie says Take your brat and get out of the house. And Florrie says Don't you worry because we would not stay here no longer if you hired us. So Florrie went in her room and I followed her in and she says Let's pack up and get out.

Then I says Yes but we won't go nowheres together after what you done to me but you can go where you dam please and I and little Al will go to Bedford. Then she says You can't take the baby because he is mine and if you was to take him I would have you arrested for kidnaping. Besides, she says, what would you feed him and who would take care of him?

I says I would find somebody to take care of him and I would get him food from a resturunt. She says He can't eat nothing but milk and I says Well he has the collect all the time when he is eating milk and he would not be no worse off if he was eating watermelon. Well, she says, if you take him I will have you arrested and sew you for a bill of divorce for dessertion.

Then she says Jack you should not ought to find no fault with me for going to them games because when a woman has a husband that can pitch like you can do you think she wants to stay home and not see her husband pitch when a lot of other women is cheering him and makeing her feel proud because she is his wife?

Well Al as I said right along it was pretty hard on Florrie to have to stay home and I could not hardly blame her for wanting to be out there where she could see what I done so what was the use of argueing?

So I told her I would think it over and then I went out and I went and seen a attorney at law and asked him could I take little Al away and he says No I did not have no right to take him away from his mother and besides it would probily kill him to be tooken away from her and then he soaked me $10.00 the robber.

Then I went back and told Florrie I would give her another chance and then her and I packed up and took little Al in a taxicab over to this hotel. We are threw with the Allens Al and let me know right away if I can get that lease for another year because Florrie has gave up and will go to Bedford or anywheres else with me now.

Yours truly,   JACK.

Chicago, Illinois, October 20.

FRIEND AL: Old pal I won't never forget your kindnus and this is to tell you that I and Florrie except your kind invatation to come and stay with you till we can find a house and I guess you won't regret it none because Florrie will livun things up for Bertha and Bertha will be crazy about the baby because you should ought to see how cute he is now Al and not yet four months old. But I bet he will be talking before we know it.

We are comeing on the train that leaves here at noon Saturday Al and the train leaves here about 12 o'clock and I don't know what time it gets to Bedford but it leaves here at noon so we shall be there probily in time for supper.

I wish you would ask Ben Smith will he have a hack down to the deepo to meet us but I won't pay no more than $.25 and I should think he should ought to be glad to take us from the deepo to your house for nothing.   Your pal,   JACK.

P.S. The train we are comeing on leaves here at noon Al and will probily get us there in time for a late supper and I wonder if Bertha would have spair ribs and crout for supper. You know me Al.

THE BUSHER
BEATS IT HENCE

◇

FRIEND AL: I guess may be you will begin to think I dont never do what I am going to do and that I change my mind a hole lot because I wrote and told you that I and Florrie and little Al would be in Bedford to-day and here we are in Chi yet on the day when I told you we would get to Bedford and I bet Bertha and you and the rest of the boys will be dissapointed but Al I dont feel like as if I should ought to leave the White Sox in a hole and that is why I am here yet and I will tell you how it come off but in the 1st place I want to tell you that it wont make a diffrence of more than 5 or 6 or may be 7 days at least and we will be down there and see you and Bertha and the rest of the boys just as soon as the N. Y. giants and the White Sox leaves here and starts a round the world. All so I remember I told you to fix it up so as a hack would be down to the deepo to meet us to-night and you wont get this letter in time to tell them not to send no hack so I suppose the hack will be there but may be they will be some body else that gets off of the train that will want the hack and then every thing will be all O. K. but if they is not nobody else that wants the hack I will pay them ½ of what they was going to charge me if I had of came and road in the hack though I dont have to pay them nothing because I am not going to ride in the hack but I want to do the right thing and besides I will want a hack at the deepo when I do come so they will get a peace of money out of me any way so I dont see where they got no kick comeing even if I dont give them a nichol now.

I will tell you why I am still here and you will see where I am trying to do the right thing. You knowed of coarse that the White

Sox and the N. Y. giants was going to make a trip a round the world
and they been after me for a long time to go a long with them but
I says No I would not leave Florrie and the kid because that would
not be fare and besides I would be paying rent and grocer;s for them
some wheres and me not getting nothing out of it and besides I
would probily be spending a hole lot of money on the trip because
though the clubs pays all of our regular expences they would be a
hole lot of times when I felt like blowing my self and buying some
thing to send home to the Mrs and to good old friends of mine like
you and Bertha so I turned them down and Callahan acted like he
was sore at me but I dont care nothing for that because I got other
people to think a bout and not Callahan and besides if I was to go
a long the fans in the towns where we play at would want to see me
work and I would have to do a hole lot of pitching which I would
not be getting nothing for it and it would not count in no standing
because the games is to be just for fun and what good would it do
me and besides Florrie says I was not under no circumstance to go
and of coarse I would go if I wanted to go no matter what ever she
says but all and all I turned them down and says I would stay here
all winter or rather I would not stay here but in Bedford. Then
Callahan says All right but you know before we start on the trip the
giants and us is going to play a game right here in Chi next Sunday
and after what you done in the city serious the fans would be sore
if they did not get no more chance to look at you so will you stay
and pitch part of the game here and I says I would think it over and
I come home to the hotel where we are staying at and asked Florrie
did she care if we did not go to Bedford for an other week and she
says No she did not care if we dont go for 6 years so I called Callahan
up and says I would stay and he says Thats the boy and now the fans
will have an other treat so you see Al he appresiates what I done
and wants to give the fans fare treatment because this town is nuts
over me after what I done to them Cubs but I could do it just the
same to the Athaletics or any body else if it would of been them in
stead of the Cubs. May be we will leave here the A. M. after the
game that is Monday and I will let you know so as you can order an
other hack and tell Bertha I hope she did not go to no extra trouble
a bout getting ready for us and did not order no spair ribs and crout
but you can eat them up if she all ready got them and may be she
can order some more for us when we come but tell her it dont make
no diffrence and not to go to no trouble because most anything she

has is O. K. for I and Florrie accept of coarse we would not want to make no meal off of sardeens or something.

Well Al I bet them N. Y. giants will wish I would of went home before they come for this here exibishun game because my arm feels grate and I will show them where they would be at if they had to play ball in our league all the time though I supose they is some pitchers in our league that they would hit good against them if they can hit at all but not me. You will see in the papers how I come out and I will write and tell you a bout it.   Your pal,   JACK.

Chicago, Ill., Oct. 25.

OLD PAL: I have not only got a little time but I have got some news for you and I knowed you would want to hear all a bout it so I am writeing this letter and then I am going to catch the train. I would be saying good by to little Al instead of writeing this letter only Florrie wont let me wake him up and he is a sleep but may be by the time I get this letter wrote he will be a wake again and I can say good by to him. I am going with the White Sox and giants as far as San Francisco or may be Van Coover where they take the boat at but I am not going a round the world with them but only just out to the coast to help them out because they is a couple of men going to join them out there and untill them men join them they will be short of men and they got a hole lot of exibishun games to play before they get out there so I am going to help them out. It all come off in the club house after the game to-day and I will tell you how it come off but 1st I want to tell you a bout the game and honest Al them giants is the luckyest team in the world and it is not no wonder they keep wining the penant in that league because a club that has got there luck could win ball games with out sending no team on the field at all but staying down to the hotel.

They was a big crowd out to the park so Callahan says to me I did not know if I was going to pitch you or not but the crowd is out here to see you so I will have to let you work so I warmed up but I knowed the minute I throwed the 1st ball warming up that I was not right and I says to Callahan I did not feel good but he says You wont need to feel good to beat this bunch because they heard a hole lot a bout you and you would have them beat if you just throwed your glove out there in the box. So I went in and tried to pitch but my arm was so lame it pretty near killed me every ball I throwed

and I bet if I was some other pitchers they would not never of tried
to work with my arm so sore but I am not like some of them yellow
dogs and quit because I would not dissapoint the crowd or throw
Callahan down when he wanted me to pitch and was depending on
me. You know me Al. So I went in there but I did not have nothing
and if them giants could of hit at all in stead of like a lot of girls they
would of knock down the fence because I was not my self. At that
they should not ought to of had only the 1 run off of me if Weaver
and them had not of begin kicking the ball a round like it was a foot
ball or something. Well Al what with dropping fly balls and booting
them a round and this in that the giants was gave 5 runs in the 1st
3 innings and they should ought to of had just the 1 run or may be
not that and that ball Merkle hit in to the seats I was trying to waist
it and a man that is a good hitter would not never of hit at it and if
I was right this here Merkle could not foul me in 9 years. When I
was comeing into the bench after the 3th inning this here smart alex
Mcgraw come passed me from the 3 base coaching line and he says
Are you going on the trip and I says No I am not going on no trip
and he says That is to bad because if you was going we would win
a hole lot of games and I give him a hot come back and he did not
say nothing so I went in to the bench and Callahan says Them giants
is not such rotten hitters is they and I says No they hit pretty good
when a man has got a sore arm against them and he says Why did
not you tell me your arm was sore and I says I did not want to
dissapoint no crowd that come out here to see me and he says Well
I guess you need not pitch no more because if I left you in there
the crowd might begin to get tired of watching you a bout 10 oclock
to-night and I says What do you mean and he did not say nothing
more so I set there a while and then went to the club house. Well
Al after the game Callahan come in to the club house and I was still
in there yet talking to the trainer and getting my arm rubbed and
Callahan says Are you getting your arm in shape for next year and
I says No but it give me so much pane I could not stand it and he
says I bet if you was feeling good you could make them giants look
like a sucker and I says You know I could make them look like a
sucker and he says Well why dont you come a long with us and you
will get an other chance at them when you feel good and I says I
would like to get an other crack at them but I could not go a way
on no trip and leave the Mrs and the baby and then he says he would
not ask me to make the hole trip a round the world but he wisht I

would go out to the coast with them because they was hard up for pitchers and he says Mathewson of the giants was not only going as far as the coast so if the giants had there star pitcher that far the White Sox should ought to have theren and then some of the other boys coaxed me would I go so finely I says I would think it over and I went home and seen Florrie and she says How long would it be for and I says a bout 3 or 4 weeks and she says If you dont go will we start for Bedford right a way and I says Yes and then she says All right go a head and go but if they was any thing should happen to the baby while I was gone what would they do if I was not a round to tell them what to do and I says Call a Dr. in but dont call no Dr. if you dont have to and besides you should ought to know by this time what to do for the baby when he got sick and she says Of course I know a little but not as much as you do because you know it all. Then I says No I dont know it all but I will tell you some things before I go and you should not ought to have no trouble so we fixed it up and her and little Al is to stay here in the hotel untill I come back which will be a bout the 20 of Nov. and then we will come down home and tell Bertha not to get to in patient and we will get there some time. It is going to cost me $6.00 a week at the hotel for a room for she and the baby besides there meals but the babys meals dont cost nothing yet and Florrie should not ought to be very hungry because we been liveing good and besides she will get all she can eat when we come to Bedford and it wont cost me nothing for meals on the trip out to the coast because Comiskey and Mcgraw pays for that.

I have not even had no time to look up where we play at but we stop off at a hole lot of places on the way and I will get a chance to make them giants look like a sucker before I get threw and Mcgraw wont be so sorry I am not going to make the hole trip. You will see by the papers what I done to them before we get threw and I will write as soon as we stop some wheres long enough so as I can write and now I am going to say good by to little Al if he is a wake or not a wake and wake him up and say good by to him because even if he is not only 5 months old he is old enough to think a hole lot of me and why not. I all so got to say good by to Florrie and fix it up with the hotel clerk a bout she and the baby staying here a while and catch the train. You will hear from me soon old pal.

Your pal,   JACK.

St. Joe, Miss., Oct. 29.

FRIEND AL: Well Al we are on our way to the coast and they is quite a party of us though it is not no real White Sox and giants at all but some players from off of both clubs and then some others that is from other clubs a round the 2 leagues to fill up. We got Speaker from the Boston club and Crawford from the Detroit club and if we had them with us all the time Al I would not never loose a game because one or the other of them 2 is good for a couple of runs every game and that is all I need to win my games is a couple of runs or only 1 run and I would win all my games and would not never loose a game.

I did not pitch to-day and I guess the giants was glad of it because no matter what Mcgraw says he must of saw from watching me Sunday that I was a real pitcher though my arm was so sore I could not hardly raze it over my sholder so no wonder I did not have no stuff but at that I could of beat his gang with out no stuff if I had of had some kind of decent suport. I will pitch against them may be to-morrow or may be some day soon and my arm is all O. K. again now so I will show them up and make them wish Callahan had of left me to home. Some of the men has brung there wife a long and besides that there is some other men and there wife that is not no ball players but are going a long for the trip and some more will join the party out the coast before they get a bord the boat but of coarse I and Mathewson will drop out of the party then because why should I or him go a round the world and throw our arms out pitching games that dont count in no standing and that we dont get no money for pitching them out side of just our bare expences. The people in the towns we played at so far has all wanted to shake hands with Mathewson and I so I guess they know who is the real pitchers on these here 2 clubs no matter what them reporters says and the stars is all ways the men that the people wants to shake there hands with and make friends with them but Al this here Mathewson pitched to-day and honest Al I dont see how he gets by and either the batters in the National league dont know nothing a bout hitting or else he is such a old man that they feel sorry for him and may be when he was a bout 10 years younger than he is may be then he had some thing and was a pretty fare pitcher but all he does now is stick the 1st ball right over with 0 on it and pray that they dont hit it out of the park. If a pitcher like he can get by in the National league and fool them batters they is not nothing I would like better then to pitch in the National league and I bet I would not get scored on in 2 to 3 years.

I heard a hole lot a bout this here fade a way that he is suposed to pitch and it is a ball that is throwed out between 2 fingers and falls in at a right hand batter and they is not no body cant hit it but if he throwed 1 of them things to-day he done it while I was a sleep and they was not no time when I was not wide a wake and looking right at him and after the game was over I says to him Where is that there fade a way I heard so much a bout and he says O I did not have to use none of my regular stuff against your club and I says Well you would have to use all you got if I was working against you and he says Yes if you worked like you done Sunday I would have to do some pitching or they would not never finish the game. Then I says a bout me haveing a sore arm Sunday and he says I wisht I had a sore arm like yourn and a little sence with it and was your age and I would not never loose a game so you see Al he has heard a bout me and is jellus because he has not got my stuff but they cant every body expect to have the stuff that I got or ½ as much stuff. This smart alex Mcgraw was trying to kid me to-day and says Why did not I make friends with Mathewson and let him learn me some thing a bout pitching and I says Mathewson could not learn me nothing and he says I guess thats right and I guess they is not nobody could learn you nothing a bout nothing and if you was to stay in the league 20 years probily you would not be no better than you are now so you see he had to add mit that I am good Al even if he has not saw me work when my arm was O. K.

Mcgraw says to me to-night he says I wisht you was going all the way and I says Yes you do. I says Your club would look like a sucker after I had worked against them a few times and he says May be thats right to because they would not know how to hit against a regular pitcher after that. Then he says But I dont care nothing a bout that but I wisht you was going to make the hole trip so as we could have a good time. He says We got Steve Evans and Dutch Schaefer going a long and they is both of them funny but I like to be a round with boys that is funny and dont know nothing a bout it. I says Well I would go a long only for my wife and baby and he says Yes it would be pretty tough on your wife to have you a way that long but still and all think how glad she would be to see you when you come back again and besides them dolls acrost the ocean will be pretty sore at I and Callahan if we tell them we left you to home. I says Do you supose the people over there has heard a bout me and he says Sure because they have wrote a lot of letters asking me to be sure and bring you and Mathewson a long. Then he says

I guess Mathewson is not going so if you was to go and him left here to home they would not be nothing to it. You could have things all your own way and probily could marry the Queen of europe if you was not all ready married. He was giveing me the strate dope this time Al because he did not crack a smile and I wisht I could go a long but it would not be fare to Florrie but still and all did not she leave me and beat it for Texas last winter and why should not I do the same thing to her only I am not that kind of a man. You know me Al.

We play in Kansas city to-morrow and may be I will work there because it is a big town and I have got to close now and write to Florrie. Your old pal, JACK.

Abilene, Texas, Nov. 4.

AL: Well Al I guess you know by this time that I have worked against them 2 times since I wrote to you last time and I beat them both times and Mcgraw knows now what kind of a pitcher I am and I will tell you how I know because after the game yesterday he road down to the place we dressed at a long with me and all the way in the automobile he was after me to say I would go all the way a round the world and finely it come out that he wants I should go a long and pitch for his club and not pitch for the White Sox. He says his club is up against it for pitchers because Mathewson is not going and all they got left is a man named Hern that is a young man and not got no experiense and Wiltse that is a left hander. So he says I have talked it over with Callahan and he says if I could get you to go a along it was all O. K. with him and you could pitch for us only I must not work you to hard because he is depending on you to win the penant for him next year. I says Did not none of the other White Sox make no holler because may be they might have to bat against me and he says Yes Crawford and Speaker says they would not make the trip if you was a long and pitching against them but Callahan showed them where it would be good for them next year because if they hit against you all winter the pitchers they hit against next year will look easy to them. He was crazy to have me go a long on the hole trip but of coarse Al they is not no chance of me going on acct. of Florrie and little Al but you see Mcgraw has cut out his trying to kid me and is treating me now like a man should ought to be treated that has did what I done.

They was not no game here to-day on acct. of it raining and the people here was sore because they did not see no game but they all come a round to look at us and says they must have some speechs from the most prommerent men in the party so I and Comiskey and Mcgraw and Callahan and Mathewson and Ted Sullivan that I guess is putting up the money for the trip made speechs and they clapped there hands harder when I was makeing my speech then when any 1 of the others was makeing there speech. You did not know I was a speech maker did you Al and I did not know it neither untill to-day but I guess they is not nothing I can do if I make up my mind and 1 of the boys says that I done just as well as Dummy Taylor could of.

I have not heard nothing from Florrie but I guess may be she is to busy takeing care of little Al to write no letters and I am not worring none because she give me her word she would let me know was they some thing the matter. Yours truly, JACK.

San Dago, Cal, Nov. 9.

FRIEND AL: Al some times I wisht I was not married at all and if it was not for Florrie and little Al I would go a round the world on this here trip and I guess the boys in Bedford would not be jellus if I was to go a round the world and see every thing they is to be saw and some of the boys down home has not never been no futher a way then Terre Haute and I dont mean you Al but some of the other boys. But of coarse Al when a man has got a wife and a baby they is not no chance for him to go a way on 1 of these here trips and leave them a lone so they is not no use I should even think a bout it but I cant help thinking a bout it because the boys keeps after me all the time to go. Callahan was talking a bout it to me to-day and he says he knowed that if I was to pitch for the giants on the trip his club would not have no chance of wining the most of the games on the trip but still and all he wisht I would go a long because he was a scared the people over in Rome and Paris and Africa and them other countrys would be awful sore if the 2 clubs come over there with out bringing none of there star pitchers along. He says We got Speaker and Crawford and Doyle and Thorp and some of them other real stars in all the positions accept pitcher and it will make us look bad if you and Mathewson dont neither 1 of you come a long. I says What is the matter with Scott and Benz and this here left hander Wiltse and he says They is not nothing the matter with none of them accept they is not no real stars like you and Mathewson and if we cant show them forreners 1 of you 2 we will feel like as if we was cheating them. I says You would not want me to pitch my best against your club would you and he says O no I would not want you to pitch your best or get your self all wore out for next year but I would want you to let up enough so as we could make a run oncet in a while so the games would not be to 1 sided. I says Well they is not no use talking a bout it because I could not leave my wife and baby and he says Why dont you write and ask your wife and tell her how it is and can you go. I says No because she would make a big holler and besides of coarse I would go any way if I wanted to go with out no I yes or no from her only I am not the kind of a man that runs off and leaves his family and besides they is not nobody to leave her with because her and her sister Allens wife has had a quarrle. Then Callahan says Where is Allen at now is he still in Chi. I says I dont know where is he at and I dont care where he is at because I am threw with him. Then Callahan says I asked him would he go on the trip before the season was over but he says he could not and if I knowed where was he I would wire a telegram to him and ask him again. I says What would you want him a long for and he says Because Mcgraw is shy of pitchers and I says I would try and help him find 1. I says Well you should ought not to have no trouble finding a man like Allen to go along because his wife probily would be glad to get rid of him. Then Callahan says Well I wisht you would get a hold of where Allen is at and let me know so as I can wire him a telegram. Well Al I know where Allen is at all O. K. but I am not going to give his adress to Callahan because Mcgraw has treated me all O. K. and why should I wish a man like Allen on to him and besides I am not going to give Allen no chance to go a round the world or no wheres else after the way he acted a bout I and Florrie haveing a room in his flat and asking me to pay for it when he give me a invatation to come there and stay. Well Al it is to late now to cry in the sour milk but I wisht I had not never saw Florrie untill next year and then I and her could get married just like we done last year only I dont know would I do it again or not but I guess I would on acct. of little Al.

Your pal,   JACK.

San Francisco, Cal., Nov. 14.

OLD PAL: Well old pal what do you know a bout me being back here in San Francisco where I give the fans such a treat 2 years ago and then I was not nothing but a busher and now I am with a team that is going a round the world and are crazy to have me go a long only I cant because of my wife and baby. Callahan wired a telegram to the reporters here from Los Angeles telling them I would pitch here and I guess they is going to be 20 or 25000 out to the park and I will give them the best I got.

But what do you think Florrie has did Al. Her and the Allens has made it up there quarrle and is friends again and Marie told Florrie to write and tell me she was sorry we had that there argument and let by gones be by gones. Well Al it is all O. K. with me because I cant help not feeling sorry for Allen because I dont beleive he will be in the league next year and I feel sorry for Marie to because it must be pretty tough on her to see how well her sister done and what a misstake she made when she went and fell for a left hander that could not fool a blind man with his curve ball and if he was to hit a man in the head with his fast ball they would think there nose iched. In Florries letter she says she thinks us and the Allens could find an other flat like the 1 we had last winter and all live in it to gether in stead of going to Bedford but I have wrote to her before I started writeing this letter all ready and told her that her and I is going to Bedford and the Allens can go where they feel like and they can go and stay on a boat on Michigan lake all winter if they want to but I and Florrie is comeing to Bedford. Down to the bottom of her letter she says Allen wants to know if Callahan or Mcgraw is shy of pitchers and may be he would change his mind and go a long on the trip. Well Al I did not ask either Callahan nor Mcgraw nothing a bout it because I knowed they was looking for a star and not for no left hander that could not brake a pane of glass with his fast 1 so I wrote and told Florrie to tell Allen they was all filled up and would not have no room for no more men.

It is pretty near time to go out to the ball park and I wisht you could be here Al and hear them San Francisco fans go crazy when they hear my name anounced to pitch. I bet they wish they had of had me here this last year.   Yours truly,   JACK.

Medford, Organ, Nov. 16.

FRIEND AL: Well Al you know by this time that I did not pitch the hole game in San Francisco but I was not tooken out because they was hitting me Al but because my arm went back on me all of a sudden and it was the change in the clime it that done it to me and they could not hire me to try and pitch another game in San Francisco. They was the biggest crowd there that I ever seen in San Francisco and I guess they must of been 40000 people there and I wisht you could of heard them yell when my name was anounced to pitch. But Al I would not never of went in there but for the crowd. My arm felt like a wet rag or some thing and I knowed I would not have nothing and besides the people was packed in a round the field and they had to have ground rules so when a man hit a pop fly it went in to the crowd some wheres and was a 2 bagger and all them giants could do against me was pop my fast ball up in the air and then the wind took a hold of it and dropped it in to the crowd the lucky stiffs. Doyle hit 3 of them pop ups in to the crowd so when you see them 3 2 base hits oposit his name in the score you will know they was not no real 2 base hits and the infielders would of catched them had it not of been for the wind. This here Doyle takes a awful wallop at a ball but if I was right and he swang at a ball the way he done in San Francisco the catcher would all ready be throwing me back the ball a bout the time this here Doyle was swinging at it. I can make him look like a sucker and I done it both in Kansas city and Bonham and if he will get up there and bat against me when I feel good and when they is not no wind blowing I will bet him a $25.00 suit of cloths that he cant foul 1 off of me. Well when Callahan seen how bad my arm was he says I guess I should ought to take you out and not run no chance of you getting killed in there and so I quit and Faber went in to finnish it up because it dont make no diffrence if he hurts his arm or dont. But I guess Mcgraw knowed my arm was sore to because he did not try and kid me like he done that day in Chi because he has saw enough of me since then to know I can make his club look rotten when I am O.K. and my arm is good. On the train that night he come up and says to me Well Jack we catched you off your strid to-day or you would of gave us a beating and then he says What your arm needs is more work and you should ought to make the hole trip with us and then you would be in fine shape for next year but I says You cant get me to make no trip so you might is well not do no more talking a bout it and then he says Well I am sorry and the girls over to Paris will be sorry to but I guess he was just jokeing a bout the last part of it.

Well Al we go to 1 more town in Organ and then to Washington but of coarse it is not the same Washington we play at in the summer but this is the state Washington and have not got no big league club

and the boys gets there boat in 4 more days and I will quit them and
then I will come strate back to Chi and from there to Bedford.

Your pal,   JACK.

Portland, Organ, Nov. 17.

FRIEND AL: I have just wrote a long letter to Florrie but I feel
like as if I should ought to write to you because I wont have no
more chance for a long while that is I wont have no more chance to
male a letter because I will be on the pacific Ocean and un less we
should run passed a boat that was comeing the other way they would
not be no chance of getting no letter maled. Old pal I am going to
make the hole trip clear a round the world and back and so I wont
see you this winter after all but when I do see you Al I will have a
lot to tell you a bout my trip and besides I will write you a letter a
bout it from every place we head in at.

I guess you will be surprised a bout me changeing my mind and
makeing the hole trip but they was not no way for me to get out of
it and I will tell you how it all come off. While we was still in that
there Medford yesterday Mcgraw and Callahan come up to me and
says was they not no chance of me changeing my mind a bout makeing
the hole trip. I says No they was not. Then Callahan says Well I
dont know what we are going to do then and I says Why and he says
Comiskey just got a letter from president Wilson the President of
the united states and in the letter president Wilson says he had got
an other letter from the king of Japan who says that they would not
stand for the White Sox and giants comeing to Japan un less they
brought all there stars a long and president Wilson says they would
have to take there stars a long because he was a scared if they did
not take there stars a long Japan would get mad at the united states
and start a war and then where would we be at. So Comiskey wired
a telegram to president Wilson and says Mathewson could not make
the trip because he was so old but would everything be all O.K. if
I was to go a long and president Wilson wired a telegram back and
says Yes he had been talking to the priest from Japan and he says
Yes it would be all O.K. I asked them would they show me the letter
from president Wilson because I thought may be they might be kiding
me and they says they could not show me no letter because when
Comiskey got the letter he got so mad that he tore it up. Well Al I
finely says I did not want to brake up there trip but I knowed Florrie

would not stand for letting me go so Callahan says All right I will wire a telegram to a friend of mine in Chi and have him get a hold of Allen and send him out here and we will take him a long and I says It is to late for Allen to get here in time and Mcgraw says No they was a train that only took 2 days from Chi to where ever it was the boat is going to sale from because the train come a round threw canada and it was down hill all the way. Then I says Well if you will wire a telegram to my wife and fix things up with her I will go a long with you but if she is going to make a holler it is all off. So we all 3 went to the telegram office to gether and we wired Florrie a telegram that must of cost $2.00 but Callahan and Mcgraw payed for it out of there own pocket and then we waited a round a long time and the anser come back and the anser was longer than the telegram we wired and it says it would not make no difference to her but she did not know if the baby would make a holler but he was hollering most of the time any way so that would not make no diffrence but if she let me go it was on condishon that her and the Allens could get a flat to gether and stay in Chi all winter and not go to no Bedford and hire a nurse to take care of the baby and if I would send her a check for the money I had in the bank so as she could put it in her name and draw it out when she need it. Well I says at 1st I would not stand for nothing like that but Callahan and Mcgraw showed me where I was makeing a mistake not going when I could see all them diffrent countrys and tell Florrie all a bout the trip when I come back and then in a year or 2 when the baby was a little older I could make an other trip and take little Al and Florrie a long so I finely says O.K. I would go and we wires still an other telegram to Florrie and told her O.K. and then I set down and wrote her a check for ½ the money I got in the bank and I got $500.00 all together there so I wrote her a check for ½ of that or $250.00 and maled it to her and if she cant get a long on that she would be a awfull spendrift because I am not only going to be a way untill March. You should ought to of heard the boys cheer when Callahan tells them I am going to make the hole trip but when he tells them I am going to pitch for the giants and not for the White Sox I bet Crawford and Speaker and them wisht I was going to stay to home but it is just like Callahan says if they bat against me all winter the pitchers they bat against next season will look easy to them and you wont be surprised Al if Crawford and Speaker hits a bout 500 next year and if they hit good you will know why it is. Steve Evans asked me was I all fixed up with cloths and I says No but I was going out and buy

some cloths includeing a full dress suit of evening cloths and he says
You dont need no full dress suit of evening cloths because you look
funny enough with out them. This Evans is a great kidder Al and no
body never gets sore at the stuff he pulls some thing like Kid Gleason.
I wisht Kid Gleason was going on the trip Al but I will tell him all
a bout it when I come back.

Well Al old pal I wisht you was going a long to and I bet we could
have the time of our life but I will write to you right a long Al and
I will send Bertha some post cards from the diffrent places we head
in at. I will try and write you a letter on the boat and male it as soon
as we get to the 1st station which is either Japan or Yokohama I
forgot which. Good by Al and say good by to Bertha for me and tell
her how sorry I and Florrie is that we cant come to Bedford this
winter but we will spend all the rest of the winters there and her
and Florrie will have a plenty of time to get acquainted. Good by
old pal.   Your pal,   JACK.

Seattle, Wash., Nov. 18.

AL: Well Al it is all off and I am not going on no trip a round the
world and back and I been looking for Callahan or Mcgraw for the
last ½ hour to tell them I have changed my mind and am not going
to make no trip because it would not be fare to Florrie and besides
that I think I should ought to stay home and take care of little Al
and not leave him to be tooken care of by no train nurse because
how do I know what would she do to him and I am not going to tell
Florrie nothing a bout it but I am going to take the train to-morrow
night right back to Chi and supprise her when I get there and I bet
both her and little Al will be tickled to death to see me. I supose
Mcgraw and Callahan will be sore at me for a while but when I tell
them I want to do the right thing and not give my famly no raw deal
I guess they will see where I am right.

We was to play 2 games here and was to play 1 of them in Tacoma
and the other here but it rained and so we did not play neither 1
and the people was pretty mad a bout it because I was announced
to pitch and they figured probily this would be there only chance to
see me in axion and they made a awful holler but Comiskey says No
they would not be no game because the field neither here or in
Tacoma was in no shape for a game and he would not take no chance
of me pitching and may be slipping in the mud and straneing myself
and then where would the White Sox be at next season. So we been

laying a round all the P.M. and I and Dutch Schaefer had a long talk
to gether while some of the rest of the boys was out buying some
cloths to take on the trip and Al I bought a full dress suit of evening
cloths at Portland yesterday and now I owe Callahan the money for
them and am not going on no trip so probily I wont never get to
ware them and it is just $45.00 throwed a way but I would rather
throw $45.00 a way then go on a trip a round the world and leave
my family all winter.

Well Al I and Schaefer was talking to gether and he says Well may
be this is the last time we will ever see the good old US and I says
What do you mean and he says People that gos acrost the pacific
Ocean most generally all ways has there ship recked and then they
is not no more never heard from them. Then he asked me was I a
good swimmer and I says Yes I had swam a good deal in the river
and he says Yes you have swam in the river but that is not nothing
like swimming in the pacific Ocean because when you swim in the
pacific Ocean you cant move your feet because if you move your
feet the sharks comes up to the top of the water and bites at them
and even if they did not bite your feet clean off there bite is poison
and gives you the hiderofobeya and when you get that you start
barking like a dog and the water runs in to your mouth and chokes
you to death. Then he says Of coarse if you can swim with out useing
your feet you are all O.K. but they is very few can do that and
especially in the pacific Ocean because they got to keep useing there
hands all the time to scare the sord fish a way so when you dont dare
use your feet and your hands is busy you got nothing left to swim
with but your stumach mussles. Then he says You should ought to
get a long all O.K. because your stumach muscles should ought to
be strong from the exercise they get so I guess they is not no danger
from a man like you but men like Wiltse and Mike Donlin that is
not hog fat like you has not got no chance. Then he says Of course
they have been times when the boats got acrost all O.K. and only a
few lives lost but it dont offten happen and the time the old Minneapolis club made the trip the boat went down and the only thing
that was saved was the catchers protector that was full of air and
could not do nothing else but flote. Then he says May be you would
flote to if you did not say nothing for a few days.

I asked him how far would a man got to swim if some thing went
wrong with the boat and he says O not far because they is a hole lot
of ilands a long the way that a man could swim to but it would not
do a man no good to swim to these here ilands because they dont

have nothing to eat on them and a man would probily starve to death un less he happened to swim to the sandwich islands. Then he says But by the time you been out on the pacific Ocean a few months you wont care if you get any thing to eat or not. I says Why not and he says the pacific Ocean is so ruff that not nothing can set still not even the stuff you eat. I asked him how long did it take to make the trip acrost if they was not no ship reck and he says they should ought to get acrost a long in febuery if the weather was good. I says Well if we dont get there until febuery we wont have no time to train for next season and he says You wont need to do no training because this trip will take all the weight off of you and every thing else you got. Then he says But you should not ought to be scared of getting sea sick because they is 1 way you can get a way from it and that is to not eat nothing at all while you are on the boat and they tell me you dont eat hardly nothing any way so you wont miss it. Then he says Of coarse if we should have good luck and not get in to no ship reck and not get shot by 1 of them war ships we will have a grate time when we get acrost because all the girls in europe and them places is nuts over ball players and especially stars. I asked what did he mean saying we might get shot by 1 of them war ships and he says we would have to pass by Swittserland and the Swittserland war ships was all the time shooting all over the ocean and of coarse they was not trying to hit no body but they was as wild as most of them left handers and how could you tell what was they going to do next.

Well Al after I got threw talking to Schaefer I run in to Jack Sheridan the umpire and I says I did not think I would go on no trip and I told him some of the things Schaefer was telling me and Sheridan says Schaefer was kidding me and they was not no danger at all and of coarse Al I did not believe ½ of what Schaefer was telling me and that has not got nothing to do with me changeing my mind but I don't think it is not hardly fare for me to go a way on a trip like that and leave Florrie and the baby and suppose some of them things really did happen like Schaefer said though of coarse he was kidding me but if 1 of them things really did happen they would not be no body left to take care of Florrie and little Al and I got a $1000.00 insurence policy but how do I know after I am dead if the insurence co. comes acrost and gives my famly the money.

Well Al I will male this letter and then try again and find Mcgraw and Callahan and then I will look up a time table and see what train can I get to Chi. I dont know yet when I will be in Bedford and may be Florrie has hired a flat all ready but the Allens can live in it by them self and if Allen says any thing a bout I paying for ½ of the rent I will bust his jaw.   Your pal,   JACK.

Victoria, Can., Nov. 19.

DEAR OLD AL: Well old pal the boat goes to-night I am going a long and I would not be takeing no time to write this letter only I wrote to you yesterday and says I was not going and you probily would be expecting to see me blow in to Bedford in a few days and besides Al I got a hole lot of things to ask you to do for me if any thing happens and I want to tell you how it come a bout that I changed my mind and am going on the trip. I am glad now that I did not write Florrie no letter yesterday and tell her I was not going because now I would have to write her an other letter and tell her I was going and she would be expecting to see me the day after she got the 1st letter and in stead of seeing me she would get this 2nd. letter and not me at all. I have all ready wrote her a good by letter to-day though and while I was writeing it Al I all most broke down and cried and espesially when I thought a bout leaveing little Al so long and may be when I see him again he wont be no baby no more or may be some thing will of happened to him or that train nurse did some thing to him or may be I wont never see him again no more because it is pretty near a cinch that some thing will either happen to I or him. I would give all most any thing I got Al to be back in Chi with little Al and Florrie and I wisht she had not of never wired that telegram telling me I could make the trip and if some thing happens to me think how she will feel when ever she thinks a bout wireing me that telegram and she will feel all most like as if she was a murder.

Well Al after I had wrote you that letter yesterday I found Callahan and Mcgraw and I tell them I have changed my mind and am not going on no trip. Callahan says Whats the matter and I says I dont think it would be fare to my wife and baby and Callahan says Your wife says it would be all O.K. because I seen the telegram my self. I says Yes but she dont know how dangerus the trip is and he says Whos been kiding you and I says They has not no body been kiding me. I says Dutch Schaefer told me a hole lot of stuff but I did not believe none of it and that has not got nothing to do with it. I says I am not a scared of nothing but supose some thing should happen and then where would my wife and my baby be at. Then Callahan says Schaefer has been giveing you a lot of hot air and they is not no more danger on this trip than they is in bed. You been in a hole lot more danger when you was pitching some of them days when you had a sore arm and you would be takeing more chances of getting killed in Chi by 1 of them taxi cabs or the dog catcher then on the Ocean. This here boat we are going on is the Umpires of Japan and it has went acrost the Ocean a million times with out nothing happening and they could not nothing happen to a boat that the N. Y. giants was rideing on because they is to lucky. Then I says Well I have made up my mind to not go on no trip and he says All right then I guess we might is well call the trip off and I says Why and he says You know what president Wilson says a bout Japan and they wont stand for us comeing over there with out you a long and then Mcgraw says Yes it looks like as if the trip was off because we dont want to take no chance of starting no war between Japan and the united states. Then Callahan says You will be in fine with Comiskey if he has to call the trip off because you are a scared of getting hit by a fish. Well All we talked and argude for a hour or a hour and ½ and some of the rest of the boys come a round and took Callahan and Mcgraw side and finely Callahan says it looked like as if they would have to posepone the trip a few days untill he could get a hold of Allen or some body and then get them to take my place so finely I says I would go because I would not want to brake up no trip after they had made all there plans and some of the players wifes was all ready to go and would be dissapointed if they was not no trip. So Mcgraw and Callahan says Thats the way to talk and so I am going Al and we are leaveing to-night and may be this is the last letter you will ever get from me but if they does not nothing happen Al I will write to you a lot of letters and tell you all a bout the trip but you must not be looking for no more letters for a while untill we get to Japan where I can male a letter and may be its likely as not we wont never get to Japan.

Here is the things I want to ask you to try and do Al and I am not asking you to do nothing if we get threw the trip but if some thing happens and I should be drowned here is what I am asking you to do for me and that is to see that the insurence co. dont skin Florrie out of that $1000.00 policy and see that she all so gets that other $250.00 out of the bank and find her some place down in Bedford to live if she is willing to live down there because she can live there a hole lot cheaper than she can live in Chi and besides I know Bertha would treat her right and help her out all she could. All so Al I want you and Bertha to help take care of little Al untill he grows up big enough to take care of him self and if he looks like as if he was going to be left handed dont let him Al but make him use his right hand for every thing. Well Al they is 1 good thing and that is if I get drowned Florrie wont have to buy no lot in no cemetary and hire no herse.

Well Al old pal you all ways been a good friend of mine and I all ways tried to be a good friend of yourn and if they was ever any thing I done to you that was not O.K. remember by gones is by gones. I want you to all ways think of me as your best old pal. Good by old pal.   Your old pal,   JACK.

P.S. Al if they should not nothing happen and if we was to get acrost the Ocean all O.K. I am going to ask Mcgraw to let me work the 1st game against the White Sox in Japan because I should certainly ought to be right after giveing my arm a rest and not doing nothing at all on the trip acrost and I bet if Mcgraw lets me work Crawford and Speaker will wish the boat had of sank. You know me Al.

CALL FOR MR. KEEFE!

◇

St. Louis, April 10.

FRIEND AL: Well Al the training trips over and we open up the sesaon here tomorrow and I suppose the boys back home is all anxious to know about our chances and what shape the boys is in. Well old pal you can tell them we are out after that old flag this year and the club that beats us will know they have been in a battle. I'll say they will.

Speaking for myself personly I never felt better in my life and you know what that means Al. It means I will make a monkey out of this league and not only that but the boys will all have more confidence in themself and play better baseball when they know my arms right and that I can give them the best I got and if Rowland handles the club right and don't play no favorites like last season we will be so far out in front by the middle of July that Boston and the rest of them will think we have jumped to some other league.

Well I suppose the old towns all excited about Uncle Sam declairing war on Germany. Personly I am glad we are in it but between you and I Al I figure we ought to of been in it a long time ago right after the Louisiana was sank. I often say alls fair in love and war but that don't mean the Germans or no one else has got a right to murder American citizens but thats about all you can expect from a German and anybody that expects a square deal from them is a sucker. You don't see none of them umpireing in our league but at that they couldn't be no worse than the ones we got. Some of ours is so crooked they can't lay in a birth only when the trains making a curve.

But speaking about the war Al you couldn't keep me out of it only for Florrie and little Al depending on me for sport and of course theys the ball club to and I would feel like a trader if I quit them

This story first appeared in *The Saturday Evening Post*, March 9, 1918; reprinted in *Some Champions* (New York: Scribners, 1976).

now when it looks like this is our year. So I might just as well make up my mind to whats got to be and not mop over it but I like to kid the rest of the boys and make them think I'm going to enlist to see their face fall and tonight at supper I told Gleason I thought I would quit the club and join the army. He tried to laugh it off with some of his funny stuff. He says "They wouldn't take you." "No," I said. "I suppose Uncle Sam is turning down men with a perfect physic." So he says "They don't want a man that if a shell would hit him in the head it would explode all over the trench and raise havioc." I forget what I said back to him.

Well Al I don't know if I will pitch in this serious or not but if I do I will give them a touch of high life but maybe Rowland will save me to open up at Detroit where a mans got to have something besides their glove. It takes more than camel flags to beat that bunch. I'll say it does.   Your pal,   Jack.

Chicago, April 15.

FRIEND AL: Well Al here I am home again and Rowland sent some of us home from St. Louis instead of takeing us along to Detroit and I suppose he is figureing on saveing me to open up the home season next Thursday against St. Louis because they always want a big crowd on opening day and St. Louis don't draw very good unless theys some extra attraction to bring the crowd out. But anyway I was glad to get home and see Florrie and litttle Al and honest Al he is cuter than ever and when he seen me he says "Who are you?" Hows that for a 3 year old?

Well things has been going along pretty good at home while I was away only it will take me all summer to pay the bills Florrie has ran up on me and you ought to be thankfull that Bertha aint 1 of these Apollos thats got to keep everybody looking at them or they can't eat. Honest Al to look at the clothes Florrie has boughten you would think we was planning to spend the summer at Newport News or somewhere. And she went and got herself a hired girl that sticks us for $8.00 per week and all as she does is cook up the meals and take care of little Al and run wild with a carpet sweeper and dust rag every time you set down to read the paper. I says to Florrie "What is the idea? The 3 of us use to get along O. K. without no help from Norway." So she says "I got sick in tired of staying home all the time or dragging the baby along with me when I went out." So I said I remembered when she wouldn't leave no one else take care of the kid only herself and she says "Yes but that was when I didn't know nothing about babys and every time he cried I thought he had lumbago or something but now I know he has got no intentions of dying so I quit worring about him."

So I said "Yes but I can't afford no high price servants to say nothing about dressing you like an actor and if you think I am going to spend all my salary on silks and satans and etc. you will get a big surprise." So she says "You might as well spend your money on me as leave the ball players take it away from you in the poker game and show their own wives a good time with it. But if you don't want me to spend your money I will go out and get some of my own to spend." Then I said "What will you do teach school?" And she says "No and I won't teach school either." So I said "No I guess you won't. But if you think you want to try standing up behind a cigar counter or something all day why go ahead and try it and we'll see how long you will last." So she says "I don't have to stand behind no counter but I can go in business for myself and make more than you do." So I said "Yes you can" and she didn't have no come back.

Imagine Al a girl saying she could make more money then a big league pitcher. Probably theys a few of them that does but they are movie actors or something and I would like to see Florrie try to be a movie actor because they got to look pleasant all the time and Florrie would strain herself.

Well Al the ski jumper has got dinner pretty near ready and after dinner I am going over North and see what the Cubs look like and I wish I pitched in that league Al and the only trouble is that I would feel ashamed when I went after my pay check.

Your old pal,   Jack.

Chicago, May 19.

DEAR FRIEND AL: Well old pal if we wasn't married we would all have to go to war now and I mean all of us thats between 21 and 30. I suppose you seen about the Govt. passing the draft law and a whole lot of the baseball players will have to go but our club won't loose nobody except 1 or 2 bushers that don't count because all as they do any way is take up room on the bench and laugh when Rowland springs a joke.

When I first seen it in the paper this morning I thought it meant everybody that wasn't crippled up or something but Gleason explained it to me that if you got somebody to sport they leave you

home and thats fair enough but he also says they won't take no left
handers on acct. of the guns all being made for right handed men
and thats just like the lucky stiffs to set in a rocking chair and take
it easy while the regular fellows has got to go over there and get
shot up but anyway the yellow stiffs would make a fine lot of soldiers
because the first time a German looked X eyed at them they would
wave a flag of truants.

But I can't help from wishing this thing had of come off before I
see Florrie or little Al and if I had money enough saved up so as
they wouldn't have to worry I would go any way but I wouldn't wait
for no draft. Gleason says I will have to register family or no family
when the time comes but as soon as I tell them about Florrie they
will give me an excuse. I asked him what they would do with the
boys that wasn't excused and if they would send them right over to
France and he says No they would keep them here till they learned
to talk German. He says, "You can't fight nobody without a quarrel
and you can't quarrel with a man unless they can understand what
you are calling them." So I asked him how about the aviators because
their machines would be makeing so much noise that they couldn't
tell if the other one was talking German or rag time and he said
"Well if you are in an areoplane and you see a German areoplane
coming tords you you can pretty near guess that he don't want to
spoon with you."

That's what I would like to be Al is an aviator and I think Gleasons
afraid I'm going to bust into that end of the game though he pretends
like he don't take me in ernest. "Why don't you?" he said "You could
make good there all right because the less sense they got the better.
But I wish you would quit practiceing till you get away from here."
I asked him what he meant quit practiceing. "Well" he said "you was
up in the air all last Tuesday afternoon."

He was refering to that game I worked against the Phila. club but
honest Al my old souper was so sore I couldn't cut loose. Well Al
a mans got a fine chance to save money when they are married to a
girl like Florrie. When I got paid Tuesday the first thing when I come
home she wanted to borrow $200.00 and that was all I had comeing
so I said "What am I going to do the next 2 weeks walk back and
forth to the ball park and back?" I said "What and the hell do you
want with $200.00?" So then she begin to cry so I split it with her
and give her a $100.00 and she wouldn't tell me what she wanted it
for but she says she was going to supprise me. Well Al I will be

supprised if she don't land us all out to the county farm but you can't do nothing with them when they cry.   Your pal,   Jack.

Chicago, May 24.

FRIEND AL: What do you think Florrie has pulled off now? I told you she was fixing to land us in the poor house and I had the right dope. With the money I give her and some she got somewheres else she has opened up a beauty parlor on 43th St. right off of Michigan. Her and a girl that worked in a place like it down town.

Well Al when she sprung it on me you couldn't of knocked me down with a feather. I always figured girls was kind of crazy but I never seen one loose her mind as quick as that and I don't know if I ought to have them take her to some home or leave her learn her lesson and get over it.

I know you ain't got no beauty parlor in Bedford so I might as well tell you what they are. They are for women only and the women goes to them when they need something done to their hair or their face or their nails before a wedding or a eucher party or something. For inst. you and Bertha was up here and you wanted to take her to a show and she would have to get fixed up so she would go to this place and tell them to give her the whole treatment and first they would wash the grime out of her hair and then comb it up fluffy and then they would clean up her complexion with buttermilk and either get rid of the moles or else paint them white and then they would put some eyebrows on her with a pencil and red up her lips and polish her teeth and pair her finger nails and etc. till she looked as good as she could and it would cost her $5.00 or $10.00 according to what they do to her and if they would give her a bath and a massage I suppose its extra.

Well theys plenty of high class beauty parlors down town where women can go and know they will get good service but Florrie thinks she can make it pay out here with women that maybe haven't time to go clear down town because their husband or their friend might loose his mind in the middle of the afternoon and phone home that he had tickets for the Majestic or something and then of course they would have to rush over to some place in the neighborhood for repairs.

I didn't know Florrie was wise to the game but it seems she has been takeing some lessons down town without telling me nothing about it and this Miss Nevins thats in partners with her says Florrie is a darb. Well I wouldn't have no objections if I thought they was a chance for them to make good because she acts like she liked the work and its right close to where we live but it looks to me like their expenses would eat them up. I was in the joint this morning and the different smells alone must of cost them $100.00 to say nothing about all the bottles and cans and tools and brushs and the rent and furniture besides. I told Florrie I said "You got everything here but patients." She says "Don't worry about them. They will come when they find out about us." She says they have sent their cards to all the South Side 400.

"Well" I said "If they don't none of them show up in a couple of months I suppose you will call on the old meal ticket." So she says "You should worry." So I come away and went over to the ball park.

When I seen Kid Gleason I told him about it and he asked me where Florrie got the money to start up so I told him I give it to her. "You" he says "where did you get it?" So just jokeing I said "Where do you suppose I got it? I stole it." So he says "You did if you got it from this ball club." But he was kidding Al because of course he knows I'm no thief. But I got the laugh on him this afternoon when Silk O'Loughlin chased him out of the ball park. Johnson was working against us and they was two out and Collins on second base and Silk called a third strike on Gandil that was down by his corns. So Gleason hollered "All right Silk you won't have to go to war. You couldn't pass the eye test." So Silk told him to get off the field. So then I hollered something at Silk and he hollered back at me "That will be all from you you big busher." So I said "You are a busher yourself you busher." So he said:

"Get off the bench and let one of the ball players set down."

So I and Gleason stalled a while and finely come into the club house and I said "Well Kid I guess we told him something that time." "Yes" says Gleason "you certainly burned him up but the trouble with me is I can't never think of nothing to say till it's too late." So I said "When a man gets past sixty you can't expect their brain to act quick." And he didn't say nothing back.

Well we win the ball game any way because Cicotte shut them out. The way some of the ball players was patting him on the back afterwards you would have thought it was the 1st. time anybody had ever pitched a shut out against the Washington club but I don't see no reason to swell a man up over it. If you shut out Detroit or

Cleveland you are doing something but this here Washington club gets a bonus every time they score a run.

But it does look like we was going to cop that old flag and play the Giants for the big dough and it will sure be the Giants we will have to play against though some of the boys seem to think the Cubs have got a chance on acct. of them just winning 10 straight on their eastren trip but as Gleason says how can a club help from winning 10 straight in that league?   Your pal,   Jack.

Chicago, June 6.

FRIEND AL: Well Al the clubs east and Rowland left me home because my old souper is sore again and besides I had to register yesterday for the draft. They was a big crowd down to the place we registered and you ought to seen them when I come in. They was all trying to get up close to me and I was afraid some of them would get hurt in the jam. All of them says "Hello Jack" and I give them a smile and shook hands with about a dozen of them. A man hates to have everybody stareing at you but you got to be pleasant or they will think you are swelled up and besides a man can afford to put themself out a little if its going to give the boys any pleasure.

I don't know how they done with you Al but up here they give us a card to fill out and then they give us another one to carry around with us to show that we been registered and what our number is. I had to put down my name on the first card and my age and where I live and the day I was born and what month and etc. Some of the questions was crazy like "Was I a natural born citizen?" I wonder what they think I am. Maybe they think I fell out of a tree or something. Then I had to tell them I was born in Bedford, Ind. and it asked what I done for a liveing and I put down that I was a pitcher but the man made me change it to ball player and then I had to give Comiskey's name and address and then name the people that was dependent on me so I put down a wife and one child.

And the next question was if I was married or single. I supposed they would know enough to know that a man with a wife dependent on him was probably married. Then it says what race and I had a notion to put down "pennant" for a joke but the man says to put down white. Then it asked what military service had I had and of course I says none and then come the last question Did I claim exemption and what grounds so the man told me to write down married with dependents.

Then the man turned over to the back of the card and wrote down about my looks. Just that I was tall and medium build and brown eyes and brown hair. And the last question was if I had lost an arm or leg or hand or foot or both eyes or was I other wise disabled so I told him about my arm being sore and thats why I wasn't east with the club but he didn't put it down. So that's all they was to it except the card he give me with my number which is 3403.

It looks to me like it was waisting a mans time to make you go down there and wait for your turn when they know you are married and got a kid or if they don't know if they could call up your home or the ball park and find it out but of course if they called up my flat when I or Florrie wasn't there they wouldn't get nothing but a bunch of Swede talk that they couldn't nobody understand and I don't believe the girl knows herself what she is talking about over the phone. She can talk english pretty good when shes just talking to you but she must think all the phone calls is long distance from Norway because the minute she gets that reciever up to her ear you can't hardly tell the difference between she and Hughey Jennings on the coaching line.

I told Florrie I said "This girl could make more than $8.00 per week if she would get a job out to some ball park as announcer and announce the batterys and etc. She has got the voice for it and she would be right in a class with the rest of them because nobody could make heads or tales out of what she was trying to get at." ·

Speaking about Florrie what do you think Al? They have had enough suckers to pay expenses and also pay up some of the money they borrowed and Florrie says if their business gets much bigger they will have to hire more help. How would you like a job Al white washing some dames nose or leveling off their face with a steam roller? Of course I am just jokeing Al because they won't allow no men around the joint but wouldn't it be some job Al? I'll say so.

                            Your old pal,   Jack.

Chicago, June 21.

DEAR AL: Well Al I suppose you read in the paper the kind of luck I had yesterday but of course you can't tell nothing from what them dam reporters write and if they know how to play ball why aint they playing it instead of trying to write funny stuff about the ball game but at that some of it is funny Al because its so rotten its good. For inst. one of them had it in the paper this morning that I flied out to Speaker in the seventh inning. Well listen Al I hit that ball right on the pick and it went past that shortstop so fast that he didn't even have time to wave at it and if Speaker had of been playing where he belongs that ball would of went between he and Graney and bumped against the wall. But no. Speakers laying about ten feet back of second base and over to the left and of course the ball rides right to him and there was the whole ball game because that would of drove in 2 runs and made them play different then they did in the eigth. If a man is supposed to be playing center field why don't he play center field and of course I thought he was where he ought to been or I would of swung different.

Well the eigth opened up with the score 1 to 1 and I get 2 of them out but I got so much stuff I can't stick it just where I want to and I give Chapman a base on balls. At that the last one cut the heart of the plate but Evans called it a ball. Evans lives in Cleveland. Well I said "All right Bill you won't have to go to war. You couldn't pass the eye test." So he says "You must of read that one in a book." "No" I said "I didn't read it in no book either."

So up comes this Speaker and I says "What do you think you are going to do you lucky stiff?" So he says "I'm going to hit one where theys nobody standing in the way of it." I said "Yes you are." But I had to hold Chapman up at first base and Schalk made me waist 2 thinking Chapman was going and then of course I had to ease up and Speaker cracked one down the first base line but Gandil got his glove on it and if he hadn't of messed it all up he could of beat Speaker to the bag himself but instead of that they all started to ball me out for not covering. I told them to shut their mouth. Then Roth come up and I took a half wind up because of course I didn't think Chapman would be enough of a bone head to steal third with 2 out but him and Speaker pulled a double steal and then Rowland and all of them begin to yell at me and they got my mind off of what I was doing and then Schalk asked for a fast one though he said afterwards he didn't but I would of made him let me curve the ball if they hadn't got me all nervous yelling at me. So Roth hit one to left field that Jackson could of caught in his hip pocket if he had been playing right. So 2 runs come in and then Rowland takes me out and I would of busted him only for makeing a seen on the field.

I said to him "How can you expect a man to be at his best when I have not worked for a month?" So he said "Well it will be more than a month before you will work for me again." "Yes" I said "because I am going to work for Uncle Sam and join the army."

"Well," he says "you won't need no steel helmet." "No" I said "and you wouldn't either." Then he says "I'm afraid you won't last long over there because the first time they give you a hand grenade to throw you will take your wind up and loose a hand." So I said "If Chapman is a smart ball player why and the hell did he steal third base with 2 out?" He couldn't answer that but he says "What was you doing all alone out in No Mans Land on that ball of Speakers to Gandil?" So I told him to shut up and I went in the club house and when he come in I didn't speak to him or to none of the rest of them either.

Well Al I would quit right now and go up to Fort Sheridan and try for a captain only for Florrie and little Al and of course if it come to a show down Comiskey would ask me to stick on acct. of the club being in the race and it wouldn't be the square thing for me to walk out on him and when he has got his heart set on the pennant.

Your pal,   Jack.

Chicago, July 5.

FRIEND AL: Just a few lines Al to tell you how Florrie is getting along and I bet you will be surprised to hear about it. Well Al she paid me back my $100.00 day before yesterday and she showed me their figures for the month of June and I don't know if you will believe it or not but she and Miss Nevins cleared $400.00 for the month or $200.00 a peace over and above all expenses and she says the business will be even better in the fall and winter time on acct. of more people going to partys and theaters then. How is that for the kind of a wife to have Al and the best part of it is that she is stuck on the work and a whole lot happier then when she wasn't doing nothing. They got 2 girls working besides themself and they are talking about moveing into a bigger store somewheres and she says we will have to find a bigger flat so as we can have a nurse and a hired girl instead of just the one.

Tell Bertha about it Al and tell her that when she comes up to Chi she can get all prettied up and I will see they don't charge her nothing for it.

The clubs over in Detroit but it was only a 5 day trip so Rowland left me home to rest up my arm for the eastren clubs and Phila. is due here the day after tomorrow and all as I ask is a chance at them. My arm don't feel exactly right but I could roll the ball up to the plate and beat that club.

Its a cinch now that the Giants is comeing through in the other
league and if we can keep going it will be some worlds serious
between the 2 biggest towns in the country and the club that wins
ought to grab off about $4500.00 a peace per man. Is that worth
going after Al? I'll say so.   Your old pal,   Jack.

Chicago, July 20.

FRIEND AL: Well Al I don't suppose you remember my draft
number and I don't remember if I told it to you or not. It was 3403
Al. And it was the 5th number drawed at Washington.

Well old pal they can wipe the town of Washington off of the map
and you won't hear no holler from me. The day before yesterday
Rowland sends me in against the Washington club and of course it
had to be Johnson for them. And I get beat 3 and 2 and I guess its
the only time this season that Washington scored 3 runs in 1 day.
And the next thing they announce the way the draft come out and
I'm No. 5 and its a misery to me why my number wasn't the 1st.
they drawed out instead of the 5th.

Well Al of course it don't mean I got to go if I don't want to. I
can get out of it easy enough by telling them about Florrie and little
Al and besides Gleason says they have promised Ban Johnson that
they won't take no baseball stars till the seasons over and maybe not
then and besides theys probably some White Sox fans that will go
to the front for me and get me off on acct. of the club being in the
fight for the pennant and they can't nobody say I'm trying to get
excused because I said all season that I would go in a minute if it
wasn't for my family and the club being in the race and I give $50.00
last week for a liberty bond that will only bring me in $1.75 per
annum which is nothing you might say. You couldn't sport a flee on
$1.75 per annum.

Florrie wanted I should go right down to the City Hall or where
ever it is you go and get myself excused but Gleason says the only
thing to do is just wait till they call me and then claim exemptions.
I read somewheres a while ago that President Wilson wanted baseball
kept up because the people would need amusement and I asked
Gleason if he had read about that and he says "Yes but that won't
get you nothing because the rest of the soldiers will need amusement
even more than the people."

Well Al I don't know what your number was or how you come
out but I hope you had better luck but if you did get drawed you

will probably have a hard time getting out of it because you don't make no big salary and you got no children and Bertha could live with your mother and pick up a few dollars sowing. Enough to pay for her board and clothes. Of course they might excuse you for flat feet which they say you can't get in if you have them. But if I was you Al I would be tickled to death to get in because it would give you a chance to see something outside of Bedford and if your feet gets by you ought to be O. K.

I guess they won't find fault with my feet or anything about me as far physical goes. Hey Al?

I will write as soon as I learn anything.   Your pal,   Jack.

Chicago, Aug. 6.

FRIEND AL: Well Al I got notice last Friday that I was to show up right away over to Wendell Phllips high school where No. 5 board of exemptions was setting but when I got over there it was jamed so I went back there today and I have just come home from there now.

The 1st. man I seen was the doctor and he took my name and number and then he asked me if my health was O. K. and I told him it was only I don't feel good after meals. Then he asked me if I was all sound and well right now so I told him my pitching arm was awful lame and that was the reason I hadn't went east with the club. Then he says "Do you understand that if a man don't tell the truth about themself here they are libel to prison?" So I said he didn't have to worry about that.

So then he made me strip bear and I wish you had seen his eyes pop out when he got a look at my shoulders and chest. I stepped on the scales and tipped the bean at 194 and he measured me at 6 ft. 1 and a half. Then he went all over me and poked me with his finger and counted my teeth and finely he made me tell him what different letters was that he held up like I didn't know the alphabet or something. So when he was through he says "Well I guess you ain't going to die right away." He signed the paper and sent me to the room where the rest of the board was setting.

Well 1 of them looked up my number and then asked me did I claim exemptions. I told him yes and he asked me what grounds so I said "I sport a wife and baby and besides I don't feel like it would be a square deal to Comiskey for me to walk out on him now." So he says "Have you got an affidavit from your wife that you sport her?" So I told him no and he says "Go and get one and bring it back here tomorrow but you don't need to bring none from Comiskey." So you see Comiskey must stand pretty good with them.

So he give me a blank for Florrie to fill out and when she gets home we will go to a notary and tend to it and tomorrow they will fix up my excuse and then I won't have nothing to think about only to get the old souper in shape for the big finish.

Your pal, Jack.

Chicago, Aug. 8.

DEAR OLD PAL: Well old pal it would seem like the best way to get along in this world is to not try and get nowheres because the minute a man gets somewheres they's people that can't hardly wait to bite your back.

The 1st. thing yesterday I went over to No. 5 board and was going to show them Florrie's affidavit but while I was pulling it out of my pocket the man I seen the day before called me over to 1 side and says "Listen Keefe I am a White Sox fan and don't want to see you get none the worst of it and if I was you I would keep a hold of that paper." So I asked him what for and he says "Do you know what the law is about telling the truth and not telling the truth and if you turn in an affidavit thats false and we find it out you and who ever made the affidavit is both libel to prison?" So I said what was he trying to get at and he says "We got informations that your wife is in business for herself and makeing as high as $250.00 per month which is plenty for she and your boy to get along on." "Yes" I said "but who pays for the rent of our flat and the hired girl and what we eat?" So he says "That don't make no difference. Your wife could pay for them and that settles it."

Well Al I didn't know what to say for a minute but finely I asked him where the information come from and he says he was tipped off in a letter that who ever wrote it didn't sign their name the sneaks and I asked him how he knowed that they was telling the truth. So he says "Its our business to look them things up. If I was you I wouldn't make no claim for exemptions but just lay quiet and take a chance."

Then all of a sudden I had an idea Al and I will tell you about it but 1st. as soon as it come to me I asked the man if this here board was all the board they was and he says no that if they would not excuse me I could appeal to the Dist. board but if he was me he wouldn't do it because it wouldn't do no good and might get me in trouble. So I said "I won't get in no trouble" and he says "All right suit yourself." So I said I would take the affadavit and go to the Dist. board but he says no that I would have to get passed on 1st. by his board and then I could appeal if I wanted to.

So I left the affadavit and he says they would notify me how I come out so then I beat it home and called up Florrie and told her they was something important and for her to come up to the flat.

Well Al here was the idea. I had been thinking for a long time that while it was all O. K. for Florrie to earn a little money in the summer when I was tied up with the club it would be a whole lot better if we was both free after the season so as we could take little Al and go on a trip somewheres or maybe spend the winter in the south but of course if she kept a hold of her share in the business she couldn't get away so the best thing would be to sell out to Miss Nevins for a good peace of money and we could maybe buy us a winter home somewheres with what she got and whats comeing to me in the worlds serious.

So when Florrie got home I put it up to her. I said "Florrie I'm sick in tired of haveing you tied up in business because it don't seem right for a married woman to be in business when their husbands in the big league and besides a womans place is home especially when they got a baby so I want you to sell out and when I get my split of the worlds serious we will go south somewheres and buy a home."

Well she asked me how did I come out with the affadavit. So I said "The affadavit is either here nor there. I am talking about something else" and she says "Yes you are." And she says "I been worring all day about that affadavit because if they find out about it what will they do to us." So I said "You should worry because if this board won't excuse me I will go to the Dist. board and mean while you won't be earning nothing because you will be out of business." Well Al she had a better idea then that. She says "No I will hold on to the business till you go to the Dist. board and then if they act like they wouldn't excuse you you can tell them I am going to sell out. And if they say all right I will sell out. But if they say its to late why then I will still have something to live on if you have to go."

So when she said that about me haveing to go we both choked up a little but pretty soon I was O. K. and now Al it looks like a cinch I would get my exemptions from the Dist. board because if Florrie says she wants to sell out they can't stop her.

                                            Your pal,   Jack.

Chicago, Aug. 22.

FRIEND AL: Well Al its all over. The Dist. board won't let me off and between you and I Al I am glad of it and I only hope I won't have to go before I have had a chance at the worlds serious.

My case came up about noon. One of the men asked me my name and then looked over what they had wrote down about me. Then he says "Theys an affadavit here that says your wife and child depends on you. Is that true?" So I said yes it was and he asked me if my wife was in business and I said yes but she was thinking about selling out. So he asked me how much money she made in her business. I said "You can't never tell. Some times its so much and other times different." So he asked me what the average was and I said it was about $250.00 per month. Then he says "Why is she going to sell out?" I said "Because we don't want to live in Chi all winter" and he said "You needn't to worry." Then he said "If she makes $250.00 per month how do you figure she is dependent on you?" So I said "Because she is because I pay for the rent and everything." And he asked me what she done with the $250.00 and I told him she spent it on clothes.

So he says "$250.00 per month on clothes. How does she keep warm this weather?" I said "I guess they don't nobody have no trouble keeping warm in August. Then he says "Look here Keefe this affadavit mitigates against you. We will have to turn down your appeal and I guess your wife can take care of herself and the boy." I said "She can't when she sells out." "Well" he said "you tell her not to sell out. It may be hard for her at first to sport herself and the boy on $250.00 but if the worst comes to the worst she can wear the same shoes twice and she will find them a whole lot more comfortable the second time." So I said "She don't never have no trouble with her feet and if she did I guess she knows how to fix them."

Florrie was waiting for me when I got home. "Well" I said "now you see what your dam beauty parlor has done for us." And then she seen what had happened and begin to cry and of course I couldn't find no more fault with her and I called up the ball park and told them I was sick and wouldn't show up this P. M. and I and Florrie and little Al stayed home together and talked. That is little Al done all the talking. I and Florrie didn't seem to have nothing to say.

Tomorrow I am going to tell them about it over to the ball park. If they can get me off till after the worlds serious all right. And if they can't all right to.　　　　Your old pal,　　Jack.

P.S. Washington comes tomorrow and I am going to ask Rowland to leave me pitch. The worst I can get is a tie. They scored a run in St. Louis yesterday and that means they are through for the week.

Chicago, Aug. 23.

DEAR AL: Well Al the one that laughs last gets all the best of it. Wait till you hear what come off today.

When I come in the club house Rowland and Gleason was there all alone. I told them hello and was going to spring the news on them but when Rowland seen me he says "Jack I got some bad news for you." So I said what was it. So he says "The boss sold you to Washington this morning."

Well Al at first I couldn't say nothing and I forgot all about that I wanted to tell them. But then I remembered it again and here is what I pulled. I said "Listen Manager I beat the boss to it." "What do you mean?" he said so I said "I'm signed up with Washington all ready only I ain't signed with Griffith but with Uncle Sam." That's what I pulled on them Al and they both got it right away. Gleason jumped up and shook hands with me and so did Rowland and then Rowland said he would have to hurry up in the office and tell the Old Man. "But wait a minute" I said. "I am going to quit you after this game because I don't know when I will be called and theys lots of things I got to fix up." So I stopped and Rowland asked me what I wanted and I said "Let me pitch this game and I will give them the beating of their life."

So him and Gleason looked at each other and then Rowland says "You know we can't afford to loose no ball games now. But if you think you can beat them I will start you."

So then he blowed and I and Gleason was alone.

"Well kid" he says "you make the rest of us look like a monkey. This game ain't nothing compared to what you are going to do. And when you come back they won't be nothing to good for you and your kid will be proud of you because you went while a whole lot of other kids dads stayed home."

So he patted me on the back and I kind of choked up and then the trainer come in and I had him do a little work on my arm.

Well Al you will see in the paper what I done to them. Before the game the boss had told Griffith about me and called the deal off. So while I was warming up Griffith come over and shook hands. He says "I would of like to had you but I am a good looser." So I says "You ought to be." So he couldn't help from laughing but he says

"When you come back I will go after you again." I said "Well if you don't get somebody on the club between now and then that can hit something besides fouls I won't come back." So he kind of laughed again and walked away and then it was time for the game.

Well Al the official scorer give them 3 hits but he must be McMullins brother in law or something because McMullin ought to of throwed Milan out from here to Berlin on that bunt. But any way 3 hits and no runs is pretty good for a finish and between you and I Al I feel like I got the last laugh on Washington and Rowland to.

Your pal,   Jack.

Chicago, Sept. 18.

FRIEND AL: Just time for a few lines while Florrie finishs packing up my stuff. I leave with the bunch tomorrow A.M. for Camp Grant at Rockford. I don't know how long we will stay there but I suppose long enough to learn to talk German and shoot and etc.

We just put little Al to bed and tonight was the first time we told him I was going to war. He says "Can I go to daddy?" Hows that for a 3 year old Al?

Well he will be proud of me when I come back and he will be proud of me if I don't come back and when he gets older he can go up to the kids that belong to some of these left handers and say "Where and the hell was your father when the war come off?"

Good by Al and say good by to Bertha for me.

Your Pal,   Jack.

P.S. I won't be in the serious against New York but how about the real worlds serious Al? Won't I be in that? I'll say so.

THE BUSHER REËNLISTS

◇

FRIEND AL: Well Al I was down to see the Dr. for the last time today as he said they wasn't no use in me comeing down there again as my arm is just as good is new though of course its weak yet on acct. of being in a sling all this wile and I haven't used it and I suppose if it was my right arm it would take me a long wile to get it strenthened up again to where I could zip the old ball through there the way like I use to but thank god its the left arm that the Dutchmens shot full of holes. But at that it wouldn't make no differents if it was the left arm or the old souper either one as I have gave up the idear of going back in to the old game.

I bet you will be surprised to hear that Al as I am still a young man just a kid you might say compared to some of the other birds that is still pitching yet and getting by with it and I figure that if I would stick in the game my best yrs. is yet to come. But that isn't the point Al but the point is that after a man has took part in the war game all the other games seems like they was baby games and after what I went through acrost the old pond how could a man take any interest in baseball and it would be like as if a man set up all night in a poker game with the sky for the limit and when they come home their wife asked them to play a hand of jack straws to see which one of them had to stick the ice card in the window. No man can do themself justice Al if you don't take your work in ernest whether its pitching baseball or takeing a bath.

Besides that Al I figure that even a man like I am that's put up like a motor Laura you might say can't last forever in baseball and why not quit wile you are young and have still got the old ambition to start out in some other line of business that a man can last in it all their life and probably by the time I got to be the age where I

The Saturday Evening Post, April 19, 1919; previously uncollected.

would half to give up pitching if I stuck at it, why by that time I can work myself up to the head of some business where I would be drawing $15000.00 per annum or something and no danger of getting kicked out of it when the old souper finely lays down on me.

And besides that when a man has got a wife and 2 kiddies that the whole 3 of them has got the world beat why should I go out and pitch baseball and be away from home ½ the year around where if I hooked up good in some business here in Chi I wouldn't never half to leave except maybe a run down to N. Y. city once or twice a yr. So in justice to them and myself I don't see nothing to it only give up the game for good in all and get in to something permerant.

Well Al I suppose you will be saying to yourself that I haven't never had no experience in business and what kind of business could I get in to that would pay me the right kind of money. Well old pal if you will stop and think I haven't never tackled no job yet where I didn't make good and in the 1st. place it was pitching baseball and I hadn't only been pitching a little over 2 yrs. when I was in the big league and then come the war game and I was made a corporal a few wks. after I enlisted and might of stayed a corporal or went higher yet only I would rather pal around with the boys and not try and lord it over them and you can bet it won't be no different in whatever business I decide to take up because they isn't nothing that can't be learned Al if a man goes at it the right way and has got something under their hat besides scalp trouble.

As for getting in to the right kind of a place I guess I can just about pick out what kind of a place I want to start in at as everybody that reads the papers knows who I am and how I went in the war wile most of the other baseball boys kept the home fires burning though I had a wife and a kid to look out for besides the baby that came since I went in and for all as I knew might of been here a long wile before that. So it looks like when I make up my mind what business I want to tackle I can just go to whoever is at the head of the business and they will say "You bet your life we will find a place for you after what you done both in baseball and for the stars and strips." Because they won't no real man turn a soldier down Al a specially 1 that erned his wound strips acrost the old pond.

So they won't be no trouble about me landing when I decide what I want to go in to and the baseball men can offer me whatever kind of a contract they feel like and I will give them 1 of my smiles and tell them they are barking the wrong tree.

Regards to Bertha.   Your pal,   JACK.

Chi, Dec. 8.

FRIEND AL: Well Al this is a fine burg where a lot of the business men don't know they's been a war or read the papers or nothing only set in front of the cash register and watch how the money rolls in or else they must of bet 20 cents on the Kaiser and have got a grudge against the boys that stopped him.

The other night I was with a couple of friends of mine that's White Sox fans and we was histing a few and 1 of them is asst. mgr. down to 1 of the big dept. stores so I told him I was going to quit the game and try and bust in to some business where I could work up to something worth wile and he says they was shy of a floor man down to their store and he would speak to the mgr. about me and if I come down maybe I could land the job, as the floor man has to be a man that can wear clothes and carry themself as most of the customers is ladys and you half to give them a smile and make them feel at home and the job pays pretty good jack.

Well I didn't think much of the job only this bird is a kind of an admire of mine on acct. of baseball so I didn't want to be nasty to him so I went down there yesterday and he introduced me to the mgr. and his name is suppose to be Kelly but I guess Heinz would be closer to what his name is. Well he asked me had I had any experience in dept. stores and I said yes I had had all the experience I wanted the times I had been in there with Florrie shoping and my feet was still sore yet where all the women in Chi had used them for a parade grounds. So he said he meant did I ever have any experience working in a store so I said do I look like a counter jumper or something? I said "I have had the kind of experience that I guess a whole lot of men would give their right eye if they could brag about it, playing in the big league in baseball and the big league in war and I guess that's enough of experience for a man of my age." So he said "Well our floor men is not suppose to hit the customers with a bat or tickle them with a bayonet either one so I don't see how we can use you right now." So I said "I have got a charge acct. here and here is where my wife does pretty near all her shoping." So he said "Well if we was to give jobs to all our customers why as soon as they had all reported for work in the A. M. we could close the doors and get along without a floor man." Well Al all as I could do was walk away from him as I couldn't very well take a wallop at his jaw on acct. of his asst. being my pal.

Well as long as I was down town I thought I might as well look up some of my other friends so I happened to remember a pal of

mine that use to work in the Gas Co. so I dropped in there and
asked for him but he wasn't there no more so I asked for whoever
was in charge and they showed me to an old bird that must of began
to work for them the day they struck gas and I told him my name
and who I was and he said about the only thing open was meter
readers so I said "Read them yourself" and come away.

That's the kind of birds we have got here Al but they can't all be
that way and the next time I will wait for them to come to me before
I go around and lay myself libel to insults from a bunch of pro German
spys or whatever you have a mind to call them.

Well they's a saloon on Adams St. that it use to be a big hang out
for the fans so I dropped in there before I started home but they
wasn't nobody in there that I knew them or they knew me and the
bunch that was in there didn't even know their own name but they
was all trying to sing tenor and that's about the way it is in all the
saloons you drop in to these days and they all seem to think that
every day is June 30. Well I couldn't stand for the noise and everybody with their arm around each other tearing off Smiles so I come
home and Florrie asked me how I had came out and I told her and
she says it looked like I better go back in to baseball. So I said if I
do go back it will be because they give me a $5000.00 contract in
the stead of the $2500.00 I was getting when I quit and enlisted and
between you and I Al that's the lowest figure I would sign up for
and of course I wouldn't have no trouble getting that if I give Comiskey the word that I was thinking about pitching baseball again. But
nothing doing in baseball for me Al when I know I can get in to
some big business with a future in it and won't never half to worry
about my arm or catching cold in it or nothing and be home every
night with the kiddies. But if I did sign up to a $5000.00 contract
in baseball it would mean our income would be around $8000.00
per annum as Florrie is kicking out pretty close to $250.00 per mo.
clear profit in her beauty parlor.

Well Florrie said if I couldn't get no $5000.00 from the White
Sox or find no job that suited me she would give me a job herself
so I said "What doing pairing finger nails over in your studio?" So
she said "No indeed I would hire you as nurse for little Al and the
baby in place of the one we have got." So I said I wouldn't mind
being a nurse for little Al as I and him can have a fine time playing
together and I would make a man out of him but I wouldn't sign no
contract to take care of little Florrie for no amt. of money as it would
mean I would half to stay awake 24 hrs. per day as this little bird

don't never close her eyes and I only wished they was a few umpires like her in the American League and maybe a man could get something like a square deal. I have often heard people that had babys brag about how good they was and slept all the wile except when they was getting their chow but little Florrie ain't no relation to them or neither is little Al as he was just as bad when he was a baby and when I hear these storys about these here perfect babys I begin to think that the husbands and wifes that owns them is the same kind that never had a cross word since they been married.

But jokeing to 1 side Al I don't see how the Swede stands it being up all day and then up again all night and sometimes I wished I could help her out by walking the floor with the kid nights but the Dr. said I wasn't to do nothing that might strain my bad arm till I was sure it was O. K.   Your pal,   JACK.

Chi, Dec. 12.

FRIEND AL: Well Al yesterday was the American League meeting and I happened to be down town so I dropped in to the hotel where the meeting was at just to see some of the boys as they's always a bunch of them hangs around in the hopes that 1 of the club owners will smile at them or something and any way I dropped in the lobby and the 1st. bird I seen was Bobby Roth that was with us a few yrs. ago and played the outfield for Cleveland last yr. So I says "Hello Bobby." So he said "Hello Jack." Well it was the 1st. time I seen him since I quit baseball for the army but I guess he hadn't never heard that I was in the war or something and any way he didn't say nothing about it but finely he said he supposed I would be back with the White Sox next yr. so then I told him I had made it up in my mind to quit the game and go in to business and he said he was sorry to hear it. So I said "Yes you are because when you was with the Cleveland club I always made you look like a monkey." So he said "I never had a chance to hit against you as they had me batting 4th. at Cleveland and by the time it come my turn to hit you was took out of the game." So I said "Yes I was" and he didn't have nothing more to say.

Well I walked around a wile and run in to some of the other boys Artie Hofman and Charley O'Leary and Jim Archer and Joe Benz but not a 1 of them mentioned about the war or me being over there and I finely figured it out that it was a kind of a sore subject with them so I walked away from them and all of a sudden I seen Rowland the mgr. and I thought sure he would ask me about signing up but I guess Bobby or somebody must of tipped him off about me going in to business so he didn't want to take a chance of me turning him down or maybe he thought he would have a better chance of landing me if he didn't say nothing at this time but just sent me a big fat contract when the time comes. Any way we didn't talk contract but he had heard about me getting shot in the left arm and he mentioned about it and smiled and said it was lucky I wasn't a left hander so you see he has got me on his mind and I suppose the contract will come along in a few days and then I will half to send it back to them and tell them I am through even if the contract meets my figure which is $5000.00 because I wouldn't go back and pitch baseball even for that amt. when I can go in to business and maybe not do that well right at the start but work myself up in to something worth wile.

Well after I left Rowland I bumped in to Hy Pond that I was with him down in the Central League and he asked me to come in and have a drink so I went with him and histed a couple beers but it was a mad house and besides wile we was over there takeing the fight out of the Germans the people that stayed home done the same thing to the beer and the way they have got it fixed now you could drink all they have got left without feeling like shock troops so finely I told Hy to make my excuses to the boys and I come along home.

Well I have had 2 or 3 pretty good chances so far to break in to some line of business and 1 of them was an ad I seen in the paper today where they wanted a young man of good appearances to represent them in Detroit with $5000.00 per annum to start out but they didn't say what line of business it was and besides I don't feel like moveing to Detroit so I decided to not answer the ad but wait till something showed up where I could stay here in Chi as they's no use of a man rushing in to something blind folded you might say when all as I half to do is play the waiting game and let them come to me with all their offers and then pick out the one that suits me best. Get them bidding against each other for you is the system Al.

Your pal,   JACK.

Chi, Dec. 23.

FRIEND AL; Well Al I just come back from down town where I and Florrie has been all P. M. buying xmas presents and she has been saying ever since I come back from France how lonesome she was

all the wile I was away but from the number of xmas presents she
had to buy for people I never seen or heard of they couldn't of been
more than a couple hours of the time I was over there when she
wasn't busy saying please to meet you. But whenever I would raise
a holler about the jack she was spending she would swell up and tell
me she would pay for it out of her own money so of course I couldn't
say nothing though when the bills comes in they will be addressed
to me and her check book will of probably got halled away with the
garbage.

Well when we got through buying for the city directory she said
she was through except for the baby as she had fixed up for little Al
last time she was down so she asked me what could I suggest for
little Florrie so I said why get her a new rattle as what else is they
for a 6 mos. old baby so she said the baby wasn't going to be 6 mos.
old all her life. How is that for a bright remark Al but of course a
woman can't expect to have the looks and everything else with it,
but any way she said she had a idear that she heard about a friend
of hers doing it that had a little baby girl and that was to start a pearl
necklace for her and 1st. buy the chain and a few pearls and then
add a couple pearls every yr. so as when she got old enough to wear
it she would have something.

Well I said why not wait till some xmas when we have got a little
more jack say in 7 or 8 yrs. and then get enough pearls to make up
for the yrs. we passed up and then give them to the little girl and
tell her we started buying them before she was a yr. old and she
wouldn't know the differents and in the mean wile we could get her
something that if she busted it we wouldn't be out no real jack. So
Florrie said "You don't suppose I am going to leave her get a hold
of the necklace now do you or even show it to her?" So I said "That
is a fine way to give a person a xmas present is to buy something
and hide it and if that is the system why don't you buy her a couple
new undershirts my size and I can wear them and when I have wore
them out you can put them away somewheres till she gets old enough
to have some sence and then you can hall them out and show them
to her and tell her that was what we give her for xmas in 1918."

Well you know how much good it done to argue and finely she
picked out a little gold chain and 4 little pearls to go with it and it
cost $47.50 but what and the he—ll is $47.50 as long as the baby
has a merry xmas.

Well we was shoping all the P. M. but you can bet we didn't go in
that smart Alex store where that smart Alex mgr. got so fresh when

they offered me that cheap job and we use to spend a lot of jack in there at that but never again and if they want to know why they haven't got no big bill against us like they usually have around xmas time I will tell them and then maybe Mr. Smart will wished he hadn't of been so smart but at that when I seen them floor men on the job today I was tickled to death I turned that job down because the way them women jousled them around I couldn't of never stood for it and I would of felt like busting them in the eye if it had of been me and of course I don't mean that Al as I wouldn't think of hitting a woman but I would of certainly gave them the elbow or accidently parked my heel on a few of their best toes.

Well of course I couldn't buy Florrie no present wile she was along and I half to go back down again tomorrow and try and find something and I haven't the lease idear what will it be and all as I know is that it won't be no pearl necklace for adults. She says she has all ready boughten my present and wait till I see it. Well I suppose it will be a corset or maybe she will give me a set of false teeth and hide them away somewheres till I come of age to put them on.

Well Al we are sending xmas cards to you and Bertha and I only wished it could be something more but we kind of feel this yr. like we shouldn't ought to spend a whole lot of money what with some of the boys still over in France yet and another liberty loan comeing along some time soon and all and all it don't seem hardly right to be blowing jack for xmas presents but maybe next yr. everything will be different and in the mean wile merry xmas to you and Bertha from the both of us.   Your pal,   JACK.

Chi, Dec. 31.

FRIEND AL: Well Al they's not much news to write as everything has been going along about like usual and I haven't made it up in my mind yet what line of business to take up though I have got several good offers hanging in the fire you might say and am just playing the waiting game till I decide which 1 looks best as I would be sorry to get in to 1 thing and then find out they was something else opened up that I would like a whole lot better.

One of the things I have got in mind is takeing up newspaper work and writeing articles about baseball or maybe army life and when the baseball season opens maybe I would go out and see the games and write up the reports and you can bet my articles would be different then some of these birds that's reporting the games as I would at lease know what I was writeing about wile you take the most of these here reporters and all the baseball they know you could carry it around in a eye dropper.

But I don't know whether the papers would pay me the kind of money I would want and if not why I am in a position to laugh at them.

Well I got tired of setting around the house today as Florrie was over to her looks garage and the Swede had both the kiddies out to get the air so I walked around a wile and then I hopped on to a 35th. St. car and rode over west and I happened to look out of the window and we was just passing the ball pk. so I didn't have nothing else to do so I give the conductor the highball and jumped off and went up in the office to see if they wasn't maybe some mail for me that some of the boys wrote from France not knowing my home address.

Well they wasn't no mail so I set down and fanned a wile with Harry the secty. of the club and he asked me all about what I seen over acrost the pond and we had quite a talk and finely I thought maybe Comiskey would be sore if he heard I had been up there and hadn't paid my respects but Harry said he wasn't in so then I thought maybe he might of left some word about me and wanted to know if I was going to come back and pitch baseball for him or not but Harry said he hadn't mentioned nothing about it so I guess when the time comes he will just send me my contract and then I will send it back and tell him I have decided to quit baseball and go in to some line of business where they's a future in it.

Because they's no use of a man killing himself pitching baseball and then when your arm gives out you haven't got no business to go in to because business men won't hire a man that's 33 or 34 yrs. old and no experience and besides if a man has got a family like mine why not stay home and enjoy them in the stead of traveling on the road ½ the yr. around you might say. So even if Comiskey should send me a contract calling for $4000.00 per annum I would send it back though that is the lease I would sign up for if I was going to sign at all.

Well Al xmas is over and I only wished you could of been here to see how little Al eat it up. Besides all the junk we give him all of Florrie's friends sent something and all together he must of got about 25 presents in the 1st. place and now he has got about a 100 as everything he got is broke in to 4 peaces and they also sent the baby a load of play things that means as much to her as the hit and run but Florrie says never mind they will be put away till some xmas when she is old enough to enjoy them and then we won't half to buy her nothing new. Well the idear is O.K. Al but it reminds me like when Sept. comes along and a man has got a straw Kelly that looks pretty good and you give it to your wife to take care of till next June and when it comes June you go and buy yourself a new hat.

Well Florrie's present to me was a phonograph and of course that's a mighty fine present and will cost her or whoever pays for it a bunch of jack but between you and I Al I wouldn't be surprised if she was thinking to herself when she bought it that maybe she might turn it on some times when I am not in the house. What I give her is 1 of these here patent shower bath attachments that you can have it put up on a regular bath tub and you can have a regular tub bath or a shower just as you feel like. They cost real money to Al but what's the differents when its your wife?   Your pal,   JACK.

Chi, Jan. 16.

FRIEND AL: Well Al I don't know if you have been reading the papers but if you have you probably seen the big news where Kid Gleason has been appointed mgr. of the White Sox. Well old pal that peace of news makes all the differents in the world to your old pal. As you know I had entirely gave up the idear of going back in to baseball and figured where I would take up some other line of business and work myself up to something big and I was just about makeing it up in my mind to accept 1 of the offers I got when this news come out.

Well old pal I haven't no idear how things will come out now as I guess you know what friends I and Gleason are. You know he was asst. mgr. when Callahan had the club and then again the yr. Rowland win the pennant and he seemed to take a fancy to me some way and I guess I may as well come out and say that I was his favorite of any man on the club and I always figured that it was because when he tried his kidding on me I always give him back as good as he sent wile the rest of the boys was a scared of him but he use to kid me just to hear what I would say back to him. Like 1 time we was playing a double header with the St. Louis club and Jim Scott lose the 1st. game and Callahan said I was to work the 2d. game so I was warming up and Gleason come out and stood behind me and I had eat something that didn't set very good so Gleason asked me how I felt and I said "Not very good. I'm not myself today." So he said "Well then it looks like we would break even on the afternoon." So I said "I will break your jaw in a minute."

But a side from all that he was the 1 man that ever give me the credit for the work I done and if he had of been mgr. of the club he would of pitched me in my regular turn in the stead of playing favorites like them other 2 birds and all as I needed was regular work and I would of made them forget Walsh and all the rest of them big 4 flushers.

Well Al Gleason lives in Philly in the winter so I expect he will either wire me a telegram and ask for my terms or else he will run out here and see me and if they give me $4000.00 per annum I am afraid they won't be nothing for me to do only sign up though I have got several chances to go in to some business at better money than that and with a future to it. But this here is a matter of friendships Al and after all Gleason done for me why if he says the word I can't hardly do nothing only say yes though of course I am not going to sacrifice myself or sign for a nickel less than $4000.00.

You see Al this will be Gleason's 1st yr. as a mgr. and he will want to finish up in the race and I don't care how good a mgr. is he can't win unless he has got the men and beleive me he will need all the pitching strenth he can get a hold of as Cleveland and N. Y. has both strenthened up and the Boston club with all their men back from the service has got enough good ball players to finish 1st. and 2d. both if they was room for all of them to play at once. So that is where friendships comes in Al and I figure that it is up to your old pal to pass up my business chances and show the Kid I am true blue and beleive me I will show him something and I will come pretty near winning that old flag single handed.

So all and all it looks like your old pal wouldn't go in to no business adventure this yr. but I will be out there on the old ball field giveing them the best I have got and I guess the fans won't holler their heads off when I walk out there the 1st. time after what I done in France.   Your pal,   JACK.

Chi, Feb. 13.

FRIEND AL: Well Al it says in the paper this A.M. that Gleason is comeing to Chi for a few days to see Comiskey and talk over the plans for the training trip and etc. but they's another reason why he is comeing to Chi and maybe you can guess what it is. Well Al that's the way to work it is to wait and let them come to you in the stead of you going to them as when you make them come to you you can pretty near demand whatever you want and they half to come acrost with it.

That's a fine story Al about him comeing to talk over plans for the training trip as I know Comiskey and you could talk to him for 3 wks. about the plans for the training trip and when you got all through talking he would tell you what the plans was for the training trip so you can bet that Gleason isn't comeing all the way out here from Philly to hear himself talk but what he is comeing for is to get some of the boys in line that lives here and when I say some of the boys I don't half to go no further eh Al?

And all the more because I dropped him a letter a couple wks. ago and said I had made all arrangements to go in to business but if he wanted me I would give up my plans and pitch for him provided he give me my figure which is $3600.00 per annum and I never got no answer to the letter and now I know why I didn't get no answer as he is 1 of the kind that would rather set down and do their talking face to face then set down and take the trouble of writeing a letter when he could just as well hop on the old rattler and come out here and see me personly.

Well Al he will be here next wk. and I have left my phone No. over to the ball pk. so as he will know how to get a hold of me and all they will be to it is he will ask me how much I want and I will tell him $3600.00 and he will say sign here.

Well Al Florrie says she don't know if she is glad or sorry that I am going to be back in the old game as she says she don't like to have me away from home so much but still and all she knows I wouldn't be happy unless I was pitching baseball but she also says that if I do get back in to harness and ern a liveing and they's another war breaks out she will probably half to go as she couldn't claim no exemptions on the grounds of a dependant husband. So I said "I guess they won't ask no women to go to war because the minute they heard 1 of them trench rats give their college yell they would all retreat to the equator or somewheres." So she said "They had women in the Russia army and they didn't retreat." So I said "Yes they did only the men retreated so much faster that the women looked like they was standing still."

Jokeing to 1 side Al I will let you know how I come out with Gleason but they's only 1 way I can come out and that is he will be tickled to death to sign me at my own figure because if he trys any monkey business with me I will laugh in his face and Comiskey to, and give up the game for good and take the best offer I have got in some other line.   Your pal,   JACK.

Chi, Feb. 20.

FRIEND AL: Well Al I have just came back from the ball pk. and had a long talk with Gleason and the most of it was kidding back and 4th, like usual when the 2 of us gets together but it didn't take no Wm. A. Pinkerton to see that he is anxious to have me back on the ball club and in a few days they will probably send me a contract at my own figures and then they won't be nothing to do only wait for the rattler to start for the sunny south land.

Well Gleason got in yesterday P.M. and I was expecting him to call up either last night or this A.M. but they didn't no call come and I figured they must of either lost my phone No. over to the office or else the phone was out of order or something and the way the phones has been acting all winter why he might of asked central to give him my No. and the next thing he knew he would be connected with the morgue so any way when they hadn't no call came at noon I jumped on a 35th St. car and went over to the pk. and up in the office and the secty. said Gleason was in talking to Comiskey but he would be through in a little while.

Well after about a hr. Gleason come out and seen me setting there and of course he had to start kidding right off of the real so he said "Well here is the big Busher and I hoped you was killed over in France but I suppose even them long distance guns fell short of where you was at." So I said "They reached me all right and they got me in the left arm and wasn't it lucky it wasn't my right arm?" So he said "Its to bad they didn't shoot your head off and made a pitcher out of you." So then he asked me all about the war and if I got in to Germany and I told him no that I got my wounds in June and was invalid home. So he said "You fight just like you pitch and they half to take you out in the 5th. inning." So I asked him if he got my letter and he said he got a letter that looked like it might of came from me so he didn't open it. So I said "Well I don't know if you opened it or not but I just as soon tell you right here what I said in the letter. I told you I was going in to some business but I would stay in baseball another yr. to help you out if you met my figure." So he asked what was my figure, so I told him $3000.00 per annum. So he said how much was I getting in the army and I told him I was getting about $30.00 per mo. most of the time. So he said

"Yes you was getting $30.00 per mo to get up at 5 G. M. and work like a dog all day and eat beans and stew and sleep in a barn nights with a cow and a pig for your roomies and now you want $3000.00 a yr. to live in the best hotels and eat off the fat of the land and about once in every 10 days when we feel like we can afford to loose a ball game why you half to go out there and stand on your feet pretty near ½ the P.M. and if it happens to be July or Aug. you come pretty close to prespireing."

So I said "You are the same old Gleason always trying to kid somebody but jokeing a side I will sign up for $3000.00 or else I will go in to business." So he asked me what business I was going in to and I told him I had an offer from the Stock Yards. So he said "How much do they offer for you on the hoof?"

Well we kidded along back and 4th. like that for a wile and finely he said he was going out somewhere with Comiskey so I asked him if he wasn't going to talk business to me 1st. So he said "I will tell you how it is boy. They have cut down the limit so as each club can't only carry 21 men and that means we won't have no room for bench lizards. But the boss says that on acct. of you haveing went to France and wasn't killed why we will take you south if you want to go and you will get a chance to show if you are a pitcher yet or not and if you are like you use to be why maybe the Stock Yards will keep open long enough to take you when we are through with you and you can tell Armour and Swift and them that I will leave them know whether I want you or not about 3 days after we get to Texas." So I asked him how about salery and he said "The boss will send you a contract in a few days and if I was you I would be satisfied with it."

So it looks now like I was all set for the season Al and Gleason said I would be satisfied with the salery which is just as good as saying it will be $3000.00 as I wouldn't be satisfied with no less, so all I half to do now is wait for the contract and put my name on it and I will be back in the game I love and when a man's heart is in their work how are you going to stop him a specially with the stuff I've got.   Your pal,   JACK.

Chi, March 8.

FRIEND AL: Well Al I am through with baseball for good and am going in to business and I don't know just yet which proposition I will take that's been offered to me but they's no hurry and I will take the one that looks best when the proper time comes.

I suppose you will be surprised to hear that I have gave up the old game but maybe you won't be so surprised when I tell you what come off today.

Well in the 1st. place when the mail man come this A.M. he brought me a contract from Comiskey and the figures amounted to $2400.00 per annum. How is that Al when I was getting $2500.00 per annum before I went to the war. Well at 1st. I couldn't hardly beleive my eyes but that was the figure all right and finely I thought they must be some mistake so I was going to call up Comiskey and demand an explanation but afterwards I thought maybe I better run over and see him.

Well Al I went over there and Harry said the boss was busy but he would find out would he see me. Well after a wile Harry come out and said I was to go in the inside office so I went in and Comiskey was setting at his desk and for a wile he didn't look up but finely he turned around and seen me and shook hands and said "Well young man what can I do for you?" So I said "I come to see you about this here contract." So he asked me if I had signed it and I said no I hadn't so he said "Well they's nothing to see me about then." So I said "Yes because I figure they must of been some mistake in the salery you offered me." So he said "Don't you think you are worth it?" So I said "This here contract calls for $2400.00 per annum and I was getting $2500.00 when I quit and enlisted in the war so it looks like you was fineing me $100.00 per annum for fighting for my country." I said "Gleason said he wanted me and would send me a contract that I would be satisfied with." Well Comiskey said "If Gleason said he wanted you he must of been kidding me when I talked to him but if he wants you bad enough to pay the differents between what that contract calls for and what you want why he is welcome but that is up to him."

Well Al it was all as I could do to hold myself in and if he was a younger man it would of been good night Comiskey but I kept a hold, of myself and asked him why didn't he trade me to some club where I could get real jack. So he said "Well I will tell you young man I have got just 1 chance to trade you and that is to Washington and if you think Griffith will pay you more money than I will why I will make the trade." Well I told him to not trouble himself as I was through with baseball any way and had decided to go in to some business so he said good luck and I started out but he said "Here

you have left your contract and you better take it along with you
because some times when you leave a contract lay around the house
a few days the figures gets so big that you wouldn't hardly know
them."

Well I seen he was trying to kid me so I said "All right I will take
the contract home and tear it up" and I walked out on him.

Well Al that's all they is to it and I am tickled to death that it has
came out the way it has and now I can take the best offer that comes
along in some good business line and can stay right here in Chi and
be home all the yr. around with Florrie and the kiddies.

As for the White Sox I wished them good luck and beleive me
they will need it the way Gleason and Comiskey are trying to run
things and they will do well to finish in the same league with Boston
and Cleveland and N.Y. but at that I don't believe its Gleason that's
doing it and the way I figure is that this is his 1st. yr. as mgr and he
is a scared to open his clam and if he had his say he would give me
the $2800.00 I am holding out for. But its Comiskey himself that's
trying to make a monkey out of me. Well god help his ball club is
all as I can say.

As for leaveing them trade me to Washington that would be a
sweet club to pitch for Al where the only time they get a run is when
the president comes out to see them and he's libel to be in France
all summer.   Your pal,   JACK.

Chi, March 20.

FRIEND AL: Well Al this is the last letter you will get from me
from Chi for a wile as I am leaveing for Texas with the White Sox
tomorrow night. The scheme worked Al and by setting pretty in the
boat and keeping my mouth shut I made them come to me.

I suppose you will be surprised to hear that I am going to get back
in to harness but wait till I tell you what come off today and you
will see where they wasn't no other way out.

Well I went over to the stores this A.M. and when I come back
the Swede said some man had called me up on the phone. So of
course I knew it must of been the ball pk. so I called them up and
the secty. answered the phone and I asked him if anybody wanted
to talk to me. So he said no but Gleason was there if I wanted to
talk to him.

So I said put him on the wire and pretty soon I heard Gleason's
voice and he said "Well Jack are you going along with us?" So I said

"What about salery?" So he said "You have got your contract haven't you?" So I said "Yes but it don't call for enough jack." So he said "Well if you earn more jack than your contract calls for you will get it." So I said "If that's a bet I'm on."

So he told me to bring my contract along and come over there and I went over and there was a whole bunch of the boys getting ready for the get away and I wished you could of heard them when they seen me stride in to the office. Well Al they was hand shakes all around and you would of thought it was a family union or something.

Well the business was all tended to in a minute and I signed up and I am going to get $2400.00 which is the same money I was getting when I quit and that's going some Al when you think of the way they have been cutting salerys in baseball.

Well Al I am going to show them that they haven't made no mistake and I am going to work my head off for Gleason and Comiskey and the rest of the boys and wile I hate to be away from Florrie and the kiddies, still and all they's nobody on this ball club that lays awake all night crying for their bottle and if Texas don't do nothing else for me it will at lease give me a chance to get a little sleep.

Your pal,   JACK.

THE BATTLE OF TEXAS

◇

On the Rattler, March 22.

FRIEND AL: Well Al I am writeing this on the old rattler bound for sunny Texas and a man has got to write letters or something or you would gap yourself to death. They don't have no more poker game Al but just some baby game like rummy that may be O. K. for birds that has spent all their life at some X roads but take a man like I that was over in France and played in the big game and it kind of sets up a man's stomach to watch a bunch of growed up men popping their eyes out for the fear that they might maybe have a picture card left in their hand when some other bird lays down their cards. So about all they's left for a real man to do is write letters or read the paper or look out at the scenery and I all ready read the papers and as for the scenery we been going through Kas. most of the day and you could pull down the shade most any minute and feel pretty sure you wasn't going to miss nothing.

Well Al we left Chi last night and the 1st. thing Kid Gleason come through the car and asked everybody if they had any bottle goods hid in their grips as he says they are getting strick and if they catch a bird carring anything in to dry territory they send you to Siberia or somewheres. So when he come along to me he said "Well you big busher I don't half to ask you if you are bringing anything along with you as my nose knows but is any of it in bottles?" So I said "No all I have got with me they would half to operate to find it."

So he said "Well you want to be sure as they are libel to go through everybody's baggage." So I said "I would like to see some fresh Alex make a move to serch my baggage and I would knock him for a gool."

Well they's 2 or 3 of the other boys besides myself that was in the service or that is they call it being in the service though I was

The Saturday Evening Post, May 24, 1919; previously uncollected.

the only 1 that got acrost the old pond outside of Joe Jenkins 1 of the catchers that's still over there yet, but Red Faber was in the navy up to Great Lakes and Ed Collins was in the marines and 1 of the young fellows is wearing a aviation uniform and I suppose he seen the war from Texas and maybe got up so high that the 1st. baseman had to jump for him. But for a wile last night they was all asking me questions about what I seen over there and this in that but every time I would tell them something Collins or 1 of the other smart Alex would say he read about it in the papers and it was different so I said "All right if you seen it in the papers that way it must be so only I kind of figured that me being right up to the front I might be in a position to know something about the war where you take the most of these here reporters and for all they seen of it they might as well of been on Pikes Peek with a pair of opera glasses looking west." So that shut them up.

Well Al we are supposed to get to Mineral Wells tomorrow noon and they can't get us there to soon to suit me as I am wild to get out there in the old ball yard and show Gleason that I have got something left and he was telling me this A.M. that he had picked up a lot of good looking young right handers and I would half to step along to hold a job or the next thing I knowed I would be up to Minneapolis wearing a white beard and pitching for Joe Cantillon. But the new recruits that I have met on the train so far that thinks they are pitchers couldn't pass the physical examination for the Portugal army so it looks like I wouldn't have much trouble if I get a square deal and if I don't I will knock somebody for a gool.

                                        Your pal,   JACK

                              Mineral Wells, March 24.
FRIEND AL: Well Al we landed here yesterday noon and it was raining when we got here and still raining and don't look like it would ever stop and a man might almost think we had came to France by a mistake. And the only differents is that the harder it rained in France why they would see that we was all out in it wile here they's nothing to do only lay around the hotel. Well Al I don't know how many people they have got in Texas but they are all stopping at this hotel and on a rainy day it would take Houdini to get through the lobby. They call this hotel the Crazy Wells on acct. of 1 of the wells that they say it cures crazy people but it would half to be some well to cure some of the birds on our club a specially after they been

jammed up together in this hotel a couple of rainy days with nothing to do only gap at each other.

Well we got in to Ft. Worth yesterday A.M. and they switched us on to the R. R. that runs over here at lease they call it a R. R. and its the Weatherford Mineral Wells and North Western but Buck Weaver says the letters stands for Whoa Mule Whoa now Whoa. So I said if you think this R. R. balks you should ought to ride around France in some of them horse cars so Buck said "I wished I was a extra catcher so as I could set down in the bull pen with you all summer and learn all about France." He said "You boys that went to France thinks you had a tough time of it but what about we birds that has to listen to it all the rest of our life." So I said shut your mouth. But any way Al this R. R. isn't only 28 miles long from 1 end to the other so even if the trains do run like old Cy Young was paceing them you get to where you was going some time, where the roads we was on in France never seemed to know where to leave off.

Well we couldn't of done no work yesterday any way on acct. of just getting in and unpacking and getting our uniforms and everything but Gleason was certainly sore when we woke up this A.M. and it was still poring rain and I set with him at the breakfast table and the waiter said this rain was makeing a big hit with the people in Texas as they hadn't had no rain for so long that pretty near everything was drying up so Gleason said "Well you better make it unanimous." He meant for the waiter to dry up to and shut his mouth.

Well Gleason said we would half to go out and work tomorrow rain or shine and he said after this everybody would half to be down for breakfast at 8 bells or they wouldn't get no breakfast and if they didn't get down for breakfast he would go up to their rooms and use his razor strap on them. That's the way he generally always does Al on the new recruits is go after them with his razor strap to show them he is in ernest but of course he wouldn't dast do that on 1 of we old timers and if he ever tried it on me I would knock him for a gool.

I told him that this A.M. and he said "Well they's no danger of you ever comeing late to a meal and the only thing I am a scared of is that you will get here before they open up the dining rm. and bust down the door and get us put out of the hotel."

Well Al I am glad of 1 thing and that is most of the people stopping at the hotel is men and very few gals not that the gals would make any differents in my young life only in most of these southern hotels they's generally always a flock of gals that wants to make a fuss over the ball players and usually 1 of them takes a kind of a shine to me but this time I have made it up in my mind to tend to business and show Gleason that he didn't make no mistake in meeting my terms so I am glad I won't have nothing to take my mind off of my work though they's 1 little gal stopping here that the boys says she is a swell heiress from St. Louis that's here with her mother that's got rheumatism and I noticed she give me a long look when I come in the dining rm. this noon but I looked straight ahead and pretended like I didn't notice it. Her name is Miss Krug and she is some looker but she is certainly wasteing them goggly eyes on me as I am down here to get my arm in shape to pitch and not hold hands or something.

The clerk tells me that she has got a big car that she drives around in it all the wile her mother is takeing the treatments but as far as I am conserned if she gets lonesome driveing she will half to talk to the spare tire.   Your pal,   JACK.

Mineral Wells, March 26.

FRIEND AL: Well Al if nerve was all that a bird needed to make good in the big league they's 1 bird down here trying to be a pitcher on our club that has all ready made good. But it takes something besides nerve Al but listen to what come off today and you will say this bird is chesty enough if he only had something to go with it.

Well this bird's name is Belden and he was a semi pro up in Chi but he got catched in the draft and went to France and he just got back from over there last month and somebody recomended him to Comiskey and so he is down here on the trip. Well he is a right hander so he is a rival of mine you might say but to look at him I guess they's no hurry about me packing up my grip and go home.

Well the rain had stopped this A.M. and Gleason said everybody must be out to the pk. at 10 bells so we started out about 9:30 and I was walking with Buck Weaver and Eddie Cicotte and this here Belden. They was about a ft. of mud on the road and Cicotte made some remark about the mud and Belden said "This isn't nothing to what it was in France and over there we would think this was a drout." Well they's a cemetery on the way out to the pk. and wile we was going past it Buck Weaver made the remark that that was where we left most of the young pitchers every spring so Belden said "You can't scare me with no stuff about cemeterys as I seen to many of them in France." So then Buck says "Is they any subject we can talk about that won't remind you of something you seen in France?" So that shut him up for a wile but after a wile Cicotte asked him what battles he was in over there and he said he was in the Marne and the Oregon forest and Bellow Woods. So Cicotte says "Its no wonder the Germans took such a licking in them places as the whole American army was there." So Belden said oh no they wasn't and what made him think that. So Cicotte said "Because every soldier I have seen that's came back from France was in the Oregon forest and Bellow Woods."

Well we finely got out to the pk. and they wasn't no chance for a real practice on acct. of the mud but Gleason found a dry spot over in 1 corner and marked off the pitching distants and had us all throw a few and honest Al my old super never felt better in my life and I cut loose a couple that pretty near knocked Schalk for a gool but Gleason finely come up and stopped me and told me to not go to strong the 1st. day. Well I watched this Belden wile he throwed a few and I was standing along side of Cicotte and he was watching him to so I asked him what he thought of him. So Cicotte said "He looks like he will make a mighty valuable man for us as when he is in there pitching Schalk can set on the bench and rest as he won't never get nothing past the batter."

Well we finely come out of the pk. and started back towards the hotel and the 1st. thing you know they was a machine come hunking up behind us and it was Miss Krug the St. Louis heiress that's stopping at the hotel and she slowed up and asked if anybody wanted a ride. Well Al she was looking right at me but I pretended like I didn't understand but I just give her a kind of a smile and the next thing you know Belden had ran out and jumped in the drivers seat with her and away they went.

How is that for nerve Al when it was me she was looking at and this other bird that's been in the league about 5 minutes you might say jumps in and rides with her and I bet the little gal felt pretty sick when she seen what she had got wished on to and she didn't come in for supper tonight as I suppose she thought some of the boys would make fun of her though she needn't have no fears on that score as if any of them tried it I would knock them for a gool.   Your pal,   JACK.

Mineral Wells, March 29.

FRIEND AL: Well old pal I guess they's no more question about
me makeing good and sticking with the club and you will say the
same thing when I tell you what Gleason said yesterday. We played
a game out to the pk. between the 1st. and 2d. clubs and the game
was to go 7 innings and Gleason told me I could pitch a part of it
for the 2d. club so my arm was feeling so good that I asked him to
let me work 4 of the 7 innings. Well Al when I got through the 1st.
club had 1 hit and never found out where 2d. base was located. So
when it was over Gleason come up to me and said "Well Jack I don't
know what the war done to you but I never seen you look better
then that in the spring and right now you look like the best man I
have got down here pitching." He said "Now don't go and swell up
but keep working hard and do like I tell you and you may turn out
to be the bird I need to round out my pitching staff." Well the club
was going over to play Ft. Worth and Dallas Saturday and Sunday
and I thought of course we would all go along but after my showing
yesterday Gleason figured he wouldn't take no chances so he left me
here to work out with Faber and Wolfgang wile the rest of the boys
is gone. He said "I wouldn't pitch you in either of them games after
working you yesterday and I want you to do a little work here with
these other 2 boys and behave just like I was here watching you."
So I said "What and the he—ll could a man do only behave himself
in this town?" Well he said "I mean for you to not try and eat for
the whole club just because they are not here to eat for themself."

So you see Al it looks like I had made good right from the start
this time and that means they will half to come acrost with more
jack before long as Gleason promised before I come south that he
would give me more then my contract calls for if I show him the
right kind of stuff.

Well the bunch went away early this A.M. and was gone before I
got up and I had breakfast with Faber and Wolfgang and we decided
to go out and work about 11 o'clock so I and the other 2 went out
to the pk. and throwed the ball around a wile and done some running
but I got tired pretty quick on acct. of pitching yesterday so pretty
soon I said I thought I would call it a day so I started back to the
hotel and I hadn't no sooner then got outside of the pk. and all of
a sudden along come Miss Krug in her machine.

Well they wasn't no getting away from her this time without turning
her down cold so I kind of waved to her and she stopped the machine
and I got in and we drove back to the hotel.

Well Al she is some gal and it is a pleasure to talk to a gal like she as you take most gals and they can't kid along with a man but about all as they can do is giggle and act silly but this baby can give you as good as you send.

Well I said "You must be pretty lonesome today with Belden gone." So she said "Oh I don't know." So then I said "He is sure some lady killer." So she said "I'll say so. But you notice I am still alive." So after a wile she said "Belden tells me you was in France too." So I said "You and Belden seems to of talked together a whole lot." "Well" she said "I haven't had no one else to talk to." So I said "Well you have got some one else to talk to now." "Yes" she says "but you always run away from me. I suppose you real stars gets tired of haveing girls run after you." So I said "Oh I don't know."

Well we kidded back and 4th. like that till we come to the hotel and then I asked her was she doing anything this P.M. and she said she had a date with her mother but I took her to the picture show tonight and tomorrow she is going to take me for another ride. Well Al it does a man good to be around with a gal like that that keeps a man on edge what to say next as she always gives you as good as you send and from what she said she must be kind of tired of hearing Belden tell how he win the battle of Bellow Woods and etc. and any way I feel like a little rest would be the best thing for me after pitching them 4 innings yesterday. So I will play around with her tomorrow and then forget her when the bunch gets back Monday A.M. and go to work in ernest but if a man works to hard right at the start you are libel to go stale.

Well Al I had a letter from Florrie today and little Florrie has got 1 tooth and another 1 showing and she says little Al misses me pretty bad and asks every day why daddy don't hurry up and come home. Well they will all be proud of daddy before this season is over eh Al.   Your pal,   JACK.

Mineral Wells, March 31.

FRIEND AL: Well Al the boys is back from Ft. Worth and Dallas and I guess they didn't show up any to good over there and any way Gleason don't look like he enjoyed the trip and he told the boys out to the pk. this P.M. that they would half to show a whole lot more pep or he would leave some of them in Texas all summer to graze.

Well he give us a long work out and he stood behind me wile I throwed a few to Schalkie and he said I didn't look as fast as when

I pitched them 4 innings last Friday but he wasn't throwing no bo-
quets at any of the boys today so I didn't pay no tension. But I
couldn't help from laughing at 1 of the young catchers name Cosgrove
that was standing up there catching in the batting practice and Joe
Jackson hit a foul ball straight up and Cosgrove throwed off his mask
and begin running a mile around a 4 ft. track and finely the ball came
down and hit him in the cheek bone and knocked him for a gool.
Well he layed there and the trainer come running out to tend to him
but Gleason says "Get away from him as he is just as good laying
there as standing up and maybe after this he will know enough to
keep his mask on after a high foul ball."

Well it was pretty near supper time when he let us off and I tried
to be 1 of the 1st. out of the pk. but they was a whole bunch out
ahead of me and when Miss Krug come along with her car they all
seen me jump in and you ought to of seen Belden when he seen us
drive away together and all the boys yelled their head off.

Well I come back here to the hotel and got dressed and come
down for supper and after a wile Gleason come in and I was setting
with 3 of the other boys but he made 1 of them get up and give him
his seat so as he could set down and kid me.

"Well Jack" he says "I hear you worked pretty hard wile we was
gone and I suppose you can pretty near run the car by this time."

Well I knew he wasn't sore at me but just sore on acct. of how
rotten the young fellows was showing up so I just give him a smile.

"After this" he says "you and all the whole rest of the club will
ride back and 4th between the ball pk. and back on your own dogs.
They's to much rideing on this club but after this I will do all of it
and everybody on this club will get rode to death if they don't quit
loafing on me. So remember every one of you will stay out of machines going to the ball pk. and comeing back and besides that when
you go up to your rms. you can use the stairs and take a load off the
elevator."

Well Al he may be my mgr. out on the old ball field but he can't
tell me how to get upstairs or from 1 place to another but I left him
get away with it rather then start trouble in the dining rm. of the
hotel in front of the other boys to say nothing of the guests.

But I wonder what he would say if he knew how I spent Sunday.
Well old pal I had some time. Miss Krug knows all the roads and
we drove pretty near all day and she is some gal Al and smart as a
whip. Everything you say to her she has got a come back and for
inst. wile we was driveing yesterday she happened to ask me where

I come from and I told her Indiana and she said "That's a good place to come from." She meant it was a good place to get away from. So I said "I guess it hasn't got nothing on St. Louis at that." "Oh I don't know" she said.

Well it looks like I had Belden's time beat and I suppose I ought to of left him a clear field on acct. of him being single but the gal says herself that she can't stand him on acct. of him talking about himself all the wile and besides his looks is against him and besides a man has got to amuse themself some way in a burg like this or it would take more then the crazy wells to stop you from turning in to squirrel meat.   Your pal,   JACK.

Mineral Wells, April 3.

FRIEND AL: Well Al tomorrow is the last day here as we leave for Houston and play there Saturday and Sunday and then Austin and Georgetown and after that we go to Dallas for a few days and play a couple games there before we start north. Gleason was kidding me again tonight and said he wanted to apologize for the schedule that takes us away from here so soon and if he had of known how I was going to enjoy Mineral Wells he would of arranged to stay here longer. But he said I was to be sure and start in saying good by soon enough so as I would be through by train time. Well Al I wonder what he would say if I told him Miss Krug is going to be in Dallas wile we are there as she is going to drive over there with her mother. It kind of looks like she hates me eh Al?

Well we played another ball game today between the 1st. and 2d club and I pitched 5 innings for the 1st. club and they got 5 runs off of me but most of them was on acct. of the way Weaver and Collins was kicking the ball around the infield and then when they had filled up the bases on me Shano Collins caught a hold of 1 that was a mile over his head and the wind blowed it down in the right field corner and the right field fence in this pk. is as far as from here to France and the ground was hard and of course the dam ball rolled and Shano could of ran around the bases twice so when the inning was over Gleason said to me "When you are pitching to a man like Collins you want to say to yourself I am pitching to Collins and not be thinking about some garbage contractor's daughter from St. Louis." So I said "He hit a ball that was over his head." So Gleason said "Yes and over Leibold's head to." He says "The next time I pick out a spot to train a ball club it will be in a man's convent where they's no gals." So I walked away from him.

But wait till you hear what this Belden pulled today Al. Dureing the game some of the boys was trying their hit and run signs and etc. and they got them all balled up so Gleason made us stay out there after the game was over and practice up on our signs and wile he was talking to some of the boys this Belden cut in and said he thought it would be a good idear if instead of slideing their hand up and down the bat or pulling their cap or something if they would learn a few French words and give their signs in French out loud and they couldn't none of the other clubs understand them and for inst. if a man was up there hitting and wanted the man on 1st. base to go down on the next ball he would holler allay at him on acct. of that being the French for go. So Cicotte said it was a great idear only about the 9th. or 10th. time we worked it on some club and they seen the man go every time they might maybe suspect what it meant and then we would half to find out the Russian word for go and use that and he thought the only Russian word for go meant go back and the base runner would get mixed up and think the batter meant he was going to hit a foul ball.

Well Miss Krug had some engagement with her mother tonight so I went with some of the boys to a picture show and Belden went along with us an 1 of the pictures was old last yr. stuff that showed a lot of different places in France and etc. and every time they would show a picture Cicotte would ask Belden if he was there and he said yes every time and finely Cicotte asked him how long he was in France all together and he said 4 mos, so Cicotte said "Well if you was only in France 4 mos. and seen all them places its no wonder you wasn't shot as you never stood still a minute."

Well Al this is the last letter you will get from me here as I will be busy packing up tomorrow and saying good by to my friends but I will try and drop you a line from Houston or somewheres along the line and let you know how things is comeing on.

Your pal,   JACK.

Georgetown, April 8.

FRIEND AL: Well I guess Gleason won't half to worry no more about at least 1 member of his pitching staff after what I done over in Houston Saturday and here again today. I worked 5 innings against the Houston club Saturday and believe me Al they have got some club but I made them look like they ought to of paid their way in. They was only 1 ball got out of the infield and Weaver could of nailed that only he didn't start in time and the rest of the wile they was popping them up in the air or missing them all together. Well Williams the left hander followed me and he was pretty good to though he didn't have anywheres near the stuff I showed but we trimmed them 6 to 0 and Gleason was all smiles.

Well of course I didn't work there again Sunday or yesterday at Austin and the boys didn't look so good behind the pitching they got but today we was up against a bunch of collegers and Gleason sent me the whole distants to see how I could stand it and I guess I showed him. Well Al I honestly felt sorry for some of these college boys and they couldn't of got a base hit off me with a shovel only their teachers and friends was watching them so I eased up in the last 2 innings and they got a couple of base hits and they felt so good about them that I wished I had of let them get some more.

Well Gleason come to me afterwards and he said "Now Jack you look like that 1st. day at the Wells and if you can just keep going like that I have got the 4 pitchers I want to work regular and you are 1 of them. You showed in Houston and here what you can do when you haven't got your mind on some millionaire janitor's daughter from St. Louis with rheumatism on the mother's side. You had a fast ball in there to-day that looked like Johnson at his best and you have pretty near got where you can slow ball them without everybody in the pk. calling it on you. You just keep pitching that way and I will get you some dough that is some dough."

So it looks like I was all set Al and the only thing now is to keep him from finding out about Miss Krug and her mother comeing to Dallas and I don't care if I see her or not only it wouldn't seem hardly fair to have she and her mother come all the way over there and then me not even take her to a picture show. But what Gleason don't know won't hurt him and that stuff about girls bothering me is all in his eye as I can pitch when my arm feels good and I can't pitch when it don't feel good girls or no girls.

Your pal, JACK.

Fort Worth, April 13.

FRIEND AL: Well Al I don't know whether to quit baseball or not and maybe I won't quit if I can get away to some other club but I can't work no more under Gleason and do myself justice.

Wait till you hear what come off in Dallas yesterday and I bet you will say I would be a sucker to stand for the kind of stuff he is trying to put over.

Well Al the second day we was there I got a phone call and it was Miss Krug and her and her mother was stopping at a certain hotel so I asked her would she like to go to a picture show or somewheres and she said she would so I said I would meet her that night and we would go somewheres and see a show. Well I was in the lobby of our hotel when the phone call come and of course they had to page me and Gleason heard them so after I got through phoneing he come up to me and asked if the bell of St. Louis was folling me around. So I said no I supposed she was in Mineral Wells. So he said where was I going that evening and I said nowheres and he said all right he wanted me to go to a picture show with him. So then I said I had forgot I had a date to go with 1 of the other boys on the club so he said all right he would go along with us. Well Al they wasn't no shakeing lose from him so finely I had to own up that I was going to take Miss Krug to a show so he said he would go along and pay for it. Well he went along all right and it was the worst picture I ever seen and when it was over Gleason asked Miss Krug and I if we wouldn't have a soda or something.

Well they wasn't nothing to do only go with him and we hadn't no sooner then give our order when he said to her "What do you think of big Jack here?" Well she said she thought I was all right. So Gleason said "Well I never thought so myself but I guess he must be or he couldn't of never got such a sweet wife like he's got up in Chi." Well I couldn't say nothing or neither could the gal. So then Gleason asked me did I have the Mrs. picture with me or either 1 of the 2 kids. Well Al they's no use telling you any more about it only we had our soda and took the gal back to her hotel and then I and Gleason come back to our hotel together and he never said a word all the way home or neither did I only just before he left me to go up to his rm. he said "You pitch tomorrow Jack" and that's all he said.

Well of course they won't be no more picture shows for Miss Krug and I and of course it don't make no differents to me as I was going to tell her about me being married and everything and her and I was just good friends and liked to talk to each other but its haveing him cut in on my private affairs and try to run them that makes me sore and he must think this is the army the way he acts.

Well Al I pitched the game in Dallas yesterday and they couldn't do nothing with me but I wouldn't of never pitched it at all only they had me advertised and I have got a whole lot of good friends there that I wouldn't disapoint them. But as for sticking with the club after that kind of business I couldn't do myself justice and as soon as we get home I will put it up to Comiskey and ask him to trade me to some other club or else I will quit and go in to some business where a man does his work and gets through and when he is through the mgr. of the store don't go noseing around in to your private affairs.   Your pal,   JACK.

Louisville, April 18.

FRIEND AL: Well Al I have only got time for a few lines as we are leaveing in a little wile for Cincy for games tomorrow and Sunday and I am going to pitch 5 innings Sunday and then rest till Wednesday when we open up the season in St. Louis. Gleason hasn't gave it out to the papers yet Al but between you and I it looks like a cinch I would pitch the opening game in St. Louis. Gleason and all the rest of the boys admits that I have been going better then any other pitcher on the club and you know how crazy every club is to win the opening game and that is why it looks like I would be the man that is chose.

Well Al I will give them everything I have got and if I only feel as good as I felt yesterday in Nashville why the St. Louis boys might just as well leave their bats in the bag.

Well I guess the last time I wrote you I was kind of on the outs with Gleason and I didn't speak to him for pretty near a wk. but a man can't stay sore at him very long on acct. of the stuff he pulls and 1st. thing you know you half to bust right out laughing and then of course its good night.

I guess I told you about Belden the young pitcher from Chi that was in France and tried to get us to give our signs in French. Well he was with the 2d. club that left us before we come away from Texas and they went up north the other way and yesterday I was setting,in the hotel at Nashville talking to Felsch and Gleason come along and Felsch asked him if he had heard how Belden was comeing along with the 2d. club. So Gleason said "He got along a whole lot faster then the club he was with as he is all ready back in Chi." He said "I wired to Shano Collins and asked him if they was anybody on his 2d. club that looked like he could get along without them so he wired back that he could rap Belden up and send him home because though they wasn't no doubt that he had beat Germany it didn't look like he would ever last 2 innings vs. Boston and Cleveland." So when Gleason pulled that I couldn't help from laughing and then he kicked me in the shins like old times and now we are pals again.

Well I haven't no more time to write from here but will try and drop you a line from Cincy but in the mean wile you can tell the boys that it looks like a cinch I will open the season in St. Louis and if any of them has a chance to get a bet down on your old pal they can't go wrong. I wasn't never as good as I am this spring Al and I will knock them for a gool.   Your pal,   JACK.

Cincy, April 20.

FRIEND AL: Well Al just a few words before we go out to the pk. and this will be my last game before the opening and Gleason says I and Lefty Williams will pitch 5 and 4 innings today for a final work out so it looks like a cinch I will open up Wednesday in St. Louis.

Speaking about St. Louis Al I guess I told you about that Miss Krug that was down to the Wells wile we was there and kind of lost her head over me and finely I had to get Gleason to tell her I was a married man. Well I had forgot all about her but this A.M. when I come down for breakfast they was a letter in my box and it was from this same gal and she is back in St. Louis and wanted to know if maybe I couldn't call her up when I get there just for old time sake and any way she said she would be out to the opening game Wednesday and pulling for us even if she is a St. Louis gal.

Well I was reading the letter at breakfast and Gleason come in and asked me what was the news from home and I said I hadn't heard nothing from home since we was in Memphis so he said who was the letter from then. So I said "You may be the mgr. of this ball club but you are not my mother." So he said "No and if I was I would give you a spanking." He says "You don't half to tell me who the letter is from because I can tell by your rosy cheeks who it is from and I can just about tell what's in it." So then I said "All right if you are such a smart Alex they's no use in me telling you anything." So then he asked me what was my home address in Chi as he said he wanted all the boys addresses and phone numbers. So I give him mine and he walked away.

Well Al I have got to get ready to go out to the pk. and give these National Leaguers a treat and I bet by the time I get through with them they will be thanking god that they don't half to look at this kind of pitching all summer or they would hit about 6 and 7-8.

Your pal, JACK.

St. Louis, April 24.

FRIEND AL: Well old pal I suppose by this time you have got a hold of the Chi papers and seen what I done yesterday and all as I have seen so far is the St. Louis papers and every 1 of them says it was 1 of the best pitched games they ever seen for an opening game.

Well Al they couldn't of nobody beat me yesterday and either 1 of the 2 hits I give them could of been scored either way and a specially Sisler's but I guess he ain't bragging much this A.M. at that as I sent him back twice for a drink of water.

Well old pal I have had lots of big days in my career both in baseball and in Uncle Sam's service but I don't believe I was ever so happy in my life as when Schalkie caught that foul ball off of Gedeon and made the last out and the way Gleason and the rest of the boys slapped me on the back.

But wait till I tell you the funny part of it Al. Gleason sent us all to bed early Tuesday night and before I went to the hay he told me to get plenty of rest as he was going to pitch me if I looked good out there before the game.

So I didn't get up till pretty near 9 o'clock and it was a quarter to 10 when I come down for breakfast and when I got in the lobby who do you think was there waiting for me? Well Al it was Florrie, all dolled up like the state fair.

Well to make a short story out of it it seems like Gleason had wrote her a letter from Cincy and asked her to come down here at the club's expense and watch me open up the season but to not say nothing to me about she was comeing and believe me Al it was some surprise and some pleasant surprise to see her and I never seen her look prettier in her life.

Well Al I guess with the stuff I had I could of beat them without her setting there in the stand but just the same I worked a whole lot harder for knowing she was up there watching me and I guess the club won't grudge the jack they spent getting her down here.

Well when we come back to the hotel for dinner last night Gleason come in the dining rm. with us and insisted on buying us a bottle of wine and I never seen nobody in my life so tickled over winning 1 ball game as him. Well of course he has got a good reason to be tickled as he will need all the pitching he can get and me makeing this showing means about half his worrys is gone.

Well you will read about the game in the papers and they isn't much more to write about only I can't help from kind of wondering if Miss Krug was out there and seen it but after all what and the he—ll do I care if she was or wasn't?   Your pal,   JACK.

ALONG CAME RUTH

◇

St. Louis, April 26.

FRIEND AL: Well Al this is our last day here and we win the 1st.
2 games and lose yesterday and have got one more game to play and
tonight we leave for Detroit. Well if we lose today we will have a
even break on the serious and a club that can't do no better than
break even with this St. Louis club better take up some other line
of business but Gleason instead of useing a little judgement sent a
left hander in against them yesterday and they certainly give him a
welcome and the more I see of left handers I am certainly glad I
pitch with my right arm the way God intended for a man.

Well the boys on our club was feeling pretty cocky the 1st. 2 days
about how they could hit but yesterday they could of played in a 16
ft. ring without no ground rules as the most of the time they was
missing the ball all together and when they did hit it it acted like a
geyser and it was Bert Gallia pitching against us and they all kept
saying he didn't have nothing but when he got through with us we
didn't have nothing either and that's the way it always goes when a
pitcher makes a sucker out of a club he didn't have nothing but when
they knock him out of the park he's pretty good.

Well any way I told Gleason last night that it looked like we
wouldn't get no better than a even break here unless he stuck me
in there to pitch the last game today. So he says "No I was figureing
on you to open up in Detroit Sunday but of course if you are afraid
of Detroit I can make different plans." So I said "I am not afraid of
Detroit or nobody else and you know yourself that they can't no
club beat me the way I am going whether its Detroit or no matter
who it is." So he said "All right then keep your mouth shut about
who is going to pitch because if you are going to manage the club I
won't have no job left." Well let him try and run the ball club the

This story first appeared in the *Saturday Evening Post*, July 26, 1919; reprinted in
Some Champions (New York: Scribners, 1976).

way he wants to but if I was running the ball club and had a pitcher
that is going the way I am going I would work him every other day
and get a start on the other clubs as the games we win now counts
just as much as the games we win in Sept.

Well Al Florrie went back to Chi last night though I wanted her
to stick with the club and go on to Detroit with us but she said she
had to get back, and tend to business at the beauty parlor so I told
Gleason that and he said he was sorry she was going to leave us as
it was a releif for him to look at something pretty once in wile when
most of the time he had to watch ball players but he admired her
for tending to business and he wished it run in the family. He says
"You should ought to be thankfull that your Mrs. is what she is as
most wifes is a drug on their husband but your Mrs. makes more
jack then you and if she give up her business it would keep you
hustleing to make both ends meet the other, where if you missed a
meal some time and died from it your family would be that much
ahead." So I said "Yes and that is because your cheapskate ball club
is only paying me a salary of $2400.00 per annum instead of some-
wheres near what I am worth." So he said "I have all ready told you
that if you keep working hard and show me something I will tear up
your contract and give you a good one but before I do it I will half
to find out if you are going to win ball games for me or just use up
1 lower birth like in old times." So I told him to shut his mouth.

Well Al I thought the war with Germany was all over but Joe
Jenkins joined the club here and now the whole war is being played
over again. He is 1 of the catchers on the club and he was in France
and if they was any battles he wasn't in its because he can't pronounce
them but anybody that thinks the U.S. troop movements was slow
over there ought to listen to some of these birds that's came back
and some of them was at Verdun 1 evening and Flanders the next
A.M. then down to Nice the next day for a couple hours rest and up
in the Oregon forest the folling afternoon and etc. till its no wonder
the Germans was dazzled. If some of these birds that was in the war
could get around the bases like they did around the western front
all as the catchers would dast do when they started to steal second
base would be walk up the base line towards third with the ball in
their hand and try to scare them from comeing all the way home.

Well its Detroit tomorrow and 3 more days after that and then
home and I haven't been there since the middle of March and I guess
they's 2 kids that won't be tickled to death to see somebody eh Al?

                                        Your pal,   JACK.

Detroit, April 28.

FRIEND AL: Well old pal I suppose you read in the papers what come off here yesterday and I guess Gleason won't have no more to say after this about me being afraid of Detroit. The shoe points the other way now and Detroit is the one that's afraid of me and no wonder.

I didn't have the stuff that I had down to St. Louis for the opening but I had enough to make a monkey out of Cobb and Veach and I couldn't help from feeling sorry for this new outfielder they have got name Flagstaff or something and I guess he was about half mast before I got through with him.

Well its a cinch now that I will open in Chi Thursday and I will give St. Louis another spanking and then I will make Gleason come acrost with that contract he has been promiseing me and if he trys to stall I will tell him he must either give me the jack or trade me to some other club and he has got good sence even if he don't act like it sometimes and they's a fine chance of him tradeing me though they's 7 other clubs in this league that would jump at it and Detroit is 1 of them though the Detroit club would be takeing a big chance if they got a hold of somebody that could realy pitch as the fans up here would die from surprise.

Well I had a letter from Florrie today and it was just like the most of her letters when you got through reading it you wondered what she had in mind and about all as she said was that she had a surprise to tell me when I got home and I use to get all excited when she wrote about them surprises but now I can guess what it is. She probably seen a roach in the apartment or something and any way I guess I can wait till I get home and not burn up the wires trying to find out before hand.   Your pal,   JACK.

Detroit, April 30.

FRIEND AL: Well Al we leave for home tonight and open up the season in Chi tomorrow but I won't be out there pitching unless Gleason apologizes for what he pulled on me last night. It was more rotten weather yesterday just like we been haveing ever since the 1st. day in St. Louis and I near froze to death setting out there on the bench so when we come back to the hotel they was a friend of mine here in Detroit waiting for me here in the lobby and he come up in the room with me and I was still shivering yet with the cold and he said how would I like something to warm me up. So I said

"That's a fine line of talk to hand out in a dry town." So he said I could easy get a hold of some refreshments if I realy wanted some and all as I would half to do would be call a bell hop and tell him what I wanted.

Well I felt like a good shot would just about save my life so I called a boy and told him to go fetch me some bourbon and he said O. K. and he went out and come back in about a half hr. and he had a qt. with him and I asked him how much did we owe him and he said $15.00. How is that for reasonable Al and I guess it was the liquor men themselfs that voted Michigan dry and you can't blame them. Well my friend seemed to of had a stroke in his arm so as he couldn't even begin to reach in his pocket so I dug down and got 15 berrys and handed it to the kid and he still stood there yet like he expected a tip so I told him to beat it or I would tip him 1 in the jaw.

Well I asked my friend would he have a shot and his arm was O. K. again and he took the bottle and went to it without waiting for no glass or nothing but he got the neck of the bottle caught in his teeth and before he could pry it loose they was about a quarter of the bourbon gone.

Well I was just going to pore some of it out for myself and all of a sudden they come a rap at the door and I said come in and who walked in but Gleason. So I asked him what did he want.

So he said "Well you wasn't the 1st. one in the dinning rm. so I thought you must be pretty sick so I come up to see what was the matter." Well it was to late to hide the bottle and he come over to the table where I was setting and picked it up and looked at it and then he pored out a couple drops in the glass and tasted it and said it tastes like pretty good stuff. So I said it ought to be pretty good stuff as it cost enough jack so he asked me how much and I told him $15.00.

So he said "Well they's some of the newspaper boys has been asking me to try and get a hold of some stuff for them so I will just take this along."

So I said I guest the newspaper boys could write crazy enough without no help from the Michigan boot legs and besides the bottle belongs to me as I payed good money for it. So Gleason said "Oh I wouldn't think of stealing it off of you but I will take it and pay you for it. You say it cost $15.00 but they's only about $11.00 and a half worth of it left so I will settle with you for $11.00 and a half." Well I didn't want to quarrel with him in the front of a outsider so

I didn't say nothing and he took the bottle and started out of the rm. and I said hold on a minute where is my $11.00 and a half? So he said "Oh I am going to fine you $11.00 and a half for haveing liquor in your rm. but instead of takeing the fine out of your check I will take what's left in the bottle and that makes us even." So he walked out.

Well Al only for my friend being here in the rm. I would of took the bottle away from Gleason and cracked his head open with it but I didn't want to make no seen before a outsider as he might tell it around and people would say the White Sox players was fighting with their mgr. So I left Gleason get away with $11.00 and a half worth of bourbon that I payed $15.00 for it and never tasted it and don't know now if it was bourbon or cat nip.

Well my friend said "What kind of a bird are you to let a little scrimp like that make a monkey out of you?" So I said I didn't want to make no seen in the hotel. So he said "Well if it had of been me I would of made a seen even if it was in church." So I says "Well they's no danger of you ever haveing a chance to make a seen in church and a specialy with Gleason but if you did make a seen with Gleason you would be in church 3 days later and have a box right up close to the front."

Well Al I have told Gleason before this all ready that I would stand for him manageing me out on the old ball field but I wouldn't stand for him trying to run my private affairs and this time I mean it and if he don't apologize this P.M. or tonight on the train he will be shy of a pitcher tomorrow and will half to open up the home season with 1 of them other 4 flushers that claims they are pitchers but if Jackson and Collins didn't hit in 7 or 8 runs every day they would be beating rugs in the stead of ball clubs.

Well any way we go home tonight and tomorrow I will be where it don't cost no $15.00 per qt. and if Gleason walks in on me he can't only rob me of $.20 worth at a time unless he operates.

Your pal, JACK.

Chi, May 3.

FRIEND AL: Well Al I have just now came back from the ball pk. and will set down and write you a few lines before supper. I give the St. Louis club another good trimming today Al and that is 3 games I have pitched and win them all and only 1 run scored off of me in all 3 games together and that was the 1 the St. Louis club got

today and they wouldn't of never had that if Felsch had of been
playing right for Tobin. But 1 run off of me in 3 games is going
some and I should worry how many runs they scratch in as long as
I win the ball game.

Well you know we was to open up here Thursday and it rained
and we opened yesterday and I was waiting for Gleason to tell me
I was going to pitch and then I was going to tell him I would pitch
if he would apologize to me for what he done in Detroit but instead
of picking me to pitch he picked Lefty Williams and the crowd was
sore at him for not picking me and before the 1st inning was over
he was sore at himself and Lefty was enjoying the shower bath. Gallia
give us another beating and after it was over Gleason come up to
me in the club house and said he was going to start me today. So I
said "How about what you pulled on me in Detroit?" So he says
"Do you mean about grabbing that bottle off of you?" So I said yes
and he says "Look at here Jack you have got a great chance to get
somewheres this yr. and if you keep on pitching like the way you
started you will make a name for yourself and I will see that you get
the jack. But you can't do it and be stewed all the wile so that is the
reason I took that bottle off of you." So I said "They's no danger of
me being stewed all the wile or any part of the wile when bourbon
is $15.00 per qt. and me getting a bat boy's salery." So he said "Well
you lay off the old burb and pitch baseball and you won't be getting
no bat boy's salery. And besides I have told the newspaper boys that
you are going to pitch and it will be in the morning papers and if
you don't pitch the bugs will jump out of the stand and knock me
for a gool." So as long as he put it up to me that way I couldn't do
nothing only say all right.

So sure enough it come out in the papers this A.M. that I was going
to pitch and you ought to seen the crowd out there today Al and
you ought to heard them when my name was gave out to pitch and
when I walked out there on the field. Well I got away to a bad start
you might say as Felsch wasn't laying right for Tobin and he got a
two base hit on a ball that Felsch ought to of caught in his eye and
then after I got rid of Gedeon this Sisler hit at a ball he couldn't
hardly reach and it dropped over third base and Tobin scored and
after that I made a monkey out of them and the 1st. time I come up
to bat the fans give me a traveling bag and I suppose they think I
have been running around the country all these yrs. with my night
gown in a peach basket but I suppose we can give it to 1 of Florrie's

friends next xmas and besides it shows the fans of old Chi have got a warm spot for old Jack.

Speaking about Florrie Al when we was in Detroit she wrote and said she had a surprise for me and I thought little Al had picked up a couple hives or something but no it seems like wile I was on the road she met some partys that runs a beauty parlor down town and they wanted she should sell her interest in the one out south and go in pardners with them and they would give her a third interest for $3000.00 and pay her a salery of $300.00 per mo. and a share of the receits and she could pay for her interest on payments. So she asked me what I thought about it and I said if I was her I would stick to what she had where she was makeing so good but no matter what I thought she would do like she felt like so what was the use of asking me so she said she didn't like to make a move without consulting me. That's a good one Al as the only move she ever made and did consult me about it was when we got married and then it wouldn't of made no differents to her what I said.

Well she will do as she pleases and if she goes into this here down town parlor and gets stung we should worry as I will soon be getting real jack and it looks like a cinch we would be in the world serious besides, and besides that the kids would be better off if she was out of business and could be home with them more as the way it is now they don't hardly ever see anybody only the Swede nurse and 1st. thing as we know they will be saying I ban this and I ban that and staying away from the bldg. all the wile like the janitor.

Your pal,   JACK.

Chi, May 6.

FRIEND AL: 4 straight now Al. How is that for a way to start out the season? It was Detroit again today and that is twice I have beat them and twice I have beat St. Louis and it don't look like I was never going to stop. They got 2 runs off of me today but it was after we had 7 and had them licked and I kind of eased up to save the old souper for the Cleveland serious. But I wished you could of heard the 1 I pulled on Cobb. You know I have always kind of had him on the run ever since I come in the league and he would as leaf have falling archs as see me walk out there to pitch.

Well the 1st. time he come up they was 2 out and no one on and I had him 2 strikes and nothing and in place of monking with him

I stuck a fast one right through the groove and he took it for a third
strike. Well he come up again in the 4th. inning and little Bush was
on third base and 1 out and Cobb hit the 1st. ball and hit it pretty
good towards left field but Weaver jumped up and stabbed it with
his glove hand and then stepped on third base and the side was out.
Well Cobb hollered at me and said "You didn't put that strike acrost
on me." So I said "No why should I put strikes acrost on you when
I can hit your bat and get 2 out at a time?" You ought to of heard
the boys give him the laugh.

Well he hit one for 3 bases in the 7th. inning with Bush and Ellison
both on and that's how they got their 2 runs but he wouldn't of never
hit the ball only I eased up on acct. of the lead we had and besides
I felt sorry for him on acct. of the way the crowd was rideing him.
So wile he was standing over there on third base I said "You wouldn't
of hit that one Ty only I eased up." So he said "Yes I knew you was
easeing up and I wouldn't take adantage of you so that's why I
bunted."

Well 1 more game with Detroit and then we go down to Cleveland
and visit Mr. Speaker and the rest of the boys and Speaker hasn't
been going any to good against them barbers that's supposed to pitch
for Detroit and St. Louis so God help him when he runs up against
Williams and Cicotte and I.   Your pal,   JACK.

Cleveland, May 9.

FRIEND AL: Well Gleason told me today he wasn't going to pitch
me here till the Sunday game to get the crowd. We have broke even
on the 2 games so far and ought to of win them both only for bad
pitching but we can't expect to win them all and you really can't
blame the boys for not pitching baseball when we run into weather
like we have got down here and it seems like every place we go its
colder then where we just come from and I have heard about people
going crazy with the heat but we will all be crazy with the cold if it
keeps up like this way and Speaker was down to our hotel last night
and said the Cleveland club had a couple of bushers from the Southren league that's all ready lost their mind and he told us what they
pulled off wile the St. Louis club was here.

Well it seems like Cleveland was beat to death 1 day and they
thought they would give some of the regulars a rest and they put in
a young catcher name Drew and the 1st. time he come up to bat
they was men on first and second and 1 out and Sothoron was pitching

for St. Louis and 1 of the St. Louis infielders yelled at him "Don't worry about this bird as he will hit into a double play." Well Drew stood up there and took 3 strikes without never takeing the bat off his shoulder so then he come back to the bench and said "Well I crossed them on their double play."

Well in another game Bagby was pitching and he had them licked 8 to 1 in the 7th inning and he had a bad finger so they took him out and sent in a busher name Francis to finish the game. Well he got through 1 inning and when he come up to hit they was a man on 3d. base and 2 out and Davenport was pitching for St. Louis and he was kind of wild and he throwed 3 balls to Francis. So then he throwed a strike and Francis took it and then he throwed one that was over the kid's head but he took a cut at it and hit it over Tobin's head and made 3 bases on it. So when the inning was over Larry Gardner heard him calling himself names and balling himself out and Larry asked him what was the matter and he said he was just thinking that if he had of left that ball go by he would of had a base on balls.

Well I had a letter from Florrie today and she has closed up that deal and sold out her interest in the place out near home and went in pardners in that place down town and she said she thought it was a wise move and she would clean up a big bunch of jack and it won't only take her a little wile to pay for her interest in the new parlor as with what she had saved up and what she got out of the other joint she had over $2000.00 cash to start in with.

Well I don't know who her new pardners is but between you and I it looks to me like she was pulling a boner to leave a place where she knew her pardners was friends and go into pardners with a couple women that's probably old hands at the game and maybe wanted some new capital or something and are libel to get her role and then can her out of the firm but as I say they's no use me trying to tell her what to do and I might just is well tell Gleason to take Collins off of second base and send for Jakey Atz.

Well Al nothing to do till Sunday and if I beat them it will make me 5 straight and you can bet I will beat them Al as I am going like a crazy man and they can't no club stop me.

Your pal,   JACK.

Chi, May 12.

FRIEND AL: Well old pal its kind of late to be setting up writeing a letter but I had a little run in with Florrie tonight and I don't feel like I could go to sleep and besides I don't half to work tomorrow as I win yesterday's game in Cleveland and Gleason is saveing me for the Boston serious.

Well we got in from Cleveland early this A.M. and of course I hurried right home and I was here before 8 o'clock but the Swede said Florrie had left home before 7 as she didn't want to be late on the new job and she would call me up dureing the forenoon. Well it got pretty near time to start over to the ball pk. before the phone rung and it was Florrie and I asked her if she wasn't going to congratulate me and she says what for and I said for what I done in Cleveland yesterday and she said she hadn't had time to look at the paper. So I told her I had win my 5th straight game and she acted about as interested as if I said we had a new mail man so I got kind of sore and told her I would half to hang up and go over to the ball pk. She said she would see me at supper and we hung up.

Well we had a long game this P.M. and it seemed longer on acct. of how anxious I was to get back home and when I finely got here it was half past 6 and no Florrie. Well the Swede said she had called up and said she had to stay down town and have supper with some business friends and she would try and be home early this evening.

Well the kids was put in bed and I tried to set down and eat supper alone and they didn't nothing taste right and finaly I give it up and put on my hat and went out and went in a picture show but it was as old as Pat and Mike so I blew it and went in Kramer's to get a couple drinks but I had kind of promised Gleason to lay off of the hard stuff and you take the beer you get now days and its cheaper to stay home and draw it out of the sink so I come back here and it was 8 bells and still no Florrie.

Well I set down and picked up the evening paper and all of a sudden the phone rung and it was a man's voice and he wanted to know if Mrs. Keefe had got home. So I done some quick thinking and I said "Yes she is here who wants her?" So he said "That's all right. I just wanted to know if she got home O. K." So I said who is it but he had hung up. Well I rung central right back and asked her where that party had called from and she said she didn't know and I asked her what and the he—ll she did know and she begun to play some jazz on my ear drum so I hung up.

Well in about 10 minutes more Florrie come in and come running over to give me a smack like usual when I get back off a trip. But she didn't get by with it. So she asked what was the matter. So I said "They's nothing the matter only they was a bird called up here a wile ago and wanted to know if you was home." So she says "Well what of it?" So I said "I suppose he was 1 of them business friends that you had to stay down town to supper with them." So she said "Maybe he was." So I said "Well you ought to know if he was or not." So she says "Do you think I can tell you who all the people are that calls me up when I haven't even heard their voice? I don't even know a one of the girls that keeps calling up and asking for you." So I said "They don't no gals call up here and ask for me because they have got better sence but even if they did I couldn't help it as they see me out there on the ball field and want to get aquainted."

Then she swelled up and says "It may be hard for you to believe but there is actually men that want to get aquainted with me even if they never did see me out there on the ball field." So I said "You tell me who this bird is that called up on the phone." So she said "I thought they was only the 2 babys in this apartment but it seems like there is 3." So then she went in her rm. and shut the door.

Well Al that's the way it stands and if it wasn't for the kiddies I would pack up and move somewheres else but kiddies or no kiddies she has got to explain herself tomorrow morning and meanwile Al you should ought to thank God that you married a woman that isn't flighty and what if a wife ain't the best looker in the world if she has got something under her hat besides marcel wavers?

Your pal,   JACK.

Chi, May 14.

FRIEND AL: Well old pal it looks like your old pal was through working for nothing you might say and by tomorrow night I will be signed up to a new contract calling for a $600.00 raise or $3000.00 per annum. I guess I have all ready told you that Gleason promised to see that I got real jack provide it I showed I wasn't no flash out of the pan and this noon we come to a definite understanding.

We was to open against the Boston club and I called him to 1 side in the club house and asked him if I was to pitch the game. So he says you can suit yourself. So I asked him what he meant and he said "I am going to give you a chance to get real money. If you win your game against the Boston club I will tear up your old contract and give you a contract for $3000.00. And you can pick your own spot. You can work against them today or you can work against them tomorrow just as you feel like. They will probably pitch Mays against us today and Ruth tomorrow and you can take your choice." Well

Al Mays has always been good against our club and besides my old souper is better this kind of weather the longer I give it a rest so after I though it over I said I would wait and pitch against Ruth tomorrow. So tomorrow is my big day and you know what I will do to them old pal and if the boys only gets 1 run behind me that is all as I ask.

That's all we got today Al was 1 run but Eddie Cicotte was in there with everything and the 1 run was a plenty. They was only 1 time when they had a chance and it looked that time like they couldn't hardly help from scoreing but Eddie hates to beat this Boston club on acct. they canned him once and he certainly give a exhibition in there that I would of been proud of myself. This inning I am speaking of Scott got on and Schang layed down a bunt and Eddie tried to force Scott at second base but he throwed bad and the ball went to center field and Scott got around to third and Schang to second and they wasn't nobody out. Well Mays hit a fly ball to Jackson but it was so short that Scott didn't dast go in. Then Hooper popped up to Collins and Barry hit the 1st. ball and fouled out to Schalkie. Some pitching eh Al and that is the kind I will show them tomorrow. And another thing Eddie done was make a monkey out of Ruth and struck him out twice and they claim he is a great hitter Al but all you half to do is pitch right to him and pitch the ball anywheres but where he can get a good cut at it.

Well they never had another look in against Eddie and we got a run when Barry booted one on Collins and Jackson plastered one out between Ruth and Strunk for 2 bases.

Well Al I am feeling pretty good again as I and Florrie kind of made up our quarrel last night. She come home to supper and I was still acting kind of cross and she asked me if I was still mopping over that bird that called her up and I didn't say nothing so she said "Well that was a man that was the husband of 1 of the girls I had supper with and he was there to and him and his wife wanted to bring me home but I told them I didn't want nobody to bring me home so his wife probably told him to call up and see if I got home all right as they was worried." So she asked me if I was satisfied and I said I guessed I was but why couldn't she of told me that in the 1st. place and she said because she liked to see me jealous. Well I left her think I was jealous but between you and I it was just a kind of a kid on my part as of course I knew all the wile that she was O. K. only I wanted to make her give in and I knew she would if I just held out and pretended like I was sore. Make them come to you Al is the way to get along with them.

I haven't told Florrie what this game tomorrow means to us as I want to surprise her and if I win I will take her out somewheres on a party tomorrow night. And now old pal I must get to bed as I want to get a good rest before I tackle those birds. Oh you $600.00 baseball game.   Your pal,   JACK.

Chi, May 16.

FRIEND AL: Well Al I don't care if school keeps or not and all as I wish is that I could get the flu or something and make a end out of it. I have quit the ball club Al and I have quit home and if I ever go back again to baseball it depends on whether I will have my kiddies to work for or whether they will be warded to her.

It all happened yesterday Al and I better start at the start and tell you what come off. Florrie had eat her breakfast and went down town before I got up but she left word with the ski jumper that she was going to try and get out to the ball game and maybe bring the rest of her pardners with her and show me off to them.

Well to make it a short story I was out to the pk. early and Gleason asked me how I felt and I told him fine and I certainly did Al and Danforth was working against us in batting practice to get us use to a left hander and I was certainly slapping the ball on the pick and Gleason said it looked like I was figureing on winning my own game. Well we got through our batting practice and I looked up to where Florrie usualy sets right in back of our bench but she wasn't there but after a wile it come time for me to warm up and I looked over and Ruth was warming up for them so then I looked up in the stand again and there was Florrie. She was just setting down Al and she wasn't alone.

Well Al I had to look up there twice to make sure I wasn't looking cock eyed. But no I was seeing just what was there and what I seen was she and a man with her if that's what you want to call him.

Well I guess I couldn't of throwed more than 4 or 5 balls when I couldn't stand it no more so I told Lynn to wait a minute and Gleason was busy hitting to the infield so I snuck out under the bench and under the stand and I seen 1 of the ushers and sent word up to Florrie to come down a minute as I wanted to see her. Well I waited and finely she come down and we come to the pt. without waisting no time. I asked her to explain herself and do it quick. So she said "You needn't act so crazy as they's nothing to explain. I said I was going to bring my pardner out here and the gentleman with me is him." "Your pardner" I said "What does a man do in a beauty parlor?" "Well" she said "This man happens to do a whole lot.

"Besides owning two thirds of the business he is 1 of the best artists in the world on quaffs." Well I asked her what and the he—ll was quaffs and she said it meant fixing lady's hair.

Well by this time Gleason had found out I wasn't warming up and sent out to find me. So all as I had time to say was to tell her she better get that bird out of the stand before I come up there and quaffed him in the jaw. Then I had to leave her and go back on the field.

Well I throwed about a dozen more balls to Lynn and then I couldn't throw no more and Gleason come over and asked me what was the matter and I told him nothing so he said "Are you warmed up enough?" and I said "I should say I am."

Well Al to make it a short story pretty soon our names was announced to pitch and I walked out there on the field.

Well when I was throwing them practice balls to Schalk I didn't know if he was behind the plate or up in Comiskey's office and when Hooper stepped in the batters box I seen a dozen of him. Well I don't know what was signed for but I throwed something up there and Hooper hit it to right field for 2 bases. Then I throwed something else to Barry and he cracked it out to Jackson on the 1st. hop so fast that Hooper couldn't only get to third base. Well wile Strunk was up there I guess I must of looked up in the stand again and any way the ball I pitched come closer to the barber then it did to Strunk and before they got it back in the game Hooper had scored and Barry was on third base.

Then Schalkie come running out and asked me what was the matter so I said I didn't know but I thought they was getting our signs. "Well" he said "you certainly crossed them on that one as I didn't sign you for no bench ball." Then he looked over at Gleason to have me took out but Gleason hollered "Let him stay in there and see what kind of a money pitcher he is."

Well Al I didn't get one anywheres near close for Strunk and walked him and it was Ruth's turn. The next thing I seen of the ball it was sailing into the right field bleachers where the black birds sets. And that's all I seen of the ball game.

Well old pal I didn't stop to look up in the stand on the way out

and I don't remember changing clothes or nothing but I know I must
of rode straight down town and when I woke up this A.M. I was still
down town and I haven't called up home or the ball pk. or nowheres
else and as far is I am concerned I am through with the both of them
as a man can't pitch baseball and have any home life and a man can't
have the kind of home life I have got and pitch baseball.

All that worrys me is the kiddies and what will become of them
if they don't ward them to me. And another thing I would like to
know is who put me to bed in this hotel last night as who ever
undressed me forgot to take off my clothes.

Your pal,   JACK.

Chi, May 20.

FRIEND AL: Well Al I am writeing this from home and that means
that everything is O. K. again as I decided to give in and let bygones
be bygones for the kiddies sake and besides I found out that this
bird that Florrie is pardners with him is O. K. and got a Mrs. of his
own and she works down there with him and Florrie is cleaning up
more jack then she could of ever made in the old parlor out south
so as long as she is makeing good and everything is O. K. why they
would be no sence in me makeing things unpleasant.

Well I told you about me staying down town 1 night and I stayed
down till late the next P.M. and finely I called up the Swede and told
her to pack up my things as I was comeing out there the next day
and get them. Well the Swede said that Gleason had been there the
night before looking for me and he left word that I was to call him
up at the ball pk. So I thought maybe he might have a letter out
there for me or something or maybe I could persuade him to trade
me to some other club so I called him up and just got him before
he left the pk. and he asked me where I was at and said he wanted
to see me so I give him the name of the hotel where I was stopping
and he come down and met me there at 6 o'clock that night.

"Well" he says "I was over to see your little wife last night and I
have got a notion to bust you in the jaw." So I asked him what he
meant and he said "She sported your kids wile you was in the war
and she is doing more than you to sport them now and she goes in
pardners with a man that's O. K. and has got a wife of his own that
works with him and you act like a big sap and make her cry and
pretty near force her out of a good business and all for nothing
except that you was born a busher and can't get over it."

So I said to him "You mind your own business and keep out of my business and trade me to some ball club where I can get a square deal and we will all get along a hole lot better." So he said where did I want to be traded and I said Boston. "Oh no" he said. "I would trade you to Boston in a minute only Babe Ruth wouldn't stand for it as he likes to have you on our club." But he said "The 1st. thing is what are you going to do about your family?" So I said I would go back to my family if Florrie would get out of that down town barber shop. So Gleason said "Now listen you are going back home right now tonight and your Mrs. isn't going to sacrifice her business neither." So I said "You can't make me do nothing I don't want to do." So he says "No I can't make you but I can tell your Mrs. about that St. Louis janitor's daughter that was down in Texas and then if she wants to get rid of you she can do it and be better off."

Well Al I thought as long as Florrie was all rapped up in this new business it wasn't right to make her drop it and pull out and besides there was the kiddies to be considered so I decided to not make no trouble. So I promised Gleason to go home that night.

So then I asked him about the ball club. "Well," he said "you still belong to us." "Yes" I said "but I can't work for no $2400.00"

"Well" he said "we are scheduled against a club now that hasn't no Ruths on it and its a club that even you should ought to beat and if you want to try it again why I will leave you pick your day to work against the Philadelphia club and the same bet goes."

So yesterday was the day I picked Al and Roth got a base hit and Burns got a base hit and that's all the base hits they got and the only 2 runs we got I drove in myself. But they was worth $600.00 to me Al and I guess Gleason knows now what kind of a money pitcher I am.   Your pal,   JACK.

THE BUSHER PULLS A MAYS

◊

N. Y., July 29.

FRIEND AL: Well old pal here we are on the gay white way but they don't nobody on this ball club feel gay and no wonder. In the 1st. place to look at our club you would think we had just came back from the Marne as Gandil was left home in a hospital with appendix and Felsch is so lame that he can't cover no more ground then where his dogs is parked and Cracker Schalk has to be wheeled up to the plate and back you might say and to cap off the climax I got stomach trouble from something I eat or something and wile I don't pitch with my stomach a man can't do themself justice when the old feed bag acts up.

To make it worse Detroit has got a hold of a couple pitchers that can do something besides make 9 men on the field and Jennings club is comeing like a house on fire and all and all it looks like we was a bad bet and will be mighty lucky to get back off of this trip in 1st. place. For inst. Cicotte pitched a nice game today and lose it because they was a couple fly balls hit to center field that Felsch only had to take 3 or 4 steps to get under them but his sick dog layed down on him and wouldn't buge and zowey they went for 3 base hits. So as I say they can call this the gay white way but they can't hardly call us the gay White Sox eh Al.

Well I suppose you seen in the paper what Carl Mays the Boston pitcher pulled off and you will half to hand it to him. He walked out on the Boston club wile they was playing us out in Chi and said he wouldn't pitch no more for the pennant though when the season

The Saturday Evening Post, October 18, 1919; previously uncollected.

opened up and they had all their men back from the service we all of us thought they would be the club we would half to beat as they had 2 stars for every position you might say and they could stick 1 club in the field 1 day and a whole different club the next day and 1 of them as good is the other but any way they blowed up like Willard and it got so as they felt cocky when they only lose 1 game per day so Mays said he was through and instead of the club suspending him why they pretty near kissed him you might say and all the other clubs in the league begun biding for him.

Well we would of had him only I guess the Boston club insisted on Gleason giveing them Cocky Collins or Schalk or myself or somebody so of course Gleason give them the razz and finely Huggins got him for the N. Y. club for 4 or 5 ball players and the liberty loan and now Mr. Mays is with a club that has got a chance to get in the world serious and it shows what a sucker a ball player is to stick with a club where you can't get nothing only the worst of it.

Well Al I guess if I was to have a run in now with Gleason or something I will know what to do as the minute he looks X eyed at me I will Mays him and I guess they wouldn't some clubs jump at the chance to get a hold of me and specially Detroit as Jennings is makeing a great fight for the old rag without hardly any pitching at all you might say and what would he do with a man like I on the club to go in there every 3d. day and take my own turn besides helping the other birds out when they begin to weaken.

Well old N. Y. is some dry town since the 1 of July and the only way a man can get a drink here is go in a saloon and the only differents between old times is what they soak you for it now which is plenty but when a man has got to have it he has got to have like today after the game for inst. my old stomach was freting pretty bad and I got myself 6 high balls on the way back from the pk. and it set me back $2.40 but as I say what is $2.40 compared to a man's health.

Your pal,   JACK.

Boston, Aug. 2.

FRIEND AL: Well Al we are haveing a fine trip and the way we been going you would think we must of clumb in to 1st. place some night after dark but we won't be there long if Gleason don't wake up and use his pitchers right. He acts like Cicotte and Williams was Adam and Eve and they wasn't nobody else in the world and he keeps yelping about what tough shape he is in on acct. of not only haveing 2 pitchers and as far is the rest of us is conserned we might as well be takeing tickets.

Well a man can't hardly blame him for going slow with birds like Kerr and Faber and Lowdermilk that when they do throw a ball somewheres close to the plate somebody's bat gets in the way but just because I lose them games to the St. Louis and N. Y. clubs in Chi with my stomach why that isn't no reason I should spend August with my feet on the water cooler and as I said to Gleason today he might as well of left me home and he says yes and the rest of the club to.

Well you don't see Jennings trying to cop the old rag with 2 pitchers but he works his staff in turn like a mgr. should and some A.M. we will wake up and find ourself a few laps behind Detroit instead of leading them and all because Jennings gives his pitchers a chance but instead of Gleason giveing me a chance he sets around and mones about what tough shape we are in and if he could only get a hold of some pitcher like Page with the Phila. club but it looks to me like if Page was so dam good the Athaletics would get rid of him. We have all ready signed up Pat Ragan that every club in the National League tried him and I don't know what and the he—ll they can expect him to do here where a man has got to have something besides acquaintences in all the big citys and it looks to me like Gleason has went plain cuckoo and it wouldn't surprise me to see him bark like a dog.

Well I suppose you seen where Ban Johnson stepped in and suspend it Mays after it come out that the N. Y. club had boughten him and I don't see what Ban has got to say about it now and I suppose we will be reading pretty soon where he has plastered a $5.00 fine on Hap Felsch for limping.

Ban said a few yrs. ago that Ty Cobb wouldn't never play another game in this league but the last time we played the Detroit club they had somebody in center field that looked a whole lot like Cobb and Jennings and the rest of the boys called him Ty.

Well this old burg isn't running as wide open as N. Y. and if a man wants a little refreshmunts they have got to go out and hunt for it like tonight I and 1 of the boys thought we better lay in a qt. to last over the sabath and 1 of the boys the Boston club told us where to go get it so we got a qt. of it and it cost $7.00 and that means $7.00 a drink as they couldn't nobody in the world take more then I swallow and I wouldn't be surprised if that is what ails the Boston club. They are poisoned. Well the qt. all but 2 drinks is standing on my burro and that is where it is going to spend the sabath and when we leave here I will give it to the chamber horse for a tip and tell her what it cost and she will know she died a high price death. In the old days when we was here on a Sunday they closed up the bars but you could walk in the hotel cafe and order up a drink as long is you ordered sandwichs with it and if they knowed you they would bring you the same sandwichs every trip.

Well 1 more game here Monday and then we go to Philly and maybe we will win 1 there as we have got 4 to play and if Mack ever win 4 in a row he would put on a auction sale.

Your pal,   JACK.

Phila., Aug. 4.

FRIEND AL: Well Al just a line to let you know I am here in Philly and the club still up in Boston yet and don't get here till tomorrow. Well that means that I am going to take my regular turn from now on and will start against this club either tomorrow or the next day and Gleason sent me on ahead to rest up along with Cicotte. You see in the old days the ball clubs use to get a party rate on the R. R. and it saved them money to all travel together from town to town but now everybody has got to pay full fare so if a mgr. wants to send a couple of his star pitchers a day or 2 ahead to the next town to rest them up why it don't cost nothing so that is how it come that I and Cicotte is here in Phila.

I didn't have no idear I was comeing on ahead till yesterday A.M. when I run in to Gleason in the hotel dinning rm. up in Boston and he motioned me to come and set down with him. Well he said how is your heart so I asked him what did he mean. "Well" he says "in them last 2 games you pitched vs. St. Louis and N. Y. out in Chi it looked to me like you was missing." So I said I guest my heart was O. K. but my stomach had been freting me on acct. of something I eat. I said "I would of made them 2 clubs look like a bum only a man can't work when your stomach aint right." "No" he says "and your stomach won't never get right on that liquid diet." So I asked him what he meant and he says you know what I mean and I should think you would get wise to yourself. So I says I guest I was wise enough so he says "Well if your wise you will cut out the rough stuff and get to work." So I asked him how could I get to work when he wouldn't give me no chance and he said "I will tell you what I will do with you. Cicotte is going over to Phila. tonight to rest up and you can go along with him and rest up includeing your stomach and if you aint in shape to pitch when I call on you it won't be nobody's fault only your own. And remember they won't be nobody over there watching you and you can behave yourself or not just as you feel like but when I get there I will know if you been behaveing."

So he had Joe O'Neill buy me a ticket and birth and I and Cicotte got here this A.M. and have the whole day to ourself and maybe we will go out this P.M. and see the game as the St. Louis club is playing here and besides we will have a chance to study Mack's batters. They are some study Al but maybe we can set where we can watch foxy Connie waggle his score card and maybe get his signs though it looks to me like he would do a whole lot better if he give up his score card long enough to have a few good ball players names printed on it.

Well 1 of the waiters here in the hotel tells me a man can get all they want to drink here in Phila. if they go at it right but nothing doing Al as I am going to be in shape to give Gleason the best I got though 3 or 4 wouldn't hurt me and what Gleason don't know won't hurt him.   Your pal,   JACK.

Phila., Aug. 6.

FRIEND AL: Well Al I guess they's no use of a man trying to go along with a mgr. that has went cuckoo and if it wasn't for the rest of the boys on the club I would pull a Mays and walk out on the club and go to some club where a man can get a square deal but if I done that it might maybe cost this club the pennant and it wouldn't be the right thing towards the rest of the boys.

Well I guess I told you that I and Cicotte was sent on here ahead of the rest of the club to rest up so as we would be in good shape for the serious here and we layed around the hotel here all Monday A.M. and after lunch Eddie said he was going out to the ball pk. and did I want to go along. Well I said I guest I seen enough of baseball without spending 2 P.M. looking at a couple clubs like Burke and Mack has got a hold of and the more a man seen of Mack's club why the lest he would know about how to pitch to them and besides the best thing for me would be to get my mind off of baseball. So Eddie went out to the game and pretty soon I got kind of lonesome so I called up a friend of mine that is quite a fan and we found a place where you can still get it and we histed a few and then he said how about running down to Atlantic City.

Well Al we went down there and seen the sights and took a dip
and my friend says he wondered why all the queens was giveing us
the double O as they didn't never pay no tension to him when he
was alone so I just laughed and didn't say nothing and didn't even
look X eyed at 1 of them as I leave the flirting game to birds that
hasn't no wife or no respect for the ones they have got so we got a
dinj to dig us up a qt. and we was comeing back here at 11 P.M. but
they must of been sleeping powders or something in that stuff we
got and any way we layed down on the beach to rest for a few minutes
after supper and the both of us overslept ourselfs and missed the
train. Well Al we finely got back here at 9 o'clock yesterday A.M.
and the club was all ready here and Gleason was setting in the lobby
when I come in. Well he said where have you been. So I told him
I had been out for a walk and he didn't say nothing so I come up to
my rm. and layed down.

Well when we got out to the ball pk. he had both Cicotte and I
take our turn in batting practice and when it come time to warm up
he said it would be me. Well I didn't feel any to good but I warmed
up pretty good and finely the game started and I hadn't pitched for
pretty near 2 wks. and no wonder I couldn't start right out as good
as ever but instead of giveing me a chance to get started he halls me
out of there after I walked the 1st. 2 men. Well Cicotte went in and
I come in to the bench and Gleason begin to rave and I said how
can a man pitch when you don't even leave him get started. "Well"
he says "you was out for 1 walk this morning and you was out for 2
walks this afternoon and I thought 3 walks a day would be enough
for you." "Where was you last night?" he says and I told him nowheres. So he said "Yes you was. You was out for a board walk
down to Atlantic City and I have got a notion to board walk you 1
in the jaw."

Well Al I don't know how he could of knew where I had been
but I am not the kind that trys to lie out of something so I says yes
I went down to Atlantic City and took a dip. So he says you mean
you took a dipper. Well they's no use argueing with a crazy man Al
so all as I could do was walk away from him before my temper got
the best of me so I went in the club house and dressed and went up
in the stand and watched the rest of the game. Well they didn't score
off of Cicotte and we got 1 run in the 11th. off of Page and beat
them 1 to 0 but I might of shut them out just the way Cicotte done
if he had of left me in there but he has went cuckoo Al and to show
you how bad he is he has signed up Mayer that has been in the

National League 20 or 30 yrs. and the next thing you know he will be sending for Geo. Van Haltren or somebody. Well I only wished I was off this club and I would walk out on them in a minute only for the rest of the boys that has got their heart set on winning.

Your pal,   JACK

Washington, Aug. 9.

FRIEND AL: Well old pal don't be surprised if you pick up a paper some A.M. and see where I have walked out on this bunch of cuckoos and pulled a Mays on them only it won't be no 2 or 3 wks. before I land somewheres else as they's a certain club in this league that would give their eye to get a hold of me as it would mean the pennant. Don't think I am bosting Al as I am just giveing you the facts and when I tell you what come off yesterday you will know who I refer. Even if the deal don't come off I can give Gleason a good scare and maybe come to some kind of a understanding with him.

Well yesterday was our last day in Philly and the Detroit club had finished up their serious in Washington the day before and their whole bunch was over in Philly yesterday and out to see our game. Well afterwards we seen the whole bunch of them and Jennings kind of smiled at me like he wanted to see me alone so I give him the chance and he says what was on my mind. So I seen he was trying to give me a opening so I said I was tired of pitching for Gleason. So he says "Well I been watching the box scores where you pitched lately and it didn't look to me like you was pitching for Gleason." He is a great kidder Al but that is just his way.

Well he humed and haud and finely he says they was no use him talking to me as Gleason wouldn't trade no pitcher to a club that was fighting him for the pennant. So I said maybe he wouldn't trade me but suppose I walked out on him like Mays done on Boston why then maybe he would give me to the club that made the best offer.

So Jennings said "Yes but we tried to get Mays but all as we could offer for him was jack and we couldn't offer nothing else for you and when a club offers money to Comiskey why it is like takeing coal to a castle."

So I said "Well it looks to me like it would be to your int. to offer something besides jack as Gleason could use a couple of your ball players." Yes said Jennings but when you begin talking trade to Gleason he can't only talk in words of 1 sylable Cobb and Bush.

Well I said if I make up my mind to walk out on him Cleveland or
N. Y. will get me either 1 and you know what that means. So he
says "I guess you won't go to neither 1 of them clubs." That is what
he said Al and they's only 1 way to take it but at that it wasn't so
much what he said as how he looked when he said it. He kind of
half smiled and give me a kind of a wink and walked away from me
and besides he was scared to make it to strong as a mgr. of a club is
not supposed to temper with a player on another club. But last night
just before we left for here I seen Bush of the Detroit club and I
told him what had came off and he says why didn't I go ahead and
pull a Mays and see what happened. He says "We are going to win
the pennant any way so you better take a chance of getting on a
live 1."

Well old pal I am not going to do nothing I will be sorry for and
if our club wakes up and begins to show something I won't leave
them in the lerch but Gleason better get help to himself or he will
wake up some A.M. and I won't be around for him to snarl at me.

Well comeing over on the train I set with 1 of the reporters that
travels with the club and he told me that Gleason had been trying
to get this here Page that pitched the 11 innings game vs. Cicotte
and Gleason wanted to pay cash for him but Mack must of been
unconscious or something and any way he turned it down so it looks
like Gleason would half to struggle along without Mr. Page and I
guess we will get along just as good without him as from what I seen
of him you could write up the game on his fast ball wile its comeing
up there but maybe he would bring us luck as a bird that can make
us go 11 innings for 1 run must have god with him.

Well I asked this reporter if Gleason had said anything about me
lately and he said nothing that could be printed so I said well maybe
I will have a story for you 1 of these mornings so he asked me what
I meant and I said well if Gleason didn't give me a square deal I
would maybe pull a Mays on him and go to some club where I can
get fair treatmunt. "Well" he says "if I was you I would cut out that
line of talk as it may get back to Gleason and he will beat you to it."
Well Al I should worry if it gets back to Gleason or not as it might
give him a scare but I don't want him to know nothing about it yet
a wile till I see how things comes along so I haven't told nobody
about my plans only a couple of the boys on the club that knows
enough to keep their mouth shut and in the mean wile mum is the
word till we see how matters comes along.

                                        Your pal,   JACK.

On Train, Aug 12.

FRIEND AL: Well old pal we are on our way back to old Chi and
everybody is happy even the Washington club though we took 2 out
of 3 from them but they made more jack out of our serious then
they ever seen before and what is 2 or 3 ball games to them you
might say. Well Gleason didn't start me but you notice he stuck me
in there yesterday in the 8th inning when Lefty Williams begin to
wilt and put the brakes on them and that ball Judge hit would have
been nuts for Gandil only for him being weak on acct. of his appendix.

Well when Gleason 1st. told me to go in there I had a notion to
go in there and dink the ball up there and let the Washington boys
get their name in the averages for once in their life and show Gleason
I didn't give a dam but then I thought of the rest of the boys and it
wasn't square to them to not give them the best I got so I cut loose
and you see what happened.

Well Gleason patted me on the back when it was over and tried
to give me the old oil but I just kind of smiled and pertended like
I fell for it but that is the way he is Al when you win you are aces
but when you have a bad day your as welcome is a gangrene.

Well it looks now like we would go right through and win the old
rag as everybody has got so as they can waggle their legs without
groaning and Gandil will soon have his strength back and then look
out as about all as we half to do is break even and Detroit will have
1 he—ll of a time catching up with us so it looks like your old pal
will get in once on the world serious dough and about time after all
I have did for this club and would of been in on it in 1917 only I
give up everything for my country wile the rest of the boys stayed
home and made nasty remarks about the Kaiser.

Speaking about the world serious Al it looks now like Cincinnati
would give the Giants some battle in the other league and if Moran
can keep his club going they have got a good chance and I guess that
old burg wouldn't go cuckoo if they win a championship. Well I
guess the ball pk. down there can't handle the crowd that we would
draw in the Polo Grounds but even if we can't make as much jack
out of a serious down there all the boys on our club would about as
leaf play them as it would save us time as we can get it over in 4
days if we play them where it would probably take 5 days vs. N. Y.
on acct. of 1 day to make the jump. The boys was talking this A.M.
about what Cicotte and Williams should ought to do to Moran's club
and they would make a bum out of them and etc. but I guess after
what I showed in Washington Gleason can't do no lest then start me

in 1 game at the outside and then we will see if Roush and Groh is such wales when they get up vs. real pitching after the dead arm Dicks they been looking at all season.

Well old pal it is pretty near time to stick the old nose in the old feed bag and we land in old Chi this P.M. and no game tomorrow but Thursday we open up vs. Boston and I suppose it will be Cicotte as Gleason sent him on ahead to get ready. Well if he can't cut her they's others on the old pitching staff that can and 1 of them is

Your pal,   JACK.

Chi, Aug 15.

FRIEND AL: Well Al I suppose you seen what the Boston club done to Cicotte yesterday and Gleason had to take him out so as Felsch and Liebold could stand still and rest a minute but when he come in to the bench all as Gleason said to him was better luck next time Ed instead of fuming at the mouth like he done to me in Philly. So I said to Gleason I says "You send this bird on ahead of the club to be ready for this game and they make a bum out of him and all as you say to him is better luck next time Ed and the same thing came off in Philly the day I started and you went cuckoo and barked like a dog." So Gleason says "Yes you big stiff but the reason they got to Eddie was because he didn't have no stuff when he got in there but your trouble was that you had to much stuff before you ever went in." So I just laughed at him.

Well it looks more then ever like Pat Moran was going to cop in the other league the way his club made a bum out of the Giants in the serious down there and I was just thinking tonight if the big show comes off in Cincinnati why couldn't you hop on a train and breeze down there for the 1st. game that is scheduled down there and maybe that will be the game I pitch or 1 of them and it would tickle me to death to know my old pal was up there in the stand pulling for me and I promise you won't be ashamed of saying your my friend when you see me out there. It wouldn't only cost you about $6.00 or $7.00 R. R. fare and you wouldn't half to bother about no ticket to the game as the boys on our club can get 2 of them a peace to every game at the regular prices and I would leave you use 1 of mine 1 day and it wouldn't only cost you $2.00 or $3.00 and after the game we could go somewheres and hist a few as its a cinch they have still got some tucked away somewheres in that old burg as even the babys would die down there without their beer.

Maybe you will think you shouldn't ought to take no trip like that and leave Bertha home but between you and I Al the ladys is a nusance when it comes to a trip like that and besides no matter how good a man and their wife gets along when you have lived with them a few yrs. its like a sweet dream to be away from them a day or 2. Think it over Al and leave me know how you feel about it and I would say come up to 1 of the games here only what with the Swede and the 2 kids we wouldn't have no place to park you and besides we could have a better time somewheres where Florrie wasn't folling us around all the wile like a caboose.

Speaking about Florrie we had a long talk last night and it seems like she is about ready to sell out her share in the beauty parlor as she don't get along very good with the Dumonts and besides as I always say a womans place is home so I guess she is about through pairing finger nails and etc. and I am glad of it as with my salery and what I pick up in the world serious and etc. I guess they won't be no over the hills to the poor house for Mr. and Mrs. Keefe yet a wile.   Your pal,   JACK.

Chi, Aug. 20.

FRIEND AL: Well Al I and Gleason had some words today and I guess he knows now where I stand and if he don't why it is his own look out. We was playing the Washington club and Nick Altrock was out on the coaching line and I begin to kid him from the bench and I hollered hello handsome at him. So he turned around and hollered why hello Carl I didn't know you was still with us. So Gleason says why is he calling you Carl and I said I didn't know so Gleason says "Yes you do he is calling you Carl after Carl Mays because you told some of the boys you was going to Mays me and walk out on the club and Nick has heard about it." So I said "Well maybe I did say that in a jokeing way." So Gleason says "What was the joke." So I said "Well maybe they wasn't no joke but I just made the remark to some of the boys that I liked to pitch and it looked like they wasn't no chance for me to pitch here so I wished I was somewheres where I could pitch." So Gleason said "Well I will send you somewheres where you can pitch." So I said "I can pitch here if you will give me a chance." "Well" Gleason says "I am not running this club to muse you but I am trying to win a pennant and I can't take no chances with a bird that has only turned out 2 good innings for me in a month." So I said "Well I can't turn out no more good innings till you stick me in there." So Gleason said "Well I will stick you in there when I get good in ready and if you want to walk out on me why walk as far is you like." So I says "I don't half to walk as the Michigan Central will take me as far is I want to go." So that shut him up Al as he knows now that if I jumped I would have a place to light and he can't afford to strengthen a club that is right on our tail you might say.

You have got to hand it to Jennings for the race they are makeing Al though we been going good to thanks to a whole lot of luck like today for inst. Cicotte was in there against a Swede name Erickson that the Washington club got from Detroit and the boys went out and got 10 runs for Eddie and a man that can't win with 10 runs better study for a janitor or something and a specially vs. the Washington club that if they ever scored 10 runs in 1 day the other clubs would ask for a recount. Well this Erickson certainly was good and the only boys on our club that could hit him was those that batted against him. Well Al you never see them pile up 10 runs behind me when I am in there pitching and about the only way as we can score at all with me in there is 3 bases on balls and a balk.

Well Al Florrie told the Dumonts today that she was going to quit them and sell out her share of the business and they wasn't no tears shed on neither side. She hasn't only payed in about $250.00 for the stock they was going to sell her so she will have that comeing besides a few dollars salery as she had drew ahead. Any way I am glad she is out of it and can stay home and pay a little tension to the kiddies and we are going to throw a party Sat. night to celebrate and as long is you can't be here Al why I suppose I will half to hist a couple for you.   Your pal,   JACK.

Chi, Aug. 25.

FRIEND AL: Well Al I am through. Not through with pitching baseball but through working for a cuckoo that treats a man like a dog. They's only 1 condition that I will go back to him Al and that is a contract calling for more money or a bonus or something and he has got to understand that I work in my regular turn which is the only way a pitcher can do themself justice. But he won't agree to my turns Al as trying to manage a ball club has went to his head and his brains has been A. W. O. L. for the last 2 mos. you might say. So it's going to be moveing day pretty soon for your old pal and I guess you know where I am going to move without me telling you.

I have all ready wired a telegram to Jennings telling him what come off and things ought to begin to pop by tomorrow at lease.

Well Al I will tell you what come off and you can judge for yourself what kind of a cuckoo this bird is. Well the last half of last wk. he had me down in the bull pen every day warming up though he didn't have no intentions of sticking me in there and God knows I was warm enough without going out and looking for it but every time I would ease up a little and try and rest he would look down there from the bench and motion to me to get busy and by the time the game was over Sat. P.M. my old souper squeeked like a rat every time I throwed a ball.

Well Sat. night we throwed a party over to the house in honor of Florrie retireing from business and I had 4 qts. of the old hard stuff layed away and I and a couple of Florrie's friends husbands finished 1 of them before supper and after supper we turned on the jazz and triped the life fantastic and I half to be oiled or I can't dance so by 11 o'clock the serch and sieze her birds could of had the run of the house and welcome. Well 1 of the husbands said he knowed a place where they had escaped from the epidemic so we went down there and they served us rat poison in tea cups and I only histed a couple to be polite but I eat something that didn't set right and when I finely got home and put on my night gown I wished it was a sroud.

Well Al I couldn't eat nothing when I got up and whatever it was I had eat the night before had gave me a fever and Florrie wanted I should call up the ball pk. and tell them I was sick but it was Williams's turn to pitch and I thought all as I would half to do would be get down in the bull pen and go through the motions but when I get to the pk. what does this cuckoo do but tell me to take my turn in the batting practice as I am going to work. So I asked him what was the matter with Williams and Gleason said he don't feel good. "Well" I said "if he felt like I do his family would be out shopping for 1 left handed casket." So Gleason said what and the he—ll is the matter with you now. So I told him my stomach. "Well" said Gleason, "get in there and give them your fast one and curve and I will tell Schalk not to sign for your stomach." So that was all as I could get out of him Al and they wasn't nothing to do only grip my teeth and try and make the best of it.

Well Al to make a short story out of it I went in there so dizzy that Vick of the N. Y. club looked like he was hitting from both sides of the plate and I tried to throw a ball between him. Well I seen him fall over but he couldn't get out of the way as I catched him right over the ear and if I had of had my regular stuff on the ball they would of been brains splashing clear up in the grand stand. Well I got 1 over for Peck and he past it up and then Schalk thought they was going to hit and run so he signed me to waist 1 and I waisted 4 and then up come Baker and I had 2 balls and nothing on him and I looked in to the bench but Gleason wasn't looking at me and I looked out to the bull pen and they wasn't nobody warming up so I pitched again and got 1 over the plate. Well I don't know what kind of baseball it is for a man to hit with 2 and 0 with birds on 1st. and 2d. and nobody out and the pitcher hog wild but that is what this bird done Al is take a lunge at the ball and Liebold couldn't of catched it without a pass out check.

Well I looked in to the bench again and Gleason didn't say I yes or no but I wasn't going to stay out there and faint away for him or no other cuckoo. So I walked in to the dug out and said I'm through. "Through with what" Gleason says. "Through with a mgr. like you that makes a man go in there and try to pitch when I am so sick I don't know what I am doing." So Gleason said "That is the way you have always pitched." So I said "Well I am not going to pitch that way or no other way for you no more but I am going to pitch for a mgr. that don't ask a man to work when he is only 2 laps this side of a corps." Who are you going to pitch for? I am going to pitch for Detroit. "Well" says Gleason "that puts them out of the race as Jennings is so crazy now that he eats grass and when you get there he will start in on his ball club." Well I said something back to him and went in the club house.

That is what come off Al and I will leave it to you if I didn't do right as how can a man work for a cuckoo that makes a bench lizard out of you for a mo. and then pitchs you 64 innings in 3 days in the bull pen and then when your sick and wore out and your souper whines every time you raise it.

Well he as much is said he wished I would go to Detroit so he can't go back on that Al or try and block the deal so as I say I wired a telegram to Jennings that I am through here and for him to hurry up with his offer.

Well Gleason and the club leaves to-night for St. Louis and I have been kind of expecting that he would call up and try and square things with me but not a peep out of him and as I say he is so cuckoo that he probably won't come down off of his horse. But I should worry Al as I will soon be with a club that can win the pennant with a little help and I am the bird that can give them the kind of help they need.

I will keep you posted Al and let you know the minute I hear news. In the mean wile come on you Tigers.

Your pal,   JACK.

Chi, Aug. 29.

FRIEND AL: Well Al no news yet and I called up the ball pk. today to see if maybe they wasn't a telegram there for me though I wired Jennings my home address. They wasn't no telegram there and I don't know what to think only it may be that Jennings is wireing back and 4th. to Gleason trying to make the trade and they can't agree on turns. Well Gleason is not a sucker enough to not make some kind of a deal when he knows that I won't never work for him again but or course its natural for him to hold out for the best man he can get and its natural for Jennings to not give more for me than he has to. But if it comes to a show down you can bet that Jennings will give up anybody he has to outside of Cobb or maybe Bush and I wouldn't be surprised if the final deal was me for Bob Veach and no money on the side. The White Sox has got room for another outfielder God knows wile on the other hand Veach's strength is hitting which is waisted in Detroit as they can all hit up there but dam few of them can pitch.

Of course Veach is in the game every day where most pitchers don't only work about every 4th. day but for a man like Jennings I would go in there every day the rest of the season if he asked me and work my head off to bring the old flag home to Detroit.

In the mean wile I should worry as news is sure to come sooner or later and I and Florrie is enjoying ourselfs and getting acquainted with the kiddies and still got enough jack to keep the wolfs from the door a couple of wks. at the outside.   Your pal,   JACK.

Chi, Aug. 31.

FRIEND AL: Well Al I suppose you seen the news in the paper Sat. and I am leaveing for the east tonight to join my new pals. Don't never get it in your head Al that I am not tickled to death to play for Connie Mack as he has always had my respect even if the Athaletics has been tail enders for the last few yrs. He has got the right idear Al and that is to build up a young ball club and learn them the game and by the time they are ready they are still young enough to play their best baseball and when they get good they don't win 1 championship and then crall back in their hole to die but they win 3 or 4 in a row and get enough jack to live in ease and luxery the rest of their life. Besides Al a man that plays ball for Mack knows that he will be treated like a gentleman and not barked at like a dog when things goes wrong.

Well Al the news come to me in a funny way. I was out late Friday night and overslept myself and when I woke up Florrie was up and dressed and I heard her in the next rm. and it sounded like she was sobing. Well I couldn't figure what and the he—ll she had to whine about so I hollered to her and she come in with the morning paper in 1 hand and her nose in the other. "Oh Jack" she says "its in the paper." So I said what was in the paper and she says "They have traded you to Philadelphia you and $5000.00 for Page."

Well for a minute I felt kind of stuned and then I snatched the paper out of her hand and read it over and over again and finely I got it through my head that it was true and Florrie was still snuffleing and I guess maybe I snuffled a little to.

Well finely I seen they wasn't no use makeing a baby out of ourselfs so I griped my teeth and I says "Well lets cut out the sob stuff as this here story don't mean nothing in our young life. They can trade me to Philadelphia for all the Pages in the book but I won't go." So Florrie spruced up to and she says "That's right you just tell them they can either send you to some decent club or you will quit the game for good."

So for a wile we talked along that line Al but Sat. P.M. I said something about going down town for supper and take in a picture show and Florrie begin to snuffle again. We can't afford no partys now she said. She says "You haven't no job and I haven't and we have got less then $200.00 to our name and what is going to become of us."

Well we stayed home and we talked things over and to make a short story out of it we seen where we was makeing a sucker out of ourselfs as when you come to think of it they's no better town in the league to live in then Phila. and its near Atlantic City so as Florrie and the kids can be down there all summer you might say and I can go down nights when the club is playing at home and Florrie thinks maybe she can get in a beauty parlor there and make enough jack to help out this winter.

So all and all Al I am tickled to death the way things has came along and wile I won't get in the world serious this yr. its the long run that counts after all and when we do get going in Philly it will still be a young ball club yet that can stand the pace and cop the old rag 2 or 3 seasons in a row. And about that time Gleason's club and Jennings's to will be in the old folks home lapping up gruel.

Well I have looked up the schedule and Detroit comes to Philly the 9 of Sept. and the White Sox the 13 and I am going to ask Connie to let me work twice against the both of them and then I will show Gleason and Jennings what a fool they made out of themself and what kind of a pitcher old Jack Keefe is when I am working for a man that can talk to you without barking like a dog.

Your pal,   JACK.

MY ROOMY

◇

I

NO—I AIN'T SIGNED for next year; but there won't be no trouble
about that. The dough part of it is all fixed up. John and me talked
it over and I'll sign as soon as they send me a contract. All I told
him was that he'd have to let me pick my own roommate after this
and not sic no wild man on to me.

You know I didn't hit much the last two months o' the season.
Some o' the boys, I notice, wrote some stuff about me gettin' old
and losin' my battin' eye. That's all bunk! The reason I didn't hit was
because I wasn't gettin' enough sleep. And the reason for that was
Mr. Elliott.

He wasn't with us after the last part o' May, but I roomed with
him long enough to get the insomny. I was the only guy in the club
game enough to stand for him; but I was sorry afterward that I done
it, because it sure did put a crimp in my little old average.

And do you know where he is now? I got a letter today and I'll
read it to you. No—I guess I better tell you somethin' about him
first. You fellers never got acquainted with him and you ought to
hear the dope to understand the letter. I'll make it as short as I can.

He didn't play in no league last year. He was with some semi-pros
over in Michigan and somebody writes John about him. So John
sends Needham over to look at him. Tom stayed there Saturday and
Sunday, and seen him work twice. He was playin' the outfield, but
as luck would have it they wasn't a fly ball hit in his direction in both
games. A base hit was made out his way and he booted it, and that's
the only report Tom could get on his fieldin'. But he wallops two

This story first appeared in *The Saturday Evening Post*, May 9, 1914; collected in
Lardner's *How to Write Short Stories*, (New York: Scribners, 1924).

over the wall in one day and they catch two line drives off him. The next day he gets four blows and two o' them is triples.

So Tom comes back and tells John the guy is a whale of a hitter and fast as Cobb, but he don't know nothin' about his fieldin'. Then John signs him to a contract—twelve hundred or somethin' like that. We'd been in Tampa a week before he showed up. Then he comes to the hotel and just sits round all day, without tellin' nobody who he was. Finally the bellhops was going to chase him out and he says he's one o' the ballplayers. Then the clerk gets John to go over and talk to him. He tells John his name and says he hasn't had nothin' to eat for three days, because he was broke. John told me afterward that he'd drew about three hundred in advance—last winter sometime. Well, they took him in the dinin' room and they tell me he inhaled about four meals at once. That night they roomed him with Heine.

Next mornin' Heine and me walks out to the grounds together and Heine tells me about him. He says:

"Don't never call me a bug again. They got me roomin' with the champion o' the world."

"Who is he?" I says.

"I don't know and I don't want to know," says Heine; "but if they stick him in there with me again I'll jump to the Federals. To start with, he ain't got no baggage. I ast him where his trunk was and he says he didn't have none. Then I ast him if he didn't have no suitcase, and he says: "No. What do you care?' I was goin' to lend him some pajamas, but he put on the shirt o' the uniform John give him last night and slept in that. He was asleep when I got up this mornin'. I seen his collar layin' on the dresser and it looked like he had wore it in Pittsburgh every day for a year. So I threw it out the window and he comes down to breakfast with no collar. I ast him what size collar he wore and he says he didn't want none, because he wasn't goin' out nowheres. After breakfast he beat it up to the room again and put on his uniform. When I got up there he was lookin' in the glass at himself, and he done it all the time I was dressin'."

When we got out to the park I got my first look at him. Pretty good-lookin' guy, too, in his unie—big shoulders and well put together; built somethin' like Heine himself. He was talkin' to John when I come up.

"What position do you play?" John was askin' him.

"I play anywheres," says Elliott.

"You're the kind I'm lookin' for," says John. Then he says: "You was an outfielder up there in Michigan, wasn't you?"

"I don't care where I play," says Elliott.

John sends him to the outfield and forgets all about him for a while. Pretty soon Miller comes in and says:

"I ain't goin' to shag for no bush outfielder!"

John ast him what was the matter, and Miller tells him that Elliott ain't doin' nothin' but just standin' out there; that he ain't makin' no attemp' to catch the fungoes, and that he won't even chase 'em. Then John starts watchin' him, and it was just like Miller said. Larry hit one pretty near in his lap and he stepped out o' the way. John calls him in and ast him:

"Why don't you go after them fly balls?"

"Because I don't want 'em," says Elliott.

John gets sarcastic and says:

"What do you want? Of course we'll see that you get anythin' you want!"

"Give me a ticket back home," says Elliott.

"Don't you want to stick with the club?" says John, and the busher tells him, no, he certainly did not. Then John tells him he'll have to pay his own fare home and Eliott don't get sore at all. He just says:

"Well, I'll have to stick, then—because I'm broke."

We was havin' battin' practice and John tells him to go up and hit a few. And you ought to of seen him bust 'em!

Lavender was in there workin' and he'd been pitchin' a little all winter, so he was in pretty good shape. He lobbed one up to Elliott, and he hit it 'way up in some trees outside the fence—about a mile, I guess. Then John tells Jimmy to put somethin' on the ball. Jim comes through with one of his fast ones and the kid slams it agin the right-field wall on a line.

"Give him your spitter!" yells John, and Jim handed him one. He pulled it over first base so fast that Bert, who was standin' down there, couldn't hardly duck in time. If it'd hit him it'd killed him.

Well, he kep' on hittin' everythin' Jim give him—and Jim had somethin' too. Finally John gets Pierce warmed up and sends him out to pitch, tellin' him to hand Eliott a flock o' curve balls. He wanted to see if lefthanders was goin' to bother him. But he slammed 'em right along, and I don't b'lieve he hit more'n two the whole mornin' that wouldn't of been base hits in a game.

They sent him out to the outfield again in the afternoon, and after a lot o' coaxin' Leach got him to go after fly balls; but that's all he

did do—just go after 'em. One hit him on the bean and another on
the shoulder. He run back after the short ones and 'way in after the
ones that went over his head. He catched just one—a line drive that
he couldn't get out o' the way of; and then he acted like it hurt his
hands.

I come back to the hotel with John. He ast me what I thought of
Elliott.

"Well," I says, "he'd be the greatest ballplayer in the world if he
could just play ball. He sure can bust 'em."

John says he was afraid he couldn't never make an outfielder out
o' him. He says:

"I'll try him on the infield to-morrow. They must be some place
he can play. I never seen a lefthand hitter that looked so good agin
lefthand pitchin'—and he's got a great arm; but he acts like he'd
never saw a fly ball."

Well, he was just as bad on the infield. They put him at short and
he was like a sieve. You could of drove a hearse between him and
second base without him gettin' near it. He'd stoop over for a ground
ball about the time it was bouncin' up agin the fence; and when he'd
try to cover the bag on a peg he'd trip over it.

They tried him at first base and sometimes he'd run 'way over in
the coachers' box and sometimes out in right field lookin' for the
bag. Once Heine shot one acrost at him on a line and he never
touched it with his hands. It went bam! right in the pit of his
stomach—and the lunch he'd ate didn't do him no good.

Finally John just give up and says he'd have to keep him on the
bench and let him earn his pay by bustin' 'em a couple o' times a
week or so. We all agreed with John that this bird would be a whale
of a pinch hitter—and we was right too. He was hittin' 'way over
five hundred when the blowoff come, along about the last o' May.

II

BEFORE THE TRAININ' TRIP was over, Elliott had roomed with
pretty near everybody in the club. Heine raised an awful holler after
the second night down there and John put the bug in with Needham.
Tom stood him for three nights. Then he doubled up with Archer,
and Schulte, and Miller, and Leach, and Saier—and the whole bunch
in turn, averagin' about two nights with each one before they put

up a kick. Then John tried him with some o' the youngsters, but they wouldn't stand for him no more'n the others. They all said he was crazy and they was afraid he'd get violent some night and stick a knife in 'em.

He always insisted on havin' the water run in the bathtub all night, because he said it reminded him of the sound of the dam near his home. The fellers might get up four or five times a night and shut off the faucet, but he'd get right up after 'em and turn it on again. Carter, a big bush pitcher from Georgia, started a fight with him about it one night, and Elliott pretty near killed him. So the rest o' the bunch, when they'd saw Carter's map next mornin', didn't have the nerve to do nothin' when it come their turn.

Another o' his habits was the thing that scared 'em, though. He'd brought a razor with him—in his pocket, I guess—and he used to do his shavin' in the middle o' the night. Instead o' doin' it in the bathroom he'd lather his face and then come out and stand in front o' the lookin'-glass on the dresser. Of course he'd have all the lights turned on, and that was bad enough when a feller wanted to sleep; but the worst of it was that he'd stop shavin' every little while and turn round and stare at the guy who was makin' a failure o' tryin' to sleep. Then he'd wave his razor round in the air and laugh, and begin shavin' agin. You can imagine how comf'table his roomies felt!

John had bought him a suitcase and some clothes and things, and charged 'em up to him. He'd drew so much dough in advance that he didn't have nothin' comin' till about June. He never thanked John and he'd wear one shirt and one collar till some one throwed 'em away.

Well, we finally gets to Indianapolis, and we was goin' from there to Cincy to open. The last day in Indianapolis John come and ast me how I'd like to change roomies. I says I was perfectly satisfied with Larry. Then John says:

"I wisht you'd try Elliott. The other boys all kicks on him, but he seems to hang round you a lot and I b'lieve you could get along all right."

"Why don't you room him alone?" I ast.

"The boss or the hotels won't stand for us roomin' alone," says John. "You go ahead and try it, and see how you make out. If he's too much for you let me know; but he likes you and I think he'll be diff'rent with a guy who can talk to him like you can."

So I says I'd tackle it, because I didn't want to throw John down.

When we got to Cincy they stuck Elliott and me in one room, and we was together till he quit us.

III

I WENT TO THE ROOM early that night, because we was goin' to open next day and I wanted to feel like somethin'. First thing I done when I got undressed was turn on both faucets in the bathtub. They was makin' an awful racket when Elliott finally come in about midnight. I was layin' awake and I opened right up on him. I says:

"Don't shut off that water, because I like to hear it run."

Then I turned over and pretended to be asleep. The bug got his clothes off, and then what did he do but go in the bathroom and shut off the water! Then he come back in the room and says:

"I guess no one's goin' to tell me what to do in here."

But I kep' right on pretendin' to sleep and didn't pay no attention. When he'd got into his bed I jumped out o' mine and turned on all the lights and begun stroppin' my razor. He says:

"What's comin' off?"

"Some o' my whiskers," I says. "I always shave along about this time."

"No, you don't!" he says. "I was in your room one mornin' down in Louisville and I seen you shavin' then."

"Well," I says, "the boys tell me you shave in the middle o' the night; and I thought if I done all the things you do mebbe I'd get so's I could hit like you."

"You must be superstitious!" he says. And I told him I was. "I'm a good hitter," he says, "and I'd be a good hitter if I never shaved at all. That don't make no diff'rence."

"Yes, it does," I says. "You prob'ly hit good because you shave at night; but you'd be a better fielder if you shaved in the mornin'."

You see, I was tryin' to be just as crazy as him—though that wasn't hardly possible.

"If that's right," says he, "I'll do my shavin' in the mornin'—because I seen in the papers where the boys says that if I could play the outfield like I can hit I'd be as good as Cobb. They tell me Cobb gets twenty thousand a year."

"No," I says; "he don't get that much—but he gets about ten times as much as you do."

"Well," he says, "I'm goin' to be as good as him, because I need the money."

"What do you want with money?" I says.

He just laughed and didn't say nothin'; but from that time on the water didn't run in the bathtub nights and he done his shavin' after breakfast. I didn't notice, though, that he looked any better in fieldin' practice.

IV

IT RAINED ONE DAY in Cincy and they trimmed us two out o' the other three; but it wasn't Elliott's fault.

They had Larry beat four to one in the ninth innin' o' the first game. Archer gets on with two out, and John sends my roomy up to hit—though Benton, a lefthander, is workin' for them. The first thing Benton serves up there Elliott cracks it a mile over Hobby's head. It would of been good for three easy—only Archer—playin' safe, o' course—pulls up at third base. Tommy couldn't do nothin' and we was licked.

The next day he hits one out o' the park off the Indian; but we was 'way behind and they was nobody on at the time. We copped the last one without usin' no pinch hitters.

I didn't have no trouble with him nights durin' the whole series. He come to bed pretty late while we was there and I told him he'd better not let John catch him at it.

"What would he do?" he says.

"Fine you fifty," I says.

"He can't fine me a dime," he says, "because I ain't got it."

Then I told him he'd be fined all he had comin' if he didn't get in the hotel before midnight; but he just laughed and says he didn't think John had a kick comin' so long as he kep' bustin' the ball.

"Some day you'll go up there and you won't bust it," I says.

"That'll be an accident," he says.

That stopped me and I didn't say nothin'. What could you say to a guy who hated himself like that?

The "accident" happened in St. Louis the first day. We needed two runs in the eighth and Saier and Brid was on, with two out. John tells Elliott to go up in Pierce's place. The bug goes up and Griner gives him two bad balls—'way outside. I thought they was goin' to

walk him—and it looked like good judgment, because they'd heard
what he done in Cincy. But no! Griner comes back with a fast one
right over and Elliott pulls it down the right foul line, about two foot
foul. He hit it so hard you'd of thought they'd sure walk him then;
but Griner gives him another fast one. He slammed it again just as
hard, but foul. Then Griner gives him one 'way outside and it's two
and three. John says, on the bench:

"If they don't walk him now he'll bust that fence down."

I thought the same and I was sure Griner wouldn't give him nothin'
to hit; but he come with a curve and Rigler calls Elliott out. From
where we sat the last one looked low, and I thought Elliott'd make
a kick. He come back to the bench smilin'.

John starts for his position, but stopped and ast the bug what was
the matter with that one. Any busher I ever knowed would of said,
"It was too low," or "It was outside," or "It was inside." Elliott says:

"Nothin' at all. It was right over the middle."

"Why didn't you bust it, then?" says John.

"I was afraid I'd kill somebody," says Elliott, and laughed like a
big boob.

John was pretty near chokin'.

"What are you laughin' at?" he says.

"I was thinkin' of a nickel show I seen in Cincinnati," says the
bug.

"Well," says John, so mad he couldn't hardly see, "that show and
that laugh'll cost you fifty."

We got beat, and I wouldn't of blamed John if he'd fined him his
whole season's pay.

Up 'n the room that night I told him he'd better cut out that
laughin' stuff when we was gettin' trimmed or he never would have
no pay day. Then he got confidential.

"Pay day wouldn't do me no good," he says. "When I'm all squared
up with the club and begin to have a pay day I'll only get a hundred
bucks at a time, and I'll owe that to some o' you fellers. I wisht we
could win the pennant and get in on that World's Series dough. Then
I'd get a bunch at once."

"What would you do with a bunch o' dough?" I ast him.

"Don't tell nobody, sport," he says; "but if I ever get five hundred
at once I'm goin' to get married."

"Oh!" I says. "And who's the lucky girl?"

"She's a girl up in Muskegon," says Elliott; "and you're right when
you call her lucky."

"You don't like yourself much, do you?" I says.

"I got reason to like myself," says he. "You'd like yourself, too, if you could hit 'em like me."

"Well," I says, "you didn't show me no hittin' to-day."

"I couldn't hit because I was laughin' too hard," says Elliott.

"What was it you was laughin' at?" I says.

"I was laughin' at that pitcher," he says. "He thought he had somethin' and he didn't have nothin'."

"He had enough to whiff you with," I says.

"He didn't have nothin'!" says he again. "I was afraid if I busted one off him they'd can him, and then I couldn't never hit agin him no more."

Naturally I didn't have no comeback to that. I just sort o' gasped and got ready to go to sleep; but he wasn't through.

"I wisht you could see this bird!" he says.

"What bird?" I says.

"This dame that's nuts about me," he says.

"Good-looker?" I ast.

"No," he says; "she ain't no bear for looks. They ain't nothin' about her for a guy to rave over till you hear her sing. She sure can holler some."

"What kind o' voice has she got?" I ast.

"A bear," says he.

"No," I says; "I mean is she a barytone or an air?"

"I don't know," he says; "but she's got the loudest voice I ever hear on a woman. She's pretty near got me beat."

"Can you sing?" I says; and I was sorry right afterward that I ast him that question.

I guess it must of been bad enough to have the water runnin' night after night and to have him wavin' that razor round; but that couldn't of been nothin' to his singin'. Just as soon as I'd pulled that boner he says, "Listen to me!" and starts in on 'Silver Threads Among the Gold.' Mind you, it was after midnight and they was guests all round us tryin' to sleep!

They used to be noise enough in our club when we had Hofman and Sheckard and Richie harmonizin'; but this bug's voice was louder'n all o' theirn combined. We once had a pitcher named Martin Walsh—brother o' Big Ed's—and I thought he could drownd out the Subway; but this guy made a boiler factory sound like Dummy Taylor. If the whole hotel wasn't awake when he'd howled the first line it's a pipe they was when he cut loose, which he done when he come to "Always young and fair to me." Them words could of been heard easy in East St. Louis.

He didn't get no encore from me, but he goes right through it again—or starts to. I knowed somethin' was goin' to happen before he finished—and somethin' did. The night clerk and the house detective come bangin' at the door. I let 'em in and they had plenty to say. If we made another sound the whole club'd be canned out o' the hotel. I tried to salve 'em, and I says:

"He won't sing no more."

But Elliott swelled up like a poisoned pup.

"Won't I?" he says. "I'll sing all I want to."

"You won't sing in here," says the clerk.

"They ain't room for my voice in here anyways," he says. "I'll go outdoors and sing."

And he puts his clothes on and ducks out. I didn't make no attemp' to stop him. I heard him bellowin' 'Silver Threads' down the corridor and down the stairs, with the clerk and the dick chasin' him all the way and tellin' him to shut up.

Well, the guests make a holler the next mornin'; and the hotel people tells Charlie Williams that he'll either have to let Elliott stay somewheres else or the whole club'll have to move. Charlie tells John, and John was thinkin' o' settlin' the question by releasin' Elliott.

I guess he'd about made up his mind to do it; but that afternoon they had us three to one in the ninth, and we got the bases full, with two down and Larry's turn to hit. Elliott had been sittin' on the bench sayin' nothin'.

"Do you think you can hit one today?" says John.

"I can hit one any day," says Elliott.

"Go up and hit that lefthander, then," says John, "and remember there's nothin' to laugh at."

Sallee was workin'—and workin' good; but that didn't bother the bug. He cut into one, and it went between Oakes and Whitted like a shot. He come into third standin' up and we was a run to the good. Sallee was so sore he kind o' forgot himself and took pretty near his full wind-up pitchin' to Tommy. And what did Elliott do but steal home and get away with it clean!

Well, you couldn't can him after that, could you? Charlie gets him a room somewheres and I was relieved of his company that night. The next evenin' we beat it for Chi to play about two weeks at home.

He didn't tell nobody where he roomed there and I didn't see nothin'
of him, 'cep' out to the park. I ast him what he did with himself
nights and he says:

"Same as I do on the road—borrow some dough some place and
go to the nickel shows."

"You must be stuck on 'em," I says.

"Yes," he says; "I like the ones where they kill people—because
I want to learn how to do it. I may have that job some day."

"Don't pick on me," I says.

"Oh," says the bug, "you never can tell who I'll pick on."

It seemed as if he just couldn't learn nothin' about fieldin', and
finally John told him to keep out o' the practice.

"A ball might hit him in the temple and croak him," says John.

But he busted up a couple o' games for us at home, beatin' Pittsburgh once and Cincy once.

V

THEY GIVE ME a great big room at the hotel in Pittsburgh; so the
fellers picked it out for the poker game. We was playin' along about
ten o'clock one night when in come Elliott—the earliest he'd showed
up since we'd been roomin' together. They was only five of us playin'
and Tom ast him to sit in.

"I'm busted," he says.

"Can you play poker?" I ast him.

"They's nothin' I can't do!" he says. "Slip me a couple o' bucks
and I'll show you."

So I slipped him a couple o' bucks and honestly hoped he'd win,
because I knowed he never had no dough. Well, Tom dealt him a
hand and he picks it up and says:

"I only got five cards."

"How many do you want?" I says.

"Oh," he says, "if that's all I get I'll try to make 'em do."

The pot was cracked and raised, and he stood the raise. I says to
myself: "There goes my two bucks!" But no—he comes out with
three queens and won the dough. It was only about seven bucks;
but you'd of thought it was a million to see him grab it. He laughed
like a kid.

"Guess I can't play this game!" he says; and he had me fooled for a minute—I thought he must of been kiddin' when he complained of only havin' five cards.

He copped another pot right afterward and was sittin' there with about eleven bucks in front of him when Jim opens a roodle pot for a buck. I stays and so does Elliott. Him and Jim both drawed one card and I took three. I had kings or queens—I forget which. I didn't help 'em none; so when Jim bets a buck I throws my hand away.

"How much can I bet?" says the bug.

"You can raise Jim a buck if you want to," I says.

So he bets two dollars. Jim comes back at him. He comes right back at Jim. Jim raises him again and he tilts Jim right back. Well, when he'd boosted Jim with the last buck he had, Jim says:

"I'm ready to call. I guess you got me beat. What have you got?"

"I know what I've got, all right," says Elliott. "I've got a straight." And he throws his hand down. Sure enough, it was a straight, eight high. Jim pretty near fainted and so did I.

The bug had started pullin' in the dough when Jim stops him.

"Here! Wait a minute!" says Jim. "I thought you had somethin'. I filled up." Then Jim lays down his nine full.

"You beat me, I guess," says Elliott, and he looked like he'd lost his last friend.

"Beat you?" says Jim. "Of course I beat you! What did you think I had?"

"Well," says the bug, "I thought you might have a small flush or somethin'."

When I regained consciousness he was beggin' for two more bucks.

"What for?" I says. "To play poker with? You're barred from the game for life!"

"Well," he says, "if I can't play no more I want to go to sleep, and you fellers will have to get out o' this room."

Did you ever hear o' nerve like that? This was the first night he'd came in before twelve and he orders the bunch out so's he can sleep! We politely suggested to him to go to Brooklyn.

Without sayin' a word he starts in on his 'Silver Threads'; and it wasn't two minutes till the game was busted up and the bunch—all but me—was out o' there. I'd of beat it too, only he stopped yellin' as soon as they'd went.

"You're some buster!" I says. "You bust up ball games in the afternoon and poker games at night."

"Yes," he says; "that's my business—bustin' things."

And before I knowed what he was about he picked up the pitcher of ice-water that was on the floor and throwed it out the window—through the glass and all.

Right then I give him a plain talkin' to. I tells him how near he come to gettin' canned down in St. Louis because he raised so much Cain singin' in the hotel.

"But I had to keep my voice in shape," he says. "If I ever get dough enough to get married the girl and me'll go out singin' together."

"Out where?" I ast.

"Out on the vaudeville circuit," says Elliott.

"Well," I says, "if her voice is like yours you'll be wastin' money if you travel round. Just stay up in Muskegon and we'll hear you, all right!"

I told him he wouldn't never get no dough if he didn't behave himself. That, even if we got in the World's Series, he wouldn't be with us—unless he cut out the foolishness.

"We ain't goin' to get in no World's Series," he says, "and I won't never get a bunch o' money at once; so it looks like I couldn't get married this fall."

Then I told him we played a city series every fall. He'd never thought o' that and it tickled him to death. I told him the losers always got about five hundred apiece and that we were about due to win it and get about eight hundred. "But," I says, "we still got a good chance for the old pennant; and if I was you I wouldn't give up hope o' that yet—not where John can hear you, anyway."

"No," he says, "we won't win no pennant, because he won't let me play reg'lar; but I don't care so long as we're sure o' that city-series dough."

"You ain't sure of it if you don't behave," I says.

"Well," says he, very serious, "I guess I'll behave." And he did—till we made our first Eastern trip.

VI

WE WENT TO BOSTON first, and that crazy bunch goes out and piles up a three-run lead on us in seven innin's the first day. It was the pitcher's turn to lead off in the eighth, so up goes Elliott to bat for him. He kisses the first thing they hands him for three bases;

and we says, on the bench: "Now we'll get 'em!"—because, you know, a three-run lead wasn't nothin' in Boston.

"Stay right on that bag!" John hollers to Elliott.

Mebbe if John hadn't said nothin' to him everythin' would of been all right; but when Perdue starts to pitch the first ball to Tommy, Elliott starts to steal home. He's out as far as from here to Seattle.

If I'd been carryin' a gun I'd of shot him right through the heart. As it was, I thought John'd kill him with a bat, because he was standin' there with a couple of 'em, waitin' for his turn; but I guess John was too stunned to move. He didn't even seem to see Elliott when he went to the bench. After I'd cooled off a little I says:

"Beat it and get into your clothes before John comes in. Then go to the hotel and keep out o' sight."

When I got up in the room afterward, there was Elliott, lookin' as innocent and happy as though he'd won fifty bucks with a pair o' treys.

"I thought you might of killed yourself," I says.

"What for?" he says.

"For that swell play you made," says I.

"What was the matter with the play?" ast Elliott, surprised. "It was all right when I done it in St. Louis."

"Yes," I says; "but they was two out in St. Louis and we wasn't no three runs behind."

"Well," he says, "if it was all right in St. Louis I don't see why it was wrong here."

"It's a diff'rent climate here," I says, too disgusted to argue with him.

"I wonder if they'd let me sing in this climate?" says Elliott.

"No," I says. "Don't sing in this hotel, because we don't want to get fired out o' here—the eats is too good."

"All right," he says. "I won't sing." But when I starts down to supper he says: "I'm li'ble to do somethin' worse'n sing."

He didn't show up in the dinin' room and John went to the boxin' show after supper; so it looked like him and Elliott wouldn't run into each other till the murder had left John's heart. I was glad o' that—because a Mass'chusetts jury might not consider it justifiable hommercide if one guy croaked another for givin' the Boston club a game.

I went down to the corner and had a couple o' beers; and then I come straight back, intendin' to hit the hay. The elevator boy had went for a drink or somethin', and they was two old ladies already waitin' in the car when I stepped in. Right along after me comes Elliott.

"Where's the boy that's supposed to run this car?" he says. I told him the boy'd be right back; but he says: "I can't wait. I'm much too sleepy."

And before I could stop him he'd slammed the door and him and I and the poor old ladies was shootin' up.

"Let us off at the third floor, please!" says one o' the ladies, her voice kind o' shakin'.

"Sorry, madam," says the bug; "but this is a express and we don't stop at no third floor."

I grabbed his arm and tried to get him away from the machinery; but he was as strong as a ox and he throwed me agin the side o' the car like I was a baby. We went to the top faster'n I ever rode in an elevator before. And then we shot down to the bottom, hittin' the bumper down there so hard I thought we'd be smashed to splinters.

The ladies was too scared to make a sound durin' the first trip; but while we was goin' up and down the second time—even faster'n the first—they begun to scream. I was hollerin' my head off at him to quit and he was makin' more noise than the three of us—pretendin' he was the locomotive and the whole crew o' the train.

Don't never ask me how many times we went up and down! The women fainted on the third trip and I guess I was about as near it as I'll ever get. The elevator boy and the bellhops and the waiters and the night clerk and everybody was jumpin' round the lobby screamin'; but no one seemed to know how to stop us.

Finally—on about the tenth trip, I guess—he slowed down and stopped at the fifth floor, where we was roomin'. He opened the door and beat it for the room, while I, though I was tremblin' like a leaf, run the car down to the bottom.

The night clerk knowed me pretty well and knowed I wouldn't do nothin' like that; so him and I didn't argue, but just got to work together to bring the old women to. While we was doin' that Elliott must of run down the stairs and slipped out o' the hotel, because when they sent the officers up to the room after him he'd blowed.

They was goin' to fire the club out; but Charlie had a good stand-in with Amos, the proprietor, and he fixed it up to let us stay—providin' Elliott kep' away. The bug didn't show up at the ball park next day and we didn't see no more of him till we got on the rattler for New York. Charlie and John both bawled him, but they give him a berth—an upper—and we pulled into the Grand Central Station without him havin' made no effort to wreck the train.

VII

I'D STUDIED THE THING pretty careful, but hadn't come to no conclusion. I was sure he wasn't no stew, because none o' the boys had ever saw him even take a glass o' beer, and I couldn't never detect the odor o' booze on him. And if he'd been a dope I'd of knew about it—roomin' with him.

There wouldn't of been no mystery about it if he'd been a lefthand pitcher—but he wasn't. He wasn't nothin' but a whale of a hitter and he throwed with his right arm. He hit lefthanded, o' course; but so did Saier and Brid and Schulte and me, and John himself; and none of us was violent. I guessed he must of been just a plain nut and li'ble to break out any time.

They was a letter waitin' for him at New York, and I took it, intendin' to give it to him at the park, because I didn't think they'd let him room at the hotel; but after breakfast he come up to the room, with his suitcase. It seems he'd promised John and Charlie to be good, and made it so strong they b'lieved him.

I give him his letter, which was addressed in a girl's writin' and come from Muskegon.

"From the girl?" I says.

"Yes," he says; and, without openin' it, he tore it up and throwed it out the window.

"Had a quarrel?" I ast.

"No, no," he says; "but she can't tell me nothin' I don't know already. Girls always writes the same junk. I got one from her in Pittsburgh, but I didn't read it."

"I guess you ain't so stuck on her," I says.

He swells up and says:

"Of course I'm stuck on her! If I wasn't, do you think I'd be goin' round with this bunch and gettin' insulted all the time? I'm stickin' here because o' that series dough, so's I can get hooked."

"Do you think you'd settle down if you was married?" I ast him.

"Settle down?" he says. "Sure, I'd settle down. I'd be so happy that I wouldn't have to look for no excitement."

Nothin' special happened that night 'cep' that he come in the room about one o'clock and woke me up by pickin' up the foot o' the bed and droppin' it on the floor, sudden-like.

"Give me a key to the room," he says.

"You must of had a key," I says, "or you couldn't of got in."

"That's right!" he says, and beat it to bed.

One o' the reporters must of told Elliott that John had ast for waivers on him and New York had refused to waive, because next mornin' he come to me with that dope.

"New York's goin' to win this pennant!" he says.

"Well," I says, "they will if some one else don't. But what of it?"

"I'm goin' to play with New York," he says, "so's I can get the World's Series dough."

"How you goin' to get away from this club?" I ast.

"Just watch me!" he says. "I'll be with New York before this series is over."

Well, the way he goes after the job was original, anyway. Rube'd had one of his good days the day before and we'd got a trimmin'; but this second day the score was tied up at two runs apiece in the tenth, and Big Jeff'd been wabblin' for two or three innin's.

Well, he walks Saier and me, with one out, and Mac sends for Matty, who was warmed up and ready. John sticks Elliott in in Brid's place and the bug pulls one into the right-field stand.

It's a cinch McGraw thinks well of him then, and might of went after him if he hadn't went crazy the next afternoon. We're tied up in the ninth and Matty's workin'. John sends Elliott up with the bases choked; but he doesn't go right up to the plate. He walks over to their bench and calls McGraw out. Mac tells us about it afterward.

"I can bust up this game right here!" says Elliott.

"Go ahead," says Mac; "but be careful he don't whiff you."

Then the bug pulls it.

"If I whiff," he says, "will you get me on your club?"

"Sure!" says Mac, just as anybody would.

By this time Bill Koem was hollerin' about the delay; so up goes Elliott and gives the worst burlesque on tryin' to hit that you ever see. Matty throws one a mile outside and high, and the bug swings like it was right over the heart. Then Matty throws one at him and he ducks out o' the way—but swings just the same. Matty must of been wise by this time, for he pitches one so far outside that the Chief almost has to go to the coachers' box after it. Elliott takes his third healthy and runs through the field down to the clubhouse.

We got beat in the eleventh; and when we went in to dress he has his street clothes on. Soon as he seen John comin' he says: "I got to see McGraw!" And he beat it.

John was goin' to the fights that night; but before he leaves the hotel he had waivers on Elliott from everybody and had sold him to Atlanta.

"And," says John, "I don't care if they pay for him or not."

My roomy blows in about nine and got the letter from John out of his box. He was goin' to tear it up, but I told him they was news in it. He opens it and reads where he's sold. I was still sore at him; so I says:

"Thought you was goin' to get on the New York club?"

"No," he says. "I got turned down cold. McGraw says he wouldn't have me in his club. He says he'd had Charlie Faust—and that was enough for him."

He had a kind o' crazy look in his eyes; so when he starts up to the room I follows him.

"What are you goin' to do now?" I says.

"I'm goin' to sell this ticket to Atlanta," he says, "and go back to Muskegon, where I belong."

"I'll help you pack," I says.

"No," says the bug. "I come into this league with this suit o'clothes and a collar. They can have the rest of it." Then he sits down on the bed and begins to cry like a baby. "No series dough for me," he blubbers, "and no weddin' bells! My girl'll die when she hears about it!"

Of course that made me feel kind o' rotten, and I says:

"Brace up, boy! The best thing you can do is go to Atlanta and try hard. You'll be up here again next year."

"You can't tell me where to go!" he says, and he wasn't cryin' no more. "I'll go where I please—and I'm li'ble to take you with me."

I didn't want no argument, so I kep' still. Pretty soon he goes up to the lookin'-glass and stares at himself for five minutes. Then, all of a sudden, he hauls off and takes a wallop at his reflection in the glass. Naturally he smashed the glass all to pieces and he cut his hand somethin' awful.

Without lookin' at it he come over to me and says: "Well, good-by, sport!"—and holds out his other hand to shake. When I starts to shake with him he smears his bloody hand all over my map. Then he laughed like a wild man and run out o' the room and out o' the hotel.

VIII

WELL BOYS my sleep was broke up for the rest o' the season. It might of been because I was used to sleepin' in all kinds o' racket and excitement, and couldn't stand for the quiet after he'd went— or it might of been because I kep' thinkin' about him and feelin' sorry for him.

I of'en wondered if he'd settle down and be somethin' if he could get married; and finally I got to b'lievin' he would. So when we was dividin' the city series dough I was thinkin' of him and the girl. Our share o' the money—the losers', as usual—was twelve thousand seven hundred sixty bucks or somethin' like that. They was twenty-one of us and that meant six hundred seven bucks apiece. We was just goin' to cut it up that way when I says:

"Why not give a divvy to poor old Elliott?"

About fifteen of 'em at once told me that I was crazy. You see, when he got canned he owed everybody in the club. I guess he'd stuck me for the most—about seventy bucks—but I didn't care nothin' about that. I knowed he hadn't never reported to Atlanta, and I thought he was prob'ly busted and a bunch o' money might make things all right for him and the other songbird.

I made quite a speech to the fellers, tellin' 'em how he'd cried when he left us and how his heart'd been set on gettin' married on the series dough. I made it so strong that they finally fell for it. Our shares was cut to five hundred eighty apiece, and John sent him a check for a full share.

For a while I was kind o' worried about what I'd did. I didn't know if I was doin' right by the girl to give him the chance to marry her.

He'd told me she was stuck on him, and that's the only excuse I had for tryin' to fix it up between 'em; but, b'lieve me, if she was my sister or a friend o' mine I'd just as soon of had her manage the Cincinnati Club as marry that bird. I thought to myself:

"If she's all right she'll take acid in a month—and it'll be my fault; but if she's really stuck on him they must be somethin' wrong with her too, so what's the diff'rence?"

Then along comes this letter that I told you about. It's from some friend of hisn up there—and they's a note from him. I'll read 'em to you and then I got to beat it for the station:

DEAR SIR: They have got poor Elliott locked up and they are goin' to take him to the asylum at Kalamazoo. He thanks you for the check, and we will use the money to see that he is made comf'table.

When the poor boy come back here he found that his girl was married to Joe Bishop, who runs a soda fountain. She had wrote to him about it, but he did not read her letters. The news drove him crazy—poor boy—and he went to the place where they was livin' with a baseball bat and very near killed 'em both. Then he marched down the street singin' 'Silver Threads Among the Gold' at the top of his voice. They was goin' to send him to prison for assault with intent to kill, but the jury decided he was crazy.

He wants to thank you again for the money.

Yours truly,   Jim——

I can't make out his last name—but it don't make no diff'rence. Now I'll read you his note:

OLD ROOMY: I was at bat twice and made two hits; but I guess I did not meet 'em square. They tell me they are both alive yet, which I did not mean 'em to be. I hope they got good curveball pitchers where I am goin'. I sure can bust them curves—can't I, sport?

Yours,   B. Elliott.

P.S.—The B stands for Buster.

That's all of it, fellers; and you can see I had some excuse for not hittin'. You can also see why I ain't never goin' to room with no bug again—not for John or nobody else!

SICK 'EM

◇

THIS IS JUST BETWEEN I and you. I don't want it to go no further. In the first place a feller that's had rotten luck as long as Red is entitled to the credit when his club fin'lly comes through and cops. In the second place if I was to tell the newspapers or the public that I was the one that really done it they'd laugh at me. They'd say: "How could you of did it when you was sittin' on the bench all summer?"

But you know I wouldn't lie to you, Jake, and you know I don't care nothin' about the honor or that bunk.

The little old World's Serious check is honor enough for me. So let 'em say that it was Red's managin' and them two guys' pitchin' that won for us, and let it go at that. I'm just tellin' you this to get it offen my chest.

Well, you must of read about Lefty Smith last fall, after we'd grabbed him. He's a wop and Smith ain't his real name, but it's the one he's went under ever since he started pitchin'. I heard his right name oncet, but I ain't got time to tell it to you to-day. It's longer'n Eppa Rixey. Anyway, the papers was full o' what him and Fogarty had did at Fort Wayne; how they'd worked a hundred games between 'em and copped the Central League pennant, and how all the scouts had went after 'em.

Pat had stopped off there when we was goin' West one trip and had saw 'em both work, and they'd looked so good to him that he'd advised Red to buy the both o' them. Well, Red told the big boss and he bought Smitty; paid five thousand for him, they say. They wanted even more for Fogarty; so we just put in a draft for him. But pretty near all the other clubs done the same and the Cubs got him.

Red thought Smitty'd fit in nice with our bunch. We needed all the pitchers we could get after what the Feds done to us. Most o'

The Saturday Evening Post, July 25, 1914; previously uncollected.

these guys with all the toutin' turns out to be dubs; but Smitty had a whale of a record, full o' no-hit games and shut-outs. He'd whiffed more guys than Rube Waddell or Johnson, and had tooken part in fifty games. Besides, he had some pitchin' sense, which is more'n you can say for most o' them bushers. Fogarty's record was just as good as Smitty's; but, o' course we wasn't so much interested in him. We figured from what Smitty'd did and from what Pat said about him that he'd come right through from the jump and show enough to make Red stick him in there in his reg'lar turn.

Well, we got down South and had a chancet to look him over. You could spot him right off the reel for a wop, but he was a handsome devil, big as a house, and with black eyes and black hair.

He didn't show nothin' for a couple o' weeks, but nobody lost no sleep over that; we thought he was takin' it easy and was one o' them careful birds that comes slow. Along in the third week we had some practice games between ourselves and Red starts Smitty agin the second club in one o' them. Say, he had a fast one like Waddell's and a cross fire like Sallee's! But he seemed to be afraid he'd show too much. He'd begin an innin' by puttin' more stuff on the ball than I ever seen, but after he'd threw two or three he'd ease up and lob 'em over. Them goofs couldn't see 'em when he was tryin'; but, say, they hit 'em across the state line when he let up. That didn't bother us none, neither, for we figured that he had the stuff when he wanted to use it, and when he got in shape he'd burn up the league.

We played a few games with them Southern clubs and Smitty kept on the same way. Maybe he'd pitch hard to one guy in a innin', but then he'd quit workin' and just float 'em up there like a balloon. Red told him one day to cut loose and see if he could go the route. He might just as well of told him to shave himself with a dish o' prunes. He went right along the way he'd been doin', pitchin' like a bear cat oncet in a while and sloppin' 'em over the rest o' the time. We was playin' the Richmond Club and they scored eleven runs, but Red wouldn't take him out.

After the game Red give him a bawlin' and ast him what was the matter. He said, Nothin'; he was doin' the best he knowed how. Red says: "You ain't doin' no such a thing. You've got the stuff, but you won't let go of it. Are you lazy or what?" Smitty didn't say a word. Then Red ast him if he wasn't in shape, and he said, Yes, he guessed he was. "Well," says Red, "you'll have to cut out the monkey business or I'll put the rollers under you!"

We stopped off in Washin'ton for a couple of exhibition games and broke even with 'em. Then we went home and tackled the Athaletics in the spring serious. Alexander trimmed 'em and they licked Mayer. Red sent Smitty at 'em in the third game and he was worse'n ever. I thought he'd be massacreed.

For two innin's they couldn't touch him and then he pulled the old stuff. Cy Young could of run to the plate as fast as the balls this bird throwed. It was just like hittin' fungoes for them Athaletics. A slow ball's all right in its place, but it's got to be mixed up with somethin' else. The way Smitty mixed 'em up was to throw one slow, and then one slower, and then one slower yet. Along in the fourth, before Red took him out, you could of went on one o' them street cars from the hotel to the ball park in St. Louis between the time he let go o' the pill and when one o' them Mackmen kissed it. Pat was crazy. He says:

"I'd give my glove to know what's the matter with him. He was the best pitcher in the world when I looked him over, and now he couldn't hold a job with a high school. He must of been full o' dope at Fort Wayne."

Meantime I got a hold o' one o' the Chi papers and seen where they was pannin' Fogarty. They said he seemed to be as fast as Johnson and to have a lot o' stuff, but he didn't show no more ambish than a horse car. I read the piece to Smitty.

"Your old sidekick don't seem to be cuttin' up much," I says.

"He ain't no sidekick o' mine," Smitty says.

"You and him was together at Fort Wayne, wasn't you?" says I.

"Yes," says Smitty; "and he's a false alarm."

I thought I'd bruise him.

"He ain't got nothin' on you," I says.

But he took it just as calm as though I'd told him his collar was dirty. Then I says:

"You and Fogarty must of pawned your pepper when you left Fort Wayne. Or maybe you can't get along without your Hoosier hops. Somethin's wrong. You couldn't of won all them games if you worked there like you're doin' here. What's the matter?"

"Matter with who?" he says.

"Both o' you—you and Fogarty," I says.

"They's nothin' the matter with me," says Smitty. "I'm all right; but that slob never had no business tryin' to pitch."

"How did he win them games?" I ast.

"I guess they felt sorry for him," says Smitty.

"They'll be feelin' sorry for you if you don't go and get some ginger," says I.

The season opened and we started off like we always do, playin' 'em off their feet and lookin' like champs. Alexander and Rixey was better'n I'd ever saw 'em, and the boys was all hittin'. It was a rotten day when Cravath or Magee or Luderus, or some o' them, didn't pole a couple out o' the park. We didn't get excited about it, though. We'd been May champions too often. We was wonderin' when the Old Jinx was goin' to hit us in the eye, and whether we'd get smashed up in a railroad wreck or have a epidemic o' lepersy. The papers was sayin' that we was up to our old tricks and that we'd blow higher'n a kite when the annual cyclone struck us.

Red had started Smitty just oncet. That was agin the Boston bunch, and he'd tooken him out in the first innin' so's we could finish the game that day. The first ball he throwed made a noise like a cannon when it hit Bill's glove. The rest o' them never got that far. One was all he had the strength to pitch. The first seven guys that come up was expresses—they didn't stop at first or second base. Paskert ast Red to send him a taxi. Smitty fin'lly was invited to the bench and sat there blinkin' while Red sprung a monologue.

"You're layin' down on me," says Red, "and it's goin' to cost you a month's pay. If you're playin' for your release you're wastin' time. I'd get rid o' you if I could, but nobody'll take you. I've ast for waivers and I know what I'm talkin' about. You're wished on to us for the summer, but you ain't goin' to do no more pitchin'. I wouldn't even let you work in battin' practice, 'cause the fellers couldn't see a real pitcher's stuff after lookin' at your'n. You can help the clubhouse boy, and you can hustle out the canvas when it rains, and you can stand and hold the bottle while the real ball players is gettin' rubbed. And you can stick round after the games and hang up the undershirts.

"We'd ought to sue the Fort Wayne club for swindlin' us! I'd like to manage a team in that league if fellers like you can win a pennant there. I'd give the ground keeper a dollar a day extra to do the pitchin' for me, and I'd go in myself when he was too busy. They give you a salary for playin' ball, but they pinch a man for stealin' a loaf o' bread! If you're the best pitcher in the Central League the rest o' them is paralytics. If we'd spent five thousand for the middle of a doughnut we'd have a better chancet o' realizin' on our investment. If pepper was worth a million dollars a ounce you'd be rated at ten cents!"

"Can I go in and dress?" says Smitty.

"I doubt it," says Red. "You better take somebody along to help you." Well, that might of been the end o' the bird if he was with any club but our'n. Red had the waivers all right, but couldn't make no deal that'd bring us within four thousand bucks of even. Still, we wasn't gettin' no service out of him and was payin' him salary all the time.

So Red was just about to sell him to a old-clo'es man when the old hoodoo hit us. Alexander strained his souper and Rixey got a pair o' busted fingers, all in the same serious. We was left with one fair pitcher and a gang o' kids that'd never saw no big-league games till last spring. The bust-up didn't surprise nobody. We figured that we'd been lucky to go till the first o' June without none o' the boys gettin' killed. It was the same old gag with us: Right up near the top and happy for a couple o' months. Then, Blooie!—and the club all shot to pieces.

It wouldn't of been sensible to turn even a rotten pitcher loose at that stage. We had to keep a hold of all o' them, so's when some got their bumps they'd be plenty to take their place. That's how Smitty happened to hang on. Red didn't start him, but he let him finish for some o' the others that wasn't much better. And he kept lookin' worse all the while.

Well, it was the second week in June when Red sent me from Cincy to Dayton to look at a big spitter.

"I ain't strong for the Central League after what they handed me," he says; "but maybe this guy's better'n most o' them, and you can see where we're up agin it. We got to get somebody or we'll go to the bottom so fast they'll pinch us for speedin'. If he's got anything at all and looks like as if he was alive we can use him; but if he's a dope, like this other boob, we don't need him. I don't want to run no lodgin' house for vagrants."

So I beat it over there and seen a double-header between the home club and Evansville. The guy I was sent after worked one game and had about as much action as a soft drink. I voted No! before he'd went two innin's. Evansville had a lefthander who knowed how to pitch, but they told me he'd been in the league six years; and, besides, he was a little feller.

Well, I spotted old Jack Barnett on the Evansville bench, so I waited to shake hands with him when the game was over. You know him and me broke in together at Utica. I found out while we rode downtown that he'd been with the Fort Wayne Club the last year and was traded to Evansville durin' the winter. I'd sort o' lost track of old Jack 'cause he hadn't been playin' enough in recent years to get his name in the book.

"I see your club's still lucky," he says. "We all thought you had a grand chancet till them two fellers got hurt."

"Yes," I says, "but we're gone now. The young guys we got ought to of been dressmakers instead o' pitchers." Then I happened to think o' Smitty. "Maybe you can tell me somethin'," says I. "How did this here Smitty ever win all them games for you?"

Barnett started to laugh.

"What's the matter?" he ast. "Ain't the big wop worth five thousand?"

"He ain't worth a cigar coupon," I says. "He's a big, lazy tramp."

Barnett kept on laughin'.

"I knowed what'd come off," he says, "I told the fellers what'd happen. I bet Punch Knoll fifty bucks that Smitty wouldn't last the season. You guys can talk about McGraw and Mack, and them other big-league managers, all you want to, but it's us fellers down here in the sticks that knows how to get the work out of a man."

I ast him what he meant.

"Well," he says, "we had Smitty two years ago and he was a bum. He was sloppin' along with us like he's doin' with you now. At that time the Grand Rapids Club had Fogarty, the guy the Cubs got now. Fogarty's a big right-hander, with a spitter and a good hook and just as good a fast ball as Smitty. He's a big, handsome brute, too, and maybe he don't know it! Up to Grand Rapids he was doin' nothin' but look pretty and draw his pay. He was just as valuable to them as Smitty was to us; but we used to have all kinds o' fun with 'em both, kiddin' 'em about their looks. We'd say to Smitty: 'You'd be the handsomest guy in this league if it wasn't for Fogarty.' And we'd pull the same stuff on Fogarty when we was playin' Grand Rapids. And the both o' them would get as sore as a boil. I never seen nothin' like it.

"At the schedule meetin' a year ago last winter, our club and Grand Rapids pulled off a trade, Bill Peck comin' to us for Joe Hammond and Bull Harper, a couple of infielders. Jack Burke, our manager, told the owner o' the Grand Rapids Club that it didn't look fair, givin' up two men for one. So he says: 'All right; I'll throw in Fogarty and then you'll have the two handsomest ball players in the business.' Jack thought he was jokin'; but, sure enough, he turned Fogarty over to us.

"We started in on the pair o' them right off the reel, tryin' to make their life miserable. When Smitty was round we'd talk about Fogarty's pretty red hair; and when Fogarty was with us we'd be wishin' we had big black eyes like Smitty's. I done the most of it, but I didn't have no idea what'd happen.

"Well, to make it short, Smitty come up to Jack a week before the season opened and ast if he could pitch the first game. Jack pretty near dropped dead, 'cause it'd been all he could do the year before to get him to put on his uniform. Mind you, we all knowed then that Smitty had the stuff if he'd only use it. Burke told him he'd think it over and was wonderin' whether to turn him down or not, when up come Fogarty and ast the same thing. Burke decided to take a chancet, so he had the two o' them toss a coin, and Smitty won the toss. He opened up for us and shut Terre Haute out with two hits. And the next day Fogarty worked and shut 'em out again, but give 'em one more hit than Smitty. They was nothin' to it after that. We kept up the good work, gettin' 'em madder and madder at each other. And the madder they got the harder they worked. Either one o' them would of pitched every day if Burke had of let 'em. While Fogarty was workin' Smitty'd slide up and down the bench cussin' to himself and pullin' his head off for the other club. And Fogarty'd do the same thing when Smitty was in there.

"Both o' them was strong for the skirts; and, o' course, a pair o' fine-lookin' slobs like them could cop one out in every town. We took up that end of it, too, tellin' Smitty that Fogarty's Marie was prettier than his Julia, and that kind o' stuff.

"You know what they done for us. We'd of finished about sixth without 'em. I never seen such pitchin' in my life, and I never seen two fellers hate each other the way them two done. When you guys bought Smitty and didn't get Fogarty I called the turn. Some o' the boys figured they both might of got the habit o' workin' and might keep it up when they was separated; but I knowed different. And that's why I made the bet with Punch Knoll. Looks like I'll win it easy, don't it?"

"Looks like it," I says. "Alexander and Rixey'd both ought to be ready again in a month and then Smitty'll lose his home sure. And we'll be absolutely last by that time."

We was goin' to Chi that night and I didn't see no use o' stickin' in Dayton when I hadn't had no orders to look at no one else but that one guy. Besides, Barnett told me they wasn't nobody else on neither club worth lampin'. I'd of liked to of listened to some more o' the stuff about the two jealous cats, but I had to beat it back to Cincy.

Well, on the way I done some thinkin'; but I was afraid to spring anything on Red for fear he'd laugh at me. We've all knew o' cases where jealousy'd helped a ball club, and a lot more cases where it'd hurt 'em; but I hadn't never heard o' no case like this here one.

We got to Chi and the Cubs proceeded to murder us. Red was desp'rate and so was the rest o' the gang. We dropped the first three and didn't have no hopes o' winnin' the fourth unless Hank lost his mind and pitched the bat boy agin us.

I hadn't never saw Fogarty. He'd been left to home when the Cubs come East in May. But I spotted him the first day out there to the Cubs' park. He sure was a nice-lookin' devil and big enough to pitch every afternoon and twicet on Sundays. He wasn't doin' no pitchin' for them, though. They was lucky enough to have their reg'lars in shape and wasn't obliged to fill up the box score with ornaments.

Well, I went up to Schulte durin' battin' practice and ast him what was the matter with Fogarty.

"Nothin' at all," says Frank. "I don't figure they can be nothin' the matter with a guy that draws his pay for sittin' on the bench and lookin' beautiful. I wisht I could get away with it."

"Don't he work none?" I ast.

"He pitches to the batters about oncet in two weeks," says Frank. "He does it when Hank can get his consent. And on the days he pitches to us I manage to hide somewheres till the practice is over."

"Why?" I ast.

" 'Cause," says Frank, "I figure that, barrin' accidents, I got many happy years before me. If he was to happen to put all his stuff on the ball oncet and hit me in the head, they wouldn't be nobody to drive the mules on my peach ranch in Georgia."

"He's got a lot o' stuff, then?" I says.

"Yes," says Frank; "and he's savin' it up for somethin'—maybe to give it away for a birthday present. All he does now is sit and wait for everybody to look away from him, so's he can pull out his pocket mirror and·enjoy himself."

This dope fit in perfect with what Jack Barnett had been tellin' me. I made up my mind right there that the thing was worth tryin'; but it took all the nerve I had to spring it on Red. My chancet soon come. He was put off the field in the second innin' and I got myself chased right afterward. He was sittin' in the clubhouse with his head in his hands when I come in.

"Red," I says, "we couldn't be worse off'n we are, could we?" He didn't pay no attention. "We'd be better off if we had somebody that could pitch, wouldn't we?" I says.

"What are you drivin' at?" he ast.

"I want you to try a experiment," I says. "It may not do no good, and then again it might. It might pull us through O.K. if you was willin' to take a chancet."

"Shoot," says Red. "I'll try anything oncet."

"Do you think you could get Fogarty offen the Cubs?" I says.

"Could I get him?" says Red. "Sure I could get him! They just give me notice that they'd ast waivers. But what do I want with Fogarty? He's another one just like this Smitty we got. I give him the oncet over to-day on their bench, and if they's anybody in the world that's lazier'n Smitty, he's him. Don't you think we're carryin' enough excess baggage?"

Then I told him what Barnett'd told me, only I made it even stronger. At first he called me a nut, and it took me pretty near till the game was over to coax him into it. He'd just gave up when the gang come in.

"How bad did they trim us?" ast Red.

"I don't know," says Magee; "but I know I chased back to that fence a hundred and sixteen times."

"Better go see Hank," says I to Red.

I had to pretty near drag him to get him out o' the clubhouse. Hank was just goin' in their door.

"Wait a minute, Hank," I says. "Red wants to see you."

"Just heard you was askin' waivers on Fogarty," says Red. "What do want for him?"

"I guess you can get him for the waiver price," says Hank; "but you'll have to see the boss."

So me and Red went up to the office and sprung it on 'em. They seemed surprised, but said Red could have him. So Red wired home and got the deal O.K.'d. And Fogarty went with us to St. Louis.

Before we got on the train, Red told me I'd have to do the funny work. I said I'd tackle it, and then I went to Pat and explained the thing to him and ast for help. He was willin' and we fixed it up that I was to room with Fogarty and Pat with Smitty.

Smitty was in his berth, gettin' his beauty sleep, when Fogarty clumb aboard that night. So they didn't see each other till next mornin'. Smitty nailed me comin' out o' the Union Station in St. Louis.

"What's that guy doin' with us?" he says.

"Who do you mean?" I says.

"That big, ugly Mick," says he.

"Ugly!" I says. "If I was you I wouldn't call him ugly. He's a big, handsome boy, and he looks handsomer'n ever alongside a homely wop like you."

He never said a word. He turned away from me like as if I'd ast him for a hundred bucks. Red told me afterward that he come and sat with him in the dinin' room at the hotel and ast if Fogarty was goin' to be with us.

"Sure!" says Red. "I thought it was about time we was gettin' a pitcher."

"A pitcher!" says Smitty. "If they sold him to you for a pitcher you got cheated. He's only a swell-headed pup that don't think about nothin' but the part in his hair."

"Well," says Red, "if I had hair as pretty as his'n I'd be proud of it too."

That shut up Smitty and he left the table without finishin' his Java; but he come to Red in the lobby an hour later and ast if he could work that afternoon! It took Red five minutes to come to. He hadn't had no such request as that from nobody for pretty near three weeks, and Smitty was the last guy on earth he expected it from. You can bet he give his consent.

When our grips come I went to my room to take a nap and a shave; but I didn't get no nap. My new roomy, Fogarty, followed me in and begin talkin' right away.

"What kind o' burg is Philly?" he says.

"Swell!" says I. "You can get anything you want there."

"How about the female population?" he ast. "Lots o' good lookers?"

"Well," I says, "I guess there's plenty o' pretty girls; but I'm a married man and I ain't got no time for 'em. If you're after information on that subject you better ast Smitty."

"Smitty!" he says. "What does he know about girls?"

"He must know how to grab 'em," says I. "All the real dolls in the burg is bugs over him."

"They must be a fine bunch!" says Fogarty. "It must be they never seen nobody."

"Well," I says, "they ain't looked at nobody since they seen him."

"I can't figure it out," he says.

"That's easy," says I. "In the first place he's a fine-lookin' boy, and in the second place he's a swell pitcher."

"Where do you get that stuff?" says Fogarty. "Don't you think I know nothin'? If he's fine-lookin' I'm a snake. And if he's a swell pitcher, why don't they never start him?"

"He's had a sore arm," I says; "but he's all O.K. now and Red's goin' to work him to-day."

He left the room right after that and I didn't see no more of him till we got out to the park; but Red tipped me that he'd came to him and ast if he could work the game. Red told him he was goin' to start Smitty.

"Good night!" says Fogarty. "They'll get a hundred runs."

But, say, I never seen such a change in a man as they was in Smitty that afternoon. He warmed up with Pat first and was so fast that Pat couldn't hardly keep his glove on. Then Red took him a while and was so pleased that he forgot to get sore when he catched one right on the meat hand.

Well, he didn't shut 'em out—he hadn't had no real work for a long time and he was hog wild; but, say, they couldn't hit him with a shovel! Two blows was what they got, an' we licked 'em, five to two. It was the first game we'd win since we left home; and all through it Fogarty was frothin' at the mouth. Every little while he'd say: "He can't keep it up—the lucky bum! He's slippin'. Better let me warm up!" But Red didn't pay no attention to him.

Maybe you think we didn't feel good in that clubhouse—'specially me and Pat and Red! We was the only ones in on the secret. We'd decided not to ask no help from the other boys for fear they'd make it too raw. I felt the best of anybody, 'cause it was my scheme and I'd been scared that it wouldn't work. It made me look good to myself and to Red too. Before we was dressed, Fogarty'd drew Red aside and got him to promise to pitch him next day.

I wasn't sure yet that success was goin' to be permanent. Still, it was up to I and Pat to go through with our end of it, and my job was to stick close to Fogarty all that evenin' and keep goadin' him. I braced him outside o' the hotel after supper and ast him to take a walk.

"Grand game Smitty pitched to-day!" I says.

"What was grand about it?" says he. "Who couldn't beat that bunch? He'd ought to of been ashamed of himself for lettin' 'em score."

"He only give 'em two hits," says I.

"Sure!" says Fogarty. "And how was they goin' to get hits when he didn't throw nothin' near the plate?"

"Well," I says, "I don't see no harm in a few walks so long's a feller can get 'em over when he has to. It's pretty hard for a guy with all that smoke to control it right along."

"Yes," he says; "but I claim it takes a lucky bird to give eight bases on balls and get away with the ball game. It don't show no pitchin' on his part; all it shows is that the other club'd ought to try some easier game than baseball. All they had to do was go up there without their bats and they'd of trimmed us; but they didn't even make him pitch. It looked to me like as if their manager'd offered a prize to the one that could miss 'em the furthest. They looked like a vaudeville team rehearsin' a club-swingin' act. At that, Smitty's got a big advantage over most pitchers. He's so dam' homely that it scares a feller to look at him."

"If that's a advantage," I says, "nobody'd never even bunt one safe off o' you."

"You're kiddin' me now," he says. "I ain't stuck on my looks, but they wouldn't be no sense in me pretendin' that I didn't have him beat. I and him was together in the Central, y'know; and I was one o' the most pop'lar if not the pop'larest feller that ever played ball in Fort Wayne. It takes the skirts to judge if a man's good-lookin' or not; and I'm here to tell you without no boastin' that I could of married any dame in that burg. So far's Smitty was concerned, he couldn't get no girl to look at him."

"Fort Wayne girls ain't like the ones in Philly, then," says I.

"Girls is the same everywheres," says Fogarty. "You can't never make me believe that they'd chase him, unless it's out o' curiosity. You'll often see a crowd round a monkey cage, but it ain't 'cause the monkeys is handsome."

"Some girls likes them big, dark fellers," I says.

"Yes," he says, "and some people likes the smell o' garlic."

"I s'pose we'll get a lickin' to-morrow," I says. "Red ain't got nobody left to work, outside of a few bushers."

"This busher right here works to-morrow," says Fogarty; "and you can bet a month's pay that he won't give no eight bases on balls."

"Maybe you won't be in there long enough," I says.

"I'll be in there just nine innin's," says he; "and at the end o' that time the St. Louis Club won't have nothin' to show they been in a ball game."

"All you need to do," says I, "is to work as good as Smitty done to-day; but that's too much to look for from most bushers."

That stung him.

"They ain't no homely wop got nothin' on me!" he says. "If I can't do no better'n he done I'll quit pitchin' and peddle bananas, which is what he'd ought to be doin'."

Well, I kept him goin' till bedtime and all the next forenoon. He was out to the park and dressed before anybody, and he warmed up enough for three games. Red ast him oncet if he wasn't workin' too hard.

"Not me," he says. "I ain't delicate like some o' these here pitchers. Work's my middle name and you'll find it out before I get through."

Say, they wasn't no kick comin' on the way he done the job! One o' the St. Louis guys got as far as second base and was so surprised that Bill caught him off o' there flat-footed. Three little singles he give 'em and not a man did he walk. Bill told me afterward that it was fast one, fast, one, fast one, and hardly three hooks or spitters all through the game. Bill said them fast ones stung right through his big mitt like he'd been barehanded.

And Smitty, on the bench, acted just like Fogarty'd did the day before. He called them St. Louis hitters everything he could think of. When the big Turk whiffed the hull side in the seventh Smitty was so sore he kicked a hole in the ball bag and throwed away his chew.

The rest o' the bunch couldn't help noticin' the way he acted, and I seen where they'd be wise to the whole game before long.

That night Pat took Smitty to a bunch o' nickel shows and entertained him with conversation about Fogarty's grand performance. The result was that the wop got Red out o' bed at seven the next mornin' and ast him whether he could pitch the game. Red stalled him, 'cause he didn't know then how strong the both o' them was—him and Fogarty.

Anyway, it rained, so Smitty'd had two days' rest before we played again, and Red sent him in to wind up the serious. Gavvy saved St. Louis another whitewashin' by droppin' a fly ball with a guy on; but that run was all they got. Fogarty's game wasn't a bit better'n this second one o' Smitty's, and I kept rubbin' that into Fogarty all the way back to Philly.

They ain't no use goin' on and tellin' you about all the rest o' the games they pitched. They was both beat a few times, but it wasn't 'cause they didn't try. Every pitcher with a arm and a glove'd cop more'n two-thirds of his games if he'd work as hard as these babies done. Some o' the papers come out and said that Red was overworkin' 'em, but the reporters that wrote that didn't know what they was talkin' about. It was all Red could do to keep either o' them on the bench. If they'd of had their way about it they'd of both been out there in the middle o' the diamond every day, fightin' for possession o' the ball.

When Red sent Mayer or one o' the other boys in, the pair o' them'd sit on the bench growlin' and makin' remarks about each other. The minute the feller in their workin' showed any signs o' weakenin', Fogarty and Smitty'd both jump up and race down to the bull pen. And when Red got ready to take the guy out and sent for one or the other o' the two handsome birds the one he didn't pick would slam his glove on the ground and start kickin' it. Everybody on the ball club kept at 'em on the bench; but Red, figurin' they might get suspicious, give orders that nobody but I and Pat was to ride 'em in private.

We was right up on the Giants' heels by the first of August. Then Rixey and Alexander joined us, but all they was ast to do was fill in when Red could persuade Fogarty and Smitty to take a rest. We was about the only club that was beatin' New York, or else we'd of had the flag cinched long before we did. We was runnin' through the rest o' the league like soup through a sieve.

One day Smitty held the Brooklyn Club to six hits in a double-header and beat 'em both games. Fogarty ast me a hundred times in the next few days when we was goin' to have another double-header. And a week before it come off he made Red promise to let him tackle it alone. It was agin the Cubs and he beat 'em clean as a whistle; but they got a couple more hits than Brooklyn'd made agin Smitty. So the big Turk was just as discontented as though he hadn't did nothin' at all. You ought to of heard Hank rave, though! He couldn't figure how Red could get so much work out of a guy who'd been on his bench two or three months and hadn't did nothin' but sleep.

But you know what they done. What I set out to tell you was how I and Pat kept 'em goin'. We soon found out that they wasn't only jealous of each other's looks and their pitchin'. Neither one o' them would let the other have anything on him at all. If I'd make a remark about what a classy necktie Smitty was wearin', Fogarty'd go out and buy the loudest one he could find. If Pat mentioned to Smitty that Fogarty always kept his shoes shined up nice, Smitty'd sneak away to a shine parlor and make the boy work his fool head off for a hour. They just naturally hated each other and acted like a pair o' grand opery stars or a couple o' schoolgirls that was both tryin' to be teacher's pet.

I and Pat would get together and figure out different things to rile 'em up with. Pat was singin' The River Shannon in the clubhouse one day. Fogarty was standin' right by me.

"Pat's got a good voice," he says.

"Fair," says I; "but the best singer on the club is Smitty."

Now I hadn't heard Smitty sing—didn't know whether he could or not. Fogarty'd ought to of knew somethin' about it, as they'd been at Fort Wayne together a hull season; but, regardless o' the fact that neither one o' the two had a voice—as we soon learned—the Turk joined right in with Pat, and it wasn't two seconds before Smitty was whinin' too. Pat quit when he seen he had competition. Everybody stopped talkin' and listened.

I wisht you could of heard it! It was like as though all the ferryboats in East River had got into trouble at once. Their idea o' singin' was to see how many sour notes they could hit and how loud they could hit 'em. The bunch give 'em a hand when they got through, and each o' them figured it was on the square and was for him personally. Well, that was a big laugh with us for a while; but it got so's it was no joke when they done it every day and yelled different songs at the same time.

Another thing we done was to write letters to both o' them and sign a girl's name. The letters was just the same, and they said that she was a great fan and was pullin' for our club, and just loved to see them two pitch. We wound them up somethin' like this:

"I think you're so handsome and I would love to meet you. I've already met Mr. Smith." We said Mr. Smith in one and Mr. Fogarty in the other. "I think he's the handsomest man I ever seen, but maybe you're just as handsome when a person sees you up close. I sit in the third or fourth row o' the stand, right back o' your bench, every afternoon."

Say, you'd ought to of seen them birds fall for that! They rubbered for that dame every day we played at home for the last two months o' the season. Sometimes, when neither o' them was workin', they'd both get up and lean on the roof o' the bench and try to get a smile from every skirt in the place, thinkin' one o' them must be the girl who'd wrote.

On the road we'd get the telephone girls in the hotels to call up

Smitty and ask him if he was Mr. Fogarty. When he'd say no she'd ring off; but she'd call him up again in about ten minutes and ask him the same question. We worked this on Fogarty, too, and both o' them pretty near went nuts 'cause the other was gettin' so many calls.

Pat pulled a hot one in Pittsburgh. He told Smitty that Fogarty was the most generous guy he'd ever met.

"Why?" says Smitty.

"He's so good to the waiters and bell hops," says Pat. "He gives the waiters a quarter tip at every meal and slips the boys two bits when they bring him ice water."

That started a battle that was pretty costly to the both o' them, but mighty sweet for the hops and waiters. If I'd of been Pat I'd of made 'em slip me a commission.

We had 'em both ridin' in taxis to and from all the parks on the last trip West. We had 'em gettin' their clo'es pressed every night, and buyin' new shirts and collars in every burg we blowed into, and gettin' shaved twicet a day, till Red made us cut some of it out, sayin' they was touchin' the club for too much dough. And all season I never seen 'em speak to each other, though neither one couldn't talk about nothin' else but the other when they was separated.

The pennant race was settled when we won a double-header in Cincy on the fifteenth o' September. When we got back to the hotel Red told us the lid was off for that night—that we could do anything we wanted to and stay out until breakfast. So they can't blame neither Pat nor I for what come off. One o' the other boys—I never found out who—told Fogarty that Smitty could hold more wine than a barrel. Then he pulled the same thing on Smitty about Fogarty.

I and Pat went to a show. When we blowed back, about eleven, they was a noise like New Year's Eve in the café. We went in to see what it was. They was a gang o' fellers at one table with Smitty, and another bunch at another table with Fogarty. They was four or five empty quart bottles in front o' each o' them. They'd had five or six more pints than they could carry comfortable and was hollerin' for more, but was broke. We got 'em both at one table and ast 'em to sing. Before they was halfway through the first verse o' whatever it was, the night clerk horned in and stopped 'em. Then we took 'em out in the street and told 'em to finish it, but they was too many coppers round.

Most of us was roomin' on the tenth floor and one o' the boys talked the pair into racin' upstairs instead of usin' the elevator. They both fell down at the first landin' and when they hit the floor they was all in. They'd of slept there for a week if we hadn't of carried 'em to the elevator and got 'em up the rest o' the way. Then what did we do but steer 'em both into Pat's room and put 'em to bed together. They was no danger o' them gettin' wise till the next day; they was dead to the world. I and Pat slept in my room and we was up bright and early so's not to miss nothin'. We walked in and found 'em both poundin' their ear. It must of tooken us fifteen minutes to get 'em roused.

"Well, boys," says Pat, "I'm glad to see you so friendly and lookin' so fresh."

They looked about as fresh as a old dray horse.

"How did you happen to be roomin' together?" I says.

It wasn't till then that they wised up. Smitty jumped out o' bed like the hotel was afire.

"I'll murder the guy that done this!" he hollered.

"What do you mean?" says Pat. "Don't you know who you went to bed with?"

"You must of been in bad shape," I says. "Fogarty was all right; he knowed what he was doin'."

Fogarty wanted to deny it, but he couldn't, 'cause if he had of he'd be admittin' that the wine was too much for him. So he just had to shut up and take it.

"I was all right too," says Smitty.

"Then what are you crabbin' about?" says Pat.

They wasn't no answer to that.

"I'm goin' to ring for some ice water," says Fogarty.

"Nobody never wants ice water at this time o' the mornin' unless they had a bad night," I says. "You don't hear Smitty askin' for no ice water."

Smitty'd of gave his right eye for a barrel of it, but he didn't have the nerve to say so.

Well, we made Fogarty get up and we stuck in there while they was dressin'. Fogarty had to go to his own room to get a clean shirt and collar, and we could hear him ringin' for water the minute he got in there. Fin'lly we took pity on Smitty and got him some too. He complained o' headache, and I says:

"That's a funny thing about Fogarty—no matter how much wine he laps up he don't never have no headache the next mornin'."

We didn't hear no more complaints from Smitty. They both went down to breakfast and tried to eat somethin', but it was hard work.

And I noticed that neither o' them bothered Red with requests to pitch that day.

They went to bed—separated—right after supper and was as good as ever the followin' mornin'. I don't s'pose neither o' them had never drank no wine before, and, so far as I know, they didn't tackle it again. They both wanted to pitch in Chi, but Red was anxious to try out some kids; so he told both o' them, on the quiet, that they was the ones he was dependin' on for the World's Serious and he didn't want to risk gettin' 'em hurt.

Well, we wound up the season in Boston, and it was the next to the last day that we got into a awful jam! You remember readin' about Davis, the infielder Red bought from the New England League? Well, he'd got married the week before he joined us— married a Boston girl. He'd left her with her folks while he went West with us and she stuck to home till we hit Boston on that last trip. She was goin' to Philly with us to take in the serious.

Davis was a fast little cuss, not much bigger'n Maranville. Red had tried him out at short agin Pittsburgh and he'd looked good; but he was usin' the reg'lars most o' the time to keep 'em in shape for the big show. Davis had more nerve than any little feller I ever seen. He wouldn't break ground for none o' them Pittsburgh guys when they come into second base. In one o' the games there big Honus had told him to keep out o' the way or he'd get killed.

"It won't be no big slob like you that'll kill me!" says Davis.

Honus had a license to get sore at that, 'cause he was just slippin' the kid a friendly warnin'; but it shows you what a game little devil Davis was.

Well, as I was sayin', it was the next to the last day up in Boston that somethin' come off that pretty near cost us the big money. Mayer was pitchin' the game and we had the reg'lar club in agin 'em.

In one o' the boxes, right down next to the field, they was the prettiest girl I ever looked at. She was all alone and she was dressed up like a million bucks. She was sittin' where we could lamp her from our bench and all the boys had gave her the oncet over before the game ever started. Fogarty and Smitty wiped the dirt offen their faces and smoothed their hair the minute they piped her.

She was a lot more interestin' than the national pastime and I guess we was all gettin' a eyeful when, all of asudden, she smiled right at us. Our club was in the field and they was only a few of us on the bench—me and Pat and Davis and the pitchers, and one or two others. Well, I was one of a number that returned the salute; but after doin' it oncet I remembered I was a old married man and cut it out. But Fogarty and Smitty give a correct imitation of a toothpaste advertisement all the rest o' the time they sat there. Every three or four minutes she'd smile and then they'd smile back. They was wise to each other and it was a battle to see which one could give her the prettiest grin.

Just before the last half o' the eighth Fogarty ast Red whether he could go in and dress. He hadn't no more'n got permission when Smitty wanted to go too. I had 'em guessed right, and I and Pat was wonderin' which one'd cop. They raced to the clubhouse and Smitty beat him in. Now them two birds was usually awful slow about gettin' their clo'es changed, 'cause they was so partic'lar; but they beat the world's record this time. They was in their street clo'es and down in front o' that box just as the game ended.

Smitty was there first, but lots o' good it done him! He tipped his hat to the girl and got a cold stare. Then Fogarty come up and spoke to her. He was gave just as much encouragement as Smitty.

I begin to laugh, but I stopped quick. Before I knowed what was comin' off, little Davis grabbed a bat and started for the stand. Smitty was leanin' agin the box, with his left hand flat on the rail. Without a word o' warnin' Davis swung the bat overhand and it come down on poor Smitty's hand like a ton o' brick. Smitty yelled and fell over on the ground. Fogarty tried to duck, but he was too late. The little busher aimed the bat at his bean and catched him square on the right arm as he throwed it up to protect himself.

That's all they was to the bout. The first punch is a lot—'specially if you use a baseball bat. Neither o' them showed signs o' fightin' back. Besides, we was all on the job by that time and grabbed Davis. Little as he was, it took three of us to hold him. But, say, they was the devil to pay in the clubhouse! Red was goin' to shoot Davis till the truth come out."

"They went too far with it," says Davis. "They ain't no man can go up and talk to my wife without a introduction! I seen 'em tryin' to flirt with her. Them big bugs is so swell-headed that they think no girl could smile at nobody but them."

"You'd ought to of tipped 'em off," says Red.

"I hadn't ought to of did no such a thing," says Davis. "They'd ought to of knew by lookin' that she wasn't the kind o' girl that'd flirt. But I didn't feel in no danger o' havin' my home broke up, so I let 'em go."

Then Red jumped on me.

"That's what you get for eggin' 'em on," he says. "Where's our chancet in the World's Serious now?"

"Have some sense!" I says. "You wouldn't be thinkin' o' no World's Serious if I hadn't of egged 'em on."

We called a doctor for Smitty and Fogarty, and the news he give us didn't cheer us up none. He said he thought Smitty's hand was broke, but he'd have to take a X ray. The mitt was swole up as big as a ham. Fogarty's souper was hangin' limp as a rag, and the doc didn't believe he'd be able to raise it for a month. Afterward he found out that they was no bones busted in Smitty's hand, but it was in such shape that he couldn't hold a han'kerchief, let alone a baseball. There we was, three days before the start o' the serious, and our pitchin' staff shot to hellangone!

Red sent me and Pat and the trainer home that night with the pair o' cripples. We was to report up to the club's offices next mornin' and have all the doctors in Philly called in. Me and Pat was so sore that we couldn't talk to each other, and I don't think they was a word said on the trip. Yes, they was too; just before Smitty went to sleep he ast me a question:

"Who was that girl?"

"You'd ought to know by this time," I says. "That wasn't nobody but Davis' wife."

"Then what was she smilin' at me for?" he says.

Well, the Philly doctors told us they was absolutely no chancet o' havin' either o' them in shape for the serious and we was gettin' ready to count the losers' share. Red'd been figurin' on alternatin' the two, 'cause none o' the rest was in real shape; but now we didn't have nothin' that you could call a air-tight pitcher.

Rixey and Alexander and Mayer would of made 'em step some if they'd been right, but they wasn't.

I says to Pat:

"Looks like as though I and you and the bat boy would have to work."

"Looks that way," he says, "unless we can bring them two fellers round."

"How can we do that?" I says. "You heard what them doctors said."

"Yes," says Pat; "but they're the only hope we got, and I ain't goin' to give up till I have to."

Red and the bunch got in the next mornin', which was a Sunday. Most o' the gang went to church, and if the Lord'd never heard o'

Fogarty and Smitty before I bet He knowed who they was when we got through prayin'. We practiced Monday and went over to Washin'ton that night.

Well, you know what come off. Johnson beat us there and Boehling beat us Wednesday in Philly. With Johnson to come back, twicet if necesary, it looked like a short serious.

And then it begin to rain. It's a wonder the District o' Columbia wasn't washed away. Four straight days of it, includin' Sunday; and I never seen it come down so hard. A cleanin' like that might do Pittsburgh or Chi some good, but it looked like wastin' it in Washin'ton. We was anxious to get the serious over with; and the more it rained, the worse we hated it. We never figured that it was the best thing that could of happened to us!

I'm the guy they'd ought to thank for coppin' the league pennant. And the rain and me together was what saved us from a awful lickin' for the big dough. On Sunday night, while we was still layin' round the hotel in Washin'ton, where we'd been stalled since Thursday, I got my hunch. I went to Red with it.

"Maybe one o' them fellers could help us out now," I says.

"What makes you think so?" says Red.

"Well," I says, "they've had time to get back in shape."

"No use," says Red. "I was just talkin' to Smitty in the dinin' room. He couldn't even hold his knife. He says his mitt feels just as bad as it did the first day."

"How about Fogarty?" I ast.

"He ain't no better off," says Red. "The worst of it is that neither one o' them seems to care."

"Maybe I can wake 'em up," I says.

"You got my permission to try," says Red.

Me and Fogarty wasn't roomin' together. The trainer was doubled up with him and they had another guy lookin' out for Smitty. Neither o' them had put on a suit, but they'd saw us get our two beatin's from the stand. I found Smitty first and took him into the bar.

"How does it look to you?" I says.

"We're licked," says he.

"Don't be too sure!" I says.

"What do you mean?" he ast me. "What chancet have we got with nobody to pitch?"

"We got somebody to pitch now," I says.

"Who?" says Smitty.

"Fogarty," says I. "The doctor says he's all right and Red's goin' to start him to-morrow."

"You're crazy!" says Smitty. "The doctor said he wouldn't be no good till next year."

"That was pretty near a week ago," I says. "Besides, that doctor didn't know nothin'. We had the best doctor in Washin'ton up to see him to-night—the doctor that looks after the President and all the congressmen. He says they's nothin' at all the matter with him."

I left Smitty then and went lookin' for Fogarty.

I found him in his room gettin' his poor souper rubbed. I spoke my piece over again. I told him Smitty'd been pronounced cured by the President's special surgeon and that he was goin' to start the next day's game.

An hour later I run into Red, and he was smilin' like Davis' wife.

"You've did it, old boy!" he says. "They both been after me till I had to duck out in the wet to get away from 'em. They both insist on workin' to-morrow, and I told 'em I wasn't goin' to decide on my pitcher till mornin'."

"I guess I don't know nothin'!" I says. "Which one are you goin' to start?"

"The one that can throw a ball with the least pain," says Red.

You know the rest of it. The sun shined on us next day, and Smitty shut 'em out and beat Johnson on the wettest grounds I ever seen! I don't know yet how he gripped a wet ball with that hand, but he done it. And Fogarty's game Tuesday was even better. If his arm hurt he kept it to himself.

Smitty come back agin Johnson Wednesday and pitched the prettiest game that was ever pitched. Milan and Gandil and them might just as well of used jackstraws as bats, for all the good their swingin' done. He whiffed plain sixteen men and Johnson's two-bagger was their only wallop. Nobody didn't grudge Walter that one, 'cause he pitched a grand game too.

Well, the honor o' coppin' the final pastime and winnin' the title went to Fogarty; and it pleased him about as much as a toothache. Do you know why? 'Cause the papers was full o' Smitty's two victories over Johnson and didn't say much about nothin' else. Fogarty told me afterward that if he'd thought at the time he'd of refused to pitch Thursday and made Red work him agin the big blond in the seventh game.

"But," I says, "s'spose Red had pitched Smitty right back and he'd of trimmed 'em and they hadn't been no seventh game anyway. Then where'd you of been at?"

"That's right!" he says. "That wop is just lucky enough to of did it, too, even if he can't pitch up an alley."

Well, I made a little speech in the clubhouse and collected a purse of a hundred and fifty bucks. I'm goin' to send it to Jack Barnett as soon as I can get his address. That'll fix him up on that bet he made with Punch Knoll and give him a little spendin' money besides. If he hadn't of told me that stuff in Dayton we'd of been fightin' the Cardinals for seventh place. And if he'd of told it to some guys they wouldn't of had sense enough to of tooken advantage of it.

One o' the Philly doctors told Red, and Red told me, that we'd prob'ly ruined both o' them guys for the next season by workin' 'em in the shape they was in. But I should worry! Between me and you, I ain't goin' to be with the Phillies next year. I'm goin' to manage the Mobile Club; and maybe I can play some in that climate. And I guess I don't know nothin' about managin' a ball club. No; I guess not!

HORSESHOES

◊

THE SERIES ENDED TUESDAY, but I had stayed in Philadelphia an extra day on the chance of there being some follow-up stuff worth sending. Nothing had broken loose; so I filed some stuff about what the Athletics and Giants were going to do with their dough, and then caught the eight o'clock train for Chicago.

Having passed up supper in order to get my story away and grab the train, I went to the buffet car right after I'd planted my grips. I sat down at one of the tables and ordered a sandwich. Four salesmen were playing rum at the other table and all the chairs in the car were occupied; so it didn't surprise me when somebody flopped down in the seat opposite me.

I looked up from my paper and with a little thrill recognized my companion. Now I've been experting round the country with ball players so much that it doesn't usually excite me to meet one face to face, even if he's a star. I can talk with Tyrus without getting all fussed up. But this particular player had jumped from obscurity to fame so suddenly and had played such an important though brief part in the recent argument between the Macks and McGraws that I couldn't help being a little awed by his proximity.

It was none other than Grimes, the utility outfielder Connie had been forced to use in the last game because of the injury to Joyce—Grimes, whose miraculous catch in the eleventh inning had robbed Parker of a home run and the Giants of victory, and whose own homer—a fluky one—had given the Athletics another World's Championship.

I had met Grimes one day during the spring he was with the Cubs, but I knew he wouldn't remember me. A ball player never recalls a reporter's face on less than six introductions or his name on less than

This story first appeared in the *Saturday Evening Post*, August 15, 1914; collected in *How to Write Short Stories*.

twenty. However, I resolved to speak to him, and had just mustered sufficient courage to open a conversation when he saved me the trouble.

"Whose picture have they got there?" he asked, pointing to my paper.

"Speed Parker's," I replied.

"What do they say about him?" asked Grimes.

"I'll read it to you," I said:

"Speed Parker, McGraw's great third baseman, is ill in a local hospital with nervous prostration the result of the strain of the World's Series, in which he played such a stellar rôle. Parker is in such a dangerous condition that no one is allowed to see him. Members of the New York team and fans from Gotham called at the hospital to-day, but were unable to gain admittance to his ward. Philadelphians hope he will recover speedily and will suffer no permanent ill effects from his sickness, for he won their admiration by his work in the series, though he was on a rival team. A lucky catch by Grimes, the Athletics' substitute outfielder, was all that prevented Parker from winning the title for New York. According to Manager Mack, of the champions, the series would have been over in four games but for Parker's wonderful exhibition of nerve and—' "

"That'll be a plenty," Grimes interrupted. "And that's just what you might expect from one o' them doughheaded reporters. If all the baseball writers was where they belonged they'd have to build an annex to Matteawan."

I kept my temper with very little effort—it takes more than a peevish ball player's remarks to insult one of our fraternity; but I didn't exactly understand his peeve.

"Doesn't Parker deserve the bouquet?" I asked.

"Oh, they can boost him all they want to," said Grimes; "but when they call that catch lucky and don't mention the fact that Parker is the luckiest guy in the world, somethin' must be wrong with 'em. Did you see the serious?"

"No," I lied glibly, hoping to draw from him the cause of his grouch.

"Well," he said, "you sure missed somethin'. They never was a serious like it before and they won't never be one again. It went the full seven games and every game was a bear. They was one big innin' every day and Parker was the big cheese in it. Just as Connie says, the Ath-a-letics would of cleaned 'em in four games but for Parker; but it wasn't because he's a great ball player—it was because he was born with a knife, fork and spoon in his mouth, and a rabbit's foot hung round his neck.

"You may not know it, but I'm Grimes, the guy that made the lucky catch. I'm the guy that won the serious with a hit—a home-run hit; and I'm here to tell you that if I'd had one-tenth o' Parker's luck they'd of heard about me long before yesterday. They say my homer was lucky. Maybe it was; but, believe me, it was time things broke for me. They been breakin' for him all his life."

"Well," I said, "his luck must have gone back on him if he's in a hospital with nervous prostration."

"Nervous prostration nothin'," said Grimes. "He's in a hospital because his face is all out o' shape and he 's ashamed to appear on the street. I don't usually do so much talkin' and I'm ravin' a little to-night because I've had a couple o' drinks; but—"

"Have another," said I, ringing for the waiter, "and talk some more."

"I made two hits yesterday," Grimes went on, "but the crowd only seen one. I busted up the game and the serious with the one they seen. The one they didn't see was the one I busted up a guy's map with—and Speed Parker was the guy. That's why he's in a hospital. He may be able to play ball next year; but I'll bet my share o' the dough that McGraw won't reco'nize him when he shows up at Marlin in the spring."

"When did this come off?" I asked. "And why?"

"It come off outside the clubhouse after yesterday's battle," he said; "and I hit him because he called me a name—a name I won't stand for from him."

"What did he call you?" I queried, expecting to hear one of the delicate epithets usually applied by conquered to conqueror on the diamond.

" 'Horseshoes!' " was Grimes' amazing reply.

"But, good Lord!" I remonstrated, "I've heard of ball players calling each other that, and Lucky Stiff, and Fourleaf Clover, ever since I was a foot high, and I never knew them to start fights about it."

"Well," said Grimes, "I might as well give you all the dope; and then if you don't think I was justified I'll pay your fare from here to wherever your goin'. I don't want you to think I'm kickin' about trifles—or that I'm kickin' at all, for that matter. I just want to prove to you that he didn't have no license to pull that Horseshoes stuff on me and that I only give him what was comin' to him."

"Go ahead and shoot," said I.

"Give us some more o' the same," said Grimes to the passing waiter. And then he told me about it.

Maybe you've heard that me and Speed Parker was raised in the same town—Ishpeming, Michigan. We was kids together, and though he done all the devilment I got all the lickin's. When we was about twelve years old Speed throwed a rotten egg at the teacher and I got expelled. That made me sick o' schools and I wouldn't never go to one again, though my ol' man beat me up and the truant officers threatened to have me hung.

Well, while Speed was learnin' what was the principal products o' New Hampshire and Texas I was workin' round the freighthouse and drivin' a dray.

We'd both been playin' ball all our lives; and when the town organized a semi-pro club we got jobs with it. We was to draw two bucks apiece for each game and they played every Sunday. We played four games before we got our first pay. They was a hole in my pants pocket as big as the home plate, but I forgot about it and put the dough in there. It wasn't there when I got home. Speed didn't have no hole in his pocket—you can bet on that! Afterward the club hired a good outfielder and I was canned. They was huntin' for another third baseman too; but, o' course, they didn't find none and Speed held his job.

The next year they started the Northern Peninsula League. We landed with the home team. The league opened in May and blowed up the third week in June. They paid off all the outsiders first and then had just money enough left to settle with one of us two Ishpeming guys. The night they done the payin' I was out to my uncle's farm, so they settled with Speed and told me I'd have to wait for mine. I'm still waitin'!

Gene Higgins, who was manager o' the Battle Creek Club, lived in Houghton, and that winter we goes over and strikes him for a job. He give it to us and we busted in together two years ago last spring.

I had a good year down there. I hit over .300 and stole all the bases in sight. Speed got along good too, and they was several big-league scouts lookin' us over. The Chicago Cubs bought Speed outright and four clubs put in a draft for me. Three of 'em—Cleveland and the New York Giants and the Boston Nationals—needed outfielders bad, and it would of been a pipe for me to of made good

with any of 'em. But who do you think got me? The same Chicago
Cubs; and the only outfielders they had at that time was Schulte and
Leach and Good and Williams and Stewart, and one or two others.

Well, I didn't figure I was any worse off than Speed. The Cubs
had Zimmerman at third base and it didn't look like they was any
danger of a busher beatin' him out; but Zimmerman goes and breaks
his leg the second day o' the season—that's a year ago last April—
and Speed jumps right in as a regular. Do you think anything like
that could happen to Schulte or Leach, or any o' them outfielders?
No, sir! I wore out my uniform slidin' up and down the bench and
wonderin' whether they'd ship me to Fort Worth or Siberia.

Now I want to tell you about the miserable luck Speed had right
off the reel. We was playin' at St. Louis. They had a one-run lead in
the eighth, when their pitcher walked Speed with one out. Saier hits
a high fly to centre and Parker starts with the crack o' the bat. Both
coachers was yellin' at him to go back, but he thought they was two
out and he was clear round to third base when the ball come down.
And Oakes muffs it! O' course he scored and the game was tied up.

Parker come in to the bench like he'd did something wonderful.

"Did you think they was two out?" ast Hank.

"No," says Speed, blushin'.

"Then what did you run for?" says Hank.

"I had a hunch he was goin' to drop the ball," says Speed; and
Hank pretty near falls off the bench.

The next day he come up with one out and the sacks full, and the
score tied in the sixth. He smashes one on the ground straight at
Hauser and it looked like a cinch double play; but just as Hauser
was goin' to grab it the ball hit a rough spot and hopped a mile over
his head. It got between Oakes and Magee and went clear to the
fence. Three guys scored and Speed pulled up at third. The papers
come out and said the game was won by a three-bagger from the bat
o' Parker, the Cubs' sensational kid third baseman. Gosh!

We go home to Chi and are havin' a hot battle with Pittsburgh.
This time Speed's turn come when they was two on and two out,
and Pittsburgh a run to the good—I think it was the eighth innin'.
Cooper gives him a fast one and he hits it straight up in the air. O'
course the runners started goin', but it looked hopeless because they
wasn't no wind or high sky to bother anybody. Mowrey and Gibson
both goes after the ball; and just as Mowrey was set for the catch
Gibson bumps into him and they both fall down. Two runs scored

and Speed got to second. Then what does he do but try to steal third—with two out too! And Gibson's peg pretty near hits the left field seats on the fly.

When Speed comes to the bench Hank says:

"If I was you I'd quit playin' ball and go to Monte Carlo."

"What for?" says Speed.

"You're so dam' lucky!" says Hank.

"So is Ty Cobb," says Speed. That's how he hated himself!

First trip to Cincy we run into a couple of old Ishpeming boys. They took us out one night, and about twelve o'clock I said we'd have to go back to the hotel or we'd get fined. Speed said I had cold feet and he stuck with the boys. I went back alone and Hank caught me comin' in and put a fifty-dollar plaster on me. Speed stayed out all night long and Hank never knowed it. I says to myself: "Wait till he gets out there and tries to play ball without no sleep!" But the game that day was called off on account o' rain. Can you beat it?

I remember what he got away with the next afternoon the same as though it happened yesterday. In the second innin' they walked him with nobody down, and he took a big lead off first base like he always does. Benton throwed over there three or four times to scare him back, and the last time he throwed, Hobby hid the ball. The coacher seen it and told Speed to hold the bag; but he didn't pay no attention. He started leadin' right off again and Hobby tried to tag him, but the ball slipped out of his hand and rolled about a yard away. Parker had plenty o' time to get back; but, instead o' that, he starts for second. Hobby picked up the ball and shot it down to Groh—and Groh made a square muff.

Parker slides into the bag safe and then gets up and throws out his chest like he'd made the greatest play ever. When the ball's throwed back to Benton, Speed leads off about thirty foot and stands there in a trance. Clarke signs for a pitch-out and pegs down to second to nip him. He was caught flatfooted—that is, he would of been with a decent throw; but Clarke's peg went pretty near to Latonia. Speed scored and strutted over to receive our hearty congratulations. Some o' the boys was laughin' and he thought they was laughin' with him instead of at him.

It was in the ninth, though, that he got by with one o' the worst I ever seen. The Reds was a run behind and Marsans was on third base with two out. Hobby, I think it was, hit one on the ground right at Speed and he picked it up clean. The crowd all got up and

started for the exits. Marsans run toward the plate in the faint hope
that the peg to first would be wild. All of a sudden the boys on the
Cincy bench begun yellin' at him to slide, and he done so. He was
way past the plate when Speed's throw got to Archer. The bonehead
had shot the ball home instead o' to the first base, thinkin' they was
only one down. We was all crazy, believin' his nut play had let 'em
tie it up; but he comes tearin' in, tellin' Archer to tag Marsans. So
Jim walks over and tags the Cuban, who was brushin' off his uniform.

"You're out!" says Klem. "You never touched the plate."

I guess Marsans knowed the umps was right because he didn't
make much of a holler. But Speed sure got pannin' in the clubhouse.

"I suppose you knowed he was goin' to miss the plate!" says Hank
sarcastic as he could.

Everybody on the club roasted him, but it didn't do no good.

Well, you know what happened to me. I only got into one game
with the Cubs—one afternoon when Leach was sick. We was playin'
the Boston bunch and Tyler was workin' against us. I always had
trouble with lefthanders and this was one of his good days. I couldn't
see what he throwed up there. I got one foul durin' the afternoon's
entertainment; and the wind was blowin' a hundred-mile gale, so that
the best outfielder in the world couldn't judge a fly ball. That Boston
bunch must of hit fifty of 'em and they all come to my field.

If I caught any I've forgot about it. Couple o' days after that I got
notice o' my release to Indianapolis.

Parker kept right on all season doin' the blamedest things you ever
heard of and gettin' by with 'em. One o' the boys told me about it
later. If they was playin' a double-header in St. Louis, with the thermometer at 130 degrees, he'd get put out by the umps in the first
innin' o' the first game. If he started to steal the catcher'd drop the
pitch or somebody'd muff the throw. If he hit a pop fly the sun'd
get in somebody's eyes. If he took a swell third strike with the bases
full the umps would call it a ball. If he cut first base by twenty feet
the umps would be readin' the mornin' paper.

Zimmerman's leg mended, so that he was all right by June; and
then Saier got sick and they tried Speed at first base. He'd never
saw the bag before; but things kept on breakin' for him and he played
it like a house afire. The Cubs copped the pennant and Speed got
in on the big dough, besides playin' a whale of a game through the
whole serious.

Speed and me both went back to Ishpeming to spend the winter—

though the Lord knows it ain't no winter resort. Our homes was
there; and besides, in my case, they was a certain girl livin' in the
old burg.

Parker, o' course, was the hero and the swell guy when we got
home. He'd been in the World's Serious and had plenty o' dough in
his kick. I come home with nothin' but my suitcase and a hard-luck
story, which I kept to myself. I hadn't even went good enough in
Indianapolis to be sure of a job there again.

That fall—last fall—an uncle o' Speed's died over in the Soo and
left him ten thousand bucks. I had an uncle down in the Lower
Peninsula who was worth five times that much—but he had good
health!

This girl I spoke about was the prettiest thing I ever see. I'd went
with her in the old days, and when I blew back I found she was still
strong for me. They wasn't a great deal o' variety in Ishpeming for
a girl to pick from. Her and I went to the dance every Saturday night
and to church Sunday nights. I called on her Wednesday evenin's,
besides takin' her to all the shows that come along—rotten as the
most o' them was.

I never knowed Speed was makin' a play for this doll till along
last Feb'uary. The minute I seen what was up I got busy. I took her
out sleigh-ridin' and kept her out in the cold till she'd promised to
marry me. We set the date for this fall—I figured I'd know better
where I was at by that time.

Well, we didn't make no secret o' bein' engaged; down in the
poolroom one night Speed come up and congratulated me. He says:

"You got a swell girl, Dick! I wouldn't mind bein' in your place.
You're mighty lucky to cop her out—you old Horseshoes, you!"

"Horseshoes!" I says. "You got a fine license to call anybody
Horseshoes! I suppose you ain't never had no luck?"

"Not like you," he says.

I was feelin' too good about grabbin' the girl to get sore at the
time; but when I got to thinkin' about it a few minutes afterward it
made me mad clear through. What right did that bird have to talk
about me bein' lucky?

Speed was playin' freeze-out at a table near the door, and when I
started home some o' the boys with him says:

"Good night, Dick."

I said good night and then Speed looked up.

"Good night, Horseshoes!" he says.

That got my nanny this time.

"Shut up, you lucky stiff!" I says. "If you wasn't so dam' lucky you'd be sweepin' the streets." Then I walks on out.

I was too busy with the girl to see much o' Speed after that. He left home about the middle o' the month to go to Tampa with the Cubs. I got notice from Indianapolis that I was sold to Baltimore. I didn't care much about goin' there and I wasn't anxious to leave home under the circumstances, so I didn't report till late.

When I read in the papers along in April that Speed had been traded to Boston for a couple o' pitchers I thought: "Gee! He must of lost his rabbit's foot!" Because, even if the Cubs didn't cop again, they'd have a city serious with the White Sox and get a bunch o' dough that way. And they wasn't no chance in the world for the Boston Club to get nothin' but their salaries.

It wasn't another month, though, till Shafer, o' the Giants, quit baseball and McGraw was up against it for a third baseman. Next think I knowed Speed was traded to New York and was with another winner—for they never was out o' first place all season.

I was gettin' along all right at Baltimore and Dunnie liked me; so I felt like I had somethin' more than just a one-year job—somethin' I could get married on. It was all framed that the weddin' was comin' off as soon as this season was over; so you can believe I was pullin' for October to hurry up and come.

One day in August, two months ago, Dunnie come in the clubhouse and handed me the news.

"Rube Oldring's busted his leg," he says, "and he's out for the rest o' the season. Connie's got a youngster named Joyce that he can stick in there, but he's got to have an extra outfielder. He's made me a good proposition for you and I'm goin' to let you go. It'll be pretty soft for you, because they got the pennant cinched and they'll cut you in on the big money."

"Yes," I says; "and when they're through with me they'll ship me to Hellangone, and I'll be draggin' down about seventy-five bucks a month next year."

"Nothin' like that," says Dunnie. "If he don't want you next season he's got to ask for waivers; and if you get out o' the big league you come right back here. That's all framed."

So that's how I come to get with the Ath-a-letics. Connie give me a nice, comf'table seat in one corner o' the bench and I had the pleasure o' watchin' a real ball club perform once every afternoon and sometimes twice.

Connie told me that as soon as they had the flag cinched he was goin' to lay off some o' his regulars and I'd get a chance to play.

Well, they cinched it the fourth day o' September and our next engagement was with Washin'ton on Labor Day. We had two games and I was in both of 'em. And I broke in with my usual lovely luck, because the pitchers I was ast to face was Boehling, a nasty lefthander, and this guy Johnson.

The mornin' game was Boehling's and he wasn't no worse than some o' the rest of his kind. I only whiffed once and would of had a triple if Milan hadn't run from here to New Orleans and stole one off me.

I'm not boastin' about my first experience with Johnson though. They can't never tell me he throws them balls with his arm. He's got a gun concealed about his person and he shoots 'em up there. I was leadin' off in Murphy's place and the game was a little delayed in startin', because I'd watched the big guy warm up and wasn't in no hurry to get to that plate. Before I left the bench Connie says:

"Don't try to take no healthy swing. Just meet 'em and you'll get along better."

So I tried to just meet the first one he throwed; but when I stuck out my bat Henry was throwin' the pill back to Johnson. Then I thought: Maybe if I start swingin' now at the second one I'll hit the third one. So I let the second one come over and the umps guessed it was another strike, though I'll bet a thousand bucks he couldn't see it no more'n I could.

While Johnson was still windin' up to pitch again I started to swing—and the big cuss crosses me with a slow one. I lunged at it twice and missed it both times, and the force o' my wallop throwed me clean back to the bench. The Ath-a-letics was all laughin' at me and I laughed too, because I was glad that much of it was over.

McInnes gets a base hit off him in the second innin' and I ast him how he done it.

"He's a friend o' mine," says Jack, "and he lets up when he pitches to me."

I made up my mind right there that if I was goin' to be in the league next year I'd go out and visit Johnson this winter and get acquainted.

I wished before the day was over that I was hittin' in the catcher's place, because the fellers down near the tail-end of the battin' order only had to face him three times. He fanned me on three pitched balls again in the third, and when I come up in the sixth he scared me to death by pretty near beanin' me with the first one.

"Be careful!" says Henry. "He's gettin' pretty wild and he's liable to knock you away from your uniform."

"Don't he never curve one?" I ast.

"Sure!" says Henry. "Do you want to see his curve?"

"Yes," I says, knowin' the hook couldn't be no worse'n the fast one.

So he give me three hooks in succession and I missed 'em all; but I felt more comf'table than when I was duckin' his fast ball. In the ninth he hit my bat with a curve and the ball went on the ground to McBride. He booted it, but throwed me out easy—because I was so surprised at not havin' whiffed that I forgot to run!

Well, I went along like that for the rest o' the season, runnin' up against the best pitchers in the league and not exactly murderin' 'em. Everything I tried went wrong, and I was smart enough to know that if anything had depended on the games I wouldn't of been in there for two minutes. Joyce and Strunk and Murphy wasn't jealous o' me a bit; but they was glad to take turns restin', and I didn't care much how I went so long as I was sure of a job next year.

I'd wrote to the girl a couple o' times askin' her to set the exact date for our weddin'; but she hadn't paid no attention. She said she was glad I was with the Ath-a-letics, but she thought the Giants was goin' to beat us. I might of suspected from that that somethin' was wrong, because not even a girl would pick the Giants to trim that bunch of ourn. Finally, the day before the serious started, I sent her a kind o' sassy letter sayin' I guessed it was up to me to name the day, and askin' whether October twentieth was all right. I told her to wire me yes or no.

I'd been readin' the dope about Speed all season, and I knowed he'd had a whale of a year and that his luck was right with him; but I never dreamed a man could have the Lord on his side as strong as Speed did in that World's Serious! I might as well tell you all the dope, so long as you wasn't there.

The first game was on our grounds and Connie give us a talkin' to in the clubhouse beforehand.

"The shorter this serious is," he says, "the better for us. If it's a long serious we're goin' to have trouble, because McGraw's got five pitchers he can work and we've got about three; so I want you boys to go at 'em from the jump and play 'em off their feet. Don't take things easy, because it ain't goin' to be no snap. Just because we've licked 'em before ain't no sign we'll do it this time."

Then he calls me to one side and ast me what I knowed about Parker.

"You was with the Cubs when he was, wasn't you?" he says.

"Yes," I says; "and he's the luckiest stiff you ever seen! If he got stewed and fell in the gutter he'd catch a fish."

"I don't like to hear a good ball player called lucky," says Connie. "He must have a lot of ability or McGraw wouldn't use him regular. And he's been hittin' about .340 and played a bang-up game at third base. That can't be all luck."

"Wait till you see him," I says; "and if you don't say he's the luckiest guy in the world you can sell me to the Boston Bloomer Girls. He's so lucky," I says, "that if they traded him to the St. Louis Browns they'd have the pennant cinched by the Fourth o' July."

And I'll bet Connie was willin' to agree with me before it was over.

Well, the Chief worked against the Big Rube in that game. We beat 'em, but they give us a battle and it was Parker that made it close. We'd gone along nothin' and nothin' till the seventh, and then Rube walks Collins and Baker lifts one over that little old wall. You'd think by this time them New York pitchers would know better than to give that guy anything he can hit.

In their part o' the ninth the Chief still had 'em shut out and two down, and the crowd was goin' home; but Doyle gets hit in the sleeve with a pitched ball and it's Speed's turn. He hits a foul pretty near straight up, but Schang misjudges it. Then he lifts another one and this time McInnes drops it. He'd ought to of been out twice. The Chief tries to make him hit at a bad one then, because he'd got him two strikes and nothin'. He hit at it all right—kissed it for three bases between Strunk and Joyce! And it was a wild pitch that he hit. Doyle scores, o' course, and the bugs suddenly decide not to go home just yet. I fully expected to see him steal home and get away with it, but Murray cut into the first ball and lined out to Barry.

Plank beat Matty two to one the next day in New York, and again Speed and his rabbit's foot give us an awful argument. Matty wasn't so good as usual and we really ought to of beat him bad. Two different times Strunk was on second waitin' for any kind o' wallop, and both times Barry cracked 'em down the third-base line like a shot. Speed stopped the first one with his stomach and extricated the pill just in time to nail Barry at first base and retire the side. The next time he throwed his glove in front of his face in self-defense and the ball stuck in it.

In the sixth innin' Schang was on third base and Plank on first, and two down, and Murphy combed an awful one to Speed's left. He didn't have time to stoop over and he just stuck out his foot. The ball hit it and caromed in two hops right into Doyle's hands on second base before Plank got there. Then in the seventh Speed bunts one and Baker trips and falls goin' after it or he'd of threw him out a mile. They was two gone; so Speed steals second, and, o' course, Schang has to make a bad peg right at that time and lets him go to third. Then Collins boots one on Murray and they've got a run. But it didn't do 'em no good, because Collins and Baker and McInnes come up in the ninth and walloped 'em where Parker couldn't reach 'em.

Comin' back to Philly on the train that night, I says to Connie: "What do you think o' that Parker bird now?"

"He's lucky, all right," says Connie smilin'; "but we won't hold it against him if he don't beat us with it."

"It ain't too late," I says. "He ain't pulled his real stuff yet."

The whole bunch was talkin' about him and his luck, and sayin' it was about time for things to break against him. I warned 'em that they wasn't no chance—that it was permanent with him.

Bush and Tesreau hooked up next day and neither o' them had much stuff. Everybody was hittin' and it looked like anybody's game right up to the ninth. Speed had got on every time he come up— the wind blowin' his fly balls away from the outfielders and the infielders bootin' when he hit 'em on the ground.

When the ninth started the score was seven apiece. Connie and McGraw both had their whole pitchin' staffs warmin' up. The crowd was wild, because they'd been all kinds of action. They wasn't no danger of anybody's leavin' their seats before this game was over.

Well, Bescher is walked to start with and Connie's about ready to give Bush the hook; but Doyle pops out tryin' to bunt. Then Speed gets two strikes and two balls, and it looked to me like the next one was right over the heart; but Connolly calls it a ball and gives him another chance. He whales the groove ball to the fence in left center and gets round to third on it, while Bescher scores. Right then Bush comes out and the Chief goes in. He whiffs Murray and has two strikes on Merkle when Speed makes a break for home—and, o' course, that was the one ball Schang dropped in the whole serious!

They had a two-run lead on us then and it looked like a cinch for them to hold it, because the minute Tesreau showed a sign o' weak-enin' McGraw was sure to holler for Matty or the Rube. But you know how quick that bunch of ourn can make a two-run lead look sick. Before McGraw could get Jeff out o' there we had two on the bases.

Then Rube comes in and fills 'em up by walkin' Joyce. It was Eddie's turn to wallop and if he didn't do nothin' we had Baker comin' up next. This time Collins saved Baker the trouble and whanged one clear to the woods. Everybody scored but him—and he could of, too, if it'd been necessary.

In the clubhouse the boys naturally felt pretty good. We'd copped three in a row and it looked like we'd make it four striaght, because we had the Chief to send back at 'em the followin' day.

"Your friend Parker is lucky," the boys says to me, "but it don't look like he could stop us now."

I felt the same way and was consultin' the time-tables to see whether I could get a train out o' New York for the West next evenin'. But do you think Speed's luck was ready to quit? Not yet! And it's a wonder we didn't all go nuts durin' the next few days. If words could kill, Speed would of died a thousand times. And I wish he had!

They wasn't no record-breakin' crowd out when we got to the Polo Grounds. I guess the New York bugs was pretty well discouraged and the bettin' was eight to five that we'd cop that battle and finish it. The Chief was the only guy that warmed up for us and McGraw didn't have no choice but to use Matty, with the whole thing de-pendin' on this game.

They went along like the two swell pitchers they was till Speed's innin', which in this battle was the eighth. Nobody scored, and it didn't look like they was ever goin' to till Murphy starts off that round with a perfect bunt and Joyce sacrifices him to second. All Matty had to do then was to get rid o' Collins and Baker—and that's about as easy as sellin' silk socks to an Eskimo.

He didn't give Eddie nothin' he wanted to hit, though; and finally he slaps one on the ground to Doyle. Larry made the play to first base and Murphy moved to third. We all figured Matty'd walk Baker then, and he done it. Connie sends Baker down to second on the first pitch to McInnes, but Meyers don't pay no attention to him— they was playin' for McInnes and wasn't takin' no chances o' throwin' the ball away.

Well, the count goes to three and two on McInnes and Matty

comes with a curve—he's got some curve too; but Jack happened to
meet it and—Blooie! Down the left foul line where he always hits!
I never seen a ball hit so hard in my life. No infielder in the world
could of stopped it. But I'll give you a thousand bucks if that ball
didn't go kerplunk right into the third bag and stop as dead as George
Washington! It was child's play for Speed to pick it up and heave it
over to Merkle before Jack got there. If anybody else had been
playin' third base the bag would of ducked out o' the way o' that
wallop; but even the bases themselves was helpin' him out.

The two runs we ought to of had on Jack's smash would of been
just enough to beat 'em, because they got the only run o' the game
in their half—or, I should say, the Lord give it to 'em.

Doyle'd been throwed out and up come Parker, smilin'. The minute I seen him smile I felt like somethin' was comin' off and I made
the remark on the bench.

Well, the Chief pitched one right at him and he tried to duck. The
ball hit his bat and went on a line between Jack and Eddie. Speed
didn't know he'd hit it till the guys on the bench wised him up. Then
he just had time to get to first base. They tried the hit-and-run on
the second ball and Murray lifts a high fly that Murphy didn't have
to move for. Collins pulled the old bluff about the ball bein' on the
ground and Barry yells, "Go on! Go on!" like he was the coacher.
Speed fell for it and didn't know where the ball was no more'n a
rabbit; he just run his fool head off and we was gettin' all ready to
laugh when the ball come down and Murphy dropped it!

If Parker had stuck near first base, like he ought to of done, he
couldn't of got no farther'n second; but with the start he got he was
pretty near third when Murphy made the muff, and it was a cinch
for him to score. The next two guys was easy outs; so they wouldn't
of had a run except for Speed's boner. We couldn't do nothin' in
the ninth and we was licked.

Well, that was a tough one to lose; but we figured that Matty was
through and we'd wind it up the next day, as we had Plank ready to
send back at 'em. We wasn't afraid o' the Rube, because he hadn't
never bothered Collins and Baker much.

The two lefthanders come together just like everybody'd doped
it and it was about even up to the eighth. Plank had been goin' great
and, though the score was two and two, they'd got their two on boots
and we'd hit ourn in. We went after Rube in our part o' the eighth
and knocked him out. Demaree stopped us after we'd scored two
more.

"It's all over but the shoutin'!" says Davis on the bench.

"Yes," I says, "unless that seventh son of a seventh son of a seventh son gets up there again."

He did, and he come up after they'd filled the bases with a boot, a base hit and a walk with two out. I says to Davis:

"If I was Plank I'd pass him and give 'em one run."

"That wouldn't be no baseball," says Davis—"not with Murray comin' up."

Well, it mayn't of been no baseball, but it couldn't of turned out worse if they'd did it that way. Speed took a healthy at the first ball; but it was a hook and he caught it on the handle, right up near his hands. It started outside the first-base line like a foul and then changed its mind and rolled in. Schang run away from the plate, because it looked like it was up to him to make the play. He picked the ball up and had to make the peg in a hurry.

His throw hit Speed right on top o' the head and bounded off like it had struck a cement sidewalk. It went clear over to the seats and before McInnes could get it three guys had scored and Speed was on third base. He was left there, but that didn't make no difference. We was licked again and for the first time the gang really begun to get scared.

We went over to New York Sunday afternoon and we didn't do no singin' on the way. Some o' the fellers tried to laugh, but it hurt 'em. Connie sent us to bed early, but I don't believe none o' the bunch got much sleep—I know I didn't; I was worryin' too much about the serious and also about the girl, who hadn't sent me no telegram like I'd ast her to. Monday mornin' I wired her askin' what was the matter and tellin' her I was gettin' tired of her foolishness. O' course I didn't make it so strong as that—but the telegram cost me a dollar and forty cents.

Connie had the choice o' two pitchers for the sixth game. He could use Bush, who'd been slammed round pretty hard last time out, or the Chief, who'd only had two days' rest. The rest of 'em—outside o' Plank—had a epidemic o' sore arms. Connie finally picked Bush, so's he could have the Chief in reserve in case we had to play a seventh game. McGraw started Big Jeff and we went at it.

It wasn't like the last time these two guys had hooked up. This time they both had somethin', and for eight innin's runs was as scarce as Chinese policemen. They'd been chances to score on both sides, but the big guy and Bush was both tight in the pinches. The crowd was plumb nuts and yelled like Indians every time a fly ball was caught or a strike called. They'd of got their money's worth if they hadn't been no ninth; but, believe me, that was some round!

They was one out when Barry hit one through the box for a base. Schang walked, and it was Bush's turn. Connie told him to bunt, but he whiffed in the attempt. Then Murphy comes up and walks—and the bases are choked. Young Joyce had been pie for Tesreau all day or else McGraw might of changed pitchers right there. Anyway he left Big Jeff in and he beaned Joyce with a fast one. It sounded like a tire blowin' out. Joyce falls over in a heap and we chase out there, thinkin' he's dead; but he ain't, and pretty soon he gets up and walks down to first base. Tesreau had forced in a run and again we begun to count the winner's end. Matty comes in to prevent further damage and Collins flies the side out.

"Hold 'em now! Work hard!" we says to young Bush, and he walks out there just as cool as though he was goin' to hit fungoes.

McGraw sends up a pinch hitter for Matty and Bush whiffed him. Then Bescher flied out. I was prayin' that Doyle would end it, because Speed's turn come after his'n; so I pretty near fell dead when Larry hit safe.

Speed had his old smile and even more chest than usual when he come up there, swingin' five or six bats. He didn't wait for Doyle to try and steal, or nothin'. He lit into the first ball, though Bush was tryin' to waste it. I seen the ball go high in the air toward left field, and then I picked up my glove and got ready to beat it for the gate. But when I looked out to see if Joyce was set, what do you think I seen? He was lyin' flat on the ground! That blow on the head had got him just as Bush was pitchin' to Speed. He'd flopped over and didn't no more know what was goin' on than if he'd croaked.

Well, everybody else seen it at the same time; but it was too late. Strunk made a run for the ball, but they wasn't no chance for him to get near it. It hit the ground about ten feet back o' where Joyce was lyin' and bounded way over to the end o' the foul line. You don't have to be told that Doyle and Parker both scored and the serious was tied up.

We carried Joyce to the clubhouse and after a while he come to. He cried when he found out what had happened. We cheered him up all we could, but he was a pretty sick guy. The trainer said he'd be all right, though, for the final game.

They tossed up a coin to see where they'd play the seventh battle and our club won the toss; so we went back to Philly that night and cussed Parker clear across New Jersey. I was so sore I kicked the stuffin' out o' my seat.

You probably heard about the excitement in the burg yesterday mornin'. The demand for tickets was somethin' fierce and some of 'em sold for as high as twenty-five bucks apiece. Our club hadn't been lookin' for no seventh game and they was some tall hustlin' done round that old ball park.

I started out to the grounds early and bought some New York papers to read on the car. They was a big story that Speed Parker, the Giants' hero, was goin' to be married a week after the end o' the serious. It didn't give the name o' the girl, sayin' Speed had refused to tell it. I figured she must be some dame he'd met round the circuit somewheres.

They was another story by one o' them smart baseball reporters sayin' that Parker, on his way up to the plate, had saw that Joyce was about ready to faint and had hit the fly ball to left field on purpose. Can you beat it?

I was goin' to show that to the boys in the clubhouse, but the minute I blowed in there I got some news that made me forget about everything else. Joyce was very sick and they'd took him to a hospital. It was up to me to play!

Connie come over and ast me whether I'd ever hit against Matty. I told him I hadn't, but I'd saw enough of him to know he wasn't no worse'n Johnson. He told me he was goin' to let me hit second—in Joyce's place—because he didn't want to bust up the rest of his combination. He also told me to take my orders from Strunk about where to play for the batters.

"Where shall I play for Parker?" I says, tryin' to joke and pretend I wasn't scared to death.

"I wisht I could tell you," says Connie. "I guess the only thing to do when he comes up is to get down on your knees and pray."

The rest o' the bunch slapped me on the back and give me all the encouragement they could. The place was jammed when we went out on the field. They may of been bigger crowds before, but they never was packed together so tight. I doubt whether they was even room enough left for Falkenberg to sit down.

The afternoon papers had printed the stuff about Joyce bein' out of it, so the bugs was wise that I was goin' to play. They watched me pretty close in battin' practice and give me a hand whenever I managed to hit one hard. When I was out catchin' fungoes the guys in the bleachers cheered me and told me they was with me; but I don't mind tellin' you that I was as nervous as a bride.

They wasn't no need for the announcers to tip the crowd off to the pitchers. Everybody in the United States and Cuba knowed that the Chief'd work for us and Matty for them. The Chief didn't have no trouble with 'em in the first innin'. Even from where I stood I could see that he had a lot o' stuff. Bescher and Doyle popped out and Speed whiffed.

Well, I started out makin' good, with reverse English, in our part. Fletcher booted Murphy's ground ball and I was sent up to sacrifice. I done a complete job of it—sacrificin' not only myself but Murphy with a pop fly that Matty didn't have to move for. That spoiled whatever chance we had o' gettin' the jump on 'em; but the boys didn't bawl me for it.

"That's all right, old boy. You're all right!" they said on the bench— if they'd had a gun they'd of shot me.

I didn't drop no fly balls in the first six innin's—because none was hit out my way. The Chief was so good that they was hittin' nothin' out o' the infield. And we wasn't doin' nothin' with Matty, either. I led off in the fourth and fouled the first one. I didn't molest the other two. But if Connie and the gang talked about me they done it internally. I come up again—with Murphy on third base and two gone in the sixth, and done my little whiffin' specialty. And still the only people that panned me was the thirty thousand that had paid for the privilege!

My first fieldin' chance come in the seventh. You'd of thought that I'd of had my nerve back by that time; but I was just as scared as though I'd never saw a crowd before. It was just as well that they was two out when Merkle hit one to me. I staggered under it and finally it hit me on the shoulder. Merkle got to second, but the Chief whiffed the next guy. I was gave some cross looks on the bench and I shouldn't of blamed the fellers if they'd cut loose with some language; but they didn't.

They's no use in me tellin' you about none o' the rest of it—except what happened just before the start o' the eleventh and durin' the innin', which was sure the big one o' yesterday's pastime—both for Speed and yours sincerely.

The scoreboard was still a row o' ciphers and Speed'd had only a fair amount o' luck. He'd made a scratch base hit and robbed our bunch of a couple o' real ones with impossible stops.

When Schang flied out and wound up our tenth I was leanin' against the end of our bench. I heard my name spoke, and I turned round and seen a boy at the door.

"Right here!" I says; and he give me a telegram.

"Better not open it till after the game," says Connie.

"Oh, no; it ain't no bad news," I said, for I figured it was an answer from the girl. So I opened it up and read it on the way to my position. It said:

"Forgive me, Dick—and forgive Speed too. Letter follows."

Well, sir, I ain't no baby, but for a minute I just wanted to sit down and bawl. And then, all of a sudden, I got so mad I couldn't see. I run right into Baker as he was pickin' up his glove. Then I give him a shove and called him some name, and him and Barry both looked at me like I was crazy—and I was. When I got out in left field I stepped on my own foot and spiked it. I just had to hurt somebody.

As I remember it the Chief fanned the first two of 'em. Then Doyle catches one just right and lams it up against the fence back o' Murphy. The ball caromed round some and Doyle got all the way to third base. Next thing I seen was Speed struttin' up to the plate. I run clear in from my position.

"Kill him!" I says to the Chief. "Hit him in the head and kill him, and I'll go to jail for it!"

"Are you off your nut?" says the Chief. "Go out there and play ball—and quit ravin'.".

Barry and Baker led me away and give me a shove out toward left. Then I heard the crack o' the bat and I seen the ball comin' a mile a minute. It was headed between Strunk and I and looked like it would go out o' the park. I don't remember runnin' or nothin' about it till I run into the concrete wall head first. They told me afterward and all the papers said that it was the greatest catch ever seen. And I never knowed I'd caught the ball!

Some o' the managers have said my head was pretty hard, but it wasn't as hard as that concrete. I was pretty near out, but they tell me I walked to the bench like I wasn't hurt at all. They also tell me that the crowd was a bunch o' ravin' maniacs and was throwin' money at me. I guess the ground-keeper'll get it.

The boys on the bench was all talkin' at once and slappin' me on the back, but I didn't know what it was about. Somebody told me pretty soon that it was my turn to hit and I picked up the first bat I come to and starts for the plate. McInnes come runnin' after me and

ast me whether I didn't want my own bat. I cussed him and told him
to mind his own business.

I didn't know it at the time, but I found out afterward that they
was two out. The bases was empty. I'll tell you just what I had in
my mind: I wasn't thinkin' about the ball game; I was determined
that I was goin' to get to third base and give that guy my spikes. If
I didn't hit one worth three bases, or if I didn't hit one at all, I was
goin' to run till I got round to where Speed was, and then slide into
him and cut him to pieces!

Right now I can't tell you whether I hit a fast ball, or a slow ball,
or a hook, or a fader—but I hit somethin'. It went over Bescher's
head like a shot and then took a crazy bound. It must of struck a
rock or a pop bottle, because it hopped clear over the fence and
landed in the bleachers.

Mind you, I learned this afterward. At the time I just knew I'd
hit one somewheres and I starts round the bases. I speeded up when
I got near third and took a runnin' jump at a guy I thought was
Parker. I missed him and sprawled all over the bag. Then, all of a
sudden, I come to my senses. All the Ath-a-letics was out there to
run home with me and it was one o' them I'd tried to cut. Speed
had left the field. The boys picked me up and seen to it that I went
on and touched the plate. Then I was carried into the clubhouse by
the crazy bugs.

Well, they had a celebration in there and it was a long time
before I got a chance to change my clothes. The boys made a
big fuss over me. They told me they'd intended to give me five
hundred bucks for my divvy, but now I was goin' to get a full
share.

"Parker ain't the only lucky guy!" says one of 'em. "But even if
that ball hadn't of took that crazy hop you'd of had a triple."

A triple! That's just what I'd wanted; and he called me lucky for
not gettin' it!

The Giants was dressin' in the other part o' the clubhouse; and
when I finally come out there was Speed, standin' waitin' for some
o' the others. He seen me comin' and he smiled. "Hello, Horseshoes!" he says.

He won't smile no more for a while—it'll hurt too much. And if
any girl wants him when she sees him now—with his nose over
shakin' hands with his ear, and his jaw a couple o' feet foul—she's
welcome to him. They won't be no contest!

Grimes leaned over to ring for the waiter.

"Well," he said, "what about it?"

"You won't have to pay my fare," I told him.

"I'll buy a drink anyway," said he. "You've been a good listener—and I had to get it off my chest."

"Maybe they'll have to postpone the wedding," I said.

"No," said Grimes. "The weddin' will take place the day after tomorrow—and I'll bat for Mr. Parker. Did you think I was goin' to let him get away with it?"

"What about next year?" I asked.

"I'm goin' back to the Ath-a-letics," he said. "And I'm goin' to hire somebody to call me 'Horseshoes!' before every game—because I can sure play that old baseball when I'm mad."

BACK TO BALTIMORE

◇

WELL, BOYS, I'm goin' right through to Pittsburgh with you if you don't mind, and I aint been traded to your bunch nor the Pirates neither. It'll be in all the papers to-night or to-morrow mornin', so they aint no use o' me keepin' it a secret. I've jumped to the Baltimore Feds, and whether Knabe is figurin' on usin' me regular or settin' me on the bench or givin' me a job washin' undershirts, I don't know or I don't givadam. I couldn't be no worse off than I was up there.

Managin' a club may be all O. K. if the directors is all bachelors and has all o' them tooken a oath not to never get married. But when a man's got a wife, they aint no tellin' when he's goin' to die, and when he dies and she gets a hold o' the ball club, *good night*. If they ever is a skirt elected President o' the United States, I'll move to Paris or Europe or somewheres, if I have to walk.

As for this here Mrs. Hayes, the dope about her lettin' the directors run the club was all bunk. She's been the boss ever since the old bird croaked, or else I'd of stuck there and finished higher with that gang than they finished since Frank Selee had 'em.

Well, sir, I'm canned out of a managin' job, and I'm through with the big league, I guess, and I'm goin' back where I started in at— Baltimore. But you don't need to waste no sympathy on me. I'm gettin' as much dough as they give me up there, and they wont be no chancet o' me bein' drove crazy by a skirt. Them Baltimore people used to like me O. K. when Dunnie had me, and I guess I aint did nothin' since to make 'em sore. I'll give 'em the best I got, and I'll let Knabe do all the worryin'. I'm off'n that stuff, and if any boob ever offers me another managin' job, I'll bean him with a crowbar or somethin'.

I bet you'll see in a few days where Mrs. Hayes gets through bein' a widow, and her next name's goin' to be Mrs. William Baker Junior.

The Red Book Magazine, November 1914; previously uncollected.

They aint no danger o' me forgettin' that name. The guy that owns
it is a ball player, but the only thing alike about he and the Baker
Connie Mack's got is that they both listen with their ears. You fellas
didn't never get a look at this bird because he was so good that we
didn't only play him in one game, and that was against the Philly
club. If him and her does hook up, he wont need to play no more.
With them runnin' the team together, they'll be enough comedy
without him puttin' on a uniform any more.

You knowed Old Man Hayes, o' course. He was a good old scout,
but he pulled a lot o' boners, one o' which was him marryin' this
doll. She's a handsome devil all right; I'll slip her that much. But he
should ought to of knew that he didn't cop her because she was a-
stuck on him. She had it doped that he was about all in, and it wouldn't
be long till the dough was all hern. His heart was bad, and they was
two or three other things the matter with him, and havin' her round
didn't make him no healthier. At that, he'd of croaked sooner or
later without no female help.

He was sure nuts over his ball club, and it hurt him every time
we lose a game. You can see where he was hurt pretty often last
year. At that, Bill Fox was gettin' by all right with the managin' job,
when you figure the bunch he had. But finishin' seventh didn't make
no hit with the old man, even if we thought we done pretty well to
stay in the league and not get arrested. Anyway, Bill got canned and
the job was gave to me. If I hadn't've needed the money pretty bad,
I wouldn't never've tooken it.

Them deals I made last winter helped us a whole lot, and when
we got down South this spring, we wasn't a bad lookin' club, barrin'
one or two positions. We was such a improvement over the old gang
that the old man lost his needle and was countin' the world's serious
receipts along in March. He kept a-askin' me who did I think would
be in the race with us. If I had of told him the truth and says we
couldn't win no pennant unless your bunch and the New York club
was killed in a railroad wreck, he'd of canned me. So what was I to
do but tell him we had a good fightin' chancet to cop, when we didn't
have no more chancet than a rabbit or somethin'. I says the luck
would have to be with us and if it was, we might surprise everybody.
That luck stuff was to be my alibi when we landed where we belonged.

The season opened and we got away good. McGraw's pitchers was
in no shape, and we skun 'em three out o' the first four. We broke

even with Philly and give Brooklyn a good lickin'. We was right out
in front along with you fellas. Then we struck a slump, and you guys
and Philly both goes ahead of us. The old man called me in and ast
me why didn't we stay in first place. I might of told him it was because
we knowed we didn't have no business there. But I stalled and says
I didn't want to have my club go too fast at first or they might maybe
get tired out.

Then we come West in May, and the old boy come along with us.
We opened up in Cincy and broke even with 'em, though they looked
like the worst club in the world. The old man wasn't feelin' well,
and a doctor told him he should ought to go home, but he says he
would go to St. Louis with us. Higgins trimmed us four straight, and
that finished the boss. He grabbed a train for home, but croaked on
the way there.

It was gave out in the papers that young Mrs. Hayes would be
president o' the club, but I didn't take no stock in that till we come
in off'n the road. I was like everybody else; I figured that Williams,
the vice president, and them other directors would run things.

But when we got home, after a rotten trip, she ast me to come
and see her at the office. I goes, and there she is, walkin' up and
down the rug just like her husband was always doin'. When we had
shooken hands, she says:

"Well, Mr. Dixon, you didn't have no success in the West."

"No," I says. "We run into some tough luck."

Then she ast me was it tough luck or rotten ball playin,' and I says
it was some o' both. Then she says:

"We'll try and stren'then your team. I and Mr. Williams, the vice
president, has decided we got to spend some dough for new players.
I have gave Mr. Sullivan orders to go scoutin' round the colleges."

"Lay off'n the college," I says. "We don't need no more ornaments.
What we should ought to have is some ball players. Besides that,
you can't buy no men off'n the colleges. They don't sell 'em."

She says; "I guess we can get a hold of 'em if we slip 'em big
sal'ries." Then she says: "I'd like to make this here club a team of
gentlemen, and they're more gentlemen in the colleges than anywheres else."

They was nuthin' for me to do then but beat it out o' the office
and get a drink o' brandy.

We kept on playin' our best, and that was about good enough to get
us beat oftener than we win. But I was satisfied with the way we was

goin'. I knowed we wasn't topheavy with class. Sullivan came in from scoutin', and I ast him where was his collegers. He says:

"I've been everywhere in the rah-rah circuit, and I aint saw no ball players that could carry bats in the Japanese League."

So I figured we wasn't goin' to be pestered with none o' them there birds that does nothin' but kick the ball round because they got the habit playin' football.

The skirt had been travelin' a lot and hadn't gave me no bother to speak of. But when she come back, my troubles begin. She come out to the games and set in a box clos't up to our bench. We was playin' Brooklyn one day, and Rucker was good. We was a couple o' runs behind along in the eighth and no hope o' catchin' up, with him goin' that way. They was two of us out, and then Rucker walks somebody and Red Smith boots one, so they was two on when it come my turn to hit. I starts up, but she calls me over to the box.

"Mr. Dixon," she says, "this would be a good place for a home run."

I says: "Yes, this is the right spot. I s'pose you'd like to see me hit one."

"You bet I would," she says.

"Well," I says, "which fence do you think I should ought to hit it over?"

"I don't care which fence," she says.

Well, I goes up there and done my best to obey orders. Nobody never swung no harder'n me, and the way I was wallopin' at 'em, I'd of knocked one o' them walls down if I had of connected. But I missed three and we didn't score.

Do you remember the day you fellas give us that awful beatin'— twelve to nothin'? Cheney worked for you and we didn't never have a look-in. What do you think she pulled after that game? She waited for me outside o' the park and says she wished I'd tell Mr. O'Day not to never let Cheney pitch there no more.

I says: "It wouldn't hurt my feelin's if he never pitched nowheres."

"Well," she says, "I hope you'll see to it, because my doctor tells me the spitball aint sanitary."

Then, one day, she ast me what made Hub's cheek bulge out so when he worked. I told her he had a ulcer on his teeth. She ast why his face was swole up that way only when he was pitchin', and I told her I didn't never work him only on days when his teeth was pretty sore, so's the batters'd feel sorry for him. She must of knew I was kiddin', but she never called me for it.

She had me worried to death with stuff like that. She wanted the suits sent to the laundry after all the games and says all of us should ought to quit slidin' because it dirtied us up so much. I got so's I stuck in the club-house a couple of hours after the games, so's to be sure and not run into her when I come out.

Well, she goes down to Yale college on some party or somethin', and when she come back, we was just finishin' up with the Western clubs. We was out in practice one day when I seen her beckonin' to me. I goes over to where she was settin', and she says:

"I've got you a new player."

"Who is he?" I says.

She says: "His name is Mr. Baker, and he has just went through Yale. He will meet you in New York."

Then I ast her what position did he play, and she says: "He aint made up his mind yet. He has been busy learnin' his lessons."

Then I ast her wasn't he on the Yale team, and she says: "No, but he could of been if he had of wanted to. The coach told him so, but he didn't have no time to play. You could tell the minute you seen him that he was a born ath-a-lete and he's a gentleman too, and I b'lieve he will help you in more ways than just one way."

"Well," I says, "they's only one way he could help us and that is to get in there and play ball. If he can do that, I don't care if he's a gentleman or a policeman."

Then I ast her what sal'ry was he goin' to get.

"Oh," she says, "you wont need to bother about that. I've already fixed that up already. I have gave him a contract for five thousand."

I ast her did she mean five thousand for five years, and she says: "No, I meant five thousand for this year."

Then I says: "That's as much as I'm gettin', and this here guy aint even made good yet."

"He'll make good all right," she says. "You can tell that from just lookin' at him, and he comes off'n a good fam'ly."

Well, we goes to New York, and I was waitin' round the lobby o' the hotel for the baggage to come in, when Kelly, the secretary, calls me over to the desk. He pointed out a name on the hotel book and ast me who was it, because the guy was registered as belongin' to us. "William Baker Junior, Boston Baseball Nine," was what it says. Do you get that? "Boston Baseball Nine." Before I ever seen him, I knowed just what he was goin' to look like, and when I seen him, he looked just like I knowed he was goin' to. But he was a big bird—

so big he couldn't get no clo'es big enough. He looked like as if he was goin' to bust right through 'em. His hair was plastered back off'n his forehead, and his shirt and tie would've made a rainbow jealous.

He come up to me and says: "Is this the head coach?"

I says: "Yes, whatever that is, I'm it."

"What time does the game start?" he says.

"Three-thirty," I says, "but we get out there about a quarter after two."

Then he ast me couldn't they start it some other time because he had a engagement. I says I would excuse him, and he says: "Thanks." Then I says: "I'll excuse you all the time if you say the word." But he says no, that wouldn't be right, because he felt like as if he should ought to do some work oncet in a while to earn his pay. Then he says he was pleased to of met me and walked away.

I guess he must of kept his date at a soda fountain or wherever it was he had a date at, because he didn't show up out to the park and I never seen no more of him till the next mornin'. Then he come to see me while I was writin' a letter and ast me could he have six passes to the game. I says: "You'd better take ten," and I writes out a pass for ten on one o' the hotel letter-heads, and I signs Otto Hess' name to it. He says "Thanks," and walked away. If I'd of signed President Bryan's name, he'd of thanked me just the same. And the pass would of been just as good.

I come out o' the hotel about one o'clock and starts for the elevated, but the colleger was standin' on the sidewalk and he hollered at me. He ast me was I goin' out and I says yes, I thought I would, because I didn't have no other date. Then he ast me would I ride out with him because he'd ordered a taxi. They wasn't none o' my ball players had ever tooken me to the park in a taxi before, but I didn't have no objection, so I and him piled in, and out we goes together.

When we got through ridin', I says, "You better let me split with you," but he says, "They aint no splittin' to be did. It's in my contract that I use cabs to and from the grounds," and he tells the driver to charge it to the club. Well, I butts in and says, "Here! You can't get by with that stuff. If you're out to give the club a trimmin', you better pull it when I aint round." Then what does he do but pull his contract out of his pocket and show it to me, and there is was, in black and white, that he was to be gave rides on the club to and from the parks where we played. Can you beat that?

We come into the grounds and I took him in the club-house and had Doc give him a unie. He made a holler because they wasn't no feet in the stockin's and I told him he was supposed to wear socks besides the stockin's. So he leaves on the reg'lar socks he'd wore with his street clo'es, and they was purple!

I wisht you could of heard the ball players ride him. They pulled some awful raw stuff, and if he hadn't of been such a boob, he'd of lost his temper and tried to lick somebody. But I don't b'lieve he never wised up that he was gettin' kidded. Even when Hub called him "Gertie," it didn't seem to make no difference to him.

We goes out to warm up and I notice that he don't have no cap on. I was goin' to tell him about it, but the boys says: "No. Let him play bareheaded and give the crowd a treat." They wasn't much practicin' done. The New York bunch come over round our bench so's they wouldn't miss nothin'. I give him a ball and a catcher's glove and told Tyler to throw him a few. George just lobbed one at him and he got it on the meat hand. He raised a holler and tells Tyler he shouldn't ought to throw so hard. I yells at him to use his mitt, but he says the ball stung his hand right through it, and after tryin' all the wrong ways they is o' catchin' a ball, he quit and set down on the bench. McGraw calls me over and ast was I startin' a chorus or what. I told him how I happened to get a-hold o' the bird, and then I ast him did he want to make a trade. He says:

"What'll you take for him?"

I says: "Oh, I'll give him to you for Matty and a piece o' money."

"No," he says, "I don't want to cheat you. Take the grandstand and a chew o' tobacco."

Well, I sends him up to take his turn in battin' practice, and he acted like as if the bat was as heavy as one o' these here steel rails. Hess slops a slow one up to him, and instead o' swingin', he ducks out o' the way and tells me he aint used to battin' at such swift balls. Hess hears him pull that and the next one he throwed was a fast one, just as fast as he could throw it. Mr. Baker turns white as a sheet and drops his bat and walks to the bench.

I stuck him in the outfield in fieldin' practice, but he looked so rotten that I took him out o' there for fear o' gettin' him killed. I called him in and says:

"You've did enough for one day, so go in and change your clo'es and you can watch the game from the stand. Maybe you'll run acrost that crowd I give you the passes for."

He was willin' to quit, all right, and the fun was over for the day.

After the game, I send a long telegram to Williams, the vice president, and tells him what a joke our new player was and that it was throwin' money away to even pay his board, let alone that Fed'ral League sal'ry he was gettin'. I didn't get no answer from Williams, but a letter come from the skirt. She give me a call for not sendin' the telegram to her instead o' Williams and ast me how could I judge if a man was a ball player when I hadn't only saw him one day.

Well, I wires to Williams that I was through, because I'd signed to manage a ball club and not to run no burlesque show, but he jumps on a train and comes over to New York to see me. He says they was tryin' to get her to sell out her stock and that him and the other directors appreciated what I'd did for the club and wanted me to stick.

So I stuck and went along the best I could. I didn't pay no more attention to "Gertie" except to tell him to beat it to the club-house before the games started. He kept on comin' out to the park, wherever we was playin', and puttin' on his unie, without no cap, and settin' on the bench till the practice was over. Then he'd go in and put on one of his eight or nine different suits o' clo'es, and go up in the stand and watch the game from there or else go to the matinée or somewheres.

I didn't hardly ever say nothin' to him, but I couldn't make the rest o' the bunch lay off. They tipped their hats whenever they seen him. While he was settin' on the bench, they'd take a shot at him with the ball, and oncet or twicet they hit him, but not wheres it hurt him bad. He thought it was a accident when he got hit, but I knowed better. Every oncet in a while, somebody'd happen to step on his feet with their spikes, and then they'd beg his pardon. Some o' them left their caps off while they was practicin' and hollered "Ouch!" when they catched the ball. And on the train they'd get together and give college yells. He didn't never get sore, and I don't s'pose I would of neither if I'd been gettin' five thousand for changin' my clo'es a couple o' times a day.

They tried to get him in the poker game, but they wasn't nothin' doin'. He says he liked to play bridge w'ist but that was all the cards he knowed. When we was on trains, he spent the time lookin' at the scenery or readin' magazines.

I remember one night when we was goin' to Philly and he was settin' acrost the aisle from I and Hub. He was readin', and pretty soon he looks up from off of his magazine and says:

"You guys should ought to read this here story in here. It's a baseball story and it's about two teams bein' tied for the pennant on the last day o' the season, and one o' the teams had a star pitcher that was sure to win the decidin' game if nothin' didn't happen to him, so they stuck him in to pitch but in the first innin' he strained his arm so it hurt him every ball he throwed but he didn't say nothin' about it, but kept on pitchin' and win his game and the pennant, though he was sufferin' terrible pain all the while. I call that nerve!"

"Nerve!" says Hub. "Say, that wasn't nothin' to what I seen come off in the Southern League the last year I was down there. The Nashville club that I was with and the New Orleans club was tied for first place, and we had to play a extra game to settle it. We had a first sacker named Smith that was the greatest I ever see. Up to the first of August he was battin' .600 and it got so's the pitchers wouldn't give him nothin' more to hit but walked him every time he come up. He offered to bat with one hand if they'd pitch strikes to him, but they wouldn't take a chancet, and finally the umps'd just give him his base every time he come up without waitin' for the four balls to be throwed.

"Well, it come time for this final game and we knowed we had it won if Smith was all right. The New Orleans club knowed it too, and they was out to get him. So when he got on in the first innin' on a base on balls, their first baseman deliberately stepped on his foot and spiked him somethin' awful. He couldn't walk on that foot no more, but he wouldn't quit, and after he'd drawed one of his bases on balls, every so often, he stole all the rest o' the bases hoppin' on his good foot.

"It come along the twenty-first innin' and the score was six to six. He'd scored every one of our six runs by walkin' to first and then hoppin' the rest o' the way. Well, he walked in the twenty-first and starts hoppin' to second. The catcher knowed they was no use to throw to second or to third neither, because Smith was so fast, even on one foot, that he was bound to beat it. So the catcher just kept a hold o' the ball, knowin' Smith wouldn't never stop till he got clear home. Along come Smith, hoppin' for the plate, and the catcher run out to meet him, but he hopped clean over the catcher's head and scored the run that beat 'em and won us the pennant. They was about sixty thousand people out there, and they tried to carry Smith off o' the field on their shoulders, but he hopped into the club-house before they could catch him. And when he took off his shoe, two toes dropped out!"

"My!" says the colleger, with his mouth wide open. "I should say that was nerve. And didn't this here Smith never get into the big league?"

"No," says Hub. "He got blood-poisonin' in that foot and they had to cut his whole leg off, and the National Commission's got a rule that you can't play in neither big league unless you got two legs."

After that, Baker and Hub hung round together all the time. He fell for everything Hub told him, no matter how raw. He was givin' Hub a good time, and it'd've been all right if we could of stayed on the road all the while, but I knowed when we got home, the doll'd ast me why wasn't I playin' him and then the trouble'd start.

Sure enough, when we come in off o' the trip, she called me to the office and put it up to me.

"Well," I says, "I don't think he's got enough experience yet. You just let me handle him and keep him on the bench awhile, and maybe he'll develop into a pretty fair ball player."

I suppose I should ought not to of gave her no encouragement about him, but I was figurin' all the time that she'd be boughten out o' the club pretty soon, and then I could can him. At that, I didn't have no objections to keepin' him except that I knowed he was cheatin' the club out of about two hundred bucks every first and fifteenth. If I had to let him go, the gang'd of missed him, especially Hub.

I run into Williams one day and ast him when was the skirt goin' to sell out, and he says they'd tried hard to get her stock away from her, but she'd made up her mind to stick it out till the end o' the season, but that Williams and the other directors was thinkin' about takin' it up with the rest o' the league and tryin' to force her out, but she'd gave 'em her promise that she'd sell in the fall if they still thought she should ought to. So they was nothin' for me to do but make as good a showin' as I could and figure on next year.

It was after the mornin' game on the Fourth o' July that she horned in again. She tells me that her brother and bunch of his friends from Yale college is comin' to the afternoon game, and they want to see their pal perform. I says I'd let him practice and they could watch him if they come out early enough, but she says, no, that wouldn't do; some o' them boys was sayin' that they didn't b'lieve he could play ball, and she wanted to show 'em that he could.

Well, I thought awhile, and then I made up my mind that if he had to be gave some position, he might as well have mine and I could take a rest. So I tells the umps about the change and then I goes back to the bench and sits in a corner where they wasn't nobody could see me.

I wisht you could of been there. The papers had a lot o' stuff about it, but they didn't tell more'n half. Hub was pitchin' and we was playin' Philly. He got the first two of 'em out, and then Cravath hits one down to the colleger on a perfect hop. I was lookin' for him to throw it wild after he got it, but Pat Moran was coachin' at first base, and he hollers to him to throw it to second. So what does he do but just like Pat tells him to, and naturally Maranville wasn't there to cover because they wasn't no play. So the ball goes out in the outfield, and Cravath got clear round to third base. Then Magee busts one, and they got a run. I thought Hub'd be sore, but he wasn't. When he come in to the bench, he was laughin' his head off, and he says:

"Don't never take me out o' this game. This is one battle I want to see all the way through."

Well, Devore leads off for us, and he walks. The colleger's up next, and I tells him to bunt. The first two Rixey throwed him was a mile outside, but he bunts at 'em just the same. Then Rixey curves one, and he tries to duck, but he can't get out o' the way. The ball hit him in the sleeve or somewheres, and Rigler tells him to take his base, but he wouldn't move.

"What's the matter?" says Rig' "Why don't you take your base? Are you hurt?"

"No," says the colleger, "but the manager says I was to bunt."

Well, we had to drive him to first base, and then he steals second, or tries to, with Devore standin' right there. Devore don't move off'n the bag, so they tagged "Gertie" out. When he comes in, I ast him what was he tryin' to pull off. He says Luderus had told him to steal. Then I says:

"Don't never pay no attention to what them Philly guys tells you. If I want you to steal a base, I'll send you a night letter."

We didn't score, and nobody hit noin' at him in their half o' the second, though they was all tryin' to, Hub was tryin' to let 'em, too.

The third innin' was a bear. Dooin hits one at him, and he jumps out o' the way. Rixey struck out, and then Dooin starts to steal. I'd told Maranville to take all the pegs, but he thought it'd be more fun to leave 'em to "Gertrude." So he hollers to him to cover. Whalin makes a perfect peg, and the colleger surprises everybody by catchin' it. But when he'd catched it, he steps on the bag instead of tryin' to tag Red. Then Red says to him:

"I bet I can beat you to third base."

Red starts runnin' with the ball right in Baker's hands, and instead o' throwin' it, he holds right on to it and goes after Red. He wasn't no slouch runner at that, and he made it a clos't race, but Red beat him. The bugs was a-hollerin' their heads off, and most o' the ball players was so sick from laughin' that they couldn't do nothin'. Rig' kept lookin' over at me to see if I wasn't goin' to take the bird out of the game, but I didn't have no stren'th left to shake my head, even.

After the sprintin' race, they took the ball away from him and throwed it back to Hub. Byrne hits one at Hub, but he jumps out o' the way so our "star" can get it, and he goes over and sticks his feet in front o' the ball and it stops right clost to him. Byrne kept on runnin' past first base and yelled at him to leave the ball lay, so he left it lay and Byrne goes all the way home. After that, when anybody got a hold o' the ball, they'd throw it to him and he catched one or two o' the throws, but most o' them he got out o' the way of, and even when he catched 'em, he held onto the ball till every-body'd scored. They made twelve runs in that one innin', and we wouldn't never of got the side out if it hadn't only of been for the umpires. They was tired from workin' the mornin' game and this one, too, so they pulled a couple o' raw ones and wound it up.

Rig' come over to me between innin's and ast me did I think this was a joke. I told him it wasn't no fault o' mine, and explained how it had came off.

"Well," he says, "I've got to catch the midnight train for New York, and we wont never get through in time if this keeps up."

"I can't help it," I says.

Then he says: "I can," and he goes back to his position.

The colleger's turn to bat come in our half, and Rixey rolls one up to him on the ground. Rig' calls it a strike, tryin' to get Baker sore, but he don't never even look round. It'd of been O. K. with him if they'd called a strike before the ball was throwed. Rixey rolled another one up, and Rig' calls it another strike. Then before Baker could say a word, and he wasn't goin' to say nothin' neither, Rig' puts him out of the game for kickin'. Most o' the crowd started home when they seen the show was over, but I didn't blame the umps none—I'd of did the same if I'd of been in their place. We finished up pretty fast after that, because they wasn't no chancet for us to ever come near catchin' up.

After I dressed, I forgot what I was doin' and walked right out o' the club-house without givin' the doll a chancet to make a get-away. There she was, layin' for me.

"What did you take him out o' the game for?" she says.

"I didn't take him out o' no game," I says. "The umps didn't like his language."

Then she ast me what was the matter with his language, and I says I didn't think the umps could understand it right.

"Well," she says, "if a umpire can't understand plain English, he should not ought to be no umpire, and I will write to the president o' the league and have both o' these here men discharged." Then she says: "Mr. Baker was doin' splendid and would of did still better if he had of been left in longer. He didn't catch all them balls that was throwed to him, but that's because he aint had no practice." Then she says: "I'm goin' out of town to-night, but I want you to keep on lettin' Mr. Baker play every day, and I'll watch the papers, and if I see where he aint playin', you'll hear from me."

Well, I couldn't see no joke in it when I got home that night. The ball players was wise and knowed it wasn't my fault. But I was a-scared that the bugs and these here reporters would get after me if I let the boob play every day. And I was a little bit proud o' the work we'd did and didn't want to have it all wasted. I figured it all out, the way I was goin' to get rid of him. I was goin' to have one o' the pitchers hit him with the ball in battin' practice—not hard enough to kill him, but just so's it would scare him out of baseball. I thought he couldn't stand the gaff and would quit in a minute.

I gets out there early the next mornin' for practice and frames it up with Young, a big busher we had that was fast as a streak and hog wild. I sends him out to pitch to us and then tells the colleger to go up there and swing till he learned how to bat. It was prob'ly a dirty trick, but I couldn't think o' no other way.

Well, I pulled a boner when I says anything to this here Young. What I should ought to of did was say nothin', but just stick him in there to pitch natural, and then he'd of hit the bird by accident. But when he was tryin' to hit him, he couldn't even come clost. He was tryin' to be wild, and he pitched more strikes than he ever done before in his life. Gertrude didn't hit nothin', and nothin' hit him. So fin'lly I give up and sent Young to the club-house and started the reg'lar practice.

Fallin' down on that made me meaner'n ever, and I doped out something else. I tells the colleger he stood too far from the plate

when he swung at a ball. I says: "When you go up to bat in the game,
keep one foot on the plate," figurin' that the guy that pitched for
Philly would try to drive him away and either wound him or scare
him to death.

Alexander worked for them, and Baker stood right on top o' the
plate. Dooin called the umps' attention, and the umps warned him,
but he wouldn't move. Fin'lly Alexander shot one up there and he
didn't duck in time. It catched him in front o' the ear, and he dropped
like as if he was shot. I bet I was the most scared guy in the world.
For a minute I felt like a murderer, and I wasn't never so glad in my
life as when I seen him get up. He staggered round a little, and I
had 'em bring him over to the bench. I stuck myself in to run for
him, and some o' the boys took him in the club-house and got him
fixed up. He wasn't hurt bad, though he got a mean lookin' bump.

We was startin' West again that night and I didn't never expect him
to show up for no trip. But there he was, down to the train, with
his wagonload o' scenery.

"Well," I says, "you got your nerve."

"Yes," he says, "I'm goin' to show Hub that they's more'n one
game ball player in the world."

He was still thinkin' about that one-legged guy in the Southern
League.

We opened up in Pittsburgh, and I kept him on the bench. I
knowed Mrs. Hayes would wire and ask me why wasn't he playin',
and when she did, I wrote to her sayin' he was hurt by that there
blow on the head. But that alibi wouldn't get by very long, and I
figured I'd have to frame somethin' new.

The first night in St. Louis, I thought up somethin' and got Doc,
the trainer, to help me pull it. I buys two tickets to a show and gives
'em to Doc with instructions to ask the colleger to go along. After
the show, they was to go to Tony's for lunch. He was to order two
beers, and then I was to drop in and catch Baker with a big stein in
front of him. Then I was to swell up and suspend him for drinkin'.
Doc done his best, but the bird says beer made him sick and he
wouldn't have nothin' to do with it. So when I come in, he was eatin'
some kind o' fancy sandwich and lappin' up a lemonade or somethin'.

He ast me the next afternoon why didn't I let him play, and I says:

"You aint no ball player and you wouldn't be no ball player if you
kept at it a thousand years. You should ought to be trimmin' hats."

"Mrs. Hayes thinks I'm all O. K.," he says.

"Yes," I says, "and you could start one o' these here Carnegie li-
berries with what she don't know about baseball." I says: "Why don't
you quit?"

Then he says: "I can't quit because I can't afford to lose this here
sal'ry."

I says: "What do you mean, you can't afford? You had plenty o'
clo'es when you joined us," I says, "and you must of had money o'
your own or you couldn't of boughten them clo'es."

Then he says his old man give him a allowance of a hundred a
month and he spent all o' that on his clo'es, and that the old man
had told him he would double this here allowance if the boy showed
he could earn five thousand bucks a year when he got out o' college,
and the old man didn't care how he earned it. So he'd told Mrs.
Hayes the whole story and she'd tooken pity on him and give him
the job. I ast him wasn't they no other way he could "earn" the
money, and he says he s'posed they was lots o' ways, only this here
way was easiest.

I says: "Yes, but you aint earnin' nothin' here. You might just as
well stick fellas up on the street as draw a sal'ry as a ball player.
You're stealin' it either way."

He just laughed, and then I says:

"Don't your old man care if you mix up with us tough boys?"

"No," he says, "the old man don't care, but the old lady does. I
told her you was a nice, polite bunch o' fellas and she fell for it, or
else she'd of made me cut this out and come home."

The hunch come to me all of a sudden, and I says:

"What's your old lady's name and where does she live at?"

He told me, and I couldn't hardly wait till I got back to the hotel.

I don't know now just what I wrote, but it was some letter. I told
her we was a bunch o' stews and that when we wan't lushin' beer or
playin' poker, we was going to burlesque shows. I says her son was
pickin' up a awful bunch o' language and drinkin' his fool head off.
I says he was stuck on a burlesque queen and was spendin' all his
dough on her. And I wound it up by sayin' that Dixon, the manager,
had killed his wife and they wasn't no tellin' when he'd cut loose and
kill somebody else. I didn't sign no name, but just put "From a Friend
in Need" down at the bottom.

It was in your town that he heard from her, and he showed me
the letter. She says he was to come home at oncet and that she'd
made the old man promise to come through with a extra allowance

without makin' him do no work for it. But if he didn't cut out the ball playin' and beat it for home, he wouldn't never get another nickel out o' none o' them. She hadn't gave no reason for writin' this way, and he was up in the air. I told him we was sorry to lose him, but maybe it was best for him to quit playin' ball, even if he hadn't never started. He left us the second night in Chi. Hub was good and sore at me. He says I'd spoiled the season for him.

I felt so good about gettin' him off'n my hands that I went out there and played like Cobb or somebody the rest o' the trip. Maybe you fellas remember how I hit ag'in' you them last two days. I done even better'n that in Cincinnati and New York. It was the best trip we'd made in a good many years, and the bugs at home went crazy over us. They was ten thousand out to the first game of our serious at home with St. Louis—on a Thursday, at that.

O' course I knowed they'd be a argument with the skirt. Our winnin' streak wouldn't make her forget to ask me what had become o' Baker. When she ast me, I sprung the stuff about him gettin' a letter from his mother, but I didn't tell her nothin' about the letter I'd wrote. She didn't say nothin', but she looked pretty sore, and she forgot all about givin' me the glad hand for what we'd did in the West.

We done pretty well at home ag'in' St. Louis and Pittsburgh. Then you fellas come along and I guess I don't need to tell you that we was goin' good. I was beginnin' to think we maybe might keep it up and throw a scare into some o' you birds.

She didn't never come out to yesterday's game, but I didn't suspect nothin' wrong till Kelly, the secretary, come into the club-house after me. He tells me that she wants to see me down to the down-town office.

"All right," I says. "I'll beat it down there right after the game."

"No," says Kelly, "she wants you right now."

So I took my unie off and beat it down there in a taxi. The girl in the front office told me to go right on in, and in I went. There was the dame, settin' at the desk where poor old Hayes used to set. And they was two big coppers with her. Without sayin' "How d'ya do" or nothin', she opens right up on me and says:

"These here officers is here to protect me. If you start somethin', you'll get nothin' but the worst of it." Then she pulls a letter out o' the desk and says: "This here letter is from Mr. Baker's mother, and in it she tells me why she made her boy come home. Somebody has tooken the trouble to tell her some fac's about this here ball club—

my ball club that I was proud of! But I aint proud of it no more. I aint proud o' no gang o' hoodlums that don't do nothin' but gamble and drink and run round with actresses and lead young men astray."

"Is that all?" I says.

"No," she hollers, "that aint all. Mr. Dixon, you killed your wife!"

"That's a whole lot o' bunk," I says. "I didn't never have no wife, so how could I kill my wife when I didn't never have none?"

"Don't lie to me!" she says. "Even if you didn't never have no wife, you killed somebody, maybe a innocent girl that was wronged."

"Cut the comedy," I says. "They's nothin' to that stuff. Somebody's went and gave the old lady a bum steer."

"What for?" she ast.

"Prob'ly," I says, "because somebody was tired o' having that boob on the ball club and figured that was the best way to get rid of him."

"We won't discuss it no fu'ther," she says. "I called you up to tell you you aint managin' the club no longer. You can stay here under the terms o' your contract and play ball if you want to, but maybe you wouldn't want to work for the new manager."

"Who is it?" I says.

"That's none o' your business," she says. "I will tell you when the proper time comes."

Then I says: "Is the seamstress comin' back?"

"The *who?*" she hollers.

"That there colleger," I says, "If I was you, I'd get him back, because you and him is certainly a grand combination. It's hard to tell which one o' you knows the most about baseball, you or that bird. Even if you couldn't use him as no ball player, you could chop up his head and build a new grandstand."

"He was smart enough to go through Yale college," she says.

"No," says I. "He didn't never go through no Yale college. If they was any college that he went through, it was this here Wellesley college."

Then I turns and beats it for the door.

Well, sir, they aint nothin' more to tell except one thing. When I come out o' the door into the outside office, I bumped right square into "Gertie." He was smilin' like a big kid, and he says: "Hello, there!" Well, I didn't say nothin' to him, but I give him a good kick in the shin, and I stepped all over his patent-leather shoes. Then I went on about my business.

I wired Knabe, and they wasn't nothin' to it. He told me to come on and join 'em in Pittsburgh, and I just had time to get my stuff together and catch this train.

I guess she wont try and get no injunction out agin' me. But I wisht she would. I'd like to tell my story to a judge, provided the judge wasn't no woman.

You know who's goin' to manage that club, don't you? And you know who's goin' to be president of it. Well, sir, I'll bet you anything you want to bet that they wont even finish in Mass'chusetts.

ALIBI IKE

◇

I

HIS RIGHT NAME WAS Frank X. Farrell, and I guess the X stood for "Excuse me." Because he never pulled a play, good or bad, on or off the field, without apologizin' for it.

"Alibi Ike" was the name Carey wished on him the first day he reported down South. O' course we all cut out the "Alibi" part of it right away for the fear he would overhear it and bust somebody. But we called him "Ike" right to his face and the rest of it was understood by everybody on the club except Ike himself.

He ast me one time, he says:

"What do you all call me Ike for? I ain't no Yid."

"Carey give you the name," I says. "It's his nickname for everybody he takes a likin' to."

"He mustn't have only a few friends then," says Ike. "I never heard him say 'Ike' to nobody else."

But I was goin' to tell you about Carey namin' him. We'd been workin' out two weeks and the pitchers was showin' somethin' when this bird joined us. His first day out he stood up there so good and took such a reef at the old pill that he had everyone lookin'. Then him and Carey was together in left field, catchin' fungoes, and it was after we was through for the day that Carey told me about him.

"What do you think of Alibi Ike?" ast Carey.

"Who's that?" I says.

"This here Farrell in the outfield," says Carey.

"He looks like he could hit," I says.

"Yes," says Carey, "but he can't hit near as good as he can apologize."

Then Carey went on to tell me what Ike had been pullin' out there.

This story first appeared in the *Saturday Evening Post*, July 31, 1915; collected in *How to Write Short Stories*.

He'd dropped the first fly ball that was hit to him and told Carey his glove wasn't broke in good yet, and Carey says the glove could easy of been Kid Gleason's gran'father. He made a whale of a catch out o' the next one and Carey says "Nice work!" or somethin' like that, but Ike says he could of caught the ball with his back turned only he slipped when he started after it and, besides that, the air currents fooled him.

"I thought you done well to get to the ball," says Carey.

"I ought to been settin' under it," says Ike.

"What did you hit last year?" Carey ast him.

"I had malaria most o' the season," says Ike, "I wound up with .356."

"Where would I have to go to get malaria?" says Carey, but Ike didn't wise up.

I and Carey and him set at the same table together for supper. It took him half an hour longer'n us to eat because he had to excuse himself every time he lifted his fork.

"Doctor told me I needed starch," he'd say, and then toss a shovelful o' potatoes into him. Or, "They ain't much meat on one o' these chops," he'd tell us, and grab another one. Or he'd say: "Nothin' like onions for a cold," and then he'd dip into the perfumery.

"Better try that apple sauce," says Carey. "It'll help your malaria."

"Whose malaria?" says Ike. He'd forgot already why he didn't only hit .356 last year.

I and Carey begin to lead him on.

"Whereabout did you say your home was?" I ast him.

"I live with my folks," he says. "We live in Kansas City—not right down in the business part—outside a ways."

"How's that come?" says Carey. "I should think you'd get rooms in the post office."

But Ike was too busy curin' his cold to get that one.

"Are you married?" I ast him.

"No," he says. "I never run round much with girls, except to shows onct in a wile and parties and dances and roller skatin'."

"Never take 'em to the prize fights, eh?" says Carey.

"We don't have no real good bouts," says Ike. "Just bush stuff. And I never figured a boxin' match was a place for the ladies."

Well, after supper he pulled a cigar out and lit it. I was just goin' to ask him what he done it for, but he beat me to it.

"Kind o' rests a man to smoke after a good work-out," he says. "Kind o' settles a man's supper, too."

"Looks like a pretty good cigar," says Carey.

"Yes," says Ike. "A friend o' mind give it to me—a fella in Kansas City that runs a billiard room."

"Do you play billiards?" I ast him.

"I used to play a fair game," he says. "I'm all out o' practice now—can't hardly make a shot."

We coaxed him into a four-handed battle, him and Carey against Jack Mack and I. Say, he couldn't play billiards as good as Willie Hoppe; not quite. But to hear him tell it, he didn't make a good shot all evenin'. I'd leave him an awful-lookin' layout and he'd gather 'em up in one try and then run a couple o' hundred, and between every carom he'd say he'd put too much stuff on the ball, or the English didn't take, or the table wasn't true, or his stick was crooked, or somethin'. And all the time he had the balls actin' like they was Dutch soliders and him Kaiser William. We started out to play fifty points, but we had to make it a thousand so as I and Jack and Carey could try the table.

The four of us set round the lobby a wile after we was through playin', and when it got along toward bedtime Carey whispered to me and says:

"Ike'd like to go to bed, but he can't think up no excuse."

Carey hadn't hardly finished whisperin' when Ike got up and pulled it:

"Well, good night, boys," he says. "I ain't sleepy, but I got some gravel in my shoes and it's killin' my feet."

We knowed he hadn't never left the hotel since we'd came in from the grounds and changed our clo'es. So Carey says:

"I should think they'd take them gravel pits out o' the billiard room."

But Ike was already on his way to the elevator, limpin'.

"He's got the world beat," says Carey to Jack and I. "I've knew lots o' guys that had an alibi for every mistake they made; I've heard pitchers say that the ball slipped when somebody cracked one off'n 'em; I've heard infielders complain of a sore arm after heavin' one into the stand, and I've saw outfields tooken sick with a dizzy spell when they've misjudged a fly ball. But this baby can't even go to bed without apologizin', and I bet he excuses himself to the razor when he gets ready to shave."

"And at that," says Jack, "he's goin' to make us a good man."

"Yes," says Carey, "unless rheumatism keeps his battin' average down to .400."

Well, sir, Ike kept whalin' away at the ball all through the trip till everybody knowed he'd won a job. Cap had him in there regular the last few exhibition games and told the newspaper boys a week before the season opened that he was goin' to start him in Kane's place.

"You're there, kid," says Carey to Ike, the night Cap made the 'nnouncement. "They ain't many boys that wins a big league berth their third year out."

"I'd of been up here a year ago," says Ike, "only I was bent over all season with lumbago."

II

IT RAINED DOWN in Cincinnati one day and somebody organized a little game o' cards. They was shy two men to make six and ast I and Carey to play.

"I'm with you if you get Ike and make it seven-handed," says Carey.

So they got a hold of Ike and we went up to Smitty's room.

"I pretty near forgot how many you deal," says Ike. "It's been a long wile since I played."

I and Carey give each other the wink, and sure enough, he was just as ig'orant about poker as billiards. About the second hand, the pot was opened two or three ahead of him, and they was three in when it come his turn. It cost a buck, and he throwed in two.

"It's raised, boys," somebody says.

"Gosh, that's right, I did raise it," said Ike.

"Take out a buck if you didn't mean to tilt her," says Carey.

"No," says Ike, "I'll leave it go."

Well, it was raised back at him and then he made another mistake and raised again. They was only three left in when the draw come. Smitty'd opened with a pair o' kings and he didn't help 'em. Ike stood pat. The guy that'd raised him back was flushin' and he didn't fill. So Smitty checked and Ike bet and didn't get no call. He tossed his hand away, but I grabbed it and give it a look. He had king, queen, jack and two tens. Alibi Ike he must have seen me peekin', for he leaned over and whispered to me.

"I overlooked my hand," he says. "I thought all the wile it was a straight."

"Yes," I says, "that's why you raised twice by mistake."

They was another pot that he come into with tens and fours. It

was tilted a couple o' times and two o' the strong fellas drawed ahead
of Ike. They each drawed one. So Ike throwed away his little pair
and come out with four tens. And they was four treys against him.
Carey'd looked at Ike's discards and then he says:

"This lucky bum busted two pair."

"No, no, I didn't," says Ike.

"Yes, yes, you did," says Carey, and showed us the two fours.

"What do you know about that?" says Ike. "I'd of swore one was
a five spot."

Well, we hadn't had no pay day yet, and after a wile everybody
except Ike was goin' shy. I could see him gettin' restless and I was
wonderin' how he'd make the get-away. He tried two or three times.
"I got to buy some collars before supper," he says.

"No hurry," says Smitty. "The stores here keeps open all night in
April."

After a minute he opened up again.

"My uncle out in Nebraska ain't expected to live," he says. "I
ought to send a telegram."

"Would that save him?" says Carey.

"No, it sure wouldn't," says Ike, "but I ought to leave my old man
know where I'm at."

"When did you hear about your uncle?" says Carey.

"Just this mornin'," says Ike.

"Who told you?" ast Carey.

"I got a wire from my old man," says Ike.

"Well," says Carey, "your old man knows you're still here yet this
afternoon if you was here this mornin'. Trains leavin' Cincinnati in
the middle o' the day don't carry no ball clubs."

"Yes," says Ike, "that's true. But he don't know where I'm goin'
to be next week."

"Ain't he got no schedule?" ast Carey.

"I sent him one openin' day," says Ike, "but it takes mail a long
time to get to Idaho."

"I thought your old man lived in Kansas City," says Carey.

"He does when he's home," says Ike.

"But now," says Carey, "I s'pose he's went to Idaho so as he can
be near your sick uncle in Nebraska."

"He's visitin' my other uncle in Idaho."

"Then how does he keep posted about your sick uncle?" ast Carey.

"He don't," says Ike. "He don't even know my other uncle's sick.
That's why I ought to wire and tell him."

"Good night!" says Carey.

"What town in Idaho is your old man at?" I says.

Ike thought it over.

"No town at all," he says. "But he's near a town."

"Near what town?" I says.

"Yuma," says Ike.

Well, by this time he'd lost two or three pots and he was desperate. We was playin' just as fast as we could, because we seen we couldn't hold him much longer. But he was tryin' so hard to frame an escape that he couldn't pay no attention to the cards, and it looked like we'd get his whole pile away from him if we could make him stick.

The telephone saved him. The minute it begun to ring, five of us jumped for it. But Ike was there first.

"Yes," he says, answerin' it. "This is him. I'll come right down."

And he slammed up the receiver and beat it out o' the door without even sayin' good-by.

"Smitty'd ought to locked the door," says Carey.

"What did he win?" ast Carey.

We figured it up—sixty-odd bucks.

"And the next time we ask him to play," says Carey, "his fingers will be so stiff he can't hold the cards."

Well, we set round a wile talkin' it over, and pretty soon the telephone rung again. Smitty answered it. It was a friend of his'n from Hamilton and he wanted to know why Smitty didn't hurry down. He was the one that had called before and Ike had told him he was Smitty.

"Ike'd ought to split with Smitty's friend," says Carey.

"No," I says, "he'll need all he won. It costs money to buy collars and to send telegrams from Cincinnati to your old man in Texas and keep him posted on the health o' your uncle in Cedar Rapids, D.C."

III

AND YOU OUGHT TO heard him out there on that field! They wasn't a day when he didn't pull six or seven, and it didn't make no difference whether he was goin' good or bad. If he popped up in the pinch he should of made a base hit and the reason he didn't was so-and-so. And if he cracked one for three bases he ought to had a home run, only the ball wasn't lively, or the wind brought it back, or he tripped on a lump o' dirt, roundin' first base.

They was one afternoon in New York when he beat all records. Big Marquard was workin' against us and he was good.

In the first innin' Ike hit one clear over that right field stand, but it was a few feet foul. Then he got another foul and then the count come to two and two. Then Rube slipped one acrost on him and he was called out.

"What do you know about that!" he says afterward on the bench. "I lost count. I thought it was three and one, and I took a strike."

"You took a strike all right," says Carey. "Even the umps knowed it was a strike."

"Yes," says Ike, "but you can bet I wouldn't of took it if I'd knew it was the third one. The score board had it wrong."

"That score board ain't for you to look at," says Cap. "It's for you to hit that old pill against."

"Well," says Ike, "I could of hit that one over the score board if I'd knew it was the third."

"Was it a good ball?" I says.

"Well, no, it wasn't," says Ike. "It was inside."

"How far inside?" says Carey.

"Oh, two or three inches or half a foot," says Ike.

"I guess you wouldn't of threatened the score board with it then," says Cap.

"I'd of pulled it down the right foul line if I hadn't thought he'd call it a ball," says Ike.

Well, in New York's part o' the innin' Doyle cracked one and Ike run back a mile and a half and caught it with one hand. We was all sayin' what a whale of a play it was, but he had to apologize just the same as for gettin' struck out.

"That stand's so high," he says, "that a man don't never see a ball till it's right on top o' you."

"Didn't you see that one?" ast Cap.

"Not at first," says Ike; "not till it raised up above the roof o' the stand."

"Then why did you start back as soon as the ball was hit?" says Ike.

"I knowed by the sound that he'd got a good hold of it," says Ike.

"Yes," says Cap, "but how'd you know what direction to run in?"

"Doyle usually hits 'em that way, the way I run," says Ike.

"Why don't you play blindfolded?" says Carey.

"Might as well, with that big high stand to bother a man," says Ike. "If I could of saw the ball all the time I'd of got it in my hip pocket."

Along in the fifth we was one run to the bad and Ike got on with one out. On the first ball throwed to Smitty, Ike went down. The ball was outside and Meyers throwed Ike out by ten feet.

You could see Ike's lips movin' all the way to the bench and when he got there he had his piece learned.

"Why didn't he swing?" he says.

"Why didn't you wait for his sign?" says Cap.

"He give me his sign," says Ike.

"What is his sign with you?" says Cap.

"Pickin' up some dirt with his right hand," says Ike.

"Well, I didn't see him do it," Cap says.

"He done it all right," says Ike.

Well, Smitty went out and they wasn't no more argument till they come in for the next innin'. Then Cap opened it up.

"You fellas better get your signs straight," he says.

"Do you mean me?" says Smitty.

"Yes," Cap says. "What's your sign with Ike?"

"Slidin my left hand up to the end o' the bat and back," says Smitty.

"Do you hear that, Ike?" ast Cap.

"What of it?" says Ike.

"You says his sign was pickin' up dirt and he says it's slidin his hand. Which is right?"

"I'm right," says Smitty. "But if you're arguin' about him goin' last innin', I didn't give him no sign."

"You pulled your cap down with your right hand, didn't you?" ast Ike.

"Well, s'pose I did," says Smitty. "That don't mean nothin'. I never told you to take that for a sign, did I?"

"I thought maybe you meant to tell me and forgot," says Ike.

They couldn't none of us answer that and they wouldn't of been no more said if Ike had of shut up. But wile we was settin' there Carey got on with two out and stole second clean.

"There!" says Ike. "That's what I was tryin' to do and I'd of got away with it if Smitty'd swang and bothered the Indian."

"Oh!" says Smitty. "You was tryin' to steal then, was you? I thought you claimed I give you the hit and run."

"I didn't claim no such a thing," says Ike. "I thought maybe you

might of gave me a sign, but I was goin' anyway because I thought
I had a good start."

Cap prob'ly would of hit him with a bat, only just about that time
Doyle booted one on Hayes and Carey come acrost with the run
that tied.

Well, we go into the ninth finally, one and one, and Marquard
walks McDonald with nobody out.

"Lay it down," says Cap to Ike.

And Ike goes up there with orders to bunt and cracks the first ball
into that right-field stand! It was fair this time, and we're two ahead,
but I didn't think about that at the time. I was too busy watchin'
Cap's face. First he turned pale and then he got red as fire and then
he got blue and purple, and finally he just laid back and busted out
laughin'. So we wasn't afraid to laugh ourselfs when we seen him
doin' it, and when Ike come in everybody on the bench was in
hysterics.

But instead o' takin' advantage, Ike had to try and excuse himself.
His play was to shut up and he didn't know how to make it.

"Well," he says, "if I hadn't hit quite so quick at that one I bet
it'd of cleared the center-field fence."

Cap stopped laughin'.

"It'll cost you plain fifty," he says.

"What for?" says Ike.

"When I say 'bunt' I mean 'bunt,' " says Cap.

"You didn't say 'bunt,' " says Ike.

"I says 'Lay it down,' " says Cap. "If that don't mean 'bunt,' what
does it mean?"

" 'Lay it down' means 'bunt' all right," says Ike, "but I understood
you to say 'Lay on it.' "

"All right," says Cap, "and the little misunderstandin' will cost you
fifty."

Ike didn't say nothin' for a few minutes. Then he had another
bright idear.

"I was just kiddin' about misunderstandin' you," he says. "I knowed
you wanted me to bunt."

"Well, then, why didn't you bunt?" ast Cap.

"I was goin' to on the next ball," says Ike. "But I thought if I took
a good wallop I'd have 'em all fooled. So I walloped at the first one
to fool 'em, and I didn't have no intention o' hittin' it."

"You tried to miss it, did you?" says Cap.

"Yes," says Ike.

"How'd you happen to hit it?" ast Cap.

"Well," Ike says, "I was lookin' for him to throw me a fast one and I was goin' to swing under it. But he come with a hook and I met it right square where I was swingin' to go under the fast one."

"Great!" says Cap. "Boys," he says, "Ike's learned how to hit Marquard's curve. Pretend a fast one's comin' and then try to miss it. It's a good thing to know and Ike'd ought to be willin' to pay for the lesson. So I'm goin' to make it a hundred instead o' fifty."

The game wound up 3 to 1. The fine didn't go, because Ike hit like a wild man all through that trip and we made pretty near a cleanup. The night we went to Philly I got him cornered in the car and I says to him:

"Forget them alibis for a wile and tell me somethin'. What'd you do that for, swing that time against Marquard when you was told to bunt?"

"I'll tell you," he says. "That ball he throwed me looked just like the one I struck out on in the first innin' and I wanted to show Cap what I could of done to that other one if I'd knew it was the third strike."

"But," I says, "the one you struck out on in the first innin' was a fast ball."

"So was the one I cracked in the ninth," says Ike.

IV

YOU'VE SAW Cap's wife, o' course. Well, her sister's about twict as good-lookin' as her, and that's goin' some.

Cap took his missus down to St. Louis the second trip and the other one come down from St. Joe to visit her. Her name is Dolly, and some doll is right.

Well, Cap was goin' to take the two sisters to a show and he wanted a beau for Dolly. He left it to her and she picked Ike. He'd hit three on the nose that afternoon—off'n Sallee, too.

They fell for each other that first evenin'. Cap told us how it come off. She begin flatterin' Ike for the star game he'd played and o' course he begin excusin' himself for not doin' better. So she thought he was modest and it went strong with her. And she believed everything he said and that made her solid with him—that and her makeup. They was together every mornin' and evenin' for the five days we was there. In the afternoons Ike played the grandest ball you ever see, hittin' and runnin' the bases like a fool and catchin' everything that stayed in the park.

I told Cap, I says: "You'd ought to keep the doll with us and he'd make Cobb's figures look sick."

But Dolly had to go back to St. Joe and we come home for a long serious.

Well, for the next three weeks Ike had a letter to read every day and he'd set in the clubhouse readin' it till mornin' practice was half over. Cap didn't say nothin' to him, because he was goin' so good. But I and Carey wasted a lot of our time tryin' to get him to own up who the letters was from. Fine chanct!

"What are you readin'?" Carey'd say. "A bill?"

"No," Ike'd say, "not exactly a bill. It's a letter from a fella I used to go to school with."

"High school or college?" I'd ask him.

"College," he'd say.

"What college?" I'd say.

Then he'd stall a wile and then he'd say:

"I didn't go to the college myself, but my friend went there."

"How did it happen you didn't go?" Carey'd ask him.

"Well," he'd say, "they wasn't no colleges near where I lived."

"Didn't you live in Kansas City?" I'd say to him.

One time he'd say he did and another time he didn't. One time he says he lived in Michigan.

"Where at?" says Carey.

"Near Detroit," he says.

"Well," I says, "Detroit's near Ann Arbor and that's where they got the university."

"Yes," says Ike, "they got it there now, but they didn't have it there then."

"I come pretty near goin' to Syracuse," I says, "only they wasn't no railroads runnin' through there in them days."

"Where'd this friend o' yours go to college?" says Carey.

"I forget now," says Ike.

"Was it Carlisle?" ast Carey.

"No," says Ike, "his folks wasn't very well off."

"That's what barred me from Smith," I says.

"I was goin' to tackle Cornell's," says Carey, "but the doctor told me I'd have hay fever if I didn't stay up North."

"Your friend writes long letters," I says.

"Yes," says Ike; "he's tellin' me about a ball player."

"Where does he play?" ast Carey.

"Down in the Texas League—Fort Wayne," says Ike.

"It looks like a girl's writin'," Carey says.

"A girl wrote it," says Ike. "That's my friend's sister, writin' for him."

"Didn't they teach writin' at this here college where he went?" says Carey.

"Sure," Ike says, "they taught writin', but he got his hand cut off in a railroad wreck."

"How long ago?" I says.

"Right after he got out o' college," says Ike.

"Well," I says, "I should think he'd of learned to write with his left hand by this time."

"It's his left hand that was cut off," says Ike; "and he was left-handed."

"You get a letter every day," says Carey. "They're all the same writin'. Is he tellin' you about a different ball player every time he writes?"

"No," Ike says. "It's the same ball player. He just tells me what he does every day."

"From the size o' the letters, they don't play nothin' but double-headers down there," says Carey.

We figured that Ike spent most of his evenin's answerin' the letters from his "friend's sister," so we kept tryin' to date him up for shows and parties to see how he'd duck out of 'em. He was bugs over spaghetti, so we told him one day that they was goin' to be a big feed of it over to Joe's that night and he was invited.

"How long'll it last?" he says.

"Well," we says, "we're goin' right over there after the game and stay till they close up."

"I can't go," he says, "unless they leave me come home at eight bells."

"Nothin' doin'," says Carey. "Joe'd get sore."

"I can't go then," says Ike.

"Why not?" I ast him.

"Well," he says, "my landlady locks up the house at eight and I left my key home."

"You can come and stay with me," says Carey.

"No," he says, "I can't sleep in a strange bed."

"How do you get along when we're on the road?" says I.

"I don't never sleep the first night anywheres," he says. "After that I'm all right."

"You'll have time to chase home and get your key right after the game," I told him.

"The key ain't home," says Ike. "I lent it to one o' the other fellas and he's went out o' town and took it with him."

"Couldn't you borry another key off'n the landlady?" Carey ast him.

"No," he says, "that's the only one they is."

Well, the day before we stared East again, Ike come into the clubhouse all smiles.

"Your birthday?" I ast him.

"No," he says.

"What do you feel so good about?" I says.

"Got a letter from my old man," he says. "My uncle's goin' to get well."

"Is that the one in Nebraska?" says I.

"Not right in Nebraska," says Ike. "Near there."

But afterwards we got the right dope from Cap. Dolly'd blew in from Missouri and was goin' to make the trip with her sister.

V

WELL, I WANT TO ALIBI Carey and I for what come off in Boston. If we'd of had any idear what we was doin', we'd never did it. They wasn't nobody outside o' maybe Ike and the dame that felt worse over it than I and Carey.

The first two days we didn't see nothin' of Ike and her except out to the park. The rest o' the time they was sight-seein' over to Cambridge and down to Revere and out to Brook-a-line and all the other places where the rubes go.

But when we come into the beanery after the third game Cap's wife called us over.

"If you want to see somethin' pretty," she says, "look at the third finger on Sis's left hand."

Well, o' course we knowed before we looked that it wasn't going' to be no hangnail. Nobody was su'prised when Dolly blew into the dinin' room with it—a rock that Ike'd bought off'n Diamond Joe the first trip to New York. Only o' course it'd been set into a lady's-size ring instead o' the automobile tire he'd been wearin'.

Cap and his missus and Ike and Dolly ett supper together, only Ike didn't eat nothin', but just set there blushin' and spillin' things on the tablecloth. I heard him excusin' himself for not havin' no appetite. He says he couldn't never eat when he was clost to the ocean. He'd forgot about them sixty-five oysters he destroyed the first night o' the trip before.

He was goin' to take her to a show, so after supper he went upstairs to change his collar. She had to doll up, too, and o' course Ike was through long before her.

If you remember the hotel in Boston, they's a little parlor where the piano's at and then they's another little parlor openin' off o' that. Well, when Ike come down Smitty was playin' a few chords and I and Carey was harmonizin'. We seen Ike go up to the desk to leave his key and we called him in. He tried to duck away, but we wouldn't stand for it.

We ast him what he was all duded up for and he says he was goin' to the theayter.

"Goin' alone?" says Carey.

"No," he says, "a friend o' mine's goin' with me."

"What do you say if we go along?" says Carey.

"I ain't only got two tickets," he says.

"Well," says Carey, "we can go down there with you and buy our own seats; maybe we can all get together."

"No," says Ike. "They ain't no more seats. They're all sold out."

"We can buy some off'n the scalpers," says Carey.

"I wouldn't if I was you," says Ike. "They say the show's rotten."

"What are you goin' for, then?" I ast.

"I didn't hear about it bein' rotten till I got the tickets," he says.

"Well," I says, "if you don't want to go I'll buy the tickets from you."

"No," says Ike, "I wouldn't want to cheat you. I'm stung and I'll just have to stand for it."

"What are you goin' to do with the girl, leave her here at the hotel?" I says.

"What girl?" says Ike.

"The girl you ett supper with," I says.

"Oh," he says, "we just happened to go into the dinin' room together, that's all. Cap wanted I should set down with 'em."

"I noticed," says Carey, "that she happened to be wearin' that rock you bought off'n Diamond Joe."

"Yes," says Ike. "I lent it to her for a wile."

"Did you lend her the new ring that goes with it?" I says.

"She had that already," says Ike. "She lost the set out of it."

"I wouldn't trust no strange girl with a rock o' mine," says Carey.

"Oh, I guess she's all right," Ike says. "Besides, I was tired o' the stone. When a girl asks you for somethin', what are you goin' to do?"

He started out toward the desk, but we flagged him.

"Wait a minute!" Carey says. "I got a bet with Sam here, and it's up to you to settle it."

"Well," says Ike, "make it snappy. My friend'll be here any minute."

"I bet," says Carey, "that you and that girl was engaged to be married."

"Nothin' to it," says Ike.

"Now look here," says Carey, "this is goin' to cost me real money if I lose. Cut out the alibi stuff and give it to us straight. Cap's wife just as good as told us you was roped."

Ike blushed like a kid.

"Well, boys," he says, "I may as well own up. You win, Carey."

"Yatta boy!" says Carey. "Congratulations!"

"You got a swell girl, Ike," I says.

"She's a peach," says Smitty.

"Well, I guess she's O.K.," says Ike. "I don't know much about girls."

"Didn't you never run round with 'em?" I says.

"Oh, yes, plenty of 'em," says Ike. "But I never seen none I'd fall for."

"That is, till you seen this one," says Carey.

"Well," says Ike, "this one's O. K., but I wasn't thinkin' about gettin' married yet a wile."

"Who done the askin'—her?" says Carey.

"Oh, no," says Ike, "but sometimes a man don't know what he's gettin' into. Take a good-lookin' girl, and a man gen'ally almost always does about what she wants him to."

"They couldn't no girl lasso me unless I wanted to be lassooed," says Smitty.

"Oh, I don't know," says Ike. "When a fella gets to feelin' sorry for one of 'em it's all off."

Well, we left him go after shakin' hands all round. But he didn't

take Dolly to no show that night. Some time while we was talkin'
she'd came into that other parlor and she'd stood there and heard
us. I don't know how much she heard. But it was enough. Dolly and
Cap's missus took the midnight train for New York. And from there
Cap's wife sent her on her way back to Missouri.

She'd left the ring and a note for Ike with the clerk. But we didn't
ask Ike if the note was from his friend in Fort Wayne, Texas.

VI

WHEN WE'D CAME TO Boston Ike was hittin' plain .397. When
we got back home he'd fell off to pretty near nothin'. He hadn't
drove one out o' the infield in any o' them other Eastern parks, and
he didn't even give no excuse for it.

To show you how bad he was, he struck out three times in Brooklyn one day and never opened his trap when Cap ast him what was
the matter. Before, if he'd whiffed oncet in a game he'd of wrote a
book tellin' why.

Well, we dropped from first place to fifth in four weeks and we
was still goin' down. I and Carey was about the only ones in the club
that spoke to each other, and all as we did was remind ourself o'
what a boner we'd pulled.

"It's goin' to beat us out o' the big money," says Carey.

"Yes," I says. "I don't want to knock my own ball club, but it looks
like a one-man team, and when that one man's dauber's down we
couldn't trim our whiskers."

"We ought to knew better," says Carey.

"Yes," I says, "but why should a man pull an alibi for bein' engaged
to such a bearcat as she was?"

"He shouldn't," says Carey. "But I and you knowed he would or
we'd never started talkin' to him about it. He wasn't no more ashamed
o' the girl than I am of a regular base hit. But he just can't come
clean on no subjec'."

Cap had the whole story, and I and Carey was as pop'lar with him
as an umpire.

"What do you want me to do, Cap?" Carey'd say to him before
goin' up to hit.

"Use your own judgment," Cap'd tell him. "We want to lose another game."

But finally, one night in Pittsburgh, Cap had a letter from his missus and he come to us with it.

"You fellas," he says, "is the ones that put us on the bum, and if you're sorry I think they's a chancet for you to make good. The old lady's out to St. Joe and she's been tryin' her hardest to fix things up. She's explained that Ike don't mean nothin' with his talk; I've wrote and explained that to Dolly, too. But the old lady says that Dolly says that she can't believe it. But Dolly's still stuck on this baby, and she's pinin' away just the same as Ike. And the old lady says she thinks if you two fellas would write to the girl and explain how you was always kiddin'; with Ike and leadin' him on, and how the ball club was all shot to pieces since Ike quit hittin', and how he acted like he was goin' to kill himself, and this and that, she'd fall for it and maybe soften down. Dolly, the old lady says, would believe you before she'd believe I and the old lady, because she thinks it's her we're sorry for, and not him."

Well, I and Carey was only too glad to try and see what we could do. But it wasn't no snap. We wrote about eight letters before we got one that looked good. Then we give it to the stenographer and had it wrote out on a typewriter and both of us signed it.

It was Carey's idear that made the letter good. He stuck in somethin' about the world's serious money that our wives wasn't goin' to spend unless she took pity on a "boy who was so shy and modest that he was afraid to come right out and say that he had asked such a beautiful and handsome girl to become his bride."

That's prob'ly what got her, or maybe she couldn't of held out much longer anyway. It was four days after we sent the letter that Cap heard from his missus again. We was in Cincinnati.

"We've won," he says to us. "The old lady says that Dolly says she'll give him another chancet. But the old lady says it won't do no good for Ike to write a letter. He'll have to go out there."

"Send him to-night," says Carey.

"I'll pay half his fare," I says.

"I'll pay the other half," says Carey.

"No," says Cap, "the club'll pay his expenses. I'll send him scoutin'."

"Are you goin' to send him to-night?"

"Sure," says Cap. "But I'm goin' to break the news to him right now. It's time we win a ball game."

So in the clubhouse, just before the game, Cap told him. And I certainly felt sorry for Rube Benton and Red Ames that afternoon!

I and Carey was standin' in front o' the hotel that night when Ike come out with his suitcase.

"Sent home?" I says to him.

"No," he says, "I'm goin' scoutin'."

"Where to?" I says. "Fort Wayne?"

"No, not exactly," he says.

"Well," says Carey, "have a good time."

"I ain't lookin' for no good time," says Ike. "I says I was goin' scoutin'."

"Well, then," says Carey, "I hope you see somebody you like."

"And you better have a drink before you go," I says.

"Well," says Ike, "they claim it helps a cold."

Ringgold Wilmer Lardner

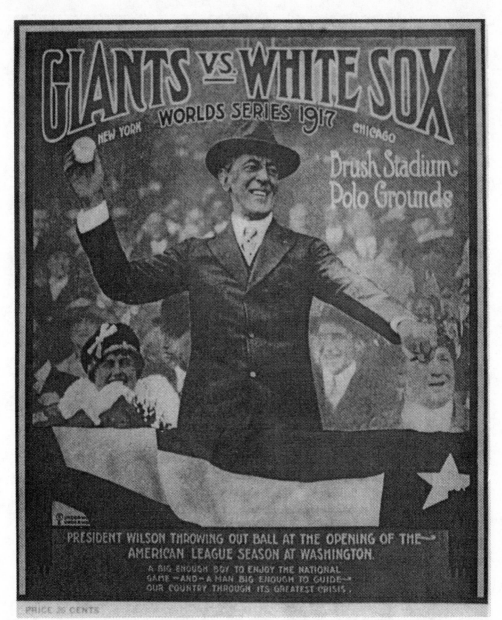

Front Cover, 1917 World Series Program (Credit: Transcendental Graphics).

YOU KNOW ME AL

RING W. LARDNER

A baseball story—*the* baseball story of the generation—batted out by a writer who hits straight to the heart of the baseball fan.

Ring Lardner's years as Sporting Writer for the *Chicago Tribune* have given him all the "inside dope" on the National game. The accurate humor in the character of his "busher" will win many a reader, from the boxes to the bleachers.

GEORGE H. DORAN COMPANY   Publishers   New York

Dust jacket for first edition (1916).

He Bawled Me Awful Illustration
by Martin Justice for the first
Jack Keefe story, "A Busher's
Letters Home."

*I Forgot All About the Game
and Cut Loose at His Bean*

I Forgot All About the Game and Cut Loose at His Bean Illustration by Martin Justice for "A
New Busher Breaks In."

"If Pepper was Worth a Million
Dollars a Ounce You'd be Rated
at Ten Cents!"

It Was Like as Though All the Ferryboats in East River Had Got Into Trouble at Once
Arthur William Brown's illustrations for "Sick 'Em."

Lardner wrote the continuity for this syndicated comic strip from 1922 to 1925; it was drawn by Will B. Johnstone and later by Dick Dorgan.

Charles A. Comiskey, the tight-fisted owner of the White Sox, was known as "the noble Roman" because of his profile.

Comiskey Park, home of the White Sox.

White Sox coach Kid Gleason became
manager in 1919.

Guy Harris "Doc" White, Lardner's
collaborator, was also a dentist.

Casey Stengel during his playing days.

Ty Cobb, the Georgia Peach

Along Came Ruth

Lardner in White Sox Uniform

HARMONY

◇

EVEN A BASEBALL WRITER must sometimes work. Regretfully I yielded my seat in the P.G., walked past the section where Art Graham, Bill Cole, Lefty Parks and young Waldron were giving expert tonsorial treatment to "Sweet Adeline," and flopped down beside Ryan, the manager.

"Well, Cap," I said, "we're due in Springfield in a little over an hour and I haven't written a line."

"Don't let me stop you," said Ryan.

"I want you to start me," I said.

"Lord!" said Ryan. "You oughtn't to have any trouble grinding out stuff these days, with the club in first place and young Waldron gone crazy. He's worth a story any day."

"That's the trouble," said I. "He's been worked so much that there's nothing more to say about him. Everybody in the country knows that he's hitting .420, that he's made nine home runs, twelve triples and twenty-some doubles, that he's stolen twenty-five bases, and that he can play the piano and sing like Carus'. They've run his picture oftener than Billy Sunday and Mary Pickford put together. Of course, you might come through with how you got him."

"Oh, that's the mystery," said Ryan.

"So I've heard you say," I retorted. "But it wouldn't be a mystery if you'd let me print it."

"Well," said Ryan, "if you're really hard up I suppose I might as well come through. Only there's really no mystery at all about it; it's just what I consider the most remarkable piece of scouting ever done. I've been making a mystery of it just to have a little fun with Dick Hodges. You know he's got the Jackson club and he's still so sore about my stealing Waldron he'll hardly speak to me.

This story first appeared in *McClure's*, August 1915; collected in *How to Write Short Stories*.

"I'll give you the dope if you want it, though it's a boost for Art Graham, not me. There's lots of people think the reason I've kept the thing a secret is because I'm modest.

"They give me credit for having found Waldron myself. But Graham is the bird that deserves the credit and I'll admit that he almost had to get down on his knees to make me take his tip. Yes, sir, Art Graham was the scout, and now he's sitting on the bench and the boy he recommended has got his place."

"That sounds pretty good," I said. "And how did Graham get wise?"

"I'm going to tell you. You're in a hurry; so I'll make it snappy.

"You weren't with us last fall, were you? Well, we had a day off in Detroit, along late in the season. Graham's got relatives in Jackson; so he asked me if he could spend the day there. I told him he could and asked him to keep his eyes peeled for good young pitchers, if he happened to go to the ball game. So he went to Jackson and the next morning he came back all excited. I asked him if he'd found me a pitcher and he said he hadn't, but he'd seen the best natural hitter he'd ever looked at—a kid named Waldron.

" 'Well,' I said, 'you're the last one that ought to be recommending outfielders. If there's one good enough to hold a regular job, it might be your job he'd get.'

"But Art said that didn't make any difference to him—he was looking out for the good of the club. Well, I didn't see my way clear to asking the old man to dig up good money for an outfielder nobody'd ever heard of, when we were pretty well stocked with them, so I tried to stall Art; but he kept after me and kept after me till I agreed to stick in a draft for the kid just to keep Art quiet. So the draft went in and we got him. Then, as you know, Hodges tried to get him back, and that made me suspicious enough to hold on to him. Hodges finally came over to see me and wanted to know who'd tipped me to Waldron. That's where the mystery stuff started, because I saw that Hodges was all heated up and wanted to kid him along. So I told him we had some mighty good scouts working for us, and he said he knew our regular scouts and they couldn't tell a ballplayer from a torn ligament. Then he offered me fifty bucks if I'd tell him the truth and I just laughed at him. I said: 'A fella happened to be in Jackson one day and saw him work. But I won't tell you who the fella was, because you're too anxious to know.' Then he insisted on knowing what day the scout had been in Jackson. I said I'd tell him that if he'd tell me why he was so blame curious. So he gave me his end of it.

"It seems his brother, up in Ludington, had seen this kid play ball on the lots and had signed him right up for Hodges and taken him to Jackson, and of course, Hodges knew he had a world beater the minute he saw him. But he also knew he wasn't going to be able to keep him in Jackson, and, naturally he began to figure how he could get the most money for him. It was already August when the boy landed in Jackson; so there wasn't much chance of getting a big price last season. He decided to teach the kid what he didn't know about baseball and to keep him under cover till this year. Then everybody would be touting him and there'd be plenty of competition. Hodges could sell to the highest bidder.

"He had Waldron out practising every day, but wouldn't let him play in a game, and every player on the Jackson club had promised to keep the secret till this year. So Hodges wanted to find out from me which one of his players had broken the promise.

"Then I asked him if he was perfectly sure that Waldron hadn't played in a game, and he said he had gone in to hit for somebody just once. I asked him what date that was and he told me. It was the day Art had been in Jackson. So I said:

" 'There's your mystery solved. That's the day my scout saw him, and you'll have to give the scout a little credit for picking a star after seeing him make one base hit.'

"Then Hodges said:

" 'That makes it all the more a mystery. Because, in the first place, he batted under a fake name. And, in the second place, he didn't make a base hit. He popped out.'

"That's about all there is to it. You can ask Art how he picked the kid out for a star from seeing him pop out once. I've asked him myself, and he'd told me that he liked the way Waldron swung. Personally, I believe one of those Jackson boys got too gabby. But Art swears not."

"That *is* a story," I said gratefully. "An old outfielder who must know he's slipping recommends a busher after seeing him pop out once. And the busher jumps right in and gets his job."

I looked down the aisle toward the song birds. Art Graham, now a bench warmer, and young Waldron, whom he had touted and who was the cause of his being sent to the bench, were harmonizing at the tops of their strong and not too pleasant voices.

"And probably the strangest part of the story," I added, "is that Art doesn't seem to regret it. He and the kid appear to be the best of friends."

"Anybody who can sing is Art's friend," said Ryan.

I left him and went back to my seat to tear off my seven hundred words before we reached Springfield. I considered for a moment the advisability of asking Graham for an explanation of his wonderful bit of scouting, but decided to save that part of it for another day. I was in a hurry and, besides, Waldron was just teaching them a new "wallop," and it would have been folly for me to interrupt.

"It's on the word 'you,' " Waldron was saying. "I come down a tone; Lefty goes up a half tone, and Bill comes up two tones. Art just sings it like always. Now try her again," I heard him direct the song birds. They tried her again, making a worse noise than ever:

"I only know I love you;
Love me, and the world (the world) is mine (the world is mine)."

"No," said Waldron. "Lefty missed it. If you fellas knew music, I could teach it to you with the piano when we get to Boston. On the word 'love,' in the next to the last line, we hit a regular F chord. Bill's singing the low F in the bass and Lefty's hitting middle C in the baritone, and Art's on high F and I'm up to A. Then, on the word 'you,' I come down to G, and Art hits E, and Lefty goes up half a tone to C sharp, and Cole comes up from F to A in the bass. That makes a good wallop. It's a change from the F chord to the A chord. Now let's try her again," Waldron urged.

They tried her again:

"I only know I love you—"

"No, no!" said young Waldron. "Art and I were all right; but Bill came up too far, and Lefty never moved off that C. Half a tone up, Lefty. Now try her again."

We were an hour late into Springfield, and it was past six o'clock when we pulled out. I had filed my stuff, and when I came back in the car the concert was over for the time, and Art Graham was sitting alone.

"Where are your pals?" I asked.

"Gone to the diner," he replied.

"Aren't you going to eat?"

"No," he said, "I'm savin' up for the steamed clams." I took the seat beside him.

"I sent in a story about you," I said.

"Am I fired?" he asked.

"No, nothing like that."

"Well," he said, "you must be hard up when you can't find nothin' better to write about than a old has-been."

"Cap just told me who it was that found Waldron," said I.

"Oh, that," said Art. "I don't see no story in that."

"I thought it was quite a stunt," I said. "It isn't everybody that can pick out a second Cobb by just seeing him hit a fly ball."

Graham smiled.

"No," he replied, "they's few as smart as that."

"If you ever get through playing ball," I went on, "you oughtn't to have any trouble landing a job. Good scouts don't grow on trees."

"It looks like I'm pretty near through now," said Art, still smiling. "But you won't never catch me scoutin' for nobody. It's too lonesome a job."

I had passed up lunch to retain my seat in the card game; so I was hungry. Moreover, it was evident that Graham was not going to wax garrulous on the subject of his scouting ability. I left him and sought the diner. I found a vacant chair opposite Bill Cole.

"Try the minced ham," he advised, "but lay off'n the sparrow-grass. It's tougher'n a double-header in St. Louis."

"We're over an hour late," I said.

"You'll have to do a hurry-up on your story, won't you?" asked Bill. "Or did you write it already?"

"All written and on the way."

"Well, what did you tell 'em?" he inquired. "Did you tell 'em we had a pleasant trip, and Lenke lost his shirt in the poker game, and I'm goin' to pitch to-morrow, and the Boston club's heard about it and hope it'll rain?"

"No," I said. "I gave them a regular story tonight—about how Graham picked Waldron."

"Who give it to you?"

Ryan," I told him.

"Then you didn't get the real story," said Cole, "Ryan himself don't know the best part of it, and he ain't goin' to know it for a w'ile. He'll maybe find it out after Art's got the can, but not before. And I hope nothin' like that'll happen for twenty years. When it does happen, I want to be sent along with Art, 'cause I and him's been roomies now since 1911, and I wouldn't hardly know how to act with him off'n the club. He's a nut all right on the singin' stuff, and if he was gone I might get a chanct to give my voice a rest. But he's a pretty good guy, even if he is crazy."

"I'd like to hear the real story," I said.

"Sure you would," he answered, "and I'd like to tell it to you. I will tell it to you if you'll give me your promise not to spill it till Art's gone. Art told it to I and Lefty in the club-house at Cleveland pretty near a month ago, and the three of us and Waldron is the only ones that knows it. I figure I've did pretty well to keep it to myself this long, but it seems like I got to tell somebody."

"You can depend on me," I assured him, "not to say a word about it till Art's in Minneapolis, or wherever they're going to send him."

"I guess I can trust you," said Cole. "But if you cross me, I'll shoot my fast one up there in the press coop some day and knock your teeth loose."

"Shoot," said I.

"Well," said Cole, "I s'pose Ryan told you that Art fell for the kid after just seein' him pop out."

"Yes, and Ryan said he considered it a remarkable piece of scouting."

"It was all o' that. It'd of been remarkable enough if Art'd saw the bird pop out and then recommended him. But he didn't even see him pop out."

"What are you giving me?"

"The fac's," said Bill Cole. "Art not only didn't see him pop out, but he didn't even see him with a ball suit on. He wasn't never inside the Jackson ball park in his life."

"Waldron?"

"No. Art I'm talkin' about."

"Then somebody tipped him off," I said, quickly.

"No, sir. Nobody tipped him off, neither. He went to Jackson and spent the ev'nin' at his uncle's house, and Waldron was there. Him and Art was together the whole ev'nin'. But Art didn't even ask him if he could slide feet first. And then he come back to Detroit and got Ryan to draft him. But to give you the whole story, I'll have to go back a ways. We ain't nowheres near Worcester yet, so they's no hurry, except that Art'll prob'ly be sendin' for me pretty quick to come in and learn Waldron's lost chord.

"You wasn't with this club when we had Mike McCann. But you must of heard of him; outside his pitchin', I mean. He was on the stage a couple o' winters, and he had the swellest tenor voice I ever heard. I never seen no grand opera, but I'll bet this here C'ruso or McCormack or Gadski or none o' them had nothin' on him for a pure tenor. Every note as clear as a bell. You couldn't hardly keep your eyes dry when he'd tear off 'Silver Threads' or 'The River Shannon.'

"Well, when Art was still with the Washin'ton club yet, I and Lefty and Mike used to pal round together and onct or twict we'd hit up some harmony. I couldn't support a fam'ly o' Mormons with my voice, but it was better in them days than it is now. I used to carry the lead, and Lefty'd hit the baritone and Mike the tenor. We didn't have no bass. But most o' the time we let Mike do the singin' alone, 'cause he had us outclassed, and the other boys kept tellin' us to shut up and give 'em a treat. First it'd be 'Silver Threads' and then 'Jerusalem' and then 'My Wild Irish Rose' and this and that, whatever the boys ast him for. Jack Martin used to say he couldn't help a short pair if Mike wasn't singin'.

"Finally Ryan pulled off the trade with Griffith, and Graham come on our club. Then they wasn't no more solo work. They made a bass out o' me, and Art sung the lead, and Mike and Lefty took care o' the tenor and baritone. Art didn't care what the other boys wanted to hear. They could holler their heads off for Mike to sing a solo, but no sooner'd Mike start singin' than Art'd chime in with him and pretty soon we'd all four be goin' it. Art's a nut on singin', but he don't care nothin' about list'nin', not even to a canary. He'd rather harmonize than hit one past the outfielders with two on.

"At first we done all our serenadin' on the train. Art'd get us out o' bed early so's we could be through breakfast and back in the car in time to tear off a few before we got to wherever we was goin'.

"It got so's Art wouldn't leave us alone in the different towns we played at. We couldn't go to no show or nothin'. We had to stick in the hotel and sing, up in our room or Mike's. And then he went so nuts over it that he got Mike to come and room in the same house with him at home, and I and Lefty was supposed to help keep the neighbors awake every night. O' course we had mornin' practice w'ile we was home, and Art used to have us come to the park early and get in a little harmony before we went on the field. But Ryan finally nailed that. He says that when he ordered mornin' practice he meant baseball and not no minstrel show.

"Then Lefty, who wasn't married, goes and gets himself a girl. I met her a couple o' times, and she looked all right. Lefty might of married her if Art'd of left him alone. But nothin' doin'. We was home all through June onct, and instead o' comin' round nights to sing with us, Lefty'd take this here doll to one o' the parks or somewheres. Well, sir, Art was pretty near wild. He scouted round till he'd found out why Lefty'd quit us and then he tried pretty near everybody else on the club to see if they wasn't some one who could hit the baritone. They wasn't nobody. So the next time we went on the road, Art give Lefty a earful about what a sucker a man was to get married, and looks wasn't everything and the girl was prob'ly after Lefty's money and he wasn't bein' a good fella to break up the quartette and spoil our good times, and so on, and kept pesterin' and teasin' Lefty till he give the girl up. I'd of saw Art in the Texas League before I'd of shook a girl to please him, but you know these left-handers.

"Art had it all framed that we was goin' on the stage, the four of us, and he seen a vaudeville man in New York and got us booked for eight hundred a week—I don't know if it was one week or two. But he sprung it on me in September and says we could get solid bookin' from October to March; so I ast him what he thought my Missus would say when I told her I couldn't get enough o' bein' away from home from March to October so I was figurin' on travelin' the vaudeville circuit the other four or five months and makin' it unanimous? Art says I was tied to a woman's apron and all that stuff, but I give him the cold stare and he had to pass up that dandy little scheme.

"At that, I guess we could of got by on the stage all right. Mike was better than this here Waldron and I hadn't wore my voice out yet on the coachin' line, tellin' the boys to touch all the bases.

"They was about five or six songs that we could kill. 'Adeline' was our star piece. Remember where it comes in, 'Your fair face beams'? Mike used to go away up on 'fair.' Then they was 'The Old Millstream' and 'Put on Your Old Gray Bonnet.' I done some fancy work in that one. Then they was 'Down in Jungle Town' that we had pretty good. And then they was one that maybe you never heard. I don't know the name of it. It run somethin' like this."

Bill sottoed his voice so that I alone could hear the beautiful refrain:

" 'Years, years, I've waited years
Only to see you, just to call you 'dear.'

Come, come, I love but thee,
Come to your sweetheart's arms; come back to me.'

"That one had a lot o' wallops in it, and we didn't overlook none
o' them. The boys used to make us sing it six or seven times a night.
But 'Down in the Cornfield' was Art's favor-ight. They was a part in
that where I sung the lead down low and the other three done a
banjo stunt. Then they was 'Castle on the Nile' and 'Come Back to
Erin' and a whole lot more.

"Well, the four of us wasn't hardly ever separated for three years.
We was practisin' all the w'ile like as if we was goin' to play the big
time, and we never made a nickel off'n it. The only audience we had
was the ball players or the people travelin' on the same trains or
stoppin' at the same hotels, and they got it all for nothin'. But we
had a good time, 'specially Art.

"You know what a pitcher Mike was. He could go in there stone
cold and stick ten out o' twelve over that old plate with somethin'
on 'em. And he was the willin'est guy in the world. He pitched his
own game every third or fourth day, and between them games he
was warmin' up all the time to go in for somebody else. In 1911,
when we was up in the race for aw'ile, he pitched eight games out
o' twenty, along in September, and win seven o' them, and besides
that, he finished up five o' the twelve he didn't start. We didn't win
the pennant, and I've always figured that them three weeks killed
Mike.

"Anyway, he wasn't worth nothin' to the club the next year; but
they carried him along, hopin' he'd come back and show somethin'.
But he was pretty near through, and he knowed it. I knowed it, too,
and so did everybody else on the club, only Graham. Art never got
wise till the trainin' trip two years ago this last spring. Then he come
to me one day.

" 'Bill,' he says, 'I don't believe Mike's comin' back.'

" 'Well,' I says, 'you're gettin's so's they can't nobody hide nothin'
from you. Next thing you'll be findin' out that Sam Crawford can
hit.'

" 'Never mind the comical stuff,' he says. 'They ain't no joke about
this!'

" 'No,' I says, 'and I never said they was. They'll look a long w'ile
before they find another pitcher like Mike.'

" 'Pitcher my foot!' says Art. 'I don't care if they have to pitch the
bat boy. But when Mike goes, where'll our quartette be?'

" 'Well,' I says, 'do you get paid every first and fifteenth for singin' or for crownin' that old pill?'

" 'If you couldn't talk about money, you'd be deaf and dumb,' says Art.

" 'But you ain't playin' ball because it's fun, are you?'

" 'No,' he says, 'they ain't no fun for me in playin' ball. They's no fun doin' nothin' but harmonizin', and if Mike goes, I won't even have that.'

" 'I and you and Lefty can harmonize,' I says.

" 'It'd be swell stuff harmonizin' without no tenor,' says Art. 'It'd be like swingin' without no bat.'

"Well, he ast me did I think the club'd carry Mike through another season, and I told him they'd already carried him a year without him bein' no good to them, and I figured if he didn't show somethin' his first time out, they'd ask for waivers. Art kept broodin' and broodin' about it till they wasn't hardly no livin' with him. If he ast me onct he ast me a thousand times if I didn't think they might maybe hold onto Mike another season on account of all he'd did for 'em. I kept tellin' him I didn't think so; but that didn't satisfy him and he finally went to Ryan and ast him point blank.

" 'Are you goin' to keep McCann?' Art ast him.

" 'If he's goin' to do us any good, I am,' says Ryan. 'If he ain't, he'll have to look for another job.'

"After that, all through the trainin' trip, he was right on Mike's heels.

" 'How does the old souper feel?' he'd ask him.

" 'Great!' Mike'd say.

"Then Art'd watch him warm up, to see if he had anything on the ball.

" 'He's comin' fine,' he'd tell me. 'His curve broke to-day just as good as I ever seen it.'

"But that didn't fool me, or it didn't fool Mike neither. He could throw about four hooks and then he was through. And he could of hit you in the head with his fast one and you'd of thought you had a rash.

"One night, just before the season opened up, we was singin' on the train, and when we got through, Mike says:

" 'Well, boys, you better be lookin' for another C'ruso.'

" 'What are you talkin' about?' says Art.

" 'I'm talkin' about myself,' says Mike. 'I'll be up there in Minneapolis this summer, pitchin' onct a week and swappin' stories about the Civil War with Joe Cantillon.'

" 'You're crazy,' says Art. 'Your arm's as good as I ever seen it.'

" 'Then,' says Mike, 'you must of been playin' blindfolded all these years. This is just between us, 'cause Ryan'll find it out for himself; my arm's rotten, and I can't do nothin' to help it.'

"Then Art got sore as a boil.

" 'You're a yellow, quittin' dog,' he says. 'Just because you come round a little slow, you talk about Minneapolis. Why don't you resign off'n the club?'

" 'I might just as well,' Mike says, and left us.

"You'd of thought that Art would of gave up then, 'cause when a ball player admits he's slippin', you can bet your last nickel that he's through. Most o' them stalls along and tries to kid themself and everybody else long after they know they're gone. But Art kept talkin' like they was still some hope o' Mike comin' round, and when Ryan told us one night in St. Louis that he was goin' to give Mike his chanct, the next day, Art was as nervous as a bride goin' to get married. I wasn't nervous. I just felt sorry, 'cause I knowed the old boy was hopeless.

"Ryan had told him he was goin' to work if the weather suited him. Well, the day was perfect. So Mike went out to the park along about noon and took Jake with him to warm up. Jake told me afterwards that Mike was throwin', just easy like, from half-past twelve till the rest of us got there. He was tryin' to heat up the old souper and he couldn't of ast for a better break in the weather, but they wasn't enough sunshine in the world to make that old whip crack.

"Well, sir, you'd of thought to see Art that Mike was his son or his brother or somebody and just breakin' into the league. Art wasn't in the outfield practisin' more than two minutes. He come in and stood behind Mike w'ile he was warmin' up and kept tellin' how good he looked, but the only guy he was kiddin' was himself.

"Then the game starts and our club goes in and gets three runs.

" 'Pretty soft for you now, Mike,' says Art, on the bench. 'They can't score three off'n you in three years.'

"Say, it's lucky he ever got the side out in the first innin'. Everybody that come up hit one on the pick, but our infield pulled two o' the greatest plays I ever seen and they didn't score. In the second, we got three more, and I thought maybe the old bird was goin' to be lucky enough to scrape through.

"For four or five innin's, he got the grandest support that was ever gave a pitcher; but I'll swear that what he throwed up there didn't have no more on it than September Morning. Every time Art come to the bench, he says to Mike, 'Keep it up, old boy. You got more than you ever had.'

"Well, in the seventh, Mike still had 'em shut out, and we was six runs to the good. Then a couple o' the St. Louis boys hit 'em where they couldn't nobody reach 'em and they was two on and two out. Then somebody got a hold o' one and sent it on a line to the left o' second base. I forgot who it was now; but whoever it was, he was supposed to be a right field hitter, and Art was layin' over the other way for him. Art started with a crack o' the bat, and I never seen a man make a better try for a ball. He had it judged perfect; but Cobb or Speaker or none o' them couldn't of catched it. Art just managed to touch it by stretchin' to the limit. It went on to the fence and everybody come in. They didn't score no more in that innin'.

"Then Art come in from the field and what do you think he tried to pull?

" 'I don't know what was the matter with me on that fly ball,' he says. 'I ought to caught it in my pants pocket. But I didn't get started till it was right on top o' me.'

" 'You misjudged it, didn't you?' says Ryan.

" 'I certainly did,' says Art without crackin'.

" 'Well,' says Ryan, 'I wisht you'd misjudge all o' them that way. I never seen a better play on a ball.'

"So then Art knowed they wasn't no more use trying to alibi the old boy.

"Mike had a turn at bat and when he come back, Ryan ast him how he felt.

" 'I guess I can get six more o' them out,' he says.

"Well, they didn't score in the eighth, and when the ninth come Ryan sent I and Lefty out to warm up. We throwed a few w'ile our club was battin'; but when it come St. Louis' last chanct, we was too much interested in the ball game to know if we was throwin' or bakin' biscuits.

"The first guy hits a line drive, and somebody jumps a mile in the air and stabs it. The next fella fouled out, and they was only one more to get. And then what do you think come off? Whoever it was hittin' lifted a fly ball to centre field. Art didn't have to move out of his tracks. I've saw him catch a hundred just like it behind his back.

But you know what he was thinkin'. He was sayin' to himself, 'If I nail this one, we're li'ble to keep our tenor singer a w'ile longer.' And he dropped it.

"Then they was five base hits that sounded like the fourth o' July, and they come so fast that Ryan didn't have time to send for I or Lefty. Anyway, I guess he thought he might as well leave Mike in there and take it.

"They wasn't no singin' in the clubhouse after that game. I and Lefty always let the others start it. Mike, o' course, didn't feel like no jubilee, and Art was so busy tryin' not to let nobody see him cry that he kept his head clear down in his socks. Finally he beat it for town all alone, and we didn't see nothin' of him till after supper. Then he got us together and we all went up to Mike's room.

" 'I want to try this here "Old Girl o' Mine," ' he says.

" 'Better sing our old stuff,' says Mike. 'This looks like the last time.'

"Then Art choked up and it was ten minutes before he could get goin'. We sung everything we knowed, and it was two o'clock in the mornin' before Art had enough. Ryan come in after midnight and set a w'ile listenin', but he didn't chase us to bed. He knowed better'n any of us that it was a farewell. When I and Art was startin' for our room, Art turned to Mike and says:

" 'Old boy, I'd of gave every nickel I ever owned to of caught that fly ball.'

" 'I know you would,' Mike says, 'and I know what made you drop it. But don't worry about it, 'cause it was just a question o' time, and if I'd of got away with that game, they'd of murdered some o' the infielders next time I started.'

"Mike was sent home the next day, and we didn't see him again. He was shipped to Minneapolis before we got back. And the rest o' the season I might as well of lived in a cemetery w'ile we was on the road. Art was so bad that I thought onct or twict I'd have to change roomies. Onct in a w'ile he'd start hummin' and then he'd break off short and growl at me. He tried out two or three o' the other boys on the club to see if he couldn't find a new tenor singer, but nothin' doin'. One night he made Lefty try the tenor. Well, Lefty's voice is bad enough down low. When he gets up about so high, you think you're in the stockyards.

"And Art had a rotten year in baseball, too. The old boy's still pretty near as good on a fly ball as anybody in the league; but you ought to saw him before his legs begin to give out. He could cover as much ground as Speaker and he was just as sure. But the year Mike left us, he missed pretty near half as many as he got. He told me one night, he says:

" 'Do you know, Bill, I stand out there and pray that nobody'll hit one to me. Every time I see one comin' I think o' that one I dropped for Mike in St. Louis, and then I'm just as li'ble to have it come down on my bean as in my glove.'

" 'You're crazy,' I says, 'to let a thing like that make a bum out o' you.'

"But he kept on droppin' fly balls till Ryan was talkin' about settin' him on the bench where it wouldn't hurt nothin' if his nerve give out. But Ryan didn't have nobody else to play out there, so Art held on.

"He come back the next spring—that's a year ago—feelin' more cheerful and like himself than I'd saw him for a long w'ile. And they was a kid named Burton tryin' out for second base that could sing pretty near as good as Mike. It didn't take Art more'n a day to find this out, and every mornin' and night for a few days the four of us would be together, hittin' her up. But the kid didn't have no more idea o' how to play the bag than Charley Chaplin. Art seen in a minute that he couldn't never beat Cragin out of his job, so what does he do but take him out and try and learn him to play the outfield. He wasn't no worse there than at second base; he couldn't of been. But before he'd practised out there three days they was bruises all over his head and shoulders where fly balls had hit him. Well, the kid wasn't with us long enough to see the first exhibition game, and after he'd went, Art was Old Man Grump again.

" 'What's the matter with you?' I says to him. 'You was all smiles the day we reported and now you could easy pass for a undertaker.'

" 'Well,' he says, 'I had a great winter, singin' all the w'ile. We got a good quartette down home and I never enjoyed myself as much in my life. And I kind o' had a hunch that I was goin' to be lucky and find somebody amongst the bushers that could hit up the old tenor.'

" 'Your hunch was right,' I says. 'That Burton kid was as good a tenor as you'd want.'

" 'Yes,' he says, 'and my hunch could of played ball just as good as him.'

"Well, sir, if you didn't never room with a corpse, you don't know what a whale of a time I had all last season. About the middle of August he was at his worst.

" 'Bill,' he says, 'I'm goin' to leave this old baseball flat on its back if somethin' don't happen. I can't stand these here lonesome nights. I ain't like the rest o' the boys that can go and set all ev'nin' at a pitcher show or hang round them Dutch gardens. I got to be singin' or I am mis'rable.'

" 'Go ahead and sing,' says I. 'I'll try and keep the cops back.'

" 'No,' he says, 'I don't want to sing alone. I want to harmonize and we can't do that 'cause we ain't got no tenor.'

"I don't know if you'll believe me or not, but sure as we're settin' here he went to Ryan one day in Philly and tried to get him to make a trade for Harper.

" 'What do I want him for?' says Ryan.

" 'I hear he ain't satisfied,' says Art.

" 'I ain't runnin' no ball players' benefit association,' says Ryan, and Art had to give it up. But he didn't want Harper on the club for no other reason than because he's a tenor singer!

"And then come that Dee-troit trip, and Art got permission to go to Jackson. He says he intended to drop in at the ball park, but his uncle wanted to borry some money off'n him on a farm, so Art had to drive out and see the farm. Then, that night, this here Waldron was up to call on Art's cousin—a swell doll, Art tells me. And Waldron set down to the py-ana and begin to sing and play. Then it was all off; they wasn't no spoonin' in the parlor that night. Art wouldn't leave the kid get off'n the py-ana stool long enough to even find out if the girl was a blonde or a brunette.

"O' course Art knowed the boy was with the Jackson club as soon as they was interduced, 'cause Art's uncle says somethin' about the both o' them bein' ball players, and so on. But Art swears he never thought o' recommendin' him till the kid got up to go home. Then he ast him what position did he play and found out all about him, only o' course Waldron didn't tell him how good he was 'cause he didn't know himself.

"So Art ast him would he like a trial in the big show, and the kid says he would. Then Art says maybe the kid would hear from him, and then Waldron left and Art went to bed, and he says he stayed awake all night plannin' the thing out and wonderin' would he have the nerve to pull it off. You see he thought that if Ryan fell for it, Waldron'd join us as soon as his season was over and then Ryan'd see he wasn't no good; but he'd prob'ly keep him till we was through for the year, and Art could alibi himself some way, say he'd got the wrong name or somethin'. All he wanted he says, was to have the kid along the last month or six weeks, so's we could harmonize. A nut? I guess not.

"Well, as you know, Waldron got sick and didn't report, and when Art seen him on the train this spring he couldn't hardly believe his eyes. He thought surely the kid would of been canned durin' the winter without no trial.

"Here's another hot one. When we went out the first day for practice, Art takes the kid off in a corner and tries to learn him enough baseball so's he won't show himself up and get sent away somewheres before we had a little benefit from his singin'. Can you imagine that? Tryin' to learn this kid baseball, when he was born with a slidin' pad on.

"You know the rest of it. They wasn't never no question about Waldron makin' good. It's just like everybody says—he's the best natural ball player that's broke in since Cobb. They ain't nothin' he can't do. But it *is* a funny thing that Art's job should be the one he'd get. I spoke about that to Art when he give me the story.

" 'Well,' he says, 'I can't expect everything to break right. I figure I'm lucky to of picked a guy that's good enough to hang on. I'm in stronger with Ryan right now, and with the old man, too, than when I was out there playin' every day. Besides, the bench is a pretty good place to watch the game from. And this club won't be shy a tenor singer for nine years.'

" 'No,' I says, 'but they'll be shy a lead and a baritone and a bass before I and you and Lefty is much older.'

" 'What of it?' he says. 'We'll look up old Mike and all go somewheres and live together.' "

We were nearing Worcester. Bill Cole and I arose from our table and started back toward our car. In the first vestibule we encountered Buck, the trainer.

"Mr. Graham's been lookin' all over for you, Mr. Cole," he said.

"I've been rehearsin' my part," said Bill.

We found Art Graham, Lefty, and young Waldron in Art's seat. The kid was talking.

"Lefty missed it again. If you fellas knew music, I could teach it

to you on the piano when we get to Boston. Lefty, on the word
'love,' in the next to the last line, you're on middle C. Then, on the
word 'you,' you slide up half a tone. That'd ought to be a snap, but
you don't get it. I'm on high A and come down to G and Bill's on
low F and comes up to A. Art just sings the regular two notes, F
and E. It's a change from the F chord to the A chord. It makes a
dandy wallop and it ought to be a—"

"Here's Bill now," interrupted Lefty, as he caught sight of Cole.

Art Graham treated his roommate to a cold stare.

"Where the h—l have you been?" he said angrily.

"Lookin' for the lost chord," said Bill.

"Set down here and learn this," growled Art. "We won't never get
it if we don't work."

"Yes, let's tackle her again," said Waldron. "Bill comes up two full
tones, from F to A. Lefty goes up half a tone, Art sings just like
always, and I come down a tone. Now try her again."

Two years ago it was that Bill Cole told me that story. Two weeks
ago Art Graham boarded the evening train on one of the many roads
that lead to Minneapolis.

The day Art was let out, I cornered Ryan in the club-house after
the others had dressed and gone home.

"Did you ever know," I asked, "That Art recommended Waldron
without having seen him in a ball suit?"

"I told you long ago how Art picked Waldron," he said.

"Yes," said I, "but you didn't have the right story."

So I gave it to him.

"You newspaper fellas," he said when I had done, "are the biggest
suckers in the world. Now I've never given you a bad steer in my
life. But you don't believe what I tell you and you go and fall for
one of Bill Cole's hop dreams. Don't you know that he was the
biggest liar in baseball? He'd tell you that Walter Johnson was Jack's
father if he thought he could get away with it. And that bunk he
gave you about Waldron. Does it sound reasonable?"

"Just as reasonable," I replied, "as the stuff about Art's grabbing
him after seeing him pop out."

"I don't claim he did," said Ryan. "That's what Art told me. One
of those Jackson ball players could give you the real truth, only of
course he wouldn't, because if Hodges ever found it out he'd shoot
him full of holes. Art Graham's no fool. He isn't touting ball players
because they can sing tenor or alto or anything else."

Nevertheless, I believe Bill Cole; else I wouldn't print the story. And Ryan would believe, too, if he weren't in such a mood these days that he disagrees with everybody. For in spite of Waldron's wonderful work, and he is at his best right now, the club hasn't done nearly as well as when Art and Bill and Lefty were still with us.

There seems to be a lack of harmony.

THE POOR SIMP

◇

I

MY HEAD ain't so heavy with brains that I walk stooped over. But I do claim to have more sense than the most o' them that's gettin' by in this league, and when I get the can it won't be because I don't know what I'm doin' out there. Ask anybody in the business what kind of a ball player I am. Some o' them will say I'm pretty fair and some o' them may say I'm rotten; but they'll all say I'm smart.

I've made my share of errors and I've hit many a perpendicular home run in the pinch, but I never lost a game by peggin' to the wrong base or by not knowin' how many was out. They ain't many can claim a record like that without gettin' called on it.

Well, that record won't buy me no round steaks when I get through here, and when I think o' the things that's happened to me and the things that's happened to fellas that didn't hardly know which was right field, I feel like I'd been better off if I'd just been born from my neck down.

Look at Jack Andrews! Bill Garwood, that batted right ahead of him, told me onct that the calves of his legs was all spike wounds, where Jack had slid into him from behind. It got so finally that every time Bill was on second and Jack on first Bill'd steal third to keep from bein' cut down. And Bill'd try to stretch every hit he made into a double so's to be two bases ahead of Jack. And now Jack's runnin' a halfway house outside of Chicago and it's a dull night when he don't take in a hundred bucks!

Then look at Red Burns!

Red never knowed how the game come out till he seen the paper next mornin', and they had to page him when it was his turn to hit.

The Saturday Evening Post, September 11, 1915; previously uncollected.

And now he's in the contractin' business in Cleveland and the hardest work he does is addin' up the month's profits.

And then look at me! S'posed to be one o' these here brainy ball players that never pulls a bone. Playin' my seventh year in fast company. Only gettin' forty-five hundred right now, because I never jumped a contract or spiked an umpire. And when they're through with me I can starve to death or pick up some nice, soft snap in a foundry.

I read the other day where some doctor says everybody should ought to have their appendixes and their tonsils and their adenoids cut out when they're still a baby yet. Well, them things didn't never give me no trouble. But I wisht I'd of had my brains removed before I ever learned to use 'em. They're the worst handicap a man can have in this business.

The less a guy knows, so much the sooner he can retire and live on his income.

You think I'm just talkin' against time? No, sir; you're listenin' to the truth now. And if you don't believe me ask Carey. Ask him to tell you about Skull Scoville. Or if you ain't too sleepy I'll tell you about him myself.

II

IT TAKES Carey to spot these boobs, and Carey wasn't with us on the spring trip last year. If you'll remember he was coachin' a college team down in Ohio and got permission to report late. Skull was with us all the wile, but I was too busy gettin' myself in shape to pay much attention to the new ones. All as I noticed about him was that he done a lot of struttin' and acted like he was more anxious to look pretty than to make good.

But Carey hadn't been round more'n a day when he braced me about Skull.

"When did we sign Francis X. Bushman?" he says.

"That's Scoville," I told him. "Skull Scoville."

"Some jealous cat must of gave him that nickname," says Carey.

"It's what they called him last year in the Carolina League," I says.

"Is he goin' back there?" ast Carey.

"I haven't been watchin' him much," I says.

"I hope he sticks," says Carey. "All our club needs is looks."

"You don't care nothin' about his looks," I says. "You're scoutin' for somebody to pick on."

"Maybe you're right," says Carey. "I wisht I could stay with them college boys all year. A couple o' them fell for all the old junk I could remember. I run out o' stale stuff finally and was goin' to write to you."

"Thanks," I says.

"But this here Skull does look promisin'," says Carey, "and I guess we'll have to try him out."

So Carey went over to where the kid was warmin' up and started in on him. After a wile he come back.

"I guess I can't pick 'em," he says. "When they get waivers on me I'm goin' scoutin'—not for no ball club, but for some circus that's shy o' clowns."

"What did you pull on him?" I ast.

"Just a couple o' feelers," says Carey. "I ast him what league he come from and he says the Carolina League. I says: 'Oh, yes, Milwaukee won the pennant, didn't they?' 'No,' he says; 'Columbia.' 'Oh, yes,' I says. 'I got it mixed up with the Utah League, where the women manages the teams.' 'Where's that league at?' he says. 'The Utah League?' I says. 'You take a westbound Hodiamont car in St. Louis and transfer twict, and then walk a block down to the wharf and get on the steamer goin' to Michigan City, only you get off when they come to Shreveport, and you can see it from there.' "

"You're goin' to have a good season," I says.

"No, it can't last," says Carey. "Some day Cap'll stick him in there and then it'll be back to the Carolina you love."

But Carey had it doped wrong. Cap give Skull a chance the second serious with the Cardinals, up home, and he got by nice. He was a little wild, but it helped him, because his fast one was fast enough to have 'em scared. They was swingin' with one foot in the bucket. Bill handled him good and Cap was tickled to death with his showin'.

"What do you think of him?" Cap ast Carey.

"Best young pitcher I've looked at in a long wile," says Carey. "You'll make a big mistake if you leave him go."

"I ain't goin' to leave him go," says Cap.

"You'd be a sucker if you did," says Carey. "But if I was you I wouldn't work him too of'en for a wile. He's nothin' but a kid and you ought to give him time to get his bearin's."

You see Carey was afraid that Skull wouldn't look as good the next time out, and he was crazy to have him stick on the club so's we could enjoy him. They wasn't no need of him bein' afraid, though, because Skull kept right on mowin' 'em down. He had everything but a noodle, and a man don't need to know nothin' about pitchin' with Bill behind the bat.

III

IT COME along May and we was goin' East. Brooklyn was the first place we was scheduled and we was leavin' home on the five-thirty, right after a game.

Well, the first thing Carey done when we got on the train was to tell the dinge to make up two berths. Then he took off his coat and collar like he was gettin' ready to undress. Some o' the boys went right into the diner and Skull was goin' to follow 'em when Carey nailed him.

"Where are you goin', kid?" he says.

"To get my supper," says Skull.

"Take a tip from me and stay where you are," says Carey. "Them other fellas ain't goin' to have nothin' to eat. They're tryin' to stall you."

"What's the idear?" says Skull.

"It's old stuff," says Carey, "but I'll explain it to you. This car ain't only got twelve lowers and they's twenty-four of us on the trip. That means they can't only twelve of us have lowers and the rest gets uppers. But the first twelve in bed gets the lowers."

"Yes," says Skull, "but the secretary give me a piece o' paper that says I'm to have a lower."

"Well," says Carey, "can you knock somebody out o' bed with that piece of paper? I'm tellin' you, kid. The paper don't make no difference; it's the fellas that gets there first."

"Are you goin' to bed yourself?" says Skull.

"You bet I am," says Carey.

"But you won't get no supper," says Skull.

"Supper!" says Carey. "I'd rather go without twenty suppers than ride in a upper through them Indiana mountains. These other birds is tryin' to put somethin' over. They'll wait till the dinge gets a couple o' berths made up and then they'll race fer 'em. He's makin' up two right now and you can bet that one is goin' to be mine."

Pretty soon Skull was peelin' his coat.

"Keep some loose change under your pillow," says Carey. "You're liable to be awake when we go through Fall River and you can send the porter out for a sandwich."

Well, Carey hid behind the curtains of his berth and waited till Skull was all set for the night. Then he put his collar and coat back on and come into the diner and told us about it. Only o' course he didn't tell Cap.

I was back in our car when Cap come in. He seen the two berths made up and got curious. First he peeked into the one Carey's been settin' in and they wasn't nobody there. Then he looked in at Skull.

"What's the matter?" he says. "Sick?"

"No, I ain't sick," says Skull.

"Been drinkin' somethin'?" says Cap.

"No," says Skull.

"Well, says Cap, "you go to bed nights after this and you won't be all in in the middle o' the afternoon."

I snuck down to Skull's berth.

"Just lay low in there," I says. "He was tryin' to get you out because he wants that berth. It's the best spot in the car—right over the front wheels. You hold on to it."

Along about nine o'clock all the berths was made up but one, the seat where the boys was playin' cards. I and Carey was up in the buffet car, but Smitty told us what come off.

Skull stuck his head out between the curtains and seen the card game. Smitty seen him lookin'.

"Ain't you goin' to bed?" says Skull.

"We can't," says Smitty. "All the lowers is gone."

"I'll set up a wile if you want to lay here," says Skull.

"Off o' that noise!" says Smitty. "Cap would fine us a hundred apiece if he catched us tradin' berths."

So Skull laid back, but pretty soon he peeked out again and ast for the porter.

"He got sore and quit at South Bend," says Smitty.

"Have we came to Fall River yet?" ast Skull.

"No, and we ain't goin' to," says Smitty.

"Why not?" says Skull.

"They's a big storm there," says Smitty. "So we're goin' round the other way, through Evanston."

"Can a man get a sandwich there?"

"Not a sandwich," says Smitty. "But they's a old lady meets this train every night with a basket o' fried chicken and mashed potatoes—four bits a throw."

"What time do we get to Evanston?"

"Can't tell; it ain't on the regular schedule," says Smitty. "But you'll know when we're pullin' in—the engine'll give one long whistle."

"They done that a wile ago," says Skull.

"Yes," says Smitty. "The engineer thought it was Evanston, but it wasn't. His mistake."

Smitty come up afterward and joined us in the buffet car. We was all back and undressin' when we slowed up for Toledo. Carey spoke up loud.

"This must be Evanston," he says.

Skull popped out of his berth.

"Where'll I find that woman?" he says to Smitty.

"Up at the head end," says Smitty. "She's the fireman's mother-in-law."

Skull started up the aisle.

"Here," I says, "you can't go callin' in your nightgown."

"You won't have time to dress," says Smitty. "We're only here two minutes."

"You better forget eatin'," says Carey. "I got hungry at Elkhart and wile I was scoutin' I lost my berth."

Skull turned to me.

"Go out and find her for me, will you?" he says. "Get two orders, one for you and one for me, and I'll pay you for the both."

"I ain't hungry," I says. "I had a pretty good dinner—soup and lake trout and a porterhouse with mushrooms and hashed brown potatoes and poached eggs and salad and apple pie and coffee."

"I'll go out for you," says Carey; "but if I get left you'll have to pay my fare from here to New York."

So Carey went out in the vestibule and stalled round till the train started up again. Then he come back, pantin' like he'd ran a mile.

"That's fine luck!" he says. "She'd just gave me the stuff when the train began to pull out. If I hadn't ran clear back here I'd of got left; they wasn't no other door open. And wile I was runnin' I dropped your supper."

Well I don't know how much more sleep Skull got that night, but I'll bet he was No. 1 in the diner next mornin'. And I'll bet when the chef seen the order he wondered where Jess Willard got on at.

IV

IT RAINED the first two days we was East. The sun was out the third mornin' and I and Carey was standin' in front o' the hotel when Skull showed up.

"Swell day," he says.

"Yes," says Carey, "and you know what it means, don't you? It means we'll have to beat it for Brooklyn as soon as we digest our breakfast. Three games."

"Three games," says Skull. "They won't play 'em all to-day, will they?"

"They're liable to," says Carey. "You can't never tell about Brooklyn."

"I ain't had no breakfast yet," says Skull.

"You better hurry it up, then," says Carey. "We was just goin' to start."

"Wait for me, will you?" says Skull.

"Not a chancet," says Carey. "I got to be there early to help direct the practice."

"You'll have to go alone," I says. "All the rest o' the boys will be gone before you're through your breakfast."

"How do I get there?" says Skull.

"They'll be a taxi to take you," says Carey. "You just come out here and look round and when you see a driver lookin' at you, hop in his car and tell him where you want to go. The club'll settle for it."

Well, as soon as Skull had went in to breakfast, Carey tipped off the rest o' the gang to keep out o' sight for a wile. I and him went over in the park acrost the street and watched for Skull to come out. Finally he come and they was two taxis standin' there. He hopped into the nearest one, told the driver to take him to the Brooklyn ball park, and off they went. It wasn't much of a trip—only from Eighty-first and Columbus to hellangone.

I s'pose he landed there about ten or ten-thirty. When we come, at a quarter to two, he was out in a suit, practicin' with the Brooklyn bunch.

Robbie seen us and came over.

"What are you fellas pullin'?" he says. "Tryin' to get our signs? This bird's been here all day; landed in a taxi this mornin'. And he had a big brawl with the chauffeur about who was goin' to settle.

Finally the chauffeur said he'd have him pinched and then the guy come acrost. But he told me that your club was payin' for the rig and he'd collect back from your secretary. Then he ast me if we was goin' to play three games to-day and I says, No, the first two had been called off. So he's been out monkeyin' with my crowd ever since. I thought at first he was lit up, but afterward I seen he wasn't."

"We was tryin' to do you a favor," says Carey. "A fella that's managin' a club in Brooklyn deserves a treat oncet in a wile. We're doin' the best we can for you, and we'll call it square if you don't pitch Rucker against us."

"But what's this bird's name?" says Robbie.

"That's Scoville," I says, "the boy that's been doin' all our winnin'."

"I'm too old to be kidded," says Robbie. "That fella's too handsome to be a good pitcher."

"If you think he can't pitch, you ain't too old to make a mistake," I says.

"It's a part of his system," says Carey, "to visit all mornin' with the club he's goin' to work against. He figures he'll do better if he knows the batters."

Well, sir, Skull pitched the game and Rucker pitched against him. Rucker outpitched him about two to one, but Skull copped.

"What do you think o' the visitin' system?" I says to Robbie, goin' out.

But he didn't have no comeback.

I and Carey and Skull rode back to the hotel together.

"Too bad you went over this mornin' for nothin'," says Carey. "As soon as we got there and found out they wasn't only goin' to play one game, we called you up to tell you about it, but you'd already left."

"I didn't go over for nothin'," says Skull. "It was eight dollars and seventy-five cents. But o' course the club'll give it back to me."

Carey seen where he was liable to get into trouble.

"Don't say nothin' to them about it," he says. "I'll go to the front for you. I know the sec. better'n you do and I can handle him."

So after supper, Carey found Skull again and broke the news to him.

"I seen the sec.," he says, "but they was nothin' doin'. If you'll remember, two taxis was settin' out there when you got ready to go, and you took the wrong one. The other one was already paid for. So you'll have to stand for it. That's what you get for bein' with a cheap club."

Skull swallowed his medicine without a whimper. But after that you couldn't get him into a taxi, not if he seen you pay for it in advance.

V

THE MORNIN' O' the first day o' the New York serious he set with us at breakfast.

"You want to get up to the Polo Grounds early," says Carey. "Maybe you'll see part o' the polo game."

"Are you fellas goin' early?" he says.

"No," says Carey, "we've saw polo played already and they won't let a man in twicet. They're afraid he'd learn the secrets o' the game."

"How do you get there without goin' in no taxi?" ast Skull.

I guess I already told you where we was stoppin'—Eighty-first and Columbus. I was just goin' to tell him to jump on the Elevated and stay on to the end o' the line, but Carey flagged me.

"Go out here on the corner," he says, "and take a car goin' south. If the motorman don't make no mistake, it'll keep goin' till it gets way down to the Battery—that's where the pitchers and catchers all starts from. But if you don't see no pitchers and catchers that you know, ask a policeman where the Sixth-Avenue Elevated is, and then get on a Harlem train. Ride forward and hold on round the curves. Set near a window if you can, only don't catch cold in your arm. Better be readin' a paper, if you can find one in the train; then they won't no girls talk to you. They's a couple o' girls here in New York that'd pick your pockets if they got a chancet. Your looks wouldn't save you. And get off when you get to the Polo Grounds."

"How'll I know when I'm there?" ast Skull.

"You'll hear a lot o' yellin'," says Carey, "the Giants practicin' what they're goin' to say to Klem."

Skull got lost somewheres, 'way down town; he couldn't tell us just where. It was afternoon when he finally got to the Polo Grounds, and o' course the polo game was all over.

"You seen the town, though, didn't you?" says Carey.

"What town?" says Skull.

"Ishpeming," says Carey.

"No," says Skull, "I was right here in New York all the wile."

He made earlier starts the next two mornin's, but he never did

manage to get there in time for polo. He was to pitch the third game
and he was restin' in the club house when I and Carey come in.

"You work to-day, don't you?" says Carey.

"Yes," he says.

"I got a message for you from Cap," says Carey. "He had to go
back to the hotel after the bag o' close decisions, and he wanted me
to be sure and tell you to have a long talk with McGraw before the
game."

"What should I talk to him about?" says Skull.

"Ask him a lot o' questions," says Carey. "He's a grand fella for a
young pitcher to talk to. He'll help you a lot. Ask him what his men
can hit and what they can't hit, and who's goin' to work for them.
Ask him anything you can think of, and try and remember everything
he tells you."

Skull got right up and went out to look for McGraw. When we
was dressed and come on the field, he was over by their bench,
obeyin' instructions. I don't know what Mac thought of him; probably
didn't think much of anything. Mac's saw so many nuts that they
don't excite him no more.

Pretty soon Skull come struttin' back to where we was.

"What'd you learn?" I ast him.

"He told me Mathewson or Marquard or Tesreau was goin' to
pitch," says Skull. "Then I ast him what his men could hit and he
says they can't hit nothin'. So I ast him what they couldn't hit and
he says everythin'. Then he ast me what I done for my complexion
and I told him I didn't do nothin' for it. And I couldn't think o'
nothin' more to ask him, so I come away."

Well, after a wile, Cap showed up and Carey stuck round to change
the subject if Skull begun tellin' about his interview with McGraw.
They wasn't nothin' said till it was time for their fieldin' practice.

"You work, Scoville," says Cap.

"All right," says Skull.

"Well, warm up with somebody," says Cap.

"I won't need much warmin' up," says Skull.

"Why not?" says Cap.

"These fellas can't hit nothin'," says Skull.

"Who told you so?" ast Cap.

"McGraw," says Skull. "He's their manager."

"Is he?" says Cap. "I thought it was George Cohan."

"No," says Skull. "It's McGraw."

"When was you talkin' with him?" ast Cap.

Then Carey horned in. "Mac was kiddin' you," he says. "He's got a good hittin' club."

"You bet he has!" says Cap. "You get that other idear out o' your head."

"What would he kid me for?" says Skull.

"Get out there and warm up!" says Cap. "McGraw's got three of 'em doin' it."

"Yes," says Skull. "He's goin' to work Mathewson or Marquard or Tesreau."

"I don't see how you can guess so good," says Cap.

"No," says Skull. "It's one o' them three."

Well, McGraw'd either been kiddin' him or he was mistaken about his own ball club. Skull didn't know which. But he knowed before he went to the shower that they could hit.

VI

SKULL PITCHED a one-hit game over in Philly. But he wasn't in there a whole innin'. He pitched to six men and the other five got bases on balls.

He went better up in Boston. He had two men out before Cap yanked him.

"What time can you get a train for Carolina?" says Carey.

"You goin' down there?" ast Skull.

"No," says Carey. "I thought maybe you was goin'."

"Oh, no," says Skull. "I'm gettin' more money up here."

"Did you get your pockets picked in New York?" says Carey.

"I guess not," says Skull.

"Just plain lost it, huh?" says Carey.

"Lost what?" asts Skull.

"Your control," says Carey.

"What's that?" says Skull.

"You had swell control in New York," says Carey. "You was hittin' their bats right in the middle. But the way you've went the last two games, you've got us all guessin'. We don't know whether you're goin' to hit the coacher at third base or kill a reporter. Pretty soon you'll have the field umpire wearin' a mask and protector. Is your arm sore?"

"No," says Skull.

"I didn't think it could be," says Carey, "on account o' the distance you get. But if your arm ain't sore, what's the matter?"

"Matter with who?" says Skull.

"You," says Carey. "You don't think the umpire's missin' 'em all, do you?"

"I'm wild," says Skull.

"Oh, that's it!" says Carey. "I've been puzzlin' my brains to find out what it was. But I see now; you're wild. And what do you s'pose makes you wild?"

"I can't pitch where I'm aimin'," says Skull. "I can't pitch no strikes. I keep givin' bases on balls."

"Funny I didn't think of that," says Carey. "I knowed they was somethin' the matter, but I couldn't put my finger right on it. I'll tell Cap and maybe we can get them to enlarge the plate."

"They wouldn't do that, would they?" says Skull.

"Well," says Carey, "they probably wouldn't in most o' the towns. But they can't stop us from doin' it on our own grounds. It's our own plate there, and I guess we can have any size we want to."

"But if I kept pitchin' too high or too low, the size o' the plate wouldn't make no difference," says Skull.

When we was through at Boston we made the cute little jump to St. Louis, and Carey was ridin' him all the way.

"This line," he told him, "is the one the James Boys works on. You see one o' the Jameses pitches for Boston and another pitches for St. Louis in the other league. And the ones that ain't ball players works back and forth between the two towns. Somebody has to set up all night and keep watch. I've been picked to set up the first night because I can shoot so good. To-morrow mornin' we'll draw lots to see who sets up to-morrow night. But if you got somethin' you don't want to lose you better sleep with one eye open and keep your suitcase right in the berth with you. O' course it's too late for 'em to steal your control, but they might get your fast ball and then you wouldn't have nothin' but your complexion."

"Oh, yes, I would," says Skull. "I got a little money and a watch and some clo'es."

"Shut up!" says Carey. "Don't be boastin' o' what you got. Maybe one o' them Jameses is right in this car now. You can't never tell where they're hidin'."

Well, the next mornin' we all ast Carey what kind of night he had and did he see anything suspicious, and so forth. He told us he had one bad scare. Somebody come through the car with a mask on. But as soon as he seen the mask he knowed it wasn't one o' the James Boys, because they wasn't none of them catchers.

"Who was it?" I says.

"Some society fella," he says, "goin' to the masquerade ball up in the day coach."

We drawed lots right after we was through breakfast. They was supposed to be all our names wrote on pieces o' paper and dropped into a hat. Then the fella that drawed his own name was to keep watch the second night.

Skull was the baby. All the rest of us drawed his name, too, only o' course he didn't know that.

"Well," says Carey, "it looks like it's up to you. And you don't want to take it as a joke. Whether we get by or not depends on how you work. You'll have to take my gun; I'll show you how it handles. If you see some stranger come into the car, shoot! Don't throw a baseball at him or you might wound the engineer. You better set up in the washroom all night with the porter, and if he asks you to help him shine shoes you go ahead and help him. Some o' these here porters is in with the James Boys and if they get sore it's good night. And be sure and don't let the robbers get the first shot."

Skull tried to sleep a little durin' the day. But he was too nervous.

"Who's keepin' watch now?" he ast Carey.

"Nobody, in the daytime," says Carey. "They're afraid of bein' seen by scouts, because, as I say, one o' them's with the Braves and another with the Browns and the next one that gets caught might be hung or sent to the Carolina League."

Carey had to borry a gun off'n the conductor.

"I'll be sure it's empty before I leave the bird have it," he says. "He's dangerous enough with a baseball in his hand, let alone a loaded gat."

Well, sir, I wisht you'd saw the porter when Skull and the gun went on watch at eleven that night. We had to call him out and put him wise or he'd of dove off the train. He told us he never seen a guy as restless as Skull. All night long he was movin' round—out on the platform, then back in the washroom, then through to the other end o' the car and then out on the platform again. And jumpin' sideways at every noise.

"Nothin' doin', eh?" says Carey in the mornin'. Not a sign o' 'em?"

"Not a sign," says Skull.

"And ain't you sleepy?" says Carey.

"Yes, I am," says Skull. "I hope I don't have to work this afternoon."

"What if you do?" says Carey. "It won't keep you up more'n ten
minutes."

VII

SKULL DIDNT PITCH that afternoon. He didn't pitch the next
day neither, but he was in there tryin'. Rigler could of umpired with
his right arm cut off. They wasn't no strikes to call.

When he'd throwed fourteen without gettin' one clost, Cap took
him out.

"I'd leave you go through with it," says Cap, "only the public likes
to see some hittin'. Did you think just because this is a bad ball town
you couldn't pitch nothin' but bad balls?"

"I'm wild," says Skull. "I can't get 'em over."

"I'd of guessed it in a few more minutes," says Cap. "Did you ever
try pitchin' left-handed?"

"Left-handed?" says Skull. "Why, I wouldn't know where a ball
was goin' if I throwed it left-handed."

"Then you must be equally good with both hands," says Cap.

Waivers was ast on Skull before we left St. Louis.

"They's no use foolin' along with him," Cap told us. "He didn't
look like he'd ever get a man out, and even if his control come back
you couldn't never learn him nothin'."

"I knowed it," says Carey. "I knowed we'd never have him the
whole year."

"It's better for you this way," I says. "Your brains would be wore
out before fall."

We went back home and the third day we was there Cap told us
that everybody'd waived.

"The next thing's placin' him," he says. "The newspaper boys has
advertised him so good that every hick town in the country is wise
to him. If I can't make no deal within a couple o' weeks I'll leave
him go outright."

The two weeks was pretty near up when Carey put over his last
one on the poor simp. I and Carey was throwin' in front o' the stand
when a couple o' girls was showed into a box right clost to us. They

was in black from head to foot; pretty as a picture too. But their
clo'es was the kind that you don't see no city-broke dames wearin'
in a ball orchard.

"Come to town just for the day?" says Carey, but they didn't pay
no attention.

Carey come over to me.

"Uncle Zeke died and left 'em three hundred iron men," he says,
"and they're goin' to blow it all in one grand good time. I bet they'll
be dancin' in Dreamland to-night; they're dressed for it already."

"The blonde's a bearcat," I says.

"Yes," says Carey, "and you can figure the other one's the class o'
the pair. That's the way it always breaks."

Skull had been shaggin' in the outfield. Carey spotted him as he
was struttin' back to the bench, and it was all off.

"You lucky stiff!" says Carey.

"What do you mean?" says Skull.

"I guess you know what I mean," says Carey. "What did you come
in for?"

"I'm tired," says Skull.

"Oh, yes," says Carey. "I s'pose you didn't see them dolls lookin'
you over."

"What dolls?" ast Skull.

"Them two in the box," says Carey.

Skull give 'em the double-o.

"Who are they?" he says.

"You don't know who they are?" says Carey. "That's Lizzie Carnegie and her sister-in-law, and they's a movin' van out-side with
their pocketbooks in it."

"Well," says Skull, "that don't get me nothin'."

"Don't get you nothin' when the richest girl in the country wants
to meet you?" says Carey.

"How do you know she wants to meet me?" says Skull.

"Didn't she call me over and tell me?" says Carey. "She says: 'Who's
that handsome bird shaggin' fungoes in the outfield?' So I told her
who you was. Then she ast if you was married and I says you wasn't.
Then she ast how she could get to talk to you, and I told her I'd find
out if you was engaged after the game, and if you wasn't you'd
probably be glad to give her a minute's time. So all as you have to
do now is go over there and make the date."

"Which is Lizzie?" ast Skull.

"The one with the earrings," says Carey.

They both was wearin' 'em.

Well, sir, Skull started over toward the box.

"He's liable to get pinched," I says.

"If he does I'll fix it," says Carey.

Skull didn't get pinched. He got two nice smiles, and Cap had to send me over to drag him away when the game started. And I and Carey came out o' the club-house after the game just in time to see Skull and the pair o' them hikin' for the exit.

When we got to mornin' practice next day, Skull had been let out already.

"I told him he was free to sign wherever he wanted to go," says Cap. "I told him to get a catcher somewheres and practice till he could pitch one or two strikes per innin'. I told him maybe he could land in the Federal. He says he guessed he would try the Utah League, where the women manages the clubs. He says women almost always gen'ally took a fancy to him."

"Yes," says Carey, "most o' them likes a good-lookin' fella all the better if he's a little wild."

We didn't see no more o' Skull till we got in from Cincinnati, the day before the Fourth o' July. He was standin' in the station, holdin' two suit cases.

"Hello there, boy," says Carey. "Where are you headin'?"

"Just downstate a ways," he says.

"Joinin' some club?" says Carey.

"No," says Skull. "I'm goin' to get married."

"Good night!" says Carey. "And who's the defendant?"

"That there blond girl," says Skull. "The girl that was out to the park that day with the other girl. Only you had her name wrong. Her name's Conahan—Mary Conahan. And the other one ain't her sister-in-law, but just a friend o' her'n."

"I must of had 'em mixed up," says Carey.

"Yes," says Skull, "you mistook 'em for somebody else. But you had one thing right: She's got the old kale."

"A lot of it?" says Carey.

"A plenty," says Skull. "Her old man makes this here Silver Tip beer; maybe you've drank it already."

"And I s'pose you're goin' to drive a wagon," says Carey.

"No," says Skull. "The old man's been feelin' bad for the last year and I'm goin' to kind-a look after the business."

"And," I says, "I bet you know just as much about brewin' beer as you do about pitchin'."

"Oh, no," says Skull. "Nowheres near."

"But you pick things up quick," says Carey.

Skull's train was gettin' ready to start.

"Well," he says, "good luck to you, and tell the boys I hope they win the pennant."

"No chancet now," says Carey.

We went over to the gate with him.

"Where to?" says the guy. "Show your ticket!"

"By cracky, I forgot about a ticket."

"I s'pose you thought the secretary'd tend to that," says Carey.

"Too late now," I says. "You'll have to pay on the train."

"You won't have no trouble," says Carey. "They's lady conductors on this road."

We persuaded the gateman to leave him through.

"Now," says Carey, "let's I and you get good and drunk."

"Yes," I says; "but let's go to a place where they keep Silver Tip, so's to help out old Skull."

"Help him out!" says Carey. "We're the ones that need help—us smart Alecks!"

WHERE DO YOU GET
THAT NOISE?

◊

I

THE TRADE was pulled wile the Phillies was here first trip. Without knockin' nobody, the two fellas we give was worth about as much as a front foot on Main Street, Belgium. And the fella we got had went better this spring than any time since he broke in. So when the news o' the deal come out I says to Dode, I says:

"What's the matter with Pat—tradin' Hawley? What's he goin' to do with them two he's gettin'—make ticket takers out of 'em? What's the idear?"

"It does look like a bad swap for us," says Dode. "Hawley's worth six like them you're givin' us, and he ain't only twenty-seven years old."

"That's what I'm tellin' you," I says. "The deal looks like you was tryin' to help us out."

"We are," says Dode. "Didn't we just get through helpin' you out o' the first division?"

"Save that for the minstrels," I says.

"Give me the inside on this business: Is they somethin' the matter with him? The trade's made now already and it won't hurt you none to come clean. Didn't him and Pat get along?"

"Sure! Why not?" says Dode. "Did you ever see a guy that Pat couldn't get along with him?"

"Well then," says I, "what's the answer? Don't keep me in suspenders."

"I ain't sure myself," says Dode, "but I and Bobby was talkin' it

The Saturday Evening Post, October 23, 1915; previously uncollected.

over and we figured that Pat just plain got sick o' hearin' him talk."

"Feed that to the goldfish," I says. "If Pat couldn't stand conversation he wouldn't of never lasted this long."

"Conversation, yes," Dode says; "but it's a different thing when a bird makes an argument out of everything that's said. They wasn't a day passed but what Hawley just as good as called everybody on the club a liar. And it didn't make no difference whether you was talkin' to him or not. If I happened to be tellin' you that my sister was the champion chess player o' Peanut County, he'd horn right in and say she wasn't no such a thing; that So-and-So was the champion. And they wouldn't be no use to argue with him because you couldn't even get a draw. He'd say he was born in the county seat o' Peanut County and empired all the chess tournaments there. They wasn't no subject that he didn't know all about it better'n anybody else. They wasn't no town he wasn't born and brought up in. His mother or his old man is first cousins to everybody in the United States. He's been operated on for every disease in the hospital. And if he's did all he says he's did he'll be eight hundred and twenty-two years old next Halloween."

"They's lots o' fellas like that," I says.

"You think so?" says Dode. "You wait a wile. Next time I see you, if you don't say he's all alone in the Argue League I'll give you my bat."

"If he's that good," I says, "he'll be soup for Carey."

"He will at first, maybe," says Dode; "but Carey'll get sick of him, just like Pat and all the rest of us did."

II

I DIDN'T LOSE no time tellin' Carey about Dode's dope, and Carey didn't lose no time tryin' it out. It was the second day after Hawley joined us. It looked like rain, as usual, and we was stallin' in the clubhouse, thinkin' they'd maybe call it off before we had to dress.

"I see in some paper," says Carey, "where the heavy artillery fire over in Europe is what makes all this duck weather."

He didn't get no rise; so he wound up again.

"It seems like it must be somethin' that does it because they wasn't never no summer like this before," he says.

"What do you mean—no summer like this?" says Hawley.

"No summer with so much rain as they's been this summer," Carey says.

"Where do you get that stuff?" says Hawley. "This here summer's been dry, you might say."

"Yes," says Carey; "and you might say the Federals done well in Newark."

"I mean," says Hawley, "that this here summer's been dry compared to other summers."

"I s'pose," says Carey, "they wasn't never such a dry summer?"

"They's been lots of 'em," Hawley says. "They's been lots o' summers that was drier and they's been lots o' summers when they was more rain."

"Not in the last twenty years," says Carey.

"Yes, in the last twenty years too," says Hawley. "Nineteen years ago this summer made this here one look like a drought. It come up a storm the first day o' May and they wasn't a day from then till the first o' September when it didn't rain one time or another."

"You got some memory," says Carey—"goin' back nineteen years.'

"I guess I ought to remember it," says Hawley. "That was the first year my old man left me go to the ball games alone, and they wasn't no games in our town from April till Labor Day. They wasn't no games nowheres because the railroads was all washed out. We lived in Cleveland and my old man was caught in New York when the first o' the floods come and couldn't get back home for three months."

"Couldn't he hire a canoe nowheres?" says Carey.

"Him and some others was thinkin' about tryin' the trip on a raft," says Hawley, "but my old lady was scared to have him try it; so she wrote and told him to stay where he was."

"She was lucky to have a carrier pigeon to take him the letter," says Carey. "Or did you swim East with it?"

"Swim!" Hawley says. "Say, you wouldn't talk about swim if you'd saw the current in them floods!"

"I'm sorry I missed it," says Carey. "I was still over in Portugal yet that year."

"It dried up in time for the world serious," says Hawley.

"The world serious between who?" ast Carey.

"The clubs that won out in the two leagues," says Hawley.

"I didn't know they was two leagues in '96." says Carey. "Who did they give the pennants to— the clubs that was ahead when it begin to sprinkle?"

"Sprinkle!" says Hawley. "Say, you'd of called it a sprinkle if you'd saw it. Sprinkle! Say, I guess that was some sprinkle!"

"I guess it must of been some sprinkle!" says Carey. "It must of made this summer look like a sucker."

"No," says Hawley; "this summer's been pretty bad."

"But nowheres near like nineteen year ago," says Carey.

"Oh, I guess they's about the same rainfall every year," Hawley says. "But, still and all, we've had some mighty wet weather since the first o' May this year, and I wouldn't be su'prised if the heavy artillery fire in Europe had somethin' to do with it."

"That's ridic'lous," says Carey.

"Ridic'lous!" says Hawley. "Where do you get that stuff? Don't you know that rain can be started with dynamite? Well, then, why wouldn't all that shootin' affect the weather? They must be some explanation."

"Did you make him?" says Carey to me afterward. "He trimmed me both ways. Some day he'll single to right field and throw himself out at first base. I seen I was in for a lickin', so I hedged to get a draw, and the minute I joined his league he jumped to the outlaws. But after this I'm goin' to stick on one side of it. He goes better when he's usin' his own stuff."

III

IN BATTIN' PRACTICE the next day Carey hit one up against them boards in right center on a line.

"Good night!" says Smitty. "I bet that's the hardest wallop that was ever made on these grounds."

"I know I didn't never hit one harder here," says Carey. "I don't never hit good in this park. I'd rather be on the road all the wile. I hit better on the Polo Grounds than anywheres else. I s'pose it's on account o' the background."

"Where do you get that stuff?" says Hawley. "Everybody hits better in New York than they do here. Do you want to know why? Because it's a clean town, without no dirt and cinders blowin' in your eyes. This town's all smoke and dirt, and it ain't no wonder a man's handicapped. The fellas that's with clubs in clean towns has got it all over us. Look at Detroit—one o' the cleanest towns in the country! And look how Cobb and Crawford hit! A man in one o' these smoke holes can't never pile up them big averages, or he can't last as long, neither."

"No," says Carey; "and that accounts for Wagner's rotten record in Pittsburgh."

Do you think that stopped him? Not him!

"Yes," he says; "and how much would Wagner of hit if he'd been playin' in New York or Detroit all the wile? He wouldn't never been below .500. And he'd of lasted just twicet as long."

"But on account of him landin' in Pittsburgh," says Carey, "the poor kid'll be all through already before he's fairly started yet. It's a crime and the grand jury should ought to take steps."

"Have you ever been to Washington?" says I.

"Have I ever been to Washington?" says Hawley. "Say, I know Washington like a book. My old man's brother's a senator there in Congress. You must of heard o' Senator Hawley."

"Oh, yes," says Carey; "the fella that made the speech that time."

"That's the fella," says Hawley. "And a smart fella too. Him and Woodruff Wilson's just like brothers. They're always to each other's houses. That's where I met Wilson—was at Uncle Zeke's. We fanned together for a couple hours. You wouldn't never know he was the President. He don't let on like he was any better than I or you."

"He ain't as good as you; that's a pipe!" says Carey.

"Where does your cousin live?" says Smitty.

"Cousin Zeke's got the swellest apartment in Washington," says Hawley. "Right next to the Capitol, on Pennsylvania Street."

"I wisht I could live there," I says. "It's the best town in the country for my money. And it's the cleanest one too."

"No factories or smoke there," says Carey.

"I wonder how it comes," I says, "that most o' the fellas on the Washington Club, playin' in the cleanest town in the country most o' the wile, can't hardly foul a ball—let alone hit it."

"Maybe the silver dust from the mint gets in their eyes," says Carey.

"Where do you get that noise?" says Hawley. "The mint ain't nowheres near the ball orchard."

"Well then," I says, "how do you account for the club not hittin'?"

"Say," says Hawley, "it ain't no wonder they don't hit in that town. We played a exhibition game there last spring and we didn't hit, neither."

"Who pitched against you—Johnson?" I ast him.

"Yes; Johnson," says Hawley.

"But that don't explain why the Washington bunch can't hit," says Carey. "He ain't mean enough to turn round and pitch against his own club."

"They won't nobody hit in that town," says Hawley, "and I don't care if it's Johnson pitchin' or the mayor."

"What's the trouble?" I says.

"The heat gets 'em!" says Carey.

"No such a thing!" says Hawley. "That shows you don't know nothin' about it. It's the trees."

"The trees!" I says. "Do they play out in the woods or somewheres?"

"No," says Hawley. "If they did they'd be all right. Their ball park's just like any ball park; they ain't no trees in it. But they's trees all over the rest o' the town. It don't make no difference where you go, you're in the shade. And then, when you get to the ball park you're exposed to the sun all of a sudden and it blinds you."

"I should think it would affect their fieldin' too," says Carey.

"They wear goggles in the field," says Hawley.

"Do the infielders wear goggles?" ast Carey.

"No; but most o' the balls they got to handle comes on the ground. They don't have to look up for 'em," says Hawley.

"S'pose somebody hits a high fly ball that's comin' down right in the middle o' the diamond," says Carey. "Who gets it?"

"It ain't got," says Hawley. "They leave it go and it gen'ally almost always rolls foul."

"If I was Griffith," says Carey, "I'd get the Forestry Department to cut away the trees in some part o' town and then make all my ball players live there so's they'd get used to the sun."

"Or he might have a few big maples planted round the home plate some Arbor Day," I says.

"Yes," says Carey; "or he might trade Johnson to the Pittsburgh Federals for Oakes."

"He'd be a sucker to trade Johnson," says Hawley.

IV

WELL, WE PLAYED down in Cincy one Saturday to a crowd that might of all came out in one street car without nobody ridin' in the motorman's vest pocket. We was discussin' it that night at supper.

"It's no more'n natural," I says. "The home club's been goin' bad and you can't expect the whole population to fight for a look at 'em."

"Yes," says Carey; "but it ain't only here. It's everywheres. We didn't hardly draw our breath at St. Louis and the receipts o' that last double-header at home with Pittsburgh wouldn't buy enough shavin' soap to lather a gnat. All over the circuit it's the same way, and in the other leagues too. It's a off year, maybe; or maybe they's reasons for it that we ain't doped out."

"Well," I says, "the war's hurt business, for one thing, and people ain't got no money to spend on box seats. And then golf's gettin' better all the wile. A man'd naturally rather do some exercisin' himself than watch somebody else do it. Besides that, automobiles has got so cheap that pretty near everybody can buy 'em, and the people that owns 'em takes their friends out in the country instead o' comin' to the ball yard. And besides that," I says, "they's too much baseball and the people's sick of it."

Hawley come in and set down with us wile I was still talkin' yet.

"What's the argument?" he says.

"We was tryin' to figure out why we can't get a quorum out to the games no more," says Carey.

"Well," says Hawley, "you know the real reason, don't you?"

"No," says Carey; "but I bet we're goin' to hear it. I bet you'll say it's on account o' the Gulf Stream."

"Where do you get that noise?" says Hawley. "If you want to know the real reason, the war's the real reason."

"That's what I was sayin'," says I. "The war's hurt business and people ain't got no money to blow on baseball."

"That shows you don't know nothin' about it," says Hawley.

"Then I got you tied," I says, "because you just sprung the same thing yourself."

"No such a thing!" says Hawley. "You're talkin' about the war hurtin' business and I'm talkin' about the war hurtin' baseball."

"What's the difference?" I says.

"All the difference in the world," says Hawley. "If everybody was makin' twicet as much money durin' the war as they made before the war started yet, the baseball crowds wouldn't be no bigger than they have been."

"Come acrost with the answer," says Carey. "The strain's somethin' awful."

"Well, boys," says Hawley, "they ain't nobody in this country that ain't pullin' for one side or the other in this here war. Is that right or wrong?"

"Which do you say it is?" says Carey.

"I say it's right because I know it's right," says Hawley.

"Well then," says Carey, "don't ask us boobs."

"No matter what a man says about he bein' neutral," says Hawley, "you can bet that down in his heart he's either for the Dutchmen or the Alleys; I don't care if he's Woodruff Wilson or Bill Klem. We all got our favorites."

"Who's yours?" I says.

"Don't you tell!" says Carey. "It wouldn't be fair to the other side."

"I don't mind tellin'," says Hawley, "I'd be a fine stiff to pull for the Dutchman after all King George done for my old man."

"What did he do for him?" says Carey.

"Well, it's a long story," says Hawley.

"That's all right," says Carey. "They's only one game to-morrow."

"I'll give it to you some other time," Hawley says.

"I hope you don't forget it," says Carey.

"Forget it!" says Hawley. "When your old man's honored by the royalties you ain't liable to forget it."

"No," says Carey; "but you could try."

"Here!" I says. "I'm waitin' to find out how the war cuts down the attendance."

"I'm comin' to that," says Hawley. "When you figure it out they couldn't nothin' be simpler."

"It does sound simple, now it's been explained," says Carey.

"It ain't been explained to me," I says.

"You're in too big a hurry," Hawley says. "If you wouldn't interrupt a man all the wile you might learn somethin'. You admit they ain't nobody that's neutral. Well then, you can't expect people that's for the Alleys to come out to the ball park and pull for a club that's mostly Dutchmen, and you can't expect Dutchmen to patronize a club that's got a lot o' fellas with English and French names."

"Wait a minute!" says Carey. "I s'pose they ain't no Germans here in Cincinnati, is they?"

"Sure!" says Hawley. "The place is ran over with 'em."

"Then," says Carey, "why don't they break all records for attendace at this park, with Heine Groh and Fritz Mollwitz and Count Von Kolnitz and Wagner and Schneider and Herzog on the ball club?"

"Because they's others on the team that offsets 'em," says Hawley. "We'll say they's a Dutchman comes out to the game to holler for some o' them boys you mentioned. We'll say that Groh kicks a ground ball and leaves three runs score and puts the club behind. And then we'll say that Clarke comes up in the ninth innin' and wins the game for Cincinnati with a home run. That makes the Dutchman look like a rummy, don't it? Or we'll say Schneider starts to pitch a game and gets knocked out, and then Dale comes in and they can't foul him. Your German friend wishes he had of stayed home and washed part o' the dashhound."

"Yes," says Carey; "but wouldn't he want to come to the game again the next day in hopes he'd get his chancet to holler?"

"No," says Hawley; "because, whatever happened, they'd be somethin' about it he wouldn't like. If the Reds win the Alleys on the club'd feel just as good as the Dutchmen, and that'd make him sore. And if they lost he'd be glad on account o' the Alleys; but he'd feel sorry for the Germans."

"Then they's only one thing for Garry Herrmann to do," I says: "he should ought to trade off all his Alleys for Dutch."

"That'd help the attendance at home," says Hawley; "but when his club played in Boston who'd go out to see 'em?"

"Everybody that could borrow a brick," says Carey.

"Accordin' to your dope," I says, "they's only one kind of a club that'd draw everywheres, and that's a club that didn't have no Dutchmen or Alleys—neither one."

"That's the idear," says Hawley: "a club made up o' fellas from countries that ain't got nothin' to do with the war—Norwegians, Denmarks, Chinks, Mongrels and them fellas. A guy that had brains enough to sign up that kind of a club would make a barrel o' money."

"A guy'd have a whole lot o' trouble findin' that kind of a club," I says.

"He'd have a whole lot more trouble," says Carey, "findin' a club they could beat."

V

SMITTY USED TO GET the paper from his home town where his folks lived at, somewheres near Lansing, Michigan. One day he seen in it where his kid brother was goin' to enter for the state golf championship.

"He'll just about cop it too," says Smitty. "And he ain't only seventeen years old. He's been playin' round that Wolverine Country Club, in Lansing, and makin' all them birds like it."

"The Wolverine Club, in Lansing?" says Hawley.

"That's the one," Smitty says.

"That's my old stampin' grounds," says Hawley. "That's where I learned the game at."

"The kid holds the record for the course," says Smitty.

"He don't no such a thing!" says Hawley.

"How do you know?" says Smitty.

"I guess I'd ought to know," Hawley says. "The guy that holds that record is talkin' to you."

"What's your record?" says Smitty.

"What'd your brother make?" says Hawley.

"Plain seventy-one," says Smitty; "and if you ever beat that you can have my share o' the serious money."

"You better make a check right now," says Hawley. "The last time I played at that club I rolled up seventy-three."

"That beats me," Smitty says.

"If you're that good," says Carey, "I'd like to take you on sometime. I can score as high as the next one."

"You might get as much as me now because I'm all out o' practice," says Hawley; "but you wouldn't of stood no show when I was right."

"What club was you best with?" ast Carey.

"A heavy one," says Hawley. "I used to play with a club that they couldn't hardly nobody else lift."

"An iron club?" says Smitty.

"Well," says Hawley, "it felt like they was iron in it."

"Did you play all the wile with one club?" ast Carey.

"You bet I did," Hawley says. "I paid a good price and got a good club. You couldn't break it."

"Was it a brassie?" says Smitty.

"No," says Hawley. "It was made by some people right there in Lansing."

"I'd like to get a hold of a club like that," says Carey.

"You couldn't lift it," Hawley says; "and even if you could handle it I wouldn't sell it for no price—not for twicet what it cost."

"What did it cost?" Smitty ast him.

"Fifty bucks," says Hawley; "and it'd of been more'n that only for the people knowin' me so well. My old man used to do 'em a lot o' good turns."

"He must of stood in with 'em," says Carey, "or they wouldn't of never left go of a club like that for fifty."

"They must of sold it to you by the pound," I says—"about a dollar a pound."

"Could you slice a ball with it?" says Carey.

"That was the trouble—the balls wouldn't stand the gaff," Hawley says. "I used to cut 'em in two with it."

"How many holes did they have there when you was playin'?" Smitty ast.

"Oh, three or four," he says; "but they didn't feaze me."

"They got eighteen now," says Smitty.

"They must of left the course run down," Hawley says. "You can bet they kept it up good when my old man was captain."

"Has your brother ever been in a big tourney before?" I says to Smitty.

"He was in the city championship last summer," says Smitty.

"How'd he come out?" Hawley ast.

"He was second highest," says Smitty. "He'd of win, only he got stymied by a bumblebee."

"Did they cauterize it?" says Carey.

"Where do you get that noise?" says Hawley. "They ain't no danger in a bee sting if you know what to do. Just slip a piece o' raw meat on it."

"Was you ever stymied by a bee?" says Carey.

"Was I!" says Hawley. "Say, I wisht I had a base hit for every time them things got me. My old lady's dad had a regular bee farm down in Kentucky, and we'd go down there summertimes and visit and help gather the honey. I used to run round barefooted and you couldn't find a square inch on my legs that wasn't all et up."

"Must of kept your granddad broke buyin' raw meat," says Carey.

"Meat wasn't so high in them days," says Hawley. "Besides he didn't have to buy none. He had his own cattle."

"I should think the bees would of stymied the cattle," says Carey.

"Cattle's hide's too tough; a bee won't go near 'em," says Hawley.

"Why didn't you hire a cow to go round with you wile you collected honey?" says Carey.

"What'd you quit golf for?" ast Smitty.

"A fella can't play golf and hit good," says Hawley.

"I should think it'd help a man's hittin'," Carey says. "A golf ball's a whole lot smaller than a baseball, and a baseball should ought to look as big as a balloon to a man that's been playin' golf."

"Where do you get that noise?" says Hawley. "Golf's bad for a man's battin'; but it ain't got nothin' to do with your swing or your eye or the size o' the ball."

"What makes it bad, then?" I ast him.

"Wait a minute and I'll tell you," he says. "They's two reasons: In the first place they's genally almost always some people playin' ahead o' you on a golf course and you have to wait till they get out o' reach. You get in the habit o' waitin' and when you go up to the plate in a ball game and see the pitcher right in front o' you and the infielders and baserunners clost by, you're liable to wait for 'em to get out o' the way for the fear you'll kill 'em. And wile you're waitin' the pitcher's liable to slip three over in the groove and you're struck out."

"I wasn't never scared o' killin' no infielder," says Carey.

"And what's the other reason?" I says.

"The other reason," says Hawley, "is still better yet than the one I give you."

"Don't say that!" says Smitty.

"When you're playin' golf you pay for the balls you use," says Hawley; "so in a golf game you're sort of holdin' back and not hittin' a ball as far as you can, because it'll cost you money if you can't find it. So you get used to sort o' holdin' back; and when you get up there to the plate you don't take a good wallop for the fear you'll lose the ball. You forget that the balls is furnished by the club."

"And besides that," says Carey, "you're liable to get to thinkin' that your bat cost fifty bucks, the same as your golf racket, and you don't swing hard because you might break it."

"You don't know nothin' about it," says Hawley.

VI

NOW I DON'T CARE how big a goof a man is, he'd ought to know better than get smart round a fella that's slumped off in his battin'. Most o' the time they ain't no better-natured fella in the world than

Carey; but when him and first base has been strangers for a wile, lay offen him!

That's how Hawley got in bad with Carey—was talkin' too much when the old boy wasn't in no mood to listen.

He begin to slump off right after the Fourth o' July double-header. In them two games a couple o' the boys popped out when they was sent up to sacrifice. So Cap got sore on the buntin' game and says we'd hit and run for a wile. Well, in the first innin', every day for the next three days, Bishop led off with a base on balls and then started down when he got Carey's sign. And all three times Carey cracked a line drive right at somebody and they was a double play. After the last time he come in to the bench tryin' to smile.

"Well," he says, "I guess that's about a record."

"A record! Where do you get that stuff?" says Hawley. "I come up four times in Philly in one game and hit into four double plays."

"You brag too much!" says Carey; but you could see he didn't want to go along with it.

Well, that last line drive seemed to of took the heart out of him or somethin', because for the next week he didn't hardly foul one— let alone gettin' it past the infield.

When he'd went through his ninth game without a blow Hawley braced him in the clubhouse. "Do you know why you ain't hittin'?" he says.

"Yes," says Carey. "It's because they don't pitch where I swing."

"It ain't no such a thing!" says Hawley. "It's because you don't choke up your bat enough."

"Look here!" says Carey. "I been in this league longer'n you and I've hit better'n you. When I want advice about how to hold my bat I'll get you on the wire."

You know how clost the clubs was bunched along in the middle o' July. Well, we was windin' up a series with Brooklyn and we had to cop the last one to break even.

We was tied up in the ninth and one out in their half when Wheat caught a-hold o' one and got three bases on it. Cutshaw raised one a little ways back o' second base and it looked like a cinch Wheat couldn't score if Carey got her. Well, he got her all right and Wheat come dashin' in from third like a wild man.

Now they ain't no better pegger in the league than this same Carey, and I'd of bet my life Wheat was runnin' into a double play. I thought he was a sucker for makin' the try. But Carey throwed her twenty feet to one side o' the plate. The run was in and the game was over.

Hawley hadn't hardly got in the club-house before he started in. "Do you know what made you peg bad?" he says.

"Shut up!" says Smitty. "Is that the first bad peg you ever seen? Does they have to be a reason for all of 'em? He throwed it bad because he throwed it bad."

"He throwed it bad," says Hawley, "because he was in center field instead o' left field or right field. A center fielder'll peg wide three times to the others' oncet. And you know why it is, don't you?"

Nobody answered him.

"I'll tell you why it is," he says: "They's a foul line runnin' out in right field and they's a foul line runnin' out in left field, and them two lines gives a fielder somethin' to guide his throw with. If they was a white line runnin' from home plate through second base and out in center field you wouldn't see so many bad pegs from out there.

"But that ain't the only reason," says Hawley. "They's still another reason: The old boy ain't feelin' like hisself. He's up in the air because he ain't hittin'."

That's oncet where Hawley guessed right. But Carey didn't say a word—not till we was in the Subway.

"I know why I ain't hittin' and why I can't peg," he told me. "I'm so sick o' this Wisenheimer that I can't see. I can't see what they're pitchin' and I can't see the bases. I'm lucky to catch a fly ball."

"Forget him!" I says. "Let him rave!"

"I can't stop him from ravin'," says Carey; "but he's got to do his ravin' on another club."

"What do you mean?" I says. "You ain't manager."

"You watch me!" says Carey. "I ain't goin' to cripple him up or nothin' like that, but if he's still with us yet when we come offen this trip I'll make you a present o' my oldest boy."

"Have you got somethin' on him?"

"No," says Carey; "but he's goin' to get himself in wrong. And I think he's goin' to do it to-night."

VII

HE DONE IT —and that night too.

I guess you know that, next to winnin', Cap likes his missus better'n anything in the world. She is a nice gal, all right, and as pretty as they make 'em.

Cap's as proud of her as a colleger with a Charlie Chaplin mustache. When the different papers would print Miss So-and-So's pitcher and say she was the handsomest girl in this, that or the other place, Cap'd point it out to us and say: "My gal makes her look like a bad day outdoors."

Cap's wife's a blonde; and—believe me, boy—she dresses! She wasn't with us on this trip I'm speakin' of. She hasn't been with us all season, not since the trainin' trip. I think her mother's sick out there in St. Joe. Anyway, Hawley never seen her—that is, to know who she was.

Well, Carey framed it up so's I and him and Cap went in to supper together. Hawley was settin' all alone. Carey, brushin' by the head waiter, marches us up to Hawley's table and plants us. Carey's smilin' like he didn't have a care in the world. Hawley noticed the smile.

"Yattaboy!" he says. "Forget the base hits and cheer up!"

"I guess you'd cheer up, too, if you'd seen what I seen," says Carey. "Just lookin' at her was enough to drive away them Ockaway Chinese blues."

"That ain't no way for a married man to talk," says Cap.

"Well," says Carey, "gettin' married don't mean gettin' blind."

"What was she like?' ast Cap.

"Like all the prettiest ones," says Carey. "She was a blonde."

"Where do you get that noise?" says Hawley, buttin' in. "I s'pose they ain't no pretty dark girls?"

"Oh, yes," says Carey—"octoroons and them."

"Well," says Hawley, "I never seen no real pretty blondes. They ain't a blonde livin' that can class up with a pretty brunette."

"Where do you get that noise?" says Carey.

"Where do I get it!" says Hawley. "Say, I guess I've saw my share o' women. When you seen as many as I seen you won't be talkin' blonde."

"I seen one blonde that's the prettiest woman in this country," says Carey.

"The one you seen just now?" says Hawley.

"No, sir; another one," says Carey.

"Where at?" Hawley ast him.

"She's in Missouri, where she first come from," says Carey; "and she's the prettiest girl that was ever in the state."

"That shows you don't know what you're talkin' about," Hawley says. "I guess I ought to know the prettiest girl in Missouri. I was born and raised there, and the prettiest girl in Missouri went to school with me."

"And she was a blonde?" says Carey.

"Blonde nothin'!" says Hawley. "Her hair was as black as Chief Meyers'. And when you see a girl with black hair you know it's natural color. Take a blonde and you can't tell nothin' about it. They ain't one in a thousand of 'em that ain't dyed their hair."

Cap couldn't stand it no longer.

"You talk like a fool!" he says. "You don't know nothin' about women."

"I guess I know as much as the next one," says Hawley.

"You don't know nothin'!" says Cap. "What was this girl's name?"

"What girl's name?" says Hawley.

"This black girl you're talkin' about—this here prettiest girl in Missouri," says Cap.

"I forget her name," says Hawley.

"You never knowed her name," says Cap. "You never knowed nothin'! We traded nothin' to get you and we got stung at that. If you want your unconditional release, all you got to do is ask for it. And if you don't want it I'll get waivers on you and send you down South where you can be amongst the brunettes. We ain't got no room on this club for a ball player that don't know nothin' on no subject. You're just as smart about baseball as you are about women. It's a wonder your head don't have a blow-out! If a torpedo hit a boat you was on and you was the only one drownded, the captain'd send a wireless: 'Everybody saved!' "

Cap broke a few dishes gettin' up from the table and beat it out o' the room.

Hawley was still settin', with his mouth wide open, lookin' at his prunes. After a wile I and Carey got up and left him.

"He ain't a bad fella," I says when we was outside. "He don't mean nothin'. It looks to me like a raw deal you're handin' him."

"I don't care how it looks to you or anybody else," says Carey. "I still got a chancet to lead this league in hittin' and I ain't goin' to be talked out of it."

"Do you think you'll hit when he's gone?"

"You bet I'll hit!" says Carey.

Cap ast for waivers on Hawley, and Pittsburgh claimed him.

"I wisht it had of been some other club," he says to me. "That's another o' them burgs where the smoke and cinders kills your battin'."

But I notice he's been goin' good there and he should ought to enjoy hisself tellin' Wagner how to stand up to the plate.

The day after he'd left us I kept pretty good track o' Carey. He popped out twicet, grounded out oncet and hit a line drive to the pitcher.

GOOD FOR THE SOUL

◇

BEFORE ME, a member of the Baseball Writers' Association of America, appeared this first day of February, 1916, one Robert Frederick Warner, alias Buck Warner, lately a professional player of the game known as baseball and now part owner of an automobile garage in Hopsboro, a suburb of Cincinnati, and voluntarily and without threat or coercion did dictate a confession, the full text of which follows:

I

THE WIFE SAYS that if I didn't quit grouchin' round the house she'd just plain leave me and go and live with her Aunt Julia. Well, the wife's a good scout and Aunt Julia's home is a farm twelve miles from Dayton, so I promised I'd try and cheer up.

"Yes, but you promised the same thing before," says Ethel; that's the wife's name. "You promised the same thing before and that's all the good it done," she says. "It's your crazy old conscience that's botherin' you. You'd ought to go to the hospital and have it took out."

"Operations costs money," I says.

"Well," says Ethel, "I'd rather be broke than have old Sidney Gloom for a husband."

"I'll try and cheer up," I says again.

"You're the world's greatest tryer," says she, "but your attempts to make everybody miserable is the only ones that's successful."

It was at breakfast yesterday mornin' that she was payin' me these

The Saturday Evening Post, March 25, 1916; previously uncollected.

compliments. At supper she pointed out a piece in the evenin'.paper and told me I should read it.

Seems like some old bird about seventy, worth a couple o' millions, had been a clerk in a grocery store when he was a kid, and one day he helped himself to twenty dollars out o' the till, and he was scared to death they'd learn who done it and send him over, but for some reason it wasn't never found out. So, as I say, he finally got rich and had everything that's supposed to make a man happy, but he hadn't been able to sleep good for several years on account o' thinkin' about his crime. So the minister o' the church where he attended at preached a sermon on what a good thing confession was for sinners, and the old boy couldn't even sleep through the sermon, so he got the drift and made up his mind to see if a confession would cure his insomnia and not bein' able to sleep. So he wrote one out, describin' what he'd did, and sent it to the minister to be read out loud in church, and that night he slept like a horse.

"Well," I says, when I was through readin', "what about it?"

"It's worth a try," says Ethel.

"You go in town to-morrow and find somebody that'll listen, and tell 'em all about your horrible crime. And then see if you can't come home to me smilin'."

"That'll be easy," I says, "if you'll leave me drink a couple o' beers."

"You can do that too," she says, "if you think it'll wash away the blues."

I thought she was kiddin' at first; I mean about the confessin'. But she made me understand she was serious.

"But I'd have to bring in the names of others that ain't entirely innocent," I says.

"Go as far as you like," says she. "You certainly don't think they're worth shieldin'; 'specially Carmody."

So here I am and she says I was to tell it all and not keep nothin' back.

It won't be necessary to start with where I was born and so forth. A year ago last August is where it really begins. Before that I'd been in the National League six years, and if they'd left me stick to short-stop all the time, they wouldn't of nobody had me beat. But they found out I could play anywheres they put me and they kept shiftin' me round like a motorcycle cop.

In the six years I'd did even worse than not save no money. I'd piled up pretty near four thousand dollars' worth o' debts. The biggest part of it I owed to fellas on the club that'd came through for me when I made a flivver out of a billiard hall in Brooklyn.

So, as I say, a year ago last August found me four thousand to the bad and that's when I met Ethel. We was playin' in Pittsburgh and she was visitin' some people I know there. She had eye trouble and liked me the first time she seen me. But she didn't like me nowheres near as much as I liked her. We both fell pretty hard, though, and the third evenin' we was together we got engaged to be married.

"I wisht I had more to offer you," I told her. "I'm flat outside o' my salary and I owe a plain four thousand."

"I don't care how much or how little you've got," she says. "Your salary'll keep us all right. But I don't want to marry you till you're clear o' debt."

"We'll do some waitin' then," I says. "A year from this fall is the best I can promise. I'll live on nothin' this winter and I won't spend nothin' next summer and I think I can just about get cleaned up. It'll be somethin' new for me to try and save, but you're worth starvin' for."

"And you're worth waitin' for," says she.

So we says good-by and I went to Chicago with the club. And the second day there I slipped roundin' first base and threw my knee pretty near out o' my stockin'.

It wasn't no common sprain or strain. The old bird just simply flew out of his cage and flew out to stay. I seen two doctors there and two more back home. They all says the same thing; that I was through playin' ball.

"After it's had a rest," they told me, "just walkin' on it won't hurt nothin'. But the minute you run you're liable to get crippled up good and proper. And if you stooped quick or made a quick turn or if your leg got bumped into, you might serve a good long sentence on the old hair mattress."

I didn't want Ethel to find out how bad it was, so all that come out in the paper was that I had a Charley horse. Mac, o' course, knowed the truth, but he couldn't do nothin' except feel sorry for me. He knowed about the girl too.

"I wisht I had a place for you," he says, "but you wouldn't be satisfied scoutin', and with the low player limit we can't carry no men that ain't goin' to do us some good. You'll get paid, o' course, up to the end o' the season. But I can't offer you no contract for next year."

"That's all right," I says. "I just want it kept quiet till I find somethin' I can do."

And w'ile I was still half dazed over the shock of it I got a letter from the girl. She had some big news, she says. Her Aunt Julia'd been told about I and her bein' engaged and had promised her a present o' $2500 on the day we was married. And we was to put this money with another $2500 that her brother, Paul, was goin' to save up, and I and her brother was goin' to buy a garage in Hopsboro from a fella that'd promised Paul he'd sell it to him in a year.

And it was the only garage in Hopsboro and done a whale of a business. And Paul was a swell mechanic and I'd take care o' the business end. And I could quit playin' ball and never be away from home. It sounded mighty good to me just then. But they was still a little trifle o' four thousand that'd have to be took care of.

I'd just mailed back an answer, as cheerful as I could write, when a call come over the phone that Mr. A. T. Grant wanted to see me at the Kingsley Hotel. I'd saw his name mentioned in connection with a club in the new league, but I didn't know if he'd bought it or not.

Well, I went down there in a taxi and was showed right up to his room.

He shook hands with me and then ast me if I was signed up for next year. I told him I wasn't.

"I've just bought the club I was after," he says. "I wanted to know if you'd consider an offer."

I done some tall thinkin'. I made up my mind that it wouldn't do no harm to sign. If I found I couldn't play nobody'd be hurt. But if the old knee wasn't as bad as the doctors thought I'd probably get a better job here than anywheres else.

"Who's goin' to be your manager?" I ast him.

"Billy Carmody," he says. "He was the shortstop on the club this year."

"I never met him, but o' course I've heard of him," I says.

Then I done some more thinkin'.

"What's your offer?" I says.

"Five thousand," says Mr. Grant.

"Where would you want me to play?" I ast him.

"Where would you want to play?" says he.

That give me a hunch. I'd heard they was one or two short fences in the league. Maybe I could play an outfield position even if my legs wouldn't stand the infield strain.

"In the outfield," I told him.

"Which field?" he says, and then I knowed he was a bug.

"Right field," says I.

"That suits me," he says, and he sent for his secretary to fix up a contract.

So I signed to play right field, and nowheres else, for Mr. Grant's club for one year at $5000.

"This business is new to me," he says, "but I believe I'll get a lot o' pleasure out of it."

"What other men have you got signed?" I ast him.

"I'm not at liberty to tell you," he says. "But I may tell you that most o' them is young men that's as new to professional ball as I am. I believe in gettin' young fellas, for enthusiasm's more valuable than experience in a sport o' this kind."

"Oh, easy," I says.

Then we shook hands again and I beat it to a train for Dayton, where the girl was stayin'. And when I seen her I give her the whole story. It looked now like they was a little bit o' hope.

II

THE PAPERS I'd saw durin' the winter hadn't wasted no space on our club and I didn't know exactly who was my teammates till I blowed into Dixie Springs, the first week in March.

I landed in the forenoon. The clerk at the hotel told me the gang was all out to the grounds, practicin'. So I planted my baggage and washed up and then set out on the porch, waitin' for the boys to come back. The beanery was on the main street, but from the number o' people that went past you'd of thought our trainin' camp had been picked out by Robinson Caruso. About one bell I got sick o' lookin' at mud puddles and woke up the clerk again.

"What do you s'pose is keepin' 'em so long?" I ast him.

"They don't never show up till after four," he says.

"Don't they come back for lunch?" I ast.

"No," he says. "You see the ball grounds is over a quarter of a mile from here and Mr. Grant, who's the proprietor o' the nine, figured it would wear his men out to make the trip four times a day."

"So they don't eat at noon?" I says.

"Oh, yes," says the clerk. "We put up a nice lunch here and send it to 'em."

"I hope you don't send 'em nothin' that's hard to chew," I says. After a w'ile I got up nerve enough to attemp' the killin' journey to the orchard.

It was an old fairgrounds or somethin', just on the edge o' what you'd call the town if you was good-natured. Waivers had been ast on a lot o' the boards on the fence and they was plenty o' places where a brewer could of walked through sideways. I was goin' in at the gate because it was handiest, but I found it locked. I give it a kick and it was opened from inside by a barber hater.

"You can't come in," he says through the shrubbery.

"Why not?" says I.

"I've got orders," he says.

"I don't wonder," I says. "You're liable to get anything in them dragnets."

"I'll fix you if you try to come in," he says.

"What'll you do?" says I. "Tickle me to death with them plumes?"

"Mr. Grant don't want no spies hangin' round," says Whiskers.

"O' course not," says I. "But I'm one of his ball players."

"Oh, no, you ain't," says the Old Fox. "If you was you'd be wearin' one o' them get-ups with the knee pants and the spellin' on the blouse."

"Look here," I says. "I don't want to cut my way through the undergrowth; they's too much danger of infection. You run along and tell Mr. Grant his star performer has arrived, and when you come back I'll give you thirty-five cents to'rds a shave."

So the old boy slammed the gate shut and locked her again and the minute it was locked I went to the nearest gap in the fence and eased in.

They was a game o' ball goin' on and I started over to where they was playin' to see if I recognized anybody. But I hadn't went more'n a step or two when Whiskers come dashin' up to me with Mr. Grant followin'.

"This is the man!" yells Whiskers. "And my suspicions was right or he wouldn't of snuck in."

Mr. Grant was gaspin' too hard to talk at first; when he catched his breath he lit into me. "A spy, eh!" he says. "Tryin' to learn our secrets, eh! That's a fine job for a big man like you! Whose stool pigeon are you?" he says. "Stop the game!" he says to Whiskers. "Don't let 'em show nothin' in front o' this sneak!"

But they wasn't no need of him givin' that order, because when the boys heard the rumpus they quit o' their own accord and come runnin' over to be in on it.

Leadin' the pack was Jimmy Boyle, that I'd busted into the game with, out in Des Moines. I'd noticed from the box scores the summer before that they was a Boyle in this league, but I hadn't never thought of it bein' Jimmy. In fac', till I seen him sprintin' to'rds me, I'd forgot they was such a guy. It was nine years since I'd saw him.

"Hello, Buck!" he hollers.

"Buck!" says Mr. Grant. "You ain't Buck Warner, are you?"

"That's me," I says, "and I guess if it hadn't been for Jimmy recognizin' me you'd of had me shot for a spy."

The Old Boy looked like he was gettin' ready to cry.

"I certainly owe you my apologies," he says. "I don't remember faces as good as I used to and besides, you're dressed different than when you and me met."

"Yes," I says, "I've changed my clo'es twice since September."

"I hope you'll forgive me," says Mr. Grant.

"I'll think it over," I says.

By this time the whole bunch was gathered round and I had a chance to see who was who. Outside o' Jimmy Boyle they wasn't only four out o' more'n two dozen that I knowed by sight. One o' the four, o' course, was Billy Carmody. Him and I hadn't never met; he'd always been in the American till he jumped. But I'd saw his picture of'en enough to spot him. Then they was Hi Boles that I'd knew in the Association. And they was Charley Wade that the Boston club had for w'ile, and Red Fulton, that had been with Philly. The rest o' them was all strangers to me and most o' them looked about as much like ball players as Mary Pickford.

I shook hands with Red and Charley and Jimmy and Hi Boles, and Mr. Grant introduced me to the gang.

"Now," he says. "I wisht you'd shake with me to show you don't bear no grudge. I wouldn't of had this thing happen for the world."

"I don't blame you at all, sir," I says. "A club owner's got to be careful these days, because if other owners will go as far as stealin' your ball players, they certainly wouldn't hesitate at hirin' spies to try and cop your club's hit-and-run signs. But," I says, "I think you're foolish not to plug them holes in the fence. A scout with a strong glass could stand way out there behind center field and find out how many fingers your catchers used to signal for a curve ball."

"Yes," he says, winkin', "but the signals we use now and the signals we're goin' to use when the season opens up is two different things."

"Oh! Deep stuff, eh!" says I. "Well, if that's the way you're workin' it you'd ought not to be scared of outsiders swipin' information. Leave as many of 'em as wants to come and look us over, and the more bum dope they take back home, the easier we'll beat 'em when we meet 'em."

"But I don't want nobody to even know my line-up," says Mr. Grant, "not till the boys runs out on the field for the openin' game. If they don't know who we got or what we got or our battin' order or nothin', they can't prepare for us, can they?"

"Ain't they no reporters along?" I ast him.

"I wouldn't have 'em," says Mr. Grant. "I don't want to have no advance news get out about this club. Takin' your enemies by su'prise is more'n half the battle."

"Yes," says I, "but after the first day they won't be no more su'prise. The whole country'll know who we are."

"But we'll be leadin' the league," he says. "They can't take that away from us."

"Not for twenty-four hours," says I.

By this time, Carmody'd took his men back to their practice. I wanted to see 'em in action and made a move to go over to where they was at, but the Old Boy flagged me.

"They'll be through in five minutes," he says. "You must be wore out with your long trip, so let's you and I walk back to the hotel and set and rest till the boys comes in. I want you to be fresh to-morrow."

So we come away together and the last thing I seen at the grounds was Whiskers. He had the gate open far enough so's his head could stick out and he could see the whole length o' the main street. They wasn't a chance for a spy to catch him off guard, unless the spy used unfair tactics and snuck up from some other direction.

"What do you think of our club?" says Mr. Grant.

"I don't know nothin' about it," I says. "Most o' them boys is strangers to me."

"But ain't they nice lookin' boys?" he says.

"Sure," says I, "but some o' the best ball players I ever seen was homelier than muskrats."

"But their bein' homely didn't make 'em good ball players," says he.

"No," I says, "but it helped 'em keep in the pink. They couldn't go girl-crazy and stay out all hours o' the night dancin'; they wasn't no girls that'd dance with 'em or be seen with 'em. And they couldn't lay against the mahogany all evenin', because all bars has got mirrors back o' them, and if a man didn't never open his eyes they'd think you'd fell asleep and throw you out."

"Your arguments may be all right for some teams," says Mr. Grant, "but they don't hold as far as we're concerned. Bein' handsome won't hurt my boys, because they can't run round nights or drink neither one."

"Why not?" I ast him.

"Because they's a club rule against it," he says.

"Oh!" I says. "O' course that makes it different. How'd you ever happen to think o' makin' a rule like that? I bet when the other club owners hears about it, they'll follow suit and thank you for originatin' the idear."

"I hope they do follow suit," he says. "It's one o' my ambitions to perjure baseball of its evils."

"I wish you luck," says I.

"And another one," he says, "is to win the pennant, and between you and I, I believe I'm goin' to realize it."

"What year?" I says.

"This year," says my boss.

"Well," I says, "I'm new in the league and I don't know what it takes to win. But from what I seen of your club and from what I read about Chicago and St. Louis and some o' the rest, I'd say you had to strengthen some."

"I'm afraid you're pessimistical, Warner," he says. "I've got the winnin' combination—yourself and Carmody and Fulton and Wade and Boles and Boyle for experience and balance, and those young-sters o' mine for speed and spirit. We'll take the League off'n their feet."

"What does Carmody think about it?"

"The same as me," he says. "And he's a great manager."

"He must be," says I.

Well, when the crowd come in, Jimmy Boyle chased up to the clerk o' the hotel and had it fixed for me to room with him.

"They had me paired with one o' the kids," he says, "but I got to have somebody to laugh with. This is goin' to be the greatest season you ever went through. I don't know what I'll hit, but I bet I giggle .380."

"What is they to laugh at?" I says.

"What ain't they to laugh at?" says Jimmy. "Wait till you get acquainted with the old man! Wait till you've saw our gang in action! Wait till you watch Carmody managin'! Dutch Schaefer couldn't of got up a better club than this."

"What have we got, outside o' you and the other fellas I know?" I ast him.

"Say, if I told you, you wouldn't believe it," says Jimmy. "In the first place, there's old Grant. If he ain't got no relatives the county'd ought to look after him. He's goin' to keep us a secret till the season opens and then we're goin' to win the first game by su'prise. And somebody tipped him off that the club that wins the first game has got the best chance for the pennant. O' course they's eight clubs in the league and four o' them'll prob'ly win their first games, but he never thought o' that. And besides, the only chance we got o' winnin' the first game or any other game is to have the other club look at us and die laughin'."

"Ain't they no stuff in them kids?" I ast.

"Just one o' them," says Boyle. "They's a boy named Steele that must of took his name from his right arm. He can whizz 'em through there faster'n Johnson. He could win with any club in the world but our'n."

"Who's the other pitchers?" I ast him.

"They ain't none," says Boyle, "none that counts. All told, we got three right-handers and three cockeyes, but outside o' Steele, I'd go up there and catch any one o' them without a mask or glove or protector or nothin'. When the balls they throw don't hit the screen on the fly they'll hit the fence on the first hop."

"Where'd he get 'em all?" says I.

"He must of bought 'em off'n Pawnee Bill," says Jimmy.

"We seem to be long on catchers," I says.

"Wade and Fulton and myself," says Jimmy, "but some of us is goin' to get switched before the season's a week old. As I say, when Steele ain't pitchin' the club don't need no catcher, and it sure does need other things. Carmody's playin' short and Boles is the first sacker and you'll be somewheres in the outfield. That only leaves four positions without nobody to fill 'em. So I and Red and Charley's

wonderin' which one of us'll be elected first. I wouldn't mind tacklin'
right field; they's some short fences in the league. But Carmody's
just crazy enough to stick me at third base where a man don't have
time to duck."

"You lay off'n right field," I says. "I got a lien on that bird."

"You'll play where Carmody puts you," says Jimmy.

"You're delirious," says I. "You ain't seen my contract. I signed
to play right field and nowheres else, and you couldn't get me out
o' there with a habeas corpus."

"Mr. Fox, eh?" says Boyle.

"You know it," I says, "and between you and I, they's a reason.
I'd just as soon tell you because they ain't no danger o' you spillin'
it. My right knee slipped out on me last August, and when it went,
it went for good. All the doctors I seen give me the same advice—
to get out o' baseball. And I had my mind all made up to quit when
old Grant stepped in with his offer. I took it, knowin' all the w'ile
that it was grand larceny."

"Don't you worry about that," says Jimmy. "They'll be only one
guy on this club that ain't a burglar. That's young Steele. The rest
of us, includin' the M.G.R., is a bunch o' bandits. But I'm not frettin'
over it. I figure that if he wasn't givin' me this dough somebody else'd
be gettin' it, maybe somebody without as much license to it as me.
If they wasn't nobody dependin' on me I might feel ashamed. But
when you got a wife and two kids, and an old bug comes along and
slips you a contract for three times what you're worth, it'd be cheatin'
your folks to not take it."

"I ain't got no folks," I says.

"But you can never tell," says Boyle.

"I can tell," I says, "if you'll listen. I met a little lady the middle
o' last July. The first week in August we got engaged. And the second
week in August Mr. Knee blowed out. So when Grant come after
me, along in September, I begin to believe in angels. But I ain't
never felt right about it."

"How bad is the old dog?" says Jimmy. "Can you run on it
at all?"

"I can run on it," I says, "but I can't get up no speed. And I don't
know when she's goin' to slip again. I can't start quick. And I'm
scared to stoop."

"You won't need to stoop; not with our pitchers," says Jimmy.
"All that'll come out your way is line drives or high boys over the
wall."

"And if I turn sudden, I'm gone," says I.

"That's easy," says Boyle. "Rest your spine against them boards and do all your runnin' to'rds the infield. You won't be the first outfielder that played that system."

"Carmody'll wise up to me," I says.

"You should worry your head off about Carmody," says Boyle. "He's pretendin' to take his job serious, but down in his heart he knows he's a thief. He's got just as much right to manage a ball club as that girl o' yours. You just stick it out and draw the old check every first and fifteenth, and remember that you got plenty o' company. Even if your two legs was cut off at the waist you'd be worth five times as much as some of us."

"Careful there, Jim," I says.

"You can hit, can't you?" he says. "And you can catch fly balls, and you can throw. There's three things you can do, and that's three more things than most of our gang can do. No, I'll that back. They's one thing they can all do."

"What's that?" I ast him.

"Eat," says Jimmy, "and if you don't believe it come down in the dinin' room. The doors is supposed to open for supper at five-thirty, but after the first day we was here, the manager seen that the only way to save the doors was to keep 'em open all the w'ile. All the other ball clubs I was ever with talked about their hittin' and their bad luck, and all that. But this bunch don't talk nothin' but meats and groceries, and when they ain't talkin' about 'em it's because they got so many o' them in their mouth that they can't talk. The kid that was roomin' with me put what he couldn't eat in his pockets or inside his shirt, and after every meal he'd come straight to the room and unload on top o' the bureau. And if I went near his storehouse to brush my hair or look in the glass, he'd growl like a dog. He had himself trained so's he wouldn't sleep more'n three hours in a row. He'd go to bed at nine and get up at twelve and three for refreshments. But no matter how hungry he was at three, he always managed to save a piece o' cold hamburger or a little fricasseed veal for when he woke up in the mornin', so's he wouldn't have to go down to breakfast in his nightgown. Our second day here it was rainin' when I rolled out o' bed. Griffin, the kid I'm tellin' you about, was puttin' on his clo'es with one hand and feedin' himself with the other. 'Well, boy,' I says to him, 'it looks like we'd loaf to-day.' He must of thought I'd mentioned veal loaf or a loaf o' bread, because all the answer I got was more things to eat. 'Fruit and cereal,' he says, 'prunes and oranges and oatmeal, bacon and eggs straight up, small tenderloin medium, sausage and cakes, buttered toast, some o' them rolls, and a pot o' coffee.' 'Well,' I says, 'your dress rehearsal goes off all right; if you don't get scared and forget your lines in front o' the waiter, you'll be the hit o' the show.' But I might as well of been talkin' to a post hole. He didn't know I was speakin' unless I spoke like a bill o' fare."

"What position does he play?" I ast.

"Third base," says Jimmy, "and for the fear everybody won't know it, he always keeps one foot on the bag. But don't get the idear that he's a bigger eater than the rest o' them. They ain't no more difference in their appetites than in their ball playin'. When they got their noses in the feed-trough, though, they look like they was at home. And when they're out there on the field, you'd think they was It for blindman's buff."

I ast him about the Old Man havin' their lunch sent out.

"Even Carmody laughed at that," he says; "but Carmody's figured that the way to get along with old Grant is to agree with him in everything. So we're relieved from two changes o' clo'es, and a half mile walk that might help some of us get down to weight."

"Is it a regular lunch?" I ast him.

"All but the tools," says Jimmy. "And that makes it the favorite meal with Griffin and them. They can throw it in faster and without near as much risk. And all you have to do to start a riot is drop a bone or part of a potato on the grass."

"How is the grounds?" I says.

"Just as good as the club," says Boyle.

"Who picked out this joint?" says I.

"The same old bug that picked up these ball players," says Jimmy. "He was lookin' for a quiet place and he got it. The burg's supposed to have a population o' twelve hundred, but I haven't even saw the twelve. Dixie Springs they call it, but the only springs is in Carmody's bed. The town and the grounds is both jokes. The hotel's all right outside o' the rooms. I'll own up the eatin's good, but that's the one thing that don't make no difference to this bunch of our'n. They'd go to it just the same if it was raw mule chops."

"How much longer do we stick?" I ast him.

"Plain five weeks," says Jimmy. "We don't play no exhibitions nowheres because they might be spies from the other clubs watchin' us. We stay right here and do all our practicin' in a park that was laid out by a steeplechase fan, and then we go straight home and win the openin' game and the pennant by su'prise. You're lucky you come a week late. If I'd knew the dope in advance I wouldn't of never reported till the day o' the big su'prise party. But leave us hurry downstairs or it'll be too late for you to get a look at a fine piece of American scenery."

"What's that?" I ast.

"The Royal Gorge," says Jimmy.

Well, he hadn't lied when he told me about their eatin'. It was just like as if they knowed the league wasn't only goin' to last this one more season, and they all o' them expected to live to be over ninety, and was tryin' to get fixed up in a year for the next sixty-five. You remember how them waiters down South come one-steppin' in with their trays balanced on their thumb a mile over their head? Well, they didn't pull that stunt with the orders these here boys give 'em. Each fella's meal took two pall-bearers, with a couple o' mourners followin' along behind to pick up whatever floral pieces fell off when the casket listed.

I and Boyle and Fulton and Hi Boles had a table to ourself, and you ought to saw them Ephs quarrel over who'd wait on us. Besides our four orders together not bein' as big as one o' them other guys', we wasn't so exhausted at the end o' the meal that we couldn't dig down in our pocket and get a dime. Mr. Grant and Carmody and the secretary set next to our table and it seemed to worry the Old Boy that our appetites was so poor. He'd say:

"Warner, I'm afraid you ain't feelin' good. You don't eat hardly nothin'."

"I'm all right," I'd tell him; "but eatin' ain't no new experience for me. I ett for several years before I broke into baseball and I been gettin' regular meals ever since."

The lunch served out to the grounds was worth travelin' south just to look at it. It always come prompt at twelve, and for a half hour before that time every ground ball was a base hit because the fielders was all lookin' up at the sun. And when the baskets full o' nourishment was drug in, no matter if we was right in the middle of an innin', everybody'd throw away their bats and gloves and race for the front. Carmody'd follow along smilin', like it was a good joke.

I was hungry my first day out. I told Jimmy I felt like eatin' a big meal.

"Well," he says, "I bet you don't eat it when you see it."

He win his bet. I was the last fella up to the baskets. They was a couple o' sandwiches and one or two pieces o' fried chicken left, but it'd all be pawed over by the early birds, and amongst the other things the grounds was shy of was a place to wash your hands. Even if they'd been one, nobody'd of had time to use it.

So that day and the rest o' the time we was there I set out on the sidelines with Hi and Jimmy and Red durin' the noon hour, and watched the performance.

"This mayn't be a big league," says Jimmy, "but our club'll be big if they don't all get lockjaw."

"It'll take two engines to pull us home," says Red.

"If them boys could hit, they'd be heavy hitters," says Hi.

Well, they couldn't hit or they couldn't field; that is, the most o' them couldn't. They was a couple that had the stuff to make pretty fair ball players if they'd knew anything. Carmody couldn't learn 'em because he didn't know nothin' himself. I done what I could to help 'em, partly because I'm kind-hearted and partly so's I'd be doin' somethin' else besides riskin' my life in that outfield. It was rough enough so's a fella with two good legs would be scared to take a chance, and it wasn't no place for a cripple to frolic round in.

We put on two ball games a day between the regulars and yannigans. The only reason for callin' our team the regulars was on account o' Carmody playin' with us. We was licked most o' the time because young Steele done most o' the pitchin' against us. He sure could buzz 'em through and he had as good control as I ever seen in a kid. He was workin' the day that I and Carmody had our first and last argument. Carmody's whole idear o' baseball was "take two strikes." That was his instructions to everybody that went up to hit. It was all right when the other fellas was pitchin' because they was all o' them pretty near sure to walk you. But I couldn't see no sense doin' it against Steele; it just helped him get you in a hole.

This day it come up to the seventh innin' and Steele had us beat four to nothin'. We was all ordered to take two strikes and most of us was addin' one onto the order. But in the seventh, one o' the kids happened to get a base hit and they was a couple o' boots, and when it was my turn to go up there, the bases was choked and two out.

"Take two strikes," yells Carmody.

"Yes," I says to myself, "I'll take two strikes."

So Steele, thinkin' I'd obey orders, laid the first one right over in my groove and I busted it out o' the ball park.

When I come in to the bench Carmody was layin' for me.

"What kind o' baseball is that?" he says.

"It's real baseball," I says. "If you think it ain't you're crazy. When a pitcher's got as good control as him, and we're four runs behind and the bases is full, I'm goin' to crack the first ball I can reach."

He called me over away from the gang.

"It's a bad example," he says, "for you not to follow instructions."

"Maybe it is," says I, "but when the instructions is ridic'lous I'm goin' to forget 'em."

"I'm managin' this ball club," he says.

"You're doin' a grand job," says I. "When you take money for managin', it's plain highway robbery."

"I suppose you're earnin' yourn," says Carmody. "I suppose you got two good legs."

That kind o' shook me up.

"Listen," he says, "I got just as much license to draw a manager's salary as you have for takin' a ball player's. You're liable to be on crutches before the middle of April. But if I don't make no crack to Grant he won't know you was crippled when you signed; he'll think, when your knee goes back on you, that it's the first time and just an accident. So," he says, "if I was you I'd play the way the manager told me and not make no fuss."

"You win," says I. "But have a heart and forget once in a w'ile to give me orders. I don't mind if the rest o' the league knows I got a bum leg, but I don't want 'em to think my head's cut off."

They wasn't never such a long five weeks as I put in down to this excuse for a trainin' camp. After the first few days I got sick o' laughin' and sleepin' and everything else. I'd promised the girl I wouldn't take a drink, but all that kept me from breakin' the promise was lack of opportunity. The burg didn't even have a soda foundry.

Nights after supper I'd write a long letter to the future Missus and then I and Boyle'd set up in the room and wish we was somewheres else. Once or twice old Grant called on us and raved about our chances to win the pennant.

"If you boys finish on top," he says, "and if the European war's over by that time, I might give you all a trip acrost the pond next fall."

When he'd went out and left us after spillin' that great piece o' news, we was as excited as a couple o' draft horses.

"I wonder what they soak a man for a steamer trunk," says Jimmy. "It'd be a grand honeymoon for you," he says. "The lady'll love you better'n ever when she knows you're goin' to take her to see the Tower o' London and the Plaster o' Paris."

"I hope," says I, "that they'll be sure and have all the dead removed before we get there."

"We'll be right to home in the trenches after practicin' all spring on these grounds," says Jimmy.

Well, the time went by one way and another and the happiest day o' my life, bar one, was when us Wellfeds clumb aboard a rattler headed north. Our trainin' season was over and we was in every bit as good shape as if we'd just left the operatin' table. Our team was picked and they was ball players in every position except two, but Carmody and Wade was the only ones in the lot that was playin' where they belonged. The two kids that acted like they had a little ability was in the outfield with me. Jimmy Boyle'd been tried at second base and third base, but he was lost both places, so they'd stuck him on first and shifted Hi Boles, a first sacker, to third. Red Fulton, another catcher, was pretendin' to play second base. Carmody was at shortstop and it looked like Charley Wade was elected to catch whenever it didn't rain. That was the club that was goin' to take the pennant by su'prise and spend the winter in Monte Carlo.

But I was too happy over leavin' Dixie Springs to be worryin' about how rotten we looked.

"Lord!" I says to Charley Wade, "I guess it won't seem great to be in a real town!"

"I don't know," he says. "I'm afraid I'll be nervous when I get where they's people."

III

THEY WASN'T ENOUGH people in the park the day we opened to bother Charley Wade or anybody else. Old Grant had made such a success o' keepin' us a secret that only about eight hundred knowed we was goin' to perform; anyway, that's all that come out to watch us, and in his great, big new stands, they looked like a dozen fleas on a flat car.

It was a crime, too, that we didn't have a crowd, because we win the ball game. The records will show that; you don't have to take my word. The Old Boy had predicted a su'prise and his prophecy come true. And the ones that was most su'prised was us and the fellas we beat.

When that Buffalo bunch first come out and seen our line-up in battin' practice, they laughed themself hoarse. But they didn't do no laughin' after the game started and they got a sample o' Steele's stuff. The weather was twice as cold as any we'd ran into down South, but it didn't seem to make no difference to him. He was lightnin' fast and steady as Matty. He didn't give 'em one real chance to score.

We trimmed 'em two to nothin' and I drove in the both of our runs. Along with that I was lucky enough to make quite a catch o' the only ball they hit hard off o' Steele.

When we got in the clubhouse afterwards, Mr. Grant was there, actually cryin' for joy. He throwed his arms round Steele and was goin' to do the same to me, but I backed off and told him I was engaged.

O' course they was reporters lookin' us over this time and the next mornin' the population was informed that Grant and Carmody'd made quite a ball club out of a bunch of misfits. So when she started that afternoon, the stands was pretty near filled.

Our whole pitchin' staff, except Steele, was in there at one time or another. The Buffalo club hadn't been able to hit Steele. They didn't have to hit these other babies. I don't know how many bases on balls was gave, but I bet it was a world's record. Charley Wade, back o' the bat, did more shaggin' than all the outfielders. When Buffalo was battin' the umps could of left his right arm in the checkroom. Fourteen to nothin' it wound up and they was no spoonin' in the clubhouse after the game.

Steele was beat his next time out, but win his third start. And one o' the cock-eyes come acrost with a win in the second series, gettin' some valuable help from an umpire that'd been let out o' the Association for bein' stone blind. I think altogether we copped four games in April. Along the last part o' May or the first o' June we grabbed two in succession, but the streak was broke up when Jimmy dropped three pegs in the eighth and ninth innin's o' the third game.

Durin' the home series in May, four or five hundred people that was fond o' low comedy come out every afternoon to get our stuff. But we pulled the same gags so often that they quit us after a w'ile. We went round the western half o' the circuit in June and our split o' the gate wouldn't of tipped the porters. Then, we come home again and was welcomed by thirty-seven paid admissions, five ushers and two newspaper men.

The Old Boy cut the price to a dime for the bleachers. The ticket takers slept peaceful all afternoon. Then he hired a band to give a concert every day, so for a w'ile we was sure of an attendance o' thirty, except when the piccolo player got piccoloed.

When August come I was leadin' the league in hittin' and Mr. Grant thought I was the most valuable man he had. He overlooked a few things about my record that would of wised up any real baseball man. For instance, though I was battin' .420, my total o' stolen bases was three, and all three o' them was steals o' second that'd been made in double steals with Hi Boles goin' from second to third. And I didn't only have about ten extra base hits, o' which five was home run drives out o' the park. In other words, I wasn't doin' no more runnin' than I had to, and I didn't try to get nowheres where they was a chance that I'd have to slide. And under this kind o' treatment, Mr. Leggo had held up good. I'd felt him wabble two different times when I was chasin' fly balls, but he'd popped back into place without me even coaxin' him.

Then, in the middle of August, everything happened at once. Charley Wade broke an ankle, Carmody's right arm went dead, and the girl had a brawl with Aunt Julia.

We was in Indianapolis. We'd just got through carryin' Charley into the club-house when a boy come down to the bench and handed me a telegram. It says I was to come at once; she must see me.

"Carmody," I says, "I got to run down to Dayton to-night."

"What for?" he says.

"Somebody wants me," I told him.

"Not as bad as I do," he says.

"Well," says I, "it's somebody that makes more difference than you do."

"I'll talk to you after the game," he says.

It was our last bats and it didn't take 'em long to get us out.

"Now," says Carmody, "you can go to Dayton to-night if you'll promise to be back in time to play to-morrow."

"I can't make no promise," I says.

"Then you can't go," says Carmody.

"What's the matter with you?" I says. "Can't you stick a pitcher or one o' them kids in right field for one day?"

"You ain't goin' to play right field no more," he says.

"I ain't going to play nowheres else," says I. "Do you think I'm goin' to catch in Charley's place?"

"No," he says. "I'm goin' to put Boyle back there."

"And me go to first?" I says.

"No," says Carmody. "I'm goin' there myself and you're goin' to take my place at shortstop."

"You're maudlin," I says. "I signed a contract to play right field and that's where I'm goin' to stick. I'm awkward enough out there; I'd be a holy show on the infield. Besides, you never played first base in your life and one o' the pitchers or that big Griffin kid could do as good as you. What's the use o' breakin' up your whole combination just because one fella's hurt?"

"We couldn't make no change that'd be for the worse," says Carmody. "But I'll come clean with you and tell you where I'm at. I'm gettin' $1800 a month for this job. But my contract says I got to play the whole season out or he can cut $2500 off'n my year's salary."

"Well," I says, "what's the difference if you play first base or stay where you're at?"

"I can't stay where I'm at," he says. "My souper's deader'n that place we trained. She quit on me in the seventh innin' to-day. I couldn't stand on the foul line and throw to fair ground."

"You hurt it in action, didn't you?" I says.

"Yes, but he's sore at me," says Carmody, "on account of our swell showin'. And the way my contract reads, he could keep my dough if he wanted to."

"But you'll have to throw when you're playin' first base," says I.

"No, I won't," he says. "You watch me and see. If I've got the ball and they's a play to make anywheres, you'll see the old pill slip right out o' my hand and lay there on the ground."

"But I don't see why you should pick on me," I says. "Boles or Red Fulton or one o' them kids could do a whole lot better job o' shortstoppin' than me."

"Boles and Fulton is bad enough where they're at," he says, "without wishin' a new bunch o' trouble on 'em. You've played there and you'd know what you was doin' even if you couldn't stoop over or cover no ground. Besides," he says, "old Grant wants you to tackle it."

"When was you talkin' to him?" I says. "You ain't seen him since Charley got hurt and your arm went."

"That's more secrets," says Carmody. "Between you and I, my

arm's been bad a long w'ile and I had the hunch it was goin' to do just what it done. So I told him a little story a couple o' weeks ago. I told him I wasn't satisfied with the way Boyle was playin' first base and I told him I was a pretty good first sacker myself and thought I'd move over there. So he ast me who'd play shortstop and I told him you'd make the best man and he says he thought so, too, but your contract read that you'd only play right field. So I told him maybe he could coax you to switch."

"It must be hard for you to shave with all that cheek," I says. "You can go and tell him now that you ast me would I play shortstop and I told you No, I wouldn't. So that's settled, and now I'm goin' to catch a train. If I can get back to-morrow I will. And if I do get back, I'll be in right field."

I left him bawlin' me out, but I knowed he couldn't do nothin' to me. I had as much on him as he had on me.

I run into a flood in Dayton, but it was salt water this time. The girl cried for two hours after I got there and couldn't quit long enough to tell me what it was about. I finally made like I was goin' away disgusted. Then she come through.

They wasn't goin' to be no $2500 from Aunt Julia. Aunt Julia'd fell in love with a G. A. R. that hadn't did nothin' since '65 but celebrate his team's victory. So Ethel, instead o' usin' her head, lost it, and ast Aunt Julia what she meant by tyin' up with a bird twenty years older than herself that hadn't shaved since Grant took Richmond. So they broke up in a riot and all bets was off.

"Well," I says, "maybe she'll get over it."

"No, she won't," says Ethel, "and even if she did, I wouldn't take her old money."

"Any high-class bank would give you new money for it," I says.

"It ain't no time for jokin'," she says. "Everything's all over. We can't get married this year; maybe not for ten years; maybe never."

"I don't have to pay all them debts right away," I says. "I can hold out $2500 and give it to Paul. The boys have waited this long for their dough; I guess they can wait a w'ile longer."

"You know what I've told you," she says. "We won't be married one minute before you're out o' debt."

"Well," I says, "it looks like they was no hurry about gettin' a license. They ain't goin' to be no post-season money for us guys."

"We'll just have to wait then," says the girl. "You'll have to save every cent o' your next year's pay."

"They ain't goin' to be no next year's pay," says I. "This league'll be past history in another season. And I couldn't carry bats anywheres else."

The more we talked the bluer things looked and I guess I'd of been cryin' myself in another minute if the big idear hadn't came to me.

"Wait a minute!" I says. "They's a chance that we can get out o' this all right."

"What's the dope?" she ast me.

But I wouldn't tell her; it wasn't clear in my own mind yet and I didn't want to say nothin' till I'd schemed it out.

"I'm goin' right back, back, back to Indiana," I says. "You'll get a wire from me to-morrow night. Maybe it'll be good news and maybe it won't. But you'll know pretty near as soon as I do."

I was up in Carmody's room at seven o'clock the next mornin'. I ast him if he'd said anything to Mr. Grant about me refusin' to play shortstop.

"No," he says. "I was hopin' you'd change your mind."

"Maybe I will," I says, "but not without he coaxes me."

Carmody didn't ask me what I was gettin' at. He dressed and went downstairs to find the Old Boy. And at half-past eight, in the dinin' room, the coaxin' commenced.

"Warner," says Mr. Grant, "Carmody's thinkin' about makin' a few changes in the team."

"Is that so?" I says. "What are they?"

"Well," he says, "he ain't satisfied with the way Boyle plays first base. And besides, now that Wade's hurt, he thinks Boyle should ought to go back and catch again. And he wants to try first base himself. So that would leave shortstop open."

"Maybe you could get a hold o' some semi-pro shortstopper," I says.

"I don't want none," he says. "I want a man that's had big league experience. I believe that with Carmody on first base and a good man at shortstop we could finish seventh yet. What do you think?"

"Very likely," I says, knowin' that they wasn't a chance in the world.

"I'd give a good deal to pull out o' last place," says he.

"Well," I says, "I'll see if I can't think o' some good shortstop that ain't tied up."

"You don't have to try and think o' one," says Mr. Grant. "I've got one in mind."

"Who's that?" I says.

"Yourself," he says. I pretended like I was too su'prised to speak.

"You can play the position, can't you?" he ast.

"Sure," says I. "That's where I was born and brought up."

"Well, then," he says, rubbin' his hands.

"Well, nothin'," I says. "I'm signed as a right fielder."

"We could make a new contract," he says.

"But listen, Mr. Grant," I says. "W'ile I know shortstop like a book, I don't want to play it. It's too hard. It keeps a man thinkin' and workin' every minute. One season at shortstop is pretty near as wearin' as two in the outfield. That's why I insisted on right field. I wanted to take things a little easier this year. That's why I was willin' to sign with you for $5000."

"What would you of wanted to play short?" he ast me.

"Oh," I says, "I wouldn't of thought of it for less than $9000."

He didn't say nothin' for a minute; a good long minute too. Finally he says:

"Well, Warner, they's only about six more weeks to go. But I'm wild to get out o' last place and I'll spend some money to do it, though spendin' money has been my chief business all season. I want to be fair with you, so if you'll finish out the season at shortstop I'll give you $2500 extra."

This time it was me that wanted to hug him. But I played safe. I considered and considered and considered and finally I give in.

"I'll do it, Mr. Grant," I says. "As a favor to you, I'll do it."

Out in the lobby Carmody was waitin' for me.

"It's fixed," I says. "He's a pretty good coaxer."

"What did you get?" he ast me.

"A November weddin'," says I.

I'd promised to wire Ethel by night, but the thing had been pulled a whole lot quicker'n I'd hoped for. I run right from Carmody to the telegraph office.

"All fixed," I says in my message. "I got $2500 extra."

At lunch time her answer come back:

"Good old boy. Did you hold somebody up?"

Well, sir, believe me or not, I hadn't thought of it that way before. But when I read her wire I had to admit to myself that she'd pretty near called the turn.

The less said about them last six weeks the better. I don't know how many games we was beat, but five was what we win. I felt worst about poor Steele. There he was, workin' his head off two to four games a week, worth four times as much as all the rest of us together, and drawin' a salary o' $400 a month. He's with a real club this year and you watch him go!

They'll always be a question in my mind about which was the biggest flivver, me at shortstop or Carmody at first base. I covered just as much ground as was under my shoes and if a ground ball didn't hop up waist high when it come to me, it kept right on travelin'.

I didn't take many plays at second base for the fear I'd get slid into. If I tagged anybody it was because they stuck out their hand and insisted on it. And I was so nervous all the w'ile that I couldn't hardly foul one up at that plate.

Carmody's dead arm wasn't half his troubles. Findin' first base with his feet was what bothered him most. Everybody in the league was ridin' him.

"Tie a bell on the bag!" they'd holler. "Look out! You'll spike yourself! Get a compass! Who hid first base?"

It was lucky for me that the Old Boy's box was on the first base side and that he couldn't see far. He could take in a lot more o' Carmody's fox trottin' than he could o' my still life posin'. He knowed, though, that I wasn't a howlin' success as a shortstopper. When he give me my extra money, he says:

"Warner, you didn't come up to my expectations."

"Mr. Grant," I says, "playin' that outfield spoiled me for an infield job. I won't never tackle it again."

And for once I was tellin' him the truth.

I ast him what his plans was for another season.

"I ain't only got the one plan," he says. "That's to get out o' baseball."

"Well," I says, "I hope you can find somebody to buy the club."

"I ain't goin' to sell it," he says. "The next man that does me a dirty trick, I'm goin' to give it to him."

IV

WELL, SIR, I paid my debts first and then I sent the girl's brother a check for my share o' the dandy little garage. The marriage nuptials

come off on schedule and I guess we wasn't su'prised when Aunt
Julia showed up with a forgivin' smile and a check for $2500.

"You can't tell if it's old money or not," I says to Ethel.

"I guess we'll keep it anyway," she says.

"Maybe," I says, "I'll send it back to old Grant."

"Maybe you won't too," says she. "This money happens to belong
to me and I never pretended I could play shortstop."

I feel better now that's off'n my chest. I know it was wrong, but
as Jimmy Boyle pointed out, if one fella didn't take it some other
fella would. And I think I got a better excuse than anybody else.
Come out to the house sometime and see for yourself.

THE CROOK

◊

TO-MORROW MORNIN' you'll see a statement in the papers, signed by Ban, sayin' that it's been learned that they was some excuse for Bull doin' what he done, and that the charge of him bein' pickled on the field wasn't true, and that he's been took back on the staff. But they won't be nothin' printed about who was the dandy little fixer; my part in it is a secret between you and I and one or two others.

I don't suppose they's a ball player in the League that Bull's chased as often as me. I don't suppose they's anybody he's pulled as much of his stuff on. I can't count the times I've got cute with him, but the times I got the best o' the repartee I can count 'em on the fingers of a catcher's mitt. Just the same, it was me that went to Ban with the real dope and was the cause of him gettin' rehired, and it was me that got him his girl back, though he don't know about that yet.

I wouldn't of took no trouble in the case if it was any other umps but Bull. But I come as near likin' him as a man could like a guy that never give a close one any way but against you. And he's a good umps, too; he guesses about a third of 'em right, where the rest o' Ban's School for the Blind don't see one in ten. And another thing: I felt sorry for him when he told me the deal he got. And besides that, he's gave me too many good laughs for me to stand by and see him canned out o' the League. Many's the time I've made a holler just to hear what he'd say, and he always said somethin' worth hearin', even if it stung; that is, up to day before yesterday, when the blow-off come.

I noticed he wasn't himself when I was throwed out at the plate in the second innin'. I wanted to stop at third, but Jack made me keep goin', and Duff Lewis all ready to shoot with that six-inch

The Saturday Evening Post, June 24, 1916; previously uncollected.

howitzer he wears in his right sleeve. Cady and the ball strolled out to meet me and I couldn't get past 'em.

"You're out!" says Bull.

"He didn't tag me," I says.

And Bull didn't say a word.

In the fourth innin' Hooper was on third base and somebody hit a fly ball to Shano. Hooper scored after the catch and big Cahill run out from the bench and made a holler that he'd left the bag too quick. The ball was throwed over to third base, but Tommy wouldn't allow the play. Then Cahill went to Bull and ast him hadn't he saw it. O' course Bull says he hadn't.

"No, I guess not!" says Cahill. "Us burglars stick together." And then, on the way back to the bench, he turned to Bull and says: "You're so crooked you could sleep in a French horn."

Bull was just puttin' on his mask, but he throwed it on the ground and tore after Cahill. He nailed him right on the edge o' the dugout, and what a beatin' he give him! It took eight or nine of us to drag him off, and he managed to wallop everybody at least once durin' the action. Some o' the boys picked Cahill up and carried him to the club-house. He was a wreck. Bull stood there a minute, starin' at nothin'; then he turned and faced the grand stand.

"Anybody else," he yelled—"anybody else that thinks I'm a crook can come down and get a little o' the same."

Well, they wasn't no need of extra police to keep the crowd back. But Ban was settin' in the stand and o' course he wasn't goin' to just set there and not do nothin'. It was too raw. So he give orders for the cops to grab Bull and get him out o' the way before he committed murder. They led him to his dressin' room and stuck with him w'ile he changed clo'es. Then they called the wagon and give him a ride. Tommy handled the rest o' the game alone and we was beat just as bad as if nothin' had happened.

Right after the game the witnesses was examined. Cahill's lips was so swelled he couldn't hardly talk. But several of us had heard the whole thing and could testify they hadn't been no profanity. Cahill hadn't no license to call Bull crooked, but if an umps was goin' to fight for a little thing like that, every ball game'd wind up in a holycaust. Besides, "a crook" was one o' the mildest things Bull'd ever been called, and till this time nobody'd ever knew him to lose his temper.

As I say, his specialty was conversation. When they was a kick made, he'd generally always pull some remark that got a laugh from everybody but the fella that was crabbin', and sometimes from he himself. He'd canned plenty o' guys out o' the ball game for tryin' too hard to show him up, but he'd did it as part o' the day's work and without displayin' any venoms. I'd heard 'em tell him he was yellow, and blind, and a jellyfish, and a "homer," and a thief, and a liar; and that he'd steal the cream off'n his mother's coffee; and that his backbone was all above the neck. I'd heard 'em call him fightin' names and saw him take it smilin'. And now, because a fella made an innocent remark about him bein' crooked, and no naughty words along with it, he'd went off his bean and all but destroyed a good Irish citizen, besides intimidatin' five or six thousand o' the unemployed.

It wasn't no wonder everybody thought what they thought, though Bull hadn't never been known to touch a drop between April and October.

"I'll uphold my umpires when they're right," Ban says to the reporters; "but when they're wrong, they got to suffer for it. They's only just the one explanation for Bull's actions. So he's discharged from the staff."

"What about Cahill?" ast somebody. "Goin' to suspend him?"

"No," says Ban. "Bull saved me the trouble."

Well, Tommy fixed it up to have Bull let out o' jail and took him back to the hotel where the two o' them was stoppin'. When Tommy told him he was canned he didn't make no comments only to say that they was one good thing about the umpirin' job—you didn't feel bad if you lost it.

On my way home from the game I got to thinkin' about Bull and what a shame it was to have him let out for just the one slip, and wonderin' what he'd do with himself, and so on. So when I'd had supper I rode down to the umps' beanery to try and find him, and maybe cheer him up.

He'd went out. Tommy told me he'd disappeared after askin' for his mail and not gettin' none.

"He'll come back with a fine package," says Tommy.

"Do you know what made him fall off?" I says.

"He didn't fall off," says Tommy. "That's the funny part of it. I and him was right up in my room readin' the papers all mornin'; then we had lunch and went out to the park together and got dressed and went on the field. I noticed he was grouchin', but I was with him

every minute o' the day up to game time and I know for a fact that
he didn't have nothin' to drink only his coffee at breakfast. Somethin's
happened to him, but I don't like to get inquisitive because we haven't
only been teamin' together a couple o' weeks."

I and Tommy didn't have nothin' else to do, so we set down in
the writin' room and chinned. Bull, o' course, was the subject o' the
conversation. You could talk about him all week and not tell half o'
the stuff.

The first game he umpired in our League was openin' day in Chi,
four or five years ago. It was our club and St. Louis. I guess he was
about twenty-six years old then, but he didn't look more'n twenty.
So the boys was inclined to ride him. Arnold, the St. Louis catcher,
started on him in the first innin'.

"Did you ever see a ball game, kid?" he ast him.

"No," says Bull, "but if I make good these four days, I'm goin' to
stay here for the Detroit series."

Arnold come up with the bases full and two out in the fourth or
fifth. He took three healthy lunges and fanned. I led off in our half
and Bull called the first one a ball. It was pretty close and Arnold,
peeved about strikin' out in the pinch, slammed the pill on the
ground.

"You're a fine umpire!" he says.

"I can't be right all the time," says Bull. "Even the best of us misses
'em sometimes. But I'll have to miss the next two in succession to
tie your score."

We was one run ahead when the ninth begin. We got two o' them
out and then Hank Douglas made a base hit and stole second. The
next fella made another base hit, but Shano fielded it clean and Hank
was called out at the plate.

"That's right," he says to Bull. "Favor the home team. You wouldn't
be umpirin' in this league if you wasn't yellow."

"No," says Bull, walkin' away, "and you wouldn't be in the League
at all if you wasn't a Brown."

In one o' the Detroit games Cobb was on second base with a man
out and Crawford hit a slow ground ball between short and third.
The ball was fielded to first base and Cobb kept right on for home.
Parker was catchin' for us and he was a little spike-shy, especially
with Cobb. So when the ball was relayed to him from first base he
backed off in an alley somewheres and give Tyrus the right o' way.
Somebody hollered from the bench that Cobb hadn't touched third.

"Yes, I seen it," says Parker to Bull, lookin' for an alibi. "He cut third base."

"I don't know about that," Bull says, "but it's a safe bet that he'll never cut you."

Bull went with us for our first series in Cleveland that year. They was a fly-ball hit to Lawton in the third and he muffed it square, lettin' in a couple o' runs. As soon as he'd dropped the ball he looked up in the sky and then stopped the game till he'd ran in and got his glasses, though it was so cloudy that we was hurryin' to beat the rain. Right afterward, when Lawton come to bat, Bull called a strike on him.

"Too high! Too high!" says Lawton.

"Maybe it was," says Bull. "I lost it in the sun."

A little w'ile later the Cleveland club had a chance to tie us up. It was some left-hand batter's turn to hit, but they was a cockeye pitchin' for us, so they sent up a kid named Brodie, a right-hander, to pinch hit. He swung at the first one and missed it. The next one was called a strike, and w'ile he was turned round, arguin' with Bull about it, another one come whizzin' over and Bull says:

"You're out!"

"It wasn't a legal delivery," says Brodie.

"Why not?" says Bull. His feet was on the slab and you wasn't out o' your box."

"You got a lot to learn about baseball," says Brodie.

"I'm learnin' fast," says Bull. "I just found out why they call your club the Naps."

He didn't put nobody out of a game till along in the middle o' that season. We was playin' Washin'ton and Kennedy was in a battin' slump. He was sore at the world and tryin' to take it out on the umps. He'd throwed his glove all over the field and tossed his cap in the air and beefed on every decision, if it was close or not. He struck out twice, and when Bull called a strike on him his third time up, he stooped over and grabbed a handful o' dirt.

"A yard outside!" he says, and tossed the dirt to'rds Bull.

"Well, Mr. Kennedy," Bull says, "if there is a yard outside, that's where you better spend the rest o' the afternoon."

"Am I out o' the game?" says Kennedy.

"Hasn't nobody told you?" says Bull. "You been out of it pretty near two weeks."

"You're about as funny as choppin' down trees," says Kennedy.

"Go in and dress," Bull told him. "Maybe you'll find your battin' eye in your street clo'es."

The next day Bull was umpirin' the bases. Kennedy didn't get suspended, and when he come to bat in the first innin' and seen that Bull had switched, he yelled to him: "Congratulations! You ought to do better out there. It's a cinch you couldn't do worse."

"Walter," says Bull to Johnson, who was pitchin', "give Kennedy a base on balls. I want to talk to him."

In the last game o' the series Kennedy finally did get a hold o' one and hit it for two bases.

"Now it's my turn to congratulate you," Bull says to him.

"Oh," says Kennedy, "I can hit 'em all right when they's a good umps behind that plate."

W'ile he was still talkin', whoever was pitchin' wheeled round and catched him a mile off'n the bag. Bull waved him out and he started to crab.

"Go on in to the bench, Kennedy," says Bull. "The game must look funny to you from here anyway."

Big Johnson worked against us in Chi one day and he had more stuff than I ever seen him have. Poor little Weber, facin' him for the first time, was scared stiff. He just stood there and took three. Next time, he struck at one and let the next two come right over. Bull, who was back o' the plate, couldn't help from laughin' and the kid got sore.

"Why don't you call 'em all strikes!" he says.

"I would," Bull says, "only they's just a few o' them I can see."

Well, Weber's third trip up there was just like his first one. He didn't even swing. And after Bull had called him out for the third time, he says:

"Fine work, umps! You ought to go to an oculist and get the dust took out o' your eyes."

"Yes," says Bull, "and you ought to go to a surgeon and have the bat removed from your shoulder."

One afternoon Jennin's started a kid named Sawyer against us. He was hog wild and he throwed ten balls without gettin' a strike.

"It looks like a tough day for us, Bull," says Stanage.

"Well, anyway," Bull says, "my right arm needs a good rest."

When two fellas had walked and they was two balls on the next one, Sawyer pitched a ball that you could of called either way. Bull called it a ball.

"What was the matter with that one?" says Sawyer.

"You pitched it," says Bull.

He was base umpire once when Walsh caught Carney flat-footed off o' third base. It was in the ninth innin' and they was only the one run behind us, so Carey begin to whine.

"Kind o' drowsy, eh?" says Bull. "I'll bet your mother was up all night with you."

Before the end of his first season he had the boys pretty well scared o' that tongue of his'n and they weren't none o' them sayin' much to him. But o' course, durin' the winter, they forgot how he could lash 'em, and when spring come again he was as good as ever. It's been that way every season since. Along about this time, and up to July, they're layin' themself wide open and takin' all he can give. Then, from July on, they're tired o' bein' laughed at and they see they can't get the best of him, so they lay off.

Not me, though. I beef on every decision he makes against me all season long. I can get as good a laugh when it's me that's the goat as when it's somebody else.

He's pulled some pippins on me. I wisht I'd wrote down even half o' them, but anyway they don't sound as good when I tell 'em as when he sprung 'em on me.

I remember we was playin' our last series with the Boston club in 1912. They'd cinched the pennant already and nobody cared a whole lot how our games come out. I've got plenty o' friends in Boston, and the first night we was there I neglected to go to bed. So the next afternoon I was kind o' logy.

I dropped a couple o' thrown balls at first base and was off the bag once when I had all the time in the world to find it. Well, Bull had three or four close ones to guess and he guessed 'em all against us.

"Are you goin' to work in the World's Series?" I ast him.

"I haven't heard," he says.

"If you do," I says, "I'm goin' to bet my season's pay on the Red Sox."

"If you're lookin' for easy money," says Bull, "why don't you go ahead and bet your season's pay on the Red Sox, and then sign with the Giants to play first base?"

In 1914 I'd been havin' a long spell o' bad luck with my hittin' and they was just gettin' ready to bench me when one day, in St. Louis, I got one safe. I tried to make two bases on it, but overslid the bag and Bull called me out.

"Oh, Bull!" I says. "Have a heart."

"They won't bawl you for this," says Bull. "You ain't been here in so long it's no wonder you forgot where the station was. I think you done pretty well to remember my name. I been umpirin' the bases for two weeks."

Then they was once in Boston, just last year. We still had a chance yet and we was crazy to take a fall out o' that bunch. I was overanxious, I guess. Anyway, it was a tight game and in the sixth or seventh innin' I got caught off o' first. "Bull," I says, "if you're with the home club, why don't you wear a white suit?"

"Larry," says he, "you ought to play ball in your pyjamas."

And in New York one day I give somebody the hit and run, and the ball fooled me and I didn't swing. The fella was throwed out at second base, and Bull called it a strike on me.

"Why, Bull!" I says. "He was wastin' that ball."

"Sure he was," says Bull. "All the good balls is wasted on you."

And once in Washin'ton, we was two runs to the good in the ninth and had two men out and it looked all over. The next man—Milan, I think it was—hit a fly ball straight up and I hollered I was goin' to take it. Well, it just missed beanin' me and Milan pulled up at second base. The next fella hit a ground ball between I and the bag. I missed it clean. Milan scored and the other fella stopped at second. Then somebody made a three-base hit. The score was tied and the winnin' run was on third base.

A slow ground ball was hit down to'rds me. I seen that Doran, who was pitchin', was goin' for the ball instead o' the bag and I seen that the ball was mine and I'd have to get it and chase back with it myself. I done it as fast as I could and the play was mighty close. Bull called the man safe. It meant the game and we was all sore, but me especially, on account o' them two flivvers.

"You blind owl!" I says to Bull. "Who told you you could umpire?"

"Who recommended you to Griffith?" says Bull.

That's the way he was. You could set up all night and figure out what you was goin' to say to him next day, and then when you said it, he'd come back with somethin' that made you wish you hadn't. That is, unless you was like me and kept after him just for the laughs he give you.

I and Tommy set there talkin' till pretty close to midnight. Then we decided they wasn't no more use waitin' for Bull. So Tommy went up to his room and I moseyed out the front door and onto the walk. I hadn't took more'n a couple o' steps when I seen the guy we'd been fannin' about. He was just goin' in to the hotel bar. I followed him.

"Hello, Bull!" I says, when we was both inside.

"What's the idear?" he says. "Did you come clear down here to tell me that Cady didn't tag you?"

"No," I says. "He tagged me all right. But I'm taggin' you to find out what's got into you."

"I guess I got plenty into me now," says he. "When a man that's cold sober gets fired from his job for bein' lit, they's only the one thing to do. I've been tryin' my best all evenin' to deserve the reputation they've wished on me."

I give him the double O. He could walk straight and he could talk straight. But he was kind of owl-eyed and his face looked like a royal flush o' diamonds.

"Let's have somethin'," he says.

"You've had enough," says I.

"That's no sign I ain't goin' to have more," he says.

"You better go to bed," I says.

"What for?" says he. "I got nothin' to do to-morrow or any other to-morrow. I'm through."

"They's other leagues," says I. "You won't have no trouble gettin' a job."

"I don't want no job," says Bull. "I haven't no use for a job."

"What are you goin' to live on?" I ast him.

"I don't want to live," he says.

"Aw, piffle!" says I. "You'll feel better for a good night's sleep."

"Well," says Bull, "they's just as much chance o' me gettin' a good night's sleep as they is o' them playin' part o' the World's Series in Peoria."

"Bull," I says, "I believe they's somethin' botherin' you outside o' losin' your job."

"You're too smart to be playin' ball," he says.

O' course I knowed then that Tommy'd been right—that the old boy had had a blow o' some kind. And I was mighty curious to learn what'd came off. But I realized it wouldn't get me nothin' to ask.

We h'isted three or four together without exchangin' a word. Then, all of a sudden, I seen a big tear streakin' down Bull's cheek and in another minute I was listenin' to his story.

Bull's parents is both dead—been dead five or six years. He never had no brothers or sisters or aunts or uncles or nothin'. He was born down South somewheres and didn't have no use for cold weather, but his old man moved to Buffalo when Bull was about sixteen, so from that time till his mother and father died he spent his winters, and the summers before he went to umpirin', up North. They wasn't no reason why he shouldn't suit himself after the old people passed out, so back South he went for his winters. He stayed in New Orleans the first couple o' years, but it cost him a pile o' money. Then he tried Montgomery, and that's where he met the lady.

Her name's Maggie, Maggie Gregory. Bull described her as the prettiest thing he ever seen, and so on. The Gregorys didn't have so much dough that they didn't know how to spend it. In fact, they was kind o' hard up. The head o' the house worked in a hardware store for somethin' like fifteen a week. He had a son named Martin; yes, sir, the same Martin Gregory that Connie Mack let go last week and we got signed up now.

Martin and Maggie was twins. Maggie was learnin' the milliner trade, but at the time Bull met 'em Martin wasn't workin' at all, except durin' meals. He was one o' the kind o' guys that'd rather go to the electric chair, where he could be sure o' settin' down, than attend the theater and take a chance o' havin' to stand up w'ile they played the Star-Spangled Banner. If he'd lived in a town where they wasn't no letter carriers he wouldn't never got no mail. He'd of starved to death in a cafeteria with a pocket full o' money.

He treated the whole of his family like they was waiters, and they treated him like he was the Kaiser. His mother was crazy over him, and Maggie used to split fifty-fifty with him on her princely salary. The old man never called him, and seemed to just take it for granted that Martin was born to have the best of it.

Bull landed in Montgomery the same time that the Gregorys made up their mind to take a boarder. They put an ad. in the paper and Bull answered it. He answered it in the evenin', when Maggie was home. After gettin' a look at her, he'd of stayed there if they made him sleep in the sink and give him nothin' to eat but catnip.

Maggie and Martin was eighteen then. They ain't no use o' me tryin' to give you Bull's description of her. Martin, accordin' to Bull, was a handsome kid and had the best clo'es his sister's money could buy. He was built like an ath-a-lete and his features was enough like the girl's to make him good-lookin'. Bull fell for him this first night; he didn't know nothin' then about the feud between Martin and Work.

Well, they all treated Bull like he was an old friend and made him feel more like it was his own house than just a place to board. Maggie smiled at him every time she seen him, though it wasn't no case o' love at first sight on her part; she was just tryin' to be friendly. The old lady worried if he didn't take nine or ten helpin's o' whatever was on the table, and kept his room as neat and clean as Martin's. The old man played rummy with him three or four times a week and give Bull good laughs on all his quick stuff. And Martin took kindly to him, too, figurin' probably that the dough Bull paid for board would mean more dude clo'es in the wardrobe. Bull says he never knowed what this here Southern hospitality was till he went to live with the Gregorys.

It wasn't till Bull had been there about three weeks that he told 'em what he done for a livin'. Well, the old people and Maggie didn't know nothin' about baseball except that Martin, when he was a kid, had been the best player in the school where he attended at. He'd told 'em so. But Martin himself, it turned out, was a nut on the national pastime. He knowed who Cobb was and who Matty was and their records, right down to little bits o' fractions. Not only that, but he went to see the Montgomery bunch perform whenever they had the courage to face the home crowd. So Bull was a hero to him, in spite of his profession.

At meals, Martin wouldn't talk nothin' but baseball, and Bull had to talk it with him. I suppose the proud parents and Maggie felt kind o' sorry for Bull, figurin' that the kid, bein' perfect, was gettin' all the best of him in the arguments. The old boy was foxy enough to see that the easiest way to win Maggie was by helpin' to make Martin look good. So when they'd got about so far in a fannin' bee, Bull'd stop dead and say, "By George! You're right," even if Martin was arguin' that Walter Johnson ought to learn to throw left-handed and play third base.

Bull thought he was just a fresh kid. He thought the reason he wasn't workin' was probably because he'd lost a job and hadn't found another. He liked Martin O. K. till he begin to suspect that he was too proud to toil. It was the old lady that give him the hunch, when she says somethin' about the kid's delicate health.

"Yes," Bull says to himself, "he's awful delicate lookin', like Frank Gotch."

Before the winter was half over, Bull was givin' 'em the time o' their lives, takin' 'em somewheres every other night. It was a pipe that Maggie liked him, and it was a bigger pipe that she had him on

her reserve list, with no chance to get away. But he was too shy to
talk to her about anything but the climate; he says she was the first
girl he was ever scared of.

Along in March, some o' the Montgomery ball players showed up
for their trainin'. Bull always took some work in the spring to get
himself hard and fix up his windpipes, so that year he joined the
local bunch and done stunts with them. Martin ast to go along with
him the third or fourth day. So out they went together to the Montgomery orchard and Bull got the biggest su'prise of his life.

Instead o' settin' up in the stand and lookin' on, Martin peeled
down to his shirtsleeves and busted right into the practice. He tackled
the high-low game first, and Bull says to see him at it you wouldn't
of never believed it was the same boy that wouldn't drink coffee
unless you held the cup to his mush. Baseball wasn't work to him—
it was fun. And that made the whole difference.

Well, Martin showed so much life the first day that Bull borrowed
a suit for him and fixed it with the Montgomery gang to leave him
frolic round their park as much as he liked. And he wasn't no joke
with the ath-a-letes. He didn't know nothin', but he had as much
mechanical ability as you ever see in a kid. He could whip the ball
round like a shot, and he was good on ground balls and he swung
the old stick like it was a lath. Bull give him a lot o' pointers and so
did the rest o' the boys, and by the time Bull was ready to go North,
Martin was good enough to hold down an infield job somewhere in
the brush.

Maggie and old Gregory was as proud as peacocks. The old woman
was proud too, but she was scared to death that the pet would get
beaned or stepped on and killed. Bull finally convinced her that
baseball was as safe as ridin' in a rockin'-chair, and Martin was allowed
to keep on with the only exercise he'd took in years, outside o'
puttin' on his pyjamas at night and pullin' 'em off in the mornin'.

Bull left Montgomery with the understandin' that he could have
his room when he come back in the fall. Maggie squeezed his hand
when she told him good-by, and that, Bull says, along with the post
cards she sent him, was all that kept him alive that summer.

In June the Gregorys sent him a clippin' from a Montgomery paper.
Martin had been signed by the Montgomery club to play second
base, and he looked like the best thing that had broke into the
Southern League in years.

The second off-season that Bull spent with the Gregorys he was

still too shy yet to make any play for the lady, outside o' blowin' all
his loose change in showin' she and her folks a time. But last fall,
after they'd gave him his bit for workin' in the big series, and he felt
like he had enough financial backin' to justify the plunge, he wired
her to meet his train and he pulled his speech on her w'ile his nerve
was still with him.

She didn't say yes or she didn't say no. She told him she liked him
a whole lot bettern'n anybody except Brother Martin, and she appreciated his kindness to all o' them, and so on. But it would take
a lot o' thinkin' to decide the question, and could he wait? So he
says he could do anything for her and they left it go at that.

As soon as they was off'n the subject, she begin to talk about
Martin and what he'd been doin' in baseball. She admitted that he
was the greatest ball player south of Alaska, but o' course the Montgomery club didn't give him a fair show on account o' bein' jealous,
and the manager kept him on the bench half the time for the fear
some big league scout'd see him and steal him away from Montgomery. What she wanted Bull to do was tell some manager in our
league about him, and have him bought. Martin would do the rest;
he'd show 'em if he ever got the chance.

Well, Bull told her it was against the rules for an umps to recommend a ball player to a club in his own league. It wouldn't be fair
to the Boston club, for instance, if Bull give Detroit first whack at
a second Cobb. O' course Bull knowed that plenty o' scouts must
of saw Martin and passed him up, and that the Montgomery club
wasn't tryin' to conceal a man for who they could get a big price.

She ast him if he couldn't get some friend to do the recommendin'
if he couldn't do it himself. He told her he was scared his part in it
would be found out. Then she says that he must care a lot about her
if he was afraid to take a little risk like that. He told her he'd try
and think of a way to swing it, but she must give him time.

He found Martin more of a dude than ever and as modest as a
wrestler. He couldn't talk about nothin' but how much better he was
than the Southern League, and it was easy to see from his clo'es that
he wasn't contributin' nothin' to the family except conversation and
his personal attendance at meals.

Hatin' yourself, though, ain't nothin' against a ball player. Take
most any real star and when the dialogue ain't about him he's bored
to death, and if he has a bad day, pitchin' or hittin' or whatever it is
he does, it's plain tough luck or rotten umpirin'.

So Bull didn't think none the less o' Martin's ability on account
o' the size of his chest, even if he did get good an' sick o' hearin'
nothin' but Martin, Martin, Martin, all day and half the night.

Bull would of gave anything if Maggie and the rest o' them had
forgot their scheme to land the pet in the big menagerie. But they
wasn't a chance. When he'd rather of been hearin' that she cared
somethin' about him, she was eggin' him on to hurry up and think
of a way to bring Brother to the attention o' the real people.

In December Bull read in the paper that Ted Pierce, the manager
o' the Montgomery club, was in town. He made a date to meet him
and find out just how good Martin was.

"He's just good enough to of pretty near drove me wild," Ted
told him. "If we're ten runs ahead and he comes up with the bases
full, he'll hit one from here to Nashville. Or if we're fifteen runs
behind in the last half o' the ninth, with two out, it's fifty to one that
he'll get to first base. But put him up to that plate when everything
depends on him and you'd think he had paralysis o' the arms. He'll
take three in the groove and then holler murder at the umps."

"Plain yellow, eh?" says Bull.

"I don't like to say that about nobody," Ted says. "But if the old
U.S. called for volunteers, I'd bet on Benedict Arnold to beat him
to the front."

"Ain't they no chance of him gettin' over it?" ast Bull.

"I've tried everything," says Ted. "I've called him all the names I
could think of. I've tried to jolly him too; I've told him the pitchers
was all scared of him and all he'd have to do was swing that club.
But he's just as bad as when he broke in."

"He's a kid yet," says Bull. "It may be just stage fright."

"It may be," says Ted. "He certainly is cocky enough most o' the
time; it's only in a pinch that he loses it."

"I'm a friend of his family," says Bull. "I'd like awful well to see
him move up."

"You wouldn't like it no better'n me," says Ted. "I'd like to see
him move anywheres. I'm sick o' lookin' at him. If you can sell him
for any kind of a price, I'll give you half of it."

"You know I couldn't sell him," says Bull. "But if somebody else
recommended him to somebody and I was ast about him, I'd do my
best."

"Well," says Ted, "I ain't goin' to recommend him nowheres, unless
it's to a fella I got no use for. I'm goin' to try him again in the spring,

and if he don't quit chokin' to death every time he's got a chance to be a hero, I'll tie a can on him whether he's a friend o' yours or Woodrow Wilson's."

"Outside o' that, he's a good ball player, is he?" says Bull.

"They ain't no man I ever seen with more natural advantages," Ted told him. "His record shows that he hit .329 and stole thirty-two bases and fielded as good as any second baseman in the league. But he didn't make none o' those base hits when we'd of gave a thousand dollars apiece for 'em, and when he could of pulled a pitcher out of a hole with a swell piece o' fieldin' he simply booted the ball all over the infield."

"They's just the one hope for him, then," says Bull, "and that's to go out and get some o' the old nervine."

"If you can make him do that," says Ted, "I'll guarantee to sell him to any club you name."

So Bull, that night, told Maggie that Martin was still shy of experience and needed at least another year in minor league ball before he could hope to stick up with the E-light. He figured that he could work on the kid all the rest o' the winter and maybe succeed in stingin' him enough with hot conversation to get that streak out of him.

But Maggie right away wanted to know where Bull'd got his information and Bull had to tell her.

"No wonder!" says Maggie. "Pierce never did have a good word for him. Him and all the rest o' them's jealous."

"You're mistaken," says Bull. "Pierce wouldn't like nothin' better than to sell him for a good price."

"All right," says Maggie, "if you think I'm mistaken, that shows you don't care nothin' about me."

So Bull didn't have no answer to that swell argument only to beg her pardon and say she was probably right.

Well, it finally come to a kind of a showdown: Bull was either to see that Martin got his chance this spring or he'd have to worry along without Maggie. She didn't come right out and say that the way I've put it, but she made it plain enough so's they wasn't much chance to misunderstand.

Bull kicked the sheets round for a few nights and then got his idear. O' course the first thing was to pick a club that was tryin' to build up, and if possible to pick one that had a manager who'd pay the right kind of attention to a kid. Bull chose Connie as the best bet. The next thing was to persuade Connie to give Martin his trial. Bull wanted to be perfectly square, as you'll see by the deal he put through. He got a fella there in Montgomery with a good Irish name to write to Connie and recommend the boy, and if Connie didn't believe Martin was a good prospect he was to ask Bull about him, and if Martin didn't make good he wouldn't cost Connie nothin', not even his railroad fare to the trainin' camp and back. Bull framed it up with Ted Pierce as a matter o' friendship to leave the boy go on trial, and if he did su'prise 'em all and make good, the Montgomery club was to get whatever Connie was willin' to pay.

Well, the letter was sent and Connie wrote back to Bull, and says a boy named Gregory had been mentioned to him, and ast Bull was he worth a trial. Bull answered that Gregory was a kid with great natural ability and one or two faults that'd have to be overcome. Then Connie fixed it with the Montgomery club, and Bull thought he'd finished his job.

But he found out different. W'ile Maggie consented to becomin' engaged, she wasn't in no hurry to get married. She says her parents was gettin' old and she didn't want to leave 'em all summer, and besides, she didn't have no clo'es, and besides, it would be a whole lot nicer to wait till fall and spend the honeymoon where they'd first met each other and when Bull was just startin' his vacation instead of endin' it. Bull coaxed and coaxed, but her rules was just like his'n—she couldn't change a decision on a question o' judgment.

In the three weeks before Martin was to report in Jacksonville, Bull done nothin' but try and shoot him full o' confidence.

"The pitchers down here have got everything you'll see in the big league," he told him. "You don't need to be afraid o' none o' them. A man that handles a bat the way you do can hit anything in the world if he'll just swing. Connie or any other manager don't care how many times you strike out in the pinch, provided you strike out tryin'. You got the stuff in you to make Cobb and Baker and them look like a rummy. Don't get scared; that's all."

Bull pulled that talk on him right up to the day the kid left Montgomery. Down at the train, Bull says to him:

"Remember, they's nothin' to be scared of. Make us all proud o' you! Make good!"

"I'll make good if they give me a square deal," he says.

"Yes," Bull says to himself, "it's a cinch it'll be somebody else's fault if he falls down. It always is."

Well, in a little w'ile it come time for Bull to leave too. And here's what the girl sprung on him at the partin':

"You'll help him all you can, won't you?" she says.

"They's not a chance for me to help him," says Bull. "A man in my place can't favor nobody."

"A man could," she says, "if a man knowed it would please the girl he was stuck on."

Now if it'd of been me that she made that remark to, I'd of ast for waivers. But you know what they say about love bein' blind. And when it's a combination o' love and an umpire—well, how can you beat it!

Bull kept close tab on the papers and he seen that Martin was at second base in the lineup o' the Ath-a-letics' regular club. This was w'ile they was still South. Then, in one o' their last exhibitions before the season started, Martin's name was left out. He wrote to the kid and he wrote to Maggie, tryin' to find out what was doin'. Maggie wrote back that she didn't know and Martin didn't answer at all.

The season begin and Bull was workin' in the West. Every mornin' he grabbed the papers and looked to see if Martin was back in. Four times in three weeks the kid went up to bat for somebody, but without doin' no good. Then come the second week in this month and the first series between the Eastern clubs and us.

Bull had the Detroit-Philadelphia series. Just before the first game he run into Connie outside o' the park. They shook hands and then Bull says:

"Didn't you ask me about a ball player this winter?"

"Yes," says Connie, "a boy named Gregory."

"How's he comin'?" says Bull.

"I don't think he's comin'," says Connie. "I think he's just gettin' ready to go."

"What's the trouble?" ast Bull.

"Well, says Connie, "once in a w'ile our club happens to not be more'n two or three runs behind, happens to have a chance to tie or win. Gregory's one o' the kind o' ball players that spoils them chances. In practice down South he looked like a find. He hit everything and fielded all over the place. But we got into some tight exhibitions on the way up and when the opportunities come to him to do somethin' big he faded away. He ain't there in a pinch; that's all."

"Is he with you yet?" Bull ast him.

"He's with us," says Connie; "he's with us for one more trial. If they's a place in this series where I can use a substitute hitter, Gregory's goin' to be the man. And if he don't swing that club the way he can swing it when it don't mean nothin', I'll hand him his transportation back to Montgomery."

"Does the kid know that?" ast Bull.

"Yes," says Connie, "and if they's any stuff in him the knowledge that this is his last chance should ought to bring it out."

"You mean," says Bull, "that if he strikes out again in a pinch he's through?"

"No, I don't," says Connie. "I mean he's through if he doesn't try to murder that ball. I don't care if he strikes out on three pitches, just so he swings."

"But suppose," says Bull—"suppose they don't throw him nothin' he can hit; suppose they walk him."

"O' course," says Connie, "if the count gets down to two and three, I'd want him to pass the ball up if it was bad. But if it was where he could reach it, I'd want him to take a wallop, just to show me he ain't scared."

So that's how Martin stood with Connie at the beginnin' o' the series between the Ath-a-letics and Detroit.

The thing didn't happen the first day. The game wasn't close and Martin watched it all from the bench. Bull talked to him, but didn't get what you could call a cordial welcome. Bull wasn't su'prised at that; they ain't no ball player that'll kid with an umps when his dauber's down. He refused Bull's invitation to come round to the hotel that night and have supper with him. And Bull decided that the best play was to leave him alone.

They was a letter from the girl waitin' for Bull that evenin'. She'd heard from her brother and she knowed that he wasn't burnin' up the League; but he'd confessed that Connie hadn't treated him good and the umpires had robbed him blind. She knew, she wrote, that Bull wouldn't cheat him; if Bull really cared for her, he'd help him if he got a chance. And it would kill her and her father and mother besides if Martin had to face the disgrace o' not makin' good.

Bull went to bed and dreamt that Martin was up in a pinch, and he was umpirin' behind the plate, and Martin turned round and looked at him just before the ball was pitched, and Bull smiled at him to encourage him, and Martin took an awful wallop at the pill and give it a ride to the fence in right center. That's what Bull dreamt before the second game o' that series. And here's what really come off:

Big Coveleskie and Bush was havin' a whale of a battle. They wasn't nobody scored till the eighth. Cobb got on then, with only one out. So that give Detroit a run. The ninth looked to be all over. Two o' the Ath-a-letics was out. Then somebody got hold o' one and lit on it for three bases, and what was left o' the crowd decided to stick round a w'ile.

Bull says he knowed Martin was comin' up before he ever looked. And he smiled at him when he announced himself as the batter.

Coveleskie come with a fast ball. Martin had to duck to keep from gettin' hit. Coveleskie come with a curve. Martin made a feeble swing and missed it. Jennin's hollered from the bench:

"Run out with the water! The boy's goin' to swoon!"

Another curve ball that broke over, and Martin left it go.

"Strike two!" says Bull.

"It was inside," says Martin.

"You'll never drive in that run with a base on balls," says Bull.

Coveleskie come with a curve that was high and outside. It was the second ball. He come with another curve, in the same spot. It was three and two.

"Give him all you got!" yelled Jennin's. "Get it over there! He's too scared to swing!"

Bull told me that w'ile Coveleskie was gettin' ready for that next pitch he could see Maggie and the old folks in front of him just as plain as if they was there, and a voice kept sayin' to him, "Call it a ball! Call it a ball!"

The ball come—a fast one. Bull knowed what it was and where it was comin', and he bit his tongue to keep from sayin' "Swing!" Right across the middle it come, as perfect a strike as was ever pitched. And Martin's bat stayed on his shoulder.

"You're out!" says Bull. "It cut the heart!"

The heart o' the plate, and Bull's too, I guess.

Bull met Connie again next day, outside o' the park.

"I've canned your friend Gregory," says Connie.

"Do you know," says Bull, "I come near callin' that last one a ball?"

"If you had," says Connie, "the kid would of been let out anyway, and you'd of fell, in my estimation, from the best umpire in the league to the worst in the world."

Now what does dear little Brother Martin do next? Instead o' goin' back to Montgomery like a man and tryin' to get a fresh start with the club that he'd been borrowed off of, he sets down and writes Maggie that Connie would of kept him only for Bull callin' him out on a ball that was so low and so far outside that the Detroit catcher had to lay down to get it, and that Bull done it because he didn't like him, and if Maggie didn't tie a can to Bull, Martin was through with her and with the old man and old lady too.

Well, the girl wrote back to Bull callin' off the engagement, sayin' how sorry her and her parents was to find out that he would stoop to such meanness and askin' him not to communicate with her no more. And Bull's bull-headed enough so as he wouldn't make a move to square things.

He got that letter from her day before yesterday, just before he left his hotel to come out to the yard. Is it any wonder he didn't say nothin' when I claimed Cady didn't tag me, and went entirely off'n his nut when Cahill called him a crook?

W'ile he was spillin' me the story I got enough into him to make a good sleepin' potion, and then helped him to the hay. The first thing yesterday mornin' I seen Ban and fixed that end of it by re-peatin' the romance. But don't never breathe that Ban knows all about it. Bull thinks he's takin' him back because it was his first offense. And he's comin' back; Ban says he's promised to be in there to-morrow.

And right here in my pocket I got somethin' to show him that'll be better news than gettin' back his job. As luck would have it, I was the first guy to get to the park yesterday, and when I blowed into the clubhouse, who was settin' there but young Mr. Gregory himself! He told me his name and wanted to know was they any chance of him gettin' a try-out with us?

"Yes," I says, "they's one chance and you'll get it if you do as I say. Connie couldn't of gave you the Montgomery club again if we hadn't waived. But I'll fix it for you to join us to-morrow and try your luck again on these conditions: In the first place, you got to go right out now and wire your sister and tell her that the ball you was called out on was right through the middle o' the plate and the best strike you ever seen, and that Connie would of released you anyway, and that if your sister don't wire right back to Bull, in my care, statin' that she's reconsidered and it's still on between she and him, you won't never recognize her as your sister."

"And what if I won't do that?" he says.

"You won't get no chance of a job here," says I, "but you'll get the worst lickin' that was ever gave."

He sent the telegram and I got a night letter this mornin'; addressed to Bull it was, but I read it. I've been tryin' to locate him all day and he's goin' to call up as soon as he gets back to his hotel. Everything's fixed and to-morrow he'll feel so good that he's liable to forget himself and give us somethin' but the worst of it.

As for Martin, if he don't make good with our club it'll be because he can't hit and not because he's too scared to try. I'll have him too scared o' me to be scared of anything else.

THE HOLD-OUT

◊

THREE PEOPLE not countin' myself, think I'm the greatest guy in the world. One o' them's my first and last wife, another's Mr. Edwards, and the other's Bill Hagedorn.

It'd be hard to pick three that I'd rather have cordial. If a person is livin' with their wife, it makes it kind o' pleasant to have her like you. Mr. Edwards, o' course, is the man I'm workin' for, so it don't hurt me at all to be his hero. And I'm glad to have Bill added to the list, because it means he'll play the bag better for me this year than he's done yet, and with a little pep on first base we're liable to be bad news to George Stallin's, Wilbert Robinson and John T. Mc-Graw.

But listen. If Mr. Edwards ever got hold o' the truth o' the Hagedorn business, him and I'd be just as clubby as Lord George and the Kaiser. If he didn't drop dead when he found it out, he'd slip me the tinware, contract or no contract, and I wouldn't have the heart to fight it in the courts, because I admit I gave him a raw deal. My only alibi is that I left my feelin's get the best o' me, and that excuse wouldn't be worth a dime with him; they's no excuse that would be, where his pocketbook's concerned, like in this case. He just simply hates money!

The worst of it is that Hagedorn didn't deserve no consideration. I like to see a fella get all that's comin' to him, provided he goes after it in the right way and puts up a real fight. Hagedorn made a hog of himself and was tremblin' all the time he did it. If he was as yellow on the ball field as when he's makin' a play for more dough, I'd take away his uniform and suspend him for life; he wouldn't be no more use to me than a set of adenoids.

He's just as game a ball player, though, as you'll find. The minute he trots out there in the old orchard he's a different guy, afraid o'

The Saturday Evening Post, March 24, 1917; previously uncollected.

nothin'. All he's lacked so far is ambish, and I figure he'll show some
o' that this year. He'll give me his best out o' gratitude. If he don't,
it'll mean his finish on the big time, family or no family.

It's part o' my agreement with Mr. Edwards that I stick on the job
all the year round, goin' to the league meetin's with him in winter,
helpin' him sign up the boys, and so forth. Well, after we was through
last fall, he called me up in the office and begin crabbin' about
finances.

"Frank," he says, "we lost $18,000 this season. I pretty near wish
I didn't have no ball club."

"You've pretty near got your wish," I says. "If some o' those
bushers don't come through next spring, or if we don't swing a couple
o' deals between now and then, the clubs that play against us won't
even get good practice."

"Bad as we are," he says, "I bet we got the biggest salary list in
the big leagues. It looks to me like not only one or two, but several
of our men were bein' overpaid."

"Yes, sir," I says; "and on their showin' the last few months some
o' them would be overpaid if they drawed a dollar a day."

"Well," he says, "I'm goin' to do some trimmin'. The boys'll kick,
I suppose, but I'm dependin' on you to show 'em they deserve cuts."

"That's a nice little job for me," I says. "It's just as easy to convince
a ball player that his pay ought to be trimmed as it is to score twelve
runs off Alexander."

"I'd just as leave pay good prices for good work," he says, "but
I'm not goin' to maintain no pension bureau. These ridic'lous Federal
League contracts have all run out, thank heavens, and from now
on my ball club'll be run on a sane basis. Look at Lefty Grant!"
he says. "He got $7000 and pitched pretty near eleven full games,
winnin' three o' them. And look at Hagedorn! A $6000 contract
and no more life in him than a wet rag! What do you suppose ailed
him?"

"Federalitis," I says. "He was gettin' soft money in the Federal, with no incentive to win and nobody to try and make him
hustle."

"A $6000 salary," says Mr. Edwards, "for a man that hit round
.220 and played first base like he was bettin' against us! Maybe we'd
better just let loose of him."

"If I was you," I says, "I'd see what the recruits is like before gettin'
rid o' Hagedorn. I'll admit he's been loafin', but he's a mighty good
ball player when he tries."

"Maybe it'll wake him up to cut him," says he. "I'm goin' to send him a contract for $4000."

"Suit youself," says I. "He'll holler like an Indian, but if he sees you're in earnest I guess he'll come round."

"He lives here in town," says Mr. Edwards. "I'll have the girl call him up sometime and tell him I want to see him."

So we discussed a few others that was gettin' way more than they earned, and the boss says he wouldn't play no favorites, but would cut 'em all from ten to forty per cent. I knew they'd be plenty o' trouble, but I didn't care a whole lot. I figured that if everybody on the pay roll quit the game and went to work it'd strengthen the team.

Well, Hagedorn accepted Mr. Edwards' invitation to call and I was in the office when Bill come in.

"Mr. Hagedorn," says the boss, "Manager Conley and myself's been talkin' things over and we come to the conclusion that several o' you boys was earnin' less than we paid you. What do you think about it?"

"Well," says Hagedorn, "some o' the boys maybe deserve cuts. But I don't see how I come in on it."

"Why not?" says Mr. Edwards. "The unofficial averages gives you a battin' percentage o' .220."

"I can't help what them dam scorers do to me," says Bill. "I never did get fair treatment from the reporters."

"But when you was in the league before," says the boss, "you always hit up round .280, and it's a cinch the scorers didn't cheat you out o' sixty points."

"They'd cheat me out o' my shirt if they had a chance," Bill says. "But even if I did have a bad year with the wood, that ain't no sign I won't do all right next season."

"That's true enough," says Mr. Edwards. "Anybody's liable to have a battin' slump. But Manager Conley and myself wasn't thinkin' about your hittin' alone. We kind o' thought that your work all round was below the standard; that you was sort o' layin' down on the job."

Hagedorn began to whine.

"Mr. Edwards," he says, "you got me entirely wrong. I wouldn't lay down on nobody. I've give you my best every minute, and if I haven't it was because things broke bad for me."

"What things?" I ast him.

"Well," he says, "for one thing, I felt rotten all summer. My legs was bad."

"Well," I says, "you can't expect Mr. Edwards to pay $3000 apiece for bad legs."

"But they're all right now," he says. "I haven't had a bit o' trouble with 'em all fall. And I'm takin' grand care o' myself and next spring I'll be as good as ever."

"Why didn't you tell me about your legs?" I ast him. "I'd of let you lay off. You certainly wasn't helpin' us much."

"I'd of told you only I don't like to quit," he says. "And besides, my legs wasn't the whole trouble."

"What else was it?" I says.

"Well," he says, "the Missus was sick and in the hospital, and I had to pay out a lot o' money and it kept me worried."

"When was she sick?" I ast him.

"Let's see," he says, "it was while we was on our last Eastern trip."

"You never ast me to let you come home," I says.

"No," he says, "I didn't know nothin' at all about it till we got back."

"That's why you worried, I suppose," says I, "and I guess your wife's illness in September was what worried you in June and July."

"She was sick on and off all season," he says.

"I noticed," says I, "that she done most of her sufferin' in a grandstand seat. Her ailment," I says, "was probably brought on by watchin' you perform."

"She's full o' nerve," he says. "She wouldn't miss a ball game if she was dyin'. And besides, her sickness wasn't all of it."

"Let's hear the whole story at once," I says. "The suspense is fierce."

"Her folks kept botherin' us," says Hagedorn. "They live in Louisville, and they're gettin' old and they wanted that she should come down there and stay with 'em."

"Couldn't they come up here?" I ast him.

"No," he says, "they got their own home and their own friends and everything down there."

"Well," I says, "that'd probably be the square thing for you to do, just pack up and move to Louisville and live with 'em."

"We'd only be there in the winter," he says.

"No," says I, "I'll fix it so's you can be there all the year round."

"What do you mean?" he says.

"I mean that if you don't want to sign at our figures Louisville'd be the ideal spot for you," says I.

"What's your figures?" he ast.

"I'm willin' to give you $4000," says Mr. Edwards. Hagedorn swelled up.

"If you think I'll take a $2000 cut, you got me wrong," he says.

"All right," says I, "and I hope the Kentucky climate agrees with your legs."

We sent Lefty Grant a contract for $5000 and after a little crabbin' by mail he signed. Joe Marsh stood for a $1000 cut, and Bones McChesney, shaved from $3500 to $3000, refused to sign and got himself sold to Toronto. I didn't cry over losin' him; he'd always been fat from his neck up, and in the last two seasons the epidemic had spread all over his body.

Now it don't often happen that a seventh-place club begins lookin' like a pennant contender between October and February. But that's what come off with us. Our worst weakness last year was at shortstop and third base and back o' the bat. Well, I talked to a lot of Association men durin' the fall, and they told me that I had a second Schalk in this young Stremmle from Indianapolis. And I got swell reports on Berner, the shortstop we drew from Dayton. Both these guys, I was told, were ready. They wouldn't need no more seasonin'.

And then along come the league meetin' in New York, and I happened to catch the St. Louis gang when they were thinkin' about somethin' else, and they traded me Johnny Gould for Hype Corliss and Jack Moran, two guys that I'd kept down in the bull pen all summer so's the bugs couldn't get a good look at 'em. There was my third base hole plugged up and the ball club was bound to be a hundred per cent better, provided Hagedorn signed and give us his best work, or that young Lahey, the first sacker we bought from Davenport, made good. I wasn't worryin' much about him, as I fig- ured right along that Hagedorn would take his $4000 when he seen we were in earnest.

O' course he had a little bit the best of us in the argument—that is, he would of had if he'd knew enough. Him and Lahey was the only candidates for first base, and no matter if he played the position in a hammock, he'd be better than an inexperienced kid from the Three Eye. Even if he wasn't never worth a nickel over $4000, here was a grand chance for him to hold us up. All he had to do was lay quiet at home, and when it come time for us to go South we'd of looked him up and met his demands. But no, he didn't have the nerve or sense to go at it the right way.

Instead o' keepin' us guessin', what does he do but hunt up excuses to come and hang round the office and try and get a hint o' whether we were goin' to stand pat or back down. I was alone the first time he showed.

"Hello, Bill," I says. "Did you bring your fountain pen?"

"What for?" he says.

"To sign that $4000 contract," says I.

"Oh, no," he says, "I wasn't thinkin' nothin' about the contract. I come up to see if they was any mail for me."

"Not now," I says, "but you may be hearin' from the Louisville club in a few days."

"What would they be writin' me about?" he says.

"Maybe they'll hear about you wantin' to move there," I says, "and they'll probably be askin' you if you'd care to take a job with 'em."

"Well," says Bill, "you won't catch me playin' ball with Louisville."

"Who was you thinkin' about playin' with?" I ast him.

"Nobody," he says. "I've decided to quit."

"That's fine, Bill!" I says. "Somebody left you money?"

"No," he says, "but I got some o' my own saved up."

"How much?" I ast him.

"Close to $2000," says Bill.

"Fine work!" says I. "You must of lived pretty simple to save $2000 in seven years."

"I never skimped," says Bill.

"Well," I says, "I don't know how you managed. But it's nice to feel that you won't never have to skimp again. If you can get six per cent for your money that'll mean $120 a year or $10 a month. That puts you on Easy Street. All you'll have to get along without is food, clothes, heat and a place to live."

He paid us another visit Christmas week, thinkin', maybe, that Mr. Edwards would be runnin' over with holiday spirits.

This was a bum guess. The old man's got more relatives than a perch, and when he was through buyin' presents for all o' them he wouldn't of paid a telephone slug for the release o' Ty Cobb.

"No mail yet," I says to Bill when he come in.

"I wasn't expectin' no mail," he says. "I was just wonderin' if I left a pair o' gloves here last time."

"A pair o' tan gloves?" I says.

"Yes," says Hagedorn.

"I didn't see 'em," I says. "I found some gray ones."

"How is everything?" he says.

"Fine!" says I. "It looks like we're goin' to have a regular ball club."

"Well, I hope you do," Bill says.

"Gould's goin' to help us a lot," says I, "and they tell me Stremmle and Berner's both good enough for anybody's team. And then, o' course, we got young Lahey."

"Who's young Lahey?" ast Bill.

"Can't be you never heard of him," I says. "He's the first sacker from Davenport that everybody was after. They say you can't hardly tell him from Hal Chase when he's in action. And he cracked the marble for about .340 last season."

"Hittin' .340 in the sticks and hittin' it up here is two different things," says Hagedorn.

"Not so different," I says. "A bird that can hit .340 anywhere can hit pretty good."

That's right, too. But the truth was that Lahey's figure had been eighty points shy o' what I credited him with. And from what I'd learned from some o' the Three Eye boys, Lahey was the eighth best first baseman in their league.

"Well," says Hagedorn, "if he makes good, you won't have no use for me."

"No," I says, "but I'd hate to see you go back in the bushes."

"Don't worry!" he says. "I'm goin' to stick right here in town."

"And live on your savin's?" I says.

"No," says Bill. "I'm just about signed up to play with the Acmes in the semi-pro league."

"How much are they givin' you?" I ast him.

"Fifty a game, and they only play Sundays," he says.

"Yes," says I, "and they're doin' well if they play twenty games a season. That nets you $1000, and you'll have somethin' like six days a week to spend it in."

"I can work at somethin' durin' the week," he says. "Maybe sell automobiles or somethin'."

"You could do that in the winter, too," I says, "if you didn't waste so much o' your time comin' for your mail and lookin' for your gloves."

"How's Mr. Edwards?" says Bill.

"Fine and dandy!" I says. "Want to see him?"

"What would I want to see him about?" says Bill.

"You might be able to sell him a car." say I. "He's right in the spendin' mood now. His nieces and nephews and Mr. Wilson's peace note has relieved him o' the few hundreds he had left after last season. I wouldn't be surprised if he'd reconsider cuttin' your contract—maybe give you a bonus just for the devil of it."

While we was talkin' Mr. Edwards come out from his private office.

"Hello, Hagedorn," he says. "Ready to sign?"

"At my own figure," says Bill.

"That's good," says Mr. Edwards. "Conley and myself was afraid you might accept the cut, and we couldn't hardly afford to keep an extra first baseman at $4000 a year."

"It's best all round," I says. "Bill's goin' to make more dough than we could possibly give him; he's goin' to sell cars durin' the week and play semi-pro ball Sundays. And maybe he can master the barber trade and pick up a few extra hundreds Saturday nights. But even if he don't make a nickel, he's got $2000 hoarded up."

"That's fine!" says the boss. "I like to see thrift in a young man. And it always seems like a pity that so many boys squander their earnin's and have to keep on slavin' as ball players till they're thirty years old and past the prime o' life."

For three or four days early in January they was an epidemic o' lockjaw in Washington, and the market come up enough for Mr. Edwards to take a trip to New Orleans. He left me in charge o' things, and my job consisted o' makin' up stories for the newspaper boys and entertainin' Hagedorn about once a week.

Once he dropped in to find out Joe Marsh's address; it'd of been impossible, o' course, to inquire by telephone. Another time he just happened to be passin', and happened to remember that he was carryin' a letter that his wife had ast him to mail, and wanted to know if I had a stamp.

I entertained him every time with dope on Lahey and what a whale of a man he was goin' to make us. But one day he come up loaded with some real facts about the guy I'd been boostin'.

"I thought you told me Lahey hit .340 with Davenport," he says.

"I did tell you that," says I.

"Well," says Bill, "somebody was stringin' you. I seen the Three Eye records the other day and they give Lahey .262."

"That don't mean nothin'," I says. "The scorers probably had it in for him."

"And he made more boots than any first baseman in the league," says Bill.

"That shows he was hustlin' " I says. "The more ground you cover, the more you're liable to kick 'em round. Besides," I says, "he was so perfect that the scorers probably thought he'd ought to make plays that would be impossible for a common first sacker."

"Another thing," says Hagedorn: "I happened to run acrost Jack Wells that played in the league with him, and he tells me Lahey's a left-hand hitter. Well, Gould's a left-hand hitter and so's young Berner, and you already had two left-hand hitters amongst the regulars. Your club's goin' to be balanced like a stew on a wild broncho. McGraw and them'll left-hand you to death."

"What do you care!" I says.

"It's nothin' to me," says Bill.

"Well, what do you suppose we better do about it?" I ast him.

"If I was you," he says, "I'd try and get myself a first baseman that hits right-handed."

"It's too late to get anybody," says I. "I guess we're just plain up against it. I wisht you hadn't made up your mind to retire."

"I'd play for you," says Bill, "if you'd meet my price."

"That's up to the old man," I says, "but I know he won't back down. He wouldn't give in to one man when he's stood pat on all the rest o' them."

"It won't be just one man," says Bill.

"What do you mean?" I ast him.

"He'll be lucky if he's got anybody when the showdown comes," says Bill. "The fraternity's give orders that nobody's to sign till you hear from them, and you won't hear from them till the leagues meets its demands."

"That don't affect our club," I says. "We got every man already signed up except yourself."

"Yes," says Hagedorn, "but signed up or not signed up, they won't report till the fraternity tells 'em to."

"You've been playin' long enough to know better'n that," says I. "If you think any ball player's goin' without his prunes to help out some other ball player, you got even less brains than I figured."

"They'll have to strike if the fraternity says so," says Bill. "They're goin' into the Federation o' Labor and be like any other union. And

if they don't strike when they're ordered to they'll be canned out o'
the fraternity."

"Well," I says, "suppose you was Ty Cobb, draggin' down a measly
$16,000 a year, or whatever he's gettin'. Which would you do if the
choice come up, go without the $16,000 or go without the frater-
nity?"

"I'd certainly stick with the fraternity," says Hagedorn. "if I didn't,
I'd be a traitor."

"If I make you out a contract for $6000, will you sign it?" I ast
him.

"Sure," he says. "I always told you I'd sign for my price."

"Well, Bill," I says, "I won't give you the contract. I'd hate to think
I'd made a traitor out o' you."

"I don't want no contract anyway," says Bill. "I'm through. I'm
goin' into business."

"What business?" I says.

"Somethin' pretty good," he says. "I and a friend o' mine's goin'
in partners in a garage.

"That's a great idear!" says I. "You won't have no competition and
it won't cost nothin' to start, and besides that, it's a game you know
more about than any other, unless it's dressmakin'."

"My friend knows all about it," says Bill. "and I can pick it up
from him."

"You better stick to pickin' up low throws," I says. "It takes years
to learn the mechanism of a car when you don't know nothin' to
start, not even what makes the front wheels run. But o' course you
won't be the only one in the garage business that has to learn, and
so long as it's other people's cars you wreck while you're learnin',
why what's the difference!"

"They's good money in a garage," says Bill.

"I know it, and a whole lot of it's mine," I says. "They's good
money in any business like that—smugglin' or counterfeitin' or
snatchin' purses. But it must be hell on a man's conscience, even
worse'n drawin' $6000 per annum for takin' a six months' nap on
the old ball field."

The first thing Mr. Edwards ast me when he got back from the
South was what was the latest dope on Hagedorn.

"He's surprised me," I says. "I thought he'd give in long before
this. But nothin' doin'."

"What will we do about it?" says the boss.

"Mr. Edwards," I says, "you're the man that's payin' me my money, and it's my business to look out for your interests. If Hagedorn had of kept away from here all winter, if we hadn't heard nothin' from him from the day he first turned down the contract, I'd say give him his $6000. But him comin' round here once a week shows that he needs us as much as we need him, and that he'll stand for the cut, if he's got to. Besides, he's showed a mighty poor opinion o' me by expectin' me to believe all that junk about him goin' into business, and so on—stuff that was old in the Noah's Ark League. He couldn't earn a dime a day in anything outside o' baseball. If he had a factory that made shells out o' lake water, he'd be bankrupt in a month. Now they's probably four better first basemen than him in the league, but I doubt if more'n one o' them's drawin' $6000. O' course with him on the ball club it looks like we'd be somewheres up in the race, and we ain't got a chance with a busher playin' the position.

"If it was a case o' givin' him his dough or gettin' along without him, I'd rather see him get the money even if it's a holdup. But if I'm any judge of a ball player, he'll come round here on his hands and knees the day before we start for the Springs, and he'll sign at whatever price you offer him."

"It's a shame," says Mr. Edwards, "when everything else looks so good for us, to have to be worryin' about a man like him, that loafed on us all last summer and that I'd get rid of in a minute if I had somebody in his place. I suppose they's no chance o' tradin' for a first baseman at this stage."

"Oh, yes, they's a chance," I says. "I suppose Matty'd let us have Chase if we'd give up our pitchin' staff and half a dozen infielders and $40,000 or $50,000 in cash. Then we'd have Chase and nothin' with him."

"Maybe young Lahey'll surprise us," says the boss.

"It won't hurt us to hope," I says, "but from what I can learn Bill Doyle was mad at you when he recommended him. And besides," I says, "Lahey's a left-hand hitter, and that'd mean five o' them in the game every day. We'd be a set-up for fellas like Schupp and Smith and Tyler. Take Hagedorn, and he can murder a left-hander even when he ain't hittin' his weight against a regular pitcher."

"Well, all we can do is wait," says Mr. Edwards.

"And I don't think it'll be long," I says.

But when the night come for us to start South, Hagedorn was still a hold-out, though he did show one more sign o' weakenin'. He was down to the station to shake hands with the boys and see us off, and he looked like he was ready to cry. I called him off to one side.

RING AROUND THE BASES

"Would you like to be goin' along, Bill?" I ast him.

"Oh, I don't know," he says.

"Why don't you take your medicine and hop aboard?" I says. "Your missus can pack up your stuff and send it after you."

"I'll go if you say the word," he says.

"You're the one that must do the talkin'," says I.

"Why couldn't I go along without signin'?" he says. "Maybe the old man would meet my figure when he seen how hard I'd work to get in shape."

"No," says I, "this ain't no charity excursion we're runnin'. We pay nobody's fare that ain't signed up and a member o' this ball club. If you want to sign at $4000, they's a contract right there in my grip. If you don't, why you can spend the rest o' the winter countin' snowflakes and cursin' the coal trust."

"Well," he says, "I'll freeze to death before I'll be robbed; starve to death, too, before I'll let old Edwards bull me out o' what's comin' to me."

"I'm sorry, Bill," I says. "But anyway, good luck to you."

"Good luck to you too," says Bill. "You'll need it."

"Oh, I don't know," I says. "I got a hunch that it's goin' to be a great year for everybody in baseball."

"Well," says Hagedorn, "I know some fellas that'll have a great year."

"Who do you mean, Bill?" I ast him.

"All the left-handers that pitches against your ball club," he says.

About half the baseball reporters on our papers know somethin' about the game. The other half's kids that can write cute stories, but don't know a wild pitch from a hit and run sign. This was the half that went on the spring trip with us. The old heads was sent with the Americans, because they'd made a fight for the pennant last year and the public was strong for 'em.

Well, I took advantage of our gang bein' green and made 'em perjure themself to their papers every day. When they'd come to me for the dope, I'd rave to 'em about what a world-beater young Lahey was, and how he'd burn up the league as soon as I'd learned him a few o' the fine points o' first-base play. If they'd been wise they could of told with one look that Mr. Lahey wouldn't do. But they were just kids and they ate it up. I bet if any o' the fellas that had played with Lahey read what I was sayin' about him in the papers they must of thought I was crazy.

My idear, o' course, was to worry Hagedorn. I knew he'd be readin' everything he could find about us, and I didn't want him to get the impression that the ball club was goin' to bust up without him.

I thought Mr. Edwards would have sense enough to get this. But no; he fell just as hard as the reporters. And when he joined us after we'd been at the Springs two weeks, he was all smiles.

"Well," he says, "I been readin' some mighty encouragin' news."

"What news?" I says.

"About Lahey," says he. "I told you he might surprise us."

"He's surprised me in one way," I says. "I'm surprised that he ever had the nerve to come on this trainin' trip. I always thought pretty well o' the Three Eye League till I seen him," I says.

"You're jokin'," says Mr. Edwards. "I've read nothin' but good reports of him."

"I'm responsible for the reports," I says, "but I thought you'd guess that I was fakin' for Hagedorn's benefit."

"Well, if you've fooled Hagedorn, he's got company," says Mr. Edwards. "I thought our troubles was all over."

"Our troubles won't never be over if Hagedorn don't give in," I says.

"But Lahey must be some good, the way he was recommended," says the boss.

"Doyle probably seen him just once," I says, "and that must of been the one good day he had. But even at that, Doyle couldn't of never watched him handle his feet and thought he was a ball player."

"Is it just his feet that's the trouble?" ast Mr. Edwards.

"No," I says, "but they'd be plenty without outside help. We've had infield practice about nine times since we been here, and that means he's got nine hundred self-inflicted spike wounds. And they must of kept first base in a different place down to Davenport. Anyway he can't find it here. And when he does happen to stumble onto it, it's always with the wrong foot. Besides that, every time Gould or Berner makes a low peg Lahey loses a tooth. Gould ast him one day why he didn't wear a mask. But you ought to see him field bunts! If experience counts for anything, he'd ought to be the most accurate thrower in the world, from a sittin' posture."

"How about his hittin'?" the boss ast me.

"He's a consistent hitter," I says. "They's a party from Kansas City stoppin' at the hotel. They come out to every practice and always set in the same place right back o' the plate, behind the grandstand screen. Well, every ball Lahey's hit so far has made 'em duck."

"Does he act like he had stage fright?" says the boss.

"Not him!" says I. "Nobody but the gamest guy in the world could cut off a few toes every day and come out the next day for more. And nobody without a whole lot o' nerve could keep diggin' after low throws when he knows that they're goin' to uppercut him in the jaw. No, sir! You can't scare Charley!"

"Charley!" says Mr. Edwards. "I thought his name was Mike."

"Gould's nicknamed him Charley," I says, "after Charley Chaplin."

Well, the boss wasn't what you could call tickled to death with my dope on Lahey, but he cheered up a little when I told him about Gould and the rest o' them. Gould was goin' even better than when he was with St. Louis. He was hustlin' like a colt and hittin' everything they throwed up there. And he kept coachin' young Berner like he'd been hired for that job. He put real pep in the infield, and I knew it was tough for him to keep it up when Lahey gummed pretty near every play that was pulled.

Berner cinched his job the first day out. He's the kind of a kid that just won't stay on the bench, as lively and full o' fight as little Bush, at Detroit, or Buck Weaver, or Rabbit Maranville. And Stremmle come up to everything they said about him. Then Joe Marsh seemed to of got over the Federal League and acted five years younger than he is. And our outfield was workin' hard. O' course this young Sheppard showin' up so good helped a lot and made the rest o' them hustle.

I told Mr. Edwards, I says:

"Outside o' first base, I wouldn't trade this ball club for McGraw's. These boys have got more spirit than any team I ever managed. They're the kind that's liable to upset the whole league. If we only just had a good reliable man on that bag, I'd almost guarantee to finish one-two-three."

"And do you still think Hagedorn's goin' to join us?" the boss ast me.

"I certainly do," I says. "I wouldn't be surprised to get a wire from him any day."

But we went along another week without hearin' from Bill. Mr. Edwards kept gettin' more and more nervous. And I guess I was beginnin' to get nervous too.

About the second day o' the third week down there, a letter come to me from Hagedorn's wife. It hit me right in the eye.

Bill, she told me, didn't know she was writin' and would probably kill her if he found it out. She'd been beggin' and beggin' him all winter to take what we offered, and she'd just about had him coaxed when the papers begin printin' the swell reports about Lahey. Those reports had took all the zip out o' Bill. Instead o' frightenin' him into signin' at our figure, they'd convinced him that he wasn't wanted on our club. And Bill was worse than broke. He was over three months behind with the rent and the meat bill and so forth, and coal was a hundred dollars a ton, and they wasn't no coal even at that price, and she was afraid he'd do somethin' desperate. And she thought if I'd just send Bill a wire and tell him that we'd carry him as an extra man, or if I'd try and trade him somewheres where he could make some kind of a salary, he'd be so tickled that he'd come to us or go wherever we sent him at whatever price he could get. And she begged me to not tell anybody that she'd wrote.

Mr. Edwards had just left us to run down to Dallas for a few days. O' course I wouldn't of let him know about the letter anyway. But him bein' away give me the idear o' keepin' Bill's comin' a secret. I was goin' to surprise him by havin' Bill blow in unexpected, because it was a cinch the old man'd be back before Bill could get there. So I didn't wire Dallas, but just sent a telegram to Bill, sayin', "If you'll sign for $4000, first-base job is yours. Answer."

The answer come the same night. It said all right, that he'd join us the followin' Thursday.

On Wednesday Mr. Edwards come back to the Springs. And that afternoon Charles C. Lahey give the funniest exhibition I ever seen on a ball field. The whole practice was a joke, because Gould and Berner and Marsh and the rest o' them was laughin' so hard they couldn't do nothin'. But the wind-up come near not bein' a joke. It'd of been a tragedy if Lahey wasn't the awkwardest guy in the world.

We was tryin' the double play, first base to second base and back. I hit a ball pretty close to the bag and it took a nice hop, so they wasn't no chance for Charley to boot it. He pegged down to Berner, and then turned round and started lookin' for his own bag. Berner took the throw and sent it back as fast as I ever seen a ball pegged. Well, sir, Lahey found out where first base was by trippin' over it. But just before he tripped he turned his head to look for the throw. If he hadn't tripped and went sprawlin', that ball would of cracked him right in the temple, and if it had, good night! To show you how much Berner had on it, it hit the grandstand on the short hop and made a noise like somewheres in France.

"That'll do, boys!" I hollered to them. "We'll quit. The express rates on caskets between here and Davenport is somethin' fierce."

I walked back to the hotel with Mr. Edwards. I never seen a guy so blue.

"He's impossible," he says.

"Never mind," says I. "He won't be with us long. One o' these days his luck'll desert him and he'll get killed."

"I think we'd better send for Hagedorn," says the boss.

"Oh, no," I says. "He'll show up before long."

"Yes," says Mr. Edwards; "but he'd ought to be here right now to get used to playin' with Gould and Berner. And I ain't so sure he'll show up, neither."

"I'd like to make you a little bet," I says. "I'd like to bet you five that we hear from him before the end o' the week."

"I'll just take that bet," says Mr. Edwards, "and I'll be glad to pay if I lose."

Well, knowin' him pretty well, I didn't hardly believe that. But I told him the bet was on.

The first train into the Springs from the North is supposed to arrive at nine in the mornin' and it don't hardly ever get in later than 3 P.M. On this Thursday it come at one-thirty. I snuck down alone to meet it, and there was Bill. "Mighty glad to see you, Hagedorn," I says.

"I'm glad to get here," says Bill.

"You don't need to work to-day if you don't want to," says I, "but we want you out there as soon as you feel like it."

"Why, what's happened to this wonderful Lahey?" says Bill.

"Not a thing," I says; "but as you pointed out, he's a left-hand hitter, and we're overloaded with 'em."

"I suppose you'll play him when they's right-hand pitchin' against us," says Hagedorn.

"No," I says, "I don't believe in switchin' on the infield. Still, you'll have to keep hustlin' to hold him on the bench. He's one o' the most remarkable first sackers in baseball."

"I'm just as good as he is," says Bill.

"You'll have to show me," I says.

"That's just what I'm goin' to do," says Hagedorn.

"And how's everything at home?" I ast him.

"Well, Frank," he says, "it's been a tough winter—the toughest I ever put in. I'm in debt so far that it scares me to think of it."

"Where was that $2000 you had saved?" I says.

"I was just stringin' you about that," says Bill. "I never had a nickel saved. But $2000 is just about what I'm behind."

"Good lord, Bill!" I says to him. "What have you done, bought a limousine?"

"No, sir," he says. "I ain't bought nothin' only clothes and food and not much o' that. But I was way in the hole before, and just this week they've ran up about $200 more on me."

"What for?" I ast him.

"Well, Frank," he says, "the wife presented me with a little boy last Sunday mornin'. If it hadn't been for that, and the way she worried about things, I'd of never been down here to sign for $4000. It was a case of have to, that's all."

I'd left orders for the boys to be out for practice at a quarter to two, and I knew Mr. Edwards would be out there with 'em. I and Bill was pretty near to the hotel by this time, but I stopped him short.

"Bill," I says, "you ain't givin' me no bull like that $2000 fortune, are you?"

"No, Frank," he says, "I'm tellin' you the truth."

"All right, Bill," I says; "I'm takin' your word. They's a northbound local train leavin' here at three bells. You go down and get aboard it and ride to Silver Creek. That's a station about twenty miles up the line. They's a hotel there, and that's about all. You go there and stay till I send for you."

"What's the idear?" he says.

"You'll find out later," I says. "I just tell you now that it's to your interest to do what I say."

"I can't go nowheres," he says. "I've got just forty cents."

"I'll stake you," says I, "and you'll hear from me in three or four days."

"But I want to get out there and see this here Lahey," says Bill. "I want to get busy showin' him up."

"He'll tend to that end of it himself," I says. "But you're on this ball club and I'm manager of it, and if you want to stick on this ball club you'll obey the manager's orders."

So Bill took the local for Silver Creek and I beat it out to the orchard to see that nobody got killed.

I set down with the boss at supper that night.

"Mr. Edwards," I says, "I've changed my mind about Hagedorn."

"What do you mean?" he says.

"I mean that I think he's through with us," I says.

"But good lord!" says the boss. "We can't get along without him."

"Well," says I, "we can get him by givin' him $6000."

Mr. Edwards shook like he had a chill.

"Give in to him now!" he says. "When he's tried to hold us up! And I thought you was so sure he'd come round."

"I did think he would," says I, "but I'm sure now that he won't. He's stuck this long, and he'll stick forever. He's gamer'n I figured."

"But I'd rather lose another $18,000 than let him hold us up," says the boss.

"Well," I says, "that's up to you. But you'll lose $18,000 all right, and maybe then some, if you don't get him. Because without him on first base we'll be the worst ball club in the league."

Mr. Edwards didn't say nothin' more for maybe five minutes. Then he give up.

"I got a lot o' confidence in you, Frank," he says. "I'll go by what you tell me. If you want to you can wire Hagedorn. Tell him we'll meet his terms, and tell him to get here on the first train."

"I think it's the best thing to do," I says. And I went out and pretended to send Bill a wire.

It takes two days and a half to get to the Springs from home. So I called Bill up at Silver Creek and had him blow into camp on the Sunday train. I met him and tipped him off. He fell all over himself thankin' me and says he was goin' to name the boy Frank. And then he made a request.

"Keep this a secret from my missus," he says. "I want her to think that I got what I was after because I insisted on it. Because she kept tellin' me all winter that I wouldn't never get it and was a sucker to try."

"Don't worry," I says, "I want it to be kept a secret from certain people myself, and I certainly ain't goin' to spill it to no woman."

Mr. Edwards was on the walk in front o' the hotel when I and Bill showed up.

"Well, Hagedorn," he says, "you got what you wanted and I hope you'll try and earn it."

"I'll earn it all right, Mr. Edwards," he says, "and I'm mighty grateful to you for comin' acrost."

The boss turned to me.

"How about our little bet?" he says.

"What bet?" says I.

"You bet me five," he says, "that we'd hear from Hagedorn before the week was over. And this is another week."

"So you want me to pay you that five?" I ast him.

"I certainly do," he says.

Well, I give him the five, and afterwards Bill told me he'd make that up to me as soon as he could. But I can't accept it from him. I'd feel like I was takin' candy from a baby, a baby named Frankie Hagedorn.

THE YELLOW KID

◊

I

THE FIRST THING we found out about Crosby was that he couldn't read. The next thing was that he was scared to death o' women and girls. It was Buck Means that give us the info, and he done it out o' spite.

You see, Buck and Crosby was with the Dallas Club together year before last, and Buck was sore because Crosby got drafted, while Buck was overlooked. And Buck didn't like to see a kid with only one year's experience go up, when Buck himself had been in the sticks four or five seasons and nobody'd paid any attention to him.

Crosby was recommended to us by Jake Atz. Jake wrote up along in July and ast if we could use the fastest young left-hander he ever seen. So the old man put in a draft and we got him.

Well, Jake was right about the kid's speed. I've faced 'em all, from Rube Waddell down, but I never hit against nobody that could zip 'em through there like Crosby. If he ever beaned a man they'd have to get along afterwards without no head. O' course that wouldn't be no hardship to most o' them. It wouldn't affect the work o' nobody on our club.

Our first exhibition game last spring was in Dallas. Buck Means was talkin' to Gilbert and I before the practice.

"How's Crosby comin'?" he ast us.

"I'm glad he's on our club," I says, "so I don't have to hit against him all season."

"He's faster'n Johnson," says Gilbert. "If he was only a little wild with it they'd all be swingin' from the bench."

"They's no doubt about his smoke," says Buck; "but he's got nothin' besides, not even a noddle. He can't even read."

The Saturday Evening Post, June 23, 1917; previously uncollected.

"Can't read!" I says. "Why, he looks brighter'n that."

"Sure!" says Means. "He's a good-lookin' kid. But, from the shoulders up, he's unimproved property."

"Not bein' able to read won't hurt him," I says. "He won't be bothered if the newspaper boys handle him a little rough once in a while."

"But if you got a joker on your club," says Buck,. "Crosby'll be pie for him. McGowan, one of our outfielders, made a monkey of him all last year. He'd buy a paper and come and set down somewheres near Crosby and make up stuff that was supposed to be in there, and read it out loud. And he didn't read no compliments, neither, except when it come to Crosby's looks. You see, that's another thing about the poor simp: He's afraid o' skirts. He's so bashful that if they's a girl under ninety stoppin' at the same hotel he'll duck out and buy a meal at his own expense rather'n take a chance o' havin' her look at him in the dinin' room. And McGowan, while pretendin' that the papers was knockin' him as a pitcher, pretended, besides, that they were always printin' how handsome he was and how all the girls was wild about him. And, to make it good, Mac'd write fake love letters to him and he'd get somebody to read 'em, and then good night! He'd lock himself up in his room for a week and never come out, only to get to the ball park. We had him believin' they was a girl in Austin that was crazy to marry him, and he was weak and sick all the times we was there, for the fear she'd call him up or he'd run into her on the street."

Well, when I and Gilbert was alone, I says that maybe we'd better keep this dope to ourself, or somebody might take advantage o' the kid and maybe spoil him as a pitcher. Gilbert was agreeable—that is, he told me he was. But he didn't lose no time spillin' the whole thing to Harry Childs, and he couldn't of picked out a worse one to tell it to.

Harry'd rather kid somebody than hit one on the pick, and him and Joe Jackson hates their base hits just alike.

So as soon as he got a chance he went after Crosby.

We was ridin' to Fort Worth and Childs had a Chicago paper. He flopped down in the seat beside Crosby.

"Well, kid," he says, "do you want to read what the reporters has sent up about you?"

"No," says Crosby, "I ain't interested in no newspaper talk. As long as I give the club the best I got, they can write anything they please."

"Yes, says Childs; "but this is a nice little boost and they's no man can tell me he don't like encouragement."

"But readin' papers on the train always puts my eyes on the bum," says the kid."

"I'll read it to you," says Harry. "I don't think your ears'll be hurt."

So Childs pulled somethin' about like this:

"One o' the most promisin' recruits is Lefty Crosby, that was drafted from the Texas League last fall. Though this boy only had one year's experience in the minors, he already handles himself like a veteran. His speed is terrific and his control a whole lot better than the average young left-hander's.

"Manager Cahill's only fear about him is that the female fans o' Chicago and New York will bother him to death with telephone calls and sweet notes. In appearance, Crosby is a great deal like Francis X. Bushman. It is a certainty that he will take the fair sex by storm, provided he gives them the slightest encouragement."

Crosby was redder'n an undershirt.

"That's bunk!" he says. "Who wrote that?"

"The guy didn't sign his name," says Childs.

"I shouldn't think he would," says Crosby.

"I don't know why not," says Childs. "He was tellin' the truth. A fella as handsome and young-lookin' as you can just about take his pick of any dame in New York or Chi."

"I wasn't thinkin' about gettin' married," says Crosby, "I'm satisfied the way I am."

"Cahill'd rather have you married, though," says Harry. "He figures a man's liable to behave himself better if he's tied down."

"I'll behave all right," says the kid. "I got no bad habits."

"But if they's a beautiful bride for you to support, you'll work harder and improve faster," Childs says.

"I always work as hard as I can," says the kid.

"Maybe you already got a girl here in Texas," says Harry. "Maybe it's some little black-eyed peacherita from acrost the Border."

"I haven't no girl at all, and don't want none," says Crosby. "I don't see why a man can't get along without thinkin' about girls all the while."

"But," says Harry, "the Lord wouldn't of made you so beautiful if he thought you was goin' to be a woman hater."

"I ain't beautiful or nothin' o' the kind," says Crosby, blushin' harder'n ever.

Childs started to tell him he was too modest; but the kid got up and moved away.

In the hotel at Fort Worth, Harry got one o' the telephone girls to call up Crosby's room and tell him she'd love to meet him. He hung up on her. In Oklahoma City, Childs had one o' the local papers print a picture o' Crosby in action. He brought the paper into the dinin' room and flopped down at the same table with the kid.

"Did you see this?" he ast him. "It's pretty fair; but it don't hardly do you justice."

"What do I care!" says Crosby.

"I'd care a whole lot if I was you," says Harry. "If I had your looks I wouldn't allow no picture to be printed that didn't give me a square deal. And you ought to read what it says under it. But maybe it affects your stomach to read while you're eatin'. I'll read it to you."

"I don't care what it says," says Crosby.

"It's only a few words," says Childs. "I don't mind readin' it at all." And he handed him this kind o' stuff: "Above is showed a likeness o' Lefty Crosby, one o' Manager Cahill's recruits from Texas. They expect him to not only break a few strike-out records in the big circuit, but also the hearts of all the girls that gets a good look at him. Crosby promises to be the Adonis o' baseball."

I guess the kid didn't know Adonis from Silk O'Loughlin; but that didn't keep him from blushin' like a beet. Childs leaned over and whispered to him.

"They's a queen over there by the window," he says, "and she's done nothin' only look at you for five minutes. Maybe if I leave you alone she'll come over and introduce herself."

"I don't feel like eatin' no more lunch," says Crosby; and he beat it out o' the room. He hadn't hardly gargled half his soup.

From then on the kid tried to duck Harry all he could. But he didn't have the nerve to offend nobody, and lots o' times Childs'd corner him where he couldn't escape without makin' it too raw.

Crosby's best pal on the club was Joe Martin. Joe's always the bushers' friend because he don't believe in ridin' 'em. Crosby tried to set with Joe at the same table on the diners and in the hotels, because Martin'd read pretty near the whole bill o' fare out loud and Crosby could pick out what he really wanted to eat. Martin, o' course, done this on purpose, knowin' Crosby couldn't read and was generally always hungry.

It's pretty tough on a kid with a good appetite to not be able to tell what's listed unless somebody reads it off to him.

But Joe couldn't spend all his time makin' things easy for Crosby, and whenever Childs could manage to set with the kid he was meaner to him than a snake. For instance, after we'd had a tough work-out and everybody was starvin', Childs'd pick up the bill and begin crabbin' about how many things had been scratched offen it.

"We're gettin' a fine deal," he'd say. "They's nothin' left only salad and ice cream." Then he'd say to the waiter: "Bring me salad and ice cream."

And Crosby'd have to say that he'd take the same. Childs was willin' to go hungry himself for the sake o' puttin' it over.

The last day we was on the spring trip, Harry bought a rule book and brought it on the train.

"They've certainly made some radical changes this year," he says to Crosby. "A left-handed pitcher can't throw to first base without turnin' round twice before he pegs. And a left-handed pitcher can't throw more'n two curve balls to the same left-handed hitter durin' one time at bat. They're tryin' to increase the hittin'. And only the first foul counts a strike. And the pitcher and catcher ain't goin' to be allowed to work with signs. And when it's a pitcher's first year in the Big League, he ain't only allowed two strikes up there at bat. That's to hurry the game. And you got to get four men out instead o' three. And you can't pitch nothin' only new balls. The minute a ball's even tipped by a bat, the umps throws it away and gives you a brand-new one. And a pitcher ain't allowed to warm up the day he's goin' to pitch. And a pitcher can't wear a glove. And a pitcher can't wind up unless they's a runner on first or second base. Then he's got to. And if a pitcher's taken out three times in three months, he's automatically released, and either he's got to go to a Class E league or quit playin' baseball."

I don't know if Crosby fell for all o' that or not; but, anyway, I got him alone a while later and told him Childs was just kiddin' and the rules was the same as ever. It'd probably been hard enough for him to learn 'em in the first place without ringin' in no long list o' changes for him to try and master.

The train was late pullin' into Chi next mornin' and Harry got one more crack at the kid before we come to Englewood.

"Well, Lefty," he says, "you're goin' to have a real try-out right away. I was talkin' to Cahill and he says he's goin' to start you Friday o' this week."

Crosby looked tickled to death.

"The reason for it," says Childs, "is because Friday is Lady's Day at our park. The womenfolks all comes in free and the boxes and stand is always full o' them. And the old man wants to get 'em well pleased with the club right from the jump. He figures that if they see you once, they'll make their husbands and sweethearts bring 'em every time you pitch."

"I don't know if I'm goin' to be right to pitch Friday or not," says the poor boob. "The old souper felt kind o' numb when I worked yesterday."

"On Fridays," says Childs, "the boxes right back of our bench is always saved for showgirls. And the ball players that looks good to them, they always talk to."

"If Friday ain't a nice hot day," says Crosby, "I'm goin' to ask him not to work me. My arm feels rotten."

II

WELL, CAHILL DIDN'T ASK the kid to pitch Friday's game; never had no intention o' doin' it, o' course! But he did start him the followin' Monday, against the Cleveland gang.

For five innin's he pitched as pretty a game o' ball as I ever seen and we had 'em licked 3 to o. Then Childs, who was warmin' the bench, got after him, either because he was sore on havin' been took out o' the outfield or just naturally couldn't resist a chance to pull somethin'.

While Cahill was coachin' at first base, Childs called Crosby up to one side o' the shed.

"Did you see her yet?" he ast him.

"See who?" says the kid.

"I guess you know who," says Childs. "They's a peach right behind the middle o' this bench. I noticed her lookin' at you ever since you warmed up. And while you was out there pitchin' last innin', she ast me your name. I told her and she says you was the handsomest man she ever looked at. So then she ast me would I introduce her to you when the game's over."

"I won't have no time," says Crosby.

"But, man," says Harry, "I promised I'd do it."

Just then the innin' was over and we went out. You never seen such a change in a pitcher. He couldn't get one near the plate. He acted like he was scared stiff. He was so wild that he had the ushers duckin'.

Cahill left him in there a few minutes to give him a chance to steady himself. But they wasn't nothin' to do but take him out after he'd walked four o' them without pitchin' a strike. Cahill was ravin' mad.

"Another yellow dog!" he says. "The next time Jake Atz recommends a man to me, I'll wire him at his own expense to take a dose o' bichloride. What do you think o' this stiff? We give him a three-run lead and they can't hit him with a board, and he's only got four innin's to go! And he blows higher'n a kite! Sixteen balls without a strike! And once he pretty near missed the whole grand stand! Go climb in the shower so you'll be clean when you start back for Texas."

Crosby was glad to sneak to the clubhouse and get out o' the park. But I and Martin was suspicious that somethin' had come off, and next time we come in we ast Childs.

"Yes," says Harry, "I suppose it's my fault. But if the poor boob is as simple as that, he'd ought to lose out."

"What did you pull on him?" ast Joe.

"I just told him," says Harry, "that they was a pretty girl setcin' right back of our bench that ast to meet him after the game."

"That ain't right, Harry," says Martin. "He looks as good as any left-hander in the league, and we can't afford to spoil him. Just lay offen him. You know he's scared o' women; but that ain't the worst fault in the world, and you got to admit that he didn't look scared o' them Cleveland boys till he blowed up. Leave him alone and he'll win a lot o' ball games for us."

"Why should I leave him alone?" says Harry. "Since they got me settin' on the bench, they's nothin' left for me to do only kid somebody."

"All right," says Joe, "if you won't do it for me I'll put it up to Cahill."

And sure enough, in the clubhouse after the game, Martin told the M. G. R. just what had come off.

"Look here, Childs!" says Cahill. "That'll be enough o' that. I don't care how much fun you have with him offen the field, but when we're playin' a game, lay off! If you don't think I'm in earnest you may soon be takin' a trip to Texas yourself!"

So Childs laid offen him entirely for a while, not even tryin' to pester him when we went on our first trip. But I knew it wouldn't never last. While it did last, though, Crosby done better work than any o' the rest of our pitchers and had the whole league stood on their heads with that fast one o' his.

III

WE LEFT CLEVELAND one evenin', goin' to St. Louis, and the boys started a game o' cards. Childs was in it and Crosby was leanin' over the back of a seat, watchin'. I was settin' in the game, too, right where I could look at Crosby.

Well, Gilbert win three pots in a row, with aces one time, aces up the next time, and the third time he beat Childs with three o' the big bulls.

"Come on, Gil!" says Harry. "Give the aces a chance to roam round the deck once in a while."

"I can't spare 'em, Harry," says Gilbert.

"You put 'em in the deck!" says Childs, just kiddin'.

"You make me put 'em in the deck!" says Gil.

Well, Harry had a gun on his hip, with nothin' in it but blanks, and he pulled it out and laid it on the table in front of him, just for a joke.

But Crosby didn't see the joke. I happened to be lookin' at him when Childs showed the gun. He turned white as a sheet and I thought for a minute he was goin' to keel over. Then he grabbed the top o' the seat to steady up, and the next thing we knew he was beatin' it for the other end o' the car as fast as he could navigate.

"What's the matter with him now?" says Harry.

"Looks like he objected to the firearms," says Gilbert.

"What the hell ain't he scared of?" says Childs.

"Well," I says, "Ty Cobb for one thing and Bob Veach for another."

"Did he think I'd be monkeyin' with a loaded gat?" says Harry. "I'll have to try him out and see which he likes best, women or artillery."

"Oh, leave him alone!" says I. "As long as he keeps winnin' ball games for us, what's the difference if he's scared o' wild cats or fishworms?"

But Harry'd been good long enough. The next mornin', when we was crossin' the bridge into St. Louis, he finds Crosby in the wash-room. Without sayin' nothin' he just simply laid his gun on one o' the sills, pointin' it straight at the kid. And Crosby begin shakin' like a leaf and staggered out o' the room without even waitin' to grab his collar.

Childs told us about it and seemed to think it was the funniest thing ever pulled off. But some o' the rest of us didn't think it was so funny, especially when we had to put Crosby to bed the minute we got to the hotel, and then get along without him all through the series with the Browns.

And Cahill made the remark, so as Childs could hear him, that the next guy that pulled a gun where Crosby was, or left one where he would see it, was through with our ball club for life.

IV

FOR A WHILE after that, Harry was satisfied to just pull the girl stuff on his victim. He begin writin' fake love letters, like the guy'd done down in the Texas League. Some o' them was wonders. I know, because I read 'em to Crosby myself, he tellin' me that the different handwritin's was so funny that he couldn't make 'em out. But this wasn't much joy for Childs, because you can bet he wasn't never ast to read 'em.

Crosby wouldn't only let me get so far when he'd make me stop, and then he'd take the letters and tear 'em up.

"I wisht all girls would leave me alone," he'd say.

"What have you got against 'em?" I'd say to him.

"Bill," he'd say, "I'd just as lief own up to you. I don't feel comfortable round 'em. I'm just plain bashful. That's what my sister used to tell me. She was the only one I could ever talk to without pretty near faintin'."

"You'd get over that soon enough, if you'd try," I'd tell him. "You won't never know what livin' is till you get married and have a home o' your own. And they's nothin' about girls to be scared of, especially for as nice a lookin' guy as you are. They wouldn't never make fun o' you."

"I ain't afraid o' that," he'd say to me. "I wouldn't mind talkin' to 'em if I thought they'd just laugh and joke with me or talk baseball.

But girls is liable to get personal and begin makin' eyes; and if they done that with me, I'd run a mile."

"Wasn't they no girls in the town you come from?"

"Too many o' them," he says. "They was only about two hundred people in the town and half o' them was girls, seemed like to me."

"How'd you get away from 'em?" I says.

"Just by runnin'," he says. "I beat it from home when I was twelve years old and that's why I didn't get no schoolin' to speak of. I joined in with a minin' gang up North, where I was sure they wouldn't be no skirts to bother me."

"You was young to be mixed up with a crowd like that," says I.

"Yes; but they treated me fine," says Crosby. "I'd of been in that game yet only for somethin' happenin'."

"What happened?" I ast.

"Oh, you'd think I was crazy if I told you," he says. "They was too rough for me. I can fight as good as the next guy when it's just usin' your fists. But I can't stand guns. Between you and I, I'm scareder o' them than I am o' girls. It started, I guess, one night when they was a scrap in a saloon. Everybody was lit up and, first thing you know, they had their gats out and was pluggin' away. And the guy that had took care o' me, when I first come to the camp, was shot dead right in front o' my eyes. I got sick at that time, watchin' it, and ever since then I get sick every time I see one o' the damn things."

"You're gunshy and girlshy," I says. "Anything else you're scared of?"

"Yes," he says; "a fast ball that's comin' at my bean. But I guess I got plenty o' company there."

"Well, Lefty," I says, "I can say one thing for you: You're brave enough when it comes to pitchin' against a .400 hitter in a pinch. And that's more than can be said for some o' the rest of our beautiful pitchers."

V

ONE O' THE PRETTIEST girls I ever seen was a telegraph operator at the hotel where we stop at in Detroit. Her name was Mary Lloyd. All the single guys on the ball club was more'n half crazy about her, and even the married ones was never heard objectin' when she give 'em a smile. To see us in that hotel, you'd of thought we was the greatest bunch o' telegram senders in the world.

Harry Childs had probably fell for her stronger than any o' the rest. When he wasn't busy talkin' base hits or kiddin' Crosby, he was tellin' somebody what a pippin she was, like nobody else had suspected it. And I guess he'd sent her enough cards from round the circuit to start a pinochle deck.

"Bill," he'd say to me, "she's the only one I ever met that I felt like I wanted to marry her."

"Go ahead!" I'd tell him. "I'd want to marry her, too, only I kind o' feel my own Missus might make a holler."

"Go ahead!" he'd say. "It's all right to say 'Go ahead'; but every time I start she says 'Back up!' She's worse'n a traffic cop."

"Keep tryin', Harry," I'd say to him. "Maybe she's heard about you bein' the world's champion joker and thinks you're just triflin' with her."

"She does all the jokin' when I'm round," he says. "She makes a regular monkey out o' me."

"Oh, I wouldn't blame that on her!" I says.

Now Mary wasn't no flirt, but she didn't mind bein' admired. She never give one guy more encouragement than another; she didn't play no favorites, or she didn't never let nobody on the club get the idear that she was to be had for the astin'. But she wasn't never too busy to talk to any of us, or to smile back when we smiled at her.

I and Gilbert was standin' there kiddin' with her the first time she seen Crosby. We'd just got in that mornin', and when he come out from breakfast he beat it through the lobby past her desk and out on the front walk.

"Who's that handsome wretch?" she ast us.

"That's the guy that made a sucker out o' Cobb and Veach over home," says Gilbert.

"Maybe if I ast him not to," she says, "he'll leave our team win a game or two this series."

"You got a sweet chance of astin' him anything," says I, "unless you got a megaphone."

"Is he deaf?" says Mary.

"When they's girls round he's deaf and dumb and blind," I says.

"He must of been disappointed in love," she says.

"Not him," says Gil. "The only time he was ever disappointed was when they postponed the game he was goin' to pitch."

"What's the trouble between him and girls?" says Mary.

"He just naturally don't like 'em—that's all," I says.

"Well," says Mary, "I don't think that's hardly fair to our sex. They ain't so many handsome men in the world that we can afford to have 'em woman haters."

"No," I says; "and they ain't so many good pitchers on our ball club that we can have him scared to death by gettin' a smile from you. So when you happen to run into him, face to face, kindly act like you didn't see him."

"I'm much obliged," she says, "for bein' told that my smile is terrifyin'. I'll keep it to myself after this."

"Not at all," says I. "I'd pretty near rather miss a hit-and-run sign than that smile o' yours. But this kid is just plain bashful; he ain't no woman hater; he's too backward to hate anything. He wants to be left alone—that's all. If a girl looks at him cross-eyed it takes him a week to get so's he can pitch again."

"I believe I'll go right out now," says Mary, "and look at him cross-eyed. You know I ought to be loyal to the Tigers."

"You ought to be loyal to this here beanery," says I; "and if you put him out o' commission, why, we'll just pass up this hotel."

"All right," she says. "I won't pay no attention to him, because I know I'd simply die if you boys stopped somewheres else and gave me a chance to do a little work."

"Has Childs been round yet?" says Gilbert.

"Foolish Question 795!" I says. "He was here even before he went in for his prunes."

"What's the matter with Harry Childs?" she ast us. "Why ain't he playin?"

"We like to win once in a while," says Gilbert.

"The reason Harry ain't playin' " I says, "is a young outfielder from the Coast, named Patrick."

"Why," says Mary, "Harry told me he was out of it with a Charley Horse."

"Yes," I says; "and a battin' average last year o' .238."

Crosby pitched the first game for us and win 2 to 1 in eleven innin's. He was goin' to wind up the series, but it begin to pour rain at noon o' the last day and the battle was off before we went out to the park. We wasn't startin' home till nine o'clock that night; so we had a lot o' time to kill. Naturally they was a reception all afternoon round Mary's desk. I and Joe Martin happened to be left there alone with her while Childs was gettin' shaved and some o' the others was celebratin'.

"Well," says Mary, "now that they ain't no more chance o' me spoilin' your trip, I think you might bring Mr. Shy round."

"She means the kid," I says to Joe. "I told her all about him."

"Have you seen him?" Joe ast her.

"O' course I seen him," she says.

"What do you think of him?" says Joe.

"Well, gentlemen," she says, "I don't want to hurt the feelin's o' the present company, so I'll just keep still."

"He is a pretty kid," says Martin, "and he's a whole lot better-lookin' since I coaxed him into some decent clothes. But he don't want to meet no girls."

"They's no sense to it," I says. "It wouldn't hurt him a bit to mingle a little with the dames. It'd do him good. And he'd get along O. K. when he found out they wasn't all tryin' to steal him."

"I'll promise not to steal him," says Mary.

"Well, it's up to Joe, here," I says. "He's his best pal."

"I guess he'd come if I ast him," says Martin. "But I don't know if I want to take a chance."

"Oh, come on!" says Mary. "I don't feel comfortable when they's one o' your boys I ain't acquainted with."

"Well," says Joe, "maybe he's up in his room takin' a nap."

"If he is in his room," says I, "that's probably what he's doin'. It's a cinch he ain't readin."

"Why not?" says Mary.

Joe give me the wink.

"He hates books," I says.

It was just then that the kid come across the lobby, toward the front windows. He looked like he was goin' to cry.

"My! He needs cheerin' up," says Mary. "Do you suppose he's sick?"

"You bet he's sick," says Martin. "He was goin' to give your Tigers another lickin' to-day, and the rain beat him out of it."

"Well, how about callin' him over?" I says.

So Martin went up to him and made the proposition. I could see the poor kid blush and then start like he was goin' to run out in the rain. Then Joe grabbed ahold of his arm and begin arguin' with him.

And finally the pair o' them come toward us. Nobody only Joe could of done it.

"Miss Lloyd," says Martin, "this is another o' the boys, Mr. Crosby. He's disappointed about the rain and I thought maybe you could cheer him up."

Mary give him her best smile.

"I'm glad to meet you, Mr. Crosby," she says. "You're the first ball player I ever seen that was disappointed about the rain."

"Except when it didn't fall," I says.

The kid didn't say nothin'; didn't even look at her. I caught him moistenin' his lips, tryin' to get a word out. But he couldn't. He seen her put her hand out to shake, and he finally managed to meet it. But he done it with the one he uses in pitchin'. And then, the minute Martin left go his arm, he backed away, pivoted on a pillar and dashed for the elevator.

"Good night!" says Mary. "Well, of all the rummies!"

"We warned you," says Martin.

"You certainly cheered him up," I says—"all the way up to his room."

"He can stay there, for all o' me," she says "I won't never try to force my acquaintance on nobody again."

"I bet he's offen me for life." says Joe.

"You ought to be glad if he is," she says.

"But you got to admit he's a handsome brute," says I.

"Yes," says Mary; "and I'd like to scratch his handsome face to pieces."

When we got on the train that night Harry Childs come up to me.

"Bill," he says, "I believe I'm goin' to win out."

"Win out what?" I ast him.

"With Mary," he says. "I took her out to supper. It was the first time she ever let me do it. And she acted like she really was fond o' me."

"Here's luck, Harry!" I says.

I didn't tell him the reason she was so friendly. It was because she'd been stung. And Harry's attentions was salve.

We was in Detroit again the first week in July. Harry took her out to supper or a picture show, or somethin', every night. I never heard her mention Crosby, and I was scared to mention him in front of her.

I did see her try to get even though. She come out from behind

her desk one mornin', just as he was walkin' in from outside. She
got right in his way, so as he either had to run into her or dodge.
And he couldn't help lookin' at her. She looked him right in the eye
and didn't speak.

And the kid looked like he was mighty glad of it.

VI

YOUNG PATRICK got hurt and Childs was back in the game when
we went East in August. Harry was full o' pep.

"I'll show 'em I can hit," he says to me. "I never felt luckier in
my life."

"You don't need no luck to hit if you take care o' yourself," I says.

"Don't worry about that," he says. "I got to keep in shape. I'm
tryin' to save the coin."

"What for?" I ast him.

"Well, Bill," he says, "I'm kind o' figurin' on gettin' married."

"Nice work, Harry!" I says. "I didn't know you'd gone as far as
that."

"They's nothin' settled," he says. "But she's writin' to me, and
when we strike Detroit next month I'll make her say yes."

Harry started to paste that pill in Philly. He broke up two games
for us there and got seven blows in three days. He was the pepper
kid when we got to Washington and he couldn't resist takin' some
of it out on Crosby.

They set at lunch together the second day.

"Lefty," he says, "looks like we're goin' to fight Germany. I was
down to the White House this mornin' to call on a friend o' mine,
a Mr. Wilson, and he says he don't think we can hold out much
longer."

"Well," says Crosby, "let 'em fight, as long as they leave us guys
out of it."

"Who says they'd leave us out of it?" Harry ast him.

"They'll leave me out of it, all right," says Crosby. "I never shot
a gun in my life."

"It ain't guns they want you to shoot. It's Germans," says Childs.
"And if the President called for volunteers I bet you'd be one o' the
first to go."

"You'd lose your bet," says the kid. "I can't take no chance o' gettin' my left arm shot off."

"Good Lord! That reminds me o' somethin'," says Harry. "I seen in the papers this mornin' that most o' the guns this country's got is left-handed guns. And they'll probably call for all the left-handed men in the United States to handle 'em."

Crosby didn't wait for no desert.

In New York, a couple o' days later, Childs was at him again.

"War's gettin' closer every minute," he says to Crosby.

"The Germans torpedoed the City o' Benton Harbor yesterday and sunk eleven bootblacks without even givin' 'em a chance to take their stands with 'em. And the Kaiser went fishin' in the mornin' and caught an American sturgeon. The President says if that kind o' thing keeps up he's offen the Kaiser and we'll all have to enlist—that is all the able-bodied guys."

"That lets me out," says the kid. "My ankles wouldn't hold up a minute if I was to try and march."

"They'd stick you in the calvary and leave you ride a motorcycle," says Childs.

"I don't know how," says Crosby; "and, besides, a man couldn't ride no motorcycle acrost the ocean."

"Oh, yes, they could," says Childs, "if the tires was blowed up tight enough. And, anyway, they's lots of us would have to do our fightin' here in this country, to keep the Germans from breakin' up the League."

I went in to breakfast with the kid the mornin' we landed in Boston. I had a paper myself and they was a piece in it sayin' that this country was thinkin' about callin' on all the young men o' nineteen and twenty, to train 'em for war—that is, all the ones that wasn't married. Childs, settin' at the next table, read it and couldn't get over to us fast enough.

"Crosby," he says, "how old are you?"

"Twenty," says the kid.

"You're in tough luck, old boy!" says Childs; and he begin readin' out loud. It was a cinch this time, because the readin' matter was really there.

"Congress," it says, "is considerin' a proposition to start universal military trainin' on account o' the strained relations with Germany and the prospects o' war. The plan is to draft every unmarried man in the United States o' the ages o' nineteen and twenty, and make 'em fit for war."

Anyway, it was somethin' like that.

"It looks like your baseball career was pretty near over," Harry says to the kid. "It's a crime too! You've had a great year, and without knowin' nothin' about pitchin' at that. But still, it ain't hard to learn to shoot and duck bullets; and they's a whole lot o' satisfaction in knowin' that you're workin' for the Stars and Stripes."

"When does this business come off?" says Crosby.

"Oh, not for a couple months," says Childs. "They'll probably leave you stick with us through the city series."

Then Childs got up and left us.

"Bill," says Crosby to me, "they ain't no kiddin' about this, is they?"

"No, Lefty," I says. "It's there in the paper, all right. But it just says they're thinkin' about it. If I was you I wouldn't start worryin' yet."

"Bill," he says, "before I'll join a army I'll walk out in Lake Michigan till my hat floats."

"Quit frettin' over it," says I. "You won't be able to pitch in this series, and you know we want some o' these games."

"But they're goin' to draft all the twenty-year-olds," he says, "and I just broke into that class. I wisht to the devil I was your age."

"Yes," I says; "or married."

"Married!" says Crosby. "That's right! It's just the single fellas that's gone."

"They ain't nobody gone," says I. "But if you don't quit worryin' you'll be just as good."

Childs spoiled whatever chance the Kid had to quit worryin' by sayin' to him, just before we started the game:

"Well, Lefty, they's one pipe: You'll be the handsomest guy in the army."

Before Crosby was taken out, Harry probably regretted that remark; because in the five innin's he pitched our outfielders must of ran back to the fence fifty times.

VII

JOE MARTIN told me about the kid bracin' him in the hotel that night.

"Joe," Crosby says to him. "I'd kind o' like to get acquainted with a girl."

"Good Lord!" says Joe. "What girl?"

"It don't make no difference," says the kid. "Some girl that ain't married, but might like to be, and ain't liable to want to spoon or make eyes or nothin' like that."

"Are you thinkin' o' gettin' married?" Joe ast him.

"Yes; only keep it quiet," says Lefty.

"And do you expect a girl to marry you for your money?" says Joe.

"You know I got no money," Crosby says.

"Well," says Joe, "if you got no money and you want to get married, you got to find a girl that's fond o' you. And a girl that's fond o' you might want to hold hands some time."

"Ain't they no sensible girl that might take me?" says the kid.

"What girls do you know?" Joe ast him.

"Joe," he says, "I ain't met a girl since I was fifteen or sixteen years old."

"Oh, yes, you have," says Joe. "How about that girl you was so nice to in Detroit?"

"Do you mean that girl you introduced me to?" says Crosby.

"Sure!" says Martin. "Mary Lloyd, the telegraph operator."

"Do you think she'd like me?" ast the kid.

"Well," Joe told him, "she ast to meet you, and she certainly was broke up the way you treated her."

"But what kind of a girl is she?" he says. "She ain't too soft?"

"I never caught her at it," says Joe.

"But she's probably sore at me," says Crosby.

"You can apologize to her," says Martin.

"But we won't be in Detroit for ten days," says the kid.

"Write her a letter," says Joe.

"I don't like to write letters," Crosby says. "Joe, will you write her a letter for me?"

"That'd make her sorer than ever," says Martin. "Besides, I don't know what you're tryin' to pull off."

"I'm on the square," says the kid. "If she'll marry me—why, I'll take her."

"That's damn' sweet o' you!" says Joe. "But what's your idear in gettin' married?"

"Never mind, Joe," says the kid. "I just feel like I want to."

"Well," says Joe, "if you want to square it with Mary, and you don't feel like writin' to her, why not send her a night letter?"

"What's that?" says Crosby.

"It's a telegram that goes at night, and you can say about fifty words for fifty cents," Joe told him.

"But I don't know no fifty words to say," says the poor kid.

To make it short, Joe done it for him, either because he was sorry for the kid or because he thought it was a joke or because he ain't none too good friends with Harry Childs. The telegram said that the kid was sorry he'd froze her, that he'd been feelin' tough that afternoon, that he apologized, and would she please forgive him, because he thought a whole lot of her.

The answer come next day, at noon. Mary wired that she'd pay more attention to him if he said all that to her face.

VIII

HARRY CHILDS' lucky spell ended when we stopped over for a game in Cleveland on the way home. He changed his mind at the last minute about makin' a slide to the plate, and they carried him off with a busted leg.

So Harry Childs didn't make the last trip to Detroit.

Young Mr. Crosby did, though he was so scared leavin' Chi that I and Gil and Martin was afraid he'd throw himself offen the train in the night.

The three of us talked it all over.

"He'll fall down, sure!" says Gil. "She'll give him an unmerciful pannin' and he'll faint dead away."

"But suppose he don't," I says. "Suppose he goes through with it and wins. Are we bein' fair to Harry?"

"Why not?" says Martin. "Childs played jokes on him all season. It's pretty near time the kid got back."

"I'm for helpin' him," says Gilbert.

"Me too," says Joe.

"All right; you're on!" I says; and we begin discussin' how to go about it.

We finally fixed it up that we'd get a taxi to come to the hotel at Mary's lunchtime. Then we'd coax 'em into it and slam the doors, and tell the driver to break all the laws o' Michigan.

Because, as Joe said, if we put 'em together where Crosby could get away, he'd get away sure!

They's nothin' more to it. They were back from their ride at one o'clock, both o' them as red as an open switch. But the smile Mary give us was an inch or so wider than we ever got before.

Crosby come blushin' acrost the lobby.

"Well?" we says.

"Well, boys," he says, "it wasn't bad."

"What do you mean—wasn't bad?" says Martin.

"Her," says the kid.

"Not half as bad as one o' them German centipede guns," says I.

"Not half!" says Crosby.

I suppose by this time she's got him through the First Reader.

THE BULL PEN

◇

CAST OF CHARACTERS

BILL CARNEY, *a pitcher, played by Al Ochs*
CY WALTERS, *a pitcher, played by Will Rogers*
JOE WEBB, *a Busher, played by Andy Toombes*

SCENE—*"Bull Pen" at the Polo Grounds during a game between the Yankees and Cleveland.* BILL *and* CY *are seated on empty boxes.*

JOE: What innings is it?

CY: Third.

JOE: What's the score?

CY: One and one. And in case you don't know who's playing, it's us and Cleveland. And you're in the American League.

JOE: I know what league I'm in and I know what league I wisht I was in. I wisht I was back in the Central League.

CY: Looks to me like you was going to get your wish.

JOE: They'll keep me longer than they will you.

CY: Well, I've got a good start on you. You only been here part of one season and I was here all last year besides.

JOE: Yes, but how many games did you pitch?

CY: Well, I pitched 154 games last year and about fifty so far this year. And I pitched 'em all right here where we're standing. Some guys gets all swelled up over pitching one no-hit game. Well, the Yankees has played over 200 games since I been with them and nobody's got a hit off me yet.

JOE: I wisht I was where they paid some attention to a man.

Performed in the *Ziegfeld Follies* of 1922.
It first appeared in *Judge*, July 29, 1922; collected in *First and Last* (New York: Scribners, 1934).

CY: That's what I wished the first part of last season. But the last part of the season, I wished they'd ignore me entirely. I used to make ugly faces at Huggins in hopes he'd get mad and quit speaking to me. But just before every game he'd say, "Go down to the Bull Pen and warm up." *WARM UP!* Say, there may be better pitchers than me in this league, but there ain't none that's hotter.

BILL (*commenting on game*): Bob was lucky to get by that inning! Did you see that one Scotty grabbed off Speaker?

JOE: Them guys don't know how to pitch to Speaker.

CY (*gives him a look*): No? How would *you* pitch to him?

JOE: First I'd give him my fast one—

CY: Hold on! Now you're pitching to the next batter. Speaker's on third base.

JOE: How would he get to third base?

CY: He'd slide.

JOE: You ain't seen my fast one when I'm right. It goes zooy! (*Makes motion with hands.*)

CY: Yes, and after it bounced off Speaker's bat, it'd go zeet! (*Makes similar motion.*) Especially this ball they're using these days with a raisin in it.

BILL: The Babe's up. (*Without raising his voice.*) Come on, Babe! Bust one!

JOE: He wouldn't bust one if I was pitching!

CY: How would you pitch to *him*?

JOE: High and on the outside.

CY: And that's just where it'd go.

BILL: No, he popped up.

JOE: Just the same, I bet Ruth's glad I ain't with some other club.

CY: He don't know you ain't.

JOE: I bet he don't break no home run record this year.

CY: Look how long he was out!

JOE: Well, it was his own fault. I bet if I'd went barnstorming, Landis wouldn't of dast suspend *me* that long!

CY: He wouldn't of suspended you at all. He wouldn't of never heard about it.

BILL: Coveleskie must *have* something in there. He made Baker pop up!

JOE: I wisht I could go in there to the bench.

CY: What for?

JOE (*with a self-conscious smile*): Well, do you remember before the game, when I was up there throwing to Schang? Well, they was a swell dame come in and set down right behind our bench. She looked like a Follies dame. And she give me *some* smile!

CY: She done well to keep from laughing outright.

JOE: She was trying to make me.

CY: She was trying to make you out.

JOE: I bet if Huggins had of left me stay on the bench, I'd be all set by now.

CY: Yes, and that's why Huggins don't let you stay on the bench. He told me the other day, he says, "Cy, old pal, I hope it won't bother you to have this gargoyle down there warming up with you all the time. But it's against the rules to have gals on the bench, and if he was there I simply couldn't keep them off." He says, "I've got a hard enough bunch to manage without adding Peggy Hopkins."

JOE: How do *you* know that's her name?

CY: Oh, I seen her looking at you and I asked one of the ushers.

JOE: Peggy Hopkins! Do you know if she's married?

CY: I can't keep track.

JOE: Do you s'pose her name's in the book?

CY: Well, seems like I've seen it in print *somewheres*.

JOE (*as if to memorize it*):   Peggy Hopkins.

BILL: Bob's wild. It's three and nothing on Sewell.

CY (*to* JOE):   You better cut loose a little, kid. This may be our day.

JOE: Not both of us.

CY: Sure, providing he picks you first. (*Slight pause.*) But, listen, kid, if I was you I'd leave the dames alone. Wait till you've made good.

JOE: I ain't after no dames. But I can't help the looks they give me.

CY: No more than you can help the looks *God* give you. And he certainly didn't spread himself.

BILL: He's walked Sewell.

JOE: The *gals* seem to think I look O.K.

CY: How do you know?

JOE: The way they act. Do you remember that poor little kid in New Orleans?

CY: What kid?

JOE: The telephone gal in the hotel. She was down to the depot when we went away. But I ducked her. And that dame in Philadelphia.

CY: What do you owe *her?*

JOE: I don't owe her nothin', but she was out to the game every day, tryin' to flirt.

CY: Oh, *that* woman!

JOE: What woman?

CY: That's the woman that goes to the games in Philadelphia. You know those Philadelphia fans? Well, she's their sister.

JOE: I don't know who she is, but she certainly made eyes at me.

CY: She don't mean to make eyes. That's a nervous disease. She's been looking at the Athletics for six years. But you want to quit thinking about the dames and pay attention to your work.

JOE: *I* pay attention to my work!

CY: Well, at that, I can see you've made quite a study of the batters. You know how to pitch to Speaker and Ruth.

JOE: Yes, and some of them other high monkey monks.

CY: Well, how would you go to work on George Sisler?

JOE: Say, that guy won't never get a hit off me.

CY: I guess you're right. He told me one day that when he was through in the big league, he was through.

BILL: There goes Gardner. Another base on balls.

JOE: But there's one guy I *could* fool, is Sisler!

CY: Oh, anybody could *fool* him.

JOE: Well, how would *you* fool him?

CY: I'd say, "Hit this one, George." And then I'd throw him an orange. Then there's another way I bet I could fool him. I could say, "George, come out to the house to dinner to-night. My wife's a great cook. We live at 450 Riverside Drive." When he got there, he'd find out I don't live at that address, and besides, I ain't married.

JOE: Well, I'd like to get a chance at him. And another guy I'd like to pitch against is Cobb.

CY: Irvin?

JOE: That ain't his name is it?

CY: You mean the man that writes the outfield for Detroit. That's Irvin.

JOE: That's right, Irvin.

BILL: He hit O'Neill in the arm. The bases is choked, boys.

CY (*to* JOE): Put something on her, kid! If he can just get Coveleskie! (*Warming up at top speed.*) Listen, kid, if you get in, don't be scared to cut loose! You got nothing to lose.

JOE: Do you think it'll be me?

CY: Well, it's one of us.

BILL (*with feeling*): Damn! Damn! And he had a double play right in front of him. Cy! He's waving to you!

CY (*jumps up and tears off his sweater*): Get out of the way, boy! He wants me in there! (JOE, *dazed, gets out of his way and mournfully goes to the bench and sits down.* CY *throws one ball.*)

CY: I'm ready. (*He picks up his sweater and goes offstage, carrying it on his arm.*)

JOE: A fine manager we're workin' for!

CURTAIN

WOMEN

◇

YOUNG JAKE UTTERED a few words which it would pain me to
repeat.

"And what are *you* crabbin' about?" asked Mike Healy from his
corner of the bench.

"Oh, nothin'!" said Jake. "Nothin' except that I'm sick of it!"

"Sick of what?" demanded Healy.

"Of settin' here!" Jake replied.

"You!" said Mike Healy, with a short laugh. "You've got a fine
license to squawk! Why, let's see: what is it? The third of June, and
your first June in the league. You ain't even *begin* to sit! Look at me!
Been on this bench since catchers started wearin' a mast, or anyway
it seems that long. And you never hear me crab, do you, Lefty?"

"Only when you talk," answered the athlete addressed. "And that's
only at table or between meals."

"But if this kid's hollerin' already," said Mike, "what'll he be doin'
along in August or September, to say nothin' about next August and
the August after that?"

"Don't worry!" said Young Jake. "I'll either be a regular by the
end of this season or I won't be on this ball club at all!"

"That-a-boy!" said Healy. "Threaten 'em!"

"I mean what I say!" retorted Jake. "I ain't goin' to spend my life
on no bench! I come here to play baseball!"

"Oh, you did!" said Healy. "And what do you think I come here
for, to fish?"

"I ain't talkin' about you," said Young Jake. "I'm talkin' about
myself."

"That's a novelty in a ball player," remarked Lefty.

This story first appeared in *Liberty*, June 20, 1925; collected in *The Love Nest and
Other Stories*, publisher (New York: Scribners, 1926).

455

"And what I'm sayin'," Jake went on, "is that I'm sick of settin' on this bench."

"This ain't a bad bench," said Healy. "They's a hell of a lot worse places you might sit."

"And a hell of a lot better places!" said Jake. "I can think of one right now. I'm lookin' right at it."

"Where at?"

"Right up in the old stand; the third—no, the fourth row, next to the aisle, the first aisle beyond where the screen leaves off."

"I noticed her myself!" put in Lefty. "Damn cute! Too damn cute for a busher like you to get smoked up over."

"Oh, I don't know!" said Young Jake. "I didn't get along so bad with them dames down South."

"Down South ain't here!" replied Lefty. "Those dames in some of those swamps, they lose their head when they see a man with shoes on. But up here you've got to have something. If you pulled that Calhoun County stuff of yours on a gal like that gal in the stand she'd yell for the dog catcher. She'd——"

"They're all alike!" interrupted Mike Healy. "South, or here, or anywheres, they're all the same, and all poison!"

"What's poison?" asked Jake.

"Women!" said Healy. "And the more you have to do with 'em the better chance you've got of spendin' your life on this bench. Why—— That's pitchin', Joe!" he shouted when the third of the enemy batters had popped out and left a runner stranded at second base. "You look good in there today," he added to Joe as the big pitcher approached the dugout.

"I'm all right, I guess," said Joe, pulling on his sweater and moving toward the water bottle. "I wished that wind'd die down."

The manager had come in.

"All right! Let's get at 'em!" he said. "Nice work, Joe. Was that a fast one Meusel hit?"

"No," said Joe. "A hook, but it didn't break."

"A couple of runs will beat 'em the way you're going," said the manager, stooping over to select his bat. "Make this fella pitch, boys," he added. "He was hog wild in Philly the other day."

The half inning wore on to its close, and the noncombatants were again left in possession of the bench. Young Jake addressed Healy.

"What's women done to you, Mike?"

"Only broke me. That's all!" said Healy.

"What do you mean, broke you! The boys tells me you ain't spent nothin' but the summer since you been in the league."

"Oh, I've got a little money," said Healy. "I don't throw it away. I don't go around payin' ten smackers a quart for liquid catnip. But they's more kinds of broke than money broke, a damn sight worse kinds, too. And when I say women has broke me, I mean they've made a bum out of my life; they've wrecked my—what-do-you-call-it?"

"Your career," supplied Lefty.

"Yes, sir," said Healy. "And I ain't kiddin', neither. Why say, listen: Do you know where I'd be if it wasn't for a woman? Right out there in that infield, playin' that old third sack."

"What about Smitty?" asked Young Jake.

"He'd be where I am—on this bench."

"Aw, come on, Mike! Be yourself! You don't claim you're as good as him!" Jake remonstrated.

"I do claim it, but it don't make no difference if I am or I ain't. He shouldn't never ought to of had a chance, not on this club, anyway. You'd say the same if you knowed the facts."

"Well, let's hear 'em."

"It's a long story, and these boys has heard it before."

"That's all right, Mike," said Gephart, a spare catcher. "We ain't listened the last twelve times."

"Well, it was the year I come in this league, four years ago this spring. I'd been with the Toledo club a couple of years. I was the best hitter on the Toledo club. I hit .332 the first year and .354 the next year. And I led the third basemen in fieldin'."

"It would be hard not to," interposed Lefty. "Anything a third baseman don't get they call it a base hit. A third baseman ought to pay to get in the park."

Healy glanced coldly at the speaker, and resumed:

"This club had Johnnie Lambert. He was still about the best third baseman in this league, but he was thirty-five years old and had a bad knee. It had slipped out on him and cost this club the pennant. They didn't have no other third baseman. They lose sixteen out of twenty games. So that learned 'em a lesson, and they bought me. Their idear was to start Johnnie in the spring, but they didn't expect his knee to hold up. And then it was goin' to be my turn.

"But durin' the winter Johnnie got a hold of some specialist some-wheres that fixed his knee, and he come South with a new least of life. He hit good and was as fast as ever on the bases. Meanw'ile I had been on a huntin' trip up in Michigan that winter and froze my dogs, and they ailed me so that I couldn't do myself justice all spring."

"I suppose it was some woman made you go huntin'," said Gephart, but Healy continued without replying:

"They was a gal from a town named Ligonier, Indiana, that had visited in Toledo the second year I played ball there. The people where she was visitin' was great baseball fans, and they brought her out to the game with them, and she got stuck on me."

"Ligonier can't be a town! It must be an asylum!" said Lefty.

"She got stuck on me," Healy repeated, "and the people where she was stayin' asked me to their house to supper. After supper the man and his wife said how about goin' to the picture show, and the gal said she was tired and rather stay home. So the man and woman excused themselves. They said it was a picture they wanted to see and would I excuse them runnin' off and leavin' we two together. They were clubbin' on me, see?

"Well, I thought to myself, I'll give this dame an unpleasant surprise, so I didn't even hold her hand all evenin'. When I got up to go she says she supposed it would be the last time she seen me as she expected to go back to Ligonier the next day. She didn't have no more intentions of goin' back the next day than crossin' Lake Erie in a hollow tooth. But she knowed if I thought it was good-by I'd kiss her. Well, I knowed it wasn't good-by, but what the hell! So that's how it started, and I went to Ligonier that fall to see her, and we got engaged to be married. At least she seemed to think so."

"Look at that!" interrupted Young Jake, his eyes on the field of action. "What could Sam of been thinkin'!"

"Thinkin'!" said Gephart. "Him!"

"What would Sam do," wondered Lefty, "if they played baseball with only one base? He wouldn't enjoy the game if he couldn't throw to the wrong one."

"That play's liable to cost us somethin'," said Gephart.

"I went up in Michigan on a huntin' trip with some friends of mine," Healy continued. "I froze my feet and was laid up all through January and February and shouldn't of never went South. It was all as I could do to wear shoes, let alone play baseball. I wasn't really myself till along the first of May. But, as I say, Johnnie Lambert had a new least of life and was lookin' better than he'd looked for years. His knee wasn't troublin' him at all.

"Well, that's how things went till around the last part of June. I

didn't get no action except five or six times goin' up to hit for somebody. And I was like a young colt, crazy to be let loose. I knowed
that if I once got in there and showed what I could do Judge Landis
himself couldn't keep me on the bench. I used to kneel down every
night and pray to God to get to work on Lambert's knee.

"The gal kept writin' me letters and I answered 'em once in a w'ile,
but we hadn't saw each other since before Christmas. She hinted
once or twice about when was we goin' to get married, but I told
her I didn't want to even disgust the subject till I was somethin'
besides a bench warmer.

"We had a serious in Chi the tail-end of June, and the first night
we was there I got a long-distance call from Ligonier. It was the gal's
sister, sayin' the gal was sick. She was delirious part of the time and
hollerin' for me, and the doctor said if she could see me, it'd probably
do her more good than medicine.

"So I said that's all right, but they ain't no off days in the schedule
right now and I can't get away. But they had looked up the time
table and seen where I could leave Chi after the ball game, spend
the night in Ligonier and get back for the game the next day.

"So I took a train from Englewood in the evenin' and when I got
off at Ligonier, there was my gal to meet me. She was the picture
of health and no more delirious than usual. They said she had been
just about ready to pass out when she learned I was comin' and it
cured her. They didn't tell me what disease she'd had, but I suppose
it was a grasshopper bite or somethin'.

"When I left next mornin', the weddin' date was set for that fall.

"Somewheres between South Bend and Laporte, the train stopped
and liked it so well that we stayed there over three hours. We hit
Englewood after four o'clock and I got to the park just in time to
see them loadin' Lambert into a machine to take him away. His knee
had broke down on him in the first innin's. He ain't never played
ball since. And Smitty, who's always been a natural second baseman,
he had my job."

"He's filled it pretty good," said Lefty.

"That's either here or there," retorted Healy. "If I'd been around,
nobody'd ever knowed if he could play third base or not. And the
worst of him is," he added, "that he never gets hurt."

"Maybe you ain't prayed for him like you done for Lambert," said
Young Jake. "What happened to the gal? Did you give her the air?"

"No, I didn't," said Healy. "When I give my word, I keep it. I
simply wrote and told her that I'd agreed to marry her and I wouldn't

go back on it. But that my feelin's towards her was the same as if
she was an advanced case of spinal meningitis. She never answered
the letter, so I don't know if we're still engaged or not."

The inning was over and the boys were coming in.

"Joe was lucky to get out of that with only two runs," remarked
Lefty. "But of course it was Sam that put him in bad."

"I'm goin' to see if he'll leave me get up on the lines," said Young
Jake, "so I can get a better look at that dame."

The manager waited for Sam to catch up.

"What the hell was the matter with you, Sam?" he demanded.

Sam looked silly.

"I thought——"

"That's where you make your mistake!" the manager broke in.
"Tough luck, Joe! But two runs are nothing. We'll get 'em back."

"Shall I go up on the lines?" asked Young Jake, hopefully.

"You? No!" said the manager. "You, Mike," turning to Healy, "go
over and coach at third base. You brought us luck yesterday."

So it was Mike who was held partly responsible a few moments
later when Smitty, who had tripled, was caught napping off the bag.

"Nice coachin', Mike!" said Lefty, as Healy came back to the bench.

"Why don't he watch hisself!" growled Mike. "And besides, I did
yell at him!"

"You're a liar!" said Lefty. "Your back was to the ball game. You
were lookin' up in the stand."

"Why would I be lookin' at the stand!" demanded Healy.

But nobody answered him. There was silence for a time. The boys
were depressed; in their own language, their dauber was down. Finally Young Jake spoke.

"She's starin' right over this way!" he said.

"Who?" asked Gephart.

"That dame I pointed out. In the tan suit. 'Way over behind third
base, the other side of the screen, in the fourth row."

"I see her. Not bad!"

"I'll say she's not bad! said Jake.

"Women!" said Healy. "You better get your mind on baseball or
you'll be back in that silo league, jumpin' from town to town in a
w'eelbarrow."

"I don't see why you should be off all women just because one of
them brought you a little hard luck."

"She wasn't the only one! Why, say, if it wasn't for women I'd be

playin' regular third base for McGraw right now and cuttin' in on
the big money every fall."

"I didn't know you was ever with McGraw."

"I wasn't," said Healy, "but I ought to been, and would of been
only for a woman. It was when I was playin' with the Dayton club;
my first year in baseball. Boy, I was fast as a streak! I was peggin'
bunts to first base before the guy could drop his bat. I covered so
much ground to my left that I was always knockin' the shortstop
down and bumpin' heads with the right fielder. Everybody was mar-
velin' at me. Some of the old timers said I reminded them of Bill
Bradley at his best, only that I made Bradley look like he was out
of the game for a few days.

"Baldy Pierce was umpirin' in our league that year. He wasn't a
bad umps, but he never left business interfere with pleasure. Many's
the time he called the last fella out in the last innin's when the fella
was safer than a hot chocolate at the Elks' convention—just because
Baldy was hungry for supper.

"He was so homely that dogs wouldn't live in the same town, and
his friends used to try and make him wear his mask off the field as
well as on. And yet he grabbed some of the prettiest gals you ever
see. He said to me once, he said, 'Mike,' he said, 'you tell me I'm
homelier than Railroad Street, but I can cop more pips than you can
with all your good looks!' "

At this point there were unprintable comments by Lefty, Gephart,
and other occupants of the bench.

"One of these gals of his," Healy went on, "was a gal named Helen
Buck from Hamilton, Ohio. She was visitin' in Dayton and come
out to the ball game. The first day she was there a lot of the boys
was hit in the face by thrown balls, and every time a foul went to
the stand the whole infield run in to shag it. But she wouldn't look
at nobody but Pierce.

"Well, McGraw had heard about me, and he sent a fella named
McDonald, that was scoutin' for him, to look me over. It was in
September and we was just about through. How the games come
out didn't make no difference, but I knowed this McDonald was
there and what he was there for, so I wanted to make a showin'. He
had came intendin' to stay two days, but he'd overlooked a skip in
the schedule that left us without no game the second day, so he said
one game would have to be enough, as he had to go somewheres
else.

"We was playin' the Springfield club. I had a good day in the field, but Bill Hutton, who started pitchin' for them, he was hog wild and walked me the first two times up. The third time they was a man on third and I had to follow orders and squeeze him home. So I hadn't had no chance to really show what I could do up there at the plate.

"Well, we come into the ninth innin's with the score tied and it was gettin' pretty dark. We got two of them out, and then their first baseman, Jansen, he got a base on balls. Bill Boone caught a hold of one just right and cracked it to the fence and it looked like Jansen would score, but he was a slow runner. Davy Shaw, our shortstop, thought he must of scored and when the ball was thrown to him he throwed it to me to get Boone, who was tryin' for three bases.

"Well, I had took in the situation at a glance; I seen that Jansen hadn't scored and if I put the ball on Boone quick enough, why the run wouldn't count. So I lunged at Boone and tagged him before Jansen had crossed the plate. But Pierce said the score counted and that Boone wasn't out because I'd missed him. Missed him! Say, I bet that where I tagged him they had to take stitches!

"Anyway, that give 'em a one run lead, and when the first two fellas got out in our half everybody thought it was over. But Davy Shaw hit one to right center that a man like I could of ran around twice on it, but they held Davy at third base. And it was up to me to bring him in.

"By this time Jim Preston was pitchin' for Springfield, and Jim was always a mark for me. I left the first one go by, as it was outside, but Pierce called it a strike. Then they was a couple of balls that he couldn't call strikes. I cracked the next one over the leftfield fence, but it was a few inches foul. That made it two and two, and the next ball he throwed, well, if I hadn't ducked my head just when I did they'd of been brains scattered all over Montgomery County. And what does Pierce do but yell 'Batter out!' and run for the clubhouse!

"Well, I run after him and asked him what the hell, and here is what he said. He said, 'Mike,' he said, 'these games don't mean nothin', but if this here game had of wound up a tie it would of meant a game tomorrow, when we got a off day. And I made a date for tomorrow to go on a picnic with my little gal in Hamilton. You wouldn't want me to miss that, would you?' "

"Why," inquired Young Jake, "didn't you break his nose or bust him in the chin?"

"His nose was already broke," said Healy, "and he didn't have no chin. I tried to get a hold of McDonald, the fella that was there

WOMEN

463

scoutin' me. I was goin' to explain the thing to him. But he'd left town before I could catch him. It seems, though, that he'd set over to the side where he couldn't see what a lousy strike it was and he told a friend of mine that he couldn't recommend a man that would take a third strike when a base hit would of tied up the game; that on top of me 'missin' ' Boone at third——"

Another half inning was over and Healy started for the third-base coaching line without waiting for the manager to reach the bench. His teammates were not in a position to see the glance he threw at a certain spot in the stand as he walked to his "work." When the side was retired scoreless and he had returned to his corner of the dugout he looked more desolate than ever.

"Women!" he said. "Why, if it wasn't for women I'd be playin' third base for Huggins; I'd have Joe Dugan's job; I'd be livin' right here in the capital of the world."

"How do you make that out?" asked Young Jake.

"It's a long story," said Healy, "but I can tell you in a few words. We was playin' the New York Club out home. Frank Baker had began to slip and Huggins was lookin' for a good fella to take his place. He was crazy to get me, but he had heard that I didn't want to play in New York. This had came from me kiddin' with some of the boys on the New York Club, tellin' 'em I wouldn't play here if they give me the town. So Huggins wanted to make sure before he started a trade. And he didn't want no one to see him talkin' to me. So he came around one night to the hotel where I was livin' at the time. I was up in my room waitin' for the phone gal to be off duty. She was stuck on me and I had a date to take her for a drive. So when Huggins come to see me she said I was out. She was afraid her date was goin' to be interfered with. So Huggins went away and his club left town that night."

"What did you do to her?" asked Jake.

"Oh, I couldn't do nothin' to her," said Healy. "She claimed she didn't know who it was."

"Didn't he give his name?"

"No."

"Then how do you know it was Huggins?"

"She said it was a little fella."

"He ain't the only little fella."

"He's the littlest fella I know," said Healy.

"But you ain't sure what he wanted to see you for."

"What *would* Huggins want to see me for—to scratch my back?

But as I say, she didn't know who it was, so I couldn't do nothin' to her except ignore her from then on, and they couldn't of been no worse punishment as far as she was concerned."

"All and all," summed up Lefty, "if it wasn't for women, you'd of been playin' third base for McGraw and Huggins and this club, all at the same time."

"Yes," said Healy, "and with Washin'ton, too. Why——"

"Mike Healy!" interrupted the voice of Dick Trude, veteran usher. "Here's a mash note and it wants an answer."

Healy read the note and crumpled it in his hand.

"Who is she?" he asked.

"Look where I point," said Trude. "It's that good-lookin' dame in the tan suit, in the fourth row, back of third base. There! She asked me who you was when you was out there coachin'. So I told her, and she give me that note. She said you could answer yes or no."

"Make it 'yes,' " said Healy, and Trude went away.

Healy threw the crumpled note under the water bottle and addressed Young Jake.

"What I want you to get through your head, boy——"

"Oh, for God's sakes, shut up!" said Young Jake.

HURRY KANE

◇

IT SAYS HERE: "Another great race may be expected in the American League, for Philadelphia and New York have evidently added enough strength to give them a fighting chance with the White Sox and Yankees.* But if the fans are looking for as 'nervous' a finish as last year's, with a climax such as the Chicago and New York clubs staged on the memorable first day of October, they are doubtless in for a disappointment. That was a regular Webster 'thrill that comes once in a lifetime,' and no oftener."

"Thrill" is right, but they don't know the half of it. Nobody knows the whole of it only myself, not even the fella that told me. I mean the big sap, Kane, who you might call him, I suppose, the hero of the story, but he's too dumb to have realized all that went on, and besides, I got some of the angles from other sources and seen a few things with my own eyes.

If you wasn't the closest-mouthed bird I ever run acrost, I wouldn't spill this to you. But I know it won't go no further and I think it may give you a kick.

Well, the year before last, it didn't take no witch to figure out what was going to happen to our club if Dave couldn't land a pitcher or two to help out Carney and Olds. Jake Lewis hurt his arm and was never no good after that and the rest of the staff belonged in the Soldiers' Home. Their aim was perfect, but they were always shooting at the pressbox or somebody's bat. On hot days I often felt like leaving my mask and protector in the clubhouse; what those fellas were throwing up there was either eighty feet over my head or else the outfielders had to chase it. I could have caught naked except on the days when Olds and Carney worked.

This story first appeared in *Hearst's International-Cosmopolitan*, May 1927; collected in *Round Up*, (New York: Scribners, 1929).
*The Yankees are and were the only American League New York team. This sentence is the same in the first magazine appearance and in Lardner's *Round Up*.

In the fall—that's a year and a half ago—Dave pulled the trade with Boston and St. Louis that brought us Frank Miller and Lefty Glaze in exchange for Robinson, Bullard and Roy Smith. The three he gave away weren't worth a dime to us or to the clubs that got them, and that made it just an even thing, as Miller showed up in the spring with a waistline that was eight laps to the mile and kept getting bigger and bigger till it took half the Atlantic cable to hold up his baseball pants, while Glaze wanted more money than Landis and didn't report till the middle of June, and then tried to condition himself on wood alcohol. When the deal was made, it looked like Dave had all the best of it, but as it turned out, him and the other two clubs might as well have exchanged photographs of their kids in Girl Scout uniforms.

But Dave never lost no sleep over Glaze or Miller. We hadn't been in Florida three days before him and everybody on the ball club was absolutely nuts about big Kane. Here was a twenty-year-old boy that had only pitched half a season in Waco and we had put in a draft for him on the recommendation of an old friend of Dave's, Billy Moore. Billy was just a fan and didn't know much baseball, but he had made some money for Dave in Texas oil leases and Dave took this tip on Kane more because he didn't want to hurt Billy's feelings than out of respect for his judgment. So when the big sapper showed up at Fort Gregg, he didn't get much of a welcome. What he did get was a laugh. You couldn't look at him and not laugh; anyway, not till you got kind of used to him.

You've probably seen lots of pictures of him in a uniform, but they can't give you no idear of the sight he was the first day he blew in the hotel, after that clean, restful little train ride all the way from Yuma. Standing six foot three in what was left of his stockings, he was wearing a suit of Arizona store clothes that would have been a fair fit for Singer's youngest Midget and looked like he had pressed it with a tractor that had been parked on a river bottom.

He had used up both the collars that he figured would see him through his first year in the big league. This left you a clear view of his Adam's apple, which would make half a dozen pies. You'd have thought from his shoes that he had just managed to grab hold of the rail on the back platform of his train and been dragged from Yuma to Jacksonville. But when you seen his shirt, you wondered if he hadn't rode in the cab and loaned it to the fireman for a wash-cloth. He had a brown paper suitcase held together by bandages. Some of them had slipped and the raw wounds was exposed. But if the whole thing had fell to pieces, he could have packed the contents in two of his vest pockets without bulging them much.

One of the funniest things about him was his walk and I'll never forget the first time we seen him go out to take his turn pitching to the batters. He acted like he was barefooted and afraid of stepping on burrs. He'd lift one dog and hold it in the air a minute till he could locate a safe place to put it down. Then he'd do the same thing with the other, and it would seem about a half-hour from the time he left the bench till he got to his position. Of course Dave soon had him pretty well cured of that, or that is, Dave didn't, but Kid Farrell did. For a whole week, the Kid followed him every step he took and if he wasn't going fast enough, he either got spiked in the heel or kicked in the calf of his hind leg. People think he walks slow yet, but he's a shooting star now compared with when he broke in.

Well, everybody was in hysterics watching him make that first trip and he looked so silly that we didn't expect him to be any good to us except as a kind of a show. But we were in for a big surprise.

Before he threw a ball, Dave said to him: "Now, go easy. Don't cut loose and take a chance till you're in shape."

"All right," says Kane.

And all of a sudden, without no warning, he whammed a fast ball across that old plate that blew Tierney's cap off and pretty near knocked me down. Tierney hollered murder and ran for the bench. All of us were pop-eyed and it was quite a while before Dave could speak. Then he said:

"Boy, your fast one *is* a fast one! But I just got through telling you not to cut loose. The other fellas ain't ready for it and neither are you. I don't want nobody killed this time of year."

So Kane said: "I didn't cut loose. I can send them through there twice as fast as that. I'm scared to yet, because I ain't sure of my control. I'll show you something in a couple more days."

Well when he said "twice as fast," he was making it a little strong. But his real fast one was faster than that first one he threw, and before the week was over we looked at speed that made it seem like Johnson had never pitched nothing but toy balloons. What had us all puzzled was why none of the other clubs had tried to grab him. I found out by asking him one night at supper. I asked him if he'd been just as good the year before as he was now.

"I had the same stuff," he said, "but I never showed it, except once."

I asked him why he hadn't showed it. He said:

"Because I was always scared they would be a big league scout in the stand and I didn't want to go 'up.' "

Then I said why not, and he told me he was stuck on a gal in Waco and wanted to be near her.

"Yes," I said, "but your home town, Yuma, is a long ways from Waco and you couldn't see much of her winters even if you stayed in the Texas League."

"I got a gal in Yuma for winters," he says. "This other gal was just for during the season."

"How about that one time you showed your stuff?" I asked him. "How did you happen to do it?"

"Well," he said, "the Dallas club was playing a series in Waco and I went to a picture show and seen the gal with Fred Kruger. He's Dallas's manager. So the next day I made a monkey out of his ball club. I struck out fifteen of them and give them one hit—a fly ball that Smitty could have caught in a hollow tooth if he hadn't drunk his lunch."

Of course that was the game Dave's friend seen him pitch and we were lucky he happened to be in Waco just then. And it was Kane's last game in that league. Him and his "during the season" gal had a brawl and he played sick and got himself sent home.

Well, everybody knows now what a whale of a pitcher he turned out to be. He had a good, fast-breaking curve and Carney learned him how to throw a slow ball. Old Kid Farrell worked like a horse with him and got him so he could move around and field his position. At first he seemed to think he was moored out there. And another cute habit that had to be cured was his full wind-up with men on bases. The Kid starved him out of this.

Maybe I didn't tell you what an eater he was. Before Dave caught on to it, he was ordering one breakfast in his room and having another downstairs, and besides pretty near choking himself to death at lunch and supper, he'd sneak out to some lunchroom before bedtime, put away a Hamburger steak and eggs and bring back three or four sandwiches to snap at during the night.

He was rooming at the start with Joe Bonham and Joe finally told on him, thinking it was funny. But it wasn't funny to Dave and he named the Kid and Johnny Abbott a committee of two to see that Kane didn't explode. The Kid watched over him at table and Johnny succeeded Bonham as his roommate. And the way the Kid got him to cut out his wind-up was by telling him, "Now if you forget yourself and use it with a man on, your supper's going to be two olives and a finger-bowl, but if you hold up those runners, you can eat the chef."

As I say, the whole world knows what he is now. But they don't know how hard we worked with him, they don't know how close we came to losing him altogether, and they don't know the real story of that final game last year, which I'll tell you in a little while.

First, about pretty near losing him: As soon as Dave seen his possibilities and his value to us, he warned the boys not to ride him or play too many jokes on him because he was simple enough to take everything in dead earnest, and if he ever found out we were laughing at him, he might either lay down and quit trying or blow us entirely. Dave's dope was good, but you can't no more prevent a bunch of ball players from kidding a goofer like Kane than you can stop the Century at Herkimer by hollering "Whoa!" He was always saying things and doing things that left him wide open and the gang took full advantage, especially Bull Wade.

I remember one night everybody was sitting on the porch and Bull was on the railing, right in front of Kane's chair.

"What's your first name, Steve?" Bull asked him.

"Well," says Kane, "it ain't Steve at all. It's Elmer."

"It would be!" says Bull. "It fits you like your suit. And that reminds me, I was going to inquire where you got that suit."

"In Yuma," said Kane. "In a store."

"A store!" says Bull.

"A clothing store," says Kane. "They sell all kinds of clothes."

"I see they do," said Bull.

"If you want a suit like it, I'll write and find out if they've got another one," says Kane.

"They couldn't be two of them," says Bull, "and if they was, I'll bet Ed Wynn's bought the other. But anyway, I've already got a suit, and what I wanted to ask you was what the boys out West call you. I mean, what's your nickname?"

" 'Hurry,' " says the sap. " 'Hurry' Kane. Lefty Condon named me that."

"He seen you on your way to the dining-room," said Bull.

Kane didn't get it.

"No," he said. "It ain't nothing to do with a dining-room. A hurricane is a kind of a storm. My last name is Kane, so Lefty called me 'Hurry' Kane. It's a kind of a storm."

"A brainstorm," says Bull.

"No," said Kane. "A hurricane is a big wind-storm."

"Does it blow up all of a sudden?" asked Bull.

"Yeah, that's it," says Kane.

"We had three or four of them on this club last year," said Bull. "All pitchers, too. Dave got rid of them and he must be figuring on you to take their place."

"Do you mean you had four pitchers named Kane?" says the big busher.

"No," said Bull. "I mean we had four pitchers that could blow up all of a sudden. It was their hobby. Dave used to work them in turn, the same afternoon; on days when Olds and Carney needed a rest. Each one of the four would pitch an innings and a half."

Kane thought quite a while and then said: "But if they was four of them, and they pitched an innings and a half apiece, that's only six innings. Who pitched the other three?"

"Nobody," says Bull. "It was always too dark. By the way, what innings is your favorite? I mean, to blow in?"

"I don't blow," says the sap.

"Then," said Bull, "why was it that fella called you 'Hurry' Kane?"

"It was Lefty Condon called me 'Hurry,' " says the sap. "My last name is Kane, and a hurricane is a big wind."

"Don't a wind blow?" says Bull.

And so on. I swear they kept it up for two hours, Kane trying to explain his nickname and Bull leading him on, and Joe Bonham said that Kane asked him up in the room who that was he had been talking to, and when Joe told him it was Wade, one of the smartest ball players in the league, Hurry said: "Well, then, he must be either stewed or else this is a damn sight dumber league than the one I came from."

Bull and some of the rest of the boys pulled all the old gags on him that's been in baseball since the days when you couldn't get on a club unless you had a walrus mustache. And Kane never disappointed them.

They made him go to the club-house after the key to the batter's box; they wrote him mash notes with fake names signed to them and had him spending half his evenings on some corner, waiting to meet gals that never lived; when he held Florida University to two hits in five innings, they sent him telegrams of congratulation from Coolidge and Al Smith, and he showed the telegrams to everybody in the hotel; they had him report at the ball park at six-thirty one morning for a secret "pitchers' conference"; they told him the Ritz was where all the unmarried ball players on the club lived while we were home, and they got him to write and ask for a parlor, bedroom and bath for the whole season. They was nothing he wouldn't fall for till Dave finally tipped him off that he was being kidded, and even then he didn't half believe it.

Now I never could figure how a man can fool themself about their own looks, but this bird was certain that he and Tommy Meighan were practically twins. Of course the boys soon found this out and strung him along. They advised him to quit baseball and go into pictures. They sat around his room and had him strike different poses and fix his hair different ways to see how he could show off his beauty to the best advantage. Johnny Abbott told me, after he began rooming with him, that for an hour before he went to bed and when he got up, Kane would stand in front of the mirror staring at himself and practising smiles and scowls and all kinds of silly faces, while Johnny pretended he was asleep.

Well, it wasn't hard to kid a fella like that into believing the dames were mad about him and when Bull Wade said that Evelyn Corey had asked who he was, his chest broke right through his shirt.

I know more about Evelyn now, but I didn't know nothing than except that she was a beautiful gal who had been in Broadway shows a couple of seasons and didn't have to be in them no more. Her room was two doors down the hall from Johnny's and Kane's. She was in Florida all alone, probably because her man friend, whoever he was at that time, had had to go abroad or somewheres with the family. All the ball players were willing to meet her, but she wasn't thrilled over the idear of getting acquainted with a bunch of guys who hadn't had a pay day in four or five months. Bull got Kane to write her a note; then Bull stole the note and wrote an answer, asking him to call. Hurry went and knocked at her door. She opened it and slammed it in his face.

"It was kind of dark," he said to Johnny, "and I guess she failed to recognize me." But he didn't have the nerve to call again.

He showed Johnny a picture of his gal in Yuma, a gal named Minnie Olson, who looked like she patronized the same store where Kane had bought his suit. He said she was wild about him and would marry him the minute he said the word and probably she was crying her eyes out right now, wishing he was home. He asked if Johnny had a gal and Johnny loosened up and showed him the picture of the gal he was engaged to. (Johnny married her last November.) She's a peach, but all Kane would say was, "Kind of skinny, ain't she?" Johnny laughed and said most gals liked to be that way.

"Not if they want me," says Kane.

"Well," said Johnny, "I don't think this one does. But how about your friend, that Miss Corey? You certainly can't call her plump, yet you're anxious to meet her."

"She's got class!" said Kane.

Johnny laughed that off, too. This gal of his, that he's married to now, she's so far ahead of Corey as far as class is concerned—well, they ain't no comparison. Johnny, you know, went to Cornell a couple of years and his wife is a college gal he met at a big house-party. If you put her and Evelyn beside of each other you wouldn't have no trouble telling which of them belonged on Park Avenue and which Broadway.

Kane kept on moaning more and more about his gal out West and acting glummer and glummer. Johnny did his best to cheer him up, as he seen what was liable to happen. But they wasn't no use. The big rube "lost" his fast ball and told Dave he had strained his arm and probably wouldn't be no good all season. Dave bawled him out and accused him of stalling. Kane stalled just the same. Then Dave soft-soaped him, told him how he'd burn up the league and how we were all depending on him to put us in the race and keep us there. But he might as well have been talking to a mounted policeman.

Finally, one day during the last week at Fort Gregg, Johnny Abbott got homesick himself and put in a long-distance call for his gal in New York. It was a rainy day and him and Kane had been just laying around the room. Before the call went through Johnny hinted that he would like to be alone while he talked. Kane paid no attention and began undressing to take a nap. So Johnny had to speak before an audience and not only that, but as soon as Kane heard him say "Darling" or "Sweetheart," or whatever he called her, he moved right over close to the phone where he wouldn't miss nothing. Johnny was kind of embarrassed and hung up before he was ready to; then he gave Kane a dirty look and went to the window and stared out at the rain, dreaming about the gal he'd just talked with.

Kane laid down on his bed, but he didn't go to sleep. In four or five minutes he was at the phone asking the operator to get Minnie Olson in Yuma. Then he laid down again and tossed a while, and then he sat up on the edge of the bed.

"Johnny," he says, "how far is it from here to New York?"

"About a thousand miles," said Johnny.

"And how far to Yuma?" said Kane.

"Oh," says Johnny, "that must be three thousand miles at least."

"How much did that New York call cost you?" asked Kane.

"I don't know yet," said Johnny. "I suppose it was around seven bucks."

Kane went to the writing table and done a little arithmetic. From there he went back to the phone.

"Listen, girlie," he said to the operator, "you can cancel that Yuma call. I just happened to remember that the party I wanted won't be home. She's taking her mandolin lesson, way the other side of town."

Johnny told me afterwards that he didn't know whether to laugh or cry. Before he had a chance to do either, Kane says to him:

"This is my last day on this ball club."

"What do you mean?" said Johnny.

"I mean I'm through; I'm going home," says Kane.

"Don't be a fool!" says Johnny. "Don't throw away the chance of a lifetime just because you're a little lonesome. If you stay in this league and pitch like you can pitch, you'll be getting the big money next year and you can marry that gal and bring her East with you. You may not have to wait till next year. You may pitch us into the world's series and grab a chunk of dough this fall."

"We won't be in no world's series," says Kane.

"What makes you think so?" said Johnny.

"I can't work every day," says Kane.

"You'll have help," says Johnny. "With you and Carney and Olds taking turns, we can be right up in that old fight. Without you, we can't even finish in the league. If you won't do it for yourself or for Dave, do it for me, your roomy. You just seen me spend seven or eight bucks on a phone call, but that's no sign I'm reeking with jack. I spent that money because I'd have died if I hadn't. I've got none to throw away and if we don't win the pennant, I can't marry this year and maybe not next year or the year after."

"I've got to look out for myself," says Kane. "I tell you I'm through and that's all there is to it. I'm going home where my gal is, where they ain't no smart Alecks kidding me all the while, and where I can eat without no assistant manager holding me down to a sprig of parsley, and a thimbleful of soup. For your sake, Johnny," he says, "I'd like to see this club finish on top, but I can't stick it out and I'm afraid your only hope is for the other seven clubs to all be riding on the same train and hit an open bridge."

Well, of course Johnny didn't lose no time getting to Dave with the bad news, and Dave and Kid Farrell rushed to the sapper's room. They threatened him and they coaxed him. They promised him he could eat all he wanted. They swore that anybody who tried to play jokes on him would either be fined or fired off the club. They reminded him that it cost a lot of money to go from Florida to Yuma, and he would have to pay his own way. They offered him a new contract with a five-hundred-dollar raise if he would stay. They argued and pleaded with him from four in the afternoon till midnight. When they finally quit, they were just where they'd been when they started. He was through.

"All right!" Dave hollered. "Be through and go to hell! If you ain't out of here by tomorrow noon, I'll have you chased out! And don't forget that you'll never pitch in organized baseball again!"

"That suits me," says Kane, and went to bed.

When Johnny Abbott woke up about seven the next morning, Hurry was putting his extra collar and comb in the leaky suitcase. He said:

"I'm going to grab the eleven-something train for Jacksonville. I got money enough to take me from here to New Orleans and I know a fella there that will see me the rest of the way—if I can find him and he ain't broke."

Well, Johnny couldn't stand for that and he got up and dressed and was starting out to borrow two hundred dollars from me to lend to Kane, when the phone rang loud and long. Kane took off the receiver, listened a second, and then said "Uh-huh" and hung up.

"Who was it?" asked Johnny.

"Nobody," says Kane. "Just one of Bull Wade's gags."

"What did he say?" Johnny asked him.

"It was a gal, probably the telephone operator," said Kane. "She said the hotel was on fire and not to get excited, but that we better move out."

"You fool!" yelled Johnny and run to the phone.

They was no gag about it. The hotel had really caught fire in the basement and everybody was being warned to take the air. Johnny tossed some of his stuff in a bag and started out, telling Kane to follow him quick. Hurry got out in the hall and then remembered that he had left his gal's picture on the dresser and went back after it. Just as he turned towards the door again, in dashed a dame with a kimono throwed over her nightgown. It was Evelyn Corey herself, almost in the flesh.

"Oh, please!" she said, or screamed. "Come and help me carry my things!"

Well, here was once that the name "Hurry" was on the square. He dropped his own suitcase and was in her room in nothing and no-fifths. He grabbed her four pieces of hand baggage and was staggering to the hall with them when a bellhop bounced in and told them the danger was over, the fire was out.

This seemed to be more of a disappointment than Evelyn could stand. Anyway, she fainted—onto a couch—and for a few minutes she was too unconscious to do anything but ask Kane to pour her a drink. He also poured himself one and settled down in the easy chair like he was there for the day. But by now she had come to and got a good look at him.

"I thank you very much," she said, "and I'm so exhausted with all this excitement that I think I'll go back to bed."

Kane took his hint and got up.

"But ain't I going to see you again?" he asked her.

"I'm afraid not," says Evelyn. "I'm leaving here this evening and I'll be getting ready from now till then."

"Where are you headed for?" Kane asked her.

"For home, New York," she said.

"Can't I have your address?" said Kane.

"Why, yes," said Evelyn without batting an eye. "I live at the Ritz."

"The Ritz!" says Kane. "That's where I'm going to live, if they ain't filled up."

"How wonderful!" said Evelyn. "Then we'll probably see each other every day."

Kane beat it down to the dining-room and straight to Dave's table.

"Boss," he said, "I've changed my mind."

"Your what!" says Dave.

"My mind," says Kane. "I've decided to stick."

It was all Dave could do not to kiss him. But he thought it was best to act calm.

"That's fine, Hurry!" he said. "And I'll see that you get that extra five hundred bucks."

"What five hundred bucks?" says Kane.

"The five hundred I promised you if you'd stay," says Dave.

"I hadn't heard about it," said Kane. "But as long as I ain't going home, I'm in no rush for money. Though I'm liable to need it," he says, "as soon as we hit New York."

And he smiled the silliest smile you ever seen.

◇   ◇   ◇

I don't have to tell you that he didn't live at the Ritz. Or that Evelyn
Corey didn't live there neither. He found out she hadn't never lived
there, but he figured she'd intended to and had to give it up because
they didn't have a suite good enough for her.

  · I got him a room in my boarding-house in the Bronx and for the
first few days he spent all his spare time looking through city directories and different telephone directories and bothering the life out
of Information, trying to locate his lost lady. It was when he had
practically give up hope that he told me his secret and asked for
help.

"She's all I came here for," he said, "and if I can't find her, I ain't
going to stay."

Well, of course if you went at it the right way, you wouldn't have
much trouble tracing her. Pretty near anybody in the theatrical business, or the people that run the big night clubs, or the head waiters
at the hotels and restaurants—they could have put you on the right
track. The thing was that it would be worse to get a hold of her than
not to, because she'd have give him the air so strong that he would
have caught his death of cold.

So I just said that they was no question but what she had gone
away somewheres, maybe to Europe, and he would hear from her
as soon as she got back. I had to repeat this over and over and make
it strong or he'd have left us flatter than his own feet before he
pitched two games. As it was, we held him till the end of May without
being obliged to try any tricks, but you could see he was getting
more impatient and restless all the while and the situation got desperate just as we were starting on our first trip West. He asked me
when would we hit St. Louis and I told him the date and
said:

"What do you want to know for?"

"Because," he says, "I'm going home from there."

I repeated this sweet news to Dave and Kid Farrell. We finally
called in Bull Wade and it was him that saved the day. You remember
Bull had faked up a note from Evelyn to Kane down at Fort Gregg;
now he suggested that he write some more notes, say one every two
or three weeks, sign her name to them, send them to Bull's brother
in Montreal and have the brother mail them from there. It was a
kind of a dirty, mean thing to do, but it worked. The notes all read
about the same——

"Dear Mr. Kane:—I am keeping track of your wonderful pitching and looking forward to seeing you when I return to New York, which will be early in the fall. I hope you haven't forgotten me."

And so on, signed "Your friend and admirer, Evelyn Corey."

Hurry didn't answer only about half of them as it was a real chore for him to write. He addressed his answers in care of Mr. Harry Wade, such and such a street number, Montreal, and when Bull's brother got them, he forwarded them to Bull, so he'd know if they was anything special he ought to reply to.

The boys took turns entertaining Kane evenings, playing cards with him and staking him to picture shows. Johnny Abbott done more than his share. You see the pennant meant more to Johnny than to anybody else; it meant the world's series money and a fall wedding, instead of a couple of years' wait. And Johnny's gal, Helen Kerslake, worked, too. She had him to her house to supper—when her folks were out—and made him feel like he was even handsomer and more important than he thought. She went so far as to try and get some of her gal friends to play with him, but he always wanted to pet and that was a little too much.

Well, if Kane hadn't stuck with us and turned out to be the marvel he is, the White Sox would have been so far ahead by the Fourth of July that they could have sat in the stand the rest of the season and let the Bloomer Girls play in their place. But Hurry had their number from the first time he faced them till the finish. Out of eleven games he worked against them all last year, he won ten and the other was a nothing to nothing tie. And look at the rest of his record! As I recall it, he took part in fifty-eight games. He pitched forty-three full games, winning thirty-six, losing five and tying two. And God knows how many games he saved! He had that free, easy side-arm motion that didn't take much out of him and he could pitch every third day and be at his best.

But don't let me forget to credit myself with an assist. Late in August, Kane told me he couldn't stand it no longer to just get short notes from the Corey gal and never see her, and when we started on our September trip West, he was going to steal a week off and run up to Montreal; he would join us later, but he must see Evelyn. Well, for once in my life I had an idear hit me right between the eyes.

The Yuma gal, Minnie Olson, had been writing to him once a week and though he hardly ever wrote to her and seemed to only be thinking of Corey, still I noticed that he could hardly help from crying when Minnie's letters came. So I suggested to Dave that he telegraph Minnie to come East and visit with all her expenses paid, wire her money for her transportation, tell her it would be doing Kane a big favor as well as the rest of us, and ask her to send Kane a telegram, saying when she would reach New York, but to be sure and never mention that she wasn't doing it on her own hook.

Two days after Dave's message was sent, Kane got a wire from El Paso. She was on her way and would he meet her at the Pennsylvania Station on such and such a date. I never seen a man as happy as Hurry was when he read that telegram.

"I knew she was stuck on me," he said, "but I didn't know it was that strong. She must have worked in a store or something since spring to save up money for this trip."

You would have thought he'd never heard of or seen a gal by the name of Evelyn Corey.

Minnie arrived and was just what we expected: a plain, honest, good-hearted, small-town gal, dressed for a masquerade. We had supper with her and Kane her first night in town—I and Johnny and Helen. She was trembling like a leaf, partly from excitement over being in New York and amongst strangers, but mostly on account of seeing the big sap again. He wasn't no sap to her and I wished they was some dame would look at me the way she kept looking at Hurry.

The next morning Helen took her on a shopping tour and got her fixed up so cute that you couldn't hardly recognize her. In the afternoon she went to the ball game and seen Kane shut the Detroit club out with two hits.

When Hurry got a glimpse of her in her Fifth Avenue clothes, he was as proud as if he had bought them himself and it didn't seem to occur to him that they must have cost more than she could have paid.

Well, with Kane happy and no danger of him walking out on us, all we had to worry about was that the White Sox still led us by three games, with less than twenty left to play. And the schedule was different than usual—we had to wind up with a Western trip and play our last thirteen games on the road. I and Johnny and Dave was talking it over one day and the three of us agreed that we would be suckers not to insist on Miss Olson going along. But Dave wondered if she wouldn't feel funny, being the only girl.

"I'll make my gal go, too," said Johnny.

And that's the way it was fixed.

We opened in St. Louis and beat them two out of three. Olds was trimmed, but Carney and Kane both won. We didn't gain no ground, because the White Sox grabbed two out of three from Washington. We made a sweep of our four games in Detroit, while the Sox was winning three from Philadelphia. That moved us up to two and a half games from first place. We beat Cleveland three straight, Kane licking them 6 to 1 and holding Carney's one run lead through the eighth and ninth innings of another game. At the same time, Chicago took three from Boston.

So we finally struck old Chi, where the fans was already counting the pennant won, two and a half games behind and three to go— meaning we had to win all three or be sunk.

I told you how Kane had the Chicago club's number. But I didn't tell you how Eddie Brainard had been making a monkey of us. He had only worked against us six times and had beat us five. His other game was the nothing to nothing tie with Hurry. Eddie is one sweet pitcher and if he had been the horse for work that Kane was, that last series wouldn't have got us nowheres. But Eddie needs his full rest and it was a cinch he wouldn't be in there for more than one game and maybe part of another.

In Brainard's six games against us, he had give us a total of four runs, shutting us out three times and trimming us 3 to 2, 4 to 1 and 2 to 1. As the White Sox only needed one game, it was a cinch that they wouldn't start Eddie against Kane, who was so tough for them, but would save him for Carney or Olds, whichever one worked first. Carney hadn't been able to finish a game with Chicago and Olds' record wasn't much better.

Well, we was having breakfast in our hotel the morning we got in from Cleveland, and Kane sent for Dave to come to the table where him and Johnny Abbott and the two gals was eating.

"Boss," he says, "I'm thinking of getting married and so is Johnny here, but they ain't neither of us can do it, not now anyway, unless we grab some of that world's series jack. And we can't get into the series without we win these three games. So if I was managing this ball club, I'd figure on that and know just how to work my pitchers."

"Maybe I've thought about it a little myself," says Dave. "But I'd like to listen to your idears."

"All right," says Kane. "I'd start Kane today, and I'd start Kane tomorrow, and I'd start Kane the day after that."

"My plan is a little different," said Dave. "Of course you start today, and if you win, why, I want to play a joke on them tomorrow. I intend to start Olds so they'll start Brainard. And if the game is anywheres near close at the end of the third or fourth innings, you're going in. It will be too late for them to take Brainard out and expect him to be as good the third day. And if we win that second game, why, you won't have to beg me to pitch the last one."

You'll think I'm getting long-winded, but they ain't much more to tell. You probably heard the details of those first two games even if you was on the Other Side. Hurry beat them the first one, 7 to 1, and their one run was my fault. Claymore was on second base with two men out in the sixth innings. King hit a foul ball right straight up and I dropped it. And then he pulled a base-hit inside of Bull, and Claymore scored. Olds and Brainard started the second game and at the end of our half of the fourth innings, the score was one and one. Hurry had been warming up easy right along, but it certainly was a big surprise to the Chicago club and pretty near everybody else when Dave motioned him in to relieve Olds. The White Sox never came close to another run and we got to Brainard for one in the eighth, just enought to beat him.

Eddie had pitched his head off and it was a tough one for him to lose. But the best part of it was, he was through and out of the way.

Well, Johnny and Kane had their usual date with the two gals for supper. Johnny was in his bathroom, washing up, when the phone rang. Kane answered it, but he talked kind of low and Johnny didn't hear what he was saying. But when Hurry had hung up, he acted kind of nervous and Johnny asked him what was the matter.

"It's hard luck," said Kane. "They's a friend of mine from Yuma here, and he's in trouble and I've got to go over on the North Side and see him. Will you take both the gals to supper yourself? Because I may not be back till late. And don't tell Min who I'm going to see."

"How could I tell her when you ain't told me?" said Johnny.

"Well," said Kane, "just tell her I'm wore out from working so hard two days in a row and I went right to bed so I'd be all right for tomorrow."

Johnny was kind of worried and tried to coax him not to go. But Kane ducked out and didn't come in till midnight. Johnny tried to find out where he'd been and what had happened, but he said he was too sleepy to talk. Just the same, Johnny says, he tossed around and moaned all night like he was having a nightmare, and he usually slept like a corpse.

Kane got up early and went down to breakfast before Johnny was dressed. But Johnny was still worried, and hustled up and caught him before he was out of the dining-room. He was hoping Hurry

would explain his getting in late and not sleeping. Kane wouldn't talk, though, and still acted nervous. So Johnny finally said:

"Hurry, you know what this game today means to me and you ought to know what it means to you. If we get trimmed, a lot of people besides ourselves will be disappointed, but they won't nobody be as disappointed as me. I wished you'd have had a good sleep last night and if you'll take my advice, you'll go up in the room and rest till it's time to go to the ball yard. If you're anywheres near yourself, this Chicago club is licked. And for heaven's sakes, be yourself, or your roomy is liable to walk out into Lake Michigan tonight so far that I can't get back!"

"I'm myself," says Kane and got up and left the table, but not quick enough so that Johnny didn't see tears in his eyes.

That afternoon's crowd beat all records and I was tickled to death to see it, because Hurry had always done his best work in front of crowds that was pulling against him. He warmed up fine and they wasn't nobody on our club, nobody but Kane himself and two others, who didn't feel perfectly confident that we were "in."

The White Sox were starting Sam Bonner and while he had beat us three or four times, we'd always got runs off him, and they'd always been lucky to score at all against Kane.

Bonner went through the first innings without no trouble. And then we got the shock of our lives. The first ball Hurry pitched was high and outside and it felt funny when I caught it. I was used to that old "zip" and I could have caught this one in my bare hand. Claymore took a cut at the next one and hit it a mile to left center for three bases. King hit for two bases, Welsh was safe when Digman threw a ground ball into the seats, and Kramer slapped one out of the park for a homer. Four runs. The crowd was wild and we were wilder.

You ought to have heard us on that bench. "Yellow so-and-so" was the mildest name Hurry got called. Dave couldn't do nothing but just mumble and shake his fists at Kane. We was all raving and asking each other what in hell was going on. Hurry stood in front facing us, but he was looking up in the stand and he acted like he didn't hear one word of the sweet remarks meant for his ears.

Johnny Abbott pulled me aside.

"Listen," he says. "This kid ain't yellow and he ain't wore out. They's something wrong here."

By this time Dave had found his voice and he yelled at Kane: "You so-and-so so-and-so! You're going to stay right in there and

pitch till this game is over! And if you don't pitch like you can pitch, I'll shoot you dead tonight just as sure as you're a yellow, quitting——!"

We'd forgot it was our turn to bat and Hildebrand was threatening to forfeit the game before he could get Bull Wade to go up there. Kane still stood in front of us, staring. But pretty soon Dave told young Topping to run out to the bull pen and warn Carney and Olds to both be ready. I seen Topping stop a minute alongside of Kane and look up in the stand where Kane was looking. I seen Topping say something to Kane and I heard Kane call him a liar. Then Topping said something more and Hurry turned white as a sheet and pretty near fell into the dugout. I noticed his hand shake as he took a drink of water. And then he went over to Dave and I heard him say:

"I'm sorry, Boss. I had a bad inning. But I'll be all right from now on."

"You'd better!" says Dave.

"Get me some runs is all I ask," says Kane.

And the words wasn't no sooner out of his mouth when Bull smacked one a mile over Claymore's head and came into the plate standing up. They was another tune on the bench now. We were yelling for blood, and we got it. Before they relieved Bonner, we'd got to him for three singles and a double—mine, if you must know—and the score was tied.

Say, if you think you ever seen pitching, you ought to have watched Kane cut them through there the rest of that day. Fourteen strikeouts in the last eight innings! And the only man to reach first base was Kramer, when Stout dropped an easy fly ball in the fifth.

Well, to shorten it up, Bull and Johnny Abbott and myself had some luck against Pierce in the seventh innings. Bull and Johnny scored and we licked them, 6 to 4.

In the club-house, Dave went to Hurry and said:

"Have you got anything to tell me, any explanation of the way you looked at the start of that game?"

"Boss," said Kane, "I didn't sleep good last night. Johnny will be a witness to that. I felt terrible in that first innings. I seemed to have lost my 'fast.' In the second innings it came back and I was all right."

And that's all he would say.

You know how we went ahead and took the big series, four games out of five, and how Hurry gave them one run in the three games he pitched. And now you're going to know what I promised to tell

you when we first sat down, and I hope I ain't keeping you from a date with that gal from St. Joe.

The world's series ended in St. Louis and naturally I didn't come back East when it was over. Neither did Kane, because he was going home to Yuma, along with his Minnie. Well, they were leaving the next night, though most of the other boys had ducked out right after the final game. Hurry called me up at my house three or four hours before his train was due to leave and asked me would I come and see him and give him some advice. So I went to the hotel and he got me in his room and locked the door.

Here is what he had to say:

On the night before that last game in Chi, a gal called him up and it was nobody but our old friend Evelyn Corey. She asked him to come out to a certain hotel on the North Side and have supper with her. He went because he felt kind of sorry for her. But when he seen her, he lost his head and was just as nuts about her as he'd been at Fort Gregg. She encouraged him and strung him along till he forgot all about poor Minnie. Evelyn told him she knew he could have his pick of a hundred gals and she was broken-hearted because they was no chance for her. He asked her what made her think that, and she put her handkerchief to her eyes and pretended she was crying and that drove him wild and he said he wouldn't marry nobody but her.

Then she told him they had better forget it, that she was broke now, but had been used to luxury, and he promised he would work hard and save up till he had three or four thousand dollars and that would be enough for a start.

"Four thousand dollars!" she says. "Why, that wouldn't buy the runs in my stockings! I wouldn't think of marrying a man who had less than twenty thousand. I would want a honeymoon in Europe and we'd buy a car over there and tour the whole continent, and then come home and settle down in some nice suburb of New York. And so," she says, "I am going to get up and leave you right now because I see that my dream won't never come true."

She left him sitting in the restaurant and he was the only person there outside of the waiters. But after he'd sat a little while—he was waiting till the first shock of his disappointment had wore off—a black-haired bird with a waxed mustache came up to him and asked if he wasn't Hurry Kane, the great pitcher. Then he said: "I suppose you'll pitch again tomorrow," and Kane said yes.

"I haven't nothing against you," says the stranger, "but I hope you lose. It will cost me a lot of money if you win."

"How much?" said Kane.

"So much," says the stranger, "that I will give you twenty thousand dollars if you get beat."

"I can't throw my pals," said Kane.

"Well," said the stranger, "two of your pals has already agreed to throw you."

Kane asked him who he referred to, but he wouldn't tell. Kane don't know yet, but I do. It was Dignan and Stout, our short-stopper and first baseman, and you'll notice they ain't with our club no more.

Hurry held out as long as he could, but he thought of Evelyn and that honeymoon in Europe broke him down. He took five thousand dollars' advance and was to come to the same place and get the balance right after the game.

He said that after Johnny Abbott had give him that talk at the breakfast table, he went out and rode around in a taxi so he could cry without being seen.

Well, I've told you about that terrible first innings. And I've told you about young Topping talking to him before he went down to the bull pen to deliver Dave's message to Carney and Olds. Topping asked him what he was staring at and Hurry pointed Evelyn out to him and said she was his gal.

"Your gal's grandmother!" said Topping. "That's Evelyn Corey and she belongs to Sam Morris, the bookie. If I was you, I'd lay off. You needn't tell Dave, but I was in Ike Bloom's at one o'clock this morning, and Sam and she were there, too. And one of the waiters told me that Sam had bet twenty thousand dollars on the White Sox way last spring and had got six to one for his money."

Hurry quit talking and I started to bawl him out. But I couldn't stay mad at him, especially when I realized that they was a fifty-three-hundred-dollar check in my pocket which I'd never have had only for him. Besides, they ain't nothing crooked about him. He's just a bone-headed sap.

"I won't tell Dave on you," I said, and I got up to go.

"Wait a minute," says Kane. "I confessed so I could ask you a question. I've still got that five thousand which Morris paid me in advance. With that dough and the fifty-three hundred from the series, I and Min could buy ourself a nice little home in Yuma. But do you think I should ought to give it back to that crook?"

"No," said I. "What you ought to do is split it with young Topping. He was your good luck!"

I run acrost Topping right here in town not long ago. And the first thing he said was, "What do you think of that goofey Kane? I had a letter from him and a check. He said the check was what he owed me."

"Twenty-five hundred dollars?" I says.

"Two hundred," said Topping, "and if I ever lent him two hundred or two cents, I'll roll a hoop from here to Yuma."

ONE HIT, ONE ERROR,
ONE LEFT

◇

Clearwater fla march 3
DEAR JESSIE well kid here it is the 3 of march and I am still in
the big league but kidding on the square things is beggin to look
pretty rosey as mgr Carey has now got Casey Stengel rooming with
me and I guest I all ready told you about Stengel he is a kind of asst
mgr and coach of the club and kind of took me in toe the 1st day
we beggin to work out and now mgr Carey has got him rooming
with me so it looks like there takeing a special interest in how I get
a long as Stengel sets and talks to me by the hr about the fine points
and gives me pointers about the fine points of the game that comes
up durn practice.

I guess that sounds pretty good hay kid on account of the promise
I give you the day I left home so you better get ready to pack up
the old bag and all a board for Brooklyn or maybe you better wait
a wile as maybe I will run a cross some kid I like better. No danger
hay kid.

Stengels name aint Casey but that is just a nick name witch he
says they call him that because he come from Kansas City but that
don't make sense but some of the boys has got nick names like wear
they come from like 1 of the pitchers Clyde Day but they call him
Pea ridge Day because he come from a town name Pea ridge and he
was the champion hog caller of Arkansaw and when he use to pitch
in Brooklyn last yr he use to give a hog call after every ball he
throwed but the club made him cut it out because the fans come
down on the field every time he give a call and the club had to hire
the champion of iowa to set up in the stand and call them back. Then

This story first appeared in *The Saturday Evening Post*, April 23, 1932; one of the
six stories collected in *Lose With a Smile*, (New York: Scribners, 1933).

there is a infielder Tommy Thompson but some times they call him Fresco and I thought it was because he come from Frisco but Stengel says his hole name is Al Fresco and his folks give him the name because he was born out doors like restrants where they got tables under a tree and 1 of the boys was asking if they call Wilson Hack because he was born in a hack but Stengel says it was 2 of them and they had to sell them to a junk dealer.

Wilson is the man who the Cubs had and 2 yrs ago he led the both leagues in home runs but last yr he had a bad yr and they trade it him to St Louis for Grimes but the St Louis club found out that the Cubs had been paying him a salery so they give him to Brooklyn as the St Louis players works on a commision base and what ever amt you get out of the world series the club leaves you keep it. Hack takes a good cut at the ball and if he meets them square it is no wonder they go for a ride as he ways as much as your piano but I can hit them just as far and maybe farther as I got more strenth in my rist but any ways we both hit right hand it and who plays center field depends on witch is socking them the hardest tho of course we will both be in there at the same time if any mgr is crazy enough to pitch a left hander. I says to Stengel last night I says to Stengel if any mgr is crazy enough to pitch a left hander again this club they would put them in a silium and Stengel says they are all ready there.

We was talking about nick names and Thompson says to me wear do you come from Warner and I says Centralia and Stengel says well we cant call him all that because he would be back a sleep before you was half threw and we all ready got a Jack Warner on the club so we better call this one bench but that was the night before last and last night we was out in front of the hotel and a couple of the boys beggin to sing and I joined in kind of soft and ever since then they don't call me nothing but Rudy on account of Rudy Valet and Thompson says if I could groon like you I would not be plain base ball and Stengel says he aint but any ways they all call me Rudy and keep asking me wear did I lern to groon.

Will close for this time kid as am all tarred out as they had me chason fly balls all day and not only that but mgr Carey makes all the boys go threw a case of calsthenics and part of it is wear you lay on your back and push your ft up in the air like you are rideing a bycycle and I says to Stengel what is the idea of that kind of practice because when we get to Brooklyn I hope to live some wear wear I wont have to ride a bycycle to the ball pk and even if I did I wouldent never get there laying on my back and pushing my ft up in the air.

Any ways am all tarred out but remember what I told you about get ready to pack up the old bag but dont breath nothing to nobody but just tell them you got a post card from me and am getting a long ok and the wether just like summer and here it is only the 3 of march.   Danny

Centralia, Ill. March 7.
DEAR DANNY—You know what a poor hand I am at writing letters and I only wish I was a better letter writer. It is hard to imajine you having summer weather and here we have had more snow than usual and it has also rained some and snowed more than usual so it is hard to imajine you having summer weather.

I am a poor hand at writing letters and I only wish I could tell you how glad I am for your sake that all the managers are all taking so much interest in your work and of course there has never been no doubts in my mind about them keeping you, but as far as what you promised me is concerned I will not hold you to no promise and of course you know how I feel towards you and will never feel no different, but I know that the promise was just in fun, but any time you realy want me you know that I will be here, but will not hold you to no promise that was just in fun.

I can imajine how those other men must enjoy hearing you sing and I almost find myself wishing that you was going to drop in for a few minutes tonight and sing for me though I know I am a poor pianist and make too many mistakes.

Things have been very quite in the store and there is no news.

Was over to see Clara and Dave and their baby last Sunday, he is a cute baby and they both think there was never no other baby like him. I guess all parents feel the same way about their first baby, he is certainly cute all right.

Be sure and take good care of yourself and dont catch cold. The weather gets cold even in Florida and if you will just keep your promise to write to me I will not hold you to no promise that was just made in fun, besides Mr. Carey may not want to have married men on his nine till they get older.   Yours,   Jessie.

Clearwater fla march 12
DEAR JESSIE don't worry about me breaking no promises and as for mgr Carey he has got a wife and family himself and most of the

men on the club has got a family and Babe Herman has got a wife and 2 kids and sells shirts and Lefty Odoul sells shoes in the winter and Jack Quinn is married and most of the other boys and mgr Carey has got a string of gas stations a round St Louis and minit rub witch is some kind of sauve that keeps the pitchers arms in shape and as for your piano plain you will do till some body better comes a long. mgr Carey calls me Rudy like the rest of the boys is calling me and he is a good singer himself but cant groon like I tho when he was in school he studed for the preist hood.

Well kid I told you to get the old bag packed and all as I ask is for you to keep your promise to not breath a word till I give you the word but between you and I it looks better then ever because last night some of the boys went to the picture and wanted I should go a long but I had all ready seen it twict and dident care nothing about seen it a 2d time so I come up in my room and who was there but mgr Carey and Stengel the both of them and I says I would go out for a walk and give them a chance to talk things over but Carey says no set down boy and maybe you will lern some thing as we got no secrets from you witch sound it like he all ready made up his mind to keep me hay kid and he says did you ever try hitting them left hand it and I says I guest I could hit them good enough 1 way and he says he was a turn a round hitter himself when he was plain base ball and it kept him in the league a long wile extra and if you could lern to hit left hand it and hit them long fly balls to right field like you hit them to left field it would not hurt you. So I says why dont you make Wilson hit left hand it and he says because Wilson can hit right hand it all the time and hit to 1 field as good as another and then Stengel says he himself was all so a turn a round hitter as he use to hit so good right hand it that the pitchers thretened to walk out unlest he would agree to hit left hand it all the time.

But he made a sucker out of them because he was even better left hand it then he had been right hand it and he says will I tell him how good I was Max and Carey says you proudly will and Stengel says well I was so good that they use to pass me on purpose in batting practice and 1 time I was in a world series again the Giants and the yankees and the empires called the game on account of darkness at 3 pm with the sun shinning and judge Landis ast them to exclaim there decision and they said they thought it must be dark because Stengel only hit for 2 bases. So I menshuned about plain night base ball in Bloomington and Stengel says that exclaims it Max how the scouts sent that report in but mgr Carey says no that dont exclaim nothing because he seen a game in Bloomington himself and they had the field all lit up and it was bright as day.

Well this pm mgr Carey ast me to just try and hit a few left hand it and Jack Quinn was pitching and he aint got nothing on the ball only he dont throw it wear you can get a cut at it so I dident even foul 1 and then Clark throwed a few and he is a left hander and that made it all the worst and Wilson hit a couple out of the pk right hand it and I could of hit them twict as far only Carey made me keep trying left hand it and I told him I couldent do nothing that way and he says nobody can lern in 1 pm and when we got back to the hotel I complaint to Stengel and he says you ought to feel pretty good because if he dident take a interest in you he wouldent care if you hit them right hand it or left hand it or back words and I says maybe he is figureing on me to take Hermans place as Herman is still holeing out but Stengel says dont worry about Herman as all of these boys has to hole out till they can remember how they spell there name so you see kid I got reasons to remind you about your promise and be ready to pack up for Brooklyn as soon as I say the word.

We had 1 bad day a wk a go when the wind blowed 50 miles a hr. and I says it was a wonder we dident all get our heads blowed off and Stengel says it was a shame because that would improve the club and must close now and turn in as we play our 1st regular game tomorrow again Cincinnati at Tampa the capitol and the boys is all talking about a trade with there club witch would give us Joe Stripp or somebody and Stengel says you better not play as bad as you can or the reds will want you in the trade. I guest he ment as good.

Danny

Centralia, Ill. March 16.

DEAR DANNY—Dave said he seen in the St. Louis paper that the Brooklyns had played Cincinnati and Newark, but it did not say who was the players on both sides, but I imajine you helped beat them, but did not know that Newark was in your league.

I am a poor hand at writing letters and there is so little news here, but the weather has been bad, rainy and snowing and it is hard to imajine you playing ball while we are having such nasty weather.

I told you in my last letter that I would not hold you to no promise that was just made in fun and just forget all about that part of it, but I know the Brooklyns will keep you and give you a good position, though I cant understand Mr. Carey wanting you to bat with your left hand when the other way comes natural to you and I know I cant do anything with my left hand, not even write my name. I told Dave about Mr. Carey once studying to be a priest and Dave said he seen a world game in Pittsburgh one time when Mr. Carey was playing there and he bet Walter Johnson wished Mr. Carey had stayed in church. Probibly you will know to what he referred to.

Things have been very quite in the store and there is very little news. Things have been going on about as usual and I guess you know I am lonesome without me telling you and I wish things were busier at the store so I would not have so much time to get blue, but the worst time is the evenings. I cant play the piano good enough to even entertain myself and besides it seems to make me all the more lonesome and I try and read, but cant get interested in nothing only your letters, and I read them over and over, though I dont understand most of it, but I love to read them just the same.

Yours, Jessie.

Clearwater fla march 23

DEAR JESSIE we been plain a game pretty near every day with some big league club ether here or some other place and I been in there pretty near every day but most of the time in right field or left field in place of Boone or Odoul and it looks like mgr Carey intend it to start the season with Wilson in center but it is a cinch they are going to keep me because they trade it Herman to Cincinnati. So remember what I told you about packing up the old bag as soon as I give you the word and it wont be more than a couple more days when I will know where I stand but after the way I been socking them it looks like I am all set. I got 4 in 4 again the As and I stared at bat again the cards. How is that again the 2 champions of the 2 big leagues but best of all is the way I been socking them to right field and when I had socked 2 over the right field wall again Newark mgr Carey quit trying to make me hit left hand it but he did make me change my stanch and Stengel says that is why I am hitting so good to right field.

Every time we go some place in a train or bus the boys start singing and next thing you know they are asking for Rudy to join in but as soon as I beggin to groon they all shet up and I wont have no voice left unlest they lay off me and night before last they was all after me to groon and I told them I was going to a picture and it happened I had promised the phone girl in the hotel to take her to a picture so I called her up and kept my promise. Her name is Vivian Duane and she was born in fla and talks with a funny drool but she calls me Rudy like the rest of the boys and she wants I should get her a job when I get up north. She is a good looker but I told her I would have to be sure of my own job before I promise to get her a job.

The other night a party of us went over to a place near here name Bellair wear they have got a caseno with a rulette wheel and 1 of the boys exclaimed on the way over there is 36 numbers and they roll a marble and half the numbers is black and half red and if you pick the right number they pay 35 to 1 and if you play red or black they pay you even money. So I seen that the way to beat it was play red 1 time and black the next time so I bought $10.00 worth of $.50 chips and wait it till they had roll the marble 1 time and it come red and then I bet $.50 on the black and sure enough it come black and then I win again on the red and I was counting how much was I a winner and forgot to bet and it come red witch was twict in a row. So I seen the game was queer so I says to the man cash me in and all the boys laughed but I was the 1 that had the laugh on the way home because I was the only 1 that win.

I guest I all ready told you about this Pea ridge Day the hog caller from Arkansaw. Well it seems that last spring he was down here and some of the boys bet him $10.00 he was scarred to jump in a fish pond with his close on and he took the bet and jumped in the pond and they had to pay him the $10.00 and the suit was too big for him when he got it and he figured it might schrink to get it wet and it only cause him $8.00 in the 1st place and he dried it out and had a man press it for $1.00 and sure enough it schrink to just the right size. So he had the laugh on them just like myself in the rulette wheel.

This pm we got a game with a club called the House of David witch aint in no league but they are members of a religious sex in Michigan and Stengel says Jack Quinn will pitch the hole game for our club because the other club all wears beards and he says they have got 4 pitchers name Mathews Mark and Luque and John and Mathews is a left hander. Well I hope he pitchs and I will give some of them outfielders a shave.

1 day last wk we was over to a place name Tarpon springs wear they are all greeks and fish for sponges in a sail boat and I bought 2 sponges and at 1st I was going to keep 1 of them for myself and male you the other and then I happened to think about your mother. So decide it to send the both of them to you only 1 of them is for

your mother but you wont get them for a few days as I dident know how to rap them up but happened to think about Vivian the phone girl and she is going to rap them up and male them.

Stengel says I am doing the right thing because just 1 of them wouldent do me no good but anyways you will know who they come from even if it is her hand writeing.

Nobody calls me Danny no more only you. So I will sine this letter Rudy.   Rudy

p.s. dont forget about packing the old bag when I give you the word.   Rudy.

Centralia, Ill., March 27

DEAR DANNY—You will never be nothing only Danny to me. I dont care what other girls call you and I certainly will not call you Rudy, as I would rather hear you sing than Rudy Vallee 100 times.

Dave seen an article on the train the other day and was going to bring it to me but forgot it, and it said Mr. Carey was delighted in your improvement since he had changed your stand up to bat and it looked like the Brooklyns were sure to keep you as a pinch man. Well Danny I knew all along that you would make good, but please dont talk about no promise to me. You know how glad I am to have you make good, but it is for your own sake and am not holding you to no silly promises. I only wish Brooklyn was not so far away, though of course you might as well be there as Bloomington as far as me seeing you is concerned.

For one thing I cant help from beleiving that Mr. Carey would not like you taking such a serious step like getting married so soon after giving you a position like pinch man and besides that there is the question about me leaving mamma and papa, though mamma has not felt as good in ten years as she feels this spring and papa dont need me in the store and says we would save money on coal bills if we closed up till business gets better, and you know how ignorant I am about things and do the player's wives travel around with them or all live together in some hotel or do they have summer homes on Coney Island or some place. I dont even know what clothes a person would have to have but I know I have not got nothing fit to wear only the dress I had last summer, and you would be ashamed of me and probibly the other player's wives would laugh when they seen my clothes.

I dont know why I am writing all this because as I told you, I am not going to hold you to no silly promise, but sometimes I get so lonesome and blue that I feel like I would go crazy, and I guess you will think I am crazy writing a letter like this.

The sponges have not gotten here yet, but it was lovely of you to think of mamma and I with so much on your mind, but maybe your friend Miss Duane got jealous because you forgot to buy her a sponge and just did not send them. I am just joking Danny but maybe you will not see the joke and I guess I better close or you will think I have gone crazy.   Yours,   Jessie

Clearwater fla march 24

DEAR JESSIE well kid I wrote you a letter yesterday am and here I am writing to you again and how is that for keeping a promise but it is regards to another promise that I am writing you this time and I mean the promise about I and you getting married if the Brooklyn club decide it to keep me.

Well kid mgr Carey told me last night that he was going to keep me and I need not worry about my job but I still got a few things to lern and he maybe will not play me regular for a wile but leave me warn the bench and use me for a pinch hitter and if I kept my eyes open and worked hard he will maybe give me a chance in place of 1 of the left hand it hitters again a left hander. So I better work out in both left and right field because he says center field is crowd it enough with just Wilson. So I thanked him and after words I and Stengel was in the room and I guest I was kind of nerves and Stengel says what is on your mind and I says I had made a promise that I would marry a little kid up home and I intend it to go threw with the promise even if it cause me my job and he says well it will cause you your job all right but if she is the right kind of a girl she will release you from your promise rather than see Max release you off of the ball club and you just tell her to do you a flavor and wait till fall or else you can check your trunk threw to Hartford.

Well kid it is all up to you and I will keep my promise if you say the word even if it cause me my job but when I made you the promise it was kind of a joke as I dident think I would make good so quick but Carey would be crazy to let me go the way I been socking them and yesterday I got 3 out of 4 off them beard it boys and 1 of there outfielders catched the other 1 in his wiskers and be sides Carey would have to get wafers and all as I am scarred of is the Reds or Phila or St Louis getting a hold of me and I would ether be with a

8 place club or put out to pasture some place all season but as I say I will go threw with my promise if you say the word but the boys is all puling for me to stay with this club so as they can lissen to me groon.

Stengel says wear does your girl live and I told him Centralia and he says you would be plain a fine trick on her makeing her leave her folks and her home town and move to a human zoo like Brooklyn and leave her there starveing to death half the time wile you travel a round the country and live in the best hotels and when your home she can come out to the ball pk and watch you in batting practice and maybe seen you march up to the plate onct a wk a mist a shower of boos. So I says how about the other boys that has got a wife and family and he says you can bet there getting more than $3000.00 a yr witch is $250.00 a mont and for 12 monts and I says how much would it cause me to live supose I was a lone and he says it wouldent cause you nothing because you eat so much on the road that you can lay off food durn the 80 days your in Brooklyn and the Brooklyn bench is a pretty good place to sleep after you get use to the rore of the animals.

Well kid I guest that is enough on that subject and I will leave it to you to say yes or no and if you hold me to my promise well in good I will go threw with my promise even if it cause me my job.

1 of the Brooklyn papers has come out with a offer of $1000.00 in cash to who ever can think of a new nick name for the club as they been calling them the robins because there mgr was Wm Robinson but Carey is the mgr now so robins dont make no sense and all the boys has been trying to think up some name and I wisht I could think up some name hay kid and knock off that $1000.00 and why dont you try it yourself kid and you might hit on some name that would be as good as I could think up myself and I ast Vivian the phone girl to try and she says why not call us the Brooks or the Bridgers on account of Brooklyn bridge but when I repeat it them to the boys they just laughed and speaking of Vivian she says she is going to come up to Brooklyn and look for a job when the season is over down here as it gets so hot durn the summer and I was out to her house for a few minutes last night and she has got a piano and can play like a street. So they was nothing to do but I must groon a few dittys so I hope she does come up to Brooklyn. That is if I have to be a lone but speaking about a name for the club I ast Carey why dident he give it a name himself and he says robins was ok with him. So I says Yes but Robinson aint mgr no more and

Carey says I wisht he was and Stengel says if you got to get a name that refers to the mgr why not call them the Max trux but the way they been looking for the last few days we ought to call them Cincinnati.

Well kid you will let me hear from you as soon as you receive this and I know you will think I am trying to walk out on my promise but I will go threw with it even if it cause me my job and I am only telling you what Stengel thinks and after all maybe you would be home sick and lone some a lone so much of the time and with your mother not feeling so good maybe you ought not to leave her a side from helping your father in the store and it will be just the same this fall and I can get some money saved up by that time. I wasent sure but what Carey would object to a young man getting married when I am just breaking in and I guest I better exclaim about them other men on the club like Wilson who has got a wife and kid but he gets a salery of $16500 witch is more then 5 times my salery and as for the boys that is all ready married why Carey cant very well tell them to get rid of there wife or he will trade them to Phila and of course in the case of a man like Jack Quinn why he was married when Carey was lerning to talk.

It is different with a man like I wear I am just breaking in and all the time I was a way on the road I would be thinking about you all a lone there in Brooklyn and you couldent even go to a picture because the place is full of gunsters and maybe the very day we picked out to get married who ever we was plain again would pick that day to pitch a left hander and Carey would lay it all on you and I if the club lose a close game.

As I say kid if you say the word I will go threw with my promise but I only made it as a kind of a joke and I dont remember if I says right away or next fall and if you think we better wait I will keep on writeing you letters and write you a letter every day all season but be sure and let me know by return male.

Rudy

Centralia, Ill. March 28

DEAR DANNY—Your letter just came and I wrote you a letter yesterday, and I hope you wont pay no attention to some of the things I said in it as it was all just a joke, and please forget that crazy promise which I took as a joke, and I dont consider it a promise for now or next fall or any other time.

The sponges came yesterday and Miss Duane has got a pretty hand writing and I am glad she is going to Brooklyn and you will have some one that can realy play the piano for you to sing.

Mamma says thanks for the sponges and we are all glad that Mr. Carey is going to keep you, but I knew he would and now you must learn all you can from he and Mr. Stengel and take care of yourself and dont imajine for a minute that I would allow you to write to me every day as I am such a poor hand at writing letters and can give you nothing in return but if you ever have a little spare time you know how I will love to hear from you, and Dave says he will keep me posted on the Brooklyn nine as soon as the season opens in earnest, and I hope you beat everybody and all I ask is that if you ever do find time to write please dont sign Rudy but your own real name.

Jessie.

WHEN THE MOON COMES
OVER THE MOUNTAIN

◊

Gulport Miss march 31

DEAR JESSIE just received your letter this am as it was ford here
from Clearwater witch we left there for good and stopped off in
mobile to play the Louisville club and I played right field the last 4
innings and was only up twict but some guy, was in there pitching
that throwed them over the plate on the 1st hop and walked me
both times and the 2d time wile I was on 1st base he wond up like
I hadent never left Fla and I stole 2d base standing up and this am
after I red your letter I told mgr Carey that you insist it on us not
getting married till next fall and he says she is the right kind of a
girl and if she still wants you next fall you marry her and all her
sisters and I will send you a present so I exclaimed that you dident
have no sisters but had a brother that died in 1928. Stengel was
standing there and he says I had sent you a sponge from Tarpon
springs so you wouldent miss me durn the summer and Carey says
I ought to slid yesterday just for practice but I told him my uniform
was to tight and was they a bigger 1 or could I have it alternated and
Stengel says it wont be so tight when you get to Brooklyn and have
to buy your own meals and be sides we will all have new uniforms
to open the season and maybe yours will have Bloomington on the
shirt but I says I would rather dress like the rest of the boys and
leave the fans fine out for there self who I am.

I told Carey that the real reason for us not getting married at this
time was so I could pay all my tension to him and he says that once
in a wile in the evening he might be tied up with the men that owns
the club or Dave Driscoll the secy and I told him that 1 of my and
your best pals was a man name Dave and he says maybe they are

The Saturday Evening Post, May 7 1932. Lose With a Smile.

brothers wear does he live and I says Centralia but his name is Burnett
and Stengel says that is funny because I use to know a man name
Gross that had a apple orchid so ask your pal did he ever meet him.
Well kid you can ask Dave when you see him but I am pretty sure
it will be no.

In the 7th innings yesterday some Louisville infielder hit a high
fly ball witch ether I or Wilson could of took but Hack says get a
way so I left him take it and when we come in to the bench Glenn
Wright says that is one thing about Hack when he says get a way
they take his word for it and what he refered to was 1 day we was
plain the As in ft Myers and I was plain left field and some body hit
a short fly ball to left center and Wright says get a way but I thot he
ment for Wilson to get out of my way so I run in to Wright and he
held on to the ball but hurt his solder and he is captain of the club
so I says I was sorry but I must of over herd him but he says dont
worry it was just my throwing arm at lease you dident hurt the arm
I tag them with.

He is a fine fella and a great short stop and 1 day in Clearwater I
complaint because I was all tarred out from chason fly balls in practice
and 1st they would hit them on 1 side of me and then the other and
he says dont mind that Rudy this is only spring training and when
we open up the regular season and you get in a regular game why
who ever we are plain again will tell you witch side they are going
to hit it and you wont only have to run 1 way till you find out if he
was trying to fool you.

This pm we play the Baltimore club and Stengel says that is wear
Connie Mack has got his farm and I says what does he raze and he
says it use to be just grapes but now we got probation he only raze
enough to keep himself and his ball players in wine because if he
makes the wine himself he knows it wont be posen and all so he can
keep tracks of how much the boys are getting a way with tho he
dont charge them only $1.00 a bbl profit.

Well tomorrow we play the Washington club at biloxi and then 2
games again Cleveland in new Orleans and then we start north and
if you feel like writeing in the next wk make it care of the Brooklyn
b b club Norfolk va and I am glad that you seen I was just jokeing
about we getting married right a way tho if you thot I ment it I
would of went threw with it even if it cause me my job but next fall
will be even better because you may be haveing good weather by
that time and I told Stengel about making you a offer to write every
day and he says make it onct or twict a wk and sent her jig sore

puzzles the rest of the time but I dont know if you like them and he says his friend Gross sold his apple orchid witch was in mexico so no use asking Dave did he know him.

I wont sine my name Rudy no more and only done it because that is what all the boys call me because the way I can groon.

Danny

Centralia, Ill. April 4.

DEAR DANNY—Was glad to get your letter but please dont bother about writing to me only when you feel like it and have the time as I am such a poor hand at writing letters that it would not be fair to expect you to spend so much time writing me such long letters when I am such a poor hand answering them and no news that would interest you and please dont bother sending me puzzles or other presents as you will need all your money to live in a place like Brooklyn.

Was sure Mr. Carey would not approve of you getting married just when you are beginning your career and please do me another favor Danny and dont say no more about you and I getting married next Fall or any other time I cant leave mamma and papa and have no intention of getting married till they are gone and by that time no one will want me or now either for that matter.

All your friends are proud of how well you are getting along and I knew you would be and I know the Brooklyns will be glad they kept you and I hope you will find a good boarding house and I hope your friend Miss Duane in Clearwater will keep her promise to move to Brooklyn so you can have some one to realy play the piano for you to sing.

Dave says to tell you that the only Gross he ever knew was a man named Schofield Gross in Chicago, but he never spoke about an orchard he thinks that he was in the insurance. Could that be the one?

Jessie.

Norfolk va apr 7

DEAR JESSIE well kid 1 more sleeper jump and I will be home I mean Brooklyn and tomorrow we play the yankees at home and the next 2 days we play them in there own pk and tomorrow I will get my 1st look at Babe Ruth and next Tues we open up the regular season with the Boston club and I am sure to be in that series as they are lucy with left hand it pitchers and I only hope they will start there star man Brant and maybe I and Wilson can fix him so he will be in shape to start the hole 4 games.

I maled you a schedule yesterday from macon a long with a list of the hotels wear we stop at in all the citys so you will all ways know wear to dress me but for a wile wile wear in Brooklyn you will have to dress me care of the Brooklyn b b club Ebbets field Brooklyn n y till I fine a place to live and maybe I will live at the St. Geo. hotel till I fine a place to live but Stengel says they sock you $4.00 a day for a room and no meals or the same amt for meals and no room. He says why dont you stop at the Aquarum in n y but Wright says they dont serve nothing only fish but Stengel says he bet I could get wait it on but I says I would get tarred of fish and supose I swallow a lot of bones and Stengel says you are bond to do that soon or latter unlest you stop eating your head off and it is just a cross the river from Brooklyn and you can make the trip by boat and I says supose I mist the boat and Stengel says they dont look nothing like a fly ball and Wright says why dont you go and live in the ground keepers tent in right field like Babe Herman done last yr because Babe walked in his sleep but when he was sure he was in right field he wouldent move no wear a sleep or a wake.

We played the Hartford club a couple games in macon and it seems the Hartford club is wear Brooklyn sends some of there ball players who they dont want and when we land it there Stengel says well Rudy you will have to groon plenty dittys for us today and tomorrow because this club needs a outfielder that hits right hand it and swings from there heels and I was kind of scarred for a minit because Carey played me all threw the 1st game and the 2 boys that worked again us was both right handers and I was scarred that Carey was maybe shown there mgr that I could hit a right hander and for a minit I thot of not hitting as good as I can but the 1st fella you couldent help from socking him and then they stuck in a boy with a fire ball and he struck 2 of the boys out and they come back to the bench sane he was faster then Vance so in the next innings I swang from my heels and the fire ball burnt up a cotton field in the next league and any ways I guest if Carey want it to show there mgr if I can sock a right hander I guest I showed them but here I am hay kid still with the Brooklyn ball club and will groon for the boys all summer as long as my grooner holes out.

Be sides your letter when we got here today they was a letter here for me from Vivian Duane that phone girl in Clearwater when we got here today and some of the other boys must of give her our root and she sent me a couple snap shots of herself in a batheing suit witch I am sending you 1 of them so as you can see what she looks like and she dident say nothing in her letter only that she was still plan to come up to Brooklyn and would I look a round for a job for her and maybe she sent me the snap shots so as I can show them to the Brooklyn phone co tho I dont beleive the phone co cares what the hell there girls looks like in a batheing suit or out of 1 till Henry Ford or some body vents a phone witch you can see threw and then they would proudly make them wear a bath road so the boys wouldent keep calling up to ask if there watch was fast.

Stengel says the Gross he referred to never sold no insurance but he used to talk about a brother who had boughten some fire insurance but he dont know the brothers name.

Well kid will close as it is about time to go out to the ball pk and knock this club off and this is wear they had the war again the north and the south and it last it 4 yrs but I guest 1 day will be enough for us to free the slaves and Stengel says when we get on the train tonight I must ask Jack Quinn to tell me about the day Grant surrend it but Jack wont never talk much and be sides the boys will proudly want me to groon.   Danny

Centralia, Ill. April 11.

DEAR DANNY—Thanks for sending me the schedule and where to address your mail, but as I am such a poor hand at writing letters I will probibly not bother you much by writing you many letters and I do wish you would not think it is your duty to write to me though I love to get them but cant help thinking that you do it because you are sorry for me.

All your friends are excited about tomorrow and the opening of the season and Dave says he will keep me posted on how the Brooklyn nine are doing as he always gets the St. Louis paper with the ball games and the player's name who are playing and he will save them up for me and I think you are very generous to hope that the Boston's best man can play every day. They brought their baby over yesterday and he is cuter than ever. Dave is pretty sure that there is no connections between Mr. Stengel's Mr. Gross and his brother unless of course they might be a more distant relation like a cousin.

Danny I think you would be crazy to live in a tent in a place like Brooklyn where they have storms and you know how easy you take cold and Danny you never used to say words like H—— though I suppose the ball men say it all the time though I hope they dont talk like that to girls.

Thanks for sending me Miss Duane's picture am sending it back though you did not say so but am afraid mamma might see it. She is very pretty and I dont blame you, but cant understand why she wants to work for the phone company when she could surely obtain a position in some musical hall where the women come out bare.

Jessie.

Brooklyn april 11.

DEAR JESSIE well kid tomorrow is the big day but they all been big days the last few days as we was plain our series with the yankees and today was the 1st real chance I had to look for a place to live and finely found a place to live and will move in there tomorrow am and the dress is 219 Parkside ave Brooklyn and you better write it down some place and then you will all ways know wear to dress me if wear home or a way from home witch we will proudly be 1 or the other most of the season and I been stain at the Ralston hotel a little hotel near the ball pk wear they only sock you $3.00 per day but no meals witch means at least $3.00 more per day unless I want to live on cat nip or some thing and lose my strenth. Now I just wisht I know if mgr Carey is going to start me tomorrow or not and my name aint in the paper this pm for the line up but he has left them guest for there self but some day they ought to hole a contest between the news paper boys and the empire behind the plate to see witch can guest the worst and of corse it pends on who the Boston club starts and if it is Brant or 1 of them other left handers I will be in there swing from my heels.

Well I was in part of 2 games again the yankees and the 1st game was here in Brooklyn and he stuck me in the 6th innings again a right hander name Ruffing and the crowd cheered when I come up and he got me 2 and 3 and throwed a fast ball or what he uses for a fast ball and I had to duck so as not dirty my cap but the empire was giveing his right arm a work out and you ought to herd the crowd bood him when I walked back to the bench and the last 2 days we road to the yankee stadium in the subway and back and that is worst then them sleeper jumps in the south because the presser stops up your ears and Stengel told me to keep my tongue out and by the time you have had your tongue out for 2 or 3 hrs you feel like a dog and hit like 1 specialy going under the river witch is twict both ways and he sent me up in the 9th innings yesterday again a left hander name Welsh and even at that I would of give it a ride if he hadent throwed wile I was rubing dirt on my hands.

Wilson had the crowd with him both here and the stadum and the cut he takes at the ball why the crowd dont care if he hits them or mist them but it is the same like myself they like to see a man swing like he was not holeing out for more money and this was my 1st look at Ruth and you ought to herd them bood him in Brooklyn but he hit a couple out of the pk durn the series but it is no wonder these left hand it hitters pile up all them home runs the way they bild these pks because if you are plain right field you got to hole your breath or the 2d base man will complain of the draft on his ears.

The place wear I am going to live is just 1 rm but it has got a wash bold with both kinds of water and a bed and 2 chairs and a burrow and of corse I dont need no tub as we got a shower in the club house and it will cause me $8.00 per wk with no meals tho I got a gas plate in the rm and a couple other of the ball players lives in the same bldg and got 2 or 3 rums but they are married and there wife cooks there meals and it cause them $60.00 a mont but the gas plate wont do me no good unlest I join the boy scouts and lern to fry eggs and coffee and I bet they will be many a time when I will wisht you was there to cook my breakfast so I could lay a round the rm with out putting on no close provide it he dont make us practice mornings all summer but I do wisht 1 thing kid and that is for you to send me your picture as I havent no picture for the burrow only a couple pictures of myself and I can remember what I look like by just looking in the glass. It dont make no difference if if is only a snap shot just any thing so as the place wont look so bare. The bldg is only a short walk to the ball pk and Stengel says to be sure and all ways walk and dont never run or the man at the players gate might think you aint with the club.

So send me your picture kid if it aint only a snap shot and will say good by for this time as am all tarred out looking for a place to live and rideing in the subway and back with my tongue out like I was a spaniel with the flu and every time we go to the polo grounds all summer it will be 1 of them rides and by may or june I will proudly be scraching flees and barking at the other passengers.

                                                    Danny.

Centralia Ill. April 15.

DEAR DANNY—Danny please dont ask me to send you a picture of myself as I have no pictures only a couple of snap shots that was taken when I visited the Prestons two years ago and they dont look like I look now as I looked so much younger then and now I look old and it would be just like sending you a picture of some other person and besides Danny I sent you back the picture you sent me of your friend Miss Duane so now you have got two pictures of her to put on your dresser though the way she dresses to have her picture taken I am afraid they wont make your room less bare but you will understand Danny that I dont want my picture along side of a girl so much prettier than I am or ever was in my life and you may think I am silly but I have still got a little pride though you may doubt it.

We read in the papers that the Brooklyns beat the Bostons and that star Boston ball man played but Dave says you did not play in the first two games and I know Mr. Carey wanted you to play against that star man so I am afraid you are sick please let me know if you are sick or been sick Danny as all your friends will want to know and I think it is terrible making you ride in those subways. Papa says that one time when he was in Chicago he went under the river in a cable car on Clark Street and had that same kind of a feeling in his ears, but he dont think it will do much good to keep your tongue hanging out, but he says he heard that if you stuff your ears with cotton you wont feel it so much will you try this Danny the next time you have to make that trip to the yankee place.

Can imajine how the crowd cheered you in Brooklyn and how mad they must have gotten at the umpire and I should think they would hire men who are fair and partial for a position like that and you know that Dave still claims that he realy won ten dollars the time he bet on Jack Dempsey, but the man called him a knock out.

I do wish you had a good boarding house where you could get your meals without going out for them and am afraid you will wake up some mornings so tired that you will go without your breakfast in a noisy place like Brooklyn where you probibly wont sleep good at first and am afraid maybe that is the reason why you did not play against Boston's star man is because you have been sick and weak from not eating regular to say nothing of your trips on the subway please take care of yourself for your friend's sake and let us know how you realy are and you will understand why I cant send you my picture.   Jessie.

Brooklyn april 15.

DEAR JESSIE well kid it took me a long wile to break in to this league and the past 3 days I beggin to think mgr Carey had forgot old Rudy and I ought to get my card print it and give him my card but he dident forget old Rudy this pm and I guest the Boston club wont forget me all season specialy there left hander Sherdel and I bet when we visit Boston next wk he will be lade up with the flu till wear safe out of town but dont supose you will see no paper so will tell you what I done.

The past 3 days I beggin to think Carey had forgot my name and I was going to ask Stengel to tell him my name but Stengel act it like he had forgot me to but I wont be no secret after today. The game beggin like we would murder them and we seen all their pitchers in the 1st 4 innings and had them beat 7 to 1 and it looked like I might as well curl up and fall a sleep on the bench like I been doing but in the 7th innings our pitchers beggin to put on there own parade and when the 8th innings beggin the score was 7 and 7 and it was Jack Quinn again this here Sherdel and they both pitch like they was trying to kid somebody but they couldent no body kid them back and we went in to extra innings for the 1st time and come to the 14th innings with the score still 7 and 7 and a cinch they would call the game on account of darkness unlest some body broke it up and of corse this would be the time to have your fireball pitcher in there but the fires had all been put out.

Well old Jack had a tough break in the 14th and Odoul lose a fly ball and I dont blame him as it was to dark to see but any ways the Boston club got a run and it looked like we was threw and all of a sudden Lopez with 1 out hit for 2 bases and Quinn was up next and all of a sudden I herd Carey holler Rudy and I jumped up and grabbed a bat and Carey come up to me from the 1st base coachers box and says remember this guy is a left hander but he will try and slow ball you to death so dont over swing and just remember you are supose to hit left handers and they cant take him out because they aint got nobody left only judge Fuchs and the sun is set so you are back in Bloomington in the moon light league and I went up and the crowd cheered and Stengel was on the 3d base coach lines and he yelled come on Rudy your at home in a night club and Sherdel throwed a curve but it was so far in side that even the empire called it a ball.

Then he throwed a dink ball and did I give it a ride hay kid a ft hire and we could of both walked a round but am glad it dident because it would of spoiled the show and it hit the fence in right center and Lopez run faster than he can and slid a cross the plate 5 ft a head of the throw and I was on 2d base with the score 8 and 8.

Well I herd Carey say wait a minit and I was scarred he was going to put some one on to run thinking I dont know nothing but he changed his mind and says go a head and Stengel hollered there just beggin to play out in Bloomington but I dident need no advice because you see kid they was only 1 out and if the next man hit a long fly what good was I on 2d base and of corse Sherdel dident give me no start but I went any ways and there catcher was so surprise that he throwed a 2 base ball over there 3d base mans head and Stengel yelled stay up keep going like he thot I was libel to stop and talk things over with him and I slid a cross the plate but they dident even make a play and the crowd would of tore me to pieces if I hadent dove in to the bench and a way from them and I wisht you could of been in the club house and herd the noise.

It was Rudy this and Rudy that and Stengel says to Carey he says what did I tell you Max all you got to do is start the games after supper and Rudy will hit 500 and steal there bench and if we could only play a double header every night beggin at 8 we would break up this league by the middle of July and then Lopez says well you give me a run a round but it was worth it and Carey shook hands and says thats a boy I was going to pull you off 2d base and put on a runner not because you aint fast but I wasen't sure you had sense enough to make the play and I would rather seen you make that play then hit 60 home runs what you done today wont hurt how you stand with me and I says I thot you had forgot me and he says I wont forget you again but that dont mean I am going to use you regular but it does mean that I can stick you in there and know you aint going to doze off and Glenn Wright says I am glad I dident do it because I am the captain and they cant no body fire me only Max and the men that owns the club but you showed you can think and you will have a tough time getting off of this club now because novelty is what the fans likes.

Then they all insist it I should groon but I says I was too tarred and I left the pk but late as it was they was a crowd hang out side waiting for I and Lopez and only for Stengel telling them to get the hell out of there and give these young fellas a chance to get home and sleep we would of been shakeing hands the rest of the night and Lopez left us and Stengel walked a long home with me and I ast him to come up and see my rm and he says aint you going to eat nothing and I says I forgot all about it and he says that is what I thot when

I seen you steal 3d base that you must of been out of your head all
day and go and eat some thing and then write a letter to that little
girl in Centralia because you certainly got enough to tell her tonight
and I says she dont understand base ball and he says you ought to
get a long fine and I says my pal Dave out there thinks they cant be
no relations between your pal Gross and his pal Gross unlest they
are cousins and he says they cant be cousins or they couldent of got
married. So leave the hole thing drop kid.

Well kid what do you think of me now and I will send you what
the Brooklyn and n y papers say in the am.   Danny

Centralia, Ill. April 19.

DEAR DANNY—I wish I could tell you how proud of you I am
winning the game with a home run and all your friends are proud
of you and would you be mad if I showed them those papers especially the two that printed your picture only I dont think neither
of them did you justice and Danny you have now said H—— twice
in your letters to me and I wish to gracious the ball men and papers
would quit calling you Rudy.

Dont you think you could get one of those couples that belong
to the Brooklyn nine and live in the same bldg to give you your
meals at least your breakfast so you would not have to go out for
breakfast supposing it was to rain and they ought to not charge you
very much when you are helping them win all those games with your
home runs. Tell Mr. Stengel I am terribly sorry about the whole
business about Mr. Gross but I don't know what we can do.

                                                    Jessie

LOSE WITH A SMILE

◇

Brooklyn april 17

DEAR JESSIE well today was a sunday and the pk was jam and big Jim Elliot was pitching for Phila and I thot sure they would be a spot wear I would go in and hit for some body as Elliot is a left hander and on account of he being so big is why they call him jumbo and 1 time we had 2 men on the bases and Cohens turn to bat and the score 4 and 3 again us so I expect it Carey to holler for me but he left Cohen hit for himself and he scrached 1 down the 3d base line for 2 bases because the hole Phila infield was over talking to there 1st base man. But any ways the crowd give me a big hand every time I come up in batting practice on account of what I done again the Boston club and when I complaint to Stengel about Carey not giveing me a chance he says it was because Carey dident want to show his full strenth again the clubs that is fighting us for 8 place and that is all so why our pitchers has been holeing themself back as McGraw is libel to have spys in the stand.

Last night I had my 1st home cook meal since I left Centralia as Frank Earl ast me to have supper with he and his wife as they live here in the same bldg only they have got 2 rms and a place wear she cooks there meals on a gas stove behind a scream and Frank is 1 of the young pitchers we got from Hartford and the only time he pitchs is in batting practice and I only wisht he was on some other club in our league and they had to use him in a regular game so I could get a sock at him. The 1st day he worked out down south Glenn Wright made the remark that some of the other young pitchers could lern 1 thing from him that no matter if he was throwing his fast ball or curve ball or slow ball why his motion was all ways the same and Stengel says yes and what makes it all the tougher is that even when it gets up to the plate you cant tell witch is witch.

The Saturday Evening Post, June 11 1932; *Lose With a Smile*.

They rent it a piano for $8.00 a mont and I hope they dident sine no all season least on it or there apt niether as all the clubs has got to cut there players to 23 in a couple monts and after that Frank wont be liveing in Brooklyn no more unlest the club needs a extra ground keeper.

They had ham for supper and after words I ast his wife to play the piano and she says I cant play nothing new as it takes me so long to lern and specialy the minors. So I says you better get use to plain in the minors and Frank seen the gag and laughed but she just looked dum. Then she says why do the boys call you Rudy and Frank says you play him some cords and you will fine out so she made a stab at you try some body else and I sung it only I had to sing in a different key then she was plain so the people next door wouldent think the Earls was entertain a bull frog. When we was threw she says well will you tell me now and I says tell you what and she says why do the boys call you Rudy and I says I guest it was because I can groon like Rudy Valet and she says well if you and Rudy was both here and we put out the lights and 1st he would groon and then you I bet I could tell when he left off and you start it. So I says yes and if we put out the lights right now and you played that same tune over I bet I could tell that it wasent Ohman and Arden so Frank says you 2 would make a good vaudeville team the way you kid each other. I says yes but when you go in vaudeville you have got to peer in the pm as well as night and his wife says maybe they would put us on right after batting practice. She is pretty but she dont get nothing you say to her and plays the piano way down in the black keys and I only wisht you was a round some wear to play for me or else Vivian Duane that phone girl down in Clearwater would keep her promise and come north for the summer tho I wouldent know how to go at it to get her a job.

2 more games here with Phila and then we go to Boston for 3 games and maybe I will get an other crack at them left handers tho I guest Carey is smart not shown our hole strenth till we play the Giants. We open with them here at home a wk from today and Stengel says he wouldent be surprise if we break a record for the biggest crowd that ever seen a game in Brooklyn. He says they will be offering all kinds of prices for seats and even the bench will be sold out and as he was going in the pk today a man offered him $50.00 for his place in the coachers box next sunday but he had to turn him down because Bancroft might want it wile the Giants is at bat.

                                                                     Danny

Centralia, Ill. April 20.

DEAR DANNY I am addressing this to your hotel in Boston with a note on the envelope to please forward it back to your Brooklyn address in case you leave Boston before this reaches you and that is why I put on the extra stamp, but maybe you wont get it anyway so please let me now if you get it or not though you wont be missing much if you dont get it at all.

I can imajine how frightened Mrs. Earl felt trying to play for you to sing as I am always nervous doing it and probibly she can play a great deal better than I can, but anyone who cant play very good is sure to feel nervous playing for a person who can sing like you can. I sincerely hope for your sake that Miss Duane will keep her promise and you will realy have some one who can realy play for you to sing. I guess I must be dumb like she is because I cant understand your pun about playing in the minors. It is not so hard when it is A minor or E minor like in the verse of "Shine On, Harverst Moon" but some of the minor keys are awfully hard for a person who is not realy a good musician. I hope it was baked ham with cloves like you like it and what else did you have?

I cant help being sorry for Mr. and Mrs. Earl if Mr. Carey is not going to keep him on the nine because if Mr. Carey waits two months before telling him it will be the middle of June and wont it be hard for him to find a position on some other nine then? I wish some one could drop him a hint in some way, but I know you are too kind hearted to do it, but I honestly believe Mr. Carey will find some way to tell him ahead of time. From Mr. Carey's pictures and all you have said about him I am positive he will find some way to drop him a hint.

Now Danny I am going to say something which I know you will say is none of my business and maybe you will be mad at me, but I have to say it just the same. Danny if some one makes you an offer to buy your seat on the bench next Sunday, please dont sell it to them at any price. It is different with Mr. Stengel because he cant play any way, but suppose it just happened that a crisis comes up like the other day when you knocked those home runs and beat the Bostons and Mr. Carey should want you to do the same thing again and could not find you among all those hundreds of thousands of people and the Brooklyns lost the game, you would never get over it Danny and neither would Mr. Carey and I know you dont care anything about money compared to keeping your friends all proud of you like they are now. I dont know what position Mr. Bancroft holds, but if he is just a coacher like Mr. Stengel and still insists on staying where they can find him, it must be a lot more important for you to keep your place because you can realy get in the game and do things.

Please dont be mad at me for saying this Danny and I am saying it as much for your own sake as my sake and the rest of your friends.

Yours,   Jessie.

Boston april 23

DEAR JESSIE your letter come today witch was just in time for me to get it here as we leave for home at midnight and play the Giants tomorrow and dont you never worry kid about me getting mad at you as I know that you all ways got my interest at heart and never your self. I am sorry you been worring over Stengels remarks but thot you would under stand that he was just kidding as mgr Carey wouldent never stand for the boys selling there seats on the bench because in the 1st place it is again the rules for any body to set on the bench unlest you are in a uniform for 1 thing and be sides that they aint enough money in the world specialy this yr to make me forget my duty to mgr Carey and the Brooklyn ball club. As for Frank Earl he knows that he is doom with out no body telling him but mgr Carey will see that he gets a job with some minor league club wear he can make good.

I only got in 1 game here but that was enough to spoil the day for the Boston club just like I done to them in Brooklyn last wk and pretty near the same play only this time it was more fun as they been rideing me and trying to kid me but I had the last laugh specialy Maranville. They call him rabbit as he is all ways trying to kid some body and track there tension off the game tho if a real rabbit lived half as long as him they would have him in a museum. Well wile we was in batting practice the 1st day here he come up to me and says well Rudy you are just 1 surprise after an other and I says I only had 1 chance to surprise you so far and he says no this is twict as we expect it you would be sined up with the Hartford glee club by this time he says you are lucky to be with a mgr that likes music. So I says well I dident groon my way a round the bases in the 14th innings last friday did I. So he says was that you danceing in the dark and I says you know who it was all right as you sword at me and called me names when I puled up at 2d base. Then he says is it in the base ball rules that you got to know a man before you sware at them and if any of the names I called you was the right 1 it was just guest work as I cant see good at that time of night and I says you are lucky if you can see good any time day or night at your age. I thot that would hole him but he kept rideing me and makeing faces at me on the bench all pm and all yesterday till the blow off come.

We was 1 run behind going in to the 8th innings and Carey sent me up to hit for Clark with 1 out tho there pitcher was a right hander named Seibold. He is an other 1 of these here pitchers that cant hardly get the ball up to the plate and you can count the seems on there fast ball and there curve beggins to break before it leaves there hand. Well it was the same catcher that throwed the ball a way when I stole 3d base in Brooklyn and he says well busher I hope you hit for 2 bases and I will dare you to steal 3d base and I says well you will proudly get your hope as it dont look like a man could hit for lest than 2 bases again this kind of pitching.

So he says I bet he strikes you out and I says that will tie up the game as you will drop the 3d strike and throw the ball over the right field stand. You see I was rideing him for the crazy throw he made in Brooklyn. Well Seibold throwed a round house curve and I was going to leave it go by and then change my mind and kind of half struck at it and hit it and the ball went over Maranvilles head and him and Bergert either 1 should of catch it in their cap but they both lose it and I come into 2d base standing up. Maranville was sore as hell and I says what is the matter is they to much day light and he called me some more names and says you was born with a spoon in your mouth and I suppose you think you socked that 1. So I says wear did you pick up that high school pitcher and he says wear did you ever see a high school or was your father the janiter and I says no your father was.

He says are you going to steal 3d base and I says no I never pull the same play twict and he says all right I wont try and hole you up so he walked a way and I led off a few ft and all of a sudden Seibold turned and throwed and there short stop had snuck up behind me and he had me but drop the ball. Well I thot Maranville would go crazy and Stengel yelled watch your self Rudy and I says dont worry and then Seibold throwed again but I was standing on the bag. Then Seibold got ready to pitch and some thing told me he was going to pitch and I just went and I dont know if I would of been out or not but there 3d base man made it sure by dropping the ball and Stengel turned a summer salt and I looked at Maranville and he was lane on the ground kicking his ft in the air. You ought to seen Carey and the boys on our bench and Frederick come threw with a fly ball so far out that I was a cross the plate before it was back in the infield and in the 9th innings Wilson and Wright got in a couple of real socks and we win the game 6 and 4.

Well I dident have no chance to get in there today but we beat them and they still kept on trying to ride me and Maranville made faces at me on the bench but all I done was waggle my thums in my ears and holler rabbit at him and sqeek at him like I was a rabbit.

Well I was scarred Hubbell would pitch for the Giants today but he dident and it is his turn tomorrow and it will be he again Dazzy and Hubbel is a left hander so maybe I will get a chance tho they say he ain't like other left handers as he has got a screw ball that breaks down and a way from a right hand it hitter but I never seen a left hander that wasent just a left hander and all as I hope is that they dont bare them out of base ball till I am as old as Maranville and kidding my way threw the league.   Danny

Centralia, Ill. April 20.

DEAR DANNY—This is the second time I wrote to you today Danny and I mailed the other one to your hotel in Boston but am afraid you wont get it there till you have left. So I am addressing this one to Brooklyn in the hopes that it will be waiting there for you when you get home.

Please dont be mad at me Danny and say it is none of my business, but I am worried about what you wrote about what Mr. Stengel said about your game with the Giants next Sunday. You said that he said there would be such a big crowd that they would probibly make you an offer for your seat on the bench and he had been offered fifty dollars for the coachman's seat, but had refused it because Mr. Bancroft might want it once in a while, and I dont know who Mr. Bancroft is, but can imajine that he is the Giant's coachman and if he wont sell his seat you ought not to sell your seat because suppose Mr. Carey should want you as a pinch man and could not find you in that big crowd, you would never get over it and neither would Mr. Carey.

So please dont sell your seat for any price Danny and please dont be mad at me for saying things that are none of my business and remember am only saying them for your own sake and my sake and the rest of your friends.   Yours,   Jessie.

Brooklyn april 25

DEAR JESSIE I got the both of your letters warming me to not sell my seat on the bench and you are a great kid worring your head off about me and pretty soon I will get mad at you for worring about me doing some thing out of the way.

Stengel was right about the crowd yesterday and it was the biggest crowd that ever seen a game in Brooklyn and it was Hubbell again Dazzy but all I side it so they was no chance for me to get in there. But I seen what this guy calls his screw ball witch is just like a nuggle ball or any of the other fancy names and I been in this league now for 2 wks and the only pitcher I seen so far that throws a fire ball and a curve ball and a change of paste is Dazzy and that dont do me no good as he is on our club. Today it was an other nuggler a right hander name Fitzsimmons and he beat us and tomorrow it will be Walker who is left handed it and maybe they will be a spot for me.

Well kid I know you dont like for me to call my self Rudy but that is what the boys calls me and never seem to get enough hearing me groon but the other day in the club house up in Boston they ast me for a song and I says I am a shame to keep sing the same old songs over and over and Stengel says dont worry about that because the way you sing them they dont sound like nothing any body ever herd before. Then Carey says your name sake writes his own songs meaning Rudy Valet and why dont you write 1 your self and I says I might write the words but how about the music and Carey says just fix up some words for music you all ready know and Stengel says why dont you write life is just a bold of cherrys only make it some other fruit or even a vegetable. So Carey says life is just a game of base ball would be a good title and you all ready got the tune and Stengel says but dont make it Brooklyn base ball unless you want a torch song.

Well kid I dident say nothing but I went up in my rm after supper that night and set down with a pencil and paper and went to work and I had to keep groon the music over to my self so as I could make up words to fit it and after a wile when Stengel come in I had it all wrote out and read it out loud to him and he says it was great but you only got the chorus and you ought to write a verse and then you will have a song hit and I says I never herd the verse and he says that dont matter as it is just the same like any other verse and cant help from fitting.

So he promise to keep a secret till I had the hole song fix up and today I sprang it on the boys in the club house and I had to just read the verse out loud as I dont know the tune but I grooned the chorus and the boys went wild and pet it me on the back and they all want it a copy. But Carey says wait till you see a publisher and get the copy rights as some of the boys may try and beat you to it so the day after tomorrow we got a day off before we go to Phila and I am going over to New York and see witch publisher will offer me the most money and wont it be funny if I turn in to a song writer as I never thot of writeing them only groon them. Well kid I know you wont cheat me so will write out the hole song and see what you think of it and will start with the verse.

> Some people take life serious
> in stead of a game to play
> If they would only not take it so serious
> But more like a game to play.
> I try and laugh at the hard knocks
> like you get in a base ball game
> so wether your with St Louis or the red Sox
> smile and dont be a shame.

Then comes the chorus.

> Life is just a game of base ball
> If you get in it
> You want to win it
> But some times the mgr dont give you a chance
> But leave you setting there on the bench.
> Just give me a left handers fast ball
> and I will sock it a mile
> And if the empire calls it a foul
> laugh and dont say your blind as a owl
> Life is just a game of base ball
> so win or lose with a smile.

I know you know the tune to the chorus and last night I was down to Frank Earls apt and his wife played it as good as she can and she says there is a couple spots where it dont come out even but Frank says the publishers will tend to that and he says he wisht he could do some thing like write a song hit be sides just pitch a base ball. So I will let you know how I come out with the publishers but I dont see how I can mist and maybe it means that I can make more money off writeing songs than plain base ball and you know kid what that means. Danny

Brooklyn april 27

DEAR JESSIE I guest I am about threw with base ball or at lease in this league wear the empires is all stone blind and the mgr dont give you a square deal and this is a off day in the schedule before we go to Phila and I was going over to New York and show them my song but I aint got the heart to show no body nothing after the raw deal I got yesterday.

It was the last game in the series with the Giants and I wasent in the 1st 2 games but yesterday I got in the game and tie it up for them like I done twict again the Boston club and here is what I get for it. They had 1 of there left handers Walker pitching and I was crazy to get in there and take a wallet at him as he dont claim to have nothing only a fast ball and curve ball and nothing fancy and I only wisht Carey would of start it me and we wouldent been behind like we all ways seem to be when it is pretty near the end of the game. Well any ways the 9th innings come a long and it was 3 and 3 and this Ott hit 1 off Hoyt for a home run and made them 4 and 3 and I wisht they would pitch that way to me and all I would have to do is touch all the bases.

Well they was 1 out in our part of the 9th and Lopez hit a 3 base hit and it was Hoyts turn and of corse Carey hollered for me and I grab a bat and thot to my self here is wear I get a chance because this baby aint no trick pitcher but just fast slow and curve. But on the way up to the plate Carey met me and says if the 1st 1 is a ball lay the 2d 1 down and I says what do you mean lay it down and he says I mean bunt and bunt tords 3d base and I says I can swing from my heels and knock this guy for a gold and he says yes he knows that and so do I but I am telling you to lay the 2d 1 down.

So I went up to the plate and give my name to the empire and Bancroft there coach come running up and ast who I was and I says you will fine out who I am and the empire told him my name and Bancroft says are you with the Brooklyn club and I says yes but I am plain for my release because McGraw wants me on your club as coach. So he says your a smart alex aint you and the empire says your holeing up the game and lets get going and Bancroft says I just want to know witch kind of pitching this baby can hit and I says the kind Walker pitchs.

So then Bancroft went back to his bench and they got a big horse name Hogan that catchs for them and he says I am giveing the sines and you tell me what you like to hit at and I will sine for it so I says I like them fast and slow and out side and threw the middle and a little bit up and he says well we will try you 1st on a curve ball in side. So he give his sine and it was a fast ball just out side and I could of socked it to Coneys island but I left it go by and it was a ball. So I says now I suppose you will give me a fast ball out side and he says all right if you want it and he give his sine and it was a curve ball in side and I bunt it tords 3d base and catch there 3d base man flat ft. So Lopez scored and I was a cross 1st base wile Vergez and Walker was still trying to kick the ball foul and Carey says that a boy Rudy what did I tell you and wile the Giants was yelling there head off about nothing he come over and wisper stay up close till I say watch your self Rudy and then go on the next pitch.

So I stood on 1st base and hollered to Bancroft do you know me now and he just made 2 or 3 different mouths at me. What else could he do. Walker got in there to pitch again and throwed for me a couple times but I was standing on the bag. Then I thot he realy was going to pitch and I led off 3 or 4 ft and Walker peg for me onct more and I could of got back only Terry there 1st base man dident leave me no rm. Rigler called me out tho I fell back and had my hand on the bag before Terry tagged me and at that he tagged me with his glove and the ball was in his bear hand. But Rigler called me out and I jump up and says what for and Rigler says for the rest of the day and I says I could slid back spikes 1st only I dident want to cut off Terrys ft. So Rigler says I dident know you was in this league to take care of Terrys ft as I thot the Giants had there own Chiropist. Then Carey says you puled a boner Rudy and now run in the club house and take a shower. I says let me sock this big blind owl 1st and Rigler says all right you sock me and then you wont need to take no shower as I will give it to you myself.

Well I was half dress when the game was over and the rest of the boys come in and the Giants win 5 and 4 in the 11th innings. I stood there groon a song like nothing hadent happen but Carey come up to me and says you aint got nothing to sing about but I wisht you would learn to bay orders and I says if you hadent order me to bunt I could of waled that 1st ball in to the eastren league. Carey says if you had you could followed it right up there and played with it all summer. I says well am I still with this club and he says I dont know. You was certainly with the Giants a wile a go.

So I aint sure if I am going to Phila with the club or not and dont care but at lease I told Carey and Rigler wear to head in.

Danny

Centralia, Ill. April 28.

DEAR DANNY—I think your song is wonderful, but I talked to Dave about it and he said you better be careful and not use anyone's else words or music without asking them first and they have lost their copy of "Life is Just a Bowl of Cherries" but he thinks a man named Bud Henderson and Brown wrote it and you better look them up in the New York phone directory and ask their permission or else you might get sued and I love your attitude about umpires so you will take their decision with a smile instead of getting mad.

Yours,   Jessie.

MEET ME IN ST. LOUIE

◇

Phila april 28

DEAR JESSIE you will proudly be surprise to lern that I am still with the Brooklyn club as I ast mgr Carey to trade me after the way he act it when I got cot off 1st base again the N.Y. Giants. He says you better do your sleeping nights and I says you was right there on the coaching lines yourself and you must of been a sleep your self or you would of warmed me that Walker was going to throw. Then I says why dont you trade me and he says all right if that is what you want I will trade you to St. Louis as they are after a man just like you to turn over to there retail branch in Alton.

He says the mgr of there Alton store is a man name Harry Splug who they are very anxius to keep a hole of him but he aint like no other mgr because he dont care how good his ball players can play base ball if they will only just talk back at him and cry and act like a baby every time they make a mistake. He aint happy unless he is in a bad tamper and the St Louis club have been hunting high in low for a man who will keep him that way. So I says I wont play for no goofy mgr like him and Carey says all right but if you insist on me tradeing you that is wear you will go.

So I ast Stengel what would he do if he was in my place and he says well Rudy if I was you I would stick a round and do what Max tells you because when he greed to manage this club it was under stood that he wouldent have to take no orders or back talk from any body who wasent with the club last yr. He says Max likes you and he has had so much tough luck this spring that if you run out on him now it would just about break his morals. On the other hand you could do a lot worst then play under Harry Splug because he is a expert at training young ball players. So I says I never herd

The Saturday Evening Post, July 2, 1932; *Lose With a Smile*.

of him and wear did he play ball and Stengel says he never played ball no wear but he use to be in charge of the forestry dept at the State reform school and took care of the boys that had fell out of trees.

Well Stengel is all ways sane things like that witch dont make no sense but I finely greed to stick with the club for mgr Careys sakes and would hate to break his morals after all he has went threw and the hole thing wouldent never happen only for Terrys ft the Giants 1st baseman and the only way I could get back on the bag was spike him and maybe cripple him for life but I guest a man must forget others peoples ft in this league.

Now kid I am going to offer you a treat if you will take it and dont say no just because you aint use to them and you will have a good time but wait till I tell you. On the 5 of may witch is a wk from yesterday we open up a series in Chicago and play them 4 games and then wear do you think we go. Well kid we go to St Louis and play there the 9 10 and 11 of may. I will be 65 miles from home but cant come and see you as we will be plain the world champions and Carey will want his full strenth. But why not you come and spend a day in St Louis and it will be a chance to see a big town and it wouldent put me out and it wont cause you nothing as it will be my treat and I will pay all the expenses. This aint just for your pleasure kid but I would like to see you kid as I been kind of home sick and you would be a site worth seen after the girls I been seen that dress themself up and powder there face.

I know it is a hard trip whether you make it by bus or train but look at the trips I have to make all the wile and if you feel tords me like last winter you wont mind the trip and I am sure your mother wont put down her ft as she knows she can trust me and can rest a sure that I will see that you get home safe in sound. If you go back and fort on the bus you might not get there till all hrs and would have to start home before the ball game and tho I may not get in the game you could watch me in batting practice and after the game we can have supper and maybe go to a picture till time for your train. So I wisht you would make the trip by train and if they aint change time you leave Centralia at 5.26 am and arrive St Louis at 7.30. I will be down to the train to meet you and take you some place wear you can wash up and then maybe take you out to the hotel and meet Stengel and mgr Carey. The train going back leaves St Louis at 11 pm at night and Carey will let me stay up late enough to see you safe on the train and you will arrive Centralia at 1.03 am.

The day you better come is Tuesday the 10 as we dont get there till Monday am and leave for Cincinnati Wednesday night. Now kid dont say no but say yes and answer right a way by air male like I am sending this and dont say you havent got no close because you wont have to see no body only I if you say the wd. Remember the trip wont cause you nothing as it is my treat and will pay all expenses.

I wisht you could see the Phila ball pk wear we played today. The right field fence is so near 1st base that Stengel says young infielders has often made a mistake and throwed ground balls to Klein in stead of Hurst.

Stengel was all so telling me about a funny play he seen here 1 time. They have got a left hander in the league name Effie Jessica Rixey and he is 7 ft tall and it was the 9th innings and the score 0 and 0 and some body socked a 3 base hit with 2 out. Well who ever was up next why Effie decide it to throw him a cross fire and in delivering it he lent so far over that he catched his little finger in the right field scream. The empire called it a balk and the fella walked in from 3d base with the winning run. Stengel is a hot skech and you will in joy meeting him so dont dissapoint me kid.

Danny

Centralia, Ill. April 30.

DEAR DANNY—Danny I wish I could express how much I appreciate your kindness and generosity in inviting me to visit St. Louis while you are there and Danny I cant think of anything that would give me a bigger thrill, but mamma and I both agree that it is out of the question. Please try and understand Danny and dont think I dont appreciate your kindness and generosity in inviting me and you can imajine how much pleasure it would give me, but it is simply out of the question.

When your letter came with the air mails stamp I was frightened at first as I thought maybe you were ill or something and papa saw it first and said it must be something important on account of the stamp and probibly the Brooklyns were selling you back to Bloomington. He was just teasing, but he held back the letter till I promised to give him the stamp so he could give it to Mr. Phillips for Joey who is still in the hospital.

I was so relieved when I opened it and learned you were not ill and then when I came to the part about you wanting me to visit St. Louis I got so excited and though I knew that it was out of the question I pretended to myself that I was realy going and of course papa and mamma wanted to know what was the news and I hated to tell them about your invitation because then I could not pretend any more. But of course I told them and papa said: "Why not?" Of course he knew how much it meant to me and always wants me to have a good time no matter how impossible it would be. Of course mamma asked him had he gone crazy and he said he guessed that he had always been that way. You know how he talks.

But Danny you will see for yourself that it is simply out of the question. In the first place people would talk and you know how they do talk in this town and make a big fuss over nothing at all. Then no matter what you say Danny a girl has to think about clothes if they are going somewhere and of course I could borrow something of Clara's, but I am so much thinner than I was and we used to wear each other's things, but now everybody would know it was borrowed and all I have got of my own is that crazy old red crepe dress with the skirt to the knees like they wore them when I got it and I might cover it up with my white coat or rather it used to be white, but if it happened to be a hot day you would smother just looking at me.

Mamma's principle objection is having me go alone because when grandma and grandfather took her to the St. Louis Fair they put up at the Planters Hotel and she was eighteen years old and they were both sick with one of those summer colds and grandfather sent her out to get them some quinine and she was no sooner on the street when a tipsy man said: "Hello Jenny." Of course her name is not Jenny so she did not speak to him, but she hurried back inside the Hotel without getting the quinine. She says of course that was World's Fair time and a good many toughs in town, but with the base ball games going on there will probibly be the same elements and besides she simply wont hear of me coming home alone on that late train because it is a through train and there is sure to be one or two traveling men on it. It would be different if Clara could go along because she is a married woman, but she cant leave the baby. Papa suggested me asking Dave to go along, but he will be on the road all that week. Then papa said: "Well ask Clara to go with you and I will spend the day at her house and take care of the baby."

Mamma said: "From five in the morning until one the next morning is twenty hours and sometimes babies get hungry in that space of time and Clara's baby is not weaned." Papa said he would wean him and then he made a joke and said that he would cook him a wiener wean her wurst sausage.

Well Danny you can see that it is simply out of the question, but I do want you to know how much I appreciate your kindness and generosity and your kind offer to pay the expenses which of course I would not allow, but it is not a question of money, but other things like mamma says. But I do thank you from the bottom of my heart and perhaps I can do it next year when you go to St. Louis if you still want me to.

I should think that the Giants base man Mr. Terry would spend the rest of his life thanking you for not cutting his foot with those sharp spikes and I think it is terrible that the ball men think that they have to wear them when tennis shoes would keep them from slipping and if one of the ball men ever cuts your foot with those horrible things I hope that you will have it seen to without delay even if it is only a scratch because there is always danger of infections. I hope that Mr. Rixey did not suffer from them when he cut his hand in the screen. Are those first names real names or just one of Mr. Stengel's jokes? Do you remember when Ernie was twelve years old and got so angry because the screen door was hooked and he punched his fist through the screen and got some bad scratches and mamma called Dr. Fred and he painted them with iodine.

Thanks again Danny and please believe that I appreciate the offer and only wish things were different. Papa is going to mail this and I know that he will buy two air mails stamps, one to put on this and one to give to Mr. Phillips for Joey so that Joey will have a new one and the used one from your letter.   Yours,   Jessie.

Brooklyn may 3

DEAR JESSIE well kid I was scarred that your mother would put down her ft and am dissapoint it as I was looking ford to seen you and at the same time give you a treat. I told you to not worry about close as you wouldent have to meet no body only my self unlest you felt like it and you would look good to me no matter what you was dressed. As for some body trying to make a mash on you drunk or sober why I would be with you all the wile only durn the ball game and every ball pk in the league has got ushers and cops who would see that you wasent molest it. When I put you on the train at night I would ask the conductor to see that you wasent molest it.

I am dissapoint it kid as I was looking ford to seen you and if Clara comeing a long would make it ok why Dave can surly ford to hire some young girl to stay with the baby just that 1 day and give him a bottle of milk every time it hollered. But I know that I wont get no wear argueing so will try and forget it.

We got home from Phila Saturday night and was suppose to play the Boston club Sunday but got rained out and yesterday we beat the Giants up at the polo grounds and go up there again this pm and then leave for Chi.

I must tell you about Stengel and I yesterday noon. Stengel told me that he was acquaint it with the mgr of Irving Berlins music Company and promise he would take me there and see what they thot of that song I wrote Life is just a game of base ball. So we stopped there yesterday noon and Stengel ast to see Mr Schwartz and the girl says they dident have no Mr. Schwartz and Stengel says what the hell kind of a music publishing Company is this. The girl ast him what did he want and he says he want it to see the mgr and she took our name and pretty soon she took us in to a private office with a piano and met the mgr Mr. Abrams and Stengel told him who we were and made me read my lyrics out loud and Abrams ast if I had a tune to it and I says not for the verse but the chorus would go to the tune of Life is just a bold of cherrys. So Abrams says yes but that tune belongs to Henderson and Brown and you cant just steal it from under there nose and besides he dident think that the public would be interest it in a base ball song.

Stengel says are you interest it in base ball and Abrams says he had only been to a couple games just to see Babe Ruth. So Stengel says well the yankees play here next Sunday and how would you like a pass to the game and Abrams says he would like it fine and Stengel says how many people would you like to take with you and Abrams says he had a wife and 2 daughters and 1 of the daughters was married and the other daughter was a Giant fan and he dident know if she would want to go or not. So Stengel took a couple pieces of Irving Berlins stationary and wrote a pass for 5 for next Sundays game at the stadum and a pass for the daughter that likes the Giants and he sined his own name to the both of them and he wrote Fridays only on the daughters pass. Well of corse that pass for 5 aint even good for 1 but the daughters pass is ok because women is admit it free to the polo grounds every Friday.

Abrams ast who the yankees are going to play Sunday and Stengel says he dident know if they had been able to get a match with a out of town club but if they couldent do that they would proudly chose up sides.

Then Abrams told me that if I am going to be a song writer I must get some body to make up the tunes and he says the tunes must be made up 1st and then write the lyrics to fit them. I thot he was kidding but he says he dident think that any body since Gilbert was good enough to write the lyrics 1st and Stengel says well it is to late to work with him as we trade it him to Cincinnati. Then Abrams says he guest he was talking about an other Gilbert. I ast if maybe I couldent get Irving Berlin to write me a tune but Abrams says no that Berlin writes his own lyrics and music both. That is to bad kid as Berlin wrote Old man Rivers and Get out of my door and 2 other big hits that I forget there name. Abrams says remember you are writeing to a radio audience and what they want is a torch song or a ballot like My Mom.

After we left the place Stengel says well now you know wear your at and got a idea all set up for you. I says what is the idea and Stengel says why just take the tune to My Mom and write some lyrics to it about your Pop. I says that I never called him my Pop but called him my Dad and he died a long wile ago in a hospital in Danville. Stengel says well you dont have to let that get out but make it sound like he was still a live and you can write it on the way to Chi and if you get stuck call on me.

So I am going to try it any ways and will say good bye for this time and will say I am dissapoint it as was looking ford to seen you.

Danny

Centralia, Ill. May 6.

DEAR DANNY—You will get this in Chicago and I hope it wont be an unpleasant surprise, but if there is any reason why it will upset your plans please Danny let me know and dont be afraid of hurting my feelings.

Well Danny I can see you in St. Louis next Tuesday after all because papa is going to make the trip with me and he suggested it himself and is going to simply close the store for the day and I realy think he wants to make the trip for his own enjoyment as well as mine because I have not seen him so happy and excited for years but he is not nearly as excited as I am. All I am afraid of is that you will be ashamed of my clothes because they are so shabby and I am going to hold you to your promise not to make me meet Mr. Carey or Mr. Stengel and it is not because I would not love to meet them, but I simply cant bear to meet them looking so shabby as I would be embarrased and so would they to say nothing of yourself.

Now you must understand Danny that this is not your treat because neither papa nor I would consider making the trip unless we pay our own way and the expenses wont amount to hardly anything outside of the railroad fare and maybe one meal in St. Louis because we will have some coffee early in the morning before we leave home and I will fix us a few sandwichs to eat on the way. Closing the store means nothing at all as there is no business and Mrs. Ferguson is going to come to our house right after her own breakfast and spend the day and the evening with mamma so that she wont be alone.

I imajine of course that you get passes to the base ball game, but papa says you must not even do that if it is any trouble because he has not seen a real base ball game for so long that he is more than willing to buy tickets. And you must not get up early and meet our train, but just say where you will meet us after your breakfast, only be sure and not make it a place where Mr. Carey or Mr. Stengel or any of the other men will see us as I would be embarrased to death.

I do hope Mr. Carey will let you play just that one day because it would make us so proud that we know you, but papa says that he will be satisfied if you can just go in as a pinch man and make one of your home run steals.

Now Danny please tell me if this upsets your plans, but if you do want us just say where we are to meet you.

I think the "Dad" song is a fine idea as "My Mom" has been so popular, but am afraid Mr. Abrams wont like it very well when he finds out that Mr. Stengel has played him a joke with that pass to the Yankee matches.

Will see you Tuesday IF——and please be honest.

Yours,   Jessie.

Chi may 8

DEAR JESSIE well kid that is surly good news and will be tickled to death to see you and your father and will try and see that you have a good time. I am going to pay your expenses kid you and your father both wether you like it or not as I know I can ford it better then you. I will stick to my promise and not make you meet mgr Carey and Stengel tho they wouldent never notice how you look and you all ways look good to me. You wont upset no plans as I havent made no plans and you wont only have to meet 1 person out side of me and that is Frank Earls wifes sister but she is just a girl about your own age and you wont care how you look in front of her.

I think I told you about Frank as him and his wife live in the same bldg with me in Brooklyn and I been down to there apt a couple times to supper and his wife plays the piano or trys to and I groon a few songs for them. He is a young pitcher and still with the club but not on this trip and I guest mgr Carey will send him to the Jersey City club witch our club has just boughten as a farm. Well any ways his wife come from St Louis and her kid sister lives there yet and I give my wd that I would look her up and treat her to lunch and take her to the ball game and Mrs. Earl wired her what day would be best and she wired back Tuesday so the 4 of us will have lunch and maybe she will set with you at the ball pk but you wont mind that and after words we can shake her off. As for wear will I meet you I will be down to the station when your train gets there and it dont make no difference if its early or not.

About the only chance I will have of plain the hole game will be if they pitch Hallahan that day as mgr Carey knows what I can do to a left hand it fire ball pitcher. I would all so like to get a sock at Rhem or Dizzy Dean and I would make him even Dizzer. Stengel says that Carey is saveing Vance to pitch again Dean so as it will be Dazzy again Dizzy.

Well kid I wrote the lyrics to the Dad song chorus on the train comeing out here and Stengel help me with them and he says I have got to end up with the wd Pop to make it the opp of Mom but I like Dad better my self and maybe will change it. Well here is the chorus.

> My dad I love him.
> My mom she loves him.
> My sister Edna she loves him my dad.
> He is a wonder
> Will live to be a hundred
> And never mind a blunder my dad.

When I was a lad
If I act it bad mom would scold me.
Then I would go to him
And on his lower limbs he would hold me.
Theys no one greater
Then my old pater.
He is my alma mater my pop.

Stengel made me put Ednas name in and told me about alma mater
but he says the line about never made a blunder dont ring true. Alma
mater and pater are greek and means the same thing.

The men that owns our club is talking about putting numbers on
our backs like some of the other clubs and Stengel says he wisht
they would hurry up and vote for it because that would give mgr
Carey and he a chance to try out a plan that would win us a lot of
ball games before the other clubs was on to it. Like say that Vance
was number 1 and Clark number 3. Well when Vance was going to
pitch they would put Clarks number on him and the other club would
see number 3 warming up and they would start the line up they use
again a left hander. Or if Frederick was number 11 and Wilson
number 12 they would change numbers and the other clubs pitcher
would pitch to Wilson like he hit left hand it.

Well I dont believe that it would fool no body but a dum bell and
it wouldent make no difference to me as I hit right handers and left
handers both a like but I bet it will be just my luck Tuesday wile
you are there watching me to have Carey send me up to hit again
Haines and his nothing ball and that is the kind of pitching wear I
look worst.

Will see you Tuesday am when your train comes in and dont get
sick or some thing between now and then.   Danny

Centralia, Ill. May 10.

DANNY—I sent you a telegram last night to your hotel in St. Louis
and I hope you got it in time so you did not get up early this morning
and go down to meet us.

As I said in the telegram mamma is not feeling so well and I know
papa and I would never forgive ourselves if we went away and left
her so long and something should happen. I also realized all of a
sudden that papa was only going to make the trip for my sake and

we cant afford it and I would feel mean making him spend his money just on account of me. It would have been nice to see you, but it is a long hard trip for a man papa's age and I even think it would have worn me out.

So I am sure that we were wise in deciding not to come and I know that you will agree with me.   Jessie.

HOLYCAUST

◇

DEAR JESSIE well kid I never thot you would throw me down and was surly dissapoint it when I received your telegram and cant understand how you come to change your mind all of a sudden. I wisht to heavens you hadent as it cause me a lot of money and am sick besides.

I told Stengel that you was going to meet me in St. Louis and all so that I had a date with Frank Earls wifes sister the same day and when your telegram come I showed it to him and he says did you tell her about your date with this other dame and I says yes and he says well your a worst sap then you look even. He says here is a real girl who you have knowed her all your life and her and her father is willing to waste there time and money comeing all the way from Centralia on your count and you have to pick out that 1 day in the hole yr to make a date with some dam fly by night flabber who you never seen before and proudly wont never want to see again and no wonder your real girl and her old man calls off there trip.

Well kid if that is the reason you dident come was because you was jellus or some thing I surly am sorry I told you about Earls sister and law because the way things turned out you wouldent had to see her at all and you being here would of give me a excuse for not seeing her myself as she called up Tuesday noon and says she couldent keep no lunch date or go to the ball game as she had a date with some movie Co to see if she screamed ok and couldent meet me till late in the evening. So I wisht you had been here so I could told her that I coudent see her at all as she insist it on me takeing her to a picture at 9 pm and it was pretty near 11 when we come out and then she says she was hungry as she had been to excite it over the scream test to eat supper. So I says she would proudly fine some

The Saturday Evening Post, July 30, 1932; *Lose With a Smile*.

531

thing at home in the ice box but no that wouldent do and she made
me take her to a place called the Nest and the way they stang me
it ought to be called the hornets Nest and I eat some schrimps
that set up my stomach with ptomanes posen and still sick from
it yet.

mgr Carey has got a rule that wear suppose to be in the hotel by
11 and I dident get in till pretty near 3 but he was out some wear
himself till midnight and went right to bed when he come in and
proudly thot I had went to bed early myself. So Stengel was a wake
when I come in the room and he balled me out and I told him about
the schrimps and how sick I was and he says your the champion
master mind of the century as you wouldent look at sea food in
Brooklyn or Boston but you wait till you get to St Louis witch is as
far a way from the ocean as they could hide it.

He says that he wouldent say nothing to mgr Carey if I would
promise to not stay out late again and I give him my promise and
will keep it. Yesterday I lade in bed till noon and Stengel made some
excuse to Carey why I dident show up for breakfast and Stengel had
a Dr come and see me with out Carey known nothing about it and
the Dr says it might be schrimps but it looked to him like I had
favored them with gin sauce. He made this remark right in front of
Stengel and I would of knock him for a Gould only I couldent raze
myself out of bed and Stengel says he suspect it when he seen me
come in because he never herd of a case wear schrimps made a man
stagger.

Well kid I dont have to tell you that I dident have no gin sauce
but I did have a couple small drinks of gin as Miss Fleming made
me buy a qt and she want it I should buy a pt but I says wait till we
see if we can get a way with the qt first. So the waiter serve us a
qt and socked me $8.00 and heavens knows what they would of
charge for a pt. They had a 4 piece orchestra and she made me tip
them a $1.00 a piece and I guest I was lucky that it wasent Susans
band.

I all so had to tip all the other employs witch ment every body in
the place as her and I was the only ones that dident work there. She
eat a hole lobster new Burke herself and all and all the bill come to
$30.00 but the tips made $12.00 more so it cause me $42.00 all
together witch leaves me with $8.00 spending money for the rest of
the trip. They was 1 item on the bill for $5.00 cover charge tho it
was hotter then hell and no body want it no covers even if they had

been a lunge to lay down and take a nap wile she was danceing with the man that owns the place name Sherry.

Earls wife had wrote her about how I can groon and the boys calling me Rudy and nothing would do but I must get up and sing so I had the orchestra play my Mom and I groon the song I made up about my Dad to the same tune and they all went wild and made me groon 2 encorps.

When I finely got her out of the place she tried to make me hire a taxi but I told her I was to sick to stand the jars and jolts and she says some thing about me being cheep and took a taxi herself and I went back to the hotel in a st car.

Fine thing her calling me cheep when she cause me $42.00. She is surly pretty enough to get in the pictures but if she goes to Hollywood they better have it in the contract that she must buy her own meals.

Well I had a break in the luck today when it rained and I dident have to go to the ball pk. So far we aint done so good on the trip specialy in Chi wear Hack Wilson tride to play the outfield lane on his stomach and all he could hit was double play balls and the crowd give him a terrible boon and mgr Carey finely had to take him out. The club sent Frank Earl to Hartford and I guest he will have a better chance there then Jersey City as he aint even a class A pitcher and never will be and I only wisht I had never seen him as then I wouldent had to spend $42.00 on his sister and law but it wouldent of happen any ways if you had kept your promise and met me in St. Louis.

Danny

Pittsburg may 16

DEAR JESSIE why dont you write and have been worried about you because you dont write and cant help from thinking maybe you been sick or ether that or your sore at me for makeing that date with Miss Fleming the day you was suppose to come to St Louis. I would give any amt of money if things hadent happen that way as I would not hurt your feelings for the world and was dissapoint it not seen you as I had looked ford to seen you and if you had kept your promise I wouldent of got sick or throwed a way $42.00 on that crazy flabber. Please let me hear from you kid and you better dress me in Brooklyn as we will be back there in a few days.

We dident have no game yesterday as it is again the law to play in Pittsburg on Sunday like Phila but maybe you read what I done the last day in Cincinnati and mgr Carey was so tickeled that I guest he would of forgive me for getting in late that night even if Stengel had sqeeled on me. You proudly dont remember but our club trade it Babe Herman and Lombardi to Cincinnati this spring and day before yesterday Lombardi socked a home run in the 2d innings with a man on and in the 8th innings we tide it up but in there part of the innings Herman cracked an other home run and the score was 3 and 2 again us going in to the 9th innings and all there runs had been drove in by men who we had give them in the trade. Well Rixey was pitching for them and he had 2 out in our 9th innings and walked Kelly and mgr Carey hollered Rudy and I went up to hit and I left the 1st ball go by and it was a strike only it was to far inside for me to hit it good and Carey hollered take your cut Rudy and he ment swing but Lombardi says dont pay no tension to him as he is talking about your salery.

Well Rixey throwed a fast ball outside witch he dident mean to throw wear I could reach it but I reached it and socked it on a line to right field and it looked for a minit like Herman couldent help catching it but he managed to run in far enough so that it cleared his head and hit the fence and when a ball gets past ether he or the left fielder on this club Douthit has to run it down but I run like a street and beat the throw home by 5 yds with Kelly a head of me and we was a run to the good 4 and 3. There left hand hitters was comeing up in there half so mgr Carey put Clark in and he set them down in orders. Nothing could of please Carey better then win the game that way and if I wasent sure of my job before I am sure of it now.

Had a letter today from Frank Earl who was sent to Hartford and he has start it 3 games for them so far and says he is doing better than last yr as he has held the other club to triples and doubles and keeps getting better all the wile as they left him in for 2 innings his 1st game and 3 innings his 2d game and the night he wrote the letter he wasent took out till the middle of the 5th innings of the game that day and they had only scored 9 runs off him but he was all in because he wasent use to going the distants. He trys to make a joke of it but I cant help from feeling sorry for him tho I wisht he hadent never been with our club and then I wouldent never had to meet his sister and law.

Now kid please set down and write me a long letter so as I will know you are ok and not sore at me and tell me all the news and how is Dave and Clara and there baby and my kind regards to your mother and father and dress me at Brooklyn and I will be worred till I hear from you.   Danny

Centralia, Ill. May 18.

DANNY—There has not been anything the matter with me Danny and I want you and Mr. Stengel to both get it out of your head that I am "jealous" or "sore" because you made an engagement with another girl and also kindly make Mr. Stengel understand that I am not your "real girl" or anybody's else. The reason why papa and I did not come to St. Louis was just exactly like I told you. I knew that papa was just sacrificing himself for what he thought was my pleasure and that he would never forgive himself if he left mamma for that length of time and anything happened and besides he could not afford the trip. Please understand Danny that I dont claim no "hold" on you and it is none of my business how many girls you see fit to entertain at speak easy music halls. It does make me feel kind of disappointed to find out that you have changed so and spend so much money on a strange girl just because she is pretty and allow her to make you disobey Mr. Carey's rules by not only staying out till all hours but drinking that boot legged gin which might easily kill you and I heard of a case in Tamaroa just the other day where a man and his wife drunk some moonlight whisky which they had boughten from a strange legger and both of them died in less than half an hour. You never used to drink Danny or care anything about it and it hurts a little to know that you are so changed.

I cant imajine why you should want a letter from me. It is probibly because you want me to think that you still feel the same towards me like you used to, but please dont try and make me believe that Danny because I am not as much of a fool as you think though I have certainly given you every reason to think so. I will answer your letter because I am still your friend if you want me to be.

Mamma and papa are both as well as usual and Dave and the baby are well, but Clara has not been feeling well, but is better. You must have read about the fire in the Pittsburgh paper or wherever you were when it happened. It started at half past one Sunday morning with a big explosion in Silvers's Furniture Store and it was so loud that they heard it as far off as Tamaroa and everybody says that if it had not been for the way the wind was blowing and the wonderful work of our fire department and fire departments that was rushed here from four other towns the whole business district would have been wiped out. All the buildings located in the 200 block on East Broadway were wiped out and there was many nearby buildings that looked like they were doomed and the merchandise and fixtures was taken out of them and damaged in the moving. Papa would not allow mamma to get up and go, but he and I went, but I only stayed a little while on account of mamma being home alone and papa had to keep quite a distance away or the smoke would have ruined his eyes. Marion Sligar saved George Cunningham from the second story of the Byrd-Watson building and there was many other brave rescues. The buildings that burned down was the Hausler and Cornell Building with Silvers's store, the Byrd-Watson Building, the Odd Fellows, the Dave Hecht Building and Edmiston-Nichols's shoe store and the E. B. Marshall Building with the Piggly-Wiggly.

Then there was other buildings that was terribly damaged, but most all of them and their tennants was pretty well insured and now the town is full of insurance adjusters that have come to adjust the insurance.

Everybody says it is the worst holycaust that has ever happened in this part of the state, even worse than the holycaust of 1909 when the Glore Lumber Co. burned up as that was about three hundred thousand dollars damages and this was about half a million dollars damages. Of course papa has to have his joke and he says that he ought to sue the different fire departments for damages for not letting the fire spread till it reached the store so we could collect the insurance and he and I could both stay home all day. Chief Archbold and three other Centralia firemen were badly burned and the other fire departments that were here were from Salem, Carlyle and Mt. Vernon and Sandoval. The people here are going to vote them a card of thanks for their help. Mr. Legried the state fire marshal, you will remember that he used to live here, he got here Sunday night and promised that there will be a sweeeping investigation and if they find out that it was larson they will be punished. I am sending you a copy of the Sentinel which will tell you the story a great deal better than I can tell it and I will let you know the results of the sweeping investigation.

Now Danny dont think that you have to write to me and dont think that I can ever feel quite the same towards you like I felt before or believe anything you tell me, and please understand and make Mr. Stengel understand that I am not your "real girl" or anybody's else.

　　　　　　　　　　　　　　　　　　　　　　　　　　　　Jessie.

P.S. Dave told me about your home runs against Cincinnati. Danny I hope you make lots of them, but you wont if you drink all that moonlight gin.

Brooklyn may 21

DEAR JESSIE I received your letter and copy of the Sentinel all about the big fire witch I had seen only a few lines in some newspaper about the big fire. Old Centralia must of had a big thrill and am sorry I mist it. But kid the rest of your letter made me feel pretty bad and you know what I mean and nothing I ever done or said could of made you feel half as bad as your letter made me feel outside of the part about the fire.

Now kid you will have to admit 1 thing and I mean that if I hadent wrote you in regards to what happen in St Louis you wouldent knew nothing about it and me writeing and telling you about it ought to show that I aint change my feelings tords you but all ways tell you just what I been doing and dont hold no secrets from you but tell you the truth. Now kid dont that look like they aint been no change on my part tords you but instead of that you write me a letter like you dident care about me no more and write like I am going to the dogs and you are threw with me and talk like I dont do nothing but drink gin wile all I done was drink 2 drinks of gin and get sick from eting schrimps and try and show Frank Earls wifes sister a good time just because I feel sorry for he and his wife.

Well kid if you want me to hide things from you when I write letters why ok and I will write about what kind of wether wear haveing and write to you like I would write to some stranger and let me know kid if that is the kind of letters you want or if you dont want no letters at all or if you want me to write like I been use to writeing and not hole back no secrets.

I was telling the boys that they had been a holycaust in Centralia and Odoul says they had 1 every yr in his home town and roast it a hole ox and Jack Quinn thot I ment the college wear Jack Barry coaches but Glenn Wright says I referd to a feast that comes a little wile after easter so I had to exclaim to them that I was talking about a big fire witch wiped out a half a million dollars worth of property.

So Stengel says wear did you say this fire took place and I says Centralia and he says do you mean to tell us that they was a half a million dollars worth of damages and I says yes. So he says why they couldent be a thousand dollars damages if they burned up the hole town and every body in it even if Greto Garba was mayor.

Well I guest I told you about the rule they had in the both big leagues witch every time 1 of the ball players talked to some body in the stand the empires was suppose to report it and it cause you a $5.00 fine. They made up the rule because it seems that 1 of the boys with the Cubs talked with Cigar face Al Capone durn a game last yr and the owners of the club was afrade the fans might expect he was trying to bride them to loose the game tho the Cubs loose plenty games with out no bride from Sigar face. Well a little wile ago the govt rest it Cigar face for not failing to pay them his hole income and sent him to a jail in Atlanta wear the club was all ready a game and a half out of last place in the southren league before he ever got there.

So they called the rule off in our league and wear loud to talk to our friends and admires and Glenn Wright says that from now on we can score from 2d base on a triple if we want to because Stengel will have his back to the play and be calling some body names in the stand behind the visiters bench.

In the American league they still wont leave the players speak to there friends but if there friends speaks to them they can wave back and Stengel says they wont be no chance of any of the Boston red sox getting a sore arm.

Well wear haveing an other series with the Giants and it is like takeing candy to a baby. They act like there trying to drop out of the bottom of this league and get in some miner league wear they can win and yet every body was picking them for the penant this spring and today Lefty Odoul made the remark that there the best club in the league on paper and Stengel says if Stoneham and McGraw was smart they would dig up the sod at the polo grounds and lay paper over the dirt so as they could at lease win some of there home games.

The Giants got a pitcher name Pearson who they use him to pitch to the batters in practice and Fresco Thompson was sane today that when it comes time to cut down to the 23 player limit this here Pearson will lead the grand march to Bridgeport. Well any ways Thompson says that he was just comeing in the ball pk today when he herd a noise that pretty near made him deef and it turned out to be this here Pearson who had drove over from n y in his own car and Thompson says it was a car with a out bord motor and Pearson had Hogan the big catcher a long with him and Hogan told Thompson he liked to ride in the car because it fixed his ears so as he cant hear McGraw or Bancroft when they ball him out.

I dont know if I wrote you about poor Hack Wilson in Chi and the crowd bood him so he couldent do nothing and was plain the outfield on his stomach and when he come up to bat and fanned we was all releived because that ment only 1 out wear as if he connect it with the ball it ment 2. Well mgr Carey took him out and some of the news paper boys that is helping manage the club had it in there paper that Hack was all threw as a regular and Carey must of not read the papers because he stuck Hack back in the game and now he catches fly balls standing up and when he connects with the ball they aint no chance to get no body out unlest the other club plays there right fielder outside of the pk and furnish him with a motor cycle. I suppose I ought to be sorry he come back so strong because if the news paper boys had of been right I might of had a chance to get in there regular myself but you cant help liking old Hack and specialy when the news paper boys is rideing him.

Well kid this is a long letter when I dont know if you want to hear from me or not but remember what I ast you at the beggin of the letter if you want me to keep on writeing like I all ways done and tell you the truth about myself or write like you was a stranger of mine or not at all. Please dont be sore at me kid or feel different tords me then you use to feel as I dont feel no different tords you and you will all ways be number 1 in my heart no matter how many flabbers make me buy gin and eat schrimps and cause me $42.00 for a stomach ake. I will be expecting a letter from you when we get back from Boston and please kid dont dissapoint me again.

Danny

Centralia, Ills. May 24.

DEAR DANNY—Danny I want to ask you to forgive me for what I wrote to you in my last letter, I dont mean the part about the fire, but saying that I could never feel the same towards you again or trust you and being cross with you like I was. Danny I realy was not feeling well when I wrote you that letter, but that is no excuse for me writing that letter. I do appreciate you always telling me the truth and not holding anything back from me and I would die if you wrote to me like I was a stranger or stopped writing to me entirely.

But if you think that you always being frank with me is a proof that you care a little, you must see that I care more than a little for you when it upset me so to know that you had drank that moonlight gin and disobeyed Mr. Carey's rules. Your last letter made me happier than anything that you ever wrote to me. From now on I will trust you Danny and will know that you are taking good care of yourself and not throwing your money away and not drinking that terrible poison.

I feel so ashamed to be such a poor hand at writing letters when you can write such nice ones to me and I am interested in every word you write though I dont understand half of what you write. Of course you realize dear that you are always seeing interesting things and having interesting experiences while the big fire is the only thing that has happened here in years that was worth writing about. But even if there was things worth writing about I would be a poor hand writing them.

I think I told you that Mr. Legried the state fire marshal had started a sweeping investigation of how the fire started the Sunday afternoon of the morning the fire started and they were going to punish them if it was larson, but it seems that they found out that the fire just started from a natural explosion or something, but Danny you cant imajine how desolate it looks with the whole 200 block on Broadway raised and most of the men who lost their property are going to rebuild, but of course it will take time and in the mean time the men who owned stores, of course they are losing money because they have no place to sell their merchandise though some of them have rented space in stores that was not raised by the fire. Papa hoped some of them would want to buy our store or at least rent it, but it seems like they think it is too far out of the way.

Well Danny there is nothing more to write about except to tell you again how happy you made me and I trust you dear to not risk your life by drinking that terrible poison like St. Louis.

Please write to me Danny and write like you always did and tell me everything you do and see.   Yours,   Jessie.

Brooklyn may 27

DEAR JESSIE well kid I thot I was going to have time to write you a long letter but it looks like I wouldent have time to write you a long letter but will write you a few lines now and write you a long letter when I get more time.

Well kid do you remember the girl I told you about name Vivian Duane who was the phone girl at the hotel wear we stade this spring in Clearwater and she ast me to fine her a job here or over in n y and of corse I couldnt fine her no job or dident even look for 1. Well when I got back from the polo grounds last night they was a telegram waiting for me and it says she had just got here from fla and was stain at the St Geo hotel here in Brooklyn and I called her up and she ast me to come down and see her and I went down and she says it was so hot in fla that she couldent stand it no longer and come up here and hopes she will get a job but any ways she all ways want it to see n y and she just couldent put it off no longer.

Well kid between you and I it looks to me like she had took a shine to me and I thot the same way when we was in Clearwater from how she act it down there but dident think it was so strong that she would follow me up here and pertend like she was looking for a job when what she is looking for is a man. Well the St Geo is wear Stengel is stain and he happen to come threw the lobby wear I and Vivian was setting and he ast her what was she doing here and she says it was to hot to stay in fla.

So Stengel says you will fine it just as hot here and if it dont get hot by its self I will make it hot for you do you get me. So Vivian says I dont get you and I dont want you and Stengel says to me remember what you promise me in St Louis and then he walked a way.

Next thing I knowed Vivian was crying and I cant stand seen no woman cry specialy in a lobby and it finely wound up by me promising to take her over to n y tonight and go to a night club or some thing.

So that is why I aint got no time to write you a long letter kid but will write more the next time and we beat the Giants yesterday but they beat us today and I come out of the polo grounds with Stengel and Bancroft the Giants coach come out at the same time and Stengel says nice work Banny and Bancroft says what do you mean and Stengel says why aint it the 1st time this yr that you fellows win a game in succession.

Must close now Jessie as it is pretty near 10 a clock and time to start out for n y as I dont know just wear to take her and may not fine a place till midnight witch is the time they get lively.

Well kid do you know that you called me dear twice in your letter besides when you said dear Danny and am going to keep your letter because it makes me feel good to read them 2 extra dears.

Danny

Centralia, Ill. May 29.

DANNY—Danny you must do something and do it right now and what I mean you must do is tear up that last letter that I wrote you as I did not mean one word I said in it. I beg your pardon for saying dear in my letter if I did say it, I certainly did not mean to.

And please dont ever write to me again except just one line to tell me you have tore up my letter, and if you write any more letters you will just be wasting your valuable time because I will tear them up unopened before I read them.   Jessie Graham.

THE IDES OF JUNE

◊

Brooklyn june 2

DEAR JESSIE I got your letter and wisht you hadent wrote me no letter at all in place of the letter you wrote me and I mean the last letter you wrote and not the letter you wrote before when you called me dear twict be sides dear Danny. Now kid when you called me dear 2 times besides dear Danny it wasent no slit of the pen and you ment it and I write you back a nice letter back and you jump all over me and pertend like wear a stranger and you sine your last name like I dident know you 21 yrs.

Well kid all I can make out of it is either the big fire went to your head and give you a fever or either your sore at me because Vivian Duane come up here chason me all the way from fla. I never told her to come but I cant help it if they come chason after me all the way from fla. I wisht that she would get home sick or some thing but she aint got money enough to pay her fair back or pay her hotel bill and stopping at the St Geo like she was Mrs. Hoover. She keeps sane that she will get a job and why dont I help her get a job but she wont go no place only to the ball pk or some night club and I guest she expects they will hire her for a empire or door man.

I took her out twict at night and the 1st time it was wear Geo Olsens band are the drawn cart and they got a great band but not worth $37.00 like it cause me and she thot Olsen was smileing at her and ast the waiter to bring him over and the waiter come back and says Olsen dident have time and Vivian says why did he smile at her and the waiter says the smile is parked there like Moon Eliza and lots of girls gets fooled by it but he is just pluging some toothe pest and the girl that sings is Mrs. Olsen under the name Ethel Schulte.

The Saturday Evening Post, September 5, 1932; *Lose With a Smile*.

Night before last was the other time and it was the Bossert roof here in Brooklyn and cause $13.00 and wouldent cause only $7.00 but I made the mistake of telling her about a pt of real absent witch I got for $6.00 off a usher at the ball pk. His brother is a rum runner on the boat that petrols the coast between here and Atlanta. She insist it on me bring it a long and I drunk 2 drinks to keep a wake and she finish the bottle and got sick and felt a sleep. I had to take her back to the St Geo in a taxi and that is wear mgr Carey and Stengel lives and Stengel was setting in the lobby when we come in and I hoped he wouldent see me as it was 10 after 12 but after she went up in the elevator he folled me out the door.

He says I got a radio in my rm and I get the base ball scores every night from the n y police Station and before they tell the scores they give out a list of missing people and most of them is missing from Brooklyn and they descry them as poor menly witch means they aint right in the head. So I says what of it and Stengel says some time about the middle of the mont I expect to hear your name on the list. Then he went back in the hotel with out exclaim what he ment and I come home but couldent sleep and yesterday I felt sick and glad that we dident have no game. It taste like lickerish and if I knowed how it taste I woudent never buy it let alone $6.00

Now kid remember what you wrote in the letter wear you called me dear twict. You wrote that you want it me to all ways tell you all I am doing and not hole nothing back like I all ways done. So dont be sore at me or rare back with an other of them letters like the last letter wear you sine your last name like you was the woman who I rent my rm. You got no need to be jellus of Vivian Duane and only wisht she would go back home and I would gladly pay her hotel bill and her fair home but I owed all but $26.00 of the pay check they give me yesterday and that will have to last till the 15th.

Must close now and go to the ball pk as we got a double header with the Boston club. Stengel says there mgr wont let none of them read a news paper even if they could because if they ever fine out that there leading the league they will get dizzy and do a nose dive like Babe Herman when some body sock a ball over his head.

Please write to me kid and write another letter like the 1 with the dears and I will promise to tear that letter up like you ast me as soon as I get 1 to take its place.   Danny

Brooklyn june 5

DEAR JESSIE well kid no letter from you yet and am scarred may be your sick. Write me a letter kid if its only a line to let me know that you aint sick or mad at me. If your mad at me on a count of Vivian Duane I hope that you will get over it when I tell you I ain't even seen her since the night she drunk up my absent but had a note from her yesterday witch it looks like I aint libel to see her again.

The hotel people was after her to pay her bill and she told them that she was waiting for some money from home but they told her that she would ether have to pay them some thing or ether leave and they would hole on to her trunk. So she ast them would they give her a job as phone girl and they said they would think it over and after a wile they called up her rm and told her ok and they are going to keep half of her salary till she gets that money from home. Her salary is $25.00 per wk.

So I told Stengel about it and he says how does she like her hrs. So I says that she hadent told me her hrs and he says well there from 10 to 2 in the day time and 6 to 12 at night. So I says who told you and he says I told them. He says I have kind of took a fancy to the girl and hotel people all ways calls on me when they got a big problem so I ranged her hrs to suit you and she both. He says she will save money on meals because she cant get off durn lunch. Then if she goes to the ball game and waits for you to scort her back to the St Geo she wont have to bother with supper unlest you want to set up till she is threw for the evening and take her to some roof. If you do that you might as well jump off the roof because the next time you do your batting after midnight Max is going to hear about it. Other wise breakfast will be the only time she can eat and no woman can eat more than 40 cts worth of breakfast if they aint a chanel swimmer or a Deligate for Al Smith.

Well kid Stengel has took the same kind of a fancy to her like he takes to the Brooklyn fans and you can bet he was telling the truth when he says that he fixed her hrs but he fixed them so her and I cant meet unlest we both get up at 7 am and go for a walk. So get her out of your head kid and write to me and tell me wear still friends at lease because when I am scarred that your sick or some thing I cant keep my mind on my work and that is what happen today in the game again phila tho how can they expect me to hear Klem talk to his self when the crowd are yelling there lunge out.

Elliot has us beat 5 and 2 in the 7th innings and Picinich let off with a 2 base hit in our half. Carey sent me up for Clark and big Jumbo wouldent throw me nothing close and give me a base on balls. Now theys a rule that with a man on 1st and 2d base and nobody out why if the man at bat hits a infield fly he is out if they catch it or not provide it the empire hollers when the ball is hit. Well Johnny Frederick took 2 balls and 2 strikes and then he swang and I thot I seen him give Picinich and I a sine so I start it with the pitch and wasent looking wear the ball went but herd the crowd holler and thot that Johnny had socked 1. Well it was a fly ball to Whitney there 3rd base man and Klem clams he hollered but all I herd was Carey and Stengel holler and I thot they ment it was a close play and slid in to 2d base and spiked Picinich who was standing on the bag. Whitney catch the ball and throwed it to 1st base and I catch hell. But as I says to Carey how and hell can you expect me to run bases when you leave me on the bench 2 wks at a time and he couldent answer. So I says to Klem have they got a new rule wear the empire dont holler but write there decision on a slit of paper and male them after the game and he says go home and put on your night shirt and finish your nap. But even with he and Carey and all of them again me the thing wouldent never happen only I been so worred about you.

Dave proudly told you wear McGraw quit as mgr of the Giants and point it Bill Terry to seed him. Bill is there 1st base man and ought to be strong for me as I left him catch me off 1st base 1 time rather then cut off his ft. So if Carey keeps on acting like today or ether him or Stengel makes a crack about sending me some wear the 15th when they got to cut down to 23 men why I will laugh in there face as they got no chance of getting wafers on me with Terry a mgr.

The reason why McGraw quit was on a count of bad helth as he cant travel no more but is still with the club as V P and got a office at the pk and Bancroft there coach quit with McGraw but will be McGraws secy and Stengel says he would like to hide in there office some time and look and lissen wile Bancroft takes down short hand mash notes witch his boss had been wanton to write to the news paper boys and empires for 30 yrs.

Stengel says that Terry ought to be a ideel mgr because the owner of the club dont speak to him only once every spring when they guarl. The owner was on speaking turns with McGraw but McGraw wouldent anser. Terry got a good start when the club win a double header and Stengel says that beats there record for a winning street by 2 games.

The rule about a 23 men limb it means bad news for some of the boys and mgr Carey has got to get rid of 4 men and it will proudly be a catcher and a pitcher and a couple infielders. Am scarred that Tommy Thompson will get sent some wear and we will surely mist him as he keeps us in a good spurts with his gags. Like today they was 1 of the young smart Alex on the phila club who he and Tommy been kidding each other all spring and he says well Thompson 10 more days and you will be in the miners and Tommy says who comes here be sides you.

Well dear this is a long letter and please write to me back so as I will know that you still like me and you aint sick or mad or some thing and you will notus I call you dear like you called it to me and will call it to you again dear and I mean it.   Danny.

Centralia, Ill. June 8

DANNY—I dont think it is quite fair for you to say that not hearing from me and worrying about my health is why you are not playing as good as you were earlier this spring, and I dont imajine that you would miss my poor letters was it was not for your friend Miss Duane being unable to keep you company. And Danny you would behave different than you have been if you was worried about me or any other of your old friends being in bad health because it certainly would not improve how they feel to know that you have forgotten yourself and become a different person and probibly would get into serious trouble with Mr. Carey was it not for Mr. Stengel doing everything to protect you.

Danny it is none of my business what happens to you and I know that you will resent me offering advice, but it does seem to me that right now is the time for you to forget everything but your duty to Mr. Carey and the Brooklyn nine and even try and forget the fascinating Miss Duane for a time and the other girls who follow you all over the country and make you go in debt and forget your duty to Mr. Carey and the Brooklyn nine.

Danny you complain of me treating you like strangers. Well Danny that is just what you have been to me lately and I cant treat or feel towards you like I used to as long as you go on like you been going on and act so different than the Danny who I thought I knew but think so no more.

I am sorry that you wont tear up my foolish letter like I asked you to, but I guess it is only people who you have known a short time who you will do anything they ask you to, including go in debt to get them intoxicated, and buy them expensive poison from a rummer employed by Uncle Sam's Navy.

Well Danny I am afraid this is not the kind of letter you want from me, though why you want any kind is more than I can imajine. And Danny there was a time when you calling me "dear" would have thrilled me through and through, but when you write it in the same letter which you write H——twice and mention nightshirts like they were nothing at all or you were writing to another man, well Danny I just wish that you had not written "dear" in that kind of a letter.   Jessie.

Brooklyn june 12

DEAR JESSIE am sorry that I fend it you by writeing hell and night shirt and will try and remember to not fend you again but you must remember that it was Klem the empire that said night shirt and not me and I dont wear them any ways but wear pajamas and dont wear the coat when its hot like last night. Today it was rain and colder and we had to call off the game with the St Louis club witch would of drew the crowd of the yr after what come off yesterday.

Well kid I guest they wont be no more kidding about Carey leaving me go after what come off yesterday. It was the 1st chance I had again Hallahans fire ball and he is the best left hander in the league and they say that he is as fast as Dazzy when Dazzy was his best. Well we was a run behind in the 8th and 1 out and Hallahan lose control and give 2 bases on balls and Carey yelled Rudy and I went up in Mungos place. I was scarred that Street would stick in 1 of his relief corpse like Lindsey and tho I could knock him for a lupe I want it a chance at the bright star. Well Street give it to me and I guest it will be my last chance as well as my 1st.

On a count of Hallahan been wild I was a frade that Carey would tell me to take 1 but he dident say nothing and it was up to me to do as I please. Well some thing told me that he would shoot that fire ball and it would be wear I could sock it and I better not leave it go by. Well kid it was his fire ball and may be it wouldent been called a strike as it was a little high and out side like the ball I hit off Rixey last mont only twict as fast. But I catch it just right and so

far over Watkins head that he never even tipped his cap to it. Glenn
Wright says it went as far as the ball Wilson hit again the Cubs and
beat them the other day and 2 or 3 of the boys greed with him.
Hallahan called me a lot of names and how lucky I was and says you
hit a wild pitch so I says when a man dont throw nothing only wild
pitchs what else do you expect me to hit. Then Street start it on me
from the bench and hollered thats your 1st and last blow off that
baby and I says yes because the next time I face him he will run and
hide in the ball box and not wait for no champion master mind to
guest himself out of a ball game. So Street says no but because Bill
wont never pitch in the eastren league. Well Jack Quinn got them
out in the 9th and my blow win the game 5 and 3 and that will keep
the boys quite about Carey leaveing me go or writeing a song like
1 of them wrote and I found it in my locker and they wrote it in
print so I wouldent know there writeing as there scarred that I could
sock who ever wrote it. I will copy it down like it is and who ever
done it cant even spell groon.

Here is what is up at the top of the paper and then the song:

For Rudy to Croon to His Favorite Tune

> Good night Rudy aint it just a pity
> Good Night Rudy sent to Jersey City
> After that old 15th of june
> Morn night and noon
> Weel miss your croon but may be
> You will lern a little sence and reason
> and be with us once again next season.
> Dont steal bases thats occupied.
> Rudy Doody good night.

How is that for a fine song for 1 of the boys on my own club and
I only hope that who ever wrote it will get sent to Jersey City or
Hartford or hell but no chance of me getting sent no wear after what
I done to Hallahan. Specialy as Carey would have to get wafers and
Terry would clam me for the Giants for thinking about his ft that
time even if I was no good.

Now kid I aint seen Vivian Duane since the last time but she has
kept writeing me notes and phone me and must tell you that I have
greed to see her for a few minits Wednesday am but it wont only

be for a few minits as she has to go to work and I got to be at the ball pk. I am going to tell her that I cant see her no more as mgr Carey has put down his ft. That will be the end of it between she and I.

Now dear can you write me a nice letter like the kind you know I want and will say again that I am sorry about the hells and it was Klem the empire that said night shirt.   Danny

Centralia, Ill. June 14

DEAR DANNY—Your letter came by the air mail and was glad to get it because it sounded so much more like the Danny who I once knew. You did say H—— again, but I suppose you hear it so much that it has become a habit for you to say it, but try and break yourself of the habit Danny. As for Mr. Klem I should think that if an umpire can put a base ball man out of the benches for using bad words, why I should think that Mr. Carey or somebody ought to be allowed to ask for another umpire when they say things like Mr. Klem.

Danny it was wonderful you hitting those three home runs and beating the St. Louis and I suppose that it was natural for Big Bill Street to get mad, but it does seem funny for people to get mad over a game, though I was at Dave and Clara's the other night and they were playing whist with the Nymeyers and Fritz and Grace got terribly mad when they beat them and Fritz said some terrible words like none of we girls were there.

Danny I hope you keep your promise about not seeing Miss Duane after tomorrow. It is none of my business, but I do believe that Mr. Carey and Mr. Stengel will be mad at you if you continue the acquaintance, for I do believe that they or at least Mr. Stengel consider her a bad influence. It is hard on her, but after all it is her own fault coming way up from Florida with no prospects and I hope that she soon receives the money from home and can go home.

I would like to tell whomever wrote that "song" what I think of them and it will be a big joke on them to find out that they were so badly mistaken.

Danny you calling me dear in this last letter did make me feel warm inside and it was because your letter sounded so much more like your old self than the other letters received from you lately. For my sake dear and your other friends try and keep the rules like Mr.

Carey wants you to and remember that Mr. Stengel cant protect you forever.   Yours,   Jessie.

Brooklyn june 15

DEAR JESSIE well kid I am threw and dont know yet if I am comeing home or stay in n y and groon songs for the radio people and wont know for a wk as the man I got to see is out of town. Who ever wrote that song knowed more than I did but I will fool him and Carey and Stengel and the rest of them by not shown up at no Jersey City or no other miner league. And Bill Terry is a fine 1 to forget me when I never would left them catch me off 1st base that time only for his ft.

When I went in the club house yesterday some of the boys was dressing and Carey was there and he called me over in a corner and set down. He says well Rudy tomorrow is the limb it wear we got to cut down to 23 men and I am going to send you over to Jersey City. Well I was so choke up that I couldent say nothing back. He says you will have a chance to get in the game every day regular and that is what you need is be in there every day under a good mgr and lern the things that you cant lern only by plain every day. I says I could play here every day if you say the wd but he says no I cant bench none of my outfield and be sides you make to many mistakes. I says I guest that was a mistake me hitting that ball off Hallahan and he says no and it is just on a count of that and some other things you done that I am turn you over to Jersey City wear I can call you back.

He says if you hadent kind of act it like your mind was logey the last couple wks I might keep you in place of 1 of the other boys but I think you need every day work to be at your best and may be next yr I will be able to start you every time they pitch a left hander again us. So I says what if I dont want to go to Jersey City. He says that will be an other of your mistakes and the biggest 1 you made yet. I says what if I dont dress this pm and he says I dont care if you dress or not and I dont care if I see you again till you get out of your present state a mind. He says I am giveing you a chance and you better take it. I says yes you surly are giveing me a fine chance and I walked out of the club house and dident even stay and watch the dam game. I come right here to my rm and lade down on the bed and cride like I was a baby or some thing. It wouldent be so bad kid if I hadent thot Carey and Stengel and the rest of the boys was my friend but I guest I got no friends a round here and only may be Vivian Duane.

I was still lain here at 6 a clock tonight when the door rapt and I dident pay no tension and Stengel walked in like it was his own home. He says well Rudy your 1 of the lucky boys. I dident anser him and he says Caldwell goes to Hartford and Max had to sell Richards right out but you go to Jersey City wear he can call you back and you will have a pal Tommy Thompson a long with you. I says I dont want to be no place where Max can call me back after what him and you done. Stengel says well may be I can fix it so as he can send Richards to Jersey and sell you right out. Then if you look good why you will proudly land with the red sox wear all men is free and eagle and some even worst. You ought to play your best base ball for them because when you feel like running from 1 base to an other you won't never fine no class mates all ready there.

I says did Carey get wafers from the Giants. Stengel says they offered him some but he dont like wafers but the Giants is full up and McGraw cant even use you in the office because he dont dictate musicle notes. I says I am threw with base ball and you can tell Carey that when you see him. Stengel say I wont have to tell him as he has thot that way for 2 or 3 wks. He says what are you going to do and I says I dont know yet so Stengel says well I will tell you. Your going to get your last check tomorrow and then your going to take that southren eye sore over to n y and both of you get lit up and bat a round till your moneys all shot and then you wont need to go to Jersey City because they all ready got there coda of bums. I says may be that is just what I will do is like you say.

Then Stengel says what is the name of that little girl in Centralia and I says what of it. He says well you dont have to tell me her name because its Jessie Graham but whats her dress and I says just Centralia and he says in a town wear they can have a half a million dollar fire they must have a street. But any ways why dont you wire and ask her to come east and see Jersey City and may be go threw with that business witch I ast you to call off last spring. I says she aint libel to want me now that Brooklyn says I aint good enough and Stengel says she is just the kind of a girl that would want you all the more and what aint good enough for Brooklyn is good enough for any body. And he says be sides that they feel different about there young ball players been married in Jersey City. I say well I aint going to no Jersey City and I aint going to ask her to marry a man that cant hole a big league job and she aint got no money to come east.

Well I met Vivian this am like I told you I had the date and she had all ready seen in the papers wear I was left out and she thinks like I do that I would be a sap to go to some miner league and she suggest it about me groon on the radio and she knows a man with the radio people who will hear me groon only he wont be back in n y till next wk. She says I ought to visit some good night club and fine out what is the new songs and lern to groon them before the man gets back. She promise to go with me Saturday night.

Well dear you see I aint no good after all and the people who I thot they were friends is turn out different. I dont care what the base ball world thinks about me as I am threw with the game but am sorry on your a count as you thot I would make good and I have felt down on the job and aint no good after all.

Good by dear and may be will see you in 10 days or may be never but will all ways feel tords you like I all ways done and only wisht I had some thing to offer but cant offer you nothing now only my love.   Danny.

Centralia, Ill. June 15

DEAREST DANNY—Well dear I wrote to you yesterday and here I am writeing to you again today, but this time I have got some news to write and I only hope it wont be bad news to you as that would make it bad news for me.

I read in the paper today that you are going to be with the Jersey City nine where you can be one of the regular fielder men and play every day and I know that you will like that better than not being active all the time. Well Danny it just happens that Jersey City has always been one of my favorite towns because papa has talked about it so much and what an interesting town it is there on the river seeing the big boats come in and go out. Dear it makes me blush to write this kind of a letter, but I am writing it just the same and taking a chance that you wont hate me for it.

Well Danny papa got some money from some one who owed him it and he asked me if I wanted to take a trip and I said yes and he said he wished that I would go to Jersey City where his step brother lives and where he paid him such a pleasant visit once.

Well dear I am coming and will arrive at the Penn station at 9:40 in New York Saturday morning and please meet me as I will be scared to death if you dont. If you still feel like you felt last winter and spring, well dear this is leap year. So good-bye till Saturday morning and dont fail me dear.   Yours,   Jessie.

TAKE A WALK

◇

IT SEEMS FUNNY working in this town without Bleat. It seems funny working anywheres without him. I don't mean funny, you know, like something to laugh at. I mean it seems lonesome and not natural. The boss had us paired off longer than most umpires, not only here, but all over the league; there was mighty few series we didn't work together from the time I broke in till the day he quit, and in the other towns we stopped at the same hotel and was hardly ever separated night or day. Yet this is where I miss him more, where I seen less of him, and where I liked to be assigned with him, even though it's the place that gave us pretty near all our trouble and finally drove him out of the game.

Maybe you're like a lot of people and think umpires are crazy, figuring that nobody would take the job if they were in their right mind. There's been times when I thought the same way. On the other hand, if you get in the big league, it's good pay for half a year's work, better than anything else for men like Bleat and I, who played baseball ourselves and didn't have brains enough to save anything. Not only that, if you make good you get quite a kick out of it, almost as much as if you're in there playing, yourself. You even enjoy an argument if you know you're right, though, whether you're right or wrong, you don't want the argument to go quite as far as it did with us and this club.

Besides, I'll bet most fans have got the idea that umpires aren't like human beings. They figure that we don't never take off our uniforms, and as soon as the game's over, we adjourn to a special little room under the stand and sit there till the next afternoon studying the rule book and figuring out what to do in case some nutty play comes up. They imagine us cooped up there half the night

The American Magazine, October 1933; previously uncollected.

struggling with our home work, preparing for the big Test that's liable to be sprung on us tomorrow.

Well, as a matter of fact, there's four or five umpires in the two leagues that have a better time than anybody I know of. The ones that ain't married, I mean. And if you seen them off the field you'd take them for picture actors. The minute they know their schedule, they wire it ahead to the different cities, and you never catch them hanging around the hotel evenings, wondering where to go or what to do with themselves; no, or worrying over a close decision they missed that afternoon.

After the game they change their clothes and they're out of the park before the fans, all of them dressed up to kill. And you don't see them again till the next day, when they've just got time enough left to holler, "Batter up!" And they like to have some pitcher in there throwing a good fire ball so the boys will foul plenty back against the screen, which gives them an excuse to look up at where the girl friend is sitting and play eyes with her.

It's different with the married brethren. They generally live at a hotel as far from the ball players as they can get. In the evenings they take in a picture or a fight or shoot some pool; or they just stay in their rooms and read or write letters. Then, of course, when you've been around the league a few years, you make friends and they invite you to their homes, and whether you go or not is up to yourself. The trouble is that most of the friends are baseball crazy and you have to earn your spareribs explaining the rule about the infield fly ball and what happened to Hornsby the last place he was at.

Bleat and I used to divide our time between the pictures and taking long walks. I always read the papers in the forenoon, and once a week I write to my wife. Even at that I have trouble filling one piece of stationery.

But with Bleat it was different; that is, anywheres except here. There was generally always a long letter from Edith, the gal he was engaged to and who I'm going to tell you about. She must have cared a lot for him to write so much and so often, though she knew that if she missed a day he would call her up from wherever we were and find out what was wrong.

When the letter arrived on schedule, he would hoard it all through breakfast, leaving it lay on the table unopened while he glanced at the box scores, which was the only thing in the paper he paid any attention to. After breakfast he would sneak over in a corner of the lobby and try to find a seat with his back to the wall, so nobody could see over his shoulder, and then read, not once but a hundred times, all the junk she had written to him a hundred times before. Between words, while he was reading, he would take his eyes off the letter and stare up at heaven with a look as blissful as if some club had just scored six runs in the fifteenth inning of one of those what-of-it games in Cincinnati or Philadelphia.

Even if the letter was only a dozen pages, it was always at least ten-thirty before he finished it; then, of course, he would have to compose the answer, which was no visiting card itself, and often on double-header days I'd have to drag him away from the writing desk by force and bribe some escaped bank president to taxi us out to the ball park in time to don the conventional blue, and go into action without as much as a hot dog under our belt to give us a feeling of authority.

I don't believe there was any other two men in the world that talked less baseball between games than myself and Bleat. Wherever we went to after the battle, it wouldn't be five minutes till he'd start raving about the gal, and all I was expected to do was say "Yes" or "No" in the right spot. Usually he'd ask me if I thought he was too old for her, and it was up to me to say "No" and convince him that I meant it. If the question had been, did I think he was too good for her, I'm not sure that my "No" would have come from the heart.

I told you I miss him more here than anywhere else, though I seen less of him, and the reason is because this is where he was always happiest and anyone around him couldn't help from being happy, too. This was his home town for fourteen years, ever since he broke in as a player and afterwards, while he played in Boston and Pittsburgh, and all the years he umpired. But you can't blame his love for the place on that. I've seen umpires and players both that would pretty near rather get suspended or crippled than perform in front of the home folks or visit the old fireside, when they can stay at a good hotel at somebody else's expense and pal around with people that don't keep asking you questions you don't want to answer or telling you things you don't want to hear. No, Bleat was happy here because his gal lived here and because her mother always kept the room for him where he lived from the day he came up from Texas, fourteen years ago.

Bleat was twenty-two years old then and Edith was nine, so of course it wasn't a case of love at first sight. He did claim she was the cutest kid that ever lived and I didn't argue with him, no more than I do with the ball players when they yell, "He missed me!" after the guy has tagged them hard enough to burst their appendix. Anyway, my experience with kids is that they're all cute, and four out of five of them are too much so. I haven't got any of my own. My wife likes dogs better, and I'm glad she does. When one of your dogs gets too cute, you can give them to some friend that's the same way. If you did that to a kid, people might begin to gossip about you.

Well, as I say, Bleat found this place the day he landed here from Texas. There was a sign in the window, "Room for Rent," and it was only a couple of blocks from the ball park, so he went up and rung the doorbell and inquired. Edith's mother told him afterwards that when she seen him she was going to name some outrageous price, because he was so big that she was scared of him and didn't want him around the house. But she changed her mind when she heard that high-pitched voice which he got his nickname from. It takes you off your feet, like the first time you hear Dempsey talk, though neither Bleat nor Dempsey need their voice to remove people's feet from under them.

She gave him the best room in the place for twelve dollars a week, and that included breakfast and supper, and he says she never would have raised it in all those fourteen years if he hadn't made her. So you can't blame him for having been fond of his home, even without the gal thrown in.

There was only one other roomer, a middle-aged spinstress that taught in some high school—that was when they were paying school-teachers—and she had two or three private sufferers on her hands in the summertime. Once she had the flu pretty bad and Bleat kept inquiring of Edith's mother how she was, and Edith asked him why he kept inquiring when he didn't care one way or the other. Edith said that it would be a nuisance to have her die on them, but that's all it would be—just a nuisance. A year ago last winter, though, she did die on them, and it turned out to be a whole lot more than a nuisance.

Now, let's see; Bleat was twenty-two when he broke in the big league. He played three seasons here and one in Boston, and part of one in Pittsburgh, before his arm went bad. He was appointed an umpire the following winter, when he was twenty-eight and Edith was fifteen. At that time he still looked on her as a kid, and treated her like one. Not till two years later did he realize all of a sudden that she wasn't just his cute "little sister" any more, or that when the schedule sent him there he was all excited for some other reason than because he was coming back to his own boarding house, or that there was a good deal more than brotherly love in the kiss he gave her when she welcomed him home. He knew he was stuck on her, and it scared him to death, and it ain't so hard to figure why.

He was thirty, and thirty sounds pretty near like a centurion to a gal seventeen. He had been a great big man the first time she seen him, when she was a little bit of a kid. By this time she probably thought of him as a grandfather, or at least a worn-out old uncle with three or four feet in the grave. He knew it was impossible to live in the same house with her all winter and not let her see that his feelings towards her had changed. The chances were that she would take it as a joke, and that would break him up. His only play was the big gamble—to tell her the truth and get it over with. Bleat is just like me in that respect as in many others: He can't stand suspense. He would rather know the worst than fear it.

Well, you can imagine how wild he went over the way she received the news—like it wasn't news at all, but the most natural thing in the world and she had been annoyed because he had held it out on her so long. She said their ages didn't make no difference, that hers might some time, but his never could; he would always be a boy just about old enough, though not bright enough, to enter high school. As for her mother, she said she had been expecting it for quite a while, but she was glad Bleat had held his proposal back till he was an umpire instead of making it while he was still playing ball, because if he took Edith to the ball park now, they wouldn't have to be separated while the game was going on. She probably had regular hired umpires mixed up with the guys that sit up in the stand, usually right behind a pillar, and not only umpire free of charge, but pay for the privilege. They are the boys that never make a mistake, though it ain't once in ten times that their decision agrees with ours. If it does, they reverse it.

There was never any question from the first in regards to where the couple were going to live. Any way you looked at it, the best idea was to stay right on at Edith's mother's. In the fall and winter, Bleat worked as a mechanic in a garage and made good money at it. And his job as umpire seemed safe as long as he wanted it. The ball players respected him and he hadn't no real trouble, just chasing a few fellows off the bench once in a while, mostly fellows that squawked on purpose so as to get chased to the clubhouse, where they could smoke. So Bleat earned enough to have a home of his own, but neither him or Edith wanted it, and Edith's mother was tickled to death to have them stay with her.

They would have been married five years now but for a break in luck. Whether the break was good or bad, only time will tell.

Bleat had a sister in Texas, and the sister and a husband who was a director of a bank in a town that you wouldn't want to call a one-horse town unless you were sore at the horse. Well, a depositor in the bank had a friend in South Dakota who had lost thirty dollars in a bank failure, so this friend wrote that banks were pretty risqué, and the depositor in Bleat's brother-in-law's bank spread the story around; and the next thing you know, he and all the other seven depositors withdrew their money, and the bank flopped and wiped out Bleat's brother-in-law's private fortune, which ran way up into four figures. While the brother-in-law was getting back on his feet, Bleat had to support him and his wife and their four kids, and that meant a postponement of Bleat's wedding.

Now, a while ago I was saying I supposed that most people considered umpires crazy and explaining why it wasn't necessarily true. But outside of special cases like Bleat (because his gal lived here) and myself (because I liked to see him happy), an umpire would have a tough time establishing his sanity if he admitted a desire to be assigned to this town, where sooner or later you're bound to get into the worst kind of a jam, no matter if the home club is struggling toothless and nailless for the tenth place and even the ushers have taken the whole week off for golf.

This ain't just talk or imagination. It's a matter of record. Ball players that were tongue-tied in other cities have flared up and been put out of games and fined and suspended here, and usually for less than no reason. Ball players that were so shy in New York and Brooklyn that you had to send out a habeas corpus for them when it was their turn to hit, they have to be brushed off the plate all the while since they joined this club. And just ask the umpires! Only be sure and ask them when they're in good humor. They'll tell you that they've seen more brawls and taken part in more real riots both with the athletes and fans of this metropolis than all the other county seats put together. The presidents of the two major loops, if they didn't want to be diplomatic, they'd testify that they hold special thanksgiving services whenever a series ends here without at least a bat boy getting soaked in the eye, and though it's been possible to economize in pretty near every item connected with baseball, the owners and managers of the two clubs, as well as the umpires that work in this fair city, are spending as much on postage for their squawks as during the years of the big boom.

Everybody has taken a shot at guessing the reason, but it sounds to me like one man's guess is as good as another, and they're all bad. Some lay it on the climate and say that nobody can live here all summer without getting crazy. But there's at least two other towns that can be just as hot and stay just as hot. Besides, that don't account for the umpires or the boys on the visiting club going haywire, too. Others claim it's because the population is made up of anarchists and reds from different countries in Europe and they learn the ball players to defy authority.

No, it's just this town, and you can't explain why, not by any logic. But it happens just the same, and it's only a question of whether you get off easy or hard. When it happens twice in half a season, like in Bleat's case, you're liable to get off hard. Personally I didn't get off so easy myself; and I don't mean what the crowd done to me physically, though a pair of swollen eyes and a broken nose and puffed lips and four loose teeth—I wouldn't recommend none of those ornaments as things a man ain't better off without. However, they're gone, which is more than I can say for the hurt of losing Bleat's company and having him suffer all he did suffer and always will suffer, just because he couldn't call a play different than he seen it—and because girls will be girls.

It was in May, a little over a year ago, when Bleat and I got our first assignment here for the season. This club had grabbed nine straight games, which everybody knew was way ahead of their speed, and they were in second place, reading down, not up. Their little third baseman from the Coast, Agnew, was hitting better than he could. Horner, the left-hander from Omaha, had won the five games he'd pitched and saved a couple for the other boys. Shayne finally got control of his knuckler and wasn't scared to throw it when he was in the hole. The way these three guys were going pepped up the whole club.

Of course, everybody with sense knew it was just a question of time till they would be fighting it out with Cincinnati for the championship of the slums, but in this town there was nobody with sense as far as baseball was concerned. They were already talking World's Series and wondering if young Agnew could be persuaded to live here all year if they gave him a house and a wife and two Sealyhams. Everybody that could get off—and there's nobody living here that can't—they were all out at the ball park every day.

Now, before I forget it, I'd better tell you that neither Edith or her mother had ever taken any interest in baseball, though Edith had attended a few games just to watch Bleat work. But now they both had the fever and went pretty near every day along with young Parvis, the boy who had rented the old schoolteacher's room when she died, which is why I said that her dying turned out to be more than a nuisance. Parvis was nineteen or twenty years old and the only way I know of to describe him is by saying that he looked just like what he was, a ukulele player. He played on the radio every day with some woman, and they both sang, and they were so good that they went on at ten o'clock in the morning. Edith liked him and felt sorry for him, because she said he was the best ukulele player in the country, but people didn't appreciate the ukulele like they did when it first came out. Bleat, of course, had to fix it for them to get seats at the ball park, and Edith was dumb enough to think he got passes.

Well, the club had won nine straight when we landed, and they were starting a series with Pittsburgh, which was leading the league by a couple of games. It was just a plain Friday, but, from the size of the crowd and the noise, you'd have thought it was the World's Series.

Bleat was working behind the plate, and he told me afterwards that before the first innings was over, he had a hunch that this young third baseman, Agnew, was another name for bad news. He was hitting way up over .400 and Snell had him batting third. The previous week he had slumped off a little, and Knowles, the Pittsburgh catcher, naturally spoke to him about it. Agnew alibied himself by laying it on the umpires, especially Rigler, claiming that Rig had it in for him and kept calling bad strikes on him, and he said there was a couple of times in Chicago when he'd had a notion to take a sock at Rigler.

Well, Agnew is back on the Coast now—the umpiring out there suits him better—so I don't know if you ever seen him or not, but he can't weigh more than a hundred and sixty, and he's five foot nine inches tall. In other words, his whole body is almost as big as Rigler's chest, and I'll tell you something more about Rig. If he had gone into professional boxing twenty-five or thirty years ago, he'd have won the heavyweight championship from whoever had it.

Anyway, Pittsburgh had French pitching. He was good, and nobody was doing much with him. Agnew had two chances to be a hero, two besides the one that caused the real misery. He came up with two out in the fourth innings and a man on second base and Pittsburgh ahead, 1 to 0. He hit the first ball a terrific blow, and it looked good for two or three bases, but Traynor made one of those impossible dives of his and it stuck in his glove. There was one out in the seventh and the score the same when Warren hit for three bases. Agnew came up whining about Traynor's lucky stab, and Bleat caught himself praying that French would strike him out. The prayer was answered, and Bleat wished he hadn't made it, because our young Agnew did his stuff in true busher style—forgetting that he had a bat until there was nothing to do with it except throw it at the bat boy as proof that Bleat was a swindler.

The next two guys got bases on balls, the only ones French gave all day, but they were more than enough to convince the bugs that Bleat had it in for Agnew, and all through the last two innings the booing was pretty near as good as Brooklyn's best. Somebody popped up to pull French out of that hole, and he wasn't in any more trouble till the rest of us were.

It was the last half of the ninth, and the score still 1 to 0 and only one guy left to get out, and the guy was Agnew. Once more he hit the first ball, and when I say he hit it, I mean he hit it. It went past half a dozen Waners and bounced off all the fences, and the kid was pretty close to third base when Lindstrom cut loose his peg. Vaughan's relay to the plate was a rifle shot, fast and true, but too late.

Oh, but wait a minute! What's this we see? It's French and Traynor and everybody else in a Pittsburgh uniform rushing at Knowles, their catcher; yelling, "Tag him! Tag him!" Knowles can't hear the command; the crowd is too noisy celebrating our hero's noble deed, the pinch home run that ties the score and saves the winning streak that was all but stopped at nine. Knowles can't hear, but his instinct tells him to look around, and the most interesting sight he sees is young Mr. Agnew, crawling towards him on his stomach, with an arm stretched out in the direction of the plate, but the hand at the end of the arm still a good eight inches short of its goal.

◇   ◇   ◇

Knowles's next instinct was to throw himself at the crawling body, and especially the outstretched arm, which pulled itself away in time to avoid a few compound fractures. Then Knowles obeyed the unheard "Tag him!" order and obeyed it in a big way. There wasn't any part of Agnew's anatomy that he didn't shove that big mitt into, beginning with the head, where it probably hurt the least. Of course, no one heard Bleat when he bleated "You're out!" either, but the motion that went with it was seen and understood, and not very well liked, so I judge.

I got to his side just as he was saying to Agnew, "But what did you come back for? Did you think you'd lost a collar button?" Then, "Take your hands off me, kid. I don't like to be petted in public."

Then I noticed that Agnew was resting his spikes on Bleat's feet. This is an old gag, but for some reason it never got popular with the guy that furnished the parking space. Bleat warned him once, but he didn't move, so Bleat spread his open hand flat against Agnew's face and pushed him, and down he went on his back. Whether he fell because he was off balance or to make it look like Bleat had hit him, is more than I know. I do know that both Agnew and Snell reported to the boss that Bleat had struck Agnew and knocked him down. I can understand Agnew making a statement like that, but not Snell. If he didn't see what happened himself, he ought to have taken somebody else's word besides Agnew's.

And you'll have to take somebody else's word besides mine for all that happened between then and the time I woke up at the hospital. What I've been telling you came off in the three or four seconds it took the crowd and the cops to reach us.

It was ten o'clock that evening before I came to for any length of time. Naturally, I asked for Bleat, and they said his face was all battered and bruised and the doctor had ordered him to stay in bed, but he had insisted on going out a little while. He got back to the hospital around eleven and came in to see me, and I was shocked at the way he looked; I don't mean the black-and-blue spots and swellings, but the expression on his face and in his eyes even when he tried to smile. I guessed that something had happened between him and Edith that hurt worse than our little afternoon lawn party. And I guessed right.

But first he told me about the telegram he'd got from the boss and the reply he'd sent. What the boss wanted to know was whether he had hit Agnew and knocked him down, as reported by Agnew and Manager Snell. There was no question, of course, about the decision at the plate. If there had been, Snell would have protested the game; at least, he'd have mentioned it.

And now, to show you how decent Bleat was, all he done was deny hitting Agnew, saying that Agnew was holding his arm and he told him to quit, and Agnew wouldn't quit, so he pushed him away with his open hand and Agnew fell down. Not a word about the names Agnew called him or about Agnew spiking his feet, and he only wanted me to send a telegram supporting his statement and denying theirs. Which you can bet I did, and I wanted to put in just a hint that Agnew had deliberately done the fall to get the crowd excited, but Bleat wouldn't let me. He said, "You might get him suspended," he said. "The longer he ain't in the game, the longer he'll be in the league," he said. "Let him pull a couple more of those 'creeping confessions' and he'll suspend himself for life."

Then he told me a little about the session with Edith. Bleat can take a joke on himself as well as anybody, and he figured that his face would give her a laugh, which it did. But he also figured on a few words of sympathy and a sigh of relief that he had escaped without any broken bones.

Well, it seems that she had always thought of Bleat as inhuman in regards to getting hurt. It hadn't worried her a bit when she seen those twenty or thirty thousand wolves run out on the field. She knew he could take care of himself. She had wanted to join the crowd herself, but Mr. Parvis wouldn't let her—Parvis is the ukulele player that took the schoolteacher's room.

As for her sympathy, she had been terribly sorry for that poor Agnew boy who had robbed himself of a home run because he was so honest. Why couldn't Bleat have pretended that he really had touched the plate even if he thought he hadn't? Those Pittsburgh men wouldn't have cared. They had been on top so often and won so many pennants and things that they must be sick of it. And Bleat was very unfair to call the Agnew boy out on strikes, when they weren't good strikes, because Mr. Parvis said they weren't, and the Agnew boy thought they weren't either, or else he wouldn't have lost his temper and thrown his bat on the ground when Bleat called him out. But the cruelest thing she had ever seen was Bleat hitting the Agnew boy and knocking him down when he was trying to explain that he had tried to be honest. It kind of scared her when she thought of marrying a man who had such poor control of his temper as Bleat.

And finally: Mr. Parvis had met the Agnew boy, and said he was awfully nice and a perfect gentleman, and not at all like a common ball player. And he was crazy about music, though he didn't sing or play any instrument, and Mr. Parvis had offered to give him ukulele lessons free, and some night soon Mr. Parvis was going to bring him to call and maybe learn him a few chords on the uke, and she would make Mr. Parvis wait till Bleat was all right again, so he could meet the Agnew boy in a social way, and when he knew how nice he was, maybe he wouldn't be so mean to him on the ball field.

There, brother, you have the explanation of the look in Bleat's eyes when he got back to the hospital that night, and never again did I see the twinkle in them that made you want to be with him and share in the good time he seemed to be having.

The doctor said positively that we mustn't work any more during the Pittsburgh series here, but we decided to defy orders and not give these hyenas the satisfaction of thinking they had done us any real damage. What with cuts and bruises and scratches from top to toe it was tough enough to change our clothes twice a day. The games were close, and the only thing that saved us was that all the hard decisions went against Pittsburgh and the other visiting clubs that followed them in.

As it was, we were booed from the minute we showed up till the game was over, and Bleat took a terrible lot of abuse, especially after one of the papers printed a picture of Agnew laying on the ground and Bleat standing over him with his fist doubled up. How that fist got doubled up I don't know, because I seen the thing happen, and I swear that Bleat's hand was open and that he pushed him, and not hard, at that. I suggested to Snell that as long as Bleat hadn't reported Agnew for calling him names or spiking him, and hadn't got him fined or suspended, it would only be fair if the kid told the newspaper boys that Bleat hadn't really socked him like the picture showed. But Snell said the kid insisted that Bleat had hit him as hard as he could. Worst of all, some young third baseman sent the picture to the boss, and when we got to New York, Bleat was called on the carpet and bawled out for socking an undersized, green, innocent boy whose mistakes were due to being young and inexperienced. What hurt Bleat most was the boss not taking his word when he swore he hadn't hit him. Bleat never sent in a false report in his life.

Well, there ain't much more to tell. The next time we came here, Snell's club was normal—only three games ahead of Cincinnati and losing four or five games a week by scores like 13 to 2, 15 to 4, and 8 to 0. Snell was shaking up his batting order every night, which seems to be a manager's pet idea of the best way to keep the other club from hitting. This series was with the New York club, then leading the league, and the attendance the first day was 122, which was also Agnew's batting average.

Bleat had left me and gone home as soon as we hit the town. When I met him at the ball park, he was lower than ever, and he told me why. Edith hadn't been up to welcome him, and it seems that she and Parvis, the ukulele strummer, had attended a party of radio people. Not only that, but when she did get up, she just had time to say hello to Bleat and grab a cup of coffee before she was off again, because she had promised Parvis to go downtown with him while he did his broadcast. And, to top it off, she had picked this night for the little gathering at home when Agnew was to come and meet Bleat socially.

Bleat said, "For his own sake and mine," he said, "I hope he behaves himself this afternoon so I can behave myself this evening."

Well, when a fresh young kid like Agnew hits around .450 for the first six weeks of his first season in the big league and then drops off to pretty near nothing inside of a month, even his mother would rather visit with a mad police dog, and this sweet youth sounded the keynote the first time he came to bat, saying to Bleat, "I hear I'm going to spend the evening with you, like hanging around all afternoon with a half-witted umpire wasn't bad enough." Bleat had decided that his best bet was to keep his mouth shut as long as he could stand it, so he didn't answer.

It was another blow when Agnew let him know later on that he had been at Edith's house before, and it took all the self-control he had not to punch him when he cracked that it was a crime for an old stiff like Bleat to ask a young girl like Edith to marry him, and that he would steal her from Bleat, himself, if he liked her style of beauty; he had made up his mind to leave her to Parvis, and Parvis was going to get her, too. And Bleat knew in his heart that this was the truth.

Agnew had a terrible day at bat, but his club was one run ahead going into the ninth innings and it took another boner on his part to give the New York club two runs and the ball game. Shayne gave the first guy a base on balls, and somebody beat out a bunt. The next guy wanted to bunt, too, but Shayne walked him and filled up the bases. The count went to two and two on Terry, and he hit the next one a mile a minute down the third base line. Agnew got it on the first hop and had a set-up double play by way of the plate and first base. But he must have thought there was one out, for he stepped on third base, making the force play there, and then pegged to first base for the double. The tying run was in and there was a man on second base with two out.

From then on, Shayne didn't know if it was cricket or billiards. He walked two more guys and filled up the bases again, and Snell yanked him and stuck in Horner. Terry sent Leslie up to hit. Horner got two strikes on him and then threw three balls. Two of them were way outside and the third was close—close enough to start some squawking. Then came the deciding one, and you could have called it either way; that is, if you weren't Bleat. It was about two inches outside and two inches low, and Bleat said, "Take a walk."

The rest of the story is in the history books. Knowing what Snell would say to him for that messed-up double play, Agnew wanted to be the first to alibi himself. He was at Bleat ahead of Horner or anybody, calling him all those pretty names and doing that spike dance on Bleat's toes. Bleat said, "I hope your photographer is here. The way this picture is going to look will prove that I didn't sock you that other day."

Agnew wanted to take a long nap after the first punch, but Bleat seemed to think he wasn't in a comfortable position. Not till about the sixth time he'd picked him up and put him down was he satisfied with the way he was laying.

Maybe I didn't tell you that Edith and Parvis were watching from up in the stand. Till Edith got sick. Parvis told me this later on, when I went to her house for some things Bleat had forgot. He also told me that he and Edith were engaged, and he hoped Bleat wouldn't have no hard feelings toward him. I don't blame him for that hope.

Bleat is working in a garage and living with his sister's family in Texas. His sister wrote me that he was spoiling those four kids, bringing them toys every time he comes home from work. He's brought them everything except a ukulele.

THE COST OF BASEBALL

◊

AS A BASEBALL FAN you may think that a major league ball club would be a money-maker in the hands of a truck gardener, that a big-league franchise is synonymous with success, and that it's all luck and no business ability.

But baseball is a business, a mighty big one, and it requires sound business sense of a peculiar kind to be successful in it. A business ignoramus will fail just as quickly and as surely in the national pastime as in any other walk of life, and a man without nerve will fail. Perhaps you can't figure how nerve is required to run a "proposition" which, as a rule, nets an annual profit of from $10,000 to $175,000 per magnate. It becomes our duty, then to do the figuring for you, to show you why a "piker" would stand no chance in the game.

If the sun always shone on holidays, Saturdays, and Sundays; if there were no such thing as a training trip; if Bakers, Benders, Schultes, McGraws, Archers, and Barrys were as thick as chop suey and as cheap as rice; if fans could be convinced that their money entitled them to seats only, and not a part in the conversation as well—what a joy ride Mr. Magnate's life would be.

Unfortunately, it is not thus. To make a barrel of money he must spend three or four barrels, and the worst of it is that the aforesaid one barrel is anything but guaranteed.

It is not difficult to understand that receipts stop with the end of the playing season. Expenses stop never. In fact, Mr. Owner is so busy digging from the first day of November until the twelfth of April that he almost forgets how to do anything else.

The past season's business is finished, between interruptions, by

It is necessary to stipulate that this article (*Collier's* March 2, 1912) is straight reportage—not travesty. In 1914 the total budget for a major-league baseball team was less than the 1991 salary of a .200 hitter.

the middle of November. Then start the preparations for the next campaign, the most important and arduous of which are the spring training plans.

If you have never planned and executed a training trip, you have not tasted of life's bitterness. The only things needed to make this jaunt artistically and financially successful are thirty-five consecutive March and April days without rain, a thermometer always above 60, a complete squad of satisfied ball players, a smooth practice field in some quiet Southern town, and a list of dates in big Southern cities, not more than a hundred miles apart, extending over three weeks, and each successive date bringing you nearer home. If only one club had to make this trip, there would be nothing to the task of schedule-making, but it must be remembered that the owners of sixteen teams are all looking for the best dates for the same three weeks. He is a wise and farsighted magnate who books some of his practice games two or three years in advance.

These dates are for the slow journey homeward. The owner must also select and secure his "permanent"training camp, where the athletes can spend three weeks, right at the start, getting into shape by practicing among themselves.

Well, your owner feels pretty good when he has completed his schedule of spring games and landed a desirable "permanent" camp. He continues to feel good till the weather begins cutting up. Bad weather is the baseball magnate's worst enemy, and it usually beats the stuffing out of him in the spring.

To show what rain and other pests can do to a training schedule, take the testimony of John I. Taylor, who thought a California trip the proper caper for his Boston Red Sox last spring. The team did succeed in getting to the Pacific Coast. When it got there it stayed over three weeks—indoors. Some of the youngsters demonstrated to the entire satisfaction of Manager Donovan that they could deal cards gracefully and shoot Kelly pool. What he learned about their ball playing ability they told him, and their accounts were naturally prejudiced.

There were plenty of good dates on the club's return schedule. About two of them were filled, rain and cold weather being on the daily menu. Mr. Taylor said to himself: "I'm certainly glad we've got those four Cincinnati games on the card. They'll give us good practice and a nice bunch of money." Three of the Cincinnati battles were called off on account of bad weather. The fourth was played in a drizzle, and the receipts for the "series" were $40.

Ball players' salaries are not paid until the beginning of the playing season. But their expenses, those which the owner must pay, start with the training trip. To begin with, there is the transportation from their homes or from the rendezvous to the Southern camp. For the average squad, with thirty-five men on its roster, this amounts to $500 or $600. Then, too, a great many big league teams "pay the freight" for newspaper correspondents. For meals on the train—and this holds good throughout the playing season as well—each athlete is given $3 a day, or $1 per meal. There are athletes who eat that case note three times daily. There are others who need sleep so badly that they don't climb out of their berths in time for breakfast, and who are so busily engaged playing cards that the dining car is taken off at noon and in the evening before they realize it. They have just time to rush into a railway eating house twice a day and grab sandwich, pie, and coffee. But the $2.50 thus saved does not go back into Mr. Magnate's purse.

The training camp reached, the players are taken to their hotel in an omnibus, an expense that is repeated every three or four days during the season while the club is on the road. It would never do for these delicate young men to walk.

The hotel bill for the athletes, from thirty to thirty-five of them, for about three weeks at $3 a day, approximates $2,000. Also to be reckoned are transportation to and from the park where the practicing is done, baths, massage, etc. Remember, gentlemen, it's all going out and nothing coming in at this stage of the game.

Once in a decade the owner gets the proper combination of good dates and good weather. Then he breaks even or makes a small profit on the training trip. As a rule, however, his loss is in the neighborhood of $5,000, and he usually counts himself fortunate if none of his valuable athletes breaks a valuable arm or leg. The trip must be made on the chance that the players will get in condition, and also for the advertising.

While the team is being thoroughly soaked in the South, repairs and changes are being made at the home park, whether it's a new one or not. Repairs and improvements on the average park aggregate between $4,000 and $5,000 a year. Counting the cost of the training trip as $5,000, a really conservative figure, and estimating the repairs at $5,000, other lesser expenditures swell the total outlay, before the season starts, to something like $13,000.

That brings us round to the opening of the playing season. The joy of opening day's receipts would be doubled but for the sickening thought that the real expenses have just begun. Of course, the biggest item is the salary list. This runs from $55,000 to $75,000 a year, depending on the make-up of the club. It is a strange fact that the highest salaried teams sometimes come nearest to setting new records for total defeats. That a club wins a pennant or finishes second is no sign that it is well paid.

The Boston Nationals, whose followers went wild with joy if they had a winning streak lasting two days, pulled down more coin for their rather feeble efforts than many of the clubs that were fattening their victory columns at Mr. Tenney's expense. In fact, two privates in the Boston ranks were getting heavier pay checks than two managers in the same league.

The team composed of two or three veterans and a bunch of kids does not part with nearly as much money on the first and fifteenth of the month as the club which boasts several seasoned performers and a few youngsters. Thus, the Chicago Cubs, as they were made up last year, were the highest paid team in either big league, and Mr. Murphy's salary list totaled just about $75,000.

Most of the major league magnates of the present day own their ball parks. Those who do not, pay from $6,000 to $25,000 annual rental, the amount depending on the size of the city, the location of the plant, etc.

The third largest item in the annual expense bill is transportation. Railroad fare is two cents per mile straight, there being no special rate. It is the aim of the schedule makers to have the annual mileage nearly equal for all clubs. Each owner figures about $12,500 for railroad and Pullman bills each year, and that is also a conservative estimate.

The athletes pay their own living expenses "at home." Their transportation and hotel bills on the road are footed by the club. The hotels alone cost each owner $8,000 annually, aside from the training trip.

Nor must it be thought that expenditures are light when the team is at home. Ticket sellers and ticket takers draw from $1.50 to $2.50 a day, to say nothing of a lot of abuse. Police protection costs $20 to $50 per day, depending on the size of the crowd. The total for the year for this protection is about $1,800 on the average. The aggregate paid out for ticket men, ushers, groundkeepers and their assistants, and "handy men" around a ball park will easily foot up to $6,500 annually.

The purchase and printing of tickets may appear a small item, but it amounts to something in a year. Advertising in the papers totals about $1,200 a month when the club is at home.

The wise magnate has new home and traveling uniforms for his players each year, and this entails an expense of about $500, figuring two uniforms for each of twenty-five men.

Each club has a secretary, a man of all work, who is virtually business manager, and an assistant secretary, the former drawing about $2,500 or $3,000 and the latter $1,800: two or more scouts, the "head" scout getting $2,500 and the others $1,500 apiece, and a trainer, whose salary is $1,000 or $1,200, but who usually is handed a bonus which brings the total stipend to $1,500.

The secretary's job is about as far from a sinecure as one can imagine. A good secretary must be a natural born actor. When he enters a railroad office, he must wear a dark frown and impress the agent as a man to be feared. In the presence of the owner, he must act the role of Shylock, varying it occasionally with a portrayal of Chesterfield. With the ball players he must appear a good fellow without actually being one. He must make them think they are stopping at swell hotels or sleeping in lower berths whether they are or not.

The trainer must be a veritable Battling Nelson or Hugo Kelly, able to stand terrible punishment. He is blamed for the loss of every game that is lost, for he is usually considered a "jinx"; held responsible for Mr. Star Pitcher's sore arm, even when the soreness was acquired by sleeping in a taxicab with the arm suspended out of the window; soundly "called" as being the cause of the short stop's headache, even though said headache is the result of the satisfaction of a pent-up thirst; and otherwise generally maltreated.

Scouts are supposed to visit minor league and college towns, discover young, undeveloped stars and secure recruits capable of making good on a big league club, and also to find glaring faults and incurable weaknesses in youngsters on whom the big leaguers have received "tips," thus saving time and money for their employers. They are supposed to do those things, but they generally do the opposite, heralding as wonders young men who can hit curve balls about as easily as they can paint landscapes, passing up as "lemons" youthful Cobbs and Tinkers, and accomplishing all manner of things designed to drive their bosses crazy.

Thus it happens that, of ten or fifteen men added to each big league roster annually, one or two show class enough to be retained. Of course, the club doesn't always suffer a total loss on the players sent back to the "bushes." Minor league owners must pay for them, but the major league magnate never profits on such a deal.

The expenditure for new material, including players bought from other big league teams, and men purchased or "drafted" from the minor leagues, averages around $20,000. The amount varies with the needs of the club and the policy of the owner. The fact that his team has won the pennant one season does not signify that the magnate can afford to stand pat for the next. The Detroit Club was champion of the American League in 1908 and paid out over $10,000 for fresh material between that season and the following one, nor did it increase its strength to any appreciable extent. The New York Giants, finishing second in the National League race the same year, spent $20,000 for three men that fall, besides paying out a lot of money in "drafts." Frequently some minor leaguer gets such a reputation that five or six big league owners are tempted to bid large sums for his release, and, very frequently also, the owner who finally secures him for $7,000 or $8,000 finds that he would have been just as well off if he had spent the money for walnut shucks.

Then, too, there is the league fund. In the American League every club sends to the president two and a half cents for each paid admission to the home grounds. From the fund thus made up are paid the salaries of the president, secretary, and umpires, rental for the executive offices and all running expenses of the organization.

It is the policy of some clubs to travel in style and of others to "go cheap." For that reason it is impossible to compile figures that fit all the big league clubs alike. The following, however, is a fair estimate of the average annual expenditure of a major league baseball club:

Players' salaries	$65,000
Purchase of players	20,000
Transportation	12,500
Rental of park	15,000
Park salaries	6,500
Hotels	8,000
Office expense (including salaries)	5,500
Repairs	4,500
Spring trip	5,000
Players' supplies (uniforms, balls, etc.)	4,000
Park police	1,800
Insurance	1,500

Taxicabs, carriages, etc	900
League fund	10,000
Trainer	1,500
Scouts	4,000
Sundries (advertising, printing, etc.)	3,300
TOTAL	$169,000

The sixteen major league owners, then, have a total annual expense of $2,704,000, and it costs each of them about $463 a day, all the year round, to run his club; or, counting only the playing days, about $1,000 per day. Barney Dreyfuss of Pittsburgh has stated that his daily outlay, during the playing season, is over $800. It is safe to say that the minimum is in the neighborhood of $750 and the maximum almost $1,200.

Ponder these things, Mr. Fan, and perhaps you will be more content with your own lot, and less envious of the gentleman who gets that dollar or half dollar of yours on a summer afternoon. Perhaps, too, you will feel a touch of sympathy for him when, on a Saturday in July, dark clouds gather above you. He's not going to the poorhouse. No, but the asylum is not so far away.

THE 1919 WORLD SERIES

◇

These syndicated articles (The Bell Syndicate, 1919) reprinted from the *San Francisco Examiner* were peppered with typographical errors which have been corrected here.

Certain Chicago White Sox players conspired to throw the 1919 World Series against the underdog Cincinnati Reds. After the second game Lardner joined other reporters in singing this version of "I'm Forever Blowing Bubbles":

> I'm forever throwing ball games
> Pretty ball games in the air.
> I come from Chi.
> I hardly try,
> Just go to bat and fade and die.
> Fortune's coming my way,
> That's why I don't care,
> I'm forever throwing ball games,
> And the gamblers treat us fair.

Although he could not print what he knew about the series, his columns convey his refusal to pretend that it was on the up-and-up.

Eight White Sox players were subsequently banned from baseball for their participation in fixing the series: Lefty Williams, Eddie Cicotte, Chick Gandil, Happy Felsch, Shoeless Joe Jackson, Swede Risburg, Fred McMullin, and Buck Weaver.

Game 1—October 1
  CHI 1
  CIN 9

Game 2—October 2
  CHI 2
  CIN 4

Game 3—October 3
  CHI 3
  CIN 0

Game 4—October 4
  CHI 0
  CIN 2

Game 5—October 6
  CHI 0
  CIN 5

Game 6—October 7
  CHI 5
  CIN 4

Game 7—October 8
  CHI 4
  CIN 1

Game 8—October 9
  CHI 5
  CIN 10

Gents: Lardner Says the Umpires Interfere With His 'Dope' on Big Series

You Never Can Tell What They Are Going to Do Declares Expert Who Compares Players of Both Teams and a Few Who Are Not

Cincinnati, Sept. 28—Gents: In doping out a conflict like the threatened world serious, an expert like myself works under a heavy strain as they's no way of telling what those d—m umpires is going to do and in the case of a couple of even matched ball clubs like the White Sox and Reds neither 1 of which has ever lose a world serious why some finicky notion of some umpire is libel to raise havioc.

An expert's 1st duty then is to make a study of the umpires that has been chose to rule or ruin the comeing serious and a comparison between the 4 of them in this case shows the advantage to be all in their favor. Suppose for inst. Heinie Groh was to hit a high fly and nobody catched it, but the umpires got it in their head to play a practical joke on the big Dane and call him out why they wouldn't be no recourses for Heinie only to walk off the field and join the New York Yanks. So as I say a man that is not in the umpires confidents and trys to make predictions may make a monkey of himself instead.

But wile it never settled a world serious 1 way or the other to figure out whether Limbo has it all over Bimbo as a bench warmer or vice versa why still and all its a habit amidst the experts, and one that don't do it lays himself open to the abuse that is always heaped onto a reformer, so I may as well try and remember who is on the different clubs and set down the facts about them in Black and White and plain water.

Reds Pitching Staff Savors of the Bible

Starting off with the cathers, Bill Rarideh was born in Bedford, Ind., and Ray Schalk was born in Litchfield, Ill., so neither one of them is libel to be dazzled by the big crowds. The edge, if any, belongs to Bill, as he has lived more different places than Ray. As for Ivy Wingo and Byrd Lynn, why Byrd has more ys in his 8 letters, but when it comes to slideing home they's very few people afraid of a Byrd wile the White Sox don't know but maybe Ivy is poison. Both clubs will miss Larry McLean.

Coming to the pitchers, I had to buy a paper to see who was the regulars on the Reds and the only name that pitched for them that day was Luque, but I suppose the others is Mathew, Mark and John. Mathew is probably Mathewson's old man and has got some of the family traits, which means he will have about as much luck in a world serious as the crown prince at Verdun. Mark, of course, has got a unfortunate name, but that don't seem to make no differents in a pitcher, as you take Ruth for inst. and you wouldn't never think it was a girl. I looked up John's record and about the only place where he mentions athaletics is where he outrun Peter and you can't judge nothing by that, as Peter may of triped over his beard or something.

It's an Even Break Between Hoblitzel and Isbell

None of the White Sox pitchers has ever wrote a gospel and any way they's only 2 of them to hear some people tell it. The 2 is Wms. and Cicotte, of which Cicotte is 1 of the most baffling pitchers in baseball, as you can't never be sure 2 days in succession how he is going to be pronounced. Wms. was baptized Claude, but has growed up normal outside of being a left hander. Of the others in the list Dick Kerr throws left handed and hits the same way, while Grover Lowdermilk throws right handed and hits seldom.

It looks like a even break between Hoblitzell and Isbell on the initial sack, as I have nicknamed 1st base, and at second base the rivals appears to be peers on paper, though they tell me Morris Rath is going to get marred this fall, but on the other hand you take a bird like Collins and they's no telling what he will do under fire, as a man like he is liable to blow sky high in a pinch. For inst. in the last game vs. the Giants 2 yrs. ago he lose his head completely and run home backwards from 3d base though Heinie Zimmerman that was chasing him is 1 of the fastest men in the Natl. League and can beat his own throws.

Moran and Gleason Widely Different Types

The shortstops can be past over, as they seldom never cut any figure in a event of this kind, and that brings us to Weaver and Groh at 3d. base both of which is the greatest 3d. baseman in the game today.

Comparisons is obvious but they tell me Heinie is libel to quit as for inst. when he was first born his old man said Heinie Groh and Heinie started but soon give it up.

The least said about the 2 outfields the better as they are about equally bad and the only chance for a argument is who has got the cutest nickname Shoeless Joe Jackson or Greasy Neale.

The rival mgrs. is widely different types as Moran gets his results by rough houseing wile Gleason is the soft spoken effeminate kind that a person would think to hear him talk that he was secretary of war or something. In the off season Moran is a Deutscher Artz at Fitchburg, Mass., wile the big Greek runs a handkerchief store in Philly. Neither 1 of them is hardily out of their teens you might say.

As far as the utility men is conserned it looks to me like it was a exageration to call them that.

Lardner Finds Cincinnati Baseball
Mad, But Purse Is Out of Danger

Our Expert Delivers Presentation Speech at Reds' Banquet and Delves Into Players' Past

Cincinnati, Sept 29—Well, gents! Several times dureing the past month I have heard people say that if Cincy win the pennant the old burg would go crazy but I didn't know how nuts they really was till they called me up and said they would pay me money to come down there and make a speech. This was after the flag was win and it seems the town wanted to give the boys some reward for their grand fight and they had decided to give them Rookwood vases and needed somebody to come down there and explain why.

Well before I went I read somewheres that this was the 1st. time Cincinnati had ever win a pennant since they's been agonized baseball but when I got there I seen plainly that it was the 1st. time any town had ever done it. The old burg was raving mad but it hadn't went to their purse and when I mentioned the jack I had on me that the boys in Chi had sent down to bet at evens why all as I could hear was 7 and 8 to 5.

Well Geo. Golde that owns a bunch of stock in the Reds give a dinner at the Business Men's Club for the athaletes and I and they had a prune colored orchestra that sung parodys about the different stars that nobody had ever heard sung before includeing the orchestra. Well I asked Sherwood Magee if the team was all there and he said all but Jake Daubert and Charley See a young outfielder and Pitcher Luque. So I says "That's one for the minstrels." So he says what did I mean. So I said well you say to me, you say: "Mis' Lahdnah, who am the playahs that isn't heah outside of Mis' Daubert"? Then I say to you "Well Mr. Magee, who are the absent players besides Mr. Daubert"? Then you say "Luque and See."

After the dinner they took us over to Music Hall that don't only hold 4 or 5000 people and they was all there and I and the ball players and Mayor Galvin set up on the stage amidst the pottery and I was as cool as a waffle iron and finely the mayor introduced me in a few well chose words quite a few of them and I got up there to talk and for the benefit of those that wasn't there to hear me as well as those who was I will tell you what I said in part.

"Ladies and Cuckoos: I hadn't no idear I would be called on for a speech tonight, but I generally always keep one in my pocket so I will read it to you. I don't know a whole lot about your ball club but I do think that while some of the ball players had something to do with the winning of the championship the greater portion of the credit should be given to the management of William A. Phelon and Pat Moran. (Applause.)

Neither Club Ever Lost a World's Series

"I presume a great many of you is wild to know how I think the serious is going to come out as I picked Willard down at Toledo. Well, cuckoos, it is impossible to tell in this case as neither of the 2 clubs ever lose a serious of this kind though back in 1843 Cincinnati played for the world's championship but it didn't count on acct. of the Natl. Commission not getting nothing out of it and I have even forgot how the games resulted though I can remember rideing out to the opening clash in a go cart pushed by Hugh S. Fullerton. (Laughter.)

"A great many of you cuckoos may resent me being here as I am supposed to be from Chicago but I want to assure you that I am so strong for the Reds that before I left old Chi I went to Ban Johnson and got him to promise that he wouldn't suspend none of your pitchers till the serious was over. (Applause.)

"The other day somebody told me they was going to be a world serious and that I was going to write something about it so I thought I better go out to a ball game and see how many men they was on a side. The game I seen was between the Cubs and Philadelphia and Philadelphia looked just like a club that Pat Moran got canned for manageing them. (Applause.)

"Well, cuckoos, when I landed here this A.M. I called up the man that had asked me to make this speech and asked him what was I to talk about and he said the Reds and I said who is on the Reds so he give me a list and I looked them over and only found 4 of them that I knowed personly outside of Pat Moran and Sallee who I give him the nickname of Slim, but I would like to meet Ring as he must be a grand fellow. The 4 I know best is Dutch Reuther and Bill Rariden and Sherwood Magee and Morris Rath. Bill Rariden was with the Boston club when I use to pretend to work there and his club use to tie up the score every day in the 9th. inning with a pop fly over the right field fence and lose out in the 13th. Bill started the season with a brand new glove and at the end of the season the glove was brand new as none of the other pitchers could throw a ball that far. (Shouts of laughter.)

Morris Proves He Must Have Been Sick

"Morris Rath was with the White Sox and 1 day we was playing in Washington and it was Walter Johnson's turn to pitch so at 11 A. M. Morris said to Manager Callahan I am sick but Manager Callahan said I don't believe it so he made Morris play and Morris got three hits off of Walter and then Cal knowed he must of been telling the truth. (Applause.)

"I bumped into Mr. Reuther in the spring of 1913 in San Francisco when he was pitching for St. Mary's College and the White Sox played them a exhibition game and murdered Dutch with a total of 1 hit which was a couple ft. foul and as for Sherwood Nottingham Magee why it was in 1872 when the Cubs was parked in Philly over Sunday and arranged a exhibition game at Atlantic City and Mac was then with the Philadelphia club and use to spend the Sabbath on the Boardwalk. Well we went down there the Saturday night before and I and Frank Schulte and Harry Steinfeldt was walking along the walk and a guy from N. Y. come along and stopped us and asked if we was members of the Cubs. So Schulte says yes this is Harry Steinfeldt the best 3d. baseman in the country. So the N. Y. bird said Arthur Devlin is the best 3d. baseman in the country so Frank hit him and knocked him for a gool. Well wile the poor bird was still laying in the ditch along come Sherwood and says what is the matter Frank are you in trouble? No trouble said Frank I just had a little fight. I will take it off your hands said Mac. (No laughter.) That is all there is to that story. (Applause).

Mayer and Mitchell Surprise of Season

"I don't know the rest of the Reds very well outside of Gary Herrmann and I read in the paper the other day where he had decided to make the serious go 9 games this yr. instead of 7 so that more people would get a chance to enjoy it but personally I think his motive was to give more of Gleason's pitchers a chance to pitch. (No applause.)

"This brings us to the business of the evening. Most presents gave to baseball players on occasions like this is absolutely useless but the gifts presented to the Reds tonight will keep them busy all winter wondering what to do with them. Gents of the Reds I take great pleasure in presenting to you on behalf of whoever is giveing them away these beautiful Rookwood vases which you should ought to pronounce vases on acct. of them being $2000.00 worth of them."

Several times dureing the speech I was interrupted by crys of Lauder on acct. of people not knowing how I pronounce my name or else they was trying to convey the idear that I am as funny as the other great Scotch comedian. Well when it was over I slipped out the stage entrance and catched an obscure train for Indianapolis and here I am safe in sound.

As for my personal feelings about the serious I have lived in Chi a No. of yrs. but always recd. fine treatment in Cincinnati so I only wished both clubs could win 5 straight and now they'se nothing more to be said till Pat and the Kid pulls the surprise of the season and sends Erskine Mayer and Roy Mitchell out to warm up for the opening of the fray.

Well, Gents: The Chisox Won't Forfeit the Series

Lardner Finds Chicago Team Diving Into Grapefruit; Then Interviews Umps.

Cincinnati, Sept. 30.—Gents: The world series starts tomorrow with a big surprise. A great many people figured that the White Sox would be scared out and would never appear. But sure enough, when we woke up this morning and came down to breakfast, here was the White Sox as big as life and willing to play.

The first bird I seen amidst them was Ray Schalk, the second catcher.

"Well, Cracker," I said, "I never expected to see you down here, as I had been told that you would quit and would never appear."

"Well, Biscuit," was his reply, "here we are and that's the best answer." So after all that is said and done the White Sox is down here and trying to win the first 2 games on their merits, so it looks like the series would not be forfeited after all.

Most of the experts went to the 2 different managers to try and learn who was going to pitch the opening game. So to be different from the rest of them as usual I passed up the two managers and went to the umpires. The first one I seen was Cy Rigler and I have known him all my life.

"Who is going to win, Cy?" I asked. "I don't know," was his ample reply. You can take that tip or leave it. Personaly I am betting on his word. He will give them the best of it if possible.

The next umpire I seen was Quigley. "My system," he said, "is to call everybody out." The two American League umpires could not be seen as they were both up writing their stuff, but you can be sure that neither of them will give anybody the best of it.

It Looks Like a Free Hitting Game

That brings us to the hotel accommodations. A large Chicago newspaper has got the price rm. of the lot, namely the smoking rm. off the ball rm. in the Gibson. This means that if anybody wakes up at

3 in the morning and wants to smoke why they can do so without moving out of their rm. and they want to dance why all as they have to do is go in the next rm. and look for a pardner.

A great many people have written in to this hotel to ask how I am going to bet so they can do the opposite and make big money. Well, Gents., I might as well tell you where I stand. I don't believe either club can win as neither one of them has got a manager. But I do know both of the so called managers personally, and I have asked them who is going to pitch the opening game and they both say everybody on the staff so it looks like a free hitting game with Gerner and Mayer in there at the start and Mitchell and Lowdermilk to relieve them, but neither has made any provisions in regards to who is going to relieve us newspaper guys.

The other day as you may remember, I tried to make a comparison of the two clubs man for man, and when I come to the shortstops why, I said the logical thing, which is, that no shortstop can win the serious as nobody ever hits to the shortstops in a big event like this. But thousands of birds wrote in personal letters to know what I thought of the two shortstops anyway, so I suppose I have got to tell them.

Two Stars of Series Have Been Overlooked

Well, of the two shortstops mentioned, Risberg and Kopf, will be in there at the start of the serious but they will both be took out before the serious is 9 games old. Comparing the both of them, Risberg is a Swede but on the other hand Kopf hits from both sides of the plate. Both of them is tricky and is libel to throw a ball to a different base than expected. Kopf is the better looking, but Risberg is the tallest and if they ever try to drive a high line drive over his head they will get fooled.

The two stars of the coming serious has both been overlooked by the experts, and I refer to Sherwood Magee and John Collins, whom a lot of you think won't be in there. Even if they are not they are both good fellows.

Another question the public keeps asking we experts is who get the advantage out of having the serious nine games instead of seven. Well, gents, all I can say is it isn't the newspaper men. Further and more I wouldn't be surprised if neither ball club liked the new regime as I have nicknamed it, as it looks to me like both mgrs. would use up all the pitchers they have got tomorrow and wouldn't know what to do next.

All together, it looks like a long serious and whoever made it nine games had it in for us.

Daubert Fools Lardner

REFUSES TO STAY DOWN

Sox Lack "Strategem"

Cincinnati (O.), Oct. 1.—Gents: Up to the eighth innings this pm. we was all setting there wondering what to write about and I happened to be looking at Jake Daubert's picture on the souvenir program and all of a sudden Jake fell over and I thought he was dead so I said to the boys:

"Here is your story. Jacob E. Daubert was born in Shamokin, Pa., on the 17 of April, 1886, and lives in Schuykill Pa. and began playing with the Kane, Pa., Club in 1907. With Cleveland in 1908 and Toledo for two years. Joined the Brooklyn Club in 1910 and remained there until this season. Then joined the Cincinnati Reds and fell dead in the 8th inning of the 1st game of the World Serious."

So everybody got up and cheered me and said that was a very funny story but all of a sudden again Jake stood up and looked at the different pts of the compass and walked to 1st base and wasn't dead at all and everybody turned around and hissed me for not giving them a good story.

Well Gents I am not to blame because when a man has got a fast ball like Grover Lowdermilk and hits a man like Jake in the temple, I generally always figure they are dead and the fact that Jake got up and walked to 1st base is certainly not my fault and I hope nobody will hold it vs me.

That was only 1 case where Mr. Gleason's strategy went amuck. His idear there was to kill the regular 1st baseman and then all Mr. Moran would have left to do would be to either stick Dutch Reuther on 1st base where he couldn't pitch or else stick Sherwood Magee over there where he couldn't coach at third base. But Jake gummed it all up by not dying.

Well another part of Mr. Gleason's strategy was dressing the White Sox in their home uniforms so as they would think they was playing on the home grounds in front of a friendly crowd but the trouble with that was that the Reds was all dressed in their home uniforms so as you couldn't tell which club was at home and which wasn't and it made both of them nervous. Then to cap off the climax Mr. Gleason goes and starts a pitcher that everybody thought he was going to start which took away the element of surprise and made a joker out of the ball game.

If he had of only started Erskine Mayer or Bill James or any of the other boys that I recommended why the Reds breath would have been took away and even if they had of hit they couldn't of ran out their hits.

The trouble with the White Sox today was that they was in there trying to back up a nervous young pitcher that never faced a big crowd in a crux before and when he got scared and blowed why it was natural for the rest of them to also blow up. But just give these young Chicago boys a chance to get use to playing before a big crowd with money depending on it and you will be surprised at how they get on their ft and come back at them.

Nobody should ought to find fault with Mr. Gleason, however, for what happened today. As soon as it was decided that they would have 9 games in this serious why the Kid set down and figured that the rules called for 9 men on a side and if 1 Red was killed per day and the serious run the full 9 games why they would only be 1 man left to play the final game and 1 man cant very well win a ball game even vs the White Sox the way they looked. But Daubert didn't die as expected and they will know better next time then to hit a left handed 1st baseman in the egg.

As for the game itself they has probably never been a thriller game in a big serious. The big thrill come in the 4th innings when everybody was wondering if the Sox would ever get the 3rd man out. They finely did and several occupants of the press box was overcome. The White Sox only chance at that pt was to keep the Reds in there hitting till darkness fell and made it a illegal game but Heinie Groh finely hit a ball that Felsch could not help from catching and gummed up another piece of stratagem.

Before the game a band led by John Philip Sousa played a catchy air called the Stars and Stripes Forever and it looks to me like everybody would be whistling it before the serious runs a dozen more games.

It now looks like the present serious would be 1 big surprise after another and tomorrow's shock will occur when the batterys is announced which will be Rube Bressler for the Reds and Lefty Sullivan for the Sox. This will be the biggest up set of the entire fiasco.

I seen both managers right after today's holy cost and Moran said hello old pal, and Gleason said hello you big bum so I am picking the Reds from now on.

'Ballyhoo' Foils Gleason

SCORE BOARD BALKS

'Happy' Felsch Is Lucky

Cincinnati (O.), Oct. 2.—Gents, the biggest scandal of a big year of baseball scandals was perpetrated down here this afternoon when the American League turned against itself and beat the White Sox out of the second game of the present horror.

Whoever is running the serious went and hired Mr. Announcer at the Washington ball park to come and announce for this serious thinking he was a fair minded American Leaguer, and what does he do today but announce Mr. Ivy Wingo as the catcher for the Reds and fool a Mr. Gleason into thinking Mr. Ivy was going to catch and he hits left-handed, so Mr. Kid started a left-hand pitcher instead of going through with his original plan, which was to pitch Mr. Red Faber.

Before the mistake could be rectified Mr. Game started.

If I was running an event as big as this I would try and get a loyal Mr. Announcer who would announce the right Mr. Catcher and not cross up his own league, and as far as that is concerned I could of got down there and told the people the right Mr. Catcher who was going to catch, and maybe nobody could of heard me, but at least they wouldn't of had to go to the expense of getting a Mr. Man from Washington to announce the wrong catcher, as some other goof is paying my expenses down here.

That was the first break of the game, and the second was the trick Mr. Score Board, which could not register strikes. This was fatal.

For instance, in the fourth inning up come Mr. Morris Rath, and Mr. Williams kept pitching to him and pitching to Mr. Rath and had him struck out at least a dozen times, but Mr. Evans would look up at Mr. Score Board and no strikes was registered there, so Mr. Evans finally got sick of looking at the left side of Mr. Morris' profile and said, "You walk, Mr.," so Mr. Morris had no choice only to walk and say thank you, Mr. Umpire, as an umpire is a czar in a event of this kind.

The next bird up, who I have forgot his name, and anyway it don't make no differents, and besides that he got out. But a man named Mr. Groh and a man named Mr. Roush kept their bat on their shoulder and watched the score board, and next thing you know they was both misters on base, and then Mr. Larry Kopf popped one up between Messrs. Felsch and Jackson for three bases and Mr. Me took a long nap, and the next time I looked at Mr. Score Board some club had three runs, which I have nicknamed Mr. Tallies.

From a baseball standpoint, if there is any such thing, the thing that impressed me most was Mr. Felsch, who I have decided that the minute we get back to old Chi we will have his first name changed from Mr. Happy to Mr. Lucky.

The first three or four times Mr. Felsch came up Mr. Felsch sacrificed, and then all of a sudden Mr. Felsch popped up a fly to Mr. Roush while Mr. Weaver was loitering on Mr. Third Base, and Mr. Roush seems to have caught it while facing Kentucky, and if he hadn't of why Mr. Felsch could of scored three times, which would of tied up the game.

Later, in Mr. Eighth Inning, up come Mr. Lucky again with Mr. Jackson on the keystone sack and knocked down Mr. Groh, but when Mr. Groh finally got up Mr. H. Groh had the baseball in his hands and threw it over to this First Mr. Baseman, who I have forgot his name. But speaking of names, it will be Mr. Lucky Felsch hereafter far as Mr. Me is concerned.

In the seventh inning a effigy was threw out of a airship and landed on the middle of Mr. Diamond, and for a minute I hoped it was me, but it turned out different.

I don't know who was playing, but I think it was Columbus and Ohio. Anyway I think Mr. Ohio won. Pay your war tax as you pass out.

Lardner Aids Chisox

KEEPS OFF 'EM

Little "Dick" Does Rest

Chicago (Ill.), Oct. 3—Gents, credit, if any, for beating the Reds today belongs to Dick Kerr and I, Dick on account of his pitching and me for not betting on the White Sox.

The very instant I made up what is left of my mind not to lay a bet on Gleason's birds, I knowed they would win and if I had of went a step further and bet on the Reds the score would of been 6 to nothing instead of half that amount.

In the place of going up in the press coop where I would of had to set next to Bud Fisher or who knows what I set this time in a box right close to the White Sox bench and as soon as the boys come out to warm up I told them I was not wagering, which gave them the added confidents needed to win.

Another advantage of me setting down there is that I could keep my ears open and overhear a lot of witty remarks which certainly would never happened up in the press coop, even setting next to Mr. Fisher.

For instants, when Heinie Groh came out to practice, a bird in the next box hollered "Hellow, you big egg," which is certainly a vivid description of Heinie, who is pretty near as big as Dick Kerr and looks more like a cucumber than an egg though he may resemble Mr. Egg in one respect, namely, being worth a whole lot of money.

On another occasion somebody hit a foul ball out in left field and Pat Duncan couldn't get to it a bird setting a couple of boxes away yelled "You couldn't catch nothing you big bum." Pat is bigger than Heinie all right but I have met him and never seen any evidents on him that he is a bum and when the man said he couldn't catch nothing he was telling a fib about him, as I seen him catch several baseballs down in Cincy.

Now, you take Charlie Risberg and Jimmie Smith and Heinie himself and if they had been calling each other eggs or bums, why it would have been just a laughing matter instead of them getting all het up and pretty near coming to blows but it must of been something else they was calling each other and I am sorry I wasn't in a position to hear all of their conversation so I could tell you birds what it was all about but the only remark I heard was when Heinie said to Charley "You will be setting on the bench next yr."

Well he shouldn't ought to say a thing like that if he don't know if its true or not and I don't believe that Mgr. Gleason has been confiding his plans for next summer to no Cincinnati ball player, even if Heinie is their captain.

From where I set I could see every decision Billy Evans made and I am pleased to state that he was right on every occasion and I wished I could say the same for the rest of the umpires but I wasn't close enough to watch them with the naked eye but will try and give a report on them later.

It looked at the start of the battle like the Reds was going to try and play a bunting game on Dickie and I guess maybe it was because perhaps they had heard that he was the best fielding pitcher in the American League and wanted to find out if it was true. Towards the finish they quit trying to bunt and some of them even went so far as to swing their bats all the way around and hit line drives to the catcher.

I suppose a great many of the other experts will criticise Ray Fisher for how he pitched, but I will say nothing about him as I expect to move down to Connecticut as soon as this holy cost is over and he teaches school down there in the winter and I might meet him some day when he had his switch on him or he might even stoop so low as to lick my kids if they happened to be wished onto his school.

So I will hafe to heap my verbal abuse on somebody else and I guess it better be Adolfo Luque, as I understand he don't read many words of English. Well then it Luques to me like he should of went to Fisher's relief earlier in the day and the score might of been 1 to 0 or 2 to 1 instead of disgraceful figures like 3 to 0.

The only unsportsmanlike thing I seen occur was in the third innings when Buck Weaver came up with Collins on first base and the Reds expected him to bunt but he hit a single over Kopf's kopf and I don't know what Cincinnati will think of Chicago's hospitality after that.

I know of no more fitting way to close than by giveing a report of the inning Luque pitched in pure Cubanola. El Lieboldo whiffoed. Si si senor Collins was outo Jako Dauberto to Adolfo. Bucko Weavero outo Ratho to Dauberto. No runos. No hittos, no bootos.

Rings Are Much Alike

JIM HAS MORE SPEED

Nine Games Hit Moran

Chicago, Oct. 4.—Gents! There is a strong family resemblance between the Rings. Both of them is tall and handsome and has beautiful curves. Both of them is inclined to be a trifle wild. Jim has a bit more speed. Neither of them has much luck, at least they told me down in Cincy that Jim was the jinx bird of the National League all summer, as the Reds never batted much behind him.

As for me, the boys has been batting around me only a trifle. Jim pitches better than I write and I pitch better than he writes. Jim is a decided blonde wile I am a kind of a dapple gray since the serious opened up.

On acct of Jim's complexion he don't look so bad when he don't have a chance to shave. Jim got a lot of praise today wile all I got was insults. For inst I was down in the hotel before the game and a Chicago man and a man from Cincy was trying to bet but they couldnt find no one to put it up with and finely the Chicago man spots me and introduces me to the Red bird and the latter said he wouldn't bet under such conditions.

As for today's game they was a scribe down town this am that 2 men asked him who was going to pitch today and the scribe said Cicotte and 1 of the men said you are crazy as Cicotte has such a sore arm that he cant wash the back of his neck so when we come out to the park this scribe told me about it and I said they wasn't nothing in the rules of Monday's game that required Cicotte to wash the back of his neck or any of the newspaper men neither.

"Well," said the other expert, "the man was just speaking figurative and meant that Eddie had a sore arm."

"Well," I said, "if he has only got one sore arm he can still wash the back of his neck as I only use 1 even when I am going to a party."

"The back of your neck looks like it," said the other expert.

"Yes," I said, "but what is the differents or not about Cicotte only having 1 sore arm as he only pitches with 1 arm."

"Yes you bum but that is the arm that the man said was sore." That is the kind clever repartee that goes on between the experts and no hard feelings on neither side.

No gents it wasn't no sore arm that beat Eddie today but just the other member of the Ring family finely getting some of the breaks and the way I seen the games you couldn't make me believe that either of the 2 birds had any impediment in the old souper as I have nicknamed it. Eddie had a sore heart when it was all over but theys other seasons comeing and may be another game in this serious which dont look like it would end for a month as I look for another 1 of them 40 day rains to begin early tomorrow am.

Gents do you remember when they decided to have the serious go 9 games instead of the conventional 7 and a whole lot of people said that was soup for the Reds as Mr. Gleason didn't have the pitchers to go 9 games.

Well now it looks like the disadvantage was vs P. J. Moran as if the serious had of only been skedoodled to go 7 games why by now he would of only had 1 more to win by now where as on the other hand Mr. Gleason has still got the same pitchers he had to begin with. The only people therefore that gets the advantage is the athaletes themselfs as they get paid for 5 games instead of 4 and I beg to assure the public that the newspaper men wishes they had kept it 4 games as we dont even get the priviledge of talking back to the umpire.

Tomorrows game will be postponed till the 4th day of November and I hope before that time they will give me a rm with bath.

Ring's Right on Rain

EVEN WITH SOOTHSAYER

Finds Hurlers Immune

Chicago, Oct. 5.—Gents: Well Gents I guess the experts who have been sniggering in their sleeve at me because maybe once in a while I make a little mistake about who is going to win a ball game or something will do their laughing on the other ft. After the little trick I showed them yesterday when I come out in print and said today's game would be postponed on account of rain.

The prediction is all the more wonderful when you set down and figure out that this is the first Sunday it ever rained in old Chi when there was a ball game skedooled at Comiskey Park, so me coming out and saying it would rain today puts me on a par with that old guy in Rome that told Caesar he was going to croke on the ideas of March and sure enough he did and it was first time in his life that he ever done it in that month or any other month in the calendar you might say.

The first thing I done when I woke up this morning was look outside of the window and the instant I looked out I seen it drooling so I ordered up the morning paper and laid down and turned to the humorous column called "Today's Weather."

Well, who ever writes it said "Probably showers with lower temperature and versatile winds." But he didn't mention nothing about postponing no ball game so if he comes forwards with the claim that he is in the same class as myself and that old Rome guy why he will get himself laughed out of the league.

Now the next thing is to predict what effect will the rain be on the remains of the worlds serious. Well, theys several ways of looking at it and a man that jumps into conclusions and says this and that the other thing about setting down and giving the matter careful thought is libel to become the Philadelphia of predicters.

So during the sermon this morning I leaned back and kind of half closed the old eyes and studied the matter from all angles and here is some of the conclusions I reached and I will give the way I arrived at them so you fans will have some idear on how a great man's mind works.

Well then to begin with there is the effect on the R. R. Companys was had their trains all fixed to start for Cincinnati tonight and either they will have to go empty or else call up all the porters and say "George, you don't need to show up tonight." This problem is out of my lines and up to the R. R. Administration.

Question No. 2—Is which club gets the benefits out of the rain. To answer this a man has got to know how rain effects the different pitchers. For inst Grover Lowdermilk always gets taller after a heavy rain. Dick Kerr usually gets cross and mean. Lefty Williams, just kind of half smiles and makes the best of it. Eddie Cicotte plays a lot of practical jokes on the rest of the boys. Bill James simply lets things take their course and waits for the clouds to roll by.

I have not yet became acquainted with Mr. Wilkinson but as they tell me he runs a farm down east I suppose he hasn't no objection to a little rain providing it dont have no heavy wind with it.

Now take the Cincinnati staff and a man stumbels on to some startling facts. On a rainy day in the regular season Slim Sallee generally most always goes to the races and the way he feels the next few days depends on who wins.

Well they wasn't no races here today or race riots neither one so I haven't no idear if Sol will be sunny and gay or morose. As for Dutch Reuther they was 1 day last summer when the Reds was supposed to play here but they was a regiment of Chi soldiers going to be welcomed home that same day so of course it poured rain and I was wading along Clark st. and met Dutch and he was wearing a rain coat so the Red fans neednt have no fear that he will come down with a heavy cold.

I never seen Jimmy Ring after a rainstorm but if he is like the rest of the Rings he will probably look like he ought to get his clothes pressed. Personally I never carry a bumbershoot and always look worse than usual when I come in out of the wet and when I look bad I get mad and bark like a dog. The one who is libel to be the most surprised is Luque as they tell me it never rains in Cuba. Eller, Fisher, Mitchell and Gerner is all good natured boys that dont allow a little thing like a rain to ruffle them up.

So all in all it looks like the rainy day would have absolutely no effect on neither club and it only remains to be seen how the umpires will take it. It will probably make them all more anxious to get the serious over in a hurry and they will begin striking everybody out.

The game was called off about 11 bells this a. m. after a consultation between Managers Gleason and Moran which run something like as follows: Moran—"Hello, is this you Bill? They tell me the grounds are too wet to play on them."

Gleason—"Well the outfield is pretty wet but we had the infield covered and we could play the game on that."

Moran—"Oh no we wont or happy and lucky Felsch might get an extra base hit."

Gleason—"Well godby old pal."

Moran—"Good luck old chum."

Ring Denies 'Hod' Rumor

DIDN'T FALL DOWN

Moran Meets Mr. Rigler

Chicago, Oct. 6.—Gents: Well, they asked me what was the feature of this game and I says I thought I heard a rumor that Hod Eller come down for breakfast this a. m. in the stead of ordering it up in his rm and wile he was struggling to get through the lobby he fell on the pavement and broke his right arm at the elbow.

Well, evidently he went and seen a dr and the next time I seen him he was out on the mound or box or what they call it pitching for the defeated Reds and I couldn't see his elbow from the where I set but dont ever let that bird brag about strikeing out 6 birds in succession because once I was pitcher for the Niles High School against New Zealand and I whiffed the whole ball club.

But speaking about the roomer of Hod Eller toppling over in the hotel lobby if he had of been a roomer at my hotel he wouldn't of never fell over because they wasnt no rm. in our lobby because the minute you try and walk through the lobby in our hotel a million bugs from Cincinnati and old Chi grabs you by either arm and ask you how to bet on the rest of the series.

Thus you get through the lobby. Now let us get back to Hod Eller. If he did fall down in the hotel lobby and break an arm it must of been the arm he pitched with because I never seen such nonsenical pitching in all my born days to use a new expression and I have seen a whole lot of pitching in my born days.

But as a matter of fact gents, you cant tell me that that bird ever fell down in a hotel lobby this morning or any other morning because he didnt fall down in a much larger place this P.M.

Please don't believe that Hod fell down either morning or afternoon either one though it was a Cincinnati baseball writer that gave me a story about him falling down which makes it exclusive between I and you and the world.

The Cincinnati baseball writer give it to me in confidence and any time they do that to me I tell it. But I really did strike out more birds the day we played New Zealand than Hod did after falling down.

Well, that disposes of the ball game and brings us to the business of the evening. A great many Cincinnati fans may think that today's game was won its merits but I ask them to consider the umpires. Why I know of a whole lot of umpires that could of win that game for the White Sox in less innings than it took to play it.

Now as for the details of the game the other experts can tell you what was visible on the field but very few can tell you what really happened in the Reds' fourth. I suppose a whole lot of you wondered what come off when Pat Moran dashed up from the first base coaching line and stopped what ever game there was going on. Well, here is the actual conversation that occurred.

"Mr. Rigeler," said Pat, "I don't believe I know you."

"I guess you don't," said Mr. Rigler, "as you have spelled my name wrong."

"Well," said Pat, "I just wanted to know if you was one of the Riglers from Crystal Falls?"

"No," said Mr. Rigler.

The game then went on as usual.

The most interesting thing I could find about the game was in the program and here is what it said in part "So and So beer has the largest sale of any beer in the loop."

"So and So beer is a case of good judgment."

Well, gents, that makes a man wonder which beer is going to advertise next.

But on the other hand it says "The pitcher who wins the game must be in perfect physical condition and the same applies to the game of life. We respectfully refer you to the following patrons, Mr. Charles A. Comiskey, Hon. Geo. Carpenter, Mr. Ban B. Johnson and Bishop C. P. Anderson"

So that puts me all up in the air again as I dont know who is going to pitch tomorrow whether it will be Charles A. Comiskey or Mr. Ban B. Johnson or Bishop Anderson, but I know it won't be a carpenter as he charges too much per hr.

Ring Tells Umps' Secret

KERR AN OIL MAGNATE

Schalk Right With Ban

Cincinnati, Oct. 7.—Gents: Instead of going to the Latonie today I sent my Jack over by a messenger and told him to throw it through the gate and in the meanwhile I went to the so-called national pastime. My first experience was trying to get into the park without showing a ticket and the guy stopped me and says where is your ticket brother?

Well I never seen this bird before in all my born days but I have got 3 perfectly good brothers so I gave him a keen glance to see maybe he was 1 of them but if he was he had changed a whole lot so I said "Which of my brothers is you?" and he kind of fumbled and stalled and couldn't answer nothing back so I simply passed it up by showing him my ticket and going into the ball park.

Up on the runway I met a lady from Philadelphia who says "Well the series will be all over today" and I asked her how did she know and she said because Cincinnati is a one night stand as all they have got to see here is Fountain Square and the Ohio River and Garfield Statue so I quit talking to her as I have seen more than that and I know for a fact that theys a whole lot more to be seen here than is visible to the nude eye if you stick around here a while which it looks like we would do so now.

After leaving the lady from Philadelphia much to her regrets I went in the banquet hall and who should I run into but the presidents of the other league. "Well Ban" I said, "are you going to suspend Cracker Schalk for what he done yesterday?"

I call Schalk Cracker because he calls me biscuit.

"What did he do?" says Ban.

"Why," says I, "he hit an umpire and didn't kill him."

"I didn't see it," says Ban, and I asked him if he was out to the game and he said he was so that makes 2 people that can go to the game and not watch them not including the umpires.

A great many of you gents may wonder why I keep bragging the

603

umpire like this. Well I don't really mean it and the real purpose is kind of subtle but I would just as leaf tell you birds what it is.

The other day I met Bill Evans and he said, "Keep putting my name in the paper," so I have to sort of pan them or how could I do it but at that I was kind of wondering around amidst the bugs in the 9th inning this pm and Bill called a strike on whoever was up to the bat and a lot of maudlins around me begin to pan Bill so i stepped up and said, "Do you know why they have the umpires down there on the field?" and one bird said "No," so I said "It's because they can see the plays much better than if they was up in the grandstand." That silenced them.

But to get back to Ban I said "If you arent going to suspend Cracker why dont you suspend Carl Mays as you ought to live up to your reputation as a suspender?" Its a wonder he didnt give me a belt in the jaw.

After banqueting on a special brand of ham recommended by Garry Herrmann but I wont mention its name in pure reading matter why I went up in the press coop and looked down on the field and some birds from Texas was just presenting Dickie Kerr with a bunch of oil stock. The differents between a bunch of oil stock and a bunch of flowers which they usually wish on a pitcher is that a bunch of oil stock waits 2 days instead of one before it withers and dies.

Well in the 5th, they was a man on third and second and first and very few out and Cocky Collins hit one by his drives which dont never seem to go safe and somebody caught it and whoever was on third scored an waffles Schalk stuck on second base but Dickie was still thinking about this here oil stock yet and he run down to second and found that somebody else had a lease on that property and along come Sheriff Groh and tagged him and said you are it you cant expect a left hander with oil stock to respect other peoples leases on bases.

Between that inning and the subsequent inning Dickie took off his shoe to rest his dogs and it took him such a long while that I was going to walk out and leave the ball game flat as I though the serious was over any way and I got down on the next floor and first thing you know Dutch Reuther wasn't in there pitching no more as Happy Go Lucky Felsch had finely got one and Pat said to himself if a man is unlucky enough to let Felsch get a base hit he is better in the clubhouse than here anyway.

I looked out there to see who was pitching and it was the other member of the Ring family, so that is why I stayed through the ball game and pretty soon I was parked right beside Dutch Reuther himself and he said "Well it ought to be over by now but I lost my stuff."

So I said let us go to the races tomorrow and he said that was my intentions but now I have got to come back here again, he acted kind of disappointed over not winning but great heavens when he gets to be my age he will be glad to be alive let alone mournin over one ball game.

Well along come the tenth inning and the Sox got a couple birds on the bases and Dutch said goodbye as I dont want to see this whatever happens as I cant stand no more strain so he left me and I promised to tell him how the game come out and I will as soon as I see him.

They tell me that the Reds went out on 3 pitched balls in their half of the tenth and that is all I would pitch in any inning if I was doing it but any way I didn't see the Red part of the tenth as I was looking up at a sign on the fence which says "Vote your protest. Vote wet November 4th." so it looks like we would be here a long while and even then I will protest by voting dry.

Lardner Has Shine Ball

PRESENT FROM UMP

Kopf Couldn't Hit It

Cincinnati, Oct. 8.—Gents: This is the most scandalous and death dealing story ever wrote about a world serious ball game. They have been a whole lot of talk in this serious about one thing and another and it finely remained for me to get at the facts.

Well, those of you who was out at todays game dont have to be explained to that in the fifth inning Eddie Cicotte pitched a baseball to Larry Kopf and Larry missed it and turned around to Mr. Quigley who was supposed to be umpiring behind the plate and asked this bird to let him (Kopf) see the ball.

Well, Mr. Quigley give Mr. Kopf the ball and he looked at it and Mr. Quigley said "Larry do you want the ball," and Larry said "No I dont want it." So Mr. Quigley said "All right throw the ball back to the pitcher. I cant stop this ball game all day to let an infielder look at a ball." Then I stepped in and said "Give me the ball" so they did.

Well, they give me the ball and here it is laying in front of me and I want to say to all infielders who of course never kep a ball long enough to look at it just what a baseball looks like and if I was an infielder I would catch a ball some time and hold on to it till after the game was lost and then I would study the ball.

Well, here is the ball right in front of me as I try to write. I will describe to you guys as I see it. Well this ball looks to me like a National League ball. That is what probably deceived them.

Well you see the reason that an infielder dont know what a baseball looks like is because the minute he gets it he has to throw it somewhere. Well as I said before here is what the baseball looks like. The National League baseball is nearly round.

This baseball which I am going to keep and give to my oldest child is a baseball that needs further description. It is the same baseball that Larry Kopf looked at and I only wished I was as nice looking as him and I wouldn't be writing this horrible stuff or working at baseball.

Well, then here is about that baseball. It is nearly round and looks nearly like an American League baseball except it has more seams and to be exact it has got 126 seams and if you take an American League ball why it has got 140 seams so why shouldnt you hit them.

But at that you take any ball and start counting seams on it and you can count all night and get innumerable seams. Well to distinguish this ball from its brothers it says John A. Heydler on it which makes it a cinch that it is a National League ball as it is a certainty that John wouldnt sign a ball that belonged to the other league.

Well as for the rest of the ball it looks soiled on the northwest side and I will worry my life away wondering who put a dirty finger on that ball which I have got and my children will still have it after me.

Now we have wrote almost a whole story about a ball. Now let us take a different angle about the game and start in on Morris Rath. At one stage of the game Morris hit a ball and broke his bat and the man setting next to me said that is the only time Morris ever broke a bat in a world's serious.

Another funny thing I heard was as follows.

A man named Wingo come up to the bat and the bird setting next to me said come on Wingo get a bingo.

Pitchers Puzzle Lardner

WHY ARE THEY PLURAL?

Ban Suspends Flingers

Chicago, Oct. 9.—Gents, the special train for Cincy wiil leave tonight at 11:30, new time, and I would advise everybody to be there with their tooth brush and typewriter. The train will leave out of the Pennsy station, and immediately on arriving in old Cincy it would be a great idear to try and get a room somewheres so as you can get shaved.

The game tomorrow will be the crucial game of the serious and it looks to me like it would be between Grover Lowdermilk and Rube Dressler. Neither mgr. dares to pitch anybody else.

Today's game here was just a exhibition between the White Sox and Reds and believe me it was some exhibition. It looked like both sides were having a battle to see which could get 3 men out the slowest. Finely Joe Jackson hit a pop fly into right field seats and broke up the game as far as I am concerned.

The first two White Sox pitchers was Williams and James, and I can't tell you why they either of them is plural, and if I was running it I would call them William and Jane. I wouldn't plural neither one of the both of them. If I was manager I would pitch a guy with a singular name like Lowdermilk. Another thing Manager Gleason did today was to change the outfield around to deceive the newspaper men. The scheme worked perfectly and I do hope he is satisfied. I know I am.

Speaking about this world serious, I will have to join the statisticians and tell you the different records I seen broke. It was the first world serious that Morris Rath ever broke a bat in. It is the only world serious which Sherwood Magee ever got a base hit. It is the only world serious that Umpire Nallin ever called a strike on Jake Daubert. It is probably the last world serious I will ever see. So much for the records.

Now to get down to facts. Here is quotations from a letter received just before the game by a Chi baseball writer:

"I have been a follower of athletics for yrs. and have taken part in athletics in my younger days. I have been greatly amused during the present series in reading the ifs, ands and buts explaining Chicago's defeat from day to day. It looks like a case of sour grapes to me. In fact, it borders on rowdyism. I suppose if you lose another game or two you will mob the Cincinnati team."

Well I know this here Chi baseball writer that the letter come to and he never mentioned sour grapes in his life or ordered them neither and as for mobbing the Cincinnati Ball Club, why this same baseball writer was standing with me when the Clubs come out of the clubhouse and Sherwood Magee come up and spoke to the both of us. If that don't prove how we stand I don't know what will or care neither one.

Now personly I don't think they will be a game tomorrow and if there is I don't know who will pitch, as I seen Ban Johnson after today's alleged game and he said he had suspended all the pitchers on both clubs.

Wile being exhausted at the game I finely set down and read the following in the afternoon paper:

"The names of the early Dukes of Normandy, as well as their family history, are known but very dimly, and it may be as well that it should be so, for their descent does not seem to have been as Orthodox as it might. Thus William 1 of England (William 2 of Normandy) was the illegitimate son of his predecessor Robert the Devil," and so on. How can a man pay attention to a ballgame like that when they's such good stuff to read in the paper.

THE COURTSHIP
OF T. DORGAN

◇

Chi, May 22.

FRIEND AL: Well Al I suppose you seen what I done to the N. Y. bunch yesterday and when it was over Gleason called me to 1 side in the club house and says he thought it was about time I was getting the real jack so if I would bring my old contract over to the pk. today he would give me a new 1 calling for $3000.00 per annum. So today I took my old contract over to the pk. and Gleason told me to take it up in the office and I took it up there and the old man give me my new 1 and says now go ahead and show me you are worth it. Well I will show him Al and when a man gets fair treatment from a club why you work all the harder for them.

Well Gleason told me to not say nothing to none of the other ball players about the matter as they might maybe take it in their head to hold up the club for more jack so I didn't tell nobody only Tom Dorgan that rooms with me when we are out on the road and the best pal a man ever had and they's no danger of him asking for more jack as he is just a 3th string catcher and all the closer he ever gets to the ball game is down in the bull pen warming up somebody but he is a regular guy and I only wished he could get in there and show them something.

Well when I told him about my new contract he said I was a lucky stiff to be getting all that jack and besides that have a beautiful wife and a couple kiddies and a nice home where all as he has got is 1 dinky little rm. over on Grand Blvd. that he can't squeeze in or out of it without barking his ears. So I told him I said "I can't get you no more jack old pal but the next gal that looks X eyed at me I will turn her over to you and welcome as 1 wife is about all as I can handle and then some."

The Saturday Evening Post, September 6, 1919; previously uncollected.

At that I would like to find him some nice gal Al as a man don't know they are liveing till you get married and I can't help from feeling sorry for a bird that has to go home nights after the ball game and open up the close closet and talk to his other suit.

Well when I told Florrie about me getting the $600.00 raise she asked me what would we do with it and I said I didn't know yet and she says why not buy a car as we could have some time rideing around old Chi in a car evenings and take in the different pks. and etc. and take our friends along and show them a time. So I said "You have got a fine idear of what cars costs these days and for $600.00 you can't even buy a tire rench." So she begin telling me about the 2d hand car the Dumonts which is her new pardners in the beauty parlor down town and they got it for $700.00 and its a 1917 5 passenger Peel and runs and looks like new and they must be a whole lot more bargains if a person would just get out and look for them so just to stall her I said I would keep my eyes open and if I seen a real bargain I would grab it off but what and the he—ll is the use of us blowing our jack on a car when the Dumonts has all ready got 1 and all as we half to do is call them up and ask for the correct time and they would probably invite us out for a spin.

Personly Al I don't see no use in anybody buying a car now as they won't be nowheres to go after the 1 of July and besides when I am out on the road with the club Florrie would want to drive it herself and we would half to hire a steeple jack to get she and the car down off in the top of the Boston store.

Well Al I won't half to work no more vs. the N. Y. club this serious but will probably work vs. the Washington club which comes next and he will save me for the game Walter pitchs as Walter is going pretty good now and a man has just about got to shut them out to beat him.   Your pal,   JACK.

Chi, May 27.

FRIEND AL: Well Al the way some people runs a ball club its a wonder we can stay in the U. S. let alone 1st place. Well yesterday Griffith started Jim Shaw against us and Gleason thought it was a good spot to try out big Lowdermilk so the 2 of them went to it but pretty soon they was both out of there and it come along the 8th inning with the Washington club a couple runs ahead and he stuck me in there to stop them and next thing you know Johnson was in there for them to try and hold the lead but we knocked his can off and beat them out.

Well of course I hadn't no idear that Gleason would send me back at them today after the work I done so the Dumonts was out to the game with Florrie and after the game I come out and the Dumonts had a mighty sweet looking doll with them named Miss Mulvihill or something so Dumont made the remark that it was pretty dry in Chi on a Sunday so why didn't we all hop in his car and go out to Lyons where they was plenty to eat and drink.

Well then Florrie said it didn't seem right for Miss Mulvihill to not have no man along when her and Mrs. Dumont both had their husband so Dumont asked me if they wasn't 1 of the ball players that was single that would like to go along. So I happened to think about Tom Dorgan so I went back in the club house and got him and you ought to seen his eyes pop out when he got a look at the Mulvihill trick. Well we went out to the car and it was the 1st time I seen it and Florrie had told me it looked like new but if it does why Jack Lapp has got a pompador. And when they said it was a 5 passenger car they meant 4 people and a weather strip.

Well the next thing was how was we going to set and Mrs. Dumont said she always set in the front seat to keep her husband from driveing to fast so that left I and Florrie and Miss Mulvihill and Tom for the soap box in back so Florrie said it looked like Miss Mulvihill would half to set on Tom's lap. Well both partys had a hemorage to the cheek when they heard that and Miss Mulvihill said she guessed not and why didn't Florrie set on my lap and Florrie said she had tried that to many times so any way the way we went was with Florrie and Miss Mulvihill squeezed along the side of me and Tom on my lap and I don't know how far it is to Lyons but by the time we got there I thought we must be all of us in the Coast League.

Well we set out on the porch of the joint out there and ordered up a few drinks and everybody acted like they had came to the morgue to identify a body till finely I begin pulling some of my stuff and I wished you could of heard Miss Mulvihill split her sides only I kind of felt sorry for poor Dorgan as he acted like the cat had his tongue or something and the gal must of thought she had been pared off with Dummy Taylor. Well we had some more drinks and a chicken dinner and when the check come around Dorgan was still speechless and Dumont was danceing with Florrie so I was elected on the 1st ballad and Miss Mulvihill made the remark that I shouldn't ought to pay for everything and just jokeing I said I was tickled to death to pay for being in her company and she blushed up like a school girl and give me a smile and I couldn't help from feeling sorry for Dorgan but I can't help it if that's the way the gals feels Al and I only wished I could be just friends with them and nothing more.

Well when it come time to go home I made the remark that I wasn't crazy about holding Tom on my lap again along with the extra load he had picked up in the mean wile so what does Miss Mulvihill do but say that if Florrie did not mind she would just as leaf set on my lap and Florrie said go ahead so that's the way we come home and even with Dumont zig zaging all over the road and hitting her up about 12 miles per hr. all the way it didn't seem more than 5 minutes when we come to where Miss Mulvihill lived and dropped her off and I seen her to the door and I said to her how did she like my friend Mr. Dorgan and she said "Why don't you speak for yourself John?" How is that Al she calling me John the 1st time she ever seen me and I didn't know they was anybody realy knew my name was John as they all been calling me Jack ever since I was a knee high grass hopper you might say.

Well when I and Florrie got home I got the silent treatmunt but she will get over it Al like they all do and anybody would think it was my fault that I wasn't born with a hair lip or something.

But wait till I tell you what come off today. It wasn't till pretty near 5 this A. M. when we rolled in this A. M. and I got up about 11 this A. M. and finely got over to the ball pk. and I felt like the supper dishs and finely it come time for batting practice and Gleason said you work today and I said what was he talking about as I worked yesterday and he said yes but it wasn't only 2 innings just long enough to warm me up so I had to get in there and try and pitch and of course it had to be the day when Weaver and Collins and all of them went to he—ll behind me and the Washington club went mad and got 4 runs which is more then they usually get all through May and Harper shut us out with 3 hits though he didn't even have a night-gown on the ball and after the game Gleason asked me where I was last night and I told him I was out and he said yes and you are out today again to the amt. of $50.00. Well Al if he makes that fine stick I will quit baseball and go in some business where a man can get fair treatmunt and sometimes I think I better get out of baseball any way as a man that is a star in the game if he has got any looks at all why the gals all loose their nut about him and bother you to death even if you turn your back every time they look at you and a man hasn't no business being before the public in a position where the gals can look you over and make a fool out of themself when you have got a wife and 2 kiddies.

Your pal,   JACK.

Chi, June 1.

FRIEND AL: Well Al I just come back from the pk. and Cleveland give us a trimming but it was about time as we win the 1st 3 we played with them. We leave for Detroit tonight and go east from there and won't be back in old Chi till the last of the mo.

Well Al they was some excitement out in the old ball yard yesterday but beleive me it wouldn't of never came off if I had of been in there pitching or even down there on the bench. The way that it come off was that I pitched the P. M. game Decoration Day and give them a good licking and Gleason called off the $50.00 fine he plastered on me last wk. and said I didn't need to dress yesterday but could set up in the stand with Florrie. Well the Dumonts and Miss Mulvihill was also out to the game and we all set together and I kind of explained the game to Miss Mulvihill and I kept talking fast for the fear she would bring up something personal. Well the game wasn't much of a game as we had them licked to death but along in the 8th inning the Cleveland bunch was sore on acct. of the way we was makeing them like it and Speaker hit a ball down towards Gandil and Chick made quite a stop of the ball and run over and stepped on the bag long before Spoke got there but Spoke was kind of sore so he slid in to the bag and that made Gandil sore and they begin barking at each other and next thing you know they was at each other and the rest of the boys was all scared and left them go to it and finely Gandil had his shirt tore off and the umps put them both off of the field. Well Al it wouldn't of never of happened if I had of been in there as the minute Speaker had of started anything I would knocked him for a gool and it would of been good night Mr. Speaker. Just like I told Jack Graney out there on the field today I said "Speaker better not never try no monkey business like that on me or Fohl will be scarring the bushs for a new center fielder."

Well Miss Mulvihill was setting next to me when the fight come off and I could feel her kind of tremble so I guess I must of kind of squeezed her hand and I told her to not worry because if I seen that either 1 of them was realy going to get hurt I would run down there and knock them both for a gool. So she give me a smile and made some remarks about how nice it must be to be so big and I kind of laughed it off and then I seen Florrie kind of looking at us so I cut it out.

Well the fight must of kind of went to Dumont's bean and any way he asked us all down to the Dearborn for supper and Mrs. Dumont said we better get Tom Dorgan along so as Miss Mulvihill would have somebody to play with and she kind of made a face but didn't say nothing so I got a hold of him and we went down there. Well Tom is a pretty fair dancer and he kept asking Miss Mulvihill to dance and of course she couldn't say no though I guess she would of rather set at the table and talk things over but I was glad he kept her danceing at that as I was afraid things might get to personal if her and I was left at the table alone. Well finely we started home and on the way she managed to ask me where we was going to stop in Detroit and I told her so I suppose she will be sending me a post card or a night letter or something and if she does why all as I can do is just pretend like I didn't get it. But any way we are on our way tonight Al and if we can come back from this trip in 1st place why the race is as good as win you might say as the way I and Cicotte and Williams is going they's no club in the league can catch us in the stretch. Personly Al wile I don't never like to leave home I am kind of glad we are going this time for Miss Mulvihill's sakes if nothing else as the less she sees of me for a wile she will be better off.

I will write to you from Detroit or somewheres in the east.

Your pal,   JACK.

N. Y., June 5.

FRIEND AL: Well Al we just got in from Detroit and we played against Jennings club like we was the Red X 2d team and if we finish up the trip like we started we will be lucky to come home in a passenger train. I suppose you read about how they beat me Al and it looks like they was enough bad breaks against me to last a whole season and the only peace of luck I had all the while we was there didn't have nothing to do with baseball but I did happen to run acrost a bird that wants to sell a car and its a 1918 Blaine that hasn't only been drove 4000 miles and it looks like it was just out of the shop. I took Cracker Schalk out to see it and he said I would be a sucker to not grab it off but the bird wants $1200.00 which is about twice as much is I figured on paying for a car so I didn't do nothing but I kind of think he took a fancy to me and if I hold off a wile he will come down to somewheres near my price. Any way I have got his name and address and if I decide I want to pay somewheres near his price why all as I half to do is wire him.

Well Al I didn't get no word from that little gal Miss Mulvihill wile we was in Detroit and I hope she finely got some sence in her head but speaking about Miss Mulvihill I have kind of got a idear that this here Tom Dorgan is stuck on her as whenever we get up in the rm. together that is about all as he can talk about and the day we left Detroit he asked me if I thought it would do any harm him writeing her and of course I said why no it wouldn't and I felt like telling him it wouldn't do no good neither one but I guess he will find that out for himself soon enough without me telling him. Only I can't help from kind of feeling sorry for the both of them and I feel sorry for him because he has fell for a gal that has left her heart run away from her to a place where it won't get her nothing and I feel sorry for her for looseing her nut over a man that has all ready got a wife and troubles of my own.

But Dorgan of course don't know nothing about what has past between her and I and wile we was setting together on the train comeing east he asked me if I thought they was anything I could do to help him get in right with her. Well I told him I would do the best I could as I would like to see them both happy but between you and I Al about the only thing I could do to help his case along would be to put myself out of the way and maybe in time she would forget me but I have got Florrie and the kiddies to think of and after all a man's family comes before your friends.

Well old pal I expect to pitch 1 of the games here and the N. Y. club is going like wild men wile we act like we was trying to see who could hit the highest foul but after the luck I had in Detroit I should ought to get some kind of luck here and all as I ask is a even break and I will make Pipp and some of the rest of them think they have got the pip eh Al?   Your pal,   JACK.

Boston, June 11.

FRIEND AL: Well old pal it looks like your old pal should ought to start a matrimony burro and charge a commission for fixing it up between couples that wants to get married though this time I guess the want to is all on 1 side and I am afraid my efforts is going to be waisted. I suppose you will wonder what am I talking about. Well

I guess I told you about Josie Mulvihill that little queen out of Chi that Tom Dorgan went nuts over her well instead of them hitting it off why she kind of lost her noodle over me without me never looking X eyed at her and of course she is waisting her time over me as I have all ready got a wife and beleive me 1 of them is enough.

Well any way Dorgan can't think of nothing else only she and this A. M. up in the rm. he asked me did I think they was any chance for him in that direction and of course I couldn't come out and tell him what I realy thought so I said "Well you can't never tell till you try." So he says "Yes but I am a busher in the lady league and I don't know how to go about it and if I was to ask her and she node me I wouldn't never dast face 1 of them again." He said "How would it be if you was to just drop her a friendily letter and kind of mention my name in it and ask her what she thinks about me and kind of give me a boost and feel her out and if she answers you back why we can come pretty close to telling if I have got a chance or have not got a chance."

Well Al I couldn't do nothing only say O. K. so I have wrote her a letter giveing Tom a boost and I am going to mail it to her special and here is what it says in it.

Dear Miss Mulvihill: Well Miss Mulvihill I suppose you will be surprised recieveing a letter from 1 who you have hardily had time to get acquainted and a specially a married man but I am writeing this in behalf of a pal of mine who I won't half to tell you his name as you can guess who it is when I say that you have been out a couple times on partys with him which I was along at the same time with the wife and the Dumonts.

This man Miss Mulvihill has not yet win his spurs in the big league yet and might do better if traded to another club as a young catcher breaking in has not got much of a chance on our club with a man like Ray Schalk a specially when you have got a couple of faults that a youngster has got to over come before they will make a big league catcher. I know you don't know a whole lot about baseball and if you seen this boy stand up there behind the plate and catch you might think he was O. K. and as good as anybody where a man that knew baseball could tell you what was the matter with him. 1 thing wile he has got a fair arm he has got to get in a certain position to peg and looses time before he can cut the ball loose and another thing he is what we call spike shy that is when a man is comeing in to the plate it seems like he has not got the nerve to block them off but trys to stand to 1 side and tag them as they are slideing past. But this boy may overcome these faults or he might make a grand catcher for some minor league club.

Well Miss Mulvihill I and this boy has been rooming together on the road ever since the season opened and wile he don't draw no star salery I wouldn't ask for a better roomy and when we have a little beer or something up in the rm. I am always glad to pay for it and I feel towards him like he was a young brother that hasn't got started yet in a money way you might say but if he keeps his eyes open and works hard he has got a chance to make good in the big league or at lease in Class A.

Now I don't want you to feel like as if I am butting in and trying to run your fairs but this boy asked me would I put in a word for him and try and find out how he stands with you and I can say to you Miss Mulvihill that you could do a whole lot worse then give this boy a chance and wile you may not like him just at the 1st he is 1 of these birds that the more you see of him he is just the same all the wile so if he gives you a ring on the phone when we get home why it won't hurt nothing if you make a date with him.

As for you and I personly girlie you know how matters stands with me and some times its to late to mend like in this case but a person can forget anybody if they try and we can be just good friends like I am with other girlies that is friends of my wife and all go out and have a good time together and no harm done. So if you will give this boy a chance and let by gones be by gones why it looks to me like it would be a good move both ways and remember that looks is not everything or money neither one.

With my personal regards and of course I don't half to tell you to not let this go no father and if you can't see your way clear why no harm done but I wished you would try and find time to write and tell me: how you feel in regards to this matter and beleive me your sinsere friend.

So that is what I wrote her Al and I signed my name and I feel like I had killed 2 birds with the same stone as she won't make no more fuss over me and she will either give this boy a chance when he gets home or else she will tell him right off in the real where to head in at and the sooner he gets the bad news he will get over it that much sooner.

Well I suppose you seen in the paper what I done to Babe Ruth yesterday and its no wonder they call him Babe Al as I had him swinging like a baby in a cradle and the only 2 times he even fouled the ball was when Liebold run back and catched the fly ball and another time when Gandil speered that line drive off in him but he would of struck out on that ball only it was a bran new ball and I tried to curve it and it didn't break like I intend it.

Well we leave here for Philly Friday night and after we get through with them we go to Washington and then Detroit for 1 game and then home. In the mean wile kindest regards to Bertha and don't take no bad money.   Your pal,   JACK.

Detroit, June 22.

FRIEND AL: Well Al we leave in a couple hrs. for old Chi and play the Cleveland club there tomorrow and I thought I was going to work here today but I guess Gleason wanted to save me up for the Cleveland club. Well I will make them like it and maybe they won't feel so cocky after I get done with them.

Well Al it looks like I would soon be a Barney Oldfield or something. I guess I told you that they was a bird here in Detroit that wants to sell me a 1918 Blaine car for $1200.00 and all the boys that seen it said I was a sucker if I didn't grab it off. Well when we got here today the 1st bird I seen was the bird that owns this car and he wanted to know if I had made up my mind or not. So I told him no I had not and he would half to give me a little more time or else cut down on the price. So he said he couldn't do neither as he had a offer from a man here in Detroit to take it off in his hands at $1200.00 and the man wants it right away and will pay cash and the only reason why he hadn't sold it to him was on acct. of takeing a kind of a fancy to me and he would rather see me get it then anybody else as he felt like we was old friends on acct. of him seeing me on the ball field so often. So I said well I only had about $800.00 in the bank and I would half to talk it over with the wife 1st any way so finely he said that if I would give him a $100.00 for a option on it he would hold on to it for a wk. before he sold it to somebody else and then I could wire him if I want it or not and that will give me plenty of time to talk it over with Florrie.

Well Al it looks like such a bargain that I would be a fool to not take it and Florrie will feel the same way when I tell her about it and I have gave the bird my check for a $100.00 and if Florrie will go in with me 50 50 why I will wire the bird and tell him the deal

is closed and then I will ask Gleason to leave me run over here from
Chi some night and drive it back the next day and that way I won't
only loose 1 day all together and when I get that old car back in old
Chi beleive me I will burn up old Michigan Ave. only they will be
1 understanding and that is that Florrie can't drive the car neither
wile I am in Chi or out on the road as I don't trust no woman to
drive a car and a specially 1 that is always looking all over the st. to
see if they's some dame that has got sporter close then her.

The bird took me out to the ball pk. this P. M. in the machine and
it run like a watch charm and he asked me if I didn't want to try and
run it a wile to see how easy it run but I don't want to take no chance
of running a machine that don't belong to me and besides it won't
take me no time to learn how to run it by myself as they's nothing
I ever tried yet that I couldn't pick it up like childs play.

Well its pretty near train time Al and besides they isn't much news
to write. I guess I told you about me writeing to Josie Mulvihill in
Chi that Tom Dorgan is nuts over her and I wrote to try and give
him a boost and see how he stood with her. Well the last day we was
in Washington I had a night letter from her and all as it said was
"Tell Mr. Dorgan the same thing I told you once why don't he speak
for himself." So I showed him the message and his face kind of fell
and I couldn't help from feeling sorry for him as it looks like he is
barking on the wrong tree but I guess he will get over it and I hope
the poor little gal will have sence enough to get over something
herself as she must know they can't be nothing only friendship
between her and I and the sooner she forgets all about me so everybody will be better off.   Your pal,   JACK.

Chi, June 24.

FRIEND AL: Well Al from all I ever seen of Bertha I wouldn't
never accuse her from being a spend drift but beleive me she has not
got nothing on Florrie. When I got back from Detroit yesterday
A. M. and told her about this here car that I had took a option on it
and could get it for $1200.00 and everybody said it was a bargain
and I would be a sucker to not grab it off so she said well why don't
you buy it. So I said that is all right to talk about buying it but I
am about $600.00 shy and I figured that as long as I and you is both
going to get the benefits out of the car you would go in with me 50
50 and pay for half of the car. So she said "All right I will pay for

half of the car if you will agree that it belongs to the both of us and not just you and I can take it out and drive it when ever I feel like." So I said nothing doing as I wouldn't trust her to drive a lawn more let alone a car and a specially in a town like Chi where its a dull day when a 100 people don't get bumped off in a automobile wreck.

So she said all right then nothing doing and you can either pay for the car yourself or go without it so I thought if she was going to be stubborn why I would be stubborn to as 2 could play in that game so it looks like we wouldn't have no car as I am not going to buy no cheap 1 for no $600.00 after seen that Blaine that is worth $2000.00 or better and the bird trying to give it to me for $1200.00 you might say. So it looks like I would do my motoring in a 60 passenger 35th st. limousine eh Al?

Well Gleason started me vs. the Cleveland club yesterday and as usual the boys wasn't hitting behind me and it come up to the 7th inning with the score 3 and 2 against us and we had a couple men on and 2 out and Gleason takes me out and sends Jack Collins up to hit and Coumbe made a monkey out of him and that's the way it always goes and some day Gleason will get wise to himself and find out that I can hit as good as anybody on the club against left handers. Any way Danforth went in to finish and they got a couple more off in him and finely beat us 5 and 3.

But beleive me Al they come near being more excitement out there then just the baseball game. I was warming up before the game and Speaker come over towards our bench and I thought he was going in the club house or somewheres but he stopped along side of me and he said "Jack Graney said you wanted to see me." So I said I hadn't told Graney nothing of the kind so he said "Well what he said was that if I ever started anything with you Fohl would half to start scarring the bushs for a new center fielder." So I said "I never said nothing like that Spoke and if Graney told you that he was just kidding." So then Speaker hollered to Graney to come over and he come over and Speaker says "This big goof says he never said what you said." So Graney says "Well he did and if he says he didn't he is a liar." So I said "You better not call me a liar or I will liar you all over the ball pk." So Graney said it looked like I and him would half to settle it but Speaker said "No I will take it off in your hands."

Well Al it was all as I could do to keep from socking the both of them and I was just going to sock Speaker when I happened to think that it would probably mean I would get put off in the field and Gleason was depending on me to work the game so I pretended like I thought they was jokeing and I said "I don't want no trouble with neither of you 2 boys out here on the field but if you are looking for trouble I will come down to your hotel tonight and we can settle it there." So Spoke said all right and don't forget where we are stopping at and the clerk will give you the rm. No.

Well what they was trying to do Al was start a fight with me and get me put off the field and Gleason is up against it for pitchers and besides he didn't have nobody else warmed up but I was to smart for them and didn't fall for it. But beleive me if it hadn't of been for us being up in the race and every game counts I would of socked the both of them.

Well finely the game started and the 1st ball I throwed come pretty close to Graney's bean and he said I better not try none of that business or he would hit me with a bat so I just laughed at him and I tried to throw the next 1 at his head but the ball kind of slipped and went right in his groove and he happened to catch it just right and hit it to left field and made 2 bases. Well I got the next bird but Speaker come up and said to throw 1 at his head and see what would happen. Well I wasn't going to leave him bluff me so I tried to get 1 close enough to scare him but I wasn't warmed up good yet and kind of wild and I got the ball outside and he hit it down the left foul line for 2 bases and at that Jackson should ought to of held him to a single but any way Graney scored and then Liebold let a fly ball get away from him and Speaker scored and that is how they got 2 of their runs. Well Graney and Speaker tried to ride me all the P. M. but I give them back what they sent and what they was trying to do was start a scrap so as I would get suspend it but I was to foxy for them. Well Al I was going down to their hotel last night and call their bluff and knock the both of them for a gool but when I got home the baby was acting kind of croopy and I was afraid to leave the house.

Well we play Cleveland here once more tomorrow and then we go to St. Louis and I will work 1 of the games there and I will make a monkey out of them.

Tom Dorgan told me tonight that he had called up Josie Mulvihill and was going to take her out somewheres tonight to a picture or somewheres and dance and I suppose she made the date so as she could tell him once in for all that they wasn't no chance for him and I only hope she lets him down easy as he is 1 of these silent birds that takes it mighty hard when the gals treats you rough.

Your pal,   JACK.

St. Louis, June 28.

FRIEND AL: Well Al it looks like I am going to be a demon motorist after all Florrie or no Florrie. I just wired a telegram to the bird in Detroit saying I would buy the Blaine for $1200.00 if he would hold on to it for me till the 7 of July. We have got a off day in the schedule that day and I can easy get leaf from Gleason to run over to Detroit and get the old boat and drive her back to Chi and won't even loose a day.

Well I suppose you will wonder what has happened to change my mind and if somebody has gave me a birthday present of $600.00 or something. Well nothing like that old pal but still and all its going to be just the same like a birthday present and instead of the whole amt. comeing out of our family I am going to spend the $600.00 like I planned and 3 poor suckers is comeing through with the rest of it.

Well I suppose you will wonder have I went crazy or what am I talking about. Well Al I have went crazy like a fox and you will say so to when I tell you what I am going to pull off. Well they's a bird here in St. Louis name Jack Casey that I have ran around with him ever since I been comeing here and maybe you have heard of him but any way he has got a stable of fighters and he has put on some bouts himself here in St. Louis and he knows the game from A to Z. Well he has gave me a steer on a whole lot of fights how to bet on them and I never loose a nickle yet on his dope. Well I was out with him last night and we was all over St. Louis lapping them up and we run in to a bunch of boxers and boys that is interested in the fight game and as soon is they heard who I was they popped their eyes out and said they had been a admirer of mine for a long wile and always wanted to meet me and if Jimmy Burke had a few pitchers like myself maybe the St. Louis club could get somewheres.

Well finely the talk got around to the Willard Dempsey fight in Toledo the 4 of July and I asked some of the boys how they thought it was comeing out and they all kind of stalled and said it looked pretty even and it looked like a even money bet and etc. but I could see they was stalling and finely Casey come out with it. Well Al these birds is all in a position to know and they couldn't have nothing only the right dope and here is what they give me.

It seems like Tex Ricketts that is running the fight has spent a whole lot of jack building the arena in Toledo and he can't expect to break better than even on the 1 fight and if Dempsey was to win why they wouldn't be nobody left for him to fight so they are going to leave the arena up and Willard is going to get the decision in this fight and then they are going to match them up again for Labor Day and get the crowd back there a 2d time and clean up a bunch of jack and the 2d time they fight it will be on the level but this time the cards is all stacked for the big fellow to win and any way he is to big for this other guy to reach him. So Casey said if he was I and wanted to clean up a peace of jack why to go ahead and bet my head off on the big fellow to win this bout and they wasn't no way I could loose unless Willard drops dead from cramps or something when they get in the ring.

Well I said I would think it over and 1 of the boys said I better not think to long as it might be to late as it is only 5 more days now before the fight and he said if I wanted to put up my jack he knew a friend of his that wasn't on the inside and he couldn't see nothing only Dempsey and this friend would take any bet I would make and this bird said he would see that I got the jack when I win. Well I said I didn't want to rob no friend of his and besides I didn't have the jack along with me to put it up and he said he would take me check but I said I would rather wait till I get to Cleveland and maybe the odds would be different and I could get some odds on the big fellow instead of even money.

Well that's the dope Al and these birds know what they are talking about and if I was you and had a few dollars to bet why I would put it up on big Jess and not say nothing about what I have told you as the more people that knows about it why it will effect the betting.

Personly when I was through with Casey and his friends I come back to the hotel and some of the boys was still setting around the lobby in the hotel and I set down with them and told them what I had found out and Buck Weaver is 1 of these smart Alex that always knows more then anybody else so he says "Well I will tell you what I think of your dope I will take all the jack you want to bet on the big fellow." So 1 word lead to another and I said I didn't want to rob no pals that was on the same club with me but they kept acting smarty and finely I kind of loose my temper and I said I would bet $600.00 even money if I didn't half to put it up and Weaver said he would take $200.00 of it and a couple more of the boys took $200.00 a peace and they covered the whole $600.00 and God help them but it will learn them not to be so smarty in the future.

So you see Al that I am going to have the big car after all and I am glad I can get it without Florrie putting in her jack as now I will own the car all myself and she won't half nothing to say only ask me to take her rideing and when I am out on the road with the club I will have the old buggy locked up in some garage where she can't get a hold of it and try to clime trees.

Well I made a monkey out of this club today and won't half to work no more till we get to Cleveland where I can get another whack at Speaker and Graney and if they try any more of their smart business on me I will give them the Jess Willard only they won't want to come back for no 2d dose on Labor Day or no other day and speaking about Cleveland reminds me that they are going to make us go there Sunday night and play a postpone game Monday and I can't see no sence to it only that is the last day before the country goes dry and I suppose they want us to spend it in a dry town for the fear we might enjoy ourself.

That is 1 place where poor Tom Dorgan has got it on us as Gleason has left him home this trip and he will be in old Chi the night of the 30 of June where he can get all as he wants to drink so he isn't so unlucky after all even if the ladys don't go nuts over him.

Well Al its time to go to bed and don't forget what I said about betting your jack on the big fellow if you have got any to spare and in the mean wile come on you big Jessica.

Your pal,   JACK.

Chi, July 5.

FRIEND AL: Well Al its good night car and good night everything else and the way I feel I don't care if school keeps or not. I am glad I didn't advise you to bet no dough on the big fellow and if you bet some on your own hook why all as I have got to say is that I am sorry and it wasn't my fault or them boys down to St. Louis neither one as I have knew Casey several yrs. and I know he wouldn't give me no bad steer and the way it looks like to me is that Dempsey double crossed the big fellow and everybody else and of course only for what they told me down there I would of bet my jack on Dempsey instead of on the other fellow as in the 1st place Jess wasn't in no shape to fight and besides when a bird 24 yrs. old fights a man pretty near 40 why its 10 to 1 he will knock him for a gool.

Well Al your old pal will do his rideing around on st. cars this summer at lease unless we win the world serious and then of course I will have enough jack to buy the finest car made and not no broke down 2d hand Blaine and they say it costs a million dollars to run a Blaine any way as they are he—ll on tires and the cylinders keeps getting gumed up. Well they's 1 good thing and that is that Florrie don't know nothing about it and if she did why I wouldn't never hear the last of it but I am not the kind to cry over sour milk and whatever is comeing to me why I take it with a smile and go on my way. I suppose that bird in Detroit will try and hold on to the $100.00 I give him for a option but he won't never get away with that Al and I have all ready wired him a telegram to send it back to me at once and if he don't why the next time we hit Detroit I will knock him for a gool.

Speaking about Detroit I suppose you seen what happened in the game yesterday P. M. and when a busher like Flagstead can get to me for 3 hits why you know I am not myself.

Well Al I am to sick in tired of everything to write you much of a letter and besides they's nothing to write about you might say only except 1 thing and that is that Tom Dorgan called me to 1 side in the club house after the game this P. M. and said to not leave till he was ready to go with me so we come down under the stand together and there was this Mulvihill dame waiting for him and grinning like a monkey and Tom couldn't hardily talk he was so fussed up but finely it come out that they are engaged to be married and they wanted to thank me for kind of helping them fix it up and she is wearing a big diamond solitary stone that he just bought for her this A. M. and he told me on the quite that he bought it with some of the jack he win on the fight down to Toledo.

Well good luck to them Al and they can have each other as far is I am concerned and I am glad she is off in my hands as she was getting to be a kind of a pest writeing me letters and night telegrams and 1 thing another and she might of knew that a married man don't want nothing to do with even a young gal let alone 1 that's way up in the paints. So I say good luck to them both Al and God help them.

Well the boys on the club has began calling me Jess and I guess they think its a joke or something but 1 of these days when I ain't feeling my best they won't think its such a joke when they pull some of their funny stuff on me and I Jess them in the jaw.

Your pal,   JACK.